Elements of
Sociology
A Critical Canadian Introduction

Sixth Edition

John Steckley

With contributions by

Angela Aujla, Liberal Arts, Georgian College

Prasad Bidaye, PhD, English, Humber College

Paige Freeborn, HBA Sociology

Kerry Potts, Liberal Arts

Scott E. Schaffer, PhD, Associate Professor of
Sociology, Western University

OXFORD
UNIVERSITY PRESS

OXFORD
UNIVERSITY PRESS

Oxford University Press is a department of the University of Oxford.
It furthers the University's objective of excellence in research, scholarship,
and education by publishing worldwide. Oxford is a registered trade mark of
Oxford University Press in the UK and in certain other countries.

Published in Canada by Oxford University Press
8 Sampson Mews, Suite 204, Don Mills, Ontario M3C 0H5 Canada

First Edition published in 2007
Second Edition published in 2010
Third Edition published in 2013
Fourth Edition published in 2017
Fifth Edition published in 2020

Library and Archives Canada Cataloguing in Publication
Title: Elements of sociology / John Steckley.
Names: Steckley, John, 1949– author.
Description: Sixth edition. | Includes bibliographical references and index.
Identifiers: Canadiana (print) 20230230091 | Canadiana (ebook) 20230230121 | ISBN 9780190165079
(loose-leaf) | ISBN 9780190165048 (softcover) | ISBN 9780190165055 (EPUB)
Subjects: LCSH: Sociology—Canada—Textbooks. | LCGFT: Textbooks.
Classification: LCC HM586 .S84 2023 | DDC 301.0971—dc23

Text and cover design: Laurie McGregor

Oxford University Press is committed to our environment.
Wherever possible, our books are printed on paper which comes from
responsible sources.

Printed and bound by Marquis, Canada

Elements

Contents

3 Doing Sociology: Social Research Methods

4 Socialization and Social Roles

⑤ Culture

6 Deviance and Crime

7 Social and Economic Inequality

⑧ "Race" and Ethnicity

⑨ Gender, Sex, and Sexuality

10 Social Organization and the Sociology of Religion

11 Family

12 Media and Society

13 Education

14 Health and Ability

⑮ Environment and Climate Change

Tables and Figures

Tables

Figures

Introducing . . .
Elements of Sociology

In preparing this new edition of *Elements of Sociology*, we have, from the start, kept in mind one paramount goal: to produce the most dynamic, accessible, and up-to-date introduction to sociology available to Canadian students.

This revision builds on the strengths of the highly acclaimed previous editions, and incorporates new material designed to make the text even more engaging, more thought-provoking, and more relevant to students and instructors alike. This edition is fortified by the involvement of an expert panel of contributing consultants—Scott Schaffer, Paige Freeborn, Angela Aujla, and Prasad Bidaye—whose diverse and compelling viewpoints have guided this revision. In addition to reviewing content and advising on changes, each contributed a POV narrative, and Scott Schaffer and Paige Freeborn engineered critical new chapters, on social theory and media, respectively. We hope that as you browse through the pages that follow, you will see why we believe *Elements of Sociology* is the most exciting and innovative textbook available to Canadian sociology students today.

Six Things That Make This a One-of-a-Kind Textbook

1. A Canadian Textbook for Canadian Students

Written by a Canadian author for Canadians readers, *Elements of Sociology* highlights the stories of the figures and events at the heart of sociological inquiry in this country: John Porter and Dorothy Smith, Aileen Ross and Daniel G. Hill, the Sixties Scoop and the Quiet Revolution, Grassy Narrows and Amber Valley, Viola Desmond, and much, much more.

2. An Inclusive, Narrative Approach

Sociology is the study of people, and in *Elements of Sociology,* the people tell their stories. Students will read first-hand accounts of what it's like to fast during Ramadan, to come out to your family, to experience racism on campus, to meet the expectations of Italian parents, and to raise daughters in an era of Lingerie Barbie and La Senza Girl.

3. A Visual, Thought-Provoking Presentation

Students are challenged on every page to adopt a sociological imagination and see the sociology in everyday life. Carefully chosen photos and captions, provocative critical thinking questions, and end-of-chapter review questions all invite readers to apply the theory and take a stance.

4. Coverage of Canada's Indigenous People

No sociology textbook can claim more extensive coverage of the issues that have affected and that continue to affect Canada's First Nations, Métis, and Inuit.

5. New! Expanded Coverage of Social Theory and a New Chapter on the Media

A new Chapter 2 on social theory explores the important contributions made by sociologists both past and present, and the new Chapter 12 on Media and Society explores how the media has played a role in Canada's growth as a nation and how social media in particular helps shape how we see ourselves.

6. Case Studies and Compelling Viewpoints

Elements of Sociology presents three different feature boxes, scattered throughout every chapter to highlight issues, events, and ideas at the centre of sociological debate and investigation.

Telling It Like It Is

The Point Is . . .

Quick Hits

Student and Instructor Resources

Elements of Sociology is accompanied by a comprehensive package of online resources for students and instructors alike, all designed to enhance and complete the learning and teaching experiences. These resources are available at **www.oup.com/he/Steckley6e**.

For Instructors

- A comprehensive **instructor's manual** provides an extensive set of pedagogical tools and suggestions for every chapter, including overviews and summaries, concepts to emphasize in class, essay and research assignments, and links to relevant videos and online resources.
- Newly updated for this edition, classroom-ready **PowerPoint slides** summarize key points from each chapter and incorporate graphics and tables drawn straight from the text.
- An extensive **test bank** enables instructors to sort, edit, import, and distribute hundreds of questions in multiple-choice, true-false, and short-answer formats.

For Students

- *Elements of Sociology* is available in various formats, including **print,** and—new for this edition—**enhanced ebook,** which includes all of the content as well as videos, and reviews throughout that further enhance the learning experience.

www.oup.com/he/Steckley6e

A Word or Two from the Author

Why Read a Sociology Text?

We live in times when it is more important than ever to be a critical consumer of social, political, medical, and environmental information. Your quality of life and the social health of your country depend on it. I know this sounds a bit extreme, but I believe it to be true. A sociology textbook (and, of course, your sociology instructor) can give you the intellectual tools that could make you such a critical consumer. Further, no matter what career you see yourself in three, ten, or eighteen years from now, you will have to be able to understand and communicate effectively with people. Again, your sociology textbook can help you here. Think of it as a literate, wise uncle/aunt, grandfather/grandmother, or elder whose opinion you value and whose advice you trust (even if you don't always take it).

Why Write a Sociology Text?

Why write a Canadian sociology textbook when there are so many out there already? I began with what I saw as an inability among introductory texts on the Canadian market to give proper voice to Indigenous and South Asian perspectives. I don't claim to have single-handedly corrected the deficiency, but by incorporating the work of authors from each group, I hope I have made a significant departure from earlier Canadian sociology textbooks.

Making "Other" Voices Heard

I realized, too, that other voices needed to be heard. While I have included the work of authors representing different ethnic backgrounds, cultures, and sexualities, I have always felt that the best way to make different voices heard is through personal narratives, which I have incorporated in each chapter. These present a variety of perspectives informed by a variety of "social locations"—trans, gay, young, old, black, Chinese, Italian, white, Muslim, Palestinian, and so on. I strongly believe that the narratives constitute one of the most important features of this textbook, and I've added more to this new edition.

> "I felt that the best way to make different voices heard was in narratives, which I have incorporated in each chapter."

Celebrating My Heroes of the Discipline

The narrative approach is not the only way in which this textbook is a little different. Some of my views are provocative, but I was tired of the dry, conservative bent of other texts, and their general failure to include much or anything about my heroes of the discipline—Dorothy Smith, Michel Foucault, Frantz Fanon, Antonio Gramsci, Albert Memmi, and (apart from a perfunctory nod to his sociological imagination) C. Wright Mills. I aimed for a more inclusive approach in covering theories and theorists, including the many women and sociologists of colour who have influenced and redirected the discipline.

> "I was tired of the dry, conservative bent of other texts."

Breaking Out of the Mould

The market imperative within the broader political economy of publishing means that there is little interest in doing something different from what has already been done. It wasn't until I began the publishing process that I realized how the conservative elements within the market influenced what materialized as the final product. A low tolerance for difference and little appetite for risk mean merely reproducing what is known to have worked before. I am fortunate that Oxford, even though constrained by its own market imperative and logic, has been so supportive of my unique views and approach.

Writing for Canadian Students

A textbook is typically considered Canadian when it uses Canadian figures, Canadian data, and Canadian research—this despite the fact the text may entirely overlook the history and emergence of sociology in this country. Canadian sociology is quite different from the sociology found in Europe and the United States. For instance, the focus of early Canadian sociology was on rural life and the resource economy, which speaks to a society that is not highly urbanized or industrialized. Moreover, from the early days, the influence of the social gospel movement and social work has oriented sociology in Canada, more than its counterparts elsewhere, around issues of social justice, even today.

I am confident that this is the most Canadian introductory sociology textbook on the market. It is not an adapted American textbook with Canadian extensions; nor is it a North American textbook co-written by American and Canadian authors. I designed this book, from the ground up, as a text for Canadian students, to teach them about what I—a Canadian sociologist—have done, am doing, have failed to do, and hope others will do in the future.

> "Canadian sociology is quite different from the sociology found in Europe and the US. . . . I am confident that this is the most Canadian introductory sociology textbook on the market."

Introducing Qualitative Research Methods

While contemporary sociology still engages in foundational methods, there has been an expansion of qualitative methodological approaches that have been influenced by feminism, queer theory, poststructuralism, postcolonialism, cultural studies, and critical disability theory, many of which had been ghettoized into other disciplines, like anthropology and women's studies. These methods are not new, but they have not been part of the methodological lexicon in sociology. In order to represent contemporary sociology accurately, I went beyond a conventional discussion of quantitative and qualitative methods to include ethnographic research, case studies, and narratives, as well as content and discourse analysis, psychoanalysis, semiotics, and genealogy. I wanted to introduce students to concepts, ideas, and themes that will be recurring throughout their education, and in this way, to inspire their imagination.

Conveying the Discipline's Vitality

To give an accurate survey of sociology today means stressing what is current, what is being done, and whom is being studied. The discipline generally and the theory specifically are exciting, yet I feel this message is not conveyed to students, who often see sociology as boring or irrelevant, buried in the past. Sociological theory has shifted immensely, with influences from queer theory, feminist psychoanalysis, postcolonialism, and poststructuralism. Whether the exclusion of these influences is the result of the status quo or the belief that they are too complex for students to comprehend, it is a misrepresentation that in the end benefits no one, and one that I have tried to correct.

> "The discipline generally and the theory specifically are exciting, yet I feel this message is not conveyed to students, who often see sociology as boring or irrelevant."

Making Students Think

A casual flip through the pages of this text will reveal an abundance of photographs and other illustrations. The photos are not just pretty distractions to keep students looking at the book. They serve a purpose. I have chosen photos and have written captions that I hope will encourage students to adopt a sociological perspective. The same objective is served by the numerous critical-thinking questions scattered throughout the chapters. Inviting students to give their views is not just a critical thinking exercise; it's a recognition that our next generation of sociologists have important ideas to share—ideas well worth listening to. I hope that student readers will later in life challenge people by asking the crucial question *How do you know that?*

My Thanks

It takes a number of people to put together a book of this size and scope. First, I would like to thank the people at Oxford University Press who made major contributions to this project. David Stover I thank for suggesting (twice) that I write this book. Ian Nussbaum, who signed me on for the new edition, deserves to be acknowledged for setting things in place, as does in-house editor Eric Sinkins, who, with amazing effort and diplomatic skill, always gets the manuscript across the goal line. For this new edition, I would thank Paige Freeborn, Angela Aujla, Prasad Bidaye, Scott Schaffer, and Kerry Potts—whose insights and honest feedback, as well as their written contributions, have helped make this sixth edition seem as fresh as the first—and Alexandrea Fiorante for taking all of the "elements of the this edition" and expertly splicing them together into the cohesive text that it is. I would like to acknowledge the following reviewers, as well as several anonymous reviewers, whose thoughtful comments and suggestions have helped to shape this edition of *Elements of Sociology*:

- **Ken Caine**, University of Alberta
- **Dana M. Cudney**, Laurentian University
- **Amber Gazso**, York University
- **David Lynes**, St. Francis Xavier University
- **Alan Paquet**, University of Prince Edward Island
- **Lina Samuel**, McMaster University
- **Mike Sosteric**, Athabasca University
- **Adam Stewart**, Crandall University
- **Dr Barret Weber**, Concordia University of Edmonton

For helping me write the initial draft of this book, I would also like to thank several of my former colleagues at Humber. Les Takahashi, Jim Jackson, John Metcalfe, and Joey Noble all contributed to this work with their support and helpful ideas. Librarians Jennifer Rayment and Marlene Beck worked major feats of magic to make obscure articles and books appear. And I would like to thank Guy Letts for his invaluable help in earlier versions of this text.

Closer to home, there is the Steckley household menagerie: Ross our new puppy and Trudy, the dogs that are, and Wiikwaas, Egwene, and Cosmo, the beloved and terribly missed dogs that were; the parrots: Quigley, Tikkifinn, Stanee, Louis, Lime, Sam, Poccopeck, and Gus, as well as Benji, Misha, Finn, Juno, and Tika, who provided support on earlier editions. No joke—I couldn't write without their wonderful distraction. And then there is Brenda, our cat, who is always on the back of the couch to greet me at the front door when I return home.

Finally, there is my wife, Angie. She supported me through the lows and highs of this project, when I was not the easiest person to live with (either low or high). When the sands of my life shift, there is always a rock I can depend on.

John Steckley,
January 2024

Knowing Sociology

What Is Sociology, and How Did It Begin?

Reading this chapter will help you to . . .

- Know your social location and explain how it shapes your perspective on the world around you.

- Understand what sociology does.

- Explain what the sociological imagination is and how it helps students of sociology understand society.

- Identify the factors that spurred the growth of sociology in Europe and North America.

- Trace the development of sociology in Canada.

- Identify and explain the five main approaches sociologists use to pursue their inquiries.

- Distinguish the four types of sociology based on audience.

For Starters

COVID-19 is both a physical and a social phenomenon. The social aspect is well within the realm of sociology, and it is an important area of research. For example, the pandemic, as we will see in later chapters, affected various groups differently. In Canada, Indigenous and Black people have had a higher rate of contracting COVID and dying from it than have those of European descent. Women were more likely than men to lose their jobs or, in the case especially of nurses, to leave their jobs because of stress. The rich (billionaires) got richer, the poor (middle and lower classes), got poorer. Amazon saw huge profits, while many small businesses suffered.

Anti-Vaccination as a Sociological Phenomenon

There has been an especially rich vein of sociological literature on anti-vaxxers over the last few years, written both by sociologists and by healthcare professionals (they must have taken a course or two in sociology at some point in their academic careers). In fact, there have been anti-vaxxers for every new vaccination since the first one in 1796, for smallpox.

The way vaccination works is poorly understood by people generally, so creating fear is easily achieved. In 1982, a television documentary created by an "investigative journalist," titled *DPT: Vaccine Roulette*, alleged incorrectly that one of the components of the combined diphtheria/tetanus/pertussis vaccine caused severe brain damage, seizures, and mental retardation in children. It led to a good number of lawsuits against some pharmacy companies, as well as an increase in whooping cough in the United States for years to come.

In 1998, a British doctor, Andrew Wakefield, (and others) published a fraudulent article in the prestigious medical journal *Lancet*. In the article, based on supposed research on 12 boys, ages 6–10 (too few for good sociological research, or for scientific research of any kind), he alleged that the measles vaccine caused autism. He had been funded by a powerful group of lawyers engaged in a lawsuit against pharmaceutical companies that produced the vaccine. Once the causal connection was proven untrue, he was struck off the medical record, meaning that he can no longer practise medicine. He has continued to be a prominent anti-vaccine activist. But the original fraudulent research led to parents living in relatively well-to-do suburbs in the state of Victoria, Australia, (where Melbourne is located) refusing to have their children vaccinated. An outbreak of measles ensued.

This goes against the stereotype of anti-vaxxers exclusively drawing from lower-class, uneducated, and generally ignorant people. Sociologists Kevin Estep and Pierce Greenberg (2020) demonstrate that parents living in certain affluent communities in California who opt out of vaccination for their children are not challenged for their actions, but have the social support of like-minded people where they live. Social support is a key factor here in being an anti-vaxxer. In Canada, the Peoples' Party of Canada had a policy that essentially supported this position and they were dead set against the vaccination passport, and Conservative Party leader Erin O'Toole refused to comment on whether all his party's candidates in the 2021 election were fully vaccinated.

Infodemic

The term "infodemic" has been coined to refer to the information, generally bad, provided in social media and on the internet about COVID-19. Donald Trump's extensive use of Twitter to communicate "fake news" was a significant source of bad information in the United States for those particularly prone to becoming anti-vaxxers, and some people died as a result of following through on the bad advice, such as ingesting bleach or taking hydroxychloroquine (an anti-malarial drug also used for rheumatoid arthritis and lupus). A "news" station supported by Trump claimed that 10,000 to 20,000 Americans had died from the COVID vaccine, and that it could make you magnetic. Social media, the internet, and the spread of counter-information sources on cable TV news have created new carnival tents where today's purveyors of snake oil can flourish.

1.1 Introduction: Why This Textbook Is a Little Different

This textbook is not like the others. It will offer candid observations, occasional humour, and lots of stories told from the perspective of the author (me), my students, and my colleagues in sociology. In keeping with contemporary sociological terminology, I call these stories narratives. Narratives make up an important branch of sociological literature, one recognizing that to properly understand someone's situation, we need to hear the person's story told in their own words, or "voice." For this reason, every chapter of this textbook will make use of narratives to illustrate key points and concepts.

Another difference between this book and others is that it will not be some mysteriously anonymous account of the discipline. I will not ask you to imagine that it tumbled out of the hands of the gods as the One True Book of Sociology. Instead, I invite you to accept it as my educated but not infallible views on the subject. So you should know some things about me before you read on. My name is John, and I will be your author for the next 15 chapters. I am a white male who has taught and written about sociology and anthropology for over 40 years. I am old enough that I was a hippie (*not* a hipster) before the word was in common use. I still have long hair and a longer beard. I was born and raised in a middle-class family in Don Mills, then a suburb of Toronto, and have lived for the last 20 some years in the village of Bolton, a little north of Toronto. I am a diabetic, but generally I am abled and healthy. Over the course of this book, you will learn several things about me—about my passion for preserving Indigenous languages, my love of parrots (we currently have eight), and my (once fraught) relationship with my two stepsons, to cite just a few examples. These details, which inform every page of this book, are important aspects of my social location, which you should be aware of. After all, how else can you read this book critically, the way you're meant to? You might occasionally find yourself saying, "It is not surprising that an old, white, middle-class man (two weeks from 70 as I write this) from suburban Toronto would say that." Assessing the context in which a piece of knowledge (like a textbook) is produced is an important part of thinking like a sociologist. At the same time, the discipline of sociology examines society—groups of people and the individuals who

Former Attorney General Jody Wilson-Raybould, testifying at a Justice Committee hearing into allegations of government interference in the judicial process, was given the opportunity to present what she called "my truth." She is an Indigenous person who traces her heritage to three of the member tribes of the Kwakwaka'wak nation, referred to historically (and inaccurately) as Kwakiutl. What is the difference between an abstract notion of "truth" and one person's own truth? Which truth would you expect to find in a narrative?

make up those groups—and thus you will encounter many other voices and perspectives in the course of this journey of discovery. You will begin to see how and why we get along as members of the society, and how and why we often fail to.

1.2 Introduction to Sociology

Sociologists notice social patterns. Things tend to happen differently to you depending on your gender, age, class, ethnicity, race, religion, sexual orientation, and ability. If you are a woman, for instance, you typically pay more in Canada for a haircut and to have your shirt dry-cleaned than you would if you were a man (Vermond, 2016). You are not paying more because the service you receive is any different: it's just that your hair and your shirt, because they are designated as "female," are subject to what we call the "pink tax," making them more expensive to cut and to clean (respectively). You may also find it hard to take a one-handed photo with a smartphone, because as several writers have noted, smartphones are built to accommodate (typically) larger male hands

The Point Is...

Your Social Location Gives You a Unique Perspective

If I were to say that television does a poor job of representing diversity, would you agree or disagree?

One of the aims in writing this textbook is to help you appreciate the importance of your social location as it relates to how you interpret events and the experiences of others. Your social location is the set of social traits that informs your views on the world around you. Consider the following questions:

- Are you over or under the age of 20? 30?
- What is your assigned sex?
- What is your gender? (Think it's the same thing? It's not, as we'll see in Chapter 9.)
- What is your ethnic background? Where are your parents from? What about your parents' parents? Indeed, what about your grandparents' grandparents and, if it matters to you personally, stretching back centuries into the past?
- Would you say you've grown up in an upper-class, middle-class, or lower-class neighbourhood? And is that neighbourhood in the city, the suburbs, or a small town?
- Do you have a medical condition that affects your everyday experience? It could be something visible like having to use a wheelchair or glasses, or something invisible like an anxiety disorder or ADHD.
- Do you feel like you're part of "the mainstream"?

Your answers to these questions combine to produce your social location, which gives you a unique set of experiences and outlook on the world around you. When one of these traits sets you apart from the mainstream—say, you identify as transgender, or you use a hearing aid—we can predict a pattern of social behaviour that involves discrimination against you because these traits tend to be negatively valued by society generally. We can also predict that the discrimination you face will be different if your social location involves two or more variables that set you apart from the mainstream—say, you identify as transgender and you use a hearing aid. At the same time, holding two or more traits that are generally valued by society—say, being white and being wealthy—can place you in a position of social privilege. The idea that two or more traits can combine, or "intersect," to increase your experience of discrimination or privilege is known as intersectionality, a topic we will consider further in Chapter 8.

Now, look around you: How many people do you think share your social location? Not too many will share your exact social location, although many of those around you will share certain aspects of it.

So, how do you think you might respond to the question above—the one about diversity and television—if you were a second-generation Iranian American? What if you were a member of a First Nations band who grew up on a reserve in Manitoba? Or an intersex person who identifies as female? Or a wheelchair athlete? See how your perspective on that question changes depending on where you're socially located?

(Ryan, 2013; Criado-Perez, 2019). If you are a young Black man, you are more likely than a young white male driver to be pulled over by the police: you are guilty of the offence known as "driving while Black"; that's another social pattern. South Asian students of mine have told me that they have been pulled over for "driving while brown," and people of South Asian and Middle Eastern descent routinely are greeted with closer scrutiny and more questioning at airport security.

What if you are a young, white, heterosexual male? If you are, you occupy a privileged social location. You have never experienced the kind of discrimination that comes from being elderly, Black, gay, or female. At the same time, you may find that in some environments—the college classroom of the twenty-first century, for instance—your experience as a white male is not always valued. And you might be economically disadvantaged, finding it difficult to pay for your education, accommodation, and food,

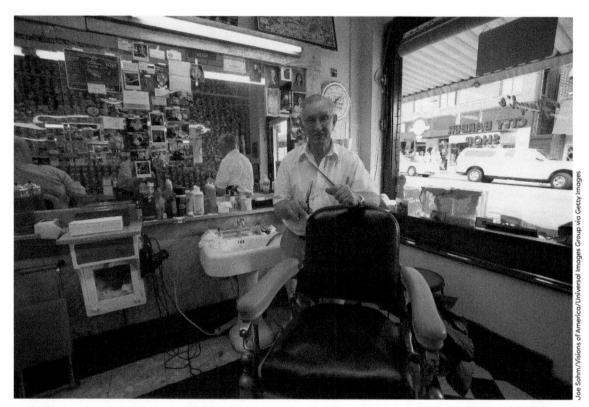

Joe Sohm/Visions of America/Universal Images Group via Getty Images

Would you take a $20 haircut from this barber? Or would you pay considerably more to receive the same haircut from a stylist at a salon? Women typically pay more than men do to have their hair cut: How do you account for this social pattern?

and don't feel particularly "privileged." That is another social pattern.

Sociologists also investigate and challenge the social patterns that other people perceive. For example, why do so many people, even some in the medical profession, assume that male nurses are gay or effeminate? This stereotype has never been demonstrated statistically, in part because it would be highly intrusive to ask a male nurse about his sexual orientation. Sociologists studying the subject might investigate the effects of movies like *Meet the Parents* (2000), starring Ben Stiller, where characters declare that all male nurses are either gay or, at the very least, "sissies." Does this stereotype discourage men from entering the nursing profession for fear of being seen as *deviant*? By this we mean simply deviating from what is seen as normal or usual, that is, that women traditionally have been ascribed the nurturing and caregiving roles in our society.

Sociology and Issues

Sociology can help students understand issues facing society today. A divisive social issue of recent years

is the legalization of marijuana for recreational use. Since October 2018, Canadians have been able to smoke marijuana legally. However, a poll conducted at the time of legalization suggested that many Canadians remained strongly opposed to the new law, but by 2021, support for legalization, nationally, stood at 64 per cent with only 28 per cent continuing to be opposed to the federal government's earlier decision to legalize cannabis (Canseco, 2021). What can sociologists tell us about this issue?

Sociology can't say what is moral, or "right," in an issue such as this. There isn't a scientific way of measuring that. But sociology *can* tell us about who tends to be in favour of Canada's new marijuana laws: younger people, those with a higher annual income, men more than women, and East and West Coast Canadians and those living from Ontario west to Saskatchewan. (Broadly speaking, people in Quebec and Alberta hold a more conservative view.) As well, sociology can speak about who tends to be against legalized marijuana, such as people 65 and older and those making between $20,000 and $40,000 annually (Forum Research, 2018). Beyond this, sociology

The Point Is . . .

If You're Reading This, You Probably Support Legal Weed

That's not just a hunch—it's based on research.

According to a poll conducted by the Canadian market research company Forum Research in October 2018—the same month that recreational marijuana became legal in this country—Canadians under the age of 35 were more likely to favour (74 per cent) than to oppose (22 per cent) legalized cannabis (Forum Research, 2018). In fact, there is a direct relationship between age and approval of legalization: the older you are, the more likely you are to disapprove of cannabis legalization (see Figure 1.1).

What does the information presented in Figure 1.1 mean? It doesn't mean that three-quarters of adults under 35 are regular pot users. In fact, only 58 per cent of those under 35 said they had tried cannabis. This means that a number of Canadians under 35 who have never tried cannabis still approve of its legalization.

What about Canadians 65 and older, 55 per cent of whom disapprove of legalization? Can we put their negativity down to bad pot experiences? Alas, the survey found that only 22 per cent of those 65 and over had used cannabis, meaning that a good number of people in this age category disapprove of marijuana without ever having tried it. I belong to the 65-and-over category, and I can state that I smoked as a teenager but haven't in decades. I approve of its legalization, but I've long been an exception to my age group on a number of issues.

What we can take from the research, I think, is that younger people are more open to the cannabis legalization in the same way they are more liberal-minded on a number of social issues, such as same-sex marriage. They have lived in times when pot use was more open and less subject to censure than it was when the 65+ generation were teenagers. In the 1950s and 1960s, society was still under the influence of a powerful and largely misleading anti-marijuana propaganda campaign that linked cannabis with crime (see Zhang, 2017).

---

might also help students understand the impact that socializing influences such as the family and the media have on their own opinions about marijuana. You can have more choice in forming your own opinion when you understand what has helped to shape it in the past.

This leads to a question that sociology students often ask: How come I got a low mark when it's just an opinion and there are no right or wrong answers? Everyone has a right to an opinion; however, people should become knowledgeable about issues before forming opinions on them. The rise in recent years

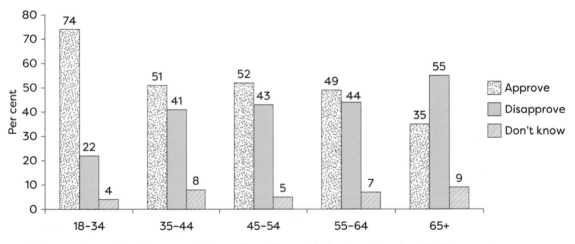

FIGURE 1.1 Canadians' Support for Legalized Cannabis by Age, October 2018

Source: Forum Research (2018).

of "fake news," "alternative facts," and conspiracy theories in Western democracies points to how insidious opinions without empirical evidence can become. Sociology gives us a means to form considered opinions on social issues. In this way, sociology helps students distinguish between a well-informed opinion and an uninformed view spouted off without careful thought (say, by peers who aren't taking sociology).

What else does the research tell us? Men are a little more likely than women to support the legalization of marijuana (56 per cent versus 48 per cent) and are more likely than women to have a somewhat or very positive view of marijuana generally (36 per cent versus 32 per cent) (Forum Research, 2018). Residents of Quebec and Alberta have the lowest opinion of cannabis and are the least likely to support its legalization (Figure 1.2).

Some of these findings may surprise you. If they don't, it's likely because you've noticed patterns in the comments you've heard people make about marijuana legalization, in the media, among your peers, at family get-togethers, and so on. If so, congratulations: noticing these social patterns is an important part of doing sociology. If not, don't worry: you'll get there.

What Is Sociology?

You may have noticed that so far I have avoided defining what sociology is. That's because it's not a straightforward thing to do, and in some ways not particularly useful. Defining something is very different from understanding it. I could give you a simple (but not terribly useful) definition by saying that *sociology is the systematic or scientific study of society*. Can you imagine the multiple-choice questions that could come from that?

Sociology is:

a) the systematic study of society
b) the unsystematic study of society
c) "statistical stuff and heavy-duty theoretical bullshit" (see Mills, below)
d) all of the above.

The answer could easily be the final one, "all of the above." I could just as easily refer you to the glossary at the back of this book, where sociology is defined as "the social science that studies the development, structure, and functioning of human society." Does that help?

The truth is, giving a precise, all-encompassing explanation of what sociology *is* would be much more difficult (and probably less useful) than explaining what sociology *does*. This is why I've begun our introduction to sociology by highlighting some of its uses. At this point it is enough to know that sociology involves looking for and looking at social patterns:

- in social variables, such as age, gender, race, ethnicity, religion, ability, and sexual orientation;
- in social institutions, such as education, religion, and the family; and
- in social interactions.

By the time you've reached the end of this textbook, I hope that you will have formed your own idea of what sociology really *is*.

Why Study Sociology?

Studying sociology helps you obtain a greater understanding of the *social world*, which encompasses the social practices, attitudes, and institutions that surround us. Studying sociology will also help you to better understand yourself in terms of whether you follow or do not follow patterns of social behaviour predicted by sociological variables. Imagine two first-year sociology students: one is an 18-year-old white woman from Montreal's wealthy Westmount neighbourhood, whose parents are both employed and hold postsecondary degrees; the other is a 30-year-old immigrant from Haiti living in the economically disadvantaged borough of Montréal-Nord who is the first member of his family to go to university. One situation is predicted by the sociological variables; the other is not.

Sociology, in this way, helps you develop an understanding about others around you in the multicultural and generally diverse social world that is Canada, as well as in the smaller social worlds of neighbourhoods, classrooms, social media sites, pubs, and workplaces. Thinking more globally, sociology helps you better understand the larger world of nations and their social institutions.

a. Support for legalized cannabis

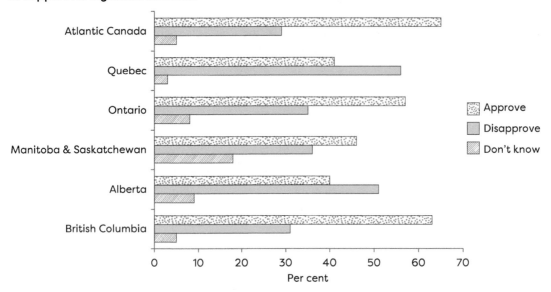

b. Support for the sale of cannabis edibles (cookies, bars, drinks, etc.)

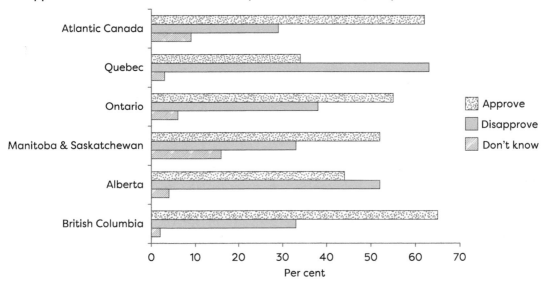

c. Feelings about cannabis generally

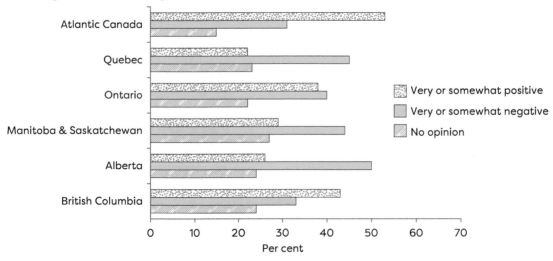

FIGURE 1.2 Canadians' Feelings about Cannabis by Region, October 2018

Source: Forum Research (2018).

Quick Hits

Sociology and Related Disciplines

Academic disciplines are artificial construc-tions. There is nothing "natural" about the borderlines that separate sociology from other established disciplines such as anthro-pology, economics, history, psychology, phi-losophy, political science, or even literature. These various fields have much in common, and there is a lot of cross-referencing in the books and articles written by specialists in each discipline. Students who have taken courses in psychology, anthropology, or philosophy will notice that sociology regularly encroaches on their territory. At the same time, you will find that people teaching such varied subjects as Canadian studies, communication, criminology, cultural studies, education, Indigenous studies, international relations, and women's studies often have degrees in sociology (Table 1.1).

TABLE 1.1 Sociology and Related Disciplines

Discipline	Emphasis
anthropology	Human societies and cultures, the way they developed, and how they function.
economics	The production and consumption of wealth, including the distribution of goods and services among individuals and groups.
literature	The fictional or quasi-fictional depiction of people living and struggling to live in society and of the relationships they share.
philosophy	Major thinkers and turns of thought in particular societies, and how they have addressed the major questions of life.
political science	Systems of government and how they serve citizens.
psychology	The human mind, the social and biological influences on it, and its functions, especially those affecting behaviour.
social work	The way our understanding of society and individuals can be applied to improving peoples' well-being.
sociology	The development, structure, and functioning of human society, especially as seen in group interaction, social relations, social institutions, and social structures.

The Heart of Sociology: The Sociological Imagination

One of sociology's most useful concepts is the **sociological imagination**. The term was coined by **C. Wright Mills** (1916–1962), who sums it up nicely as:

> the capacity to shift from one perspective to another—from the political to the psycho-logical; from examination of a single family to comparative assessment of the national budgets of the world. . . . It is the capacity to range from the most impersonal and re-mote transformations to the most intimate features of the human self—and to see the re-lationship between the two. (Mills, 1959, p. 4)

Mills argues that when we create and communicate sociological knowledge, our ideas must show "how society works" in terms of our own personal lives. If you go to buy a good pair of rubber boots, and the only ones you can get are yellow and relatively flimsy, then you are likely a woman, and your own frustrating shopping experience reflects the way so-ciety thinks of and treats women in general.

What happens when we fail to exercise our so-ciological imagination is discussed by Henry Giroux in *Beyond the Spectacle of Terrorism: Global Uncertainty*

Telling It Like It Is

An Author's Point of View

Not a Sociological Phenomenon?

In August 2014, after 15-year-old Tina Fontaine's lifeless body was found wrapped in a bag in the Red River in Winnipeg, Indigenous rights groups and women's rights activists called on the government to hold an inquiry into why Indigenous women are disproportionately targeted for murder and other violent crime. In response, then Prime Minister Stephen Harper said that violent crime involving Indigenous women was not a "sociological phenomenon" but a series of more or less isolated incidents best left to the police. Sociology instructors across the nation said, "Thank you, Stephen, for helping me write my first lecture of the semester."

Sociology, as we have just seen, involves looking for patterns predicted by sociological variables—age, race, sex, gender, class, and ability. When we consider Indigenous women living in Canada, we can say that they have at least three strikes against them: they are Indigenous, they are usually poor, and they are women, embodying three traits that mainstream society judges negatively. This makes it easier for people to treat them violently and to exploit them

sexually; it makes it easier for politicians and the media to neglect their problems and for police to treat them like non-humans. It makes it easy for someone like Stephen Harper, who is white, wealthy, male, and powerful, to say that the killing of Tina Fontaine was just an isolated crime; after all, the variables that make up his social location rule. Imagine if powerful white men started to disappear and turn up dead in disproportionate numbers. Would these be treated as isolated crimes?

Indigenous women are far more likely than other women, and other Canadians, to be victims of homicide, domestic violence, and violence generally; they are more likely to go missing or enter the sex trade; they are more likely to have grown up in foster care; and they are more likely to be teenage parents and lone (i.e., single) parents. That Indigenous women are represented in unusually large numbers in these statistical findings is an example of what sociologists call **disproportionate representation**. This is a sociological phenomenon. It does not take a lot of sociological imagination to realize that.

---

and the Challenge of the New Media (2006). Commenting on the lack of sociological imagination in the post-9/11 political posturing of George W. Bush, Giroux warned that "democracy begins to fall and political life becomes impoverished when society can no longer translate private problems into social issues" (Giroux, 2006, p. 1). He spelled this out in detail in a chapter called "Acts of Translation":

> As the very idea of the social collapses into the private realm of the self and its fears, it becomes more difficult for people to develop a vocabulary for understanding how individual insecurity, dread, and misery could be translated into concerns of an engaged and critical citizenry. Instead, they

are told that their privately held misery is a fall from grace, a flaw in character that must be suffered in isolation. Poverty, for example, is now imagined to be a problem of individual failing. Racism is rationalized and represented as simply an act of individual discrimination or prejudice. Homelessness is reduced to a freely chosen decision made by lazy people. (Giroux, 2006, p. 4)

In other words, without the sociological imagination, the individual, not society, becomes the primary focus of blame. The sociological imagination enables us to see an individual's circumstances in the context of broader social forces that affect us all and warrant our attention.

The Point Is . . .

C. Wright Mills Was a Rebel with a Cause

In my first year of university, the sociologist who fed my imagination was C. Wright Mills. He took on the rich and powerful and challenged his conservative colleagues and his country's government in the staid and stuffy 1950s. His public critique of American society caught the attention of the FBI, who started a file on him. He rode a motorcycle to work, and dressed in plaid shirts, old jeans, and work boots. Mills became my first sociologist hero.

Mills published seven books. These include two trilogies and an important stand-alone volume that gave its name to a way of viewing the world that sociologists and sociology students should aspire to: *The Sociological Imagination* (1959). His first trilogy, a study of the three main socioeconomic classes in the United States, comprises *The New Men of Power: America's Labor Leaders* (1948), *White Collar: The American Middle Classes* (1951), and *The Power Elite* (1956). The last of these found a wide and varied audience that included the then young Cuban revolutionary Fidel Castro, who, after he had overthrown the American-backed dictator Fulgencio Batista, invited Mills to visit so they could discuss his ideas. After the book was translated into Russian, Mills was asked to visit Moscow.

In the early 1950s, Mills issued a challenge to those writing sociology. Responding in a letter to a question about whether sociology writing could be improved, Mills wrote:

> It doesn't look good. I think for two reasons: First, there is no real writing tradition in sociology, as there is, for example, in history. It just doesn't exist. Second, the field is now split into statistical stuff and heavy duty theoretical bullshit. In both cases, there's no writing but only turgid polysyllabic slabs of stuff. So, because that is now the field, no men get trained, have models to look up to; there is no aspiration to write well. (Mills, 2000, pp. 154–5)

While Mills himself has disproved the first point, the second critique stands. So much of sociological writing is mired in jargon and fails to resonate with a broad audience. So sociologists and sociology students, your duty is clear. Prove him wrong and aspire to write well, avoiding the "theoretical bullshit" and "polysyllabic slabs"!

1.3 The Origins of Sociology

People since ancient times have contemplated social systems and looked for patterns in human social relationships. Perhaps the earliest person whose recorded writings reflect a true sociological imagination is the Chinese philosopher **Confucius** (c. 551–479 BCE). A strong proponent of role modelling—a topic discussed often in sociology today—Confucius believed it was better for leaders to engage in moral practices that modelled the principles they wanted their citizens to follow than to overuse laws to enforce morality. In his words:

> If you use laws to direct the people, and punishments to control them, they will merely try to evade the laws, and will have no sense of shame. (Kaizuka, 2002, p. 126)

We can all think of politicians who would have benefited from following the wise sociological advice of Confucius.

While Confucius's teachings touched on some important sociological themes, the first person to carry out a systematic study of sociological subjects and set his thoughts down in writing is most likely Arab scholar **Ibn Khaldûn** (1332–1406). In his *Kitāb al-'Ibār*, or "Book of Lessons" (which is actually seven books), he examined various types of societies and their histories, cultures, and economies. The introductory volume, *Al Muqaddimah* ("An Introduction to History"), contains a wealth of research on, and insights into, the cyclical rise and fall of powerful tribes and nations. From his travels across North Africa, from Tunisia, where he was born and educated, to Egypt and the Arabian Peninsula, and

Photo by Yaroslava Mills

Consider this photo of C. Wright Mills: Does he look like an educator to you? Why or why not?

from his work as a teacher and political adviser to tribal and national leaders, Khaldûn developed his evolutionary theory of history, politics, and society. This influential theory, which has found increased support in recent centuries, involves social cohesion and how, as a society achieves strength, it inevitably reaches a point of decay and is overtaken by outside forces or by disgruntled factions from within.

The Development of Sociology in Europe

Sociology became an area of academic interest in nineteenth-century Europe, specifically in France, Germany, and Britain. Table 1.2 lists a number of these earlier European scholars and theorists who sought to describe and understand the shifting world of their time. This work developed in response to the dramatic social and economic changes that had taken place as a feudal landholding system finally gave way to industrialization, urbanization, and significant population increases. Cities were growing

What do *you* think?

Even if you're new to sociology, you might have heard of people like Marx, Durkheim, and Weber before picking up this textbook, yet you probably hadn't heard of Ibn Khaldûn. Why do you think Ibn Khaldûn has been less recognized in Western Europe and North America for his contributions to the development of sociology?

rapidly, both because of natural population growth and because of the dramatic influx of people from the countryside looking for jobs in newly minted factories. Concerned scholars like the economist **Thomas Malthus** (1766–1834) began to wonder whether Europe's cities could cope with such tremendous population growth. The politics of the time were also favourable to the growth of sociology, with the French Revolution in particular providing evidence that citizens could bring about social change swiftly and on a massive scale.

Max Weber: A Founder of Modern Sociology

An example of the intellectual impact of early sociology is seen in the work of German sociologist **Max Weber** (pronounced VAY-ber; 1864–1920). One of his most important and well-known contributions was his identification of a set of values embodied in early Protestantism, which he called the **Protestant (work) ethic**. For Weber, these values contributed significantly to the development of modern capitalism.

Weber's theory was based on a number of related ideas. One is the notion, popular among early Protestants, that there is a predestined "elect," a group of people who have been chosen to be "saved" during the Second Coming of Christ. Naturally, it was important to early Protestants to be seen as part of this exclusive group. Success through hard work was considered one proof of membership; another was

TABLE 1.2 Some Early European Sociologists and Their Contributions

Sociologist (years, nationality)	Key Works	Contribution
Auguste Comte (1798–1857, French)	• *The Course in Positivist Philosophy* (1830–42) • *A General View of Positivism* (1848)	A proponent of positivist philosophy, he aimed to develop a social science that could be used for social reconstruction.
Harriet Martineau (1802–1876, British)	• *Illustrations of Political Economy* (1834) • *Society in America* (1837)	Widely viewed as the first woman sociologist, she wrote extensively on social, economic, and historical topics and translated several of Comte's works.
Karl Marx (1818–1883, German)	• *The German Ideology* (1846) • *The Communist Manifesto* (1848, with Friedrich Engels) • *Capital* (1867)	The founder of modern communism, he viewed social change in terms of economic factors.
Herbert Spencer (1820–1903, British)	• *Social Statistics* (1851) • *First Principles* (1862) • *The Study of Sociology* (1873)	Social evolutionist sought to apply Darwin's theory of natural selection to human societies and coined the term **survival of the fittest**.
Friedrich Nietzsche (1844–1900, German)	• *Human, All Too Human* (1878) • *Beyond Good and Evil* (1886) • *On the Genealogy of Morals* (1887) • *The Will to Power* (1901)	Philosopher rejected Christianity's compassion for the weak and championed the "will to power" and the *Übermensch* ("superman"), who could rise above the restrictions of ordinary morality.
Émile Durkheim (1858–1917, French)	• *The Division of Labour in Society* (1893) • *The Rules of the Sociological Method* (1895) • *Suicide* (1897) • *The Elementary Forms of the Religious Life* (1912)	Among the first to consider society as a legitimate subject of scientific observation, he studied society in terms of **social facts** such as ethics, occupations, and suicide.
Georg Simmel (1858–1918, German)	• *On Social Differentiation* (1890) • *The Philosophy of Money* (1900) • *Sociology: Investigations on the Forms of Sociation* (1908)	Father of microsociology studied the way people experience the minutiae of daily life.
Max Weber (1864–1920, German)	• *The Protestant Ethic and the Spirit of Capitalism* (1904–5) • *Economy and Society* (1922)	Identified a set of values, the "Protestant (work) ethic," to which he attributed the rise of capitalism.
Antonio Gramsci (1891–1937, Italian)	• *Prison Notebooks* (1948)	Marxist theorist and co-founder of Italy's Communist Party developed a theory of hegemony and power while in prison for political activism.

Note: We have identified all works by their English titles, although several of these works first appeared, in the years indicated, in languages other than English.

the accumulation of **capital** (money and other assets used to generate money, like factories). Working hard, making profitable use of one's time, and living a materially *ascetic* (self-denying) life by acquiring property and saving rather than spending lavishly are all principles of Weber's Protestant work ethic. As Weber explained:

The span of human life is infinitely short and precious to make sure of one's own election. Loss of time through sociability, idle talk, luxury, even more sleep than is necessary for health . . . is worthy of absolute moral condemnation. . . . [Time] is infinitely valuable because every hour lost is

What do you think?
Marianne Weber, the wife of Max Weber, was a sociologist in her own right, a public figure in German social and political circles, well known for her writings on marriage and divorce, women's work inside and outside the home, and the changing role of women in a patriarchal society. She outlived Max Weber by over 30 years, and edited 10 volumes of his work for posthumous publication. Why do you think her own work is only now beginning to receive critical attention in the English-speaking world?

lost to labour for the glory of God. Thus inactive contemplation is also valueless, or even directly reprehensible if it is at the expense of one's daily work. For it is less pleasing to God than the active performance of His will in a calling. (Weber, [1904]/1930, pp. 157–8)

Weber later elaborated on how demonstrating these values represents proof of being one of God's chosen few, and how these values supposedly fuelled the rise of capitalism:

The religious valuation of restless, continuous, systematic work in a worldly calling, as the . . . surest and most evident proof of rebirth and genuine faith, must have been the most powerful conceivable lever for the expansion of . . . the spirit of capitalism. (Weber, [1946]/1958, p. 172)

Although the idea of the Protestant (work) ethic took hold firmly enough that it entered popular thought and speech, it was never demonstrated sociologically that capitalism developed primarily in Protestant rather than in Catholic countries, or that the work ethic Weber associated with Protestantism was somehow missing from other religions. Latin American and other postcolonial scholars argue that the rise of capitalism began with colonialism, a movement in which Catholic Spain and Portugal were major early players. Weber paid little attention to the

What do you think?
Look at the list of early sociologists in Table 1.2. Why are most of them men?

role that colonialism played in the rise of capitalism as an instrument for exploiting colonized countries. Spain looted Aztec and Inca gold to become, for a time, the richest empire in Europe. Weber, by attributing the development of capitalism to the strength of the Protestant will, might have been trying too hard to account for the relatively recent economic and political superiority of European Protestants.

1.4 The Spread of Sociology to North America

During the late nineteenth and early twentieth centuries in North America, the emergence of conditions similar to those that existed already in Europe—the arrival of millions of immigrants, the development of cities and urban life, and the growing impact of technology on the daily lives of individuals—spurred the growth of sociology. **Social change** happened quickly in the United States, which was undergoing a rapid transition from an essentially rural society to a nation of fast-growing urban centres revolving around industry and commerce. This development came with considerable human costs, as people were pressed into severely inadequate living and working conditions, and large cities were divided into ethnic communities or ghettos. Social scientists in the United States were inspired to study the new ways that Americans were living, working, and sharing space, and the country's oldest sociology department, at the University of Chicago, arose primarily as a way of understanding the problems associated with the rapid immigration of thousands of Europeans to the American city (Table 1.3).

Canada underwent urbanization and industrialization at a slower rate and, as we will see shortly, had a different set of social concerns that fuelled the growth of sociology in this country. But like Canadian politics, Canadian entertainment media, and Canadian culture generally, our sociology was not untouched by what was happening south of the border, and several of Canada's early sociologists had ties to what became known as the "Chicago school," which had a significant influence on the development of sociology across the continent.

Chicago: The City as Training Ground for Aspiring Sociologists

In the latter half of the nineteenth century, Chicago exemplified the conditions conducive to the birth

TABLE 1.3 Some Early American Sociologists and Their Contributions

Sociologist	Key Works	Contribution
William Graham Sumner (1840–1910)	• *Folkways: A Study of the Sociological Importance of Usages, Manners, Customs, Mores, and Morals* (1906)	Yale professor taught the first American course in sociology and explored the social significance of manners, mores, and taboos.
Thorstein Veblen (1857–1929)	• *The Theory of the Leisure Class* (1899) • *The Theory of the Business Enterprise* (1904)	Economist and social critic attacked American "conspicuous consumption."
Jane Addams (1860–1935)	• "The Subjective Necessity for Social Settlements" (1893) • *Hull-House Maps and Papers* (1896)	Social worker/activist, sociologist, and intellectual established America's first settlement house, in Chicago.
George Herbert Mead (1863–1931)	• *Mind, Self, and Society* (1934)	Father of "symbolic interactionism" looked at how the self is constructed through personal exchanges with others.
Charles Horton Cooley (1864–1929)	• *Human Nature and the Social Order* (1902) • *Social Organization: A Study of the Larger Mind* (1909)	Symbolic interactionist advanced the idea of the looking-glass self, asserting that the self is created and reinforced through social interaction.
Robert Park (1864–1944)	• *Introduction to the Science of Sociology* (1921) • *The City: Suggestions for the Study of Human Nature in the Urban Environment* (1925)	Urban sociologist was a founding member of the Chicago school of sociology.
W.E.B. Du Bois (1868–1963)	• *The Souls of Black Folk* (1903) • *Black Reconstruction in America* (1935)	Documented African American experience and introduced the concept of "double consciousness" whereby colonized people are forced to see the world from the viewpoint of the colonizer, which creates internal conflict.
Edwin Sutherland (1883–1950)	• "White Collar Criminality" (1940) • *White Collar Crime* (1949)	Criminal sociologist and symbolic interactionist introduced the idea of white-collar crime.
E. Franklin Frazier (1894–1962)	• *The Negro Family in the United States* (1939)	Baltimore-born sociologist performed pioneering studies of African American families.
Everett C. Hughes (1897–1983)	• *French Canada in Transition* (1943) • "Dilemmas and Contractions of Status" (1945)	Chicago school sociologist studied the ethnic division of labour in the French Canadian province of Quebec.

and growth of academic sociology. It became the second largest city in the United States, thanks to spectacular rates of immigration both from Europe and from the American rural South, which fostered the growth of ethnic communities. At the same time, working conditions, particularly in the city's notorious stockyards, were spectacularly bad. Chicago was, in the words of poet Carl Sandberg (1914), "hog

butcher to the world," and socialist author Upton Sinclair's 1906 novel, *The Jungle*, detailed the miserable living and work conditions of immigrant workers in the meat-packing industry, where packing plants processed into sausages and lard "everything about the hog except the squeal."

It is little surprise, then, that Chicago was central to much of the early history of sociology not just in the United States but in North America. With its founding in 1892, the University of Chicago's Department of Sociology became the first sociology department in North America, and during the 1920s and 1930s the Chicago school became synonymous with both the specialized subdiscipline of urban sociology and a number of prominent sociologists, including Robert Park, Ernest Burgess, Everett C. Hughes, George Herbert Mead, Edwin Sutherland, and Jane Addams.

The Chicago School: Park, Burgess, and Addams

Robert E. Park

The leading figure of the Chicago school of sociology, Robert Park (1864–1944), travelled a long road before settling down as a sociologist. He taught for a year at Harvard but left the university to work with the African American educator and activist Booker T. Washington (1856–1915) at the Tuskegee Institute in Alabama. It was not until 1914 that Park joined the faculty of the University of Chicago, where he taught until his retirement in 1933. There, with Ernest Burgess, he wrote what was considered at the time the authoritative text of introductory sociology, *Introduction to the Science of Sociology* (1921). It continued to exert a tremendous impact on the discipline long after the two authors had died.

Park was a pioneer in urban sociology, based largely on his work in Chicago. His research was focused on the concept of human ecology, which views the city as the main habitat for the human species, the same way that an African jungle may be home to the needle-clawed bush baby or the Senegal parrot (my examples). The city was Park's laboratory, and he was a consummate observer. As the German sociologist René König wrote: "You must imagine Park as a tireless pedestrian, roaming through Chicago in every direction, this way and that, noting down his observations as he goes" (1978; quoted in Lindner, 1996, p. 1). König's description captures the spirit of ethnography, the main research method used by Park and the Chicago school. (There will be more on ethnography in Chapter 3.)

Ernest Burgess

A formative member of the Chicago school, Ernest Burgess (1886–1966) was, like Park, an urban sociologist. His field of study is surprising when you consider that he was born and raised in tiny Lidbury, Ontario, a village that was not even incorporated as a town until 1910. As well as co-authoring *Introduction to the Science of Sociology*, Burgess collaborated with Park and Roderick McKenzie to produce a classic study of urban sociology, *The City: Suggestions for the Study of Human Nature in the Urban Environment* (Park, Burgess, & McKenzie, 1925).

Burgess was one of those sociologists who added a physics-like statistical precision to the field, particularly when it came to making predictions (something sociologists are often hesitant to do). In his research in criminology, one of sociology's subfields, he developed a 21-point scoring system to measure the likelihood that an inmate on parole would reoffend (Burgess, 1928). Modified versions of Burgess's criminology scale are still used, but not all of his statistical measures have survived the test of time. In *Predicting Success or Failure in Marriage* (Burgess & Cottrell, 1939)—an interesting project for a man who never married—he introduced a rubric for gauging the strength of a marriage; neither love nor affection was among the variables taken into account in this system.

Jane Addams

Though she was never a member of Chicago's Department of Sociology, Jane Addams (1860–1935) had close and influential ties with the faculty there. But her interest in Chicago's urban neighbourhoods was beyond academic: she was a pioneering social reformer and worked tirelessly to improve the welfare of those living in poverty in the inner city.

In 1889, Addams, with Ellen Gates Starr (1859–1940), turned a run-down mansion in one of Chicago's poorest communities into North America's first settlement house. With help from a number of local sponsors, Addams paid for rent and repairs to the mansion, and established Hull House as an innovative outreach and research centre, offering social and educational services to people of different ethnic backgrounds and social classes. The residents of Hull House—the middle-class, university-educated women who volunteered at the centre—led courses in a range of domestic and cultural subjects for families in Hull House's predominantly working-class immigrant community. At the same time, the centre served as a training ground for social workers. The first of its kind in North America, it set the model for settlement houses established in other cities around the world.

Addams today is recognized for her accomplishments as an activist, author, community organizer, university lecturer, and public intellectual, a leading figure in what was termed the Progressive Era. However, with the establishment of Hull House, she made studying the relationship of poverty, pollution, sanitation, and diseases such as typhoid fever and tuberculosis a central pillar of the house's mission, and for this reason we can add sociologist to the list of roles in which she distinguished herself.

1.5 The Development of Canadian Sociology

While there is no distinctly Canadian approach to sociological research and practice, the way the discipline developed in this country and its focal points are unique. The relationship between French and English, the development of the Canadian West, the connection between class and ethnicity, and a close working relationship with anthropology have all been fundamental to the development of a Canadian perspective on sociology, as has, more recently, the relationship between Indigenous people and settlers and the colonial state.

McGill University: Dawson, Hughes, and Miner

The first professional, university-based sociologist in Canada was **Carl Addington Dawson** (1887–1964). Born in Prince Edward Island, Dawson completed his MA and PhD at the University of Chicago. In 1922, shortly after joining the faculty at McGill, he founded the university's sociology department, an accomplishment not without opposition. Senior administrators worried about the left-wing political leanings of sociologists (they still do), and academics in other departments did not want their scholarly territory infringed upon. Dawson succeeded in spite of these objections. McGill's remained the only independent department of sociology until 1961.

Dawson's work reflected two elements of early Canadian sociology: (1) the **social gospel** movement and (2) hands-on social work. The social gospel movement developed as an attempt by people trained for the ministry to apply Christian principles of human welfare to the treatment of social, medical, and psychological ills brought on by industrialization and unregulated capitalism, not just in Canada but in the United States, Britain, Germany, and other European countries during the late nineteenth century. Out of the social gospel movement came the Social Service Council of Canada (1912), which through various churches carried out the first sociological surveys of Canadian cities.

Dawson's affinity with the social gospel movement was natural—his first degree was in divinity—but his inspiration to become involved in social work came from his time studying at the University of Chicago. The Chicago school put an emphasis on going out into communities—what Park called "living laboratories"—to observe them first-hand. Dawson took this approach and, with his students, applied it to the living laboratory of Montreal. Their research was given a jump-start in 1929, when they were awarded a $110,000 Rockefeller Foundation grant to study unemployment in the city.

That same year, Dawson and Warren E. Gettys became the first Canadians to write a sociology textbook (Dawson & Gettys, 1948). The text was an instant success, adopted by over 150 colleges and universities across North America within a year. While there was not a great deal of Canadian content, it helped legitimize the study and practice of sociology in Canada.

Another figure vital to the development of sociology at McGill was **Everett C. Hughes** (1897–1983). Like Dawson a graduate of the University of Chicago, the Ohio-born Hughes joined the sociology department at McGill in 1927. Hughes was a firm believer in community research. While at McGill, Hughes focused on the "ethnic division of labour," a situation that enabled English Canadians to rise above French Canadians in large companies, creating a disparity that he wished to correct. Out of this research came *French Canada in Transition* (1943). By the time the landmark study was published, Hughes had already returned to the States to take a position in the faculty of his alma mater.

Horace Miner (1912–1993) was another American sociologist who put the study of French Canada at the forefront of Canadian sociology. As a graduate student at Chicago, he came to Quebec to study the parish of St Denis. His book *St Denis: A French-Canadian Parish* (1939) shows the blurred distinction between sociology and anthropology in Canada. His

McCord Museum

What kind of work do you think is being performed at this Montreal office c. 1920? Are the people you see here more likely to be anglophones or francophones?

work is best described as an **ethnography**, a study of a community based on extensive fieldwork, whose primary research activities include direct observation of and interaction with the people observed. Ethnography is the main research method used in social anthropology. Miner described the rural peasants and farmers of his study as a **folk society**, following the model of University of Chicago anthropologist Robert Redfield, who coined the term. The close connection between sociology and anthropology can still be seen in Canadian universities where the two disciplines are joined in the same department.

University of Toronto: Harold Innis and S.D. Clark

Around the same time, a different sociological tradition, that of **political economy**, was beginning at the University of Toronto. Political economy is an interdisciplinary approach involving sociology, political science, economics, law, anthropology, and history. It looks primarily at the relationship between politics and the economics of the production, distribution, and consumption of goods. It is often Marxist in nature, pointing to the tensions that arise in the extraction and distribution of goods.

A Canadian pioneer in this field was **Harold Innis** (1894–1952), who joined the University of Toronto in 1920. Innis was more economic historian than sociologist, but his work has exerted a strong influence on Canadian sociology. He argued that the availability of *staples*—resources such as fish, animal fur, minerals, and wheat—shaped the economic and social development of Canada. I wonder what he would think of the oil projects in northern Alberta today.

Innis was also a mentor to the first person hired at the university specifically as a sociologist, **Samuel Delbert Clark** (1910–2003). Born in Alberta, S.D. Clark received his first two degrees from the University of Saskatchewan before joining the Department of Political Economy at the University of Toronto in 1938. Sociology remained a branch of that department until 1963, when it became a stand-alone department, with Clark as its chair. Summarizing

Clark's influence, sociologist Deborah Harrison wrote:

> The importance of S.D. Clark within the development of Canadian sociology is universally recognized. Clark's publications span more than forty prolific years, with at least the first fifteen occurring when almost no other sociologists were writing in Canada; he is generally acknowledged as the father of the Canadian approach to the discipline. ... For reasons of both his scholarly engagement and his articulation of a "Canadian" sociology, Clark is the most important sociologist Canada has yet produced. (Harrison, 1999)

Clark can be considered a "sociological historian": consider a selection of his chapter headings in *The Developing Canadian Community* (1962):

- The Farming–Fur-Trade Society of New France
- The Rural Village Society of the Maritimes
- The Backwoods Society of Upper Canada
- The Gold-Rush Society of British Columbia and the Yukon
- The Prairie Wheat-Farming Frontier and the New Industrial City
- The Religious Influence in Canadian Society
- The Canadian Community and the American Continental System
- History and the Sociological Method

Social Class and Ethnicity: John Porter

Fundamentally missing from the work of both Innis and Clark are the themes of class and ethnicity. These themes received their definitive treatment in what is generally recognized as the best-known work of Canadian sociology, *The Vertical Mosaic: An Analysis of Social Class and Power in Canada* (1965), by **John Porter** (1921–1979). Porter joined the faculty of Carleton University in 1949, becoming the university's first full-time appointment in sociology. The title of his book plays on the term **cultural mosaic**, a metaphor frequently used to characterize Canada's multicultural society. A mosaic is a type of artwork composed of many small tiles that lend different

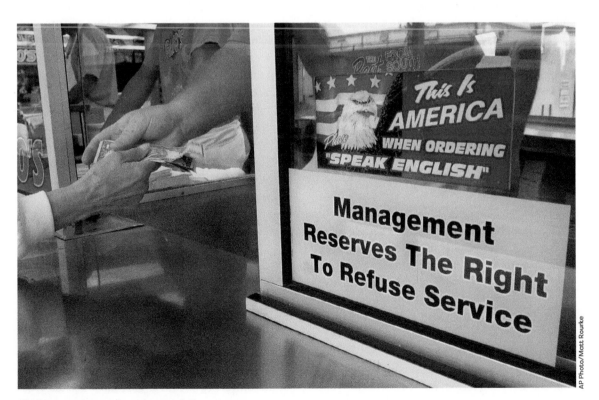

AP Photo/Matt Rourke

Melting pot or cultural mosaic?

colours to the picture. A society that is a cultural mosaic is one "in which racial, ethnic, and religious groups maintain a distinct identity, rather than being absorbed into a 'melting pot'" (Lundy & Warme, [1986]/1990, p. 583). A **melting pot** encourages the "rapid assimilation of recent immigrants into their new society" (Lundy & Warme, 1990, p. 586).

Porter coined the term **vertical mosaic** to describe the situation he observed in Canada, in which systemic discrimination produced a hierarchy of racial, ethnic, and religious groups. Keeping with the metaphor of the mosaic, we can say that the different tiles were stacked and not arranged evenly. Tiles representing white Anglo-Saxon Protestants were at the top of the hierarchy, followed by French Canadian tiles, the tiles of the more successful ethnic groups (notably Jewish, Chinese, and Italian), and finally those of everyone else, with the racially marginalized groups, notably Indigenous peoples and recent immigrants, at the bottom. Porter concluded that ethnicity was the main factor determining how the tiles were ranked.

Four Early Women Sociologists and the Writing of Gender in Canada

Early Canadian sociology was largely a male domain, and these Canadian sociologists were what we might call "big-picture" sociologists whose focus was on the whole of a society rather than on fractions within it. Consequently, their sociology took on a male gaze, because society was dominated by males and, need we say, they were men. There were, however, some outstanding exceptions, and the focus of several women sociologists helped to broaden the scope of the discipline in Canada, especially by including women as subjects worthy of sociological study.

Annie Marion MacLean

Annie Marion MacLean (c. 1870–1934) was the first Canadian woman to obtain a PhD in sociology. Born in Prince Edward Island, she received her first two degrees from Acadia University before earning her PhD at the University of Chicago. She also taught there, although, despite her excellent qualifications, in a very subordinate position.

MacLean pioneered the sociological study of working women, especially in *Wage-Earning Women* (1910), which was based on a survey of some 13,500 women. She conducted her research in department stores, in "sweat shop" factories, and among hop-pickers in rural Oregon. Though born in Canada, she was never hired by a Canadian university.

Aileen Ross

The first woman hired as a sociologist at a Canadian university was Aileen Ross (1902–1995), a Montrealer, who taught sociology at the University of Toronto for three years before joining the faculty at McGill. She earned her first degree at the London School of Economics and her MA (in 1941) and PhD (in 1950) from the University of Chicago.

Ross devoted her books to two of her foremost concerns: women and India. She published *The Hindu Family in an Urban Setting* (1962) after carrying out several years of research in India. *The Lost and the Lonely: Homeless Women in Montreal* (1982) was the first study of homeless women in Canada. Her research strategy for that study is discussed in Chapter 3.

Helen C. Abell

Alberta-born Helen C. Abell (1917–2005) has been called the founder of rural sociology in Canada. After receiving a degree in human nutrition at the University of Toronto (1941), she worked as a nutritionist for the Ontario Department of Agriculture, and then as an officer in the Canadian Women's Army Corps during World War II. She received her PhD in rural sociology (the first Canadian to do so) in 1951. She then established a rural sociology research unit in the federal Department of Agriculture. Her research, notes Jenny Kendrick,

> played an important role in identifying systematically the roles women played on the farm. This was an invaluable contribution to the policy arena, virtually forcing society and policymakers to lay aside their stereotypes of the marginal contributions of farm women to agriculture. (quoted in Eichler, 2001, p. 382)

Dorothy Smith

Dorothy Smith (1926–2022) was born in England and trained in England and the United States, where she received her doctorate in sociology from the University of California, Berkeley. Upon graduation and following a divorce, Smith took a position at the University of British Columbia, and later was associated with the University of Toronto and the

Ontario Institute for Studies in Education before returning to British Columbia. She is best known for developing two important theoretical stances: feminist **standpoint theory** (Smith, 1987), which views knowledge as developed from a particular lived position, or "standpoint," making **objectivity** impossible; and **institutional ethnography** (Smith, 2005), which challenges the need—or, indeed, the possibility—for a neutral stance in sociological research. Smith's theories were drawn from the mundanities of her own lived experience: viewing a group of apparently Indigenous Canadians from her own comfortable position in a passing train; walking her dog and determining which lawns she would allow the dog to defecate on.

The Growth of Sociology in Canada

In 1958, there were fewer than 20 sociology professors in Canada, teaching in just nine universities (Clark, 1976, p. 120). Sociology did not become a significant area of study and teaching in Canada until the 1960s and 1970s, as baby boomers entered universities and colleges. The growth of sociology during that time is astounding. Hiller and Di Luzio, for example, report that the University of Alberta "had no sociology majors in 1956–57, but a year later had nine, followed by 24 (1957–58), 44 (1959–60), and 62 (1960–61). The number of majors there reached a peak for the twentieth century at 776 in 1987" (Hiller & Di Luzio, 2001, p. 490).

During this era of growth in sociology, most of the sociologists hired to teach in Canadian postsecondary institutions were from the United States and Britain. Of those with doctorates teaching sociology and anthropology in Canada in 1967, 72 per cent had PhDs from the United States, 10 per cent from Britain, and only 6 per cent from Canada (Gallagher & Lambert, 1971, p. vii). In 1973–4, 45 per cent of the full-time sociology faculty in Canada was made up of non-Canadians (Hofley, 1992, p. 106). This should not be surprising given that only 22 doctorates in sociology were conferred at Canadian universities between 1924 and 1967 (Gallagher & Lambert, 1971, p. vi).

The lack of Canadian sociologists meant that sociology textbooks lacked a Canadian perspective. When John Hofley was hired to teach sociology at Carleton University in 1966, he saw "very little about Canada in the sociology texts that were available" (Hofley, 1992, p. 104). The 1970s saw a big movement to "Canadianize" sociology textbooks. Today most introductory sociology textbooks used in Canadian schools are either Canadian in origin or "Canadianized" versions of American textbooks.

Still missing from Canadian sociology textbooks is an adequate representation of Indigenous sociologists. In my doctoral dissertation, "Aboriginal Voices and the Politics of Representation in Canadian Sociology Textbooks" (2003), I argued that the production of Canadian introductory textbooks involved a general failure to create an Indigenous sociology, though there were Indigenous writers in the 1970s whose work could correct that flaw—Harold Cardinal, George Manuel, and Howard Adams, to name just three. I have made an effort in this book to correct that omission, but more work needs to be done. There are Canadian perspectives, not a Canadian perspective. Different voices—those of the many "visible minorities" in Canada—need to be heard.

> **What do you think?**
> How might an introductory sociology textbook written in Canada be different from a "Canadianized" one originally written in the United States?

Wrap It Up

Summary

In this chapter, you have gained a sense or overview of what sociology looks like. You've learned a bit about what my approach to writing sociology is like, and my aim of making this a textbook not like the others. You have been introduced to a couple of the main players who will strut the stage in the chapters that follow: Max Weber and his hypothesis of a "Protestant ethic" and C. Wright Mills and his contribution of "the sociological imagination." Some others you have met only in passing, but you can expect to read a lot more about them in later chapters.

In this chapter, also, you have seen how sociology relates to other disciplines and have learned something about the origins of the discipline and its spread in North America, especially through what came to be called the Chicago school, and at McGill and the University of Toronto in Canada. You have tasted some of sociology's Canadian flavours. Expect plenty more Timbits and maple syrup in the chapters to come. In the following chapters you will be introduced more formally to some of the discipline's key figures, and will discover more about the different approaches and theories that continue to drive the discipline forward.

Think Back

Questions for Critical Review

1. What is the relationship between a sociological narrative and a person's social location? Why are narratives important to the study of sociology?
2. What sociological and political explanations can you give for Quebec and Alberta residents being less supportive of legalized marijuana?
3. What case can you make for the failings of modern societies and states being attributable to people's lack of sociological imagination? Explain.
4. What are some of the factors that gave rise to the birth and growth of sociology in Europe and the United States? To what extent was sociology in Canada shaped by the same factors?
5. How did the Chicago school influence sociology in Canada?
6. List as many reasons as you can for why Chicago was especially fertile ground for sociology and its spread in North America. What Canadian city today might best fit these criteria?
7. Explain the term "vertical mosaic." Who coined it, and what situation did it apply to?

Read On

Suggested Print and Online Resources

Mary Jo Deegan, *Jane Addams and the Men of the Chicago School, 1892–1918* (New York: Transaction, 2009)
The author explores Addams's influence in America's leading sociology department.

"From Cradle to Cane: The Cost of Being a Female Consumer," www1.nyc.gov/assets/dca/downloads/pdf/partners/Study-of-Gender-Pricing-in-NYC.pdf
New York City's Department of Consumer Affairs commissioned a study of gender pricing in 800 products sold at over two dozen retailers in the Big Apple. Released in December 2015, the report documented evidence of the "pink tax" on everything from toys and children's clothing to adult apparel and personal care products.

FrontPage: *Sociology through Documentary* Film, http://sociologythroughdocumentaryfilm.pbworks .com/w/page/17194965/FrontPage
A PhD student at Hunter College and CUNY created this wiki list of sociology-themed documentaries. The films are organized by category ("Culture," "Family," "Education," and so on), so you can pick out something that suits your mood, or you can create an account to add to the list yourself.

C. Wright Mills [1916–1962], www.genordell.com/ stores/maison/CWMills.htm
This very useful website features a short profile of the eminent sociologist, as well as lists of works by and about Mills and links to online copies of some of his books and articles.

Dorothy Smith, *The Everyday World as Problematic: A Feminist Sociology* (Boston: Northeastern University Press, 1987)
This is probably the most often read work by the Canadian pioneer of standpoint theory.

Tanya Talaga, *Seven Fallen Feathers: Racism, Death, and Hard Truths in a Northern City* (Toronto: House of Anansi, 2017)
An award-winning sociological investigation into the deaths of seven Indigenous youths in Thunder Bay from 2000 to 2011, by Anishinaabe journalist Tanya Talaga.

Max Weber [1864–1920], www.sociosite.net/topics/ weber.php
Created by Dutch sociologist Albert Benschop, this site contains links to books and articles by and about Max Weber.

Mona Zang, "The Crimes of Reefer Madness," High Times, September 30, 2017, https://hightimes.com/ culture/crimes-reefer-madness
This piece discusses the history and nature of the anti-marijuana campaign.

② Thinking Sociologically
An Introduction to Theory

Reading this chapter will help you to . . .

- Think sociologically about the behaviour of people you observe interacting.
- Look for patterns in the ways people interact.
- Think about the historical and immediate social influences on people's behaviour.
- Learn more about the metalanguage of sociological terms for describing your social observations.
- Understand Durkheim's sociological concept of "normative."
- Learn Auguste Comte's concepts of "stasis" and "kinesis."
- Distinguish the *levels of analysis* in sociological studies.
- Learn how sociological theory is constructed "from the ground of observations."
- Use Martinussen's elements of social situations for constructing explanations of social events.
- Know what a social paradigm is and the three main types of sociological paradigms.
- Recognize the main forms of sociological practice and their importance in Canada.
- Learn more about sociologists' contribution to theory and to social projects in Canada.

For Starters

Doughnut Shops, Drive-Throughs, and the Value of Sociology

I am a big fan of coffee. When I go to a coffee shop, I savour the experience: I park my car, walk in, chat with the server, and enjoy the social aspect of the transaction. I try not to use a drive-through (or a "drive-thru") because that would limit my overall experience—the socializing with fellow patrons, the customer service, the ritual of surveying the assortment of doughnuts and being unable to choose the perfect one because of gluten issues. For that matter, the drive-through doesn't really save time, based on my informal observations. I often wondered why some people use it instead of parking and coming into the shop. Who would rather interact over an intercom and receive their orders through a pickup window? I long thought it was either young men too attached to their cars to leave them unattended in the parking lot, or else lazy, unfit, older men who drive everywhere rather than walk.

My opinion changed because of a student in one of my sociology classes. He carried out his own study in Newmarket, north of Toronto. He spent an hour one morning in the parking lot of the local doughnut shop, taking notes on who was using the drive-through and who was walking in through the front door. Over that period, he observed 91 people walk in and 95 people drive through. And he did notice a gender difference in the two groups, but not the one I had predicted: in terms of the counter sales, 42 of the customers were women and 49 were men, but of the drive-through patrons, 70 were women and just 25 were men. The student also observed that compared with middle-aged and older women, *young* women were much more likely—by a ratio of nearly 7 to 1—to use the drive-through. This was in stark contrast to the male drive-through customers, among whom there was a roughly 1 to 1 ratio of the two age-determined groups.

Another statistic enabled the student to come up with a hypothesis to account for the results of his research. He observed that compared with the parked cars of the walk-in clientele, the cars entering the drive-through were more likely to have child car seats in them. Further, he often identified young children among the passengers of the drive-through vehicles. The student's hypothesis was that at that hour and at that location, young mothers with infants and toddlers were significantly more likely to use the drive-through because it was easier than going through the complicated process of unbuckling their children and bringing them into the restaurant to order food and carry it back to the car. To be really convincing, his hypothesis would have to be tested for other times and locations, but it presented a compelling example of how sociology can be used to challenge assumptions (mine, in this case) and better understand the social world around us.

2.1 Introduction: Observing Social Behaviour

What has this student done that makes this observation at a doughnut shop "sociological"? At first, it seems as if all he did was count cars, drivers, and child car seats—interesting, yes, but not really worthy of notice, until you get to the next step of his thinking: the identification of *patterns of actions that are socially relevant*, such as finding that young mothers with children were more likely to drive through to get their orders. That observation led this student to think about the experience of mothers in the morning rush hour, which could then lead to thinking about the role of young mothers in childcare, the expectations Canadian society has of young mothers (to be both workers and parents), and other social factors.

The first part of learning to think sociologically is to look for patterns in how people do things in relation to others. By noticing that the drive-through customers had certain characteristics in common, our student could identify one important, socially relevant category—that of mothers of young children—which seemed to explain or predict the differences in people using the drive-through service. *But*, we didn't observe any of the other parts of this situation that I just mentioned, so how can we presume that they have anything to do with these data? It could be that instead of drive-through patrons being unfit older men, they're actually lazy younger women. Or it could be coincidence that many of those cars had car seats and children in them—it was the morning and maybe observing customers later in the day would reveal something else.

What allows us to think about how other social elements might be producing this situation is, as we saw in the previous chapter, Mills's idea of the sociological imagination. For Mills, what made sociology unique as a discipline wasn't simply the things that we chose to study, but rather *the ways in which we thought about them*. By learning how to think about the historical, the societal, and the individual elements in every situation, we can begin to see that what we do on a daily basis is not simply a matter of free will or "because we want to," but rather that forces beyond us as individuals and that operate outside of us on others—and through us—shape nearly every element of our daily lives.

What makes sociology different from other social sciences, and from merely documenting things that happen in the world, is that we want to be able to explain events in the social world in terms of factors aside from any one individual; to understand why some things matter for most or all individuals and how they shape people's lives. Ultimately, we want to assess whether or not how social events happen is "good" or "bad" for people in our society—and which ones are helpful and which ones are not helpful to the society as a whole.

2.2 Social Theory: The Paradox of Sociology

An important thing to remember is that many of the things we want to explain in the social world cannot be viewed directly by an observer. *Wait, what?* you might say. *You want me to think that we can explain and understand things that we can't see? Whatever happened to that idea from the last chapter that social science studies the development, structure, and functioning of human society?* This is one of the most interesting and challenging things about learning to think like a sociologist, and we call it "the sociological paradox." The things that we want to observe, explain, and understand *can't normally be directly observed*. The student above counted the apparent sex of drivers and whether or not there were child car seats in the cars of drivers that chose the drive-through. But is that what we are trying to learn? We really wanted to understand the social factors that made people choose to use the drive-through, but the factors we identified through noticing the patterns of behaviour could not be seen directly. There is nothing obvious about a young woman in Timmy's drive-through with kids in the car that would lead us to explain her choice to use the drive-through in terms of motherhood or the roles and expectations that our society places on mothers.

How do we arrive at sociological understanding? How can we figure out what's happening sociologically without being able to see it? One of the uses of sociological theory is *to help us to identify the historical and societal forces influencing our daily lives*. Sometimes it's helpful to think of theory as a kind of frame that helps us contain the types of things we would be looking for in a sociological study. Or we can use the metaphor of eyeglasses to talk about theory bringing certain social forces into focus. Perhaps a microscope is a better image, because it allows us to zoom in and look at things we can't see with the naked eye. The role of theory in sociology is to give us a "right logic" (Martin 2015) for figuring out the motivating forces in a social situation and how to link them to sociologically valuable ideas.

Two other aspects of sociological theory help us to explain and understand events in the social world. Social theory offers us the *kinds of questions* to ask in a study of social behaviour. Social theory also gives us a specialized language of terms and a grammar for building sociological explanations of human behaviour. You can see that other disciplines in the humanities and social sciences tend to overlap with sociology. Psychology examines individual behaviour from the standpoint of physiological and relational causes and effects. History looks at the interactions of individuals and social groups over the time of recorded information. Archaeology looks back further in time to what can be learned about individual and group behaviour from the artifacts left to us from before the time when written records existed. Medicine focuses primarily on human physiology, which is important for understanding the physical limits and possibilities for human behaviour, both individually (anatomically) and socially (epidemiologically). Students of language and literature preserve and promote the means of communication relied on by the other metalanguages, including sociology. You can think of further specialties that contribute to the sociologist's toolkit for studying and reporting on human social behaviour.

Telling It Like It Is

A Student's Point of View

You're Not Learning Sociology Like Other Sociology Students

You may have friends in other sociology courses, or know people who have taken sociology before. If you talk with them about what you're learning in this chapter, they will probably say something like, "Oh yes, I know the three or five sociological theories," and then they'll proceed to list them all out.

We're not starting there. Part of it has to do with the history of sociology, some of which you read in Chapter 1. Sociology did not take on a uniform appearance as it grew as a discipline during the nineteenth century: instead, it diversified. European and North American social thinkers had differing views of what sociology was, what it could do, and how it should be applied. Consequently, sociology developed into several different schools that varied according to their particular applications and the perspectives (historical, political-economic, feminist, and so on) of those who were using it. Over the course of the twentieth century, it became accepted wisdom among those who teach sociology that the discipline consisted of a rather fixed set of schools of thought, or viewpoints, that together described all of the sociology that was then being practised.

But the main reason is that learning about that list of three, five, or seven sociological "theories" doesn't necessarily allow you to learn about what theory is supposed to do for sociology—to explain, to understand, and to evaluate the things that happen in the social world. It can be easy, even for professional sociologists, to get trapped by these schools of thought, or what I think are better called sociological paradigms, particular ways of viewing and understanding the social world.

These paradigms, as Reynolds tells us, provide us with the guiding language, framework, and questions we can use to gain a better sense of how the world works around us (Reynolds, 2016). They give us a nice heuristic, or way of learning something for ourselves, with some core assumptions about what is relevant for building sociological explanations. But it's better to consider other things that theory is supposed to accomplish before discussing these sociological paradigms.

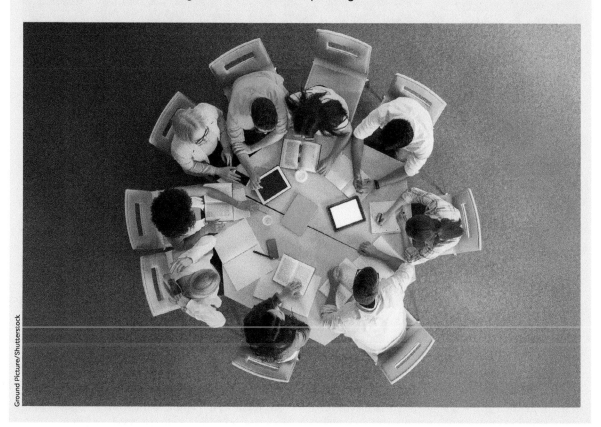

Ground Picture/Shutterstock

Bugs versus Features: Social Life as Pattern or Problem

One of the first thinkers to use the word "sociology" was Auguste Comte (France, 1798–1857), who as you saw in Table 1.2 in Chapter 1 wanted to build a social science that could be used to heal society. Growing up in the midst of a turbulent period of French history in which there were many changes in the form of government and the dominant social norms, Comte sought a way of understanding society that would help prevent the kinds of upheaval France had seen. His solution was to focus sociological eyes on two forces: *stasis*, or how social institutions were able to remain largely the same over time; and *kinesis*, how and why societies change. These two aspects of Comte's social physics made it possible, he argued, for

humans to control the future of society by enabling them to analyze the causes and potential effects of social change so they could propose solutions for keeping the peace.

What's embedded in this approach—and typical of sociology as a discipline—is what I would call a "bug versus feature" way of thinking about things. This phrase comes from the world of computer programming, in which features are things that an app is intentionally supposed to do while "bugs" are glitches or problems with the app (Feature Upvote, 2022). What an app developer would want to know is whether or not something happening in their app was there by design or a clue that things in the app are not working as intended. Another way of thinking about this is to consider Stephanie Labbé's

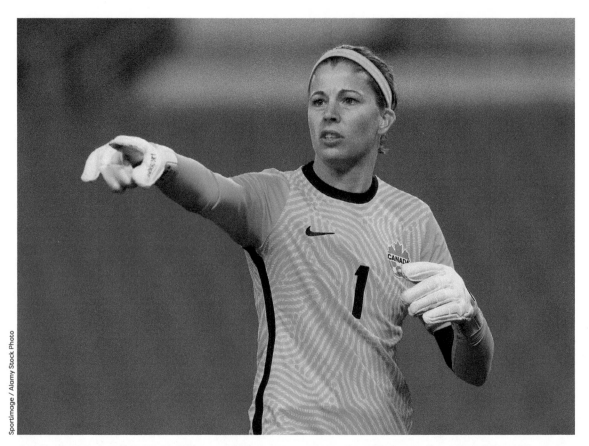

Sportimage / Alamy Stock Photo

Goalkeeper Stephanie Labbé for the Canada Women's National Team in the 2020 Tokyo Olympics

performance as goalkeeper for the Canada Women's National Team in the 2020 Tokyo Olympics gold medal soccer game. When the match went to a penalty shootout, rather than keeping a serious "game face" on, Labbé grinned at the Swedish players and team before every shot was taken on her. She went on to stop four of the six penalty kicks to help win the match and the medal for Canada. *But why smile,* she was asked? Her response: "There's no pressure on me; I'm not supposed to make saves. And if I can make a save, it's great" (Williams, 2021). For Labbé, making the save was the odd thing out, the bug; the player taking the kick is *supposed* to score (the feature). Baseball players' batting averages show the same thing: the best batters in the world only get a hit one out of every three at-bats. *That's the bug.* The strikeout and pop fly and infield groundout are the feature, what you'd normally expect.

This "bug or feature" mindset among sociologists shows in how we pursue our research studies. Some fields in sociology focus on understanding the normal operation of society—how society reproduces itself through socialization, or how cultures remain roughly the same over time even though the people

practising them are different. Other areas and theoretical perspectives in sociology—crime and deviance, for example, and social problems—study events as if they are "bugs," showing that something isn't working correctly or as it ought to be. For instance, we could imagine a sociological study where the researcher is trying to figure out how, in a society that claims all people are equal, some people do not have the same access to resources as others. And other theorists in sociology think of these same things as "features," that is, as how social life is *supposed* to work. Some scholars of poverty, for example, see poverty as the necessary and normal outcome of how our economy works and they try to understand how such a thing can remain a "feature" in our time when people are considered to be "equal" (Piven and Cloward, 1993).

Durkheim's Normative

Émile Durkheim, whom we've encountered before, was one of the early sociologists who attempted to define the "bug versus feature" approaches in sociology. In his *Rules of Sociological Method*, Durkheim identified two kinds of social phenomena or social facts: those that are "normal," average, typical, or

Science History Images / Alamy Stock Photo

Émile Durkheim

expected things that happen in a society; and those that are "pathological," pointing us toward examining the not-normal, atypical, and unexpected things that suggest societal dysfunction. Notice that Durkheim isn't attributing a *normative* value (or a claim that something is "good" or "bad") to the terms "normal" and "pathological," but rather a *statistical* one. The "normal phenomenon" is "normative," that is, it usually happens, while the pathological one is relatively rare. The phenomenon Durkheim most famously dealt with on these terms was crime. Durkheim argued that, even though we as members of society view crime as "abnormal" and "pathological," criminal acts actually fulfill very important functions in a society, most notably by unifying people to the moral code that society upholds. Crime is, to put it another way, *normal*. Yes, it's a "bad thing" for all of the affected individuals that people commit crimes; but for the society as a whole, crime isn't an abnormal "bad thing," because it reminds everyone what the rules are.

One of the keys that social theory gives us is an *orientation* to the phenomenon we want to study. By "orientation" I mean "how we approach it." Do we see this type of behaviour that we are interested in as a problem or more simply as interesting? Is it something that we think needs to be fixed? Or is it a traditional practice that needs to be resuscitated? Two different sociology students studying, for example, the so-called freedom convoy protests that occupied Ottawa in February 2022 during the COVID-19 pandemic might have completely different orientations. Geneviève might want to look for the ways in which those protests happened in order to compare them with other kinds of protests about "hot button" issues in recent years, while Samuel wants to explore the ways in which the "freedom convoy" represents a lack of social integration in Canadian society. Knowing these orientations, we can already see a couple of differences in the understandings they'll reach. They are taking different positions with regard to the "bug versus feature" issue: the first may be looking at the occupation of Ottawa as a "normal" or typical kind of "feature" in a democratic society, albeit one that disturbed the peace of a great many people; while the second is seeing the protests as a sign that there is a significant "bug" in Canada that needs to be addressed.

The theoretical position we choose will draw our attention to different aspects of Canada's history, social structures and processes, and Canadian culture as the basis of the explanation we develop. Geneviève's approach might lead her to study Canadian protest culture, or characteristics of the protestors, or, perhaps, the response of law enforcement agencies to the "freedom convoy" as compared with their response to Black Lives Matter protestors. Samuel, on the other hand, would likely head toward understanding the protestors' reasons for participating in the protest, and perhaps would lead to questions about the protestors' goals, their motivations, or some socially valued characteristics about them, such as their class position or religious background. *Both* researchers are using the sociological imagination as Mills explains it. They're *both* studying the same set of events. But by way of their respective choices of theory, Geneviève and Samuel will find different things of interest and of explanatory value in the events of the Ottawa protests. Furthermore, they are able to do so because, thanks to the complexities and vagaries of human beings and their social lives, *all of these things are present in the situation, even if they can't be directly seen.*

Finally, when choosing a theoretical stance, it is possible to imagine the presence of things that actually are not present in the situation. One of the pitfalls is assumptions so ingrained in the culture that you, too, may take them for granted, although some research would show you that they were never proven. Some of Sigmund Freud's theories about family relationships were inventions rather than observations. Some feminist viewpoints do not represent the views of all women or even a majority. It is a good idea to do preliminary research before settling on a topic and designing a project.

Being Traffic or Being In Traffic: The Levels of Analysis

What helps our ability to be able to see all of these different practices, values, and social forces at work in the same situation is a tool that sociologists call the **levels of analysis**. Tying in nicely with Mills's idea of the sociological imagination, levels of analysis give us a way of focusing on a particular set of things when observing a social situation, and are linked as well to the frame of reference we're using for our observations.

Let's return to Geneviève and Samuel and the Ottawa protests. Geneviève wants to explore the police response to the protests and to compare this with police responses to Black Lives Matter protests and the US Capitol insurrection in 2021. She has chosen her frame of reference here: how and why the police acted as they did vis-à-vis these three different groups of protestors and three different types of protests in two different countries. She isn't necessarily interested in why particular police officers acted as they did; her interests are in the way in which the organizations responded in each situation. She is interested neither in the institution of policing nor in law enforcement in Canada and the United States or how each approach came into existence. It's not that those historical things don't matter to Geneviève—they do. They just don't matter for what Geneviève is studying in her current research. The reverse of Geneviève's frame holds for Samuel, who's trying to understand the background of reasons and social contexts of different people who would go and occupy the nation's capital for three weeks. Samuel isn't going to focus on the institution of policing or police organizations in Ottawa or across Canadian history. Rather, for Samuel, the police don't matter in the research because they're only interested in the individuals who protested.

The work that Geneviève and Samuel are doing provides us with a means of discussing the levels of analysis. Samuel's research tries to capture the individual level of experience of social phenomena, which is the idea of the *micro* level of analysis. Micro-level studies are generally about individuals and small groups of people and their patterns of action or senses of self. Some of the people you will read about in this book considered themselves micro-sociologists. Jane Addams, George Herbert Mead, Charles Horton Cooley, and W.E.B. Du Bois all could be seen as working on questions about how individuals come to be social beings or members of society, the ways in which societal issues such as race or poverty affect how we think of ourselves, and even how we learn how to follow social rules. By asking sociological questions about how they came to join the Ottawa protests—the reasons they joined, the feelings they experienced, and so on—Samuel is working on questions of **subjectivity**, or a social sense of self, a typically microsociological object of study. However, if he were to discover physiological or social factors common to all of the protesters—say, an ingrained *wanderlust* from their jobs as truckers coupled with significant deafness from their constant exposure to the sounds of their vehicles' diesel engines that makes them unable to comprehend the impacts of their extremely noisy protest on the people of Ottawa—Samuel might be on to something with much wider social applications that rockets his subjective study into a *meso* or even a *macro* level of study.

Geneviève, on the other hand, isn't trying to explore individual-level phenomena but the social forces at work that produced three different kinds of police responses to three different protests. This type of study is higher on what we could call "the ladder of analysis," in part because of the *complexity* of what Geneviève is looking at—a highly organized group of people who operate in particular ways for particular socially agreed-upon purposes—and in terms of the *scale* at which she's looking (larger groups of people acting in concert, as opposed to individuals deciding to joining a group that is much less organized) (Jepperson and Meyer, 2011). However, she's not looking at policing as a kind of institution—just what these particular policing organizations did in these particular situations. We could say, then, that Geneviève is holding to a *meso*, or middle, level of analysis of groups or organizations. Had she wanted to research how the institution of policing handles protests and the factors that go into institutional decisions about police practices, then Geneviève would be working at a *macro* level of analysis, one that brings our attention to structural phenomena. (You will spend more time on the differences between organizations and institutions in Chapter 10.)

Imagine that you're driving down the highway, alone, on the way to meet up with friends, while blasting your stereo and singing poorly at the top of your lungs to one of your guilty-pleasure songs. Suddenly, the sea of red brake lights in front of you compels you to slow down and soon stop, completely crushing your groove. You sit. And sit. And scream that you have the worst luck with traffic. And sit. Eventually, after you've turned the volume on your stereo down—and yes, I know that you have done that for what are probably good social-psychological reasons—you call your friends to tell them that you are going to be late because you are "stuck in traffic." You can clearly imagine this situation by the view through your windshield and windows. It's you against the 401, and every other driver is an obstacle between you and your concert. Just above you, a couple is walking on an overpass. They saw you come to your screeching halt, start calling your friends to report you're stuck in traffic, and pound your fists against the steering wheel in frustration. During the many times they've been walking on the overpass, they've seen tens, if not hundreds, of people in shiny, metal, wheeled boxes do exactly the same thing you've just done, including the statement that they're "stuck in traffic." Because of their ability to see more of the situation than you, they're able to see the entire pattern of action, as well as the cause of the traffic jam (an accident just up ahead and over a hill, so you're unable to see it). From this couple's overhead, more distant, and more complex view, you and every other driver around you are not stuck in traffic. You *are* traffic.

Meanwhile, a traffic reporter, flying overhead at this time in a helicopter, sees all of this as well. But where the couple on the overpass sees you and each of the cars slamming on the brakes and the steering wheel out of frustration, the traffic reporter sees only a ribbon of cars on the 401, stuck behind an accident that is now sparking traffic jams on multiple streets and two additional superhighways. From the chopper, the whole highway and traffic system is blocked; this one accident has brought thousands of people to

a standstill. It's a normal Thursday evening rush hour for them—nothing out of the ordinary; and, the reporter thinks, "exactly what happens when you build a highway system and metropolitan area in such a haphazard way." In other words, where you and the other drivers see the traffic tie-up only through your individual windshields, the traffic reporter can see the entire picture—not your frustration at being late (though they certainly imagine and sympathize with it), but the causes and the consequences of this particular incident. From 500 metres up not only are you traffic, but you're also stuck in a systemic problem, one that happens nearly every day in a predictable way and that won't let up for hours—or decades.

All of these events are occurring simultaneously, and they're all true. Each of them indicates a different frame of reference, an ability to see particular bits of information about what's going on (the couple on the overpass knows more than you do), and an inability to focus on other aspects of the situation (the couple could tell you where the accident is ahead of you, but not how it's impacting the whole highway system). From your *micro*-level perspective through your windshield, you see just what's in front of or around you—the traffic you're stuck in. The couple's *meso*-level perspective provides them with more information (they can see the accident) but less detail (they see you as the driver of your car, but not as *you*, concert-goer). They see that you are traffic, just like all the other people around you.

Toronto Transit Commission advertisements along the notoriously busy Allen Road

The *macro*-level perspective of the traffic reporter affords the broadest possible view of all of the pieces of the complex puzzle that is the highway system, but with even less of the detail. The reporter doesn't know you're going to miss your musical idol, only that you're not going anywhere any time soon.

A Story Always Has a Point of View

You will have noticed that *three* things are happening in how I presented this traffic situation: the level of analysis; Mills's distinction between private troubles and public issues; and the "bug versus feature" question. At the micro level, you were screaming about "bad luck" and cursing everyone. Traffic is a bug for you. It's not supposed to happen when you have front-row centre seats. The traffic reporter in the helicopter, though, sees the city-wide traffic jam as a "feature"—traffic like this is the normal, expected, and predictable result of urban sprawl and poor decisions made by city planners that elevate automobiles over mass transit (see, among other places, Arnott and Small, 1994; Sweet, 2011). One of the things that we need to be aware of, and we'll come to this later in this chapter, is the *value* that we give analytic terms such as "normal," "pathological," "bug," or "feature." While we like to think that the social sciences can be conducted in a bias-free way, it does not mean that values do not appear in the research, analysis, and writing process but rather that we do not necessarily prejudice our findings and analyses in order to "support" an already decided-upon conclusion. Just because something is a feature of a social formation doesn't necessarily mean that it's a *good* or *beneficial* feature.

Likewise with something being a bug. For example, CEOs really like the "bug" in our economy—the pay structure of corporate executives being in both salary and stock—that allows them to earn the average annual salary of a Canadian worker in the first day and a half of the year (Benchetrit, 2023). One could easily imagine the average Canadian worker being pretty upset about this "bug."

What we've begun to do through these examples is to put together *sociological explanations* of phenomena—that is, explanations of something happening in the social world that takes into account primarily factors and forces that we consider "sociological," which happen mostly outside of individual minds. As we've seen already, our explanation contains as its starting point "a documented social regularity or pattern of stability or change" (Martinussen,

2017, p. 160). We have identified a level of distance from which we plan on studying the thing. We've begun to think about whether or not we see this pattern as being normal, beneficial, or harmful. Our goal as sociologists is to provide a clear explanation of how and why these social patterns happen in the ways that they do. As well, we hope that our one instance can be tested against other instances of this kind of social pattern so that our explanation—our *sociological theory*—actually explains what we think it explains.

Willy Martinussen has provided one of the clearest ways of thinking about the unique nature of sociological explanations. Martinussen (2017) organizes the variety of modes of sociological explanation in terms of two dimensions: the level of analysis they focus on, or the complexity of the social phenomenon being analyzed; and whether or not the explanation emphasizes *structural* aspects of the situation or the **agency** the actors have within that situation. The difference between structure and agency here has to do with whether or not we are interested in understanding the broader conditions in which something happens (structure), or the intentions of the people acting within that situation. And as with other aspects of sociology that you'll discover, a tension exists between thinking of the "social" as being something that is merely the collection of individual behaviours (known as *atomism* or *methodological individualism*), or as something that transcends us, or exists beyond us, as a kind of system (a more holistic approach). Martinussen goes on to identify four particular components of a social situation that we can turn to for clues as to what is making our object of study happen in the way that it does:

1) *Systems explanations*, which hone in on how the internal dynamics and relations of social systems impact on sociological phenomena;
2) *Communities explanations*, which look to the *relations and interactions between individuals acting in a particular position* in a social formation;
3) *Opportunities explanations*, which focus on the ways in which *groups of individuals assess and access resources*, as well as what they define as "a resource"; and
4) *Meaningful behaviours*, which see the explanatory factor in the *collection of individual actions and the motives* behind those actions.

TABLE 2.1 Types of Sociological Explanations

Type of explanation	Level of analysis	Structure-focused	Action- or intention-focused	How we think of "the social"
Systems	**Macro—systems and institutions**	Functional explanations	Linkage explanations	Social whole
Communities	**Meso—group level**	Social integration explanation	Joint/collective action explanation	
Opportunities	**Meso/micro— how individuals deal with social formation**	Social context explanation	Situation logic explanation	
Meaningful behaviour	**Micro—how individuals operate**	Adjustment explanation	Choice explanation	Sum total of individuals

Adapted from Martinussen (2017, p. 163).

Perhaps viewing them in a different format gives us a better sense of how Martinussen's ideas line up with what we have said about sociological explanations thus far (see Table 2.1).

Returning to our student sociologists, Samuel and Geneviève now have a clearer direction in which to look for evidence in their analyses of the Ottawa protests. Samuel's interest in the subjectivity of the "freedom convoy" protestors might lead toward "meaningful behaviour" explanations, requiring questions about the choices that protestors made, the motivations behind those choices, and the consequences of those choices. Geneviève's interest in comparing the three different policing responses to the Ottawa, Black Lives Matter, and US Capitol protests is more likely to direct her toward "communities" explanations. Her desire to understand the societal factors that impacted how *these* particular police departments acted in response to *these* particular protests would lend itself nicely to a joint or collective action explanation.

We've now pulled together most of the components of a sociological explanation. First, we figured out the starting point—the pattern of social actions or conduct that we've identified as being important; the level of analysis or complexity that we believe this pattern demands; whether we will think of society as simply the sum total of the individuals who make it up, or as something that exists outside of us and operates on all of us; and the kinds of places where we will look for evidence. But we're not quite at *theory*, yet. Even though we know *where* to look for

insights into why social phenomena happen as they do, we still are neither sure of *what* would constitute "evidence," nor are we sure of *how* we should interpret or analyze that evidence.

2.3 Sociological Paradigms: Umbrella Theories

While most introductory textbooks simply state a theory, we have taken the time to learn how to *build* a theory. Often, students who make their way through an introduction to sociology course latch onto the idea of "three theories" (or five, or seven) and don't necessarily get past the labels and into developing an ability to build sociological insights. Being able to work through all of the components of a sociological theory will actually make your understanding of the rest of the ideas in this book easier. You now have a way of categorizing sociological ideas in terms of whether they are looking at groups or individuals, as well as the kinds of explanatory factors sociologists look at. You have concepts of the direction you'd head in to identify the objects of your analysis or the evidence for your theory. And you have brought to light the often hidden perspective of "bug" versus "feature" in the issues you want to investigate.

A sociological theory is better thought of as a **paradigm**, which is a particular philosophical or theoretical way of thinking about the world. Thomas Kuhn, best known for his book *The Structure of*

Scientific Revolutions ([1962] 2012), gives us the core components of a paradigm:

- what is to be observed;
- the kinds of questions to be asked;
- how these questions should be structured;
- what predictions would be made by these paradigms; and
- how to interpret the results of these investigations.

What we've said so far about sociological theory aligns with these characteristics, but we have yet to deal with the issue of *interpretation*—and that is where the sociological paradigms come in. The theoretical approaches that lie at the forefront of every introduction to sociology can guide us in terms of how we interpret the things we observe. When combined with the other elements of sociological explanations that we have covered thus far, they give us the ability to actually build sociological theories to understand, explain, and evaluate the social world around us, and sometimes even to identify pathways to positive social change.

Structural Functionalism

The **structural-functionalist** approach has deep roots in sociology, going all the way back to Auguste Comte. As the name suggests, the approach contains two dimensions. *Functionalism* focuses on how social systems, in their entirety, operate and produce consequences of stability or of change. The functionalist approach was fused with *structuralism* as a way of explaining social forms and their contributions to social cohesion. It uses an *organicist*—biological—analogy for society. When nursing, medical, and physiotherapy students study anatomy and physiology, they have to learn all the different *structures* of the human body as well as the *functions* each one performs. The structural-functionalist approach treats society in a similar way: *This is the part of society we call "organized religion." This is what it does for society* . . .

You can see in Table 2.2 the early sociologists who were concerned with righting the social order. The kinds of questions that structural-functionalist theorists ask about how society works tend to be questions about social reproduction and the management of social change and of societal transformations. Their research is directed toward making sure

Auguste Comte

Historia/Shutterstock

that the humans within a society are acting in ways that society needs them to act in order to ensure its reproduction. The types of explanations it produces, therefore, will be those near to the top of Table 2.1: "functional explanations." Such explanations rely on an element of "feedback" so that the result of the phenomenon is seen as positive for society. However, "linkage explanations," which show how different institutions in society impact one another and how that process shapes the society, and "social integration explanations," that deal with how social systems produce or constrain action so that members of that society are fully integrated into it (Martinussen, 2017), are more open-ended in their values and conclusions. They are less interested in reproducing the past than in finding better ways forward.

While the structural-functionalist approach was popular for much of sociology's early history in North America, it has lost favour in recent decades. Part of the problem with structural functionalism is that it makes a number of assumptions about societal phenomena that do not necessarily align with how we have seen things work in the world since then. For example, Kingsley Davis and Wilbert E. Moore (1945), two researchers on social stratification

TABLE 2.2 Structural Functionalists and What They Study

Author (years, nationality)	Key Works	Key Contributions
Auguste Comte (1798–1857, French)	*The Course in Positivist Philosophy* *A General View of Positivism*	Aims to develop a science of society that could be used for social reconstruction.
Herbert Spencer (1820–1903, British)	*Social Statistics* *First Principles* *The Study of Sociology*	Social evolutionist who seeks to apply Darwin's theory of natural selection to human societies; coins the term "survival of the fittest."
Émile Durkheim (1858–1917, French)	*The Division of Labour in Society* *The Rules of the Sociological Method* *Suicide* *The Elementary Forms of Religious Life*	Among the first to consider society scientifically in terms of "social facts"; sees the relationship between economy, social solidarity, and ideas of morality.
Talcott Parsons (1902–1979, American)	*The Structure of Social Action* *Politics and Social Structure* *The System of Modern Societies*	Works toward a systematic and generalizable theory of social systems based on how social structures constrain social actions.
Robert Merton (1910–2003, American)	"Social Structure and Anomie" *Social Theory and Social Structure* *The Sociology of Science*	Identifies three types of functions (manifest, latent, and latent dysfunction), which helps to develop his theory of anomie and bridges functionalist and conflict paradigms.

and inequality, assumed that a society could encourage its most qualified members to pursue the most difficult and important jobs through ensuring the highest rewards for those positions, a theoretical position known as "functional necessity." However, this idea comes into direct conflict with one of the major belief systems in North America, namely the idea of "meritocracy," which is the allocation of rewards based on merit. When it comes to thinking about social inequality, we are left either questioning the ideology of meritocracy or accepting Davis and Moore's functional necessity theory. In such conflicts, over the course of time, what is proven in the real world wins the paradigm contest. Furthermore, functionalism is not good at promoting an understanding of conflict or of social change. In some ways, it actually presumes that any kind of social change is a problem that is the result of some sort of "bug," or failure of the social system to maintain itself. We might think otherwise when we consider some of the more beneficial changes that have happened in the last 100 years. We can see that

structural-functionalist approaches tend to take the most conservative interpretation of the findings of a study. When I say "conservative" in this context, I don't necessarily mean politically conservative, but rather an interpretation that will privilege the conservation of the existing social order and treat other changes as unnecessary bugs. Such an attitude can also influence a political position, of course.

Symbolic Interactionist Paradigms

Symbolic interactionism is an approach that looks at the meaning or "symbolism" of our daily social interactions and the ways in which we communicate these interactions that produce or reproduce the social order. Max Weber was one of the first sociologists to examine how the meanings of actions and interactions related to social institutions. He defined the most fundamental concept of his sociological approach, the "social action," as behaviour that is oriented to, or wishing to express some meaning toward, the conduct of others, whether in the past, the present, or the future (Weber, 1962). Because social

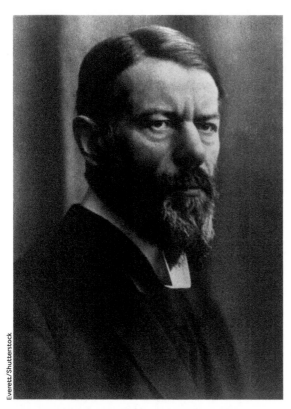

Everett/Shutterstock

Max Weber

action involves subjective or personal elements, Weber argues that a special kind of interpretive analysis, which he called *Verstehen* or "deep understanding," is needed to be able to analyze behaviour, though it needs to be tempered with a mental "distancing" approach, so that sociology becomes for him "the objective study of subjective phenomena." **Georg Simmel**, a student of Weber's, examined the ways in which particular styles of fashion and architecture operated as expressions of how groups of people envisioned themselves as "members of a society." He took this granular level of analysis to every type of person in the society.

Later sociological thinkers we consider in this paradigm include **George Herbert Mead** (1863–1931), who examined the way the individual self is constructed as we interact with others and how the self allows us to take on social roles, reflect on ourselves, and internalize social expectations. **Herbert Blumer** (1900–1987), a pupil of Mead's, coined the term "symbolic interaction." He (1969) argues that social systems are simply abstractions that do not exist independently of individual relations and interactions. In other words, social systems (friendship patterns,

education, the economy, etc.) are simply by-products of our personal dealings with one another.

While structural-functionalist paradigms are almost always **macrosociological** in nature, as they focus on society-wide mechanisms, symbolic-interactionist paradigms are much more interested how individuals become social creatures (or develop their subjectivity), how they produce, reproduce, and change social institutions through their interactions, and how they make meaning out of the world. The forms of explanation that thinkers in this paradigm build usually focus on explanatory factors that have to do with *individual choices* and adjustments to situations, the *contexts* that people find themselves in, and the *kinds of logic* they use to make sense of and to make choices within those situations. The questions that symbolic interactionists generally ask, as you might expect, are those relating to the production, transmission, usage, and implications of particular kinds of *symbols*. And as this paradigm is concerned with what goes into the relationship between social orders, meaning systems, and individual and group interactions, symbolic-interactionist sociologists do not necessarily take one position or the other with regard to the "bug versus feature" question—which means that unlike structural functionalists (and the conflict-oriented paradigm we will discuss next), symbolic interactionists can take *either* "bug" positions, "(good) feature" positions, *or* a "(bad) feature" stance with regard to the object of their study. In Table 2.3, Weber appears again as an anchor: one of the early symbolic interactionists introduced in Table 1.2, and other sociologists whose work is within that same paradigm.

Conflict-Oriented Paradigms

Conflict-oriented paradigms are interested in answering questions about what we could call the "four Cs": *conflict; classifications; contestation;* and *change.* The approach is based, first, on the idea that *conflict* exists in all large societies. While this may not be an overt form of conflict such as a civil war, it does contain the idea that societies create social groupings that are in conflict with other groups. Second, conflict paradigms draw our attention to forms of social *classification,* the ways in which the institutions in a society put people in particular positions in a social order based upon some valued set of characteristics, and then allocate a variety of resources based on

TABLE 2.3 Symbolic-Interactionist Thinkers and Their Explanations

Author (years, nationality)	Key Works	Key Contributions
Max Weber (1864–1920, German)	*The Protestant Ethic and the Spirit of Capitalism* (1904–5) *Economy and Society* (1922)	Identified the ways in which meaning and belief systems could be translated into action and ultimately social institutions.
George Herbert Mead (1863–1931, American)	*Mind, Self, and Society* (1934) *The Philosophy of the Act* (1938)	Understood how the self is constructed through learning to anticipate how we will be viewed through personal exchanges with others.
Herbert Blumer (1900–1987, American)	"Race Prejudice as a Sense of Group Position" (1958) *Symbolic Interactionism: Perspective and Method* (1969) "Social Problems as Collective Behavior" (1971)	Devised the term "symbolic interaction" to examine the role of meaning in how people relate to things and others; explored how sociologists developed and studied concepts.
W.I. Thomas (1863–1947, American)	*Sex and Society: Studies in the Social Psychology of Sex* (1907) *The Child in America: Behavior Problems and Programs* (1928)	Developed with Dorothy Swaine Thomas (the first woman president of the American Sociological Association) the Thomas theorem that "if men [*sic*] define situations as real, they are real in their consequences."
Erving Goffman (1922–1982, American)	*The Presentation of Self in Everyday Life* (1956) *Asylums: Essays on the Social Situation of Mental Patients and Other Inmates* (1961)	Developed the dramaturgical perspective, understanding social interactions as if in a dramatic play; gave us the idea of the "total institution."

that classification (Bourdieu, 2019). The stress lines of these classifications tend to be factors such as sex and gender, race and ethnicity, religion, age, and class—the sociological ingredients of a group or individual social position in a social formation. **Conflict theory** is usually associated with Marxism; however, as Alan Sears (2008) points out, the basic structure of conflict theories also is the foundation for "feminist, post-modernist, anti-racist, and lesbian-gay liberationist theories" (Sears, 2008, p. 36). Third, it contends that the functions of society, as laid out in traditional structural-functionalist theory, can be *contested* or challenged based on the question, *What group does this function best serve?* Or, to put it another way, conflict paradigms argue that what might appear to be a *bug*—such as gender inequality in a society that claims to be equal—may actually be a *feature* of that society that benefits or advantages certain groups more than others. Finally, the approach

involves the assumption that society either will or should be *changed*.

Because of their emphasis on forms of social inequality, conflict-oriented paradigms also prioritize the position and perspective of those groups who are subordinated in a society, or what we might call *the subaltern*. I mentioned above that societies—or some social groups who are dominant in a society—tend to allocate or distribute resources, such as wealth, political or cultural influence, health, and even physical safety, to other groups on the basis of some characteristic that a society values, whether positively or negatively. For example, as a meritocracy, Canadian society values educational achievement as an indicator of merit. This becomes the basis for a classification structure, in which people who have a high degree of educational achievement such as one or more university degrees are positioned more favourably in a social order than those who do not.

Particular kinds of societal resources—perhaps comfortable, relatively easy jobs, a larger paycheque, or the ability to work safely at home during a global pandemic—are then distributed to people based on how they are positioned in this classification system. If we see things only from the position of those who get to control resources, then we may think that the people who get them *deserve* them. However, if we look at these structures from below, or from a subaltern standpoint as was undertaken notably by Dorothy Smith in her institutional ethnography (see "The Point Is" box), we are able to see that gaps between the reality of social phenomena and the narratives we construct to explain them can emerge—that the inequalities that appear from the top of the social order to be bugs are actually *features*.

This complacency with social structures doesn't just happen on the basis of one particular classification. As we'll see shortly, the social hierarchies based on these classification schemes very often intersect with other classification schemes to produce even more positions in that social order, which can very often have the effect of leading groups who are subordinated on the basis of different classification schemes to fight among themselves about which form of inequality is "most harmful" or "most impactful"—which, as a conflict-oriented sociologist would point out, is a very beneficial feature for the groups of people at the top of these hierarchies.

What can sometimes confuse new sociology students is that in many ways, the types of explanations and the explanatory factors that conflict-oriented sociologists study are very often the same ones that structural-functionalists would study. So, the kind of explanations that conflict theorists develop tend to be those that happen at macro levels of analysis, much like the explanatory factors that each type of sociologist looks to. The foundation of most conflict theories has to do with the structural classification of groups of people according to some set of socially valued qualities—frequently, qualities that are out of the control of the people who are being classified— such as their biological sex, the expression of their gender identity, their physiognomic characteristics such as stature and skin colour, and where they were born, for example, whether outside of Canada or on a First Nations reserve within Canada. Examples of the types of classifications that provoke these societal conflicts appear in Table 2.4.

However, it is easier for conflict-oriented sociologists also to discuss behaviours that are closer to smaller social groups and people, partly because these perspectives are less preoccupied with questions of the maintenance of the social order and more

The Point Is . . .

Dorothy Smith's Institutional Ethnography

Institutional ethnography is a relatively new method of research, based on the theories of Dorothy Smith. This research differs from traditional sociological research in that it does not reflect the view that a neutral stance is necessarily more scientific than an approach that explicitly involves "taking sides" (Campbell & Gregor, 2002, p. 48). Institutional ethnography recognizes that any organization can be seen as having two sides, each associated with a different kind of data. One side represents ruling interests: the interests of the organization, particularly its administration, and/or the interests of those who hold power in society. The data associated with this side are text-based, comprising the institution's written rules and practices.

When the workers in the institution follow these rules and practices, they are activating ruling relations: that is, they are helping to serve the needs of the organization, often at the cost of their clients and themselves. The other side of an organization is that of the informant, someone who works in the institution outside of management. The data associated with the informant's side are experiential, based on the informant's experience. Institutional ethnography recognizes a disjuncture, or separation, between the knowledge produced from the perspectives of these two sides. In pointing out this disjuncture, institutional ethnographers generate information that they hope will lead to institutional change.

TABLE 2.4 A Selection of Conflict Theorists and Their Work

Author (years, nationality)	Basis (or Bases) of Conflict in Society	Key Works	Key Contribution
Karl Marx (1818–1883, German)	class	*The German Ideology* (1846) *The Manifesto of the Communist Party* (1848, with Friedrich Engels) *Capital*, 4 volumes (1867)	Developed a historical materialist perspective, viewing social structure, culture, and change in terms of economic factors.
Jane Addams (1860–1935, American)	class, gender	*Democracy and Social Ethics* (1902) *The Spirit of Youth and the City Streets* (1909) *Twenty Years at Hull-House* (1910)	Established Hull House, a settlement house to foster independent thinking and social improvement; closely connected with the founding of sociology within the Chicago school of sociology.
Georg Simmel (1858–1918, German)	general shape of conflict	"The Sociology of Conflict" (1904) "The Expansion of the Group and the Development of Individuality" (1908) *The Philosophy of Money* (1907)	Provided a social geometry to map social forms; examined the role that conflict plays in unifying social groups
C. Wright Mills (1916–1962, American)	class	*The Power Elite* (1956) *The Causes of World War Three* (1958) *The Sociological Imagination* (1959)	One of the first public sociologists; developed concept of the "sociological imagination"; very concerned with the removal of power from everyday members of society.
W.E.B. Du Bois (1868–1963, American)	race	"The Souls of White Folk" (1920) *The Souls of Black Folk* (1930) *Black Reconstruction in America* (1935)	Demonstrated the ways in which structural inequalities based on race impacted the sense of self of those who are discriminated against; built some of the first infographics based on his research.
Paul Gilroy (b. 1956, British)	race + nation	*There Ain't No Black in the Union Jack* (1987) *Darker Than Blue: On the Moral Economies of Black Atlantic Culture* (2011)	Examines the ways in which the legacy of the Atlantic trade in enslaved persons constructs ideas of cultural membership, diasporic consciousness, and ultimately modernity itself.
Simone de Beauvoir (1908–1986, French)	gender	*An Ethics of Ambiguity* (1947) *The Second Sex* (1949)	Makes the existentialist claim that "existence precedes essence" to demonstrate how women are made "the second sex" and therefore Other in society.
Nancy Fraser (b. 1947, American)	class + gender	*Unruly Practices: Power, Discourse, and Gender in Contemporary Social Theory* (1989) *Fortunes of Feminism: From Stage-managed Capitalism to Neoliberal Crisis* (2013) *Cannibal Capitalism* (2022)	Highlights the differences between recognition justice (the recognition of difference between identities and groups) and distributive justice (emphasizing a more equitable distribution of resources).

(Continued)

TABLE 2.4 Continued

Author (years, nationality)	Basis (or Bases) of Conflict in Society	Key Works	Key Contribution
Kimberlé Crenshaw (b. 1959, American)	gender + race	"Demarginalizing the Intersection of Race and Sex: A Black Feminist Critique of Antidiscrimination Doctrine, Feminist Theory, and Antiracist Politics" (1989) *Words That Wound: Critical Race Theory, Assaultive Speech, and the First Amendment* (with Mari J. Matsuda, 1993)	Develops intersectionality as a theoretical perspective, calling us to understand forms of inequality as intersecting to position people differently within a social order; one of the first scholars to work on critical race theory.
Himani Bannerji (b. 1942, Bengali-Canadian)	class + gender + race + nation	*Dark Side of the Nation: Essays on Multiculturalism, Nationalism, Racism* (2000) *Inventing Subjects: Studies in Hegemony, Patriarchy, and Colonialism* (2002) *Demography and Democracy: Essays on Nationalism, Gender, and Ideology* (2011)	Studies the ways patriarchy and class formation operate in India and transnationally; writes on intersection of nationalism, cultural identity, and gender.
Glen Sean Coulthard (b. 1974, Yellowknives Dene, Canadian)	Indigeneity	*Red Skin, White Masks: Rejecting the Colonial Politics of Recognition* (2014) "From 'Wards of the State' to Subjects of Recognition?" (2014)	Uses anti- and postcolonial theorists to analyze the idea of state-based recognition of First Nations peoples; develops the idea of "grounded normativity."
Tanya Talaga (b. unknown, Ojibwe, Canadian)	Indigeneity	*Seven Fallen Feathers: Racism, Death, and Hard Truths in a Northern City* (2017) *All Our Relations: Indigenous Trauma in the Shadow of Colonialism* (2020)	Explores the ways Indigenous people are excluded for written narratives of colonist nations.
Frantz Fanon (1925–1961, Martiniquan)	Race + nation (anti-colonial)	*Black Skin, White Masks* (1952) *The Wretched of the Earth* (1961)	Uses psychoanalytic and socio-therapeutic techniques to understand colonialism's destruction of people's agency and humanity.
Edward Said (1935–2003, Palestinian)	nation (postcolonial)	*Orientalism* (1978) *Covering Islam: How the Media and the Experts Determine How We See the Rest of the World* (1981) *Culture and Imperialism* (1993)	Studies the ways Western culture creates false cultural representations of the Middle East; expands that analysis to describe ongoing relations between metropolitan and colonial countries.
Trinh T. Minh-Ha (b. 1952, Vietnamese)	nation + gender	*Reassemblage* (film, 1982) *Women, Native, Other: Writing Postcoloniality and Feminism* (1989)	Critiques the Western and male-centric nature of anthropological knowledge; uses oral traditions to open up ideas of who counts as a valid knower.

Author (years, nationality)	Basis (or Bases) of Conflict in Society	Key Works	Key Contribution
Adrienne Rich (1929–2012, American)	sexuality	*Of Woman Born: Motherhood as Experience and Institution* (1976) "Compulsory Heterosexuality and Lesbian Existence" (1986)	Poet and theorist who grounds her "women's liberatory" theory in the lived experiences of being a mother and a lesbian.
Michael Warner (b. 1958, American)	sexuality	*The Trouble with Normal: Sex, Politics, and the Ethics of Queer Life* (1999) *Publics and Counterpublics* (2002)	Student of the public sphere; argues that queer theory and the ethics of a queer life actively critique all social structures, not just those around heterosexuality.
Srila Roy (b. unknown, Indian)	sexuality + nation	*Remembering Revolution: Gender, Violence and Subjectivity in India's Naxalbari Movement* (2012) *Changing the Subject: Feminist and Queer Politics in Neoliberal India* (2022)	Scholar of gender, gender-based violence, queerness, and cultures of resistance in a transnational context.
Christopher Bell (1974–2009, American)	(dis)ability + race	"Introducing White Disability Studies: A Modest Proposal" (2006) *Blackness and Disability: Critical Examinations and Cultural Interventions* (2012)	Argues that mainstream disability studies is primarily the study of white bodies by white scholars.
Rosemarie Garland-Thomson (b. 1946, American)	(dis)ability + gender	*Extraordinary Bodies: Figuring Disability in American Culture and Literature* (1996) *Staring: How We Look* (2009)	One of the first disability studies scholars, treating disability as a socially marginalizing discourse instead of using a medical approach.

Note: The selection should not be taken as indicative of the breadth of scholarship in these areas. I have tried to balance them on the basis of a variety of characteristics to provide an equitable entrée into these various fields.

Karl Marx

Kimberlé Crenshaw

Tanya Talaga

concerned with how social institutions and structures normally operate to create inequalities. We can imagine, as Pierre Bourdieu does, a conflict approach to pose questions about how particular social institutions produce social contexts and situation logics for people that roughly constrain them to particular types of cultural activities, educational pursuits, and goals for living based upon their class position (Bourdieu, 1984). Bourdieu does exactly this in his book *Distinction*, where he develops a social mapping of the relationships between class positions of people based on the occupations they pursue and their cultural activities, such as musical preferences, newspapers, television shows, and types of sports and food choices, and finds that the best explanation for these types of behaviour has to do with how members of occupational groupings view themselves in relation to others ("situation logic," which also reaches into choice explanations) as well as the availability of cultural choices to people based on their economic capital (social context + adaptation + social integration explanations). The key difference between conflict paradigms and structural-functionalist thinking, then, has to do with what counts as the societal feature that's worth studying and whether that feature is positively or negatively valued. Is it what makes society remain the same—if it appears to be a good thing to be conservative in this way? Or is it that society's efforts to conserve itself have a harmful impact on people and, therefore, the structure needs to be changed?

Intersectionality

As you begin to think about these conflict-oriented paradigms, you will notice that each of these perspectives is closely connected to particular forms of inequalities, or ways in which the operation of social institutions lead to unequal outcomes for different groups of people based upon their group membership. These perspectives also are linked frequently to particular kinds of social movements dealing with these inequalities. It becomes easy, then, to slide from the theoretical perspective dealing with conflict X to the form

of inequality Y, to the social movement Z addressing them, and to think of all of these as necessarily bound up together. Feminist theoretical perspectives, for example—those built from understanding social structures from the position of certain women within them—are very often discussed at the same time as feminist social movements and as dealing only with "women's issues." It's important to be able to separate those two types of activity: the development of theory and the social activism of a movement.

A theoretical perspective can be applied to various situations, issues, and structures. For example, a class-conflict perspective can be used to study the production of mass culture, which we examine in Chapters 5 ("Culture") and 12 ("Media and Society"), and as Max Horkheimer and Theodor Adorno (2002) do. A feminist theoretical position can be focused on international migration from countries formerly colonized by Europe to the countries that colonized them (Tudor, 2018). An Indigenous perspective can be applied to studying how class identities operate in conjunction with Indigenous identities in urban settings in Canada (Peters, 2011). As you study aspects of these and other themes, you can practise applying various sociological paradigms for further study in these social areas.

Another issue to consider when thinking about conflict-oriented paradigms is the ways social conflicts can overlap or become exaggerated as they interact. Economic class position does not operate alone. It produces effects in conjunction with, say, gender and/or national origin and/or age, so that the forms of inequality observed in one model invade other inequalities, which "fractionates" the disbursement available to that particular social group. For example, consider how *gender* inequalities in *income* in a workplace are intersected by *racial classifications* so that women as a group earn 90 per cent of what men make as a group, but prejudicially racialized women as a group earn even less in relation to other women and to men. This multifactor approach to social research is called **intersectionality**, the analytic position that recognizes forms of inequality operating layer upon layer to differentially distribute advantages for and discrimination against a group of individuals based on their complex identities. You could make the analysis in terms of factors other than money. Prestige, respect, privileges, opportunities for advancement, favours, or subtleties like tones of voice, social inclusion, offers of assistance, and sharing of information can produce intersecting factors in a workplace. Moving away from the workplace to a broader social location, white, able-bodied, cisgendered heterosexual women using urban transportation and access to public buildings, for example, have a different set of experiences from physically impaired or disabled queer women who also are white. To be adequate for understanding the ways in which these forms of inequality affect groups of individuals, the theoretical stance needs to take into account how these axes (like the vectors illustrated on a graph) of inequality operate *together*. And because forms of inequality and *oppression* intersect in various ways, theories addressing those social activities can intersect as well. Sociologists can combine elements of these theoretical perspectives in a variety of ways to address the problems in the social groups they are researching.

Paradigms and Theories

Our examination of these sociological paradigms provides an overview of how sociologists have studied many of the factors contained in the vague phrase "social life." At our starting point in this chapter, we noted that the paradox of sociology is that "the social" can seem nebulous, vague, and ephemeral, perhaps too fuzzy and brief to matter. In any situation we can agree on as being "social" or having to do with "society," we could hone in on many features or factors that point to some idea of what society is. These paradigms have given us methods for sorting these factors into three broad types of social elements:

- Patterns of action that exist outside of any one individual but exert forms of social control over all people, such as how Durkheim conceptualizes social facts;
- Social interactions between people or groups of people in which meaning and interpretation occur and are transmitted through their interactions; and
- Social institutions' classification and categorizing of people that marks their involvement in social processes, which very often leads to inequalities.

Having a grasp of the kinds of factors sociologists study allows us (1) to develop an explanation and

understanding of how particular social processes or events work that we want to study further, and (2) provides some guidance as to why processes work that way and what they mean for the people involved.

The second reason for focusing on what goes into sociological theories or paradigms is to understand how sociologists explain behaviour and events. Sociologists generally do not take a *particular* individual as a starting point for figuring out what's happening around them socially. They look, instead, at many people, watching for patterns and commonalities in the ways that these social interactions occur. Doing so also involves identifying the site where these patterns of interaction take place. Now, we are equipped to examine the types of explanations sociologists develop. Table 2.1 above shows that each of these broad types of explanation—meaningful behaviour, opportunities, communities, or systems—draws our attention to different social patterns. They streamline the number of factors we have to contend with by privileging one type of phenomenon as more important than others in an analysis, whether it will be (1) meaning, (2) access to resources, (3) relationships between individuals, or (4) something systemic. Deciding on the most suitable type of explanation in a study can help us to assess whether we want to privilege the study of human individuals and their "agency"—and hence the possibility for social change; or if we prefer to analyze how a social setting stays the same.

The third reason for studying sociological paradigms brings us back to the "bug versus feature" viewpoint. Despite their individual differences, theoretical paradigms are more likely to prioritize looking for *static* aspects of a social setting or for aspects able to *change*. They have different ideas about the ability of people in that setting to change circumstances, if they knew how. Assessing whether or not a sociological phenomenon is beneficial or detrimental—for the social structure as a whole, for all the persons within it, or for some group or groupings of people—highlights the ways that people *are* the way society operates. Our assessment implicates us or makes us recognize our responsibility for how social life happens. And that awareness is the sociological imagination and the sociological endeavour.

Audiences, Intentions, and Values

Another way of thinking about sociological theory and the reason for doing sociology is to find out who sociologists do their research and write up their reports, as well as what they hope to accomplish with their research. From the foundations of the discipline, a struggle has created tension between those who want to build a science of society and those whose goal it is to effect some kind of change in society. Auguste Comte's primary goal, as influenced by the political economist Henri de Saint-Simon and by his growing up in postrevolutionary France, was to analyze and fix the societal disarray left by the French Revolution, the Terror, and the Restoration of the monarchy. While Max Weber believed that politics and science should be separate vocations (he even delivered two lectures on the dangers of crossing these endeavours), **Harriet Martineau**, Karl Marx and Friedrich Engels, Jane Addams, and even Émile Durkheim were interested in their analytic understandings of societal ills bringing about a positive form of social change.

Burawoy's Sociology Categories

A more recent way of thinking about the "who for" and "why" of sociology comes from Michael Burawoy (2004), who identified four predominant positions with regard to these questions: professional sociology, critical sociology, policy sociology, and public sociology.

Professional Sociology

Professional sociology targets the academic world of sociology departments, scholarly journals, professional associations, and conferences. The research carried out by professional sociologists typically is designed to generate very specific information, often with the aim of applying it to a particular problem or intellectual question. These articles address specific sociological questions, centring around the current key issues of gender, work, culture, and the state of sociology in Canada. Written in technical or specialized language, they target an academic or professional readership, but can usually be read by interested students. The primary goal of professional sociology is the development of a scientific understanding of a social phenomenon, and the development of scientific theories to explain those phenomena that other sociologists can test. They may be very interested neither in having their research make an impact outside of universities nor in being explicit about the "bug versus feature" question, except insofar as it would frame their specific research question.

sirtravelalot/Shutterstock

Critical Sociology

According to Burawoy (2004), *critical sociology* is mainly to be "the conscience of professional sociology." It performs this role in two ways:

> Critical sociology reminds professional sociology . . . of its value premises and its guiding questions. It also proposes alternative foundations upon which to erect sociological research. In other words, critical sociology is critical in two senses, first in bringing professional sociology into alignment with its historical mission and second in shifting the direction of that mission. (Burawoy, 2004)

Critical sociology, then, addresses the same audience as professional sociology does, but with a different purpose. Its aim is to make sure that professional sociologists do not lose sight of the goals of sociological inquiry, specifically to bring about meaningful social change. To that end, critical sociologists might use the scientific findings developed by professional sociologists in order to highlight some kind of societal problem, flaw, or bug/feature that needs to be addressed, understood, and explained. As you might imagine, the majority of critical sociologists tend to work within conflict-oriented paradigms because these approaches are explicitly value-oriented, whereas professional sociologists can come from the other two main paradigms, in part because they do not have such a reliance on a normative evaluation of the findings.

Policy Sociology

Policy sociology generates sociological data for governments and large corporations, to be used in developing laws, rules, and long- and short-term plans. Education, health, and social welfare are three main areas that policy sociology serves, but they are by no means the only ones. For example, a government might commission a study on crime prevention to see whether tougher sentences or better rehabilitation programs are more likely to reduce the rate of criminals reoffending. Not all works of policy sociology are initiated by government lawmakers. Think tanks are policy organizations that try to bring about social change by persuading governments to adopt or to amend certain laws. The right-wing Fraser Institute and the left-leaning Broadbent Institute are examples of two such think tanks that commission studies to generate findings that support their lobbying efforts.

Public Sociology

Finally, and possibly the most important category of sociological work, is **public sociology**, which addresses an audience apart from the academic world of colleges and universities or the political establishment. Herbert Gans (1989) has identified three key traits of public sociologists:

> One is their ability to discuss even sociological concepts and theories in the English of the college-educated reader. . . . Their second trait is the breadth of their sociological interests, which covers much of society even if their research is restricted to a few fields. That breadth also extends to their conception of sociology, which extends beyond research reporting to commentary and in many cases social criticism. . . . Their work is intellectual as well as scientific. A third, not unrelated, trait is the ability to avoid the pitfalls of undue professionalism. (Gans, 1988, p. 7)

By "undue professionalism" Gans is referring to professional sociology's overly cautious style, its tendency to footnote almost everything, and its inclination to bury analysis in statistics—or as C. Wright Mills, perhaps the quintessential public sociologist, more pungently put it, not characterized by "statistical stuff and heavy-duty theoretical bullshit." Instead, their goal is to contribute to public discussions and debates about policies, social forces, and other important issues, so that members of the general public can contribute to collective decision-making processes in a more informed manner.

Of course, none of these "faces" of sociology is completely separate from the others. The German sociologists Max Horkheimer and Theodor Adorno, for example, generally looked down on professional sociology as merely reproducing the status quo. But they also had to turn to professional sociological findings to have the data they needed to be able to explain particular societal problems and identify paths for social change. Policy sociologists have at

What do _you_ think?

What different "faces" of sociology have you encountered in your community? Do you know people who interact with researchers or with "case workers" for a municipality or institution? Are those jobs you have considered preparing for?

least a segment of the public in mind when they produce their analyses. As we see in Chapter 15 on the environment and climate change, they also need to make sure that their research meets the scientific standards of environmental scientists as well as of professional sociologists. Critical sociologists very often worry about reaching their publics, about having any kind of policy-related impact, and about being taken seriously as "scientific" sociologists. We should focus, therefore, on the reasons that motivate sociologists to pursue their research and the values they see their research as embodying. The values with which they imbue their work and the purposes to which they pursue their research can give us a further piece of the puzzle of figuring out their theoretical approach and goals.

Wrap It Up

Summary

In this chapter, we have come to see how sociology is a habit of mind or form of imagination (to use Mills's term) that can be used to build a particular kind of understanding of the world around us and that it differs from those perspectives on human behaviour that one finds in other social science disciplines. Sociologists look to social interactions to understand how society functions. One of the core concerns of the discipline, since the days of Auguste Comte, has been to assess whether or not society _ought_ to function in those ways. Deep at the heart of the sociological imagination is both an acceptance of the responsibility human beings have for how they live with and relate to other human beings, _and_ a firm belief in the fundamental value that knowledge about how the world works can empower human beings to improve that world. And while that hasn't always been the case in human history, it does give us an opportunity to improve the world if we choose that path forward.

Think Back

Questions for Critical Review

1. Name three historical and four contemporary influences on your parent's choice of habitation in Canada or in whatever country they happen to be living. Use your sociological imagination to compare their choices with the historical and contemporary influences on the choices of people who live where your parents would not or could not consider living.
2. Explain Durkheim's concept of "normative." Describe three social situations in your life that are "normative" for other Canadians your age.
3. When do the rules behind "normative" values for crime need to be changed? (Hint: the laws regarding marijuana use and possession have been changed within your lifetime.) How would you design a sociological study to prove a law needs to be changed in those social circumstances?
4. Much is said about "feminist" viewpoints on certain kinds of "normative" social behaviour. Does something need to be said about masculinist viewpoints on other kinds of "normative" social behaviour, such as, for example, child custody following a divorce?
5. If you were to earn a degree in sociology, which of the four specialties would you like to work in and why? Explain how at least three intersecting social forces are acting on you to contribute to your choice.
6. Make a list of seven social problems you feel you know something about through your personal experience or reading, including problems related specifically to both urban and

rural Canadians. Arrange these in order of your idea of the urgency to address and solve them. Then, arrange them in the order of how you think they actually are being addressed and solved. Find out if sociologists are actively involved in solving any of these problems.

Read On

Suggested Print and Online Resources

Jenna Benchetrit, "By 9:43 a.m., Canada's Richest CEOs Have Already Earned the Average Worker's Annual Salary," *CBC News*, January 3, 2023, https://www.cbc.ca/news/business/canada-richest-ceo-average-salary-1.6701407 and "Top CEOs Raked in Average Worker's Salary Before Noon Tuesday" (video), *The National*, https://www.cbc.ca/player/play/2157803075862.

Émile Durkheim, *The Rules of Sociological Method*. Steven Lukes (ed.) (New York: Free Press, 1982)
Durkheim's classic work, first published in 1895, in which he elucidates the significance of "social facts" and, essentially, tells us as sociologists and as humans how to go about our business.

The Durkheim Pages, http://durkheim.uchicago.edu/
Created by University of Illinois historian and sociologist Robert Alun Jones, this site contains abundant information on the French sociologist, including a biography, summaries of some of his works, and a glossary of terms important to understanding Durkheim's work, which we will encounter throughout this book.

Feature Upvote. "Bug vs Feature: What's the Difference and Which to Prioritise?" Feature Upvote blog (2022, last updated May 9), https://featureupvote.com/blog/bug-vs-feature/.

Willy Martinussen, "Explanatory Practices in Sociology: An Overview," in Peter Sohlberg and Håkon Leiulfsrud (eds.), *Theory in Action: Theoretical Constructionism*, pp. 160–79. (Leiden and Boston: Brill, 2017)
A useful approach to understanding social situations.

Doing Sociology
Social Research Methods

Reading this chapter will help you to . . .

- Articulate the difference between fact, theory, and hypothesis.
- Understand the role of the scientific method in social science research.
- Name some strengths and limitations of insider and outsider perspectives.
- Distinguish between qualitative and quantitative social research.
- Outline the value of narratives to sociological research.
- State the significance of operational definitions in quantitative research.
- Recognize and give examples of spurious reasoning.
- Explain why care must be taken when you use statistics.
- Respect the importance of treating research subjects ethically.

For Starters

Fact, Theory, Hypothesis, and Wondering Why People Speed Up When I Pass Them

It's easier to observe than it is to explain. I can observe people speeding up on the highway when I pass them, but I can't really explain why they do it. Is it because the bee-like buzz of my car's engine wakes them up from a semi-sleeping state? Or is it their competitive spirit that awakens when I—an aging hippie in a Toyota Corolla—pass them in their shiny, high-priced, high-powered vehicles?

That people speed up when I pass them is a **fact**: an observation that, as far as can be known, is true. It does not happen all the time. I have observed it often enough to call it at least a tentative fact. But if I want to use important qualifiers such as "almost all of the time," or "most of the time," or the easier to prove "often," then I have to find a way to quantify this fact—for example, by saying: "I passed 100 vehicles, and 37 were observed to speed up." I should also be more specific about the situation involved by adding "on Highway 50, northwest of Toronto"; "while driving in the slow lane, passing someone who is in the passing lane"; "commuting from work, travelling north around four o'clock." This is how I quantify and qualify my fact: by giving details about how often it occurs and under what conditions.

Now I need a **theory**. A theory is an attempt to explain a fact or observed phenomenon. My theory of why people speed up when I pass them is that I make them aware that they are travelling more slowly than they thought they were. My theory becomes a **hypothesis** when I set out to verify it by providing some kind of concrete test of its validity. What kind of test can I provide? Obviously I can't pull people over on the highway and

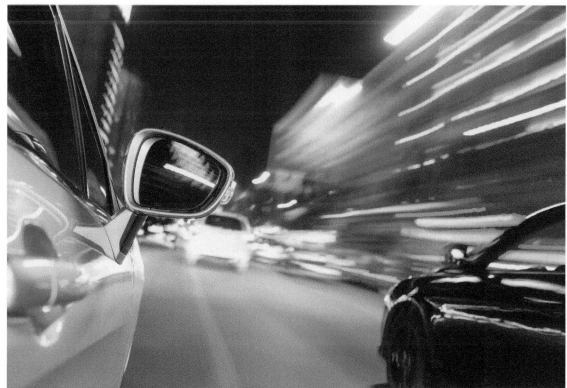

ask them why they just sped up when I passed them. However, I could develop a questionnaire for people who use that highway. First, I might ask a question such as, "Do you frequently speed up when people pass you on a highway?" I might follow up with a multiple-choice question such as the following:

What is your best explanation for speeding up when people pass you on a highway?

a) Being passed makes me realize that I am driving slower than I thought.
b) I do not like people passing me.
c) I am very competitive.
d) Other (explain): _____. (e.g., I use the highway to re-create my favourite movie scenes from *The Fast and the Furious*.)

Then I would proceed to test the hypothesis.

3.1 Introduction: Research Methodology Is No Joking Matter

Nothing is more contentious in sociology than **research methodology**, the system of methods a researcher uses to gather data on a particular question. There's a running joke:

(*Q*) How many sociologists does it take to change a light bulb?

(*A*) Twenty: one to change the light bulb and nineteen to challenge that person's methodology.

I didn't say it was a *funny* joke. The point is, there is no single best way to do sociological research. In fact, researchers often combine several research methods in their work.

In this chapter we'll take a look at some of the different methods used in sociological research, pointing out the pluses and pitfalls of each one. We begin, though, with a few comments about the history of sociology research and some challenges to be aware of.

3.2 How Do You Know That? Generating Knowledge in the Social Sciences

A question I have repeatedly asked my students—and one that I encourage them to ask me—is simply, *How do you know that?* It can sound confrontational. But in an age of "alternative facts" and the notion that a 9 could easily be a 6 if you just looked at it differently,

it is an important way to distinguish sociological fact from ill-formed opinion.

Here's an example. Several years ago a friend of mine asserted that "all Americans love guns." In Canada we can sometimes be a little smug and self-righteous when it comes to discussing our southern neighbours' attitudes to gun control and gun ownership. In this case, my friend was off base, and I knew it.

How do you know that? I challenged.

"Just look at the news," he replied. But "the news" over-communicates (to borrow a phrase from Erving Goffman) certain events, making them seem more common than they actually are.

How do *I* know my friend's declaration was false? I have my own anecdotal evidence, based on discussions I have had with a good number of Americans who do not love guns, but I also came to the conversation armed (sorry) with statistics. Drawing on a Pew Research Center survey (2016), I could claim that as of August 2016, only 52 per cent of Americans believed it was more important to protect the right to own guns than to control gun ownership. Moreover, certain groups prioritized gun control over gun rights more than others:

- women (54 per cent) over men (37 per cent)
- Hispanics (67 per cent) and Blacks (65 per cent) over whites (37 per cent)
- liberals (70 per cent) over conservatives (29 per cent)
- urban residents (59 per cent) over rural residents (29 per cent).

Of course, such poll results vary depending on current events, such as the school shooting at Uvalde, Texas, in 2022, but they have remained relatively stable in recent years, with many people supporting gun control. An April 2021 *Washington Post*–ABC News poll, for example, found that 50 per cent support new laws to curb gun violence while 43 per cent said protecting gun rights is a greater priority (Guskin & Clement, 2021). These statistics come from just one research company and from news organization polling, and as we shall see, not all statistics are created equal, but thanks to these findings my opinion on this matter is more fact-based, and therefore is a position with more truth value.

A related question concerns the distinction between "many" and "most." Students of mine over the years have seen the dreaded stroke of the red pen crossing out the *most* in an exam paper or essay and replacing it with a *many*. Why? *Many* is easily observed, and is difficult to challenge. *Most* is a statistical statement, and usually requires some kind of numbers behind it. In classroom discussions, I have often challenged a student who says "most" with the question, *How do you know that it is "most"?* It can be a nasty question, and it may sound picky, but sociology is, after all, a social science, and it must be held to scientific standards of evidence or it loses credibility.

The Scientific Method

As a social science, sociology employs the **scientific method**, a series of steps leading to proof. A first step is observation, which involves noticing a repeated action or situation. Cars in the fast lane will speed up when I pass them: that is an example of an observation. Here is another example, which I touched on briefly in Chapter 1.

At the college where I worked, I frequently taught the introductory sociology course to nursing students. It was a required course for them, as it should be, since we expect nurses to treat patients as social beings, not just bodies.

The first thing I would observe—and it was obvious—was the gender imbalance in the classroom. The vast majority of the students were female. This observation was expected, and would be easily proved by a simple head count. The next observation concerning gender involved the social characteristics of the male students. When compared with female students, the male students were more often older than the typical college student. I also observed that the male students were more likely to speak with a non–North American accent, usually eastern European. (I was often able to confirm this

observation in speaking with them, since they would tell me something of their personal history.)

So, I had observed a pattern of behaviour, which led me to a question: How does the background of male nursing students differ from the background of female nursing students? This question is important because it helps to define the hypothesis, or the prediction we make about what we have observed. In this case, my hypothesis was that male nursing students in my North American classroom are generally older and more likely to be of eastern European background than are female nursing students. Had I been engaged in a formal sociological study of the subject, I would have needed to prove the hypothesis by generating statistics on both male and female nursing students over, probably, a 10-year period at least. I should also have consulted the sociological literature to see whether anyone had already written on the subject.

Let's assume I had been able to generate enough data to substantiate my hypothesis. I would now have been prepared to answer the question *How do you know that?* should anyone have challenged my hypothesis. But if I were engaged in a formal study, I would have gone on to the next step in the scientific method: theory. A theory is not an observation but an explanation, and it is more difficult to validate than an observation is. Think about how easily we make casual observations with respect to other humans. Girls talk more than boys do. Boys are more aggressive than girls are. Women in their thirties who are named Jennifer are often involved with yoga (personal observation). Gathering data to prove our observations is hard, but explaining our observations—and testing that explanation—is even more difficult.

In the case of my sociological look at male nursing students, I do have a theory: I believe there is a strong social factor that keeps young men born and raised in North America from wanting to become nurses. I think a strong association exists in the minds of many (you'll notice I didn't say most) North Americans between male nurses and femininity. It is an association that is reflected in and perpetuated by film and television representations of male nurses. As mentioned in Chapter 1, Ben Stiller's character in *Meet the Parents* (2000) and *Meet the Fockers* (2004) is a male nurse named Gaylord, who is teased by his in-laws for his "sissy" career choice.

Quick Hits

Steps in the Scientific Method

My doctor's office is next door to a large, fancy coffee shop, where people often sit with their laptops. The same people who are there when I go into my doctor's building are usually there when I leave. Are they working? Are they looking for work? Are they just passing time with social media? How much time do they spend there? Does length of time relate to seriousness of purpose? Let's apply the scientific method to this situation.

1	**Make an observation**	We notice that patrons of a coffee shop sit for long periods with their laptops.
2	**Identify a research question**	We articulate the main question we are trying to answer. It could be *What percentage of patrons use laptops at the coffee shop?* or *What is the main reason people use laptops at the coffee shop?*
3	**Conduct background research**	We need to see if anyone has already investigated this situation. If so, their findings might help us refine our research question, or we might see if our own experiment replicates their findings. If our experiment records something different, we should attempt to explain it in terms of possible social differences between our group and the group in their study.
4	**Formulate a hypothesis**	Here we come up with a prediction that we wish to test. It is a tentative answer to our research question. It could be *25 per cent of patrons at our coffee shop use laptops* or *Length of time spent in the coffee shop correlates with the seriousness of their laptop activity.*
5	**Select a research design**	How will we test our hypothesis? We could sit in the coffee shop from 8 a.m. to 5 p.m. and count how many people use their laptops and for how long. We could ask some of the people with laptops what they're doing, or we could try peeking at their screens to avoid having to ask them, but this would be performing research without their consent, which is unethical (as we will see later in the chapter).
6	**Gather data**	We have selected a research design to test our hypothesis, and now we can carry out our research.
7	**Analyze data**	After we have completed our experiment, we summarize the results to see if they confirm the prediction we made with our hypothesis. Were we right? Were we close? Were we way off base?
8a	**Revise hypothesis** **or**	If our results do not confirm the prediction we made, we need to go back to step 4 and revise our hypothesis, performing more research until we get results that align with what we predicted.
8b	**Present results**	Once we have results that confirm our hypothesis, we can write them up and share them with other sociologists who may find our research useful.

Our research may uncover a group of reluctant freelance workers who do not have the infrastructure—the office space and internet access—to work from home; they spend long hours at the coffee shop because it is the only place where they can do work. Or it may show us a group of people who stop in at the coffee shop to check social media on their way from one activity to another. Either way, our findings should help us formulate some theories about the situation and open up avenues for further research. As you read about the methods described throughout this chapter, try to imagine how each might be used to investigate this example.

A 2014 study published in the *Journal of Advanced Nursing* provides more evidence to substantiate this theory. The study found that male nurses on American TV "were often subject to questions about their choice of career, masculinity, and sexuality, and their role [was] usually reduced to that of prop, minority spokesperson, or source of comedy" (Weaver, Ferguson, Wilbourn, & Salamonson, 2014). The researchers note that even the programs that apparently set out to challenge misconceptions about men in nursing actually "reinforced stereotypes in more implicit ways."

This research doesn't really prove my theory; it merely gives it some weight. In other cases, research findings may cause us to re-evaluate or even discard our theory. In this way, the scientific method is a cycle in which theories are proposed, tested, revised, and retested many times over, with each step generating a new understanding of the research topic and bringing us closer to truth.

Social Science Debate #1: Insider versus Outsider Perspectives

The French philosopher **Auguste Comte** (1798–1857) coined the word "sociology" and established the discipline as a social science. Comte's sociology was rooted in **positivism**, a belief that the social sciences could be studied using the methods of the natural sciences, namely experiment, measurement, and systematic observation—in other words, the steps that make up the scientific method (Comte, 1853, 1877). Positivism also assumes that the supposed objectivity of these methods can be applied just as well to the social sciences with no accommodation made for the biases of the social scientist.

Although the positivist mode of thinking had a long run, many sociologists today do not believe it is possible for an "outsider" to study a group with complete objectivity. Indeed, one way to contrast the different methods of sociology research is to look at how researchers treat **insider** and **outsider perspectives**. In Comte's view, the outsider was the "expert" and occupied a privileged position over the subjects of study. Most of sociology's history reflects this privileging of the outsider perspective. Of the four audience-based types of sociology discussed in Chapter 1—professional, critical, policy-based, and public—policy sociology is the one most likely to reflect the outside expert ideal.

By contrast, critical sociology, particularly feminist sociology, rates the insider view highly while questioning the outsider's presumed objectivity. Dorothy Smith's standpoint theory, also introduced in the last chapter, states that social characteristics such as gender, race, ethnicity, age, and sexual orientation strongly condition both the questions sociologists ask and the answers they receive. **Michel Foucault**, in volume 1 of *The History of Sexuality* (1978), criticized the outsider approach in his discussion of the "sexual confession." Foucault described the sexual confession as an approach to treating sexual deviance in which the "deviant" patient admits to "impure" thoughts, fantasies, and taboo sexual practices in the presence of an "expert"—typically a doctor or psychotherapist. The people being treated provide information based on personal experience. But according to Foucault, this information is not recognized as "authentic" until it has been interpreted by an "objective" outsider expert. The subject is not allowed to have a **voice** that is heard without translation from the outsider/expert. This is how sociologically important messages get lost.

To see how an outsider perspective can be flawed, imagine yourself as a non-Indigenous sociologist studying a First Nations reserve. Taking an outsider approach, you conduct your study by looking only at statistics, covering such subjects as unemployment, housing, crime rates, and suicide. Not including the voice of the people who live on that reserve means that you will miss key elements of interpretation. First, some definitions could be problematic. Take "unemployed." Is someone "unemployed" who provides for their family by hunting, trapping, fishing, gathering plants for food and medicine, and cutting wood for home heating and cooking? Technically, yes, because supplying country food and heating is not part of the market economy—no money is earned that shows up in the statistics. Second, typical statistical surveys of Indigenous communities leave unanswered the questions about why so many people choose to live on reserves when there is so much more unemployment, crime, and overcrowding than in non-Native communities of comparable size. You need to hear the people's voices to answer these questions.

Brian Maracle is a Kanienkehaka (Mohawk) who left his home reserve when he was five years old but returned as an adult. *Back on the Rez: Finding*

Quick Hits

The Weaknesses of the Insider View

Have you ever been told you were too close to a situation to judge it fairly? Many of Maracle's insights come from his position as both an insider *and* an outsider. Imagine the perceptual weaknesses of an investigation of the Prime Minister's Office conducted by the prime minister or a cabinet minister. Think of how a marriage counsellor can see the flaws in a marriage that are invisible to the couple. The point is, while insider views are vital to a proper sociological understanding of a situation, a critical view often requires a certain measure of distance.

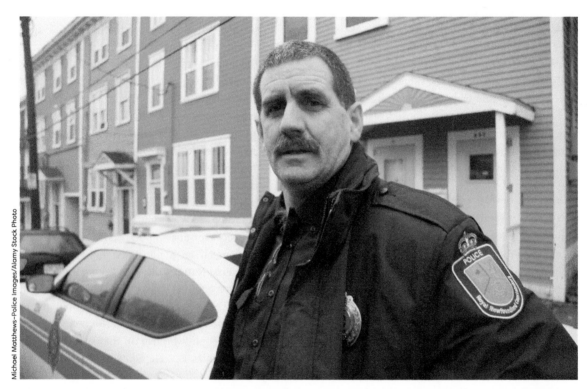

Michael Matthews–Police Images/Alamy Stock Photo

Do you find the sight of a police officer on your street comforting or alarming? Your perspective is likely to be shaped by your age, your race, your class, sex, sexual orientation, and other social characteristics. How would you overcome this challenge as an outsider sociologist studying the relationship between the police and a particular community?

What do *you* think?

Think of a community that you are particularly involved in—a club or team, a religious group, your college or university residence, or some other. How easily could it be studied by an outsider? Which insider voices would an outsider need to listen to in order to get an accurate picture of it? What biases would be reflected if they asked only you?

the Way Home (1996) is his account of the first year of his return to the Six Nations reserve near Brantford, Ontario. This reserve is very different from more troubled Indigenous communities—Grassy Narrows and Attawapiskat, for example—commonly described in sociology textbooks. The people of the Six Nations reserve have lived there for about 240 years, since the land was granted to them for siding with the British during the American Revolution.

In the introduction to *Back on the Rez*, Maracle points out that reserves can be considered homelands because they function as refuges from non-Indigenous society:

> The reserves mean many things. . . . On one level, these postage-stamp remnants of our original territories are nagging reminders of the echoing vastness of what we have lost. On another, they are the legacy and bastion of our being. They are a refuge, a prison, a madhouse, a fortress, a birthplace, a Mecca, a resting-place, Home-Sweet-Home, Fatherland and Motherland rolled into one. (Maracle, 1996, p. 3)

Maracle writes of the importance of the reserve as the home of the Mohawk elders, who interpret past traditions and adapt them to the present. In this way, he emphasizes that the reserve is the home of Indigenous culture. However, reserves are not always a homeland or refuge to everyone. They can be places where men with physical strength and social connections can oppress women and sexually abuse children. They can be places where young people feel despair and alienation, caught between the ancient traditions that make up their heritage and the rapidly modernizing practices of a globalizing world. They can become places of high suicide rates and unspeakable tragedy, such as the stabbing deaths in September 2022 on the James Smith Cree Nation in Saskatchewan. Thus, while recognizing the importance of the insider's view in sociological research, we must remember that a range of voices have to be heard.

My position is that complete objectivity is impossible whenever one human being studies others. However, complete subjectivity can be blind. A judicious balance of insider and outsider vision is the ideal.

Social Science Debate #2: Quantitative versus Qualitative Research

Another debate in sociology concerns the relative merits of quantitative research and qualitative research. **Quantitative research** focuses on social elements that can be counted or measured, which can therefore be used to generate statistics. It often involves working with surveys, questionnaires, and polls. **Qualitative research** involves the close examination of characteristics that cannot be counted or measured. Unlike quantitative research, which is typically used to find the patterns governing whole structures or systems, communities, and so on, qualitative research may be used to study those smaller cases that don't fit into the larger model.

Proponents of quantitative research argue that a qualitative approach relies on data that are "soft," "anecdotal," or "too subjective." On the other hand, those more inclined to a qualitative approach tend to dismiss quantitative research as "number-crunching" and point out that it is not possible for humans to study other humans with complete objectivity. This debate relates to a distinction between macrosociologists, with a big-picture approach to social issues and an emphasis on statistics that help to describe large groups of people, and **microsociologists**, who are more concerned with the actions and behaviours of individuals and small groups and consequently take a qualitative approach.

So which side is better? In true twenty-first-century fashion, everyone gets a medal. Quantitative research and qualitative research both have merits, and sociologists can draw valuable insights from each. It's wrong to think that the two methods are mutually exclusive. Good quantitative researchers know that their research always has a subjective component to it and always involves choice and some personal bias; they usually acknowledge as much in the abstracts or introductory comments of their research articles. Qualitative researchers, similarly, often benefit from using quantitative data to provide some context for the cases they are focusing on.

Many researchers today embrace **triangulation**, or a **mixed-methods approach**, in which qualitative research is used to confirm or expand on the results of quantitative research, or vice versa (Gephart, 1988). For example, a researcher might poll all of the students in the sociology department to measure their level of support (on a scale from 1 to 5) for online textbooks, and then supplement those findings with open-ended interviews of a sample of the students.

We will spend the next few sections of this chapter taking a closer look at different methods of qualitative and quantitative research. We will see how they measure up and how they can be used together.

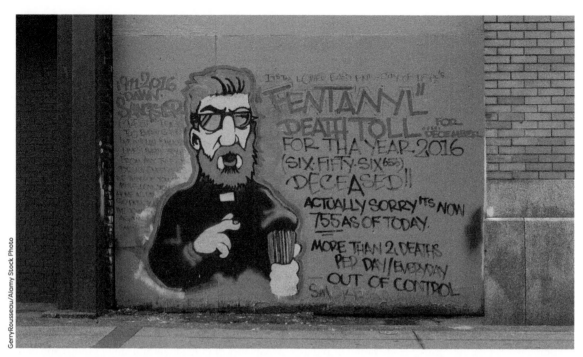

GerryRousseau/Alamy Stock Photo

Imagine you wanted to study the impact of fentanyl use on a community like Vancouver's Downtown Eastside. How would you use quantitative data in your study? What insights could qualitative data (e.g., interviewing drug users, police officers, doctors, and therapists) give you?

3.3 Qualitative Research

Qualitative research permits—often encourages—subjectivity on the part of both researcher and research subject in a way that quantitative research oriented around "hard data" does not. Among the various qualitative methods are ethnography and the **case study approach**, which differ mainly in their breadth of focus. The former typically takes a broader view by attempting to describe the entirety of a culture, while the latter adopts a narrower focus to study individual cases.

Ethnography

A classic example of the ethnographic approach in sociology is William Whyte's *Street-Corner Society: The Social Structure of an Italian Slum (1955)*. Beginning early in 1937, Whyte spent three-and-a-half years living in the neighbourhood of Boston that he called "Cornerville," following a standard research practice of assigning a fictitious name to the community studied in order to preserve the anonymity of the subjects. Whyte spent 18 months living with an Italian American family. His research methodology involved

semi-structured interviews—informal, face-to-face interviews designed to cover specific topics without the rigid structure of a questionnaire but with more structure than an open interview—and **participant observation**, which entails both observing people as an outsider would and actively participating in the various activities of the studied people's lives. Participant observation enables the researcher to achieve something resembling an insider's perspective.

Researchers engaged in ethnography typically depend as well on **informants**, insiders who act as interpreters or intermediaries while helping the researcher become accepted by the community studied. Whyte's informant was a gang leader in his late twenties who went by the name "Doc." Whyte describes his first meeting with Doc and the cooperation that was offered:

> I said that I had been interested in congested city districts in my college study but had felt very remote from them. I hoped to study the problems in such a district. I felt I could do very little as an outsider. Only if I could get to know the people and learn their

problems first-hand would I be able to gain the understanding I needed. (Whyte, 1955, p. 291)

Doc replied:

Well, any nights you want to see anything, I'll take you around. I can take you to the joints—gambling joints—I can take you around to the street corners. Just remember that you're my friend. That's all they need to know. I know these places, and, if I tell them that you're my friend, nobody will bother you. You just tell me what you want to see, and we'll arrange it. (Whyte, 1955, p. 291)

Doc and Whyte would discuss Whyte's research interests and findings to the point where Doc became "in a very real sense, a collaborator in the research" (Whyte, 1955, p. 301). Whyte learned to speak Italian so that he could talk directly to the older generation from Italy. He participated in the second generation's activities of going to "gambling joints," bowling, and playing baseball and cards. He called his work "participatory action research" because he wanted his research to lead to actions that would improve the lives of the people studied.

In Canada, Whyte's study influenced Carl Dawson's work with Prairie communities, as well as the Quebec community studies of Everett Hughes (*French Canada in Transition*, 1943) and Horace Miner (*St. Denis: A French-Canadian Parish*, 1939).

Institutional Ethnography

Institutional ethnography is a method of research based on the theories of Dorothy Smith. This differs from traditional sociological research in that it does not reflect the view that a neutral stance is necessarily more scientific than an approach that explicitly involves "taking sides" (Campbell & Gregor, 2002, p. 48).

Institutional ethnography recognizes that any organization can be seen as having two sides, each associated with a different kind of data. One side represents **ruling interests**: the interests of the organization, particularly its administration, and/or the interests of those who hold power in society. The data associated with this side are text-based, comprising the institution's written rules and practices. When the workers in the institution follow

> **What do *you* think?**
> William Whyte's *Street-Corner Society* was published without a co-author, despite the fact that Doc's involvement was instrumental to the research. What does this say about the power imbalance between research subject and researcher? Or might it say something else?

these rules and practices, they are activating **ruling relations**: that is, they are helping to serve the needs of the organization, often at the cost of their clients and themselves.

The other side of an organization is that of the informant, someone who works in the institution outside of management. The data associated with the informant's side are **experiential**. Institutional ethnography recognizes a **disjuncture**, or separation, between the knowledge produced from the perspectives of these two sides. In pointing out this disjuncture, institutional ethnographers generate information that they hope will lead to institutional change.

Schools offer a good example of the kind of organization that institutional ethnographers study. York University professor Alison Griffith asserts that teachers rely on parents (typically mothers) to get children to do the work and acquire the skills necessary to succeed at school. Campbell and Gregor refer to this reliance on parents as "downloading educational work" (2002, p. 43). This practice serves the ruling interests of boards of education and provincial governments, who can then spend less on schools and teachers. Teachers and parents, by complying with the demands of school administrators, are activating ruling relations. At the same time, they are also biasing the system in favour of students from upper- and middle-class households, whose parents are in a better position to provide the resources (including their own time and knowledge, as well as computers and high-speed internet access and a quiet study space) to best serve this end. Lower-class students are poorly served by the system, as they are more dependent on the school and its resources.

The problem is made worse in provinces like Ontario, where it is illegal for school boards to pass deficit budgets. Local boards, meeting the ruling interests of the provincial government, have been forced to consider closing pools and cutting music and athletic programs, putting more pressure for children's health and enrichment onto the parents. This creates a second disjuncture—between the provincial government and its boards—in addition to the one between boards and administrators and parents/children. This kind of information, generated through institutional ethnography, can be used to recommend improvements to the school system.

An Example of Institutional Ethnography: Aileen Ross's Research on Homeless Women in Montreal

In 1977–8, Canadian sociologist Aileen Ross engaged in pioneering sociological research in two women's shelters in Montreal, one run during the day, the other at night. Both shelters had just opened when she began her research in the summer of 1977. The methodology she chose, and her reasons for choosing it, are instructive in understanding the limits of sociological research as she saw them:

> This study began without case histories that could be analyzed in terms of the usual neat hypotheses gleaned from previous studies. One reason for this omission was that very

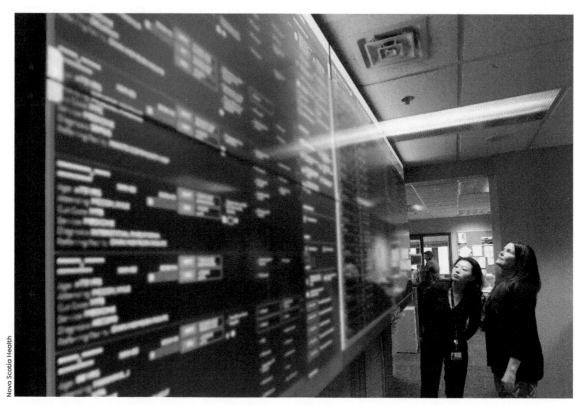

Nova Scotia Health

Nova Scotia Health implemented Canada's first province-wide care coordination centre, which uses data, health information, and available resources to deliver care efficiently and cut down on patient wait times. The hospital is a common subject for institutional ethnography, given the enormous pressure on front-line health professionals and administrators to fix problems in real time. Who in a hospital represents the ruling interests? Who is responsible for ensuring that those ruling interests are met? Who introduces innovations like the one shown here? Who benefits?

little sociological research has been done which throws light on Skid Row men, still less on homeless women. Another reason was that the staff of the day shelter held tenaciously to their basic philosophy that the women would not be questioned about themselves. . . . "Don't sit eyeball to eyeball with them. If they think the shelter is being researched, they won't come back. No questions, please, and <u>no</u> questionnaires" (Staff member).

The data were collected through careful observation of and informal interviews with, the women and through accounts of their behaviour by the staffs of the two shelters and several other shelters. Interviews also were obtained from the directors of the Women's Shelter Foundation and from many professionals, including psychiatric, medical, and other social workers. . . . The records kept at the night shelter and the log written up each night at the day shelter were other sources of information. (Ross, 1982, p. 107)

In the description of her methodology Ross notes that she gathered information not just from observations and interviews but from logs kept by the staff of the shelter. These kinds of records can be valuable to social research as they provide clues to what goes on in a person's life. Consider "Lily," one of the homeless women Aileen Ross wrote about. Lily was a 30-year-old anglophone resident of Montreal. She had held a steady job until she injured her leg skiing. During a painful recovery, she became addicted to painkillers, which led her to homelessness. Table 3.1 outlines some of her interactions with local institutions during the period of Ross's study.

> **What do *you* think?**
> 1. What can you learn from examining the record of Lily's interactions with institutions? What questions does it leave unanswered? Does it only show the negative side of her life?
> 2. In what ways can Ross's study be considered an institutional ethnography?

TABLE 3.1   Subject's Interactions with Social and State Institutions, June–September 1977

Date	Institution	Problem	Result
1977			
19 June	hospital	drugs—couldn't speak	discharged
2 July	hospital	stomach pains	discharged
6 August	night shelter	crying at door in early morning frightened, scratches and bruises	—
7 August	hospital	stoned, shaky, grave condition	discharged
19 August	night shelter	strongly medicated, couldn't stand	—
23 August	hospital	drug overdose	discharged next day
26 August	hospital	could not stand, poor respiration	discharged next day
28 August	detention centre	upset as she had to go to court	did not show in court
29 August	hospital	stomach ulcers	discharged
2 September	jail	one day for shoplifting	sent to hospital
9 September	hospital	drugs and sore legs	discharged next day
23 September	hospital	suicide attempt (set fire to room)	sent to another hospital
28 September	hospital	drug overdose	left

Nature's Charm/Shutterstock

Why might a homeless person fear being questioned by someone in a position of authority?

The Case Study Approach

British sociologist Gordon Marshall describes the case study approach as:

> [a] research design that takes as its subject a single case or a few selected examples of a social entity—such as communities, social groups, employers, events, life-histories, families, work teams, roles, or relationships—and employs a variety of methods to study them. (Marshall, 1998, p. 56)

The case study approach is often used to investigate or compare situations that are considered either very typical or very different from the norm. The approach is a key tool of policy sociology, used to identify and describe **best practices**—strategies with a proven history of achieving desired results more effectively or consistently than similar methods used in the past by a particular organization or currently by similar organizations. The case study typically begins by introducing an organization or department that exemplifies the best practices under review, before describing the practices in terms of the organization's success. The case study is often geared to finding out whether certain best practices can be applied with comparable success elsewhere.

Case Study of a Best Practice: First Nations Policing in Kitigan Zibi Anishinabeg

Located about 130 kilometres north of Ottawa, Kitigan Zibi Anishinabeg, with a registered population of 3,466 (as of April 2019), is the largest of nine communities that make up the Algonquin Nation in Quebec. The community first had its own policing services in 1981, when, like other Quebec First Nations, it began operating a community police force under the auspices of the Amerindian Police Service (the APS). The APS is usually seen as a failure by Quebec's First Nations, whose officers were typically given limited, second-class roles as "special constables." In 1985, Kitigan Zibi moved ahead of other Indigenous communities by transferring police services to its own independent force.

Following the introduction of the federal First Nations Policing Policy in April 1992, the community entered into a three-year tripartite agreement that allowed the Kitigan Zibi Police Department (KZPD) to become a fully functional force, with powers equivalent to those of any non-Indigenous force in Canada. By 2002, the KZPD had a chief of police, five full-time officers, and one part-time officer. Community satisfaction with the department's work was high: in a 2002 survey, 91 per cent of community members surveyed felt that the KZPD was the best police organization to meet the needs of the community. This compares favourably to the 55 per cent of community stakeholders who, in a First Nations Chiefs of Police Association survey, felt the self-administered police services in their communities were effective.

There are four keys to the success of the KZPD. Unfortunately, two of them cannot be replicated in most other First Nations. First, Kitigan Zibi has a very stable political environment. At the time of the study, the chief councillor of the band had been in the position for over 20 years. During that time there had been few changes in the makeup of the band council. Further, there were no apparent political factions within the community. Second, the KZPD has a reasonably harmonious relationship with the Quebec provincial police, a rarity for a First Nations force in Quebec.

Two remaining keys to the KZPD's success offer lessons for police forces operating in other First Nations. One is the strong relationship between the KZPD and the youth of the community. In 1995, the KZPD took part in a pilot project with Indigenous youths aged between 12 and 24, who were paired with police officers to ride in cruisers, observe police duties first-hand, and visit the homes of their police mentors. Commenting on the mentoring experience, one officer said, "I took great pride in seeing the barriers fall and the sense of openness that developed in our communication" (Aboriginal Policing Directorate, 1995, p. 3).

The final key is the KZPD's dedication to training. One condition of the 1992 tripartite agreement signed with federal and provincial governments was that constables already in the force would earn the basic training equivalency diploma. This would enable the officers to assume powers equal to those of any other officer in Quebec. All of the KZPD's officers successfully completed the training. The chief of police went beyond the qualifications required in the agreement, taking managerial courses for senior officers and additional courses offered at the Canadian Police College in Ottawa. When the Quebec Police Act was amended to include more training for provincial officers, the chief of police prepared a five-year forecast of the training needs of his force.

Narratives

The narrative is perhaps the purest form of the insider view. Narratives are the stories people tell about themselves, their experiences, and the others around them. They have long been part of sociology. An early Canadian example of narrative research is Aileen Ross's *Becoming a Nurse* (1961), based on her analysis—for an introductory sociology course—of 259 term papers written by nursing students between 1948 and 1959.

In spite of their history and the value of narratives to sociological inquiry, the positivism of early sociology and the discipline's emphasis on statistical evidence kept narrative study in a minor role until the late 1980s. In 1993, D.R. Maines proclaimed the growing interest in narratives among sociologists as "narrative's moment." He saw in this trend a dual focus for sociological study, aimed at both examining the narratives of the subjects of study and at the same time "viewing sociologists as narrators" (Maines, 1993, p. 17). The use of narratives in research is important because it can give voice to people whose voices have been excluded in research. Voice is the expression of *a* (not *the*) viewpoint of a particular subject that comes from occupying and experiencing a particular social location.

Consider the two narratives presented in the following boxes. Both give voice to viewpoints not often

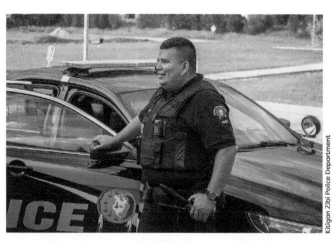

Kitigan Zibi Police Department.

Justin Petonoquot is an Algonquin police corporal and investigator with the Kitigan Zibi Police Department. What makes the KZPD a good subject for a case study? How does the study combine qualitative and quantitative research?

heard in mainstream media. In the first, a young, male, Muslim college student talks about fasting. His voice is different from the voices of other Muslims—those of young women, or of local religious leaders—but it speaks a truth because it reflects the speaker's life experience. It carries value because it gives the non-Muslim reader a sense of what it is like to be a young, male Muslim living in Canada. The second narrative provides a perspective on what it is like to be a young Palestinian Canadian woman growing up in a small suburban community in Ontario. Consider the factors shaping her *social location*, the vantage point from which she speaks: age, gender, ethnic background, nationality, the site of her upbringing, her status as a student, even the political climate at the time of writing. All contribute to her unique perspective.

What do *you* think?
Consider an issue raised in one of the two narratives in the following boxes. What further research could you do to deepen your understanding of the topic?

Content Analysis

Content analysis involves studying a set of **cultural artifacts** or events and interpreting the themes they reflect. Cultural artifacts may include children's books, billboards, novels, newspaper articles, advertisements, artwork, articles of clothing, clinical records—even textbooks. These items all have two

Telling It Like It Is

A Student's Point of View

Fasting

"Hey Moe, come join us for lunch."

"I can't, guys. I'm fasting."

"Fasting, what's that?"

This passage may be heard every year, asked by anyone and almost everyone. It bothers me to consider that the average person doesn't know what fasting for Muslims is. Fasting is an Islamic tradition practised for centuries, where a Muslim is subjected to no food or drink from sunrise to sunset. This is done to remind Muslims where we came from, to remind us that we started with nothing. It teaches us to value what we have and to value our gracious religion. There is fasting in almost every religion, yet the people who know

the basic term of fasting don't know what type of fasting Muslims commit to. Many people [I have spoken to] were shocked to hear that during Ramadan [fasting month] not only can you not eat, but you also cannot drink [from sunrise to sunset]. Many people thought that water was allowed in any fasting, but it isn't for the Muslim type of fasting. When someone asks me what fasting is for Muslims, I reply with such fatigue from saying it over and over that I simply reply, "Well, we (Muslims) basically can't eat or drink anything when the sun is up." I simply gave a quick answer because I get that question asked every year, by anyone and almost everyone.

—Mohamed Abseh

Telling It Like It Is

A Student's Point of View

Canadian by Birth, Palestinian by Culture

My name is Nadine and I am Canadian-born, but Palestinian by culture. My father was born in Palestine and my mother was born in Egypt to Palestinian refugees. Nowadays, being of Palestinian origin is quite difficult, even when you're living in a so-called multicultural nation. I guess it's not as hard for me as it has been for my parents because I am Canadian-born, and my parents came to Canada knowing little about the country. However, the difficult aspect in my life was that I grew up in a one-cultured town [the predominantly Italian Canadian town of Woodbridge, in southern Ontario] which made it extremely difficult for my brothers and I to fit in. I have never been able to have any close relationship with anyone. Why? I guess that children needed a common ground in order to establish a relationship, and not possessing the same culture as those around me made my assimilation even more difficult. Within homogeneous groups one can be easily singled out and that happened to me. Furthermore, as I grew up it became harder

for me to engage in any real relationship with boys or girls because my culture became stronger for me and as well for them, which made us even grow farther apart. Maybe it was because I didn't speak or dress like them, or because I was darker than them, it didn't matter—basically I was just different.

Entering college, it was a bit easier for me to make acquaintances, though I realized how uneducated and ignorant people could be. It was particularly difficult for me after the events of 9/11 because, automatically, the Arab world would get blamed for it and most people, ignorant as they are, believed everything that the media's propaganda had been telling them. I was in college at that time, and explaining to people my point of view was tremendously challenging. Media brainwash had its toll on the majority of those around me. Furthermore, getting into debates with individuals about what's occurring in Palestine and my views as a Palestinian was almost impossible. Right now my oppressed and displaced people who have been legitimately re-sisting occupation since 1948 are the bad guys. Maybe in a couple of years it will be another group, but for me now it's hard because I'm still singled out by my friends and the media. Maybe it would be a little bit easier if individuals would become open-minded about what goes on in the world. Then people could understand who we are and who I am. Knowledge is responsibility and to most, responsibility is a heavy burden to take. It is pretty sad what's going on in the twenty-first century is that people like me, Canadian-born, have difficulties growing up because of who they are and where they're from!

—Nadine Dahdah

distinct properties not normally found in the subjects studied using other types of qualitative methodology. First, they have a "found" quality because they are not created specifically to be studied. Second, they are *non-interactive:* no interviews are used or behaviours observed in gathering data (Reinharz, 1992, pp. 146–8). Content analysis of online material and internet-based community ethnographies comprise a fertile area for sociological research, just as this has become an important research area for investigative journalists and law enforcement in their combing the "dark web" for those involved in criminal activities such as child pornography, terrorism, and other anti-state conspiracies.

Feminist approaches to content analysis investigate the way gender is portrayed in the media, particularly as it reflects a culture of persistent **patriarchy** (male domination) and misogyny (hatred of women). At the same time, feminist analysis often has drawn in other issues, such as race and queerness.

In *Gender Advertisements* (1976), Erving Goffman undertook a content analysis of commercial pictures depicting gender in print media. The women in the magazine ads he examined were overwhelmingly shown as subordinate and submissive. The magazines, both mass media and popular culture, were selected on the basis of their availability and their circulation size. Taken together, these magazines (available in supermarkets, convenience stores, and drugstores) act as cultural objects, reflecting the social world. This relationship, however, is bi-directional: cultural objects such as magazines reflect the social world, and the social world, in turn, is influenced by cultural objects (Griswold, 1994, pp. 22–3). Popular magazines give us a snapshot of the social world and also, if we look carefully, an indication of how the social world is being constructed through mass media.

Sut Jhally (1990) argues that magazine ads are neither completely true nor completely false reflections of social reality. They are partial truths and falsehoods. Ads depicting gender do not truly or falsely represent "real" gender relations or **ritualized** gender displays. Rather, for Jhally, they are "hyper-ritualizations," exaggerations that emphasize certain aspects of gender display and de-emphasize others (1990, p. 135).

While content analysis is considered a qualitative method of research, it can often involve some quantification of the data. Elements may be systematically counted to see which ones dominate. Consider Alan J. Sofalvi's content analysis of 39 condom ads, in print and online. Affiliated with the Health Department at the State University of New York at Cortland, Sofalvi believed that his study could help high school and college educators begin a discussion about media literacy and health literacy. Underlying his study was the question of whether advertising succeeds in delivering messages about public health. To answer this question, Sofalvi looked for the benefits touted in the condom ads and tallied them up. His results are summarized in Table 3.2.

One of Sofalvi's main conclusions was that, compared with condom ads from an earlier time, the emphasis of the 39 ads he studied was decidedly more on pleasure for the two participants (a theme often presented with humour) than on disease and pregnancy prevention (topics that, frankly, aren't as funny). Only 12 ads—less than one-third of the total sample—mentioned safe sex. One reason for this, he explained, was that some American media outlets, more conservative by nature, would not air commercials addressing pregnancy prevention.

A topic that Sofalvi did not fully explore in his study was how condom ads varied in their messaging depending on the target audience—male versus

TABLE 3.2 Features or Benefits Specified in Condom Advertisements, 1997–2007

Condom feature/benefit	Number
Pleasure	26
None specified	9
Protection (unspecified)	9
Disease prevention	8
Sensitivity	6
Lubricated	5
Comfort	4
Larger size	4
Pregnancy prevention	4
Thinness	3
Strength	2
Low latex odor	1
Non-lubricated	1

Source: Sofalvi, (2008, p. 12).

female, gay versus straight, North American versus Russian or Indian, and so on. This sort of research could be carried out without too much difficulty by students with the time, inclination, and internet access to do so.

Discourse Analysis

For French theorist Michel Foucault, **discourse analysis** focuses on social power relationships. These are expressed through practices and behaviour, and, certainly, through language. There are two types of discourse analysis used by sociologists. One analyzes discourse as the term is commonly understood: that is, as a conversation, a speech, or a written text. Sociologists may examine the **discourse** found in a given ethnography, in an open-ended interview, or in a narrative. They might also focus on other kinds of "text," such as court transcripts, newspaper stories, movie trailers, and advertisements.

Another type of discourse analysis considers a broader definition of "text," going beyond individual works and authors to include large "fields" of presentation of information over a period of time, such as movies in general or in the early twenty-first century, reality shows, introductory sociology textbooks, Canadian historical writing, and so on.

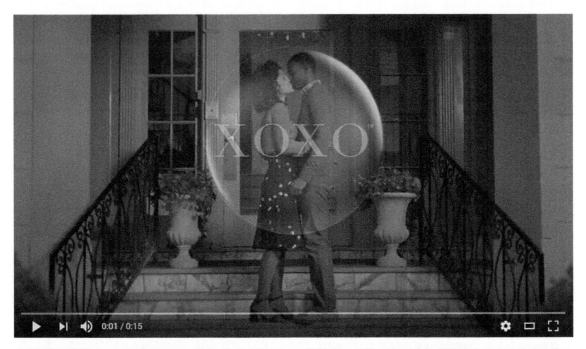

In 2017, Trojan introduced a new line of condoms marketed to women, with pretty purple packaging and a wholesome ad campaign empowering female consumers to "trust themselves" and "have the confidence to be who they want to be." Wait, aren't women interested in novelty-flavoured warming lubricants and a pleasure-enhancing configuration of riffles and dots? Why should ads targeting men and women be different when the principal aim of the product—prevention of disease and unwanted pregnancy—should be of equal importance to both sexual partners?

A "field" comprises all known discourse on a particular cultural concept or idea—"masculinity," for instance.

The role of the researcher is to examine a discourse through time and to decode it, looking at it as a way of constructing knowledge that benefits its creator. A discourse analysis could, for instance, focus on a government's messages around immigration—in ads, in speeches, in press briefings, in tweets—to understand how that discourse advances a political agenda by conditioning a segment of the voting public to view outsiders in a particular way.

In discourse analysis, **genealogy** is a method of examining the history of the second type of discourse defined above. Foucault, in his later works, used a genealogical method to trace the origins and histories of modern discourses as they collide, fragment, and adhere to other cultural practices and discourses over time. Foucault's genealogical work captures the dynamic nature of such discourses as mental illness (1961), the penal system (1975), and sexuality (1978).

Edward Said's study of Western attitudes toward Eastern culture, *Orientalism* (1979), offers another example of genealogical research. The Palestinian-born Said (1935–2003) developed the genealogy of **Orientalism**, broadly defined as a Western fascination with or romanticization of the "exotic" cultures of Asia, from Islamic societies to Pacific Rim nations, especially those societies that were colonized by European powers. For Said, Orientalism could not be studied or understood without the concept of discourse:

> My contention is that without examining Orientalism as a discourse one cannot possibly understand the enormously systematic discipline by which European culture was able to manage—and even produce—the Orient politically, sociologically, militarily, ideologically, scientifically, and imaginatively during the post-Enlightenment period. (Said, 1979, p. 3)

Orientalism, for Said, refers to "a corporate institution for dealing with the Orient—dealing with it by making statements about it, authorising views of it, describing it, by teaching it, settling it, ruling over it: in short . . . a Western style for dominating, restructuring, and having authority over the Orient" (Said, 1979, p. 3).

Mary Evans / Grenville Collins Postcard Collection

JIM WATSON/AFP/Getty Images

(*a*) **What does this 1904 postcard from Constantinople (present-day Istanbul, Turkey) tell us about how Westerners thought of "the Orient" at this time? Compare it with a more recent reflection of Orientalist thought (*b*). In each case, how does the discourse of Orientalism reflect, in Said's words, "a Western style for dominating, restructuring, and having authority over the Orient"?**

What do you think?
Now decidedly old-fashioned, "Oriental" was once the common term to describe what many people today consider "Asian." But what does "Asian" mean to you? If you're North American, it likely refers mostly to China, Japan, and Korea. If you're British, you probably associate it with India and Pakistan (countries of the former British Empire that we in Canada might refer to as "South Asian"). What countries do the terms "Southeast Asian" and "East Asian" suggest to you? What term might you use for someone from Siberia or Mongolia?

Orientalism, then, refers to the ways in which the "Orient" was, and continues to be, constructed in the western European and North American imagination. What is important to understand is that the discourse of Orientalism was created and has been revised over time to further expansionist goals of Western powers by dominating and controlling this part of the world. It also has been central in the West to the othering of and violence toward those from the Orient—from the dispossession and internment of Japanese Canadians during World War II to violence and threats of violence directed at those from the Arab/Muslim world in the wake of the 9/11 attacks on the United States, to the physical and verbal abuse faced by Chinese Canadians during the COVID-19 pandemic because of the Chinese origin of this coronavirus.

3.4 Quantitative Research

Understanding Statistics

Sociologists have mixed feelings about **statistics**, a science that, in sociology, involves the use of numbers to map social behaviour and beliefs. Statistics, some would argue, are what lend the "science" to "social science." At the same time, sociologists are also critical of other people's statistics. There are more jokes about the science of statistics than about any other kind of sociological research method—and we can prove that statistically. But here is some anecdotal evidence:

- "It shames me some to hear the statistics about us in class. The shame burns holes in whatever sympathy I may have for Indians, not my mom though."—the Indigenous protagonist of Stó:lō writer Lee Maracle's novel *Sun Dogs* (Maracle, 1992, p. 3)

- "There are three kinds of lies: lies, damned lies, and statistics."—Benjamin Disraeli, nineteenth-century British Prime Minister

- "There are two kinds of statistics: the kind you look up, and the kind you make up."—Rex Stout, twentieth-century American mystery author

- "An unsophisticated forecaster uses statistics as a drunk man uses lamp-posts—for support rather than illumination."—Andrew Lang, nineteenth- and twentieth-century Scottish folklorist, anthropologist, and poet

- "Smoking is one of the leading causes of statistics."—Fletcher Knebel, twentieth-century American journalist and author of political fiction

- "Statistician: A man who believes figures don't lie, but admits that under analysis some of them won't stand up either."—Evan Esar, *Esar's Comic Dictionary*

- "Statistics: The only science that enables different experts using the same figures to draw different conclusions."—Esar

In the sections that follow we will look at the ways that statistics can either enhance or impair good sociological research.

Measuring the Centre: The Median, the Average, and the Mean

Let's take a moment to consider that last statement above and the idea that experts can draw different conclusions from the same statistics. How is that possible? One way is by using different measures of centre to analyze the statistics. A *measure of centre* is a way of taking all of the data you have gathered on a particular subject and finding the most representative result. Two of the most common measures of centre are the median and the average. The **median** represents the number, score, or result that separates the higher half of all results from the lower half of results in a given set of data. If you have a set of five scores, in order from lowest to highest, the median will be the one in the third position. In the series 6, 8, 10, 11, 14, 16, 18, the median is 11: it is the number in the fourth position, separating the bottom three scores from the top three scores.

How is the median different from the **average**? You find the average by adding up all the scores and dividing the total by the number of scores you have. In the series above, the average would be 6 + 8 + 10 + 11 + 14 + 16 + 18 = 83 ÷ 7 = 11.9. The average is not always higher than the median. For the sequence 4, 7, 9, 11, 12, 14, 16, the median—the score in the middle—would be 11, and the average would be 10.1. Another measure of centre is the **mean**, which is usually calculated in the same way as the average. However, for weather (and other purposes), it can be determined by taking the two extremes and dividing by two. If the daily low is 0 degrees Celsius and the daily high is 10, then the daily mean is 5.

To see why this matters, let's consider an example. A small hardware store employs seven sales associates to help customers with their purchases. Two of the sales associates believe they are significantly underpaid: they both make $14.75 an hour. They pluck up the courage to talk to the store's owner, who explains that the median salary of the seven

employees is $15.00—not much more than what the two employees make. End of story? Not quite.

The two employees decide to ask their co-workers what their hourly wages are, and this is what they discover:

Employee	Hourly Wage
1	$22.50
2	$21.00
3	$19.75
4	$15.00
5	$14.75
6	$14.75
7	$14.00

The median hourly wage, represented by Employee 4, really is $15.00. However, the average salary, found by adding all of the wages and dividing the

Quick Hits

The Value of Using the Median: All those "Indian Chiefs" Making So Much Money

Members the news media suspicious of the way First Nations bands manage their funds have occasionally drawn attention to the exorbitant salaries of band chiefs. An analysis in the *Toronto Star* gave me material for a good reply to these criticisms, and a teaching moment for readers. The numbers shown in Table 3.3 come from the former federal Department of Indigenous and Northern Affairs.

What you can expect from critics of Canada's First Nations would be a focus on all of the band chiefs getting paid $240,000, or else the $180,000+ earned by the list's top 10. However, when analysts at the *Star* looked for the median salary earned by First Nations chiefs, they arrived at a figure of $64,697. Other figures could have been used to get across the same idea: for instance, 79 per cent received less than $80,000, and about 67 per cent (or roughly two-thirds) received between $20,000 and $79,999. This approximates the pay of a low-level bureaucrat or a lower-middle manager in a large company—or even less.

TABLE 3.3 **Median Pay for First Nations Band Leaders**

Salary Range ($)	Number of First Nations Chiefs	Running Total
0	8	8
1–9,999	34	42
10,000–19,999	41	83
20,000–39,999	100	183
40,000–59,999	140	323
60,000–79,999	190	513
80,000–99,999	70	583
100,000–119,999	28	611
120,000–139,999	14	625
140,000–159,999	8	633
160,000–179,999	4	637
180,000–199,999	5	642
200,000–209,999	2	644
210,000–219,999	0	644
220,000–239,999	0	644
240,000+	3	647

Source: Smith (2015, pp. A1, A8).

total by 7, is $17.39—quite a bit more than what the two employees make. The employees would make good sociologists: they did their own analysis of the data and came up with a different interpretation to the one they were given. The average is not necessarily more reliable than the median: the two scores can be very different, though, so it's good to look at both if you can.

Using Operational Definitions

Knowing that different measures of centre can produce different interpretations of the data is one area of quantifiable research in which a sociology student can learn to challenge the research of professionals. Another involves the use of **operational definitions**. These definitions take abstract or theoretical concepts—"poverty," "abuse," or "middle class," for example—and transform them into concrete, observable, and measurable entities. But "operationalizing" abstract concepts can be difficult to do.

The *Handbook for Sociology Teachers* (1982), by British sociologists Roger Gomm and Patrick

> **What do *you* think?**
> 1. How would you define "single parent"?
> 2. Do you think that "single-parent family" is a category that would be easy to do research with? Why or why not?

McNeill, contains a brilliant exercise illustrating the importance of operational definitions. Students are presented with a table showing the number of thefts that have occurred at a number of schools. Included in the table are the following factors that may have a bearing on the findings:

- size of the school
- social class of the school's students
- whether the school is single-sex or co-educational.

Students are asked to determine if there may be a cause-and-effect relationship between any of these factors and the number of thefts. Having given the students a chance to reach tentative conclusions, the teacher gives them a handout showing that each school in the study defined "theft" differently. With no consistency in the operational definition, the students' efforts to compare schools were sociologically worthless (although pedagogically rewarding).

Measuring Poverty: Operational Definitions in Action

To get a sense of how operational definitions are used, consider **poverty**. There is no standard definition for "poverty" or "poor." There are, however, various conventional methods for defining poverty. One is to establish a **poverty line**, an income level

Quick Hits

So You Think You Know What a Single Parent Is?

Arriving at an operational definition for a concept that appears to be obvious can sometimes be difficult. Take a category as seemingly self-evident as "single parent" (or "lone parent"). Identify which of the following you would count as a single parent, and then address the questions below.

a) a mother whose husband is dead

b) a 41-year-old separated mother who lives with her 22-year-old son

c) a father whose four-year-old daughter sees her mother every weekend

d) a mother whose 10-year-old son lives with his father every summer

e) a father whose two daughters live with their mother every other week

f) a mother whose husband lives in the same house but contributes nothing financially or in services to the raising of her children from a previous marriage

g) a gay man who, along with his live-in partner, is raising his two sons without any assistance from the children's mother

h) a mother who, along with her son, is completely supported financially by her ex-husband

i) a mother whose husband is in the armed forces and stationed overseas for most of the year

TABLE 3.4 MBM Thresholds for Saskatchewan, 2015

MBM region	Persons not in economic families	2 persons	3 persons	4 persons	5 persons
Rural areas	$18,779	$26,558	$32,526	$37,558	$41,991
Small population centres with less than 30,000 persons	$19,329	$27,335	$33,479	$38,658	$43,221
Medium population centres with a population between 30,000 and 99,999 persons	$18,216	$25,761	$31,550	$36,431	$40,731
Saskatoon	$19,055	$26,948	$33,004	$38,110	$42,608
Regina	$18,807	$26,569	$32,574	$37,613	$42,053

Source: Statistics Canada, Income Statistics Division, www12.statcan.gc.ca/census-recensement/2016/ref/dict/tab/t4_5-eng.cfm

below which a household is defined (for statistical or governmental purposes) as being "poor."

How is a poverty line established? There is no universally accepted procedure, though a few methods are prevalent. One is to link it to the availability of basic material needs: food, clothing, and shelter. Anything below the minimum income level needed to secure these necessities is considered **absolute poverty**. But this varies across countries and provinces. Consider, for example, how housing costs vary across Canada. It costs more for a resident of Vancouver to pay rent on an apartment than it costs a citizen of Moncton living in a comparable dwelling.

Since 1997 Statistics Canada has used the **Market Basket Measure** (MBM) to establish a poverty line for different regions across the country. As Giles explains:

> The MBM estimates the cost of a specific basket of goods and services for the reference year, assuming that all items in the basket were entirely provided for out of the spending of the household [i.e., that none of the items were purchased for the householders by family or friends]. Any household with a level of income lower than the cost of the basket is considered to be living in low income. (Giles, 2004)

The "basket" includes five types of expenditures for a reference family of two adults and two children:

- food
- clothing and footwear
- shelter
- transportation
- "other" (school supplies, furniture, recreation and family entertainment, personal care products, and phone and internet access).

Different levels are calculated for specific communities in Canada and theoretical communities based on province and population size (Statistics Canada, 2013). To give you an idea of what the Market Basket Measure looks like, Table 3.4 shows the MBM thresholds for Saskatchewan in a given year, to show how they differ.

In 2020, following an extensive review and in light of the 2019 Poverty Reduction Act, Statistics Canada updated and revised the MBM to better account for certain changes in basic costs for a family of four, especially in regard to the rising costs of urban transportation and phone/internet service. Notable in Table 3.5 are the minimal changes from 2016 to

TABLE 3.5 MBM for a Family of Four, Saskatchewan, 2016 and 2020

	2016	2020
Rural	$41,690	$41,473
Population under 30,000	$43,452	$43,236
Population 30,000–99,999	$43,630	$43,489
Saskatoon	$47,234	$47,025
Regina	$46,242	$46,188

Notes: Measured in 2020 constant dollars. The base year is 2018.
Source: Adapted from Statistics Canada (2022).

2020, although the effects of the COVID-19 pandemic and rising food and gas prices caused by the Russia–Ukraine war that began in 2022 may alter this.

Another way to define "poor" is to use a **relative poverty** scale, which defines poverty relative to average, median, or mean household incomes. An example is the **low income cut-off**, which is calculated based on the percentage of a family's income spent on food, clothing, and shelter, whereby any household spending 20 percentage points more of its after-tax income than does the median family on these basics is considered to be below the low income cut-off. A household is considered simply "low income" when its income is below 50 per cent of median household incomes (Government of Canada, 2022), a measure mostly used for international comparisons.

What Difference Does It Make?

Poverty measures are used to determine how government assistance is distributed. You can imagine, then, that groups with different views on how much government funding should go to reducing poverty might adopt different definitions of what it means to be poor.

Take conservative-minded analyst Christopher Sarlo, who argues that measures of relative poverty are merely measures of inequality, a condition that exists even in prosperous societies. The focus, he argues, should be not a person's standard of living compared to that of a neighbour but rather a person's "absolute level of well-being and ability to acquire basic necessities" (Sarlo, 2013, p. 3). With that in mind, Sarlo developed the Basic Needs Poverty Line (BNL), which is favoured by the Fraser Institute, a conservative think tank. Like the Market Basket Measure, the BNL is a measure of absolute poverty based on a household's ability to purchase a certain set of necessities. In this case, regional variations are not considered. This differs from MBM thresholds, which are adjusted higher for families living in larger cities and lower for those living in rural areas. Table 3.6 shows the BNL thresholds for households of 1 to 5 people compared with the MBM thresholds for the most and least expensive regions, according to Statistics Canada.

The table shows that Statistics Canada considers a family of four in Toronto to be living in poverty if its total household income after taxes is less than $36,861. The Fraser Institute considers the same family to be in poverty only if its total household income is less than $26,619. That's a difference of over $10,000. Why? Statistics Canada is a government agency that gathers and supplies statistics for public policy makers—and for researchers. The Fraser Institute is a private think tank appealing to conservative policy makers with policy recommendations that promote free enterprise and limit spending on social programs. The lower the poverty line, the lower the number of people considered poor in the analysis of statistics, and the lower the need for social programs such as social assistance.

Research Surveys and a Lesson in Interpreting Poll Results

Polls, surveys, and questionnaires are frequently used in both quantitative and qualitative research. Quantitative research uses *closed-ended questionnaires*, in which respondents are asked to reply to set questions by selecting the best answer from a list of possibilities. "What college or university do you presently attend?" would be an example of a closed-ended question, and you can see how the results

TABLE 3.6 **MBM and BNL Thresholds for Households of 1 to 5 Members**

Household Members	Statistics Canada's Market Basket Measure (2015)		Fraser Institute's Basic Needs Poverty Line (2014)
	High[a]	Low[b]	
1	$19,976	$16,436	$13,310
2	$28,250	$23,243	$18,824
3	$34,599	$28,467	$23,054
4	$39,951	$32,871	$26,619
5	$44,667	$36,751	$29,762

[a] Province of British Columbia, Vancouver census metropolitan area
[b] Province of Quebec, medium population centre with a population between 30,000 and 99,999

Source: Statistics Canada, Income Statistics Division, www12.statcan.gc.ca/census-recensement/2016/ref/dict/tab/t4_5-eng.cfm; Lammam & MacIntyre (2016, p. 3, Table 1).

would be easy to summarize in numbers. Closed-ended questionnaires can be administered online, over the phone, or in person. They are generally administered to a sample, a selection of the population under investigation, such as a sample of college and university students or a sample of Canadians. The sample must be representative of the broader population so that the results of the survey can be extrapolated and applied to the whole. You could not do a study of student debt by interviewing only students from families with a total household income of over $175,000: that would not be a representative sample.

Qualitative research relies on open-ended questionnaires, in which respondents are encouraged to answer freely to each question without having to select a predetermined response from a list. Open-ended questions are most effective when they cannot be answered with a simple *yes* or *no*. "How would you describe your first year of college or university?" is an open-ended question. You can see how this question might give you a more informative response than one that asks you to rate your first year of college or university on a scale from 1 to 5, although it can be more difficult to summarize the results of open-ended questionnaires. Such questionnaires, because they are more nuanced, are often best-suited to face-to-face interviews.

The term "poll" usually refers to a quantitative survey designed to measure respondents' views on a particular topic or set of topics. The wording of poll questions is important, since polls may be manipulated for political ends rather than scientific accuracy. Consider the following example. In 2015, Conservative member of Parliament Lawrence Toet sent a pamphlet out in his Winnipeg riding to promote the federal Conservatives' anti-terrorism legislation, Bill C-51. The mailer included the following poll question designed to be answered by the recipient and returned to the riding office:

What do you think?
How would you turn the question in Lawrence Toet's pamphlet into an unbiased poll question?

Can you see the problem with this question? In logic terms it represents the fallacy known as a false dichotomy, where two positions are presented as though they were opposites and mutually exclusive, so that if you disagree with one premise, you must naturally agree with the other. In fact, this is not a choice between two opposites. In other words, polls can be used to guide or shape, rather than gauge, public opinion. As a sociologically aware consumer of polls, you should always ask yourself, *who funded this poll?*

Variables and Correlations

Here are a few concepts necessary for understanding and carrying out quantifiable research (and even certain forms of qualitative research). The first one is **variable**: a concept with measurable traits or characteristics that can vary or change from one person, group, culture, or time to another. One variable can cause another variable to change, or it can be affected by another. The average temperature of Nunavut's capital, Iqaluit, can be a variable, as can the average amount of clothing a resident of Iqaluit wears. Clearly the first variable can affect the second one.

Sociologists commonly refer to two different types of variables: independent variables and dependent variables. **Independent variables** are presumed to have some effect on another variable. In the example given above, the average temperature of Iqaluit is the independent variable. **Dependent variables** are those that are assumed to be affected by an independent variable. In our example, the average amount of clothing worn by the Iqalungmiut ("people of Iqaluit") would be the dependent variable. Table 3.7 presents a list of possible independent and dependent variables from examples presented in this chapter.

Another key term is **correlation**. A correlation exists when two variables are associated more frequently than could be expected by chance. Both variables might increase together, or one might increase while the other decreases. A **direct or positive correlation** exists when the independent variable and the dependent variable increase or decrease

The Point Is . . .

How to Survey the Public on Government COVID-19 Responses

On 4 February 2022, the results of a survey on government responses to the COVID-19 pandemic were published in the newspaper *The Tyee* under the title "Most Disagree with Convoy Truckers on Vaccine Mandates and Lockdowns" (Van der Linden & Beyer, 2022). Thinking sociologically, you should wonder about who did the survey, how many Canadians did they consult, and how were those people chosen.

The researchers were two sociologically savvy political scientists, Clifton Van der Linden of McMaster University and Alexander G.W. Beyer of Simon Fraser University. The research was conducted online from 4 to 10 January 2022. It involved 2,339 respondents randomly selected from the Vox Pop online respondent panel. To achieve a broad-based representative sample, Van der Linden and Beyer ensured that there was diversity in age, education, region, and vote choice in the 2021 federal election. The questions asked in the survey related to vaccine passports, vaccine mandates, and government-imposed restrictions. Needless to say, given the title of the article, survey respondents by sizable majorities disagreed with the anti-vaxxer, anti-restriction views of the convoy truckers and their supporters, who swarmed and largely shut down the centre of the nation's capital in early 2022. The following questions were asked:

Vaccine Passports
Do you agree or disagree that vaccinations against COVID-19 should be mandatory for each of the following? (see below for some results)

Vaccine Mandates
Do you agree or disagree that proof of COVID-19 vaccination should be required in order to engage in the following activities? (see below for some results)

Restrictions
Given present circumstances, how supportive are you of the government imposing restrictions on each of the following? (see below for results)

Answer choices included strongly agree, somewhat agree, don't know, somewhat disagree, and strongly disagree for passports and mandates, and for restrictions the choices were very supportive, somewhat supportive, not very supportive, and not at all supportive. Of note, when people said they agreed, the vast majority of them answered with "strongly agree." Likewise, when people said they disagreed, the vast majority of them answered with "strongly disagree."

On vaccine passports (i.e., proof of vaccination), agreement was especially high. Roughly 80 per cent agreed this was necessary for health and long-term care workers; roughly 75 per cent for government workers, politicians, teachers, and professors; and roughly 70 per cent for university students. Support diminished in regard to age groups, so that for those five years and under there was little more than 50 per cent agreement.

For vaccine mandates, agreement was also high. A little over 75 per cent supported vaccine mandates for travelling by plane and cruise ships, slightly less than that for movie theatres, indoor public gatherings, and restaurants, bars, and gyms. The lowest agreement was on grocery stores, with just about 50 per cent supporting mandates.

Support was high as well, at around 75 per cent, for restrictions being placed on international travel, bars and nightclubs, stadiums, and nursing homes. For colleges and universities, the supportive response was at about 70 per cent. There was less than 50 per cent support for restrictions placed on playgrounds and parks, with the lowest figure, at 25 per cent, for curfews.

As an aside, a CBC report revealed that, as of 10 February 2022, more than half of the donors to the so-called freedom convoy came from the United States, and these largely right-wing donors had provided US$3.6 million or about 44 per cent of the money raised to support this brief but consequential Canadian anti-governance effort (Thompson, Rocha, & Leung, 2022).

TABLE 3.7 Independent and Dependent Variables: Three Examples

Study	Independent Variable		Dependent Variable
opening narrative	Car passes another car.	⇨	The passed car speeds up.
schoolwork	Middle-class parents take an active role in children's education.	⇨	Middle-class children achieve better results.
fasting	Muslim student mentions Ramadan.	⇨	Non-Muslim classmates ask what fasting is.

TABLE 3.8 Direct Correlation of Independent and Dependent Variables: Three Examples

Independent Variable		Dependent Variable
smoking	⇨	rates of lung cancer
education level	⇨	(1) income level; (2) tolerance for difference (e.g., regarding race and ethnicity, sexual orientation, etc.)
parents' income level	⇨	likelihood of child becoming a dentist, doctor, or lawyer

TABLE 3.9 Inverse Correlation of Independent and Dependent Variables: Three Examples

Independent Variable		Dependent Variable
average temperature	⇨	average amount of clothes worn
woman's education	⇨	number of children she will have
age (of an adult)	⇨	support for legalizing cannabis

together. Table 3.8 shows some examples. An **inverse or negative correlation** exists when the two variables change in opposing directions—in other words, when the independent variable increases, the dependent decreases, and vice versa. Table 3.9 gives examples of inverse correlation.

Spurious Reasoning: Correlation Is Not Causation

In the discussion of correlations above I've said nothing about **causation**, the linking of effects to causes. We may *observe* that women with postsecondary education have fewer children than those who do not have any postsecondary education, but we can't assume, based on that correlation, that being engaged in postsecondary education *causes* them to have fewer children. We have to prove it, by testing hypotheses

about why this is so (for example, women who attend college and university delay childbirth while they complete their studies and begin a career).

While correlation is relatively easy to prove, causation is not. Claiming that a cause-and-effect relationship exists based on correlation alone, without sufficient evidence, is known as *spurious reasoning*. Spurious reasoning is a concept that's hard to grasp with just the definition. Sociology instructors are challenged to explain and identify it. It usually takes lots of examples. So I'll begin here with the definition and then present several examples.

Spurious reasoning exists when someone sees *correlation* and falsely assumes *causation*. Remember that a correlation is easy to determine; causation is not. The journey from one to the other is long and difficult. It involves proving—or else disproving—the existence of the critical **third variable**, the outside factor that influences both correlating variables.

Here are the examples, some silly, some serious.

Example #1: Birds and Leaves

There is a correlation in Canada between birds flying south and leaves falling. We can see both phenomena occurring roughly at the same time. It would be spurious reasoning to say that the birds see the leaves falling and therefore decide to migrate. If we look for a third factor, we'll find that the angle of the sun's rays affects both dependent variables.

Example #2: Fire Trucks and Fire Damage

There is a direct correlation between the number of fire trucks that go to a fire and the amount of damage that takes place at the fire. The greater the number of fire trucks, the greater the amount of fire damage. It would be spurious reasoning to say that the large number of fire trucks *causes* the extensive damage done at the site of the fire. Seek out the third variable: the seriousness of the fire affects both the number of fire trucks that appear and the amount of damage caused.

Example #3: Cohabitation and Divorce

There is a direct (but not strong) correlation between a couple's living together prior to marriage and the likelihood of divorce. People who live together first are more likely to divorce than those who go directly from living apart to living together in marriage. It would be spurious reasoning to say that a couple's greater likelihood of divorce comes from the fact that they lived together first. Seek out the third variable and you will find it in social liberalism and social conservatism (the latter possibly a cause or effect of that difficult-to-pin-down social factor "religiosity"). Socially liberal people are more likely *both* to live together *and* to leave a marriage if they feel it is bad. More socially conservative people are *both* more likely to begin living together with marriage *and* more likely to stay in a marriage, even if it is horrible.

Example #4 Divorce and Suicide

Durkheim detected a direct correlation between divorce rates and suicide rates during a 10-year period from 1870 to 1880; some of his findings are recorded in Table 3.10.

There was a positive correlation between divorce rates and suicide rates over this period. However, it would be spurious reasoning to say that greater rates of divorce produced higher suicide rates. For Durkheim, the third variable was **anomie**, a societal state of breakdown or confusion, or a more personal

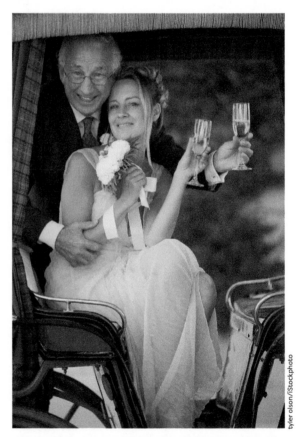

tyler olson/iStockphoto

TABLE 3.10 Correlation between Divorce and Suicide Rates in Four Countries, 1870–89

Country	Divorce Rate (per 1,000 marriages)	Suicide Rate (per 1 million people)
Italy	3.1	31.0
Sweden	6.4	81.0
France	7.5	150.0
Switzerland	47.0	216.0

Source: Durkheim ([1897] 1951).

Older men who marry significantly younger women tend to live longer. Spurious reasoning might lead us to conclude that this man will live long because he is married to this younger woman. What do you think? What "third variable" might help to explain the correlation between marrying a younger woman and living longer? Or do you believe such a correlation even exists? How might you prove/disprove this?

one based on an individual's lack of connection to society. Anomie, concluded Durkheim, was the real cause of increases in both divorce and suicide rates.

Critical Thinking and Statistics

Sociologist Joel Best, author of *Damned Lies and Statistics: Untangling Numbers from the Media, Politicians, and Activists* (2001), presented the following example illustrating why we should approach statistics critically. He was on the PhD dissertation committee of a graduate student who began his dissertation with a questionable statistic. The student cited the following stat from an article published in 1995:

> Every year since 1950, the number of American children gunned down has doubled.

This certainly gains the reader's attention. But wait a minute, said Best: do the math. Say the 1950 figure was 1. Here is how it would add up from 1950 to 1995:

1950	**1**
1951	**2**
1952	**4**
1955	**32**
1957	**128**
1959	**512**
1960	**1,012**
1961	**2,058**
1965	**32,768** (there were 9,960 homicides in total that year)
1970	**1 million +**
1980	**1 billion** (approximately more than four times the total population of the United States at the time)
1983	**8.6 billion** (nearly one-and-a-half times the world's population at that time)

What the author of the original article—the one cited by the PhD student—had done was misquote a 1994 document stating (accurately) that the number of American children killed each year by guns had doubled since 1950; the number itself had not doubled *each year*.

Best advises us to approach statistics critically. That involves recognizing that all statistics have flaws, and that some flaws are more significant than others. Best presents the following useful series of questions for sociology students to consider when encountering a statistic in a news report, magazine, newspaper, or conversation:

> What might be the sources for this number? How could one go about producing the figure? Who produced the number, and what interests might they have? What are the different ways key terms might have been defined, and which definitions have been chosen? How might the phenomena be measured, and which measurement choices have been made? What sort of sample was gathered, and how might that sample affect the result? Is the statistic properly interpreted? Are comparisons being made, and if so, are the comparisons appropriate? Are there competing statistics? If so, what stakes do the opponents have in the issue, and how are those stakes likely to affect their use of statistics? And is it possible to figure out why the statistics seem to disagree, what the differences are in the ways the competing sides are using figures. (Best, 2001)

Joel Best's point that statistical claims need to be evaluated critically is borne out by a 2022 study of possible racist hiring practices by the Chipotle Mexican Grill food chain in the United States (see Melendez, 2022). The study, undertaken by the Equal Rights Center and sponsored by a fast-food workers' union, involved sending out 624 fake job applications (bearing the names of people who did not exist) in pairs for real jobs of general manager and assistant or apprentice manager, one with a first name and surname that gave the appearance of the individual being Black, the other of the person being white. These racial name associations were obtained through an investigation published in 2021 by the National Bureau of Economic Statistics. The study determined racial bias by looking at which one of the pair received responses or callbacks.

One example was of applications sent in by "Antwan Braxton" and "Neil Klein." They sent in 12 applications to different Chipotle restaurants over a three-day period. "Braxton's" resumé included one more year of general manager experience, plus

The Point Is . . .

Misreading Statistics Can Have Grave Consequences

Failing to give proper scrutiny to a statistic is not just a student mistake: journalists, politicians, and other professionals have been guilty of misinterpreting, misusing, or placing too much trust in reported evidence, sometimes with devastating consequences.

According to the US Centers for Disease Control and Prevention (CDC, 2018), over 183,000 people in the United States died from overdoses related to opioid-based prescription narcotics between 1999 and 2015. The situation has been just as grave here in Canada, where, according to the federal Public Health Agency, there were over 9,000 opioid-related deaths in a two-and-a-half-year period from January 2016 to June 2018 (Special Advisory Committee, 2019).

Opioid painkillers such as oxycodone are highly effective but highly addictive: up to one in four people using prescription opioids subsequently experience long-term struggles with addiction (CDC, 2018). So why are opioids so widely prescribed if they carry such risks? It is possible the risks may have been misunderstood, thanks in part to a one-paragraph letter

published in a 1980 issue of the *New England Journal of Medicine* (Porter & Jick, 1980, p. 123). A recent American study found that the letter, published under the headline "Addiction Rare in Patients Treated with Narcotics," was cited "heavily and uncritically . . . as evidence that addiction was rare with long-term opioid therapy . . . even though no evidence was provided by the correspondents" (Leung, Macdonald, Dhalla, & Juurlink, 2017).

The problem is that the letter's claim was based on an informal, unsystematic study of patients in hospital (whose use of medication is easier to monitor and regulate; patients outside of hospital are much more likely to misuse prescribed medications). The letter was cited as evidence that opioid addiction was rare in 439 separate articles, some of which "grossly misrepresented the conclusions of the letter" (Leung, et al., 2017). Greater scrutiny of the original letter might have prompted additional research on the subject, or at least reduced the propensity for prescribing opioid-based narcotics for chronic pain.

having a ServSafe Food Protection Manager Certificate, plus a Manager of the Quarter Award. "Klein" did not have these enticements in his resumé. "Klein" received an email, voicemail, and text message from the recruiters. "Braxton" got no reply. Needless to say, the former was the "white name" and the latter the "Black name."

The general figures for the entire study were as follows:

General Manager	58% of fake applications get a callback
White	64%
Black	53%
Assistant/ Apprentice Manager	25%
White	30%
Black	20%

There were, however, some potential and real limitations to this study. First, it did not undergo any "peer review," as would have been the case prior to publication in most academic journals; in other words, it had not received the critical eye of one or more scholars engaged in research on the same subject. Another possible limitation is that it was sponsored by an organization—a trade union—that would have a distinct interest in criticizing management. Significantly, in the larger study there were quite different scores for different sections of the United States:

Northeast	more responses to "white" names
South	more responses to "Black" names for assistant and apprentice managers
Midwest	more responses to "Black" names for general managers
West	more responses to "Black" names for general managers

3.5 Ethics and Research

An important consideration in sociological research today, and one that is more important now than it once was, is the **ethics** of research. Practising good research ethics largely involves demonstrating respect for the research subjects, specifically concerning their privacy, their understanding of what the research will require of them, and their capacity to choose to be researched or not. When participants indicate their understanding and acceptance of the research conditions, they are providing what is known as **informed consent**. Colleges and universities now have research committees or entire departments responsible for vetting the research that sociologists and other faculty members engage in. In times before such oversight was common, breaches of ethics might not have been detected until after the research had been completed, if they were detected at all.

The Ethics of Deception: Tales of Covert or Undisclosed Research

The following cases—one well known, the other considerably less so—involve sociological research conducted during the 1960s and 1970s in a way that could be considered, particularly by today's standards, as unethical. As you read the cases, you can consider how the research would have been different had it been proposed today.

Laud Humphreys and the Tearoom Trade

Robert Allen "Laud" Humphreys (1930–1988) was an American sociologist best known for his published PhD dissertation *Tearoom Trade* (1970), which has been viewed both as a pioneering study of male homosexuality and as an egregiously unethical case of sociology gone wrong. For his doctoral thesis Humphreys engaged in ethnographic research of anonymous male–male sexual encounters in public

toilets. ("Tearoom" was a code word for these meeting places; a quick search of *Urban Dictionary* suggests it's not in common use today.) Fairly obviously, Humphreys did not disclose to the men he encountered that he was performing sociological research; instead, he posed as a voyeur and "watch queen"—a scout keeping a lookout for approaching police.

Conducting research without advising his subjects, much less gaining their consent, was already an ethical no-no, but Humphreys went a step further. By recording their licence plate numbers, he was able to find the names and addresses of the men he was studying. Disguising himself as a public health official performing a social survey, he interviewed about 50 of the men. The research yielded interesting findings. Humphreys discovered that many of his research subjects appeared to the world to be heterosexual. Many were married, with wives who apparently knew nothing about their husbands' extramarital activity. Humphreys's thesis was that the people he studied used a conservative public persona that conformed to societal norms and values to conceal a private self that was participating in a deviant (at the time, illegal) practice. Interestingly, Humphries was in a position similar to that of many of his research subjects: he was married for 20 years before coming out as gay.

The deceptive, or covert, nature of Humphreys's research turned out to be a divisive issue in the Department of Sociology at Washington University in St. Louis, where he received his PhD in 1968. Some faculty members wanted to rescind his doctorate. It was one of the issues that ultimately caused the disbanding of the department in 1989.

"Unethical" Fieldwork in Religion: 1972–3

This case is not as well known. It concerns my own work as an undergraduate, when I applied the theories of Erving Goffman to a newly formed religious group as part of my honours thesis. The group was known as the Process Church, or the Church of the Final Judgement. The *Toronto Sun* had labelled them

The Point Is . . .

Ethnographic Research Can Turn a Sociologist into a Witness

Alice Goffman (b. 1962), Erving's daughter, is a sociologist whose book *On the Run: Fugitive Life in an American City* (2014) draws on fieldwork she carried out to study the impact of policing on the lives of young Black men in Philadelphia. Positive reception came quickly from both the academic world (her thesis, the basis for the book, received the American Sociological Society's Dissertation Award for 2011) and the popular press (the *New York Times* listed it as one of the 100 most notable books of 2014). But the academic world is intensely competitive, and with the accolades came fierce scrutiny and harsh criticism of Goffman's research methodology. An unsigned, untraceable 60-page document (single-spaced!) was sent to hundreds of sociologists across the country, detailing what the document's author felt were the flaws, big and small, of the book. Two stand out because of how they relate to current ethical practices.

The first is that Goffman did not begin her work with a discussion of *positionality* (her social

a Satanist cult. They weren't, as it turned out, but the rumour alone was enough to make them particularly interesting to me.

My research method was *undisclosed* participant observation. This means that I did not tell them that I was doing research. I was working "undercover." I presented myself as an unemployed drummer (which I was); I did not tell them I was also an undergraduate sociology student. My research subjects were not willing participants who knew they were being studied. I felt that my research had to be undisclosed because the Process Church had received negative publicity from the local media, and its members were nervous about outsiders, especially if they felt they might be reporters posing as faithful congregants to observe their meetings.

The Process Church was located in downtown Toronto, where they operated a soup kitchen and held different services every night. Once a week from September to February, I would participate in the evening activities, which could include their own music (no choir or church organ here; think sitars and bongos) and a sermon. The speaker did his best to "keep it real," in the words of the day. He would be hip and funny, but he also dispensed good advice. On some nights there would be workshop sessions in which people in groups would talk to each other, sometimes at a very personal level. I grew close to a

Speed Bump

When the need for informed consent gets in the way of research progress, it can be tempting to forgo or lessen ethical standards in order to get things done. Why is it important to retain your ethical integrity, even at the cost of potential sociological insight? Who do ethics policies benefit?

What do *you* think?

1. Why might this kind of research be considered unethical today?
2. How would the research have changed if informed consent had been sought? Do you think that the information gathered would have as useful?

location, essentially). In other words, she did not address the limits of her understanding (i.e., that she could not know from her own life experience what poverty and racism feel like), nor did she acknowledge the exercises of privilege that came from her being a rich, white sociologist studying a mixed-income Black community (i.e., she could invade their lives, but they could not invade hers).

The second issue relates to illegal practices she observed. During her fieldwork, she heard about and may have witnessed plans to break the law. She even drove with a young man who was armed and out for revenge on an individual he suspected of killing one of his gang members. This presented her with an ethical dilemma: protect the confidentiality of her research participants or prevent the commission of a crime (or several crimes). The guidelines for sociological research at the University of Pennsylvania, where Alice Goffman studied, were clear: she was not to divulge the identity of the individuals she was writing about, and she was expected to burn her field notes (which ran to thousands of pages).

number of people there, including those who worked in the soup kitchen, where I often hung out. Once the evening's session was over, I would head to the subway, take a pad of paper out of my pocket, and write notes like crazy.

3.6 Social Research Methods: A Final Word

In this chapter we've considered a number of ways to carry out sociological research. In all the talk about quantitative and qualitative methods, independent and dependent variables, correlation and statistics, it's easy to lose sight of an important point: the subjects under investigation are people, and the moment you begin to study them, you start a relationship that will not always be equal. Students, soldiers, and inmates of prisons and asylums are often studied because they have little power to say no. If I can ask questions about your life but you can't ask questions about mine, then I have a kind of power over you that you do not have over me. People who are poor or who belong to racialized (e.g., Black) or colonized (e.g., Indigenous) groups have often been studied by white, middle-class researchers for purposes that serve more to control or exploit the subjects of the research than to give them power over their lives. The Maori of New Zealand have been through that experience. Maori researcher Linda Tuhiwai Smith, in *Decolonizing Methodologies: Research and Indigenous Peoples* (1999), wrote:

> **What do *you* think?**
> Which do you consider a greater breach of ethics: failing to report illegal activity or failing to protect an informant's confidentiality? When would you stop being a sociologist to honour your civic duty as a citizen?

From the vantage point of the colonized . . . the term "research" is inextricably linked to European imperialism and colonialism. The word itself, "research," is probably one of the dirtiest words in the indigenous world's vocabulary. When mentioned in many indigenous contexts, it stirs up silence, it conjures up bad memories, it raises a smile that is knowing and distrustful. . . . The ways in which scientific research is implicated in the worst excesses of colonialism remain a powerful remembered history for many of the world's colonized peoples. . . . It galls us that Western researchers and intellectuals can assume to know all that it is possible to know of us, on the basis of their brief encounters with some of us. It appalls us that the West can desire, extract and claim ownership of ways of knowing, our imagery, the things we create and produce, and then simultaneously reject the people who created and developed those ideas and seek to deny them further opportunities to be creators of their own culture and own nations. (Smith, 1999, p. 1)

If your interest in sociology comes from a desire to effect positive social change, the critical tone of this statement might shock you. Let it serve as a reminder. Treat research participants with respect and represent the data fairly. You will go a long way toward sociology's goal of bringing clarity to social issues.

Wrap It Up

Summary

This chapter has taken you on a flight over a large piece of land known as Sociology's Contested Ground—otherwise known as "the things over which sociologists argue the most." Among the main fault lines along which sociologists differ are theories, approaches, and perhaps most bitter of all, social research methods. If sociologists worked with Santa Claus, they would challenge him on his operational definitions of "naughty" and "nice."

Ideally, the study of sociological research can lead students to develop reliable "fact check-ers" or "bullshit detectors" that will automatically kick in when it comes to assessing the many forms of social information they receive through a variety of media. Asking such questions as *How did they define . . . ?*, *What social voices or locations were being heard or excluded?*, *How do they know that?*, and *Who paid for the research?* should enable you to be critical of even professional researchers. Keep these questions in mind as you read the chapters that follow.

As you encountered the diverse and, at times, opposing research strategies presented here, it has hopefully become clear to you that the facts do *not* speak for themselves. Knowledge is created: social "facts" and hypotheses are tested by human researchers with human biases who occasionally (and perhaps unintentionally) allow these biases to manufacture distortions rather than the ever-elusive "facts" or "proof." In short, be critical.

Think Back

Questions for Critical Review

1. Distinguish between qualitative and quantitative research. Give examples of each.
2. What value do narratives bring to sociological research?
3. Explain the relationship between insider views and qualitative research, on the one hand, and outsider views and quantitative research, on the other.
4. How could you combine qualitative and quantitative research methods in an institutional ethnography of your school's sociology department?
5. COVID-19 brought to the fore a number of long-term problems among Canada's nursing workforce: burnout, low pay, job stress, and mental health issues such as PTSD. From late 2019 to the end of 2021 nursing vacancies increased across Canada by 133 per cent, and in 2022 fully one-half of nurses were reported as considering leaving their jobs (Coutts, 2022).

As a political leader, what would you do to make nursing a more attractive profession, and how would you determine priorities in executing your plan of action? (For a start, see the report prepared for the Canadian Federation of Nurses Unions: Jane Coutts, "Half of Our Nurses Are Thinking of Quitting," available online.)
6. In 2016, N'we Jinan Artists recorded a video for their song "Home to Me," about their connection to Grassy Narrows First Nation in northern Ontario. You can view the video on YouTube: search "Grassy Narrows Home to Me." What could you learn from a content analysis of the 500+ comments on YouTube?
7. According to a report from the province's Road Safety Research Office in the Ministry of Transportation (2016), there are more fatal traffic accidents in Ontario during the

N'we Jinan Artists - "HOME TO ME" // Grassy Narrows First Nation

summer (June–September) than during the winter (December–March). Can we conclude that road conditions in Ontario are safer in winter than in summer? What other variables might affect this relationship?

8. Imagine you wanted to study binge drinking on campus among students. How would you go about operationalizing your key terms?

Would you distinguish between female and male subjects? Why or why not?

9. You have received scores of 30/40, 22/30, and 20/30 in three sociology tests. Which would you rather have as your mark: Your average percentage or your median? And shouldn't you have studied harder for the third test?

Read On

Suggested Print and Online Resources

Joel Best, *Damned Lies and Statistics: Untangling Numbers from the Media, Politicians, and Activists,* updated edition (Berkeley: University of California, 2012)
Now in an updated edition, this relatively lighthearted but helpful sociological guide to understanding the manipulation of statistics was so popular that it spawned a sequel, *More Damned Lies and Statistics: How Numbers Confuse Public Issues* (2004).

Michael Blastland & Andrew Dilnot, *The Tiger That Isn't: Seeing through a World of Numbers* (London: Profile Books, 2007)
A Scottish journalist and an English economist teamed up to produce this useful guide to interpreting statistics.

Marie Campbell & Frances Gregor, *Mapping Social Relations: A Primer in Doing Institutional Ethnography* (Aurora, ON: Garamond, 2002)

The insights of Dorothy Smith inform this insightful work on institutional ethnography.

James Paul Gee, *How to Do Discourse Analysis: A Toolkit,* 2nd edition (London: Routledge, 2014)
A relatively accessible introduction to discourse analysis by a professor of literature.

Ginger Gorman, *Troll Hunting: Inside the World of Online Hate and Its Human Fallout* (Richmond, Australia; Hardie Grant, 2019)
After being trolled online, Gorman, an Australian journalist, decided to investigate the phenomenon, first by studying the incidence of trolling (with help from the Australia Institute), and then by speaking with psychologists, victims, and trolls themselves, whom she met by embedding herself in their online world. The work offers a good example of a sociological study combining qualitative and quantitative research methods.

Government of Canada Panel on Research Ethics (2018), Tri-Council Policy Statement: Ethical Conduct for Research Involving Humans, https://www.ethics .gc.ca/eng/policy-politique_tcps2-eptc2_2018.html
This policy statement defines ethical research in the social sciences, natural sciences, health sciences, and humanities in Canada. It is long, but you should know where to find it for guidelines on such topics as consent, confidentiality, and conflicts of interest.

Orientalism: How the West Views the Rest of the World, www.youtube.com/watch?v=NExfbX7E42o

This 13-minute video, posted in 2017, gives a good explanation of Orientalism and how it shapes Western ideas of "the East" today.

John L. Steckley, *White Lies about the Inuit* (Toronto: University of Toronto Press, 2008)
This genealogical work puts to rest three discourse myths about the historic Inuit: that Inuit elders are sometimes abandoned on ice floes; that there are blond, blue-eyed Inuit descended from Norse ancestors; and that the Inuit have 52 (or more) words for snow.

4

Socialization and Social Roles

Reading this chapter will help you to . . .

- Define socialization and describe the role it plays in human lives.

- Explain how the concepts of agency, biological determinism, and social determinism relate to our understanding of socialization.

- Explain, with examples, what it means to be an agent of socialization.

- Outline the basic ideas of Freud, Mead, and Cooley as they apply to sociology.

- State the difference between broad and narrow socialization.

- Explain the relationship between primary socialization, secondary socialization, and resocialization.

For Starters

Playing for Fun vs Playing to Win: Sports as an Agent of Socialization

"Straight from Canada, the land of loonies, politeness, and socialized medicine, comes the latest concept to baffle Americans—a youth sport that doesn't keep score." (John Keilman, Chicago Tribune)

Organized sports have long been a way of socializing Canadian children. As well as promoting fitness through exercise, organized sports provide an environment for children to learn certain social values from their peers and from adults. These values include teamwork, cooperation, work ethic, practice, friendship, and competitiveness. Parents and coaches and the community anticipate the socialization of these qualities into the children growing up in their community.

However, these adults may not practise anticipatory socialization in some of their behaviour. Parents and coaches sometimes model unhealthy competitive behaviour. They may holler abuse at players, officials, and each other. I have seen riled-up parents confront one another in the stands. I have heard a mom vehemently shout, "Kill her!" at a girls' house league hockey game. When fistfights break out in the stands, they can become news stories, as in February 2019, when the Ontario Provincial Police were called to break up a 30-parent brawl in Simcoe. When parental rage is not isolated but becomes a pattern of devastating abuse, someone may write a book about it, as former NHL player Patrick O'Sullivan (2015) did.

Incidents of abusive competition have caused some people to question the value of organized sports as a socializing agent for children. As a result, some youth athletic associations in Canada have made the move to no-score sports. In 2013, the Ontario Soccer Association announced that it would stop keeping score in matches involving under-12 teams in its recreational, or "grassroots," leagues. Many associations across the country followed suit, adopting the "festival" format and the philosophy of "No scores, no standings, no trophies" (OSA, 2015). The aim of no-score programs is to lower the stress associated with the pressure to win (see the discussion of hurried child syndrome later this chapter) and to focus instead on fostering skills and love of the game in child athletes.

The immediate response to no-score programs was predictable. Newspaper editorials supported by online comments warned that no-score sports would blunt the "natural" human trait of competitiveness and encourage young people to believe in a world with no winners and losers, setting them up for failure when they encounter "real world" hardships and adversity. "They'll just keep score anyway," some critics argued. This is true. Kids, living in a culture that stresses "better" and "best," will "naturally" compete and measure themselves against their peers: this is an important part of their socialization into Canadian culture. They will do this with or without adults bellowing encouragement from the sidelines or the stands. Kids will know who the best and the worst teams are and whether their team is winning or losing. They will still have to learn how to take failure well, how to lose with pride, and how to win with grace. And while end-of-season participation awards can seem meaningless to a 15-year-old tired of hearing that everyone's a winner, they matter a great deal to the five-year-old earning that first trophy. My son once received an award in hockey not for first place or MVP but for being the most improved player on his team. That gave him a sense of pride and showed that real achievement can be celebrated without keeping score.

> **What do *you* think?**
> 1. Did you ever participate in competitive activities? What values did you learn from activities such as chess club, gymnastics, tennis, baseball, video games, robotics? Who reinforced those values? Your peers? Your parents? Your coaches? Someone else? How did those activities expand your social network?
> 2. John Keilman, quoted above, writes: "I'm hard pressed to identify anything good that comes from sorting [kids] into winners and losers at so young an age." Can you? Do you think the no-score policy makes athletic programs more beneficial or less beneficial to young people? How would you design a sociological study to research the issue?

4.1 Introduction: Socialization Is a Learning Process

Socialization is an area of sociological study that intersects with psychology. In fact, a number of the leading socialization theorists are psychologists.

Socialization is something we all experience. It is a learning process that involves figuring out or being taught how to interact with other people in a given society. It brings changes to an individual's sense of self. This applies in the earliest socialization we undergo in infancy and childhood, generally known as **primary socialization**, and in socialization that occurs later in life, which is sometimes known as **secondary socialization**.

If socialization is a learning process, who are the teachers? You have probably had many schoolteachers before now, some that you preferred over others. So it is with **agents of socialization**, the people and institutions who contribute to our socialization. We will meet these agents shortly, but first we will look at some of the ideas underpinning theories of socialization.

4.2 Determinism: Nature versus Nurture

Central to any discussion of socialization are two contentious topics:

- *determinism versus free will* and
- *biological determinism versus social determinism*.

When we speak of **determinism**, we are talking about the degree to which an individual's behaviour, attitudes, and other "personal" characteristics are *determined*, or caused, by something specific. Is that specific cause your genetic makeup or the people in the environment in which you were raised? Has anyone ever told you that "you're just like your mother," or like your father or a grandparent? If so, they were implying that your behaviour was caused either through genetic inheritance or through upbringing, and that you had little or no role in shaping your own character. In other words, they were endorsing a deterministic view of personality formation.

Most sociologists and social psychologists think that determinism plays a role in socialization. Champions of "hard determinism" claim that we essentially are programmed to think and act in a particular way, either by our biology ("nature") or by the society we live in ("nurture"). Proponents of "soft determinism" believe biology and society play a part, but they also believe there is some room in everyone's life for "free will," which is the exercise of agency. Agency implies that all people have a certain amount of choice above and beyond the effects of nature or nurture. Agency is related to the degree of social power a person may exert. Some such power comes from being able to manage how others think of us. To continue the sports example, a child may not only strive to prove herself more skilled than the opposing team members in order to win but to be the blue-ribbon winner she thinks her mother wants to see. First, we take a closer look at the kinds of determinism based on biology and society.

Biological Determinism

Biological determinism ("nature") states that the greater part of who we are is determined by our 26,000 genes that create particular physiological characteristics, for example, perfect eyesight or the eyeball shape that causes short-sightedness; healthy reproductive organs or a likelihood of ovarian cancer; normal growth during adolescence or the swift growth of the tibia in the legs that stretches the quadricep muscles attached below the knee, causing acute pain in the knees, especially during exercise (Osgood-Schlatter's syndrome). Biological determinism has become a popular subject of discussion and debate in the mainstream media, owing to the rise of human genetic research generally and to the Human Genome Project in particular, which involves a painstaking count of the number of genes we have and investigation into what each of those genes is a code for (if anything), either singly or in combination.

However, the popularity of this recently birthed field of research may lead to a neglect of other aspects of biological research that may be safer routes to human enhancement than tinkering with the building blocks of the human (or other genetic) matrix. For example, the invention of spectacles—eyeglasses—around the thirteenth century to improve sight had revolutionary effects on individuals and societies without risking other aspects of the person's health. A parallel interest in the ear's ability to transmit (or failure to transmit) sound frequencies through the ear has been eclipsed by a preoccupation with the brain, which is not the first recipient of sound that enters the body through the complex ear mechanism and then reaches the brain and flows through the nervous system along particular routes. As social scientists, we must be alert to assumptions and to speculation that can flaw some of the most prestigious work.

Certain abilities seem to fall into the "nature" category. We all know of people who are "naturally good" at sports, music, art, and so on. However, we have to be very careful in making even tentative statements about biological determinism and the influence of nature. A cautionary tale in two parts comes from a notorious research study into **XYY males** that began in 1962. The standard pattern of chromosomes in men is XY; the corresponding pattern for women is XX. During the 1960s, the atypical XYY chromosome pattern was found in some men studied in hospitals for dangerous, violent, or criminal patients with emotional/intellectual problems, first in England and then in the United States and Australia (see Jacobs et al., 1965; Price & Whatmore, 1967; Telfer, 1968). The XYY pattern was hastily declared the "criminal gene."

The problem was that researchers at first studied only people institutionalized in prisons or special security hospitals after being convicted of crimes. When the study was extended to the general population, researchers discovered that roughly the same percentage of men outside the institutionalized population (about 1 in 1,000) were XYY (Brown, 1968). There remain some well-documented associations of XYY males with above-average height, a tendency to have acne, and somewhat more impulsive and anti-social behaviour and slightly lower intelligence, but there is no evidence that XYY males are more likely than XY males to engage in criminal activity.

"Softer" forms of biological determinism focus on predispositions for personality characteristics (e.g., for shyness, for aggressiveness, and so on). These findings tend to have a stronger social foundation and are easier to support than the more sensational claims of "hard" determinism—the ones beginning "*We have found the gene for . . .*" that sometimes make the news. Who we are is based on too complex a mixture of social and biological factors for any one gene to be an absolute determinant of behaviour or of personality. One of the ways sociologists get around the intricacies of individual personalities is by studying them as a group, gathering information from "samples" of a population and analyzing it using statistical methods to make an educated guess about the characteristics of the entire population. Of course, care must be taken so that the sample will be representative of the group.

Sigmund Freud: Balancing the Biological and the Sociocultural

I mentioned that socialization is a meeting point for sociology and psychology. Let's take a moment, then, to consider **Sigmund Freud** (1856–1939), the founder of **psychoanalysis**, whose ideas about the processes that shape human nature influenced other theorists and generations of people worldwide, who have sought to understand the role of socialization in personality development. We also take note of the work of his granddaughter, Sophie Freud (1924–2022), a psychosociologist, educator, and author, who was less impressed by her famous ancestor whose socializing effects on family members were completely familiar to her.

Central to Freud's psychodynamic theory was his belief that the human mind has three parts: the id, the superego, and the ego. Think of it as a team with three players, but three players who don't get along and are often in conflict. Human personality is shaped, supposedly, by that conflict and how it is resolved (or not) in childhood and adolescence.

The **id** is the driving force of personality, an expression of two motives that demand gratification in all humans. The two motives (which you can think of as i̲nstinctive d̲rives) are *eros* and *thanatos*.

Eros (related to the word "erotic") is the drive that tends to be stressed by Freud's fans and critics. It is a "life drive" that is dedicated to seeking pleasure—particularly, but not exclusively, sexual pleasure. **Thanatos**, the less celebrated of the two drives, is the "death wish," an instinct for aggression and violence.

In order to get along in society, humans must learn to control the instinctive drives for pleasure and aggression, and this is where the **superego** comes in. It is the part of the mind that polices the id. Some people would think of it as your reasoning or conscience. It takes in the messages about right and wrong thinking and behaviour that parents, family, friends, teachers, and other socializing agents teach the child, and *internalizes* them as "normative" moral concepts. In other words, children adopt them as a personal code of moral behaviour. Picture a caped crusader with a big "S" on its chest, saying "Don't hit your sister!" or "Don't even think about locking your brother in the basement!" so you learn that those acts or thoughts are "wrong."

In Freud's thinking, the id and superego often come into conflict. Failure to manage the conflict can take years of psychotherapy to resolve. If one of the drives is too strong, a person may grow to become either too unrestrained or too controlled. The **ego**, meanwhile, is the main agent of personality, driven by the id and its demands but restrained by the superego. As the ego matures, it learns and develops strategies to satisfy the id's demands in socially acceptable ways. This "maturation" occurs through a sequence of stages that begin in infancy and end in adolescence. Freud called them *psychosexual stages* because he imagined each one to be associated with sexual pleasure from a different part of the body.

Freud saw biological and social factors as contributing equally to the development of human personality. But personality, Freud decided, was pretty well set by the end of the last psychosexual stage, when the superego is fully formed and sexual maturity is achieved (Freud, 1977). He also considered women of secondary importance to men. Psychoanalysts who followed in Freud's footsteps agreed that early experiences were critical to personality formation, but they believed that the ego continued to grow over the lifespan. **Erik Erikson** (1902–1994), for instance, recognized that society influences ego development well into old age. He believed that each stage of life, from infancy to maturity, is defined by a central crisis (trust versus mistrust, intimacy versus isolation, etc.) that has a significant bearing on individual personality development. A pivotal stage is adolescence, from about age 12 to the early twenties, which is defined by a conflict between identity (self-concept) and identity confusion. During this stage, humans engage in anticipatory socialization: they chart the course for their adult lives by choosing high school subjects that will lead to a career track in apprenticeships or in college or university, by thinking about selecting a mate, and by developing a worldview. These are weighty decisions, but Erikson warned that putting them off will produce an *identity crisis*, a state of doubt and uncertainty resulting from the failure to resolve the conflict between identity and identity confusion.

Sophie Freud, granddaughter of Sigmund Freud, knew her famous grandfather from when she was young and into her teens and was thoroughly familiar with his ideas as well as with all the relatives in that family. She escaped with her mother from the Nazi invasion of France by bicycling 400 miles to the south. She was educated in the United States, graduating in psychology, but later turned to sociology and how cultures shape personality. She criticized her grandfather's ideas to the point of ridicule. She decried aspects of psychoanalysis as "narcissistic indulgence" (*Boston Globe*, 2022). Her criticism of his theories about women's sexuality? "His ideas on women's sexuality were all wrong." She brought feminism into her discipline and into her family. Her children accompanied her to protests so they would become aware of social wrongs that people can act in various ways to change. She rejected Sigmund Freud's theory of the Oedipus complex. She thought her illustrious grandfather did not allow his son to become a doctor, perhaps fearing the competition. She was painfully aware of his arrogant demeaning of his wife. Although he thought women were not worth the trouble of complete psychoanalysis, he spent four years analyzing her Aunt Anna, who turned her experiences into a career in England, psychoanalyzing children. In fact, Freud's attitude to and treatment of women was everything that contemporary women reject as "patriarchal" (Lazarus, 2022).

She ratcheted up her criticism in an interview for a Canadian television film, *Neighbours: Freud and Hitler in Vienna* (2003), saying, "In my eyes, both Adolf Hitler and my grandfather were false prophets of the 20th century." They shared, in her words, "the ambition to convince other men of the one and only truth they had come upon." In her words, "Never could he be wrong" (*Boston Globe*, 2022).

The great difficulty with Freudian theory is that it has never been proven through scientific research. During the early years of its emergence, it relied for its popularity on the "shock value" of Freud's outspoken sexual theory in a historical period of social reticence to discuss intimate matters publicly. Authors who adopted Freudian "explanations" for their fictitious characters derived some of the same publicity from their plots and characters, for example, D.H. Lawrence in *Sons and Lovers* (1913) and *Lady Chatterley's Lover* (1928). The Freudian legacy includes the lowering of barriers to sexual discourse in public, which may be necessary to effect change, but which some feel has opened a door to abusive uses of sexual language in a social atmosphere that is becoming increasingly litigious about sexual assault. Freud has been faulted for refusing to believe the stories of sexual abuse disclosed to him by some female patients, relegating them to neurotic "fantasies" and persuading the women that they had imagined their abuse.

Social (or Cultural) Determinism, a.k.a. Behaviourism

Behaviourism is a school of thought in psychology that takes a strongly cultural-determinist position. It emphasizes the power of learning through behavioural modification ("nurture") in the development of behaviour. For the behaviourist, the social environment is the prime mover in the development of personality. Biology and agency count for less. One cautionary aspect of this school of thought is that much of the research on which it is based involved non-human animals: Pavlov's dogs, Thorndike's cats, B.F. Skinner's rats and pigeons. Critics say that the theory disallows the existence of choice or agency, which even a dog, pigeon, or rat can be seen as possessing (for example, try training a dachshund, if you doubt the existence of agency in dogs).

One of the earliest principles of behaviourism is the **law of effect**, introduced by **Edward Thorndike** (1874–1949) in his book *Animal Intelligence* (1911). The law of effect has two parts. The first says that if you do something and it is rewarded, the likelihood that you will do it again increases. The rewarded behaviour is said to be "reinforced." According to the second part of the law of effect, if you do something and it is ignored or punished, the likelihood of your doing it again decreases. The law of effect boils down to the idea of the carrot (reward) and the stick (punishment). Accordingly, if the screaming child in the grocery store lineup is given a lollipop to be quiet, the reward reinforces in the child's mind the benefit of screaming. You can expect it to scream for what it wants again. If a student is ridiculed when giving an answer in class, that student may never raise their hand in that class again.

There are debates about what constitutes a reward for an individual, and about what behaviour is or is not being rewarded. For example, if you punish a child who is acting out at school by making her sit in the corner and the objectionable behaviour persists, could it be that she experiences the "punishment" as a reward? Children who act out usually succeed in getting attention. Is that their goal? If so, what kind of attention do they actually need? If you pick up crying babies, does that teach them that they can get anything they want by crying? Or does it reward communication, which, once they learn to speak, becomes words and not tears? Attempting to change someone's behaviour using positive or negative reinforcement is called **behaviour modification**.

"Hard" social determinism claims that just about any behaviour can be taught and learned. A powerful expression of this view comes from **John B. Watson** (1878–1958), the founder of behaviourist psychology:

> Give me a dozen healthy infants, well-formed, and my own specified world to bring them up in and I'll guarantee to take any one at random and train him to become any type of specialist I might select—doctor, lawyer, artist, merchant-chief and yes, even beggar-man and thief, regardless of his talents, penchants, tendencies, abilities, vocations, and race of his ancestors. There is no such thing as an inheritance of capacity, talent, temperament, mental constitution and behavioral characteristics. (Watson, 1925, p. 82)

If this approach sounds like it comes from a scary science fiction movie: *Attack of the Rat Psychologists*, indeed, some of Watson's research methods now are considered unethical. His most famous experiment, the "Little Albert" study (Watson & Rayner, 1920), involved conditioning fear of a white rat in an 11-month-old infant ("Little Albert" was the infant, not the rat), who had not responded initially to the animal with fear. The mother, who had been paid $1.00 for the loan of her child, probably did not understand that part of the experiment would entail frightening her baby. (See ethics issues for researchers in Chapter 3.) The child was not deconditioned by his manipulators and died at six years of age so that further investigations of the effect of this experiment could not be made by later research. It is hardly surprising that someone who manipulated humans so easily would write popular books and articles on parenting and eventually enter a career in advertising, as Watson did.

Jeff Harper/Starmetro File Photo

A parking ticket is a negative sanction issued to someone who has violated a norm. What role do negative and positive sanctions play in behaviour modification? Who is doing the socializing in this case, and what is the lesson being taught?

What do *you* think?
How much of your own behaviour do you think is influenced by your social environment—by friends, family, your charismatic sociology professor—and how much were you born with?

The Point Is . . .

Socialization Encourages Good and Bad Habits

I am not a gambler, but I am no stranger to casinos. When I visit Oklahoma to teach the Wyandotte language, the hotel I stay at is attached to a casino. It has a decent restaurant where I go for breakfast. When I arrive and sit down, usually around 7:00 a.m., I see people playing the slot machines. I wonder why, but I know that the answer has a lot to do with Edward Thorndike's law of effect.

The first slot machine, called the Liberty Bell, was invented by San Francisco native Charles Fey. Depositing a coin and pulling a lever would set three reels spinning, each one decorated with the same set of colourful symbols. The aim for players from the beginning was to get three matching symbols to line up when the reels stopped spinning. Over the years, different kinds of fruit, especially cherries, became common symbols on the machines. In Britain, where the machines are often found in pubs, they are called "fruit machines."

Obviously, the odds have always been against the players—hence the term "one-armed bandits"—but for most of the twentieth century these were "natural odds" having to do with the mechanics of the machines. During the last few decades, the machines have been computer-programmed, their levers replaced by buttons or touch screens. This technology has allowed manufacturers of the machines to manipulate the results. The newer machines, known informally as "cherry dribblers," are behaviourist-driven socializing agents. They offer a reassuring number of rewards, small payouts, and bonus rounds in which the possible prizes are higher. They also serve a relatively high number of two-of-a-kind "near wins," so that people will think that they are "*this* close" to winning. They are not. There is no payout for "almost winning." There is only winning and losing.

The Oversocialized View of Human Behaviour

Critics of the social determinist perspective argue that it is important not to view humans as merely passive recipients of socialization. Canadian sociologist **Dennis H. Wrong** (1961), for example, warned against taking an **oversocialized** view of people. Wrong argued that people do not completely conform to the lessons of their socialization, automatically doing what socializing agents dictate. Rather, they can elect to resist their socialization. Put another way, they have a greater degree of agency—the power to influence the outcomes of one's life—than a behaviourist like Thorndike would acknowledge.

Wrong's critique of the social determinist position came during the 1950s, a period associated with growing commercialism and conformity to norms in North America. His arguments resonate in the **branding** days of the twenty-first century, as advertisers tried to socialize children at younger and younger ages into thinking that they can acquire social acceptance through branded products. It is also worth considering this point in terms of the debate (discussed in Chapter 5) between proponents of mass culture, who see individuals as passive recipients of cultural messages, and champions of popular culture, who view individuals as having agency in producing and interpreting culture.

In the debate between determinism and agency, consider the story of Luis Aguiar, who teaches sociology at the Okanagan campus of the University of British Columbia. Born in the Azores, off the coast of Portugal, Aguiar grew up in Montreal and experienced the "working-class socialization" of his parents, who encouraged him to adopt a trade rather than to pursue a postsecondary education. They could not understand the idea of "finding a career,"

What do *you* think?

How does the law of effect apply to someone sitting at a casino slot machine? In what other situations are humans trained to behave a certain way by the promise of an occasional, small reward?

and they considered boys who preferred mental to physical work "sexually suspect" and "unmanly" (Aguiar, 2001, pp. 187–8). Aguiar's father even supplied his son with examples of men "who became insane as a result of too much reading and studying" (p. 180).

Ultimately, Aguiar did go to university, demonstrating agency by overcoming his parents' attempts to socialize him into entering a trade. However, he was not unaffected by their efforts that left him with feelings of guilt, since he could not, because of the length of his schooling, help the family financially until relatively late in their lives:

Today I still feel terribly guilty because of my selfish educational pursuits that deprived my parents from owning a home or car or having some higher level of comfort in their retirement years. My parents never complained about my lack of financial contribution to the family, but my sense is that they are extremely disappointed at not achieving the immigrant dream of owning their own home. To my mind, only immigrant students of working-class background feel this heavy load of class guilt. (Aguiar, 2001, p. 191)

The Point Is . . .

Cold Mothers Don't Cause Autism

The tendency to adopt an oversocialized view of certain behaviours has caused experts to ascribe biological conditions to ineffective socialization, usually blaming the parents. Male homosexuality was once commonly attributed to poor socialization involving a smothering, over-attentive mother and a weak or absent father. Joseph Nicolosi is a clinical psychologist who still holds this outdated view. In a 2002 handbook for parents, he warns that

> if a father wants his son to grow up straight, he has to break the mother-son bond that is proper to infancy but not in the boy's best interest afterward. In this way, the father has to be a model, demonstrating that it is possible for his son to maintain a loving relationship with this woman, his mom, while still maintaining his own independence. (Nicolosi & Nicolosi, 2002, p. 27)

Though not many clinical psychologists today subscribe to this oversocialized view, such ideas have become embedded in cultural notions of "masculinity" development.

Ineffective parenting and faulty socialization also were blamed for the behaviours associated with autism. Autism spectrum disorder encompasses several conditions and may be associated with social communication difficulties, repetitive or fixated behaviours, and sensory problems.

Autism appears to have a strong biological and/or genetic component. The influence of the effects of socialization is strongly contested. There was a time, though, when it was widely believed that so-called refrigerator mothers, described as "cold" women who withheld affection from their sons, were responsible: they had supposedly socialized their children into not expecting warmth from a parent. This oversocialized view developed from Freudian foundations in the 1940s, when autism was first described, and then expounded single-mindedly with worldwide influence by a Viennese devoté of Freud (who believed mothers caused their children's mental illness): the self-styled child psychologist Bruno Bettelheim (1903–1990). Bettelheim perpetrated academic fraud at the University of Chicago Orthogenic School for disturbed children. He is reported to have been a compulsive liar. He claimed to have academic degrees and qualifications that he did not have. He perpetrated and encouraged abuses on the autistic children in care. His assistant and successor in the school, Jacquelyn Sanders, later confessed:

> "We became abusers of abused children"; that "children who had aggressive tendencies identified with this aspect of our approach"; and that "we became actors in sexual-sado-masochistic fantasies." The biographer who published these findings

(Continued)

concludes that "physical and emotional abuse was a part of everyday life at the Orthogenic School," with children feeling like frightened prisoners, some of whom were incarcerated for longer than Bettelheim himself had been [at Dachau and Buchenwald concentration camps during World War II]. (Badcock, 2010)

Bettelheim's oversocialized explanation of autism has been rejected, but only after three generations of women were blamed for their children's autism or other mental illnesses through ineffective socialization.

The Canadian physician Gabor Maté gained a large audience for a less strident version of the same belief: that inadequate parenting creates trauma that predisposes their children to addiction, dyslexia (attention deficit disorder [ADD/ADHD]), autism, and other "mental" problems. He describes heart-wrenching mental illness in addicts and claims to "see trauma" in everyone (Maté, 2009, ch. 3). Yet why should that trauma be ascribed to a parent, let alone to the mother? When parents have several children, only one of whom develops a mental illness, might not the illness lie in the child rather than in the parent? Or perhaps hereditary factors cause intergenerational illness.

By contrast, the noted Canadian psychiatrist (former Chair in Psychiatry at the University of Toronto) and writer Norman Doidge (2015) showcases accounts of an autistic child, a suicidally depressed child, and a dyslexic teen healed with the Tomatis Method of music therapy developed by French otolaryngologist Alfred Tomatis. In addition, although Guy Bérard, another French otolaryngologist who initially collaborated with Tomatis, claimed to have healed only one autistic child, his binaural music treatment significantly helped a great many autistics. He also had consistent results with his 1,800 dyslexic syndrome patients, healing all of them of their principal symptom, which was not being able to learn to read. And Bérard cured 97.7 per cent of his suicidal patients: all but five of the 233 suicidal patients he diagnosed and treated. Four were not cured following treatment. One committed suicide at the beginning of treatment (Bérard and Brockett, 2011, p. 101).

4.3 Agents of Socialization

Luis Aguiar's parents were among his most influential agents of socialization, meaning the people who had a significant impact on his socialization. Many individuals, groups, and institutions can act as agents of socialization—and the list varies from person to person—but the following are most likely to be highly influential agents of socialization for most people:

- family
- peer group
- neighbourhood/community
- school
- mass media and pop culture
- the legal system
- culture, including religion

The relative impact of each of these agents is greatly contested in the sociological literature and in psychology and other academic studies in the humanities. Yet theories about all of them prevail in popularized versions in bestselling books. You will notice most of them in the day-to-day conversations of people in society. In the following sections, we'll take a closer look at some of the debates surrounding their influence.

Significant Other, Generalized Other, and Sense of Self

The American psychologist George Herbert Mead saw all agents of socialization falling into one of two categories he named "significant other" and "generalized other." He believed that children develop their sense of self by internalizing values and behaviours modelled by these "others" in their lives (Mead, 1934).

Significant others are those key individuals—primarily parents but, to a lesser degree, older siblings and close friends—that young children imitate and after whom they model themselves. Picture a mother or father doing yardwork with a young child imitating their clearing of leaves but with a toy rake. The parent, in this case, is a significant other to the child. (Note that your boyfriend/girlfriend, your spouse, or your partner is not your "significant other" in the sociological sense.)

Mead's concept of the **generalized other** is a bit harder to grasp. The generalized other is not one person. It's more like a composite of all the people who make up a group, such as a team, a local community, or a larger section of society. As children grow up, they become aware of the attitudes and expectations of various others, and as they do so, they adjust their own behaviour to conform to the generalized social expectations of these groups. How, for example, do you think your social media profiles and posts are shaped by the audience you imagine is or might be interested, that is, by the generalized other?

Mead also identified a developmental *sequence* for socialization, just as Freud and Erikson did.

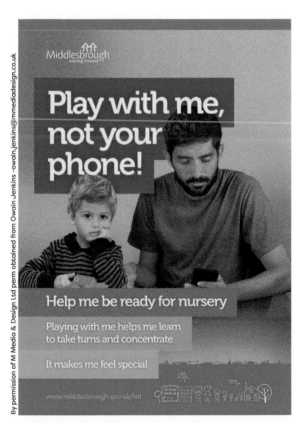

By permission of M Media & Design Ltd perm obtained from Owain Jenkins –owain_jenkins@mmediadesign.co.uk

A British campaign warned parents of the harm their cellphone use might be doing to their children. What lessons might the child in this ad be internalizing from his significant other? How might that affect his behaviour as he grows older?

Mead's sequence begins with the **preparatory stage**, which involves simple imitation by the child. The next step is the **play stage**, where the child engages in **role-taking**. At this stage, children are aware of the viewpoints of significant others—parents, grandparents, siblings, and so on—and can imagine what those others are thinking about them as they act. The third stage is the **game stage**, in which a child is able to consider several roles and viewpoints simultaneously. A seven-year-old playing soccer, for instance, will understand that the goalie has a different role from other players on the team, and that players on an opposing team will have different objectives than those of the players on their own team. Whereas younger children tend to make up rules as they play, children at this stage can understand and follow the socially recognized rules for organized sports, board games, card games, and so on.

Significant and generalized others continue to exert strong socialization influences later in the life of an individual, with important consequences for the individual's self-concept. Mentors and other role models can be important significant others to an adolescent or adult. The media, meanwhile, is a leading source of generalized others that can have a powerful impact on the individual's sense of self. Advertisers cultivate generalized others to great effect. When a commercial presents a group of young, attractively dressed people dancing and having a good time, the advertising agency is trying to tell you that these shoes/shirts/jeans and the drinks, snacks, and media devices are what your cool, young community likes, and you should, too. At the same time, advertisers also use celebrity spokespersons—a star athlete, the latest musical pop sensation—who they hope will be viewed as significant others by consumers in their target market. This ploy can backfire, of course: when celebrities transgress the moral norms of a society, they lose their marketability as role models. In May 2018, Vancouver's transit authority, TransLink, suspended announcements broadcast over its SkyTrain system when the reader of those announcements, actor Morgan Freeman, was accused of sexual harassment. Two months later, TransLink announced that a native of Vancouver, Seth Rogen, was the new voice of a series of etiquette tips for its SkyTrain riders. Why do you think a public transit system needs a celebrity to remind passengers to keep their feet off the seats?

Another symbolic interactionist, **Charles Horton Cooley** (1864–1929), presented the idea of the **looking-glass self**. This notion of the individual's self-image is based on how people think they are viewed by others (see Cooley, 1902, 1909). In Cooley's

poetic words, "each to each a looking glass / Reflects the other that doth pass" (quoted in Marshall, 1998, p. 374). The looking-glass self has three components:

1. how you imagine you appear to others
2. how you imagine those others judge you according to your appearance
3. how you feel as a result (proud, ashamed, self-confident, embarrassed).

The relationship between body image and self-esteem, especially in young women, illustrates this idea. Harvard educational psychologist and feminist **Carol Gilligan** notes how the self-esteem of girls declines during their teenage years (Gilligan, 1990). Studies show that this happens more with girls and young women than with boys. The harsher standards of body type that we apply to women have rightfully been associated with this difference in self-esteem. However, people with very low self-esteem may go to great lengths to present themselves as beautiful, polished, groomed, careful about their clothing, using polite language, and so on.

Family

The family is an individual's first agent of socialization, and often the most powerful one. Just as families differ across cultures, so do the means and goals of families in socializing the child. Consider the Telling It Like It Is feature describing the research conducted among the Rajput of Khalapur in northern India by John T. Hitchcock (1917–2001) and Ann Leigh Minturn (1928–1999) in the early 1960s. Their work was part of a classic study of cross-cultural socialization, Beatrice Whiting's *Six Cultures: Studies of Child Rearing* (1963).

Class and the Passing on of Parental Values to Children

In a classic study of socialization, American sociologist Melvin Kohn (1959) investigated the relationship between social class and the way parents socialize their children. The study was done in Washington, DC, with children aged 10 and 11. Kohn drew his research subjects from 11 census tracts: four were predominantly working-class, four were mostly middle-class, and the remaining three were made up of working-class and middle-class households in roughly equal numbers. His sample contained 200 families in which the father had a white-collar job,

Plus-size model Tess Holliday's appearance on the UK edition of *Cosmopolitan* was seen as a positive step for a magazine better known for its tips on how to achieve a standard of beauty represented by much skinnier models. Praise for the magazine was not universal, though. English commentator Piers Morgan called the cover "dangerous & misguided," viewing Holliday as a negative role model in light of Britain's "ever-worsening obesity crisis." As an agent of socialization, is Tess Holliday a positive or a negative role model? What about Piers Morgan?

Telling It Like It Is

The Point of View of Two Anthropologists

The Rajputs: Child-Rearing and Personality in a North Indian Village, c. 1960

Although Rajput infants will be picked up and attended to when they are hungry or fussing, for the most part they are left in their cots, wrapped up in blankets. . . . Except for anxieties about a baby's health, it is not the centre of attention. A baby receives attention mainly when it cries. At that time, someone will try to distract it, but when it becomes quiet, the interaction will stop. Adult interaction with babies is generally aimed at producing a cessation of response, rather than stimulation of it. Infants and children of all ages are not shown off to others. . . . Children are also not praised by their parents, who fear that this will "spoil" them and make them disobedient.

Rajput children . . . are never left alone, yet neither are they the centre of interest. The child learns that moodiness will not be tolerated. Few demands are put on Rajput children; they are not pressured or even encouraged to become self-reliant. Weaning, which generally occurs without trouble, takes place at two to three years; but if the mother does not become pregnant, a child may be nursed into its sixth year. There is no pressure for toilet training. . . . Babies are not pressured, or even encouraged to walk. They learn to walk when they are ready, and mothers say they see no reason to rush this. . . .

Village women do little to guide children's behaviour by explaining or reasoning with them. There is also little direct instruction to small children. Small children learn . . . the customs and values of the group through observation and imitation. In the first five years of life, the child moves very gradually from observer to participant in village and family life. . . .

Children are not encouraged in any way to participate in adult activities. The chores a child is given are mainly directed to helping the mother. . . . There is little feeling that children should be given chores on principle in order to train them in responsibility. . . . Rajput children take little initiative in solving problems by themselves. Instead, they are taught whom they can depend on for help in the web of social relations of kin group, caste, and village. . . . Although chores increase somewhat as the child gets older, it is not a Rajput custom to require children to work if adults can do it. Children are not praised for their work, and a child's inept attempt to do an adult job is belittled. Thus children are reluctant to undertake what they cannot do well.

Source: Excerpted from Hitchcock and Minturn (1963).

What do you think?
1. How would this style of child-rearing be interpreted by a behaviourist?
2. What values are being taught with this form of socialization?
3. How does this parenting style compare with your upbringing?
4. How do survival strategies in an Indian village six decades ago compare with the socialization needs of a family in a Canadian big-city suburb today?

and 200 families in which the father had a "manual occupation" (Kohn, 1959).

Parents were presented with a set of 17 value-based characteristics and asked to indicate which characteristics they most valued in their fifth-graders. While some characteristics were valued by middle-class and working-class parents, certain qualities were valued more highly by one class or the other (see Table 4.1).

An important conclusion of the study was that middle-class parents valued self-control or inner control, while working-class parents put a higher valuation on external control. As Kohn himself put it in a reassessment of the work (Kohn, 1977), "Middle-class parents . . . are more likely to emphasize children's *self-direction*, and working-class parents to emphasize their *conformity to external authority*" (p. 34). What does this mean? Essentially, Kohn believed that

TABLE 4.1 Areas of Significant Difference in Working-Class and Middle-Class Rankings of Values

As Judged by Mothers					
Valued in Boys ("That he . . .")		Valued in Girls ("That she . . .")		Valued Overall ("That he or she . . .")	
Middle Class	Working Class	Middle Class	Working Class	Middle Class	Working Class
• is happy • is curious about things	• obeys his parents well	• is considerate of others	• is neat and clean	• is happy • is considerate of others • has self-control • is curious about things	• is honest • obeys his/her parents well
As Judged by Fathers					
Valued in Boys ("That he . . .")		Valued in Girls ("That she . . .")		Valued Overall ("That he or she . . .")	
Middle Class	Working Class	Middle Class	Working Class	Middle Class	Working Class
• is happy • is considerate of others • is dependable	• obeys his parents well	• is considerate of others • is dependable • has self-control • is ambitious	• is honest • obeys her parents well • is able to defend herself • is popular with other children • is a good student • is liked by adults	• is happy • is considerate of others • is dependable • has self-control	• obeys his/her parents well • is a good student • is able to defend him/herself

Source: Kohn (1977, Tables 2.1 and 2.2).

working-class families were raising their children to value qualities that would make them successful members of that class—notably, obedience to authority and conformity—while middle-class families were socializing their children into white-collar occupations by emphasizing self-reliance, independence, and curiosity. Kohn noted that wives of the men with the better-educated jobs (professionals and highly educated businessmen) put the highest value on these characteristics. Kohn later carried out comparative studies in Poland, Ukraine, and China to see if he could replicate his findings there, which he did.

What do *you* think?

1. What is the significance of Kohn's finding similar results in Poland, Ukraine, and China? What other variables are at play in socialization that Kohn does not address in his research?
2. How would you expect Kohn's findings to be different if he were conducting the same study today, among twenty-first-century families in Washington, DC, with its predominantly Black demographic? How might those results differ from a parallel study in a large Canadian city?

Family Socialization through the Lens of Culture and Personality

I mentioned that the impacts of certain agents of socialization are contested. One of the more debated mechanisms of socialization is the focus of the **culture and personality** school of thought, which emerged during the first half of the twentieth century, drawing on sociology, anthropology, and psychology. Proponents of this school attempted to identify and describe idealized personalities or "personality types" for different societies, attaching to each one a particular form of family socialization. During World War II and in the early years of the Cold War standoff between the West and the Soviet Union, the scope of these studies broadened to examine **national character**, the personality type of entire nations. These studies typically drew conclusions about how the primary socialization of child-raising was linked to a country's national character.

An example is *The People of Great Russia* (1949), in which Geoffrey Gorer and John Rickman proposed the **swaddling hypothesis**. They identified moodiness as a supposedly typical Russian character trait, citing extremes of controlled and out-of-control behaviour (for example, intense bouts of alcoholism), and attributed it to the *swaddling*—snug bundling—of infants commonly practised among Russian families. Theories that attempt to generalize about such large populations are extremely difficult to prove. Alcoholism is extremely widespread and by no means exclusive to Russia. Furthermore, other cultures swaddle their children, many using traditional cradle boards in use for centuries or millennia. Canadian Indigenous people find them multifunctional as cradles, carriers, high chairs, and baby seats. Many are beautifully decorated. Swaddling is not dangerous if done properly and infants usually enjoy the comfort of close wrapping.

Studies attempting to link child socialization practices to national character could have faded from thought if it weren't for violent aggression. A desire to understand personality traits of certain populations assumes there is such a thing as a "national character." Since the 11 September 2001 attacks on the United States and the rise of groups like Daesh (the self-styled Islamic State), al-Qaeda, and al-Shabaab, the media and Western political and military leaders have focused particular attention on the "Arab mind."

Of course, an awareness of social dichotomies existed long before 9/11. Raphael Patai's *The Arab Mind*, first published in 1973, gained new attention after the 9/11 attacks, and replicates the negative excesses of the "national character" studies by oversimplifying the psychological makeup of very diverse societies and by tying that broad portrait to over-generalized child-raising practices. Think of the significant class differences and life experiences between, say, oil-wealthy Saudi princes and Arab shop-owners and camel-herders. Families in different cultures and classes may socialize their children differently, but no culture exhibits complete uniformity in its socialization practices.

As we will see in Chapter 5, people commonly mistake their own culture as complex and dynamic while viewing others as fixed and easy to caricature in stereotypes. All cultures have elements that are contested, and a population of many millions cannot be reduced to a single set of personality traits or a unified mindset. While such stereotyping can lead to racism, it is important to notice that elements within cultures also can be racist toward each other. For example, cracks in the United States political system are turning the Republican Party into a fascist movement against the Democrats, and especially against immigrants, the Other, and people of colour. Similarly, the religious divide between Shiite and Sunni Muslims has been transplanted into the nations of their diaspora.

Peer Group

An important agent of socialization is the **peer group**, a social group sharing characteristics such as age, social position, and interests. The term usually is applied to children and adolescents.

The term **peer pressure** refers to the social force exerted on individuals by their peers to conform in behaviour, appearance, or externally demonstrated values, such as not appearing excited about something that isn't deemed acceptable and important to the group. Peer pressure is a highly visible type of socialization.

A classic sociological study that argues for the strength of the influence of the adolescent peer group is Paul E. Willis's *Learning to Labour: How Working Class Kids Get Working Class Jobs* (1977). Willis studied the informal culture of a group of 12 teenage boys attending a working-class, all-male school in the industrial town of Hammerstown, England. Willis wanted to know why working-class boys chose labouring jobs rather than aiming for the kinds of jobs obtained by middle-class boys in their cohort. He believed the boys were not passive recipients, through socialization, of the informal working-class culture. Rather, he speculated that, through acts of minority-culture resistance to the dominant culture, they were active participants in the creation of their own culture—with its belief and values systems and rules

> **What do you think?**
> 1. Do you think the power held by the Hammerstown peer group was related more to the fact that the students attended a single-gender school or to the fact that they were from working-class families?
> 2. Do you think these individuals had as much agency as Willis claimed they had? If not, what sort of determinism were they subject to?

Telling It Like It Is

An Author's Point of View

Experiencing Peer Pressure

Almost everyone is exposed to peer pressure while growing up. How we respond to the powerful influence exerted by our peer group helps to mould us into the adults we become.

When I was 10, I hung out with a small group of classmates. I felt they were "cooler" than I was, so I was susceptible to pressure from that peer group. I was up for pretty much any of their hijinks, even when I knew they weren't the wisest things to do. We never caused serious harm but we took risks that could have had terrible outcomes. We begged candy from a local candy manufacturer and stole chocolate bars from the neighbourhood drug store. We played "chicken" with trains on the railroad tracks. We threw snowballs at passing cars. Peer pressure prompted me

do things I knew were wrong and would never have done in a different social group.

But it's important to recognize that peer pressure plays a vital role in forging personality. By encouraging a degree of conformity, peer pressure helps children develop friendships and find acceptance among others their own age, fostering self-confidence and independence. I belonged to a class of smart kids culled from various schools in the district. At first, we felt separate, different. Before long, we formed a close circle from which we all gained a sense of belonging. Our solidarity gave us a fairly safe place to test norms and values. By remembering these stories, I become less critical of younger people who do similar things with worse consequences.

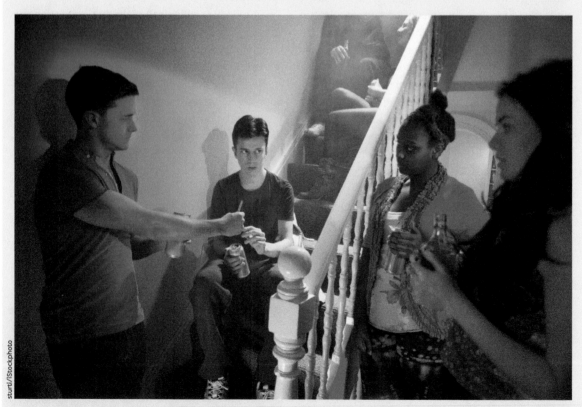

sturti/iStockphoto

How does the peer group you interact with in person differ from the peer group you interact with online? What kinds of socializing influences does your online community exert on you? Is the peer pressure you experience online different from the peer pressure pictured above? If so, how?

of behaviour—and in socializing newcomers into their culture. Among the evidence Willis found to support his theory were vocalized disdain for and humour directed against more conformist middle-class peers, ridicule of the "effeminate" nature of the mind-centred work done in school and in offices, and denunciation of middle-class values in general. The minority-culture resistance also involved manipulating the classroom (by controlling attendance and the quality of work done, for example) and educational figures of authority in ways that the youths would repeat in the "shop floor" environments of factories and warehouses and in opposition to the middle-management people they would encounter there. Their classroom behaviour prepared them for their future.

Community and Neighbourhood

Risk Behaviour

Community and neighbourhood can be important agents in child and adolescent socialization. With that awareness, families debate whether they should live in the city or in a town or suburb outside the big city where they work. Urban planners in this generation are concerned about creating mixed-class urban neighbourhoods rather than ghettoizing the economically disadvantaged in government-assisted housing projects, which was the trend in the twentieth century. However, people living in cities ghettoize themselves without help from urban planners.

Studies of young people living outside large cities late in the twentieth century revealed that they were at lower risk of becoming involved in crime, drug and alcohol abuse, and other high-risk behaviour. **Risk behaviours** include driving at dangerous speeds, engaging in unsafe sexual activities, drinking to excess, experimenting with different drugs, and so on. Much of this research was carried out in the United States, although American developmental psychologist Jeffrey Arnett and Danish-born sociologist Lene Balle-Jensen (1993) performed a cross-cultural study of adolescents in the United States and in Denmark. Their findings showed a correlation between risk behaviour and city size (1993). As the authors explained:

> City size was related to adolescents' reports of sex without contraception, sex with someone known only casually, marijuana use, heavy marijuana use, shoplifting, vandalism, and cigarette dependency. For most types of risk behavior, adolescents in the larger city were more likely to report the risk behavior than adolescents in the smaller city. (Arnett & Balle-Jensen, 1993, p. 1849)

More recent research suggests that rates of drug and alcohol use in rural areas of North America have caught up to and in some cases surpassed the rates in cities. A 2015 review of the literature for the Canadian Centre on Substance Abuse reports that "Among American youth, those living in a rural setting are more likely to report use of alcohol, compared to those living in urban areas," and that "the former group is also more likely to report heavy drinking on one occasion and risk behaviours, such as drinking and driving, or driving under the influence of illicit drugs" (McInnis, Young, et al., 2015, p. 4). Drawing on studies of Canadian students from across the country, the researchers found that students in rural schools in Canada were more likely than students in urban schools to report alcohol use, heavy drinking, and driving while under the influence of alcohol or cannabis (McInnis, Young, & Student Drug Use Surveys Working Group, 2015, p. 17). The greater necessity for having a car or truck in a rural location, where there is little or no public transportation, may affect those figures. There were no significant differences in rural and urban rates of using illicit or prescription drugs.

Broad and Narrow Socialization

Let's return to Arnett and Balle-Jensen's study to see how they accounted for the fact that adolescents in certain communities were especially prone to engaging in risky behaviour. The authors recognized that there is a biological component to such behaviour—a predisposition to certain kinds of behaviour that is present prenatally, from birth, or acquired early in infancy in certain individuals—but they also stressed the large role that socialization plays in encouraging or discouraging risk behaviours. In presenting their

What do you think?
How might you account for the correlation between risk behaviour and type of community (big city, small city, rural)?

Marc Taylor for Maclean's

In Kamsack, Saskatchewan, population 1,825, two men wait for a drug store to open so they can pick up their methadone. What other resources for opioid addicts may be scarce in a small, rural community?

argument, they made an important distinction between **narrow socialization** and **broad socialization**, describing them as follows:

> In cultures characterized by *broad socialization*, individualism and independence are promoted, and there is relatively less restrictiveness on the various dimensions of socialization. This allows for a broad range of expression of individual differences on the developmental tendencies (such as sensation seeking) that contribute to risk behaviour, and leads to higher rates of risk behaviour. Cultures characterized by *narrow socialization*, in contrast, consider obedience and conformity to the standards and expectations of the community to be paramount (enforced through the parents and the school as well as through members of the community), and punish physically and/or socially any deviation from the norm. The result is greater obedience and conformity, a narrower range of expression of individual differences, and low rates of antisocial adolescent risk behaviour (although risk-taking tendencies may be directed by such cultures into avenues that serve a culturally approved purpose, such as warfare). (Arnett & Balle-Jensen, 1993, p. 1843)

In other words, young people in cultures characterized by broad socialization have greater freedom to act independently and make choices—about what they will study at school, how they will spend their time when they're not at school, where they will work, with whom they will socialize, and so on. By contrast, in cultures based on narrow socialization, young people face greater pressure—from families, from the authorities, and from society in general—to act a certain way and to conform to widely held expectations regarding behaviour. Adolescents in these societies, therefore, are less likely to participate in risky activities.

To test this hypothesis, Arnett and Balle-Jensen undertook a cross-cultural study of adolescent socialization in Denmark. While that country has a tendency toward broad socialization, the researchers noted ways in which Denmark has narrower socialization than the United States. For instance, they cite the fact that the legal driving age in Denmark is 18, reflecting narrow socialization elements in the legal system and in the cultural belief system. It reflects, too, a different cultural consensus concerning the balance between ensuring the individual autonomy of the teenager who wants to drive a car and the good of the community, through fewer traffic fatalities and fewer cars on the road. According to these researchers, then, this narrower socialization means that in Denmark fewer adolescents engage in the risk behaviour of unsafe driving than in North America.

Mass Media

Questions about the role communication for the masses plays in socializing young people go back at least as far as the ancient Greek philosopher Plato, who felt that art (in his day, plays) aroused primal instincts, stimulating violence and lust. Plato's student Aristotle believed that violence depicted in art actually produced among those viewing it an experience of *catharsis*, a release of hostile or violent emotions during the theatrical experience that leads to a rational sense of resolution and to emotional peace. Theatre, of course, is replicated exponentially in mass media, and so it wasn't until the middle of the twentieth century, after television arrived on the scene, that researchers began to wonder about and investigate the socializing effects of media drama, which extends to news reporting and other "real" programming.

A Canadian-born clinical psychologist, Albert Bandura, made a major contribution to the research with a series of experiments he conducted in the 1960s. Recall Edward Thorndike, the "rat psychologist" we met earlier in this chapter. The central tenet of his behaviourism is that behaviour is learned through rewards and penalties. If someone compliments you on your new leather pants, you may wear them again tomorrow. If someone laughs or disapproves, you may not.

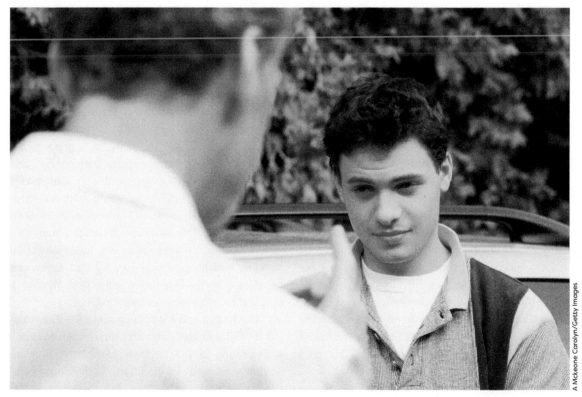

A McIeone Carolyn/Getty Images

Growing up, you might have felt as though your parents were on your back *all the time*. Overall, would you say your upbringing was characterized by narrow socialization or broad socialization?

Bandura wanted to see if behaviour could be learned without rewards and penalties. He set up an experiment in which children were placed individually in a room with an adult, an inflatable clown (a "Bobo doll"), and an assortment of toys, including stickers, tops, mallets, and bats. Children in the "control group" were invited to play with the toys while the adult sat in an opposite corner. Children in the "experimental group" watched as the adult abused the Bobo doll physically and verbally. In both scenarios, the adult left the room for a period, leaving each child alone in the room with the doll.

Can you guess what happened? Children in the control group paid little attention to the doll. Children who had witnessed the doll being struck or shouted at repeated these behaviours when left alone. In variations of the experiment, the adult was either praised or scolded by the experimenter for their treatment of the doll, and this reinforcement of the adult's behaviour had an effect on how the children behaved. The important point is that the children were not receiving any direct rewards or penalties. These findings become an important part of Bandura's social cognitive learning theory. First, people (children and adults) learn by observing the behaviour of other people—that's the social part. Second, we are able to assess the rewards and penalties implied by demonstrated actions and to make judgments about how and when we "should" perform those learned behaviours.

Bandura's research wasn't designed to test the effects of watching violent images on television, but you can see why people made that link. His research helped touch off a debate that has yet to be settled: Do mass media—through action movies that make heroes out of vicious criminals, video games that promote war and crime, and TV shows that glorify death and murder—socialize young people, especially adolescent males, into committing violence, or at least into being desensitized to violence and the pain of others? Or do they provide a safe outlet for pent-up hostile emotions? Competing viewpoints in the contentious debate are offered in the following passages. First up, arguing for a link between media violence and criminal activity, are Brad Bushman and Rowell Huesmann:

True, media violence is not likely to turn an otherwise fine child into a violent criminal.

But, just as every cigarette one smokes increases a little bit the likelihood of a lung tumor someday, every violent show one watches increases just a little bit the likelihood of behaving more aggressively in some situation. (Bushman & Huesmann, 2001, p. 248)

Arguing for the other side is communications professor and sociologist Jib Fowles, in *The Case for Television Violence*:

Television is not a schoolhouse for criminal behavior. . . . Viewers turn to this light entertainment for relief, not for instruction. Video action exists, and is resorted to, to get material out of minds rather than to put things into them. . . . Television violence is good for people. (Fowles, 1999, pp. 53, 118)

Huesmann's Longitudinal Studies

Huesmann's pioneering work on the effects of television violence on children involved the use of **longitudinal studies**, which examined data gathered on research subjects over an extended period of time. His first was a 22-year study of 856 youths in New York State. At the beginning of his study, the participants were in Grade 3, about 8 years of age. Huesmann interviewed them again when they were 19, and again at 30 (Huesmann & Eron, 1986). Among male subjects, the relationship between viewing television violence and engaging in aggressive behaviour roughly 10 years later was both positive and highly significant—in other words, the link was a strong one. These findings were consistent for males of different social classes, IQ scores, and levels of aggressiveness at the start age. When the male subjects were checked again at age 30, the relationship between violent television viewing and aggressive behaviour—both self-reported and as documented in criminal records—was just as strong.

Huesmann and his colleagues (2003) also studied 557 Chicago-area children from Grade 1 to Grade 4, beginning in 1977. Fifteen years later, they interviewed as many of them (and their spouses and friends) as they could. They also looked at public records and archival material. The researchers were able to gather reasonably complete data for

329—roughly 60 per cent—of the original research participants (153 men and 176 women, all in their early twenties by then). The results of this study were similar to those of the earlier study, with the only difference being that the link between TV violence and aggressive behaviour was evident among women as well as among men. The researchers concluded their study as follows:

> Overall, these results suggest that both males and females from all social strata and all levels of initial aggressiveness are placed at increased risk for the development of adult aggressive and violent behavior when they view a high and steady diet of violent TV shows in early childhood. (Huesmann et al., 2003, p. 218)

Huesmann proposed two theories to explain the data. One, **observational learning theory**, states that children acquire what he termed "aggressive scripts" for solving social problems through watching violence on television. The other, **desensitization theory**, states that increased exposure to television violence desensitizes or numbs the natural negative reaction to violence.

Fowles's Defence of Television Violence

Jib Fowles has argued that sociologists and others who condemn violence on television are really using TV violence as a pretext to tackle other issues: class, race, gender, and generation. He calls television violence a "whipping boy, a stand-in for other clashes":

> The attack on television violence is, at least in part, an attack by the upper classes and their partisans on popular culture. In this interpretation . . . the push to reform television is simply the latest manifestation of the struggle between the high and the low, the dominant and the dominated. (Fowles, 2001, p. 2)

Fowles draws upon the work of **Pierre Bourdieu** (1930–2002), a French thinker best known for his work on the connection between class and culture. Fowles applies two of Bourdieu's concepts: habitus and reproduction. **Habitus** (more comprehensive in meaning than the word "habits") is a set of socially acquired behaviours, including definitions of "manners," "good taste," leisure pursuits, and ways of walking in public. Each social class has its own habitus, its set of shared characteristics. **Reproduction**, in Bourdieu's definition, is the means by which classes, particularly the upper or dominant class, preserve status differences among classes. As Fowles phrases it, "the reproduction of habitus is the key work of a social class" (Fowles, 2001, p. 3).

Fowles's main point is that sociologists who condemn television violence are merely fighting proxy wars aimed at reproducing the habitus of the dominant class by condemning the habitus of the dominated class. It is ironic that he uses Bourdieu's writing in his argument, as Bourdieu (1996) was a severe critic of television.

Education

The Teacher's Role in Socialization

Education can be a powerful socializing agent. Schools often are the first source of information that children receive about social groups other than their own. Teachers, curriculums, textbooks, and the social experience of being in the classroom and in

What do *you* think?

In what ways do you think violence is "normalized" in Canadian culture? Is violence a natural way to solve problems? If it is "natural," is it also justifiable? In domestic disputes, are women or men more likely to become violent? Is gender identification a factor in violent reactions to interactional problems?

What do *you* think?

1. Do you think that Fowles's arguments are valid? Do you think TV news reporting about violence, whether distant wars or paramilitarism in the United States or individual's violent crimes in Canada, should be part of this discussion?
2. In a number of cities, police forces put more officers on duty on nights when the latest instalment of *The Fast and the Furious* franchise is opening. Is this a statement about the socialization potential of these movies? If speeding is thought to be incited by a movie, why not violent behaviour in response to violence in movies?

Online video games like the hugely successful *Fortnite: Battle Royale*, in which players fight one another to the death, are attracting younger and younger participants. Which is more likely: That this young man is becoming desensitized to violence, or that he is ridding himself of aggression?

the playground all play a part. We will focus here on the role teachers play in the socializing function of education.

What we call the "social location" of the teacher—the teacher's gender, age, ethnicity, and so on—can have a powerful effect on the educational socialization of the student. The fact that the early years of schooling are dominated by women teachers will have different effects on girl and boy students. The fact that science and math courses in high school usually are taught by men and English courses by women also will have different effects on girls and boys. Being of the same ethnic background or race as the teacher can have a positive effect on a child's socialization experience, as Kristin Klopfenstein points out in her discussion of Black teachers as role models:

> Poor [in terms of income] Black students, amongst whom teachers are often the only college-educated people they know, are in particular need of role models who (a) are interested in their educational progress; (b) understand the school system as an institution [i.e., as being located in the middle class and more in "white culture" than in "Black culture"]; and (c) actively encourage academic excellence and the pursuit of a challenging curriculum. Culturally similar teachers may take more interest in mentoring Black students and have more credibility with those students. Given the importance of a rigorous mathematics curriculum and that math is frequently a gate-keeper subject for Black students [i.e., success in math determines whether or not they will advance to post-secondary education], same-race math teachers play a potentially vital role in preparing Black students for their academic and working futures. (Klopfenstein, 2005, p. 416)

Klopfenstein looked for a correlation between having a Black math teacher in Grade 9 and the kinds of math courses a Black student would take the following year. She found that Black students who had had a Black math teacher in Grade 9 were more likely to enroll in a more challenging math class in Grade 10. These students, she found, also had a greater chance of postsecondary entry and success than students who had not had a Black math teacher.

The socialization effect of having Black teachers does not end there. Klopfenstein quotes P.R. Kane and A.J. Orsini's assertion that "Teachers of color are important role models to white students, as they shape white students' images of what people of color can and do achieve" (Kane & Orsini, 2003, p. 10). Though you may not have noticed, the prevailing demographics of the teachers you had growing up—their age, sex, ethnic background, and so on—played a role in your socialization.

Gendered Achievement in Reading, Writing, and Arithmetic

A common belief among parents and educators is that boys have a greater aptitude for the so-called STEM subjects—science, technology, engineering, and math—while girls have a higher ability in language and literature. Concerns that young female students are not succeeding at math and that boys are falling behind in reading have generated a large body of research into the accuracy of these assumptions and the causes.

The Organisation for Economic Co-operation and Development (OECD) tracks student achievement in its 35 member countries with its Program for International Student Assessment, more commonly known as PISA. The program tests 15-year-old students every three years in math, science, and reading, to see how different countries compare in turning their academic policies and funding into success. According to the results of the 2015 PISA survey, Canadian girls outperformed Canadian boys by an average of 26 points on the reading literacy scale; however, boys outperformed girls by 1 point on the science literacy scale and by 9 points on the literacy scale for mathematics (OECD, 2016, pp. 383, 328, 395). This appears to confirm the belief that boys do better in math and (by a narrow margin) science, while girls do better in reading.

PISA also generates some interesting findings on the career expectations of participating students. The 2015 survey found that 33.9 per cent of Canadian

> ### What do *you* think?
> How do you think the social location of a teacher might affect a student's socialization? Can you give personal examples? How do you think this might differ for male and female students, especially during the early years when, typically, most of the teachers are women?

students expected to be working in a science-related field by the time they were 30. That's well above the OECD average score of 24.5 per cent and well ahead of student scores for such countries as Germany (15.3 per cent), Israel (27.8 per cent), Japan (18.0 per cent), and Sweden (20.2 per cent). In fact, the only OECD countries with a higher percentage of students expecting to find work in the science professions were Chile (37.9 per cent), the United States (38.0 per cent), and Mexico (40.7 per cent). The Canadian results are notable also for the difference in male and female students' expectations. Across the OECD, male and female students expected to find work in the sciences in roughly equal percentages (25.0 per cent for boys, 24.0 per cent for girls). Among Canadian 15-year-olds, girls (36.5 per cent) were more likely than boys (31.2 per cent) to expect to work in science-related professions (OECD, 2016, p. 364). As Figure 4.1 shows, much of the difference has to do with girls expecting to enter health professions, as doctors, dentists, veterinarians, nurses, and so on.

To what extent does socialization influence these results? Sociologists and educators today recognize that socialization plays a big part in shaping student academic success and expectations. Beyond the actual instruction they provide, parents and teachers give cues to children about what is expected of them in these subjects. Some of these cues are fairly explicit, as when a parent tells a girl struggling in the supposedly male STEM subjects not to worry: "You aren't expected to do well in math," or "You won't need to know it." Other cues can be subtle, as when a teacher gives a male student a graphic novel to read instead of the traditional, unillustrated novel his female classmates are reading.

However, US studies regarding children of parents who hold postsecondary degrees show that those children are more successful at going to college or university and at completing their degree.

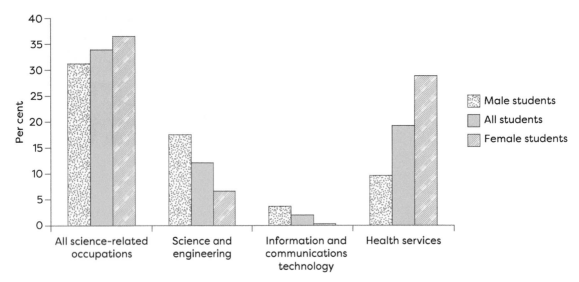

FIGURE 4.1 Percentage of 15-Year-Old Canadian Students Who Expect to Work in Science-Related Occupations at Age 30

Source: OECD (2016, Table 1.3.10b, Table 1.3.11a–c).

Thus, the greatest influence parents have on their children's learning may be whether or not they themselves excelled in a line of study and/or pursued it through postsecondary education.

A study published in the online journal *Psychological Bulletin* offers some interesting thoughts on the role of socialization in female students' math and science marks. The authors, Daniel Voyer and Susan Voyer (2014), performed a meta-analysis on grades awarded by teachers in 30 countries between 1914 and 2011. The researchers examined year-end grades awarded by teachers and found that girls (particularly in middle school) performed consistently better than boys not just in language and literature but also—by a smaller margin—in math and science (Voyer & Voyer, 2014, p. 1194). They acknowledge that these findings contradict analyses based on the results of standardized "performance tests" like the PISA assessment, but suggest that school marks provide a broader measure of long-term overall success than point-in-time tests.

Another study suggests that well-meaning parents can actually make their children's struggles worse. Researchers Ruchi Bhanot and Jasna Jovanovic (2005) found that when parents offer their children unsolicited help with homework, they may be undermining their children's confidence. As the researchers explain, "parents tend to provide such unsolicited—or intrusive—support when they perceive that their child is not doing well in school" (p. 598). Since many parents expect male students to struggle with English and female students to struggle with math, they will provide their uninvited assistance accordingly, reinforcing the stereotypes.

Considering the facts (see Jantz, 2014) known at present about the differences between the male and the female brains, such as the differences in the distribution and use of grey and white matter, how might that account for the differences in boys' and girls' success in particular academic subjects or in applied sciences? Is it possible that parents' and educators' approach to socialization in order to diminish the gender differences in literacy and math

What do *you* think?

1. Why do you think so many more Canadian girls than boys expect to enter the health professions? What socializing agents could be shaping female students' expectations about their future roles as doctors, veterinarians, dentists, and nurses?

2. Blaming the parents seems to be a recurring theme in our chapter on socialization. Do you think the criticism is fair when it comes to gender differences in classroom performance? What other socializing influences are at play? Which one do you think has the greatest bearing on academic performance?

The Point Is...

Parents May Be to Blame for the "Disappearance of Childhood"

David Elkind studies culture as an agent of socialization. One of his interests is the negative effects on children whose lives have been over-programmed by their parents, with little free time built in for spontaneous play. On this topic, Elkind's tone is dire: "[The] traditional culture of childhood is fast disappearing," he warns. "In the past two decades alone, according to several studies, children have lost 12 hours of free time a week, and eight of those lost hours were once spent in unstructured play and outdoor pastimes" (Elkind, 2003).

Spontaneous play, Elkind argues, has been replaced by a programmed schedule of organized sports and extracurricular learning. Technology is partly to blame: digital communication enables us to do more, faster, giving us a false feeling that we can accomplish much more than we used to. We extend this push for accomplishment to our children, putting pressure on them to take part in more after-school activities, play more organized sports, do more homework, and learn languages and other academic subjects at an earlier age. All of this contributes to what Elkind (2001) calls the **hurried child syndrome**, which causes kids to feel adult-like levels of stress and guilt. It also contributes to the sometimes crippling apprehension that postsecondary students feel about deadlines and about choosing their career—"I'm 21 and I don't know what I want to be." It doesn't help that television and the movies often present people in their twenties as being financially successful.

Elkind was expressing concerns similar to those of media commentator and cultural critic Neil Postman (1931–2003), who made an important contribution to the discussion of primary socialization with his book *The Disappearance of Childhood* (1982). Early in the book, Postman speaks of the disappearance of children's games. By "children's games" he means the kind of game that "requires no instructors or umpires or spectators . . . uses whatever space and equipment are at hand . . . [and] is played for no other reason than pleasure" (Postman, 1982, p. 4). Examples he cites include jacks, blind man's buff, hide-and-seek, and rhyming games played with a bouncing ball, to which I would add skipping games (which my sisters did all the time), marbles, capture-the-flag, and tag. He contrasts these kinds of games with organized sports such as Little League Baseball and peewee football, which are played by children following adult practices: maximizing adult-level competence through professional-style coaches and trainers. This leads him to the following series of questions, and a tentative conclusion:

> Why should adults encourage this possibility [i.e., adult-level competence]? Why would anyone wish to deny children the freedom, informality, and joy of spontaneous play? Why submit children to the rigors of professional-style training, concentration, tensions, media-hype? . . . What we have here is the emergence of the idea that play is not to be done for the sake of doing it but for some external purpose, such as renown, money, physical conditioning, upward mobility, national pride. For adults, play is serious business. As childhood disappears, so does the child's view of play. (Postman, 1982, p. 131)

and science skills is neutralized by some biological differences?

Many education experts recognize that boys and girls have different learning styles, and this view has led to experiments with single-sex classrooms and schools. However, the benefits of single-sex learning environments are difficult to assess. A 2012 report by a council of educators concluded that "the existing research on single-sex schooling is inconclusive and too tenuous to support a widespread move to single-sex classrooms or schools" (Ungerleider, Thompson, & Lavin, 2012).

If classroom socialization is not the source of differences, what is? Ungerleider et al. suggest that

What do *you* think?

1. The children Postman was writing about in 1982 have grown up to become the "helicopter parents" sometimes criticized for over-scheduling their children's lives today. Do you think this trend in the way parents are socializing their children is changing? If so, why do you think that is? Do you think the COVID-19 pandemic raised or lowered the pressure from "helicopter parents"?
2. Elkind also warned that advances in technology were affecting socialization by dissuading children from enjoying "traditional games" and thereby stifling opportunities to exercise imagination, originality, and autonomy. Do you agree or disagree with his assessment?

"Parents may play a role in the different performance levels achieved by boys and girls in math and reading," adding that "girls may be doing better in reading and boys may be doing better in math because of parents' own beliefs about boys' and girls' natural abilities. . . . Children absorb their parents' beliefs about their own abilities and then those beliefs become powerful determinants of their school success" (Ungerleider, Thompson, & Lavin, 2012).

4.4 COVID-19 and Schooling

Everything we have said about teachers' influence and parental influence in socialization and social roles was severely disrupted by the COVID-19 pandemic, not just in Canada but globally. At the time of this writing, not enough sociological research has

What do *you* think?

1. How did your school experience change during the September 2020 to August 2021 year?
2. How was your family affected by the first pandemic year?
3. How did your school experience change during the September 2021 to August 2022 year?
4. Do similarities and differences during the second year suggest helpful adjustments to the situation by the school board, administrators, and teachers? How did the issues of those people differ from yours?
5. Do you think you were advantaged or disadvantaged in relation to most of your peers? In what ways?

been done on those disruptions to report to you. Everyone has their own experiences of this enormously impactful event and has formed opinions based on their own experience, including their reading about what has been happening to others similarly impacted. Those sources are as varied as your friends (available mostly on your cellphone), the TV, internet, radio, podcast, and word-of-mouth in your local community. Governments at every level have taken a stance about the disease, its importance socially and economically, and its significance politically. However, those stances have differed from province to province and within municipalities. Individuals have been impacted differently within provinces, within economic strata, within municipalities, and even within neighbourhoods. News media, some of them highly politicized, have done a great deal of reporting. In fact, at times it has seemed as though COVID-19 and its ramifications were the only news topics.

The vast majority of readers of this text fall into the age bracket of the population least likely to fall gravely ill from COVID-19. Unless you have grandparents or other relatives over the age of 65, the responses of governments and other major social systems may look to you like over-reactions. If you or anyone in your family has worked in the medical professions or in any of the services deemed "essential," you doubtless will have been affected more comprehensively by the pandemic and may have developed much stronger opinions on those who hold positions of authority. While safety measures such as wearing masks in public, hand sanitizing, and social distancing have been relaxed, the COVID-19 virus continues to mutate and still is killing three times as many people as the flu.

4.5 Secondary Socialization and Resocialization

At the start of the chapter, we saw the difference between *primary socialization*, which occurs early in childhood, and *secondary socialization*, which usually occurs in adolescence and early adulthood. Secondary socialization also differs from primary socialization in that:

a) it typically involves a group that is smaller than society in general, such as a new school or a new neighbourhood; and

b) it usually takes place outside of the family (unless it involves a new "blended" family with step-parents and step-siblings).

Secondary socialization involves learning life lessons from a different source—from classmates at school or teammates on the ice instead of from parents at home. What you learn during secondary socialization may contradict some of what you've learned in primary socialization. Any time you switch from one experience of socialization to another—whether as a child or as an adult—you undergo **resocialization**. This process typically involves unlearning and learning. In extreme cases, the individual rejects all of the behaviours, attitudes, and values deemed appropriate in the previous social environment while accepting those that make it possible to socialize in the new situation.

Karen Armstrong describes her process of "unlearning" values in *Through the Narrow Gate*, which chronicles the period when, as a teenager, she joined a strict order of nuns in Britain. In the following passage she recollects what the Mother Superior said to her and others who had just joined the order as *postulants*, candidates seeking admission to the order:

> Novices and postulants are kept in a particularly strict seclusion. They may not speak at all to seculars [i.e., to those who are neither nuns nor priests]. If a secular speaks to you, you must never reply. It is only by severing yourself absolutely from the world that you can begin to shed some of its values. Again no novice or postulant may ever speak to the professed nuns unless she is working with them and those few necessary words are essential for the job. The professed are in contact with the world, and even that indirect contact might seriously damage your spiritual progress. . . .

> You have to be absolutely ruthless in your rejection of the world, you know, Sisters. So many of its attitudes, even in really good people, are permeated with selfish values that have nothing at all to do with the self-emptying love of God. You yourselves are riddled with these ideas; you can't help it—it's not your fault. (Armstrong, [1982]/2005, pp. 92–3)

Resocialization can be voluntary, as the extract from Armstrong's book implies. But one can question how ethical any total institution is, even when it is endorsed by a mainline religious organization, when a 17-year-old with some psychological issues is subjected to severe silencing in an order that encourages self-flagellation and self-injury as a form of "mortification." Humans deprived of sufficient sound energy become mentally ill because the left half of the brain requires sufficient high-frequency sound to maintain the rationality of that half of the brain. At the least, sound deprivation can induce sleep and produce hallucinations (Daniel & Mason, 2015; Leggett, 2009). Extensive sound deprivation causes psychosis. In fact, Armstrong had psychotic episodes before she broke free of the oppressive monastic lifestyle. Her earliest books are about how she escaped from that "brainwashing" environment.

Randall De Trinis, another 17-year-old who entered monastic life—the total institution of an American Trappist monastery—had the exceptional experience of gaining Thomas Merton, the celebrated Roman Catholic contemplative and mystic, as his spiritual advisor. Rules of silence similar to those in Armstrong's convent prevailed. De Trinis preserved a letter Merton wrote in 1968 that states in part:

> It is true that we were told absurd things, made to behave with a stupid and artificial formality, and put through routines that now, as we look back, seem utterly incredible. How did we ever stomach such atrocious nonsense? It must even be admitted that the climate of Catholic spirituality, perhaps especially in contemplative . . . life has proved for many to be unhealthy, both physically and mentally. We carry deep wounds which will prevent us from ever forgetting it. (De Trinis, 2010)

Such stories underscore the ignorance and abusiveness sequestered in traditions and rituals that have yet to be addressed (although Merton certainly had been for many years when he died at the age 53 in Thailand in 1968 while attending a monastic conference).

Voluntary resocialization occurs when someone starts school or moves to a new school, when someone begins a job with a new company, when

The Point Is ...

The Vision Quest: A Modern Indigenous Rite of Passage

A traditional rite of passage for Indigenous people is the **vision quest**, which once marked the passage from childhood to adulthood. After receiving months of informal instruction from elders, the individual would embark on a journey away from the home community to an isolated location. Then, they would fast for days, and possibly go without sleep, in the process of seeking a vision. A vision could be a song that comes to mind, or the appearance in dreams of an animal or other spirit who instructs the dreamer and initiates a connection with him or her that will continue until death.

More recently, adults have used the vision quest as a way of resocializing themselves with traditional ideals following a period of difficulty. The following is a generalized example of the Ojibwa vision quest as practised recently in northeastern Ontario. It begins in a sweat lodge, a dome-shaped structure built around overlapping willow poles, covered with skins or tarpaulins, and used like a sauna. The participants throw sacred tobacco on a fire to thank the Creator. They are told the story of how the sweat lodge came to the people from a little boy who was taught about healing from the seven grandfather spirits. Water is poured onto the seven stones that represent those spirits. The Elder sings ceremonial songs.

After the sweat, the participants are led to their own small lodges, where they fast and meditate. The Elder visits them to ask about their spiritual experiences. The participants fast for three nights and four days. What they learn changes with each night:

> The first is described as the night of doubt, where participants pray but are uncertain about what will happen. Hunger is mitigated by a feeling of excitement.

The second night is one of fear, sometimes known as the dark night of the soul. Participants realize that their bodies are beginning to weaken, and they may question their resolve. The third night is the night of the spirit. It is often said that if something meaningful is going to happen, it will occur between the beginning of the spirit night and when the fast is finished. (Steckley & Rice, 1997, pp. 226–7)

After a final sweat ceremony, there is a feast with gift-giving to the Elder and to those who have assisted the individuals in their resocialization.

Involuntary resocialization can take place with brutal violence, such as occurred in First Nations residential schools, like the one in Shubenacadie discussed in the Telling It Like It Is box that follows, where the language, religion, and customs of Indigenous children literally were beaten out of them. Other examples of involuntary resocialization include being drafted into military service, being imprisoned, being committed to a psychiatric hospital, being subjected to anti-homosexual "conversion therapy," and being subjected to mandatory retirement. Goffman (1961) called institutions where involuntary resocialization takes place **total institutions**, as they regulate all aspects of an individual's life. A significant part of involuntary resocialization is a **degradation ceremony**, a ritual that strips the person of his or her individuality. Hazing, whether of Grade 9 students, first-year college or university students, or rookies on amateur and professional sports teams, is a degradation ceremony in which being made to perform acts of minor (sometimes major) humiliation informs the initiates that they are in a new social world where they are mere beginners.

someone retires from work (willingly), or when someone undergoes a religious conversion (which, in extreme circumstances such as cults, can be involuntary). Associated with this kind of resocialization is the **rite of passage**, which is a ritual marking a life change from one status to another, typically following some form of training. A wedding is a rite of passage; so is a funeral. Other examples include the Christian practices of baptism and **confirmation**, and the Jewish **bar mitzvah** (for boys) or **bat mitzvah** (for girls), when adolescents, after a period of instruction, are deemed to have become "adults in the faith."

Hazing as Resocialization

Hazing is a semi-ritualized initiation ceremony to resocialize new members of some group or organization, such as a high school, a university fraternity or sorority, a sports team, or a military unit. Hazing is viewed as a test in which the initiate must demonstrate, by stoically enduring a demeaning or uncomfortable experience, that they are "committed enough" or "tough enough" to be a member.

Hazing rituals have long been practised in amateur, professional, and collegiate athletics. They typically involve some form of degradation ceremony imposed on the team's rookies by the veterans, who as first-year members survived the same trial. For instance, male players might have to shave their heads, or wear women's clothing, or dress like a chicken to go on display in a public place. Increasingly, hazing rituals involve violence and cause serious harm to the individuals being hazed, particularly when the activity involves nudity and sexual activities. In 2005, sports hazing made national headlines when a member of the McGill University football team quit after he and other rookies were forced to participate in a hazing ritual: nude and gagged, they were made to bend over while being prodded up the backside with a broom. This sexual abuse was vigorously protested by the victim and led to consequences for the team. At around the same time, a 16-year-old rookie on the Windsor Spitfires of the Ontario Hockey League became the subject of media attention after refusing to go through a hazing ritual called the "sweat box." This entailed crowding, naked, with other rookies into the washroom at the back of the team bus, with the heat turned up high enough to make the participants perspire.

Hazing, historically, has been much more a male than a female activity. Establishing one's toughness has long been viewed as a manly thing to do. But this cultural value may be changing. In September 2009, the Carleton University's women's soccer team was suspended by the university for holding a rookie initiation party that ended up with a player becoming so drunk that she had to be rushed to hospital by ambulance. While the suspension made the national news, the ensuing decision to reduce the suspension to just two games did not.

The last three decades have seen the emergence of a solid body of sociological literature on hazing, including why it exists, the various forms it can take, its harmful consequences, and (rarely) its benefits as an instrument of socialization (see, e.g., Kirby & Wintrup, 2002; Waldron & Kowalski, 2009). Sociologists have addressed several questions. The first is whether hazing has always existed at the same level. Is it more out of control today, or has the privacy lid been opened up so that it simply is reported more often? Michelle Finkel (2002, p. 231) argues that victims of hazing, like victims of domestic violence, are difficult to identify and may not come forward "out of

Photo by Doug Pensinger/Getty Images

As part of its anti-hazing and anti-bullying policy, Major League Baseball no longer permits teams to force players to dress up in costumes they may find demeaning. How do you distinguish joking behaviour from abusive behaviour? Does age or athletic ability matter? Do hyper-athletic women have rituals comparable to those of "hyper-masculine" males in professional sports? Why are athletic women not called "hyper-feminine"? Who benefits from hazing rituals in professional sports? Who might be offended by a highly publicized ceremony such as the one illustrated? (Consider not only players but fans, journalists, and others involved in the game.)

embarrassment or the desire to protect their perpetrator(s)." Greater social awareness is emboldening victims to report cases of hazing in greater numbers than in the past.

The second is whether hazing rituals are becoming more dangerous and more widespread, as some observers claim. If so, why? Does hazing perform a useful or necessary socializing function? If we consider hazing to be a form of resocialization, what norms of behavior does hazing encourage in initiates?

A final question comes from a finding by Waldron and Kowalski (2009) that, among athletes who reported engaging in risky hazing behaviours, "both the values of sports as well as the desire to be accepted by teammates encouraged hazing." What are the "values of sports" that hazing supposedly promotes? How do they overlap with the values of organized sport we identified in the box at the start of the chapter? If those values are worth promoting, what is a healthier way to promote them in clubs, teams, and organizations for adolescents and emerging adults?

4.6 Social Status and Social Roles

Socialization, as we have seen, is the process of learning how to behave in society. That process is set in motion by some preexisting conditions—what kind of environment we're born into, for instance—and conditioned by various agents of socialization, such as family, peers, teachers, coaches, and so on. Along the way we also occupy various statuses and roles, which may come with social scripts that influence the way we act. We will spend the remainder of this chapter looking at social statuses and roles.

Unlike some of the sociological concepts we've encountered so far, *status* is a term that probably has meaning for you already. You might think of it as something along the lines of high social standing, credibility, or a favourable reputation. In this sense, status is something you either have or don't have, something you can gain or lose. You might also think of status in terms of the update you post to your favourite social media site to give followers some insight into your condition, state of mind, or romantic

Telling It Like It Is

A First-Hand Point of View

Resocializing the Mi'kmaq

The Shubenacadie Indian Residential School operated for 45 years, beginning in the early 1920s, under the auspices of two Roman Catholic orders in the small Nova Scotia community of Shubenacadie. Mi'kmaw students at the school suffered terrible abuse at the hands of the staff, whose mission was to resocialize students by beating their traditional culture out of them—literally, if necessary. The abuse is illustrated graphically in the words of anthropologist and former student at the school Isabelle Knockwood, who provides the following account of a young girl caught speaking in her native language:

The nun came up from behind her and swung her around and began beating her up. . . . Then the Sister pinched her cheeks and her lips were drawn taut across her teeth and her eyes were wide with terror. . . . Then the nun picked the little girl clean off the floor by the ears or hair and the girl stood on her tiptoes with her feet dangling in the air. . . . The nun was yelling, "You bad, bad girl." Then she let go with one hand and continued slapping her in the mouth until her nose bled. (Knockwood, 1992, p. 97)

What do you think?

1. Where would the nun have learned such abusive behaviour?
2. Has this type of abuse occurred in the public school system?
3. What are the consequences today for a teacher who abuses a child?
4. How are professionals, such as teachers and physicians, supported in lawsuits brought against their members?

Resocialization at the Shubenacadie Indian Residential School. Notice that the boys have more freedom in what they can wear than the girls do. Why do you think that was so?

relationships. In this sense, status is something singular that can change as often as you post to your preferred social media.

To a sociologist, status is something different. "Status" isn't something you have or you don't. Everyone has a status. In fact, everyone holds *several* statuses at the same time. Moreover, some statuses can change and be replaced, while others do not change, or they change very infrequently. I gained a status when I became a stepdad over 35 years ago, and I still have that status. In 2019, I gained the status of grandfather.

Our statuses are vitally important to how we see ourselves and how others see us. When we interact with people, much of what goes on in thoughts and in behaviour relates to the statuses we hold and the way we perform the *roles* attached to those statuses. When the status expectations are well understood by both parties, the interaction may be relatively simple. But if the set of expectations attached to a complex status is not well established, the social exchange may be more difficult. I found that to be the

case as a stepfather with stepchildren. Sometimes, the expectations associated with one status interfere with those of another.

The sociological concept of status is important to understanding how people interact in pairs and in small groups. Later, we can broaden our understanding of individual statuses to look at the social dynamics existing in large groups and organizations. We will see that small- and large-group dynamics differ in a very important way: while the statuses we hold help us establish ourselves as individuals in small groups, the principles at play in large social organizations seem designed to strip our individuality away entirely.

4.7 Social Status

Status and role concepts are critically important to helping us establish social identities. A **status** is a recognized social position a person occupies. It contributes to a person's social identity by imposing responsibilities and expectations that help define that person's relationships to others. You don't have just one status. You have many over your lifetime and several statuses at once—daughter, mother, wife, CEO, volunteer board member, soccer coach, and so on. The collection of statuses you have is your **status set**. For instance, you could have the statuses of son, brother, uncle, teacher, drummer (for your band), neighbour, taxpayer, and Black person—all at the same time. These would make up your status set. We gain and lose some statuses as we age. We possess dozens of statuses over our lifetimes, some of them only briefly, others for as long as we live.

Ascribed and Achieved Status

One way of classifying our many statuses is to distinguish between statuses that are *achieved* and those that are *ascribed*. A status is considered **achieved** if you have entered into it at some stage of your life but were not born into it. For example, if a person is a high school graduate, that is an achieved status. If the person becomes a college or university student, that is another achieved status. A professional position (assuming it's not a job in the family business), a role in a hobby or recreational activity, and a brief stint as a contestant on *Jeopardy* are examples of achieved statuses. Those achievements assume some personal ability, accomplishment, or voluntary act, although very few statuses are entirely achieved—for instance, an accomplished drummer has *some* natural or ascribed ability.

An **ascribed** status is one that you were born into ("daughter" or "son," "Black" or "Latino," etc.) or one you have entered into involuntarily ("teenager," "elderly person," "cancer survivor," "unemployed person"). Circumstances trump choice in ascribed statuses.

Some statuses can be simultaneously achieved and ascribed. The degree to which a status is achieved or ascribed often depends on how much **social mobility** exists. Consider a professional position or role, like "doctor" or "prime minister." A status of this kind usually is achieved. However, in a society with little social mobility, where a small elite class dominates, the statuses of president, judge, or rich business owner may be more "ascribed" than "achieved." Some Hindu villages of South Asia have traditionally been organized socially according to a system called "varna," that is, of ranked social classes, or *castes*, that people are born into and that are associated with different occupations. Cities are not organized that way now. The colonial perception was that Brahmans are people born into the highest caste, associated with priesthood; Vaisyas occupy the third caste, comprising merchants, farmers, and craftspeople. People traditionally have found it very difficult to move beyond their caste, but the restrictions are overcome by some people in a society that is increasingly flexible.

Your race in North America—white, Black, Asian, Latino, and so on—is primarily an ascribed status. However, people from a racialized group who want to avoid discrimination and whose appearance makes them difficult to categorize sometimes can claim—or "achieve"—a racial status that the larger society judges to be more "favourable." They do so by allowing their appearance to provide assumptions that they do not correct. This process is known as **passing**. Especially historically, it was not unusual for some fair-skinned Indigenous people in Canada to "pass" (i.e., to pass unidentified by skin colour under the scrutiny of the social bigots) for white, or at least to try, so they might receive some of the privileges intrinsic to being white in a predominantly white (and significantly racist) society.

Sexual Orientation and Status

Sexual orientation is primarily an ascribed status. Heterosexuality is natural for some, and homosexuality is natural for others. Other people feel naturally *asexual* (having no feelings of sexual attraction), bisexual, *demisexual* (sexually attracted only to someone with whom one has a strong emotional bond), *sapiosexual* (sexually attracted to people with high intelligence), and so on.

There are those who believe that being gay or lesbian is a "lifestyle choice," one that can be overcome with determination or with heavy doses of therapy (see The Point Is: Cold Mothers Don't Cause Autism, earlier in this chapter), drugs, religion, or conservative politics. Homosexuality was against the law in Canada until 1969. In January 2022 Bill C-4 came into effect banning conversion therapy. Since the cause of homosexuality has not been established scientifically, what sociological change has occurred? History and literature present many different social and cultural accommodations to non-heterosexual individuals. Without yet being able to identify physiological causes, contemporary scholarly literature nevertheless strongly argues that sexual orientation is a physical/psychological predisposition, whether or not it is acted upon at some point in an individual's life. According to this position, regardless of whether you live in a gay or lesbian relationship, you are homosexual if your sexual fantasies are overwhelmingly about people who are of the same sex as yourself. The notion of "sexual fantasies" determining anything is, of course, Freudian.

Sexual orientation is much more complicated sociologically than its label. One problem with characterizing any orientation as either an achieved or as an ascribed status has to do with the way one's sexuality is acknowledged by others. A gay male who marries into a heterosexual relationship in order to not be socially recognized as homosexual is another example of "passing" (as described in the section above). In such a circumstance, the *status* of "heterosexual orientation" is achieved, at least partially, because a person has decided not to behave in a way that conforms with social norms and expectations about how a gay man (or a straight woman) should act. Status, then, to some extent, lies in what you do that is observed, not in how you feel. In some cases, choice can trump less visible circumstances. The complexities of this issue of status as it relates to sexual orientation is examined in two Canadian autobiographical novels whose focal point is the same straight woman, a young Canadian scholar who was murdered. Richard Teleky (a gay man) takes a wistful, longing view in *Pack Up the Moon* (2001) about learning of the death of someone he cared deeply about, and Richard Tallman (a straight man) in *The Turning Year* (2012) explores the details of the death of the woman he intended soon to marry and its broader meaning for himself and others, including the woman's gay, estranged husband.

Born in Inuvik, Northwest Territories, Darcie Bernhardt grew up in Tuktoyaktuk and was the first Inuk from that town to participate in the RCMP's pre-cadet training program for Indigenous people. She later studied at the Yukon School of Visual Arts and the Nova Scotia College of Art and Design in Halifax, taking on the more "traditional" status of Inuk artist. Why might the achieved status of "artist" put less pressure on an Inuk than the achieved status of "police officer"?

Master Status

Everett C. Hughes (1897–1983) introduced the concept of master status when he worked at the University of Chicago. He applied the term in the context of race in the United States:

> Membership in the Negro race, as defined in American mores and/or law, may be called a master status–determining trait. It tends to overpower, in most crucial situations, any other characteristics [i.e., statuses] which might run counter to it. (Hughes, 1945, p. 357)

The term **master status** signifies the status that dominates all of an individual's other statuses in most social contexts, and plays the greatest role in the formation of the individual's social identity. You can learn a lot about people by asking them what they consider to be their master status. Canadians, upon being introduced to someone, often will ask: "What do you do?" This perhaps implies that a person's occupation is their master status. Ethnicity and gender can be master statuses, even when someone doesn't

Telling It Like It Is

A Student's Point of View

Being Casually Queer in a Heteronormative World

There's a weird sort of liminality to being "out" as bisexual. A lot of LGBTQ2+ people know that coming out is never just one moment, you're constantly coming out to everyone you meet. But when you're bi, I feel like you don't even get those moments in a satisfying way, either. You just kind of exist, not sure if you're saying too much or too little about yourself.

I've had people know me for months, and be surprised when it comes out that I'm bisexual. "Well, the subject just never came up," I can say, and shrug it off. But it still feels like I've been hiding something from them. This part of myself, which I never try to conceal—no big deal, right? just let it come up naturally—has suddenly become this really personal thing that you only get to unlock with a high enough friendship level. But if I bring it up too soon, who knows how they might react? With lots of people, you can tell what they would say if you told them you were gay. But telling them you're bi? It's way harder to gauge. Lots of times, even they don't know. They know what they think about gay people, but they still don't know what to make of bisexuality. It's confusing. It's a lot of things at once. "Wait, so how do you choose, then?" they might ask. "Do you think you'll end up gay or straight?"

I'll listen to my gay and lesbian friends talk among themselves, and wonder if I'm allowed in that conversation. I'll listen to my straight friends talk about their relationships, and wonder if I'm allowed in that conversation. I'll hear a female friend gush about how gorgeous she thinks a female celebrity is, and I'll wonder if she's like me, or if this is just the way that straight girls appreciate aesthetic beauty (usually it is). I'll try to find a way to casually tell people—colleagues, friends, people I trust—"hey, by the way, this is who I am! But also, it's no big deal!" But if it's no big deal, then I shouldn't have to say anything, right? But if I don't, then why do I feel like I'm hiding something?

If anyone ever asked me if I'm bi—anyone at all—I'd say yes. I have no problem telling people, whoever they are. So I guess that means I'm "out." But I don't really feel "out," because no one ever really asks. They make their assumptions one way or another, and I just don't deny them. But it's hard to put into words what it feels like to be so separate from who people think I am. Sometimes it's enough to make me wonder who I am at all.

What do *you* think?

1. Why is bisexuality a complicated status for the student writer of this narrative?
2. Sexual orientation is said to be an ascribed status, but as the writer explains, it is largely invisible. How, then, is it "ascribed"? What are some other ascribed statuses that are "invisible"? How might they complicate the lives of people who hold them in ways that visible statuses (such as race) do not?

What do *you* think?

1. Hughes called "Black" a master status because in most interactions it was more significant than statuses based on sex, age, or class. Do you think that "white" only exists as a master status for white nationalists? Do you think that your race affects your answer to this question?
2. Has there ever been a time in your life when your race or ethnicity was your master status? How did you know?

want them to be. During his presidential campaign, Barack Obama's master status was his race. In the opinion of some conservative Americans, it still is.

Status Hierarchy

Statuses can be ranked from high to low based on prestige and power; this ranking is referred to as **status hierarchy**. For each of the basic social categories—gender, race, ethnicity, age, class, sexual orientation, and physical ability—one status tends to

Quick Hits

Labelling Theory

Sociologist **Howard Becker** (b. 1928) developed labelling theory in the 1960s to explain the negative effects a label can have when applied to a group outside of the majority. Part of this theory states that when negative labels are attached to a status, a powerful master status can be created and internalized both by the individual and by others. The process is illustrated in the following excerpt from a study of drug culture:

> If people who are important to Billy call him a "druggie" this name becomes a powerful label that takes precedence over any other status positions Billy may occupy. Even if Billy is also an above-average biology major, an excellent musician, and a dependable and caring person, such factors become secondary because his primary status has been recast as a "druggie." Furthermore, once a powerful label is attached, it becomes much easier for the individual to uphold the image dictated by members of society, and simply to act out the role expected by significant others. (Hanson et al., 2009, p. 76)

A label like "druggie" thus becomes a master status that can follow a person for their entire life, despite the person's efforts to change it.

---

be valued above the others. In Canadian society we tend to rank male over female, white over Black or brown, British heritage over eastern European and Asian, upper-class over middle- and working-class, heterosexual over LGBTQ2+, and able-bodied people over people with disabilities.

Applying the status hierarchy to age is complicated. Power is concentrated in the hands of those who are middle-aged, yet because we live in a society that promotes the cult of youth—the desire to look, act, and feel young—youth also attracts some prestige. Middle-aged men and women often risk their health with surgeries, Botox (a potentially deadly poison) injections, liposuction, and facelifts. Others fight to hold onto their youthful appearance through fitness regimes, dieting, surgically implanted hair replacement, breast enlargement or reduction surgeries, and so on. We do not usually speak of cultivators of youthful appearance as "passing," although women hoping to ensure their social and labour statuses in relationships and in jobs with ceilings may be the principal consumers of cosmetic surgeries.

Status Inconsistency

Some people seem to hold all the favoured social statuses. For example, federal and provincial governments have tended to be clubs for people who are male, white, of British heritage, rich, heterosexual, and able-bodied: a winning set of mostly ascribed statuses. By contrast, many Black or Indigenous women live at or below the poverty line in a status set where the power and prosperity deck is stacked against those born into it.

Status consistency is the condition a person experiences when all of their statuses fall in the same range in the social hierarchy. However, there are cases in which a person holds social statuses that are ranked differently and do not align; this condition is known as **status inconsistency**. An Indigenous woman who is a lawyer and was a high-ranking federal cabinet minister—such as Jody Wilson-Raybould—exemplifies such inconsistency.

When a person's statuses do not add up—when an individual holds one highly valued status and other less-valued ones, or vice versa—the situation that results can cause social tension. Similar tension can occur when the value of statuses shifts over time. Everett Hughes noticed this pattern in Quebec during the 1930s. He found that when people of "lower" status moved into occupations typically held by people with more favoured statuses, they became targets of certain strategies their colleagues used to reduce the apparent inconsistency. One strategy was to modify

The Point Is . . .

Statuses Change through Time

Norman Kwong (1929–2016) was born in Canada six years after the Chinese Exclusion Act was passed. Though it did not stop Chinese immigration to Canada, it required all Chinese people—even those born in Canada—to register with the government. It diminished the status of Chinese Canadians compared with other Canadians. The Act was in place until 1947, when Normie Kwong was 18 years old. As a child, his master status was Chinese Canadian, among his other statuses as son, brother, and student.

The year the Act was repealed, Kwong became a star junior football player. The next year, he began his professional football career, first, playing for the Canadian Football League's Calgary Stampeders (1948–50) and then for the Edmonton Eskimos (1951–60). During this time, professional football player was his master status in a status set that also included Chinese Canadian, husband, and father.

When he retired from football, Kwong became involved in sports management, both for the Calgary Stampeders and for the National Hockey League's Calgary Flames, a team he helped bring to the city and part-owned. This enterprise was but one of his several business interests during this time. It is harder to define his master status then, although Chinese Canadian still was prominent.

From 2005 to 2010 Kwong served as lieutenant-governor of Alberta. His appointment was not surprising, given his high profile as an athlete and sports executive and his connections with the then-ruling provincial Conservative Party. His political position was his master status at the time.

When we look at Norman Kwong's life, we can see that he held many different statuses, some ascribed and some achieved, as well as at least three different master statuses (Chinese Canadian, professional football player, provincial lieutenant-governor).

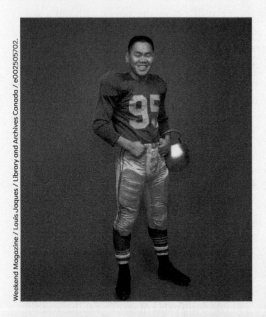

Weekend Magazine / Louis Jaques / Library and Archives Canada / e002505702.

CP PHOTO/Jeff McIntosh

What do *you* think?

1. Norman Kwong had at least three master statuses. In each case, how did it become his master status? Did he choose it?
2. Under what circumstances does racial identity lose its master status? In Kwong's case, does he really lose the master status of being racialized as a "Chinese Canadian" as he achieves the status of football player? When he achieves the status of lieutenant-governor?

the stereotype surrounding the lowly regarded status. As Hughes explained:

> The idea that French-Canadians were good only for unskilled industrial work was followed by the notion that they were especially good at certain kinds of skilled work but were not fit to repair machines or to supervise the work of others. In this series of modifications, the structure of qualities expected for the most-favoured positions remains intact. But the forces which make for mobility continue to create marginal people on new frontiers. (Hughes, 1945, p. 356–7)

In other words, these upwardly mobile people would become alienated from others sharing their low ascribed status and from people defined by the more highly regarded, achieved status. When he called these individuals "marginal people," Hughes

was drawing on the work of Robert E. Park, who described the figure he called "marginal man." The male bias implied in the term is the main reason it's no longer used; however, it is historically important and preserved in the commonly used term **marginalization**, which refers to the process by which groups are assigned into categories that set them at or beyond the margins of the dominant society.

Status Inconsistency and White Male Violence

Let's consider an example of how changing status values can lead to tension, the rise of white nationalism and the alt-right movement, and blatant or creeping populism and fascism. These have become central concerns of the white, working-class, Christian male in the United States and, it can be argued, in Canada. Thirty years ago, this type of person held a highly valued status set, likely to translate into prosperous employment, a place at the head of the

Courtesy of the Northern Alberta Institute of Technology

There is a high demand in Canada for workers in skilled trades, such as electrical work, plumbing, construction, heavy equipment operation, and so on. What would cause young people to shy away from careers in these well-paying industries? What role could status inconsistency play in career decisions?

household, and a secure position within the middle class. Higher education was not a prerequisite for success, but with the offshoring of manufacturing jobs outside the United States and Canada it became more so. In 1990, about 20.6 million Americans were employed in manufacturing, most of them men without college degrees; by 2020 the number stood at 13.9 million employees, and this was an increase over more recent years (see Grundy, 2020; Statista, 2022). Overall, work has shifted toward lower-paying jobs in the service sector, where women without degrees have fared better than men without degrees, and white Americans in recent years are far less likely than Americans of other ethnicity "to think their children will be better off than they themselves are now" (Fletcher & Cohen, 2011). As Thompson (2016) puts it, "Many of these first beneficiaries of the franchise now feel disenfranchised. The original middle class feels cut out of the American Dream."

The devaluation of the status set representing the white, working-class, Christian male has had a profound effect on American society. This group became the target audience for Donald Trump's "Make America Great Again" speeches during the 2016 election campaign. As Robert Jones (2017) explains, "Trump's promise to restore a mythical past golden age—where factory jobs paid the bills and white Protestant churches were the dominant cultural hubs—powerfully tapped evangelical anxieties about an uncertain future." The insecurity of white Americans has fuelled the rise of movements opposing immigration, feminism, globalism—in short, any "-ism" that might threaten the privileged status of white, Christian men. White men without a university degree also make up the group most likely to own guns, and while there are many reasons for owning a firearm, some have drawn a link between gun ownership and the declining status of the American male. In an interview, Canadian-born conservative political commentator David Frum made the following observation:

> The typical man finds himself less needed than he was 20 or 30 years ago. . . . [He] is less likely to be married, less likely to be supporting a family. In many ways he's become superfluous to society. But there's

one thing he can do. For just a few hundred bucks, he can pick up godlike power to dispense death . . . to dozens or hundreds of people. And he may or may not do that, but you know that you can. And how can you be a loser if you can kill so many people? (Frum, 2017)

Following Trump's vocal xenophobia, expressed and demonstrated repeatedly at rallies and broadcast by the media, racists among the police and in the general population—including a small percentage of people with severe mental problems—felt they had "permission" to perpetrate crimes against non-white individuals, against women, against children, and against society more generally. Frum's economic analysis may not explain the mass murderers who show signs of psychosis and other severe mental illness. But he provides a description of the fertile ground where Trump sowed the seeds of discontent that "normalized" bigotry, social polarization, greater recourse to violence, and an interior discourse of irrationality (his constant stream of lies) and asocial values to a large proportion of the American electorate. Like a wildfire leaping from grass to the forest, anti-social elements in society, whether acting individually or already armed with military-grade weapons in their paramilitary groups, stood ready to answer the call of their leader. Millions of people were affirmed in their paranoid, xenophobic feelings, whether or not they fit the profile Frum describes.

Thus, a businessman in his sixties, sufficiently well-paid to become a high-stakes gambler, plots a massacre against a cross-section of the population attending a music festival (59 deaths and hundreds injured, many severely) in Las Vegas in October 2017. A 45-year-old truck driver, anti-Semitic xenophobe, and dupe of online neo-Nazis and white supremacist conspiracy cultists, who had been asocial from his teens, attacks worshippers at the Tree of Life Synagogue in Pittsburgh, for the delusional and paranoid "reason" that the Hebrew Immigrant Aid Society "likes to bring invaders in that kill our people. I can't sit by and watch my people get slaughtered," he posted online, just before killing 11 and wounding six on 27 October 2018. The internet makes neighbours of the world's population. A virulently anti-Muslim 29-year-old Australian man attacks people in two mosques in Christchurch, New Zealand, killing 51 and injuring another 50 on 15 March 2019. He described himself as an ordinary white man, born to a working-class but low-income family, and the product of a "regular childhood." But his weapons were emblazoned with neo-Nazi symbols and the names of those who had acted violently against Muslims, including that of the killer in the 2017 attack at a mosque in Quebec City. "Even the music playing in the gunman's car as he arrives to the mosque had meaning; it was a nationalist Serb song from the war that tore apart Yugoslavia in the 1990s, glorifying Serbian leader Radovan Karadzic, who is currently jailed for genocide and other war crimes against Bosnian Muslims" (CBS News, 2019). The man who claimed responsibility for the attack, which he livestreamed on social media, wrote a manifesto referencing "white genocide" driven by "mass immigration." Notably, he called President Trump a "symbol of renewed white identity."

New Zealand's parliament acted swiftly in an almost unanimous vote (119 to 1) to ban military-style semi-automatic weapons and parts that could be used to construct banned firearms. In the United States, the absence of such political will has fostered increased violence against people of colour, both individually and in mass—in their homes, on the streets (especially by police), in their churches, schools, malls, grocery stores. And always it is the Black, the immigrant, the Latino, the Jew—the alien Other—who is targeted, including in some instances women, as was the case in Toronto in April 2018 when a self-identifying "incel" (involuntarily celibate) young man drove a rented van through a crowd of shoppers, killing 10. Even in Canada, hate crimes in some instances have explicitly invoked Donald Trump (e.g., the Islamic Cultural Centre assailant in Quebec City). A contingent of the neo-Nazi protestors in Charlottesville, Virginia, that killed one woman and paraded through the streets in August 2017 chanting "Jews will not replace us" came from the Canadian Prairie provinces. In fact, other participants in the Charlottesville protest included the Proud Boys, a far-right militia group founded by Canadian Gavin McInnes, who relocated to the United States. They were prominent again in Washington on 6 January 2021, during the armed insurrection against the US Capitol. In February 2021, the Canadian government declared the Proud Boys to be a terrorist entity. While having "dispersed" and claiming to disband in Canada, some of the leaders remain vocal neo-Nazis (Hart & Davies, 2022), and diehards within the group—the most radical—were expected to continue their activities. In addition, local Proud Boys chapters in Canada had considerable autonomy from the national umbrella organization and some continue to be active under one guise or another.

A summary of Canadian police-reported hate crime (Wang & Moreau, 2022) noted 2,669 criminal incidents motivated by hate in 2020. This was the largest number recorded since comparable data became available in 2009. The first year of the pandemic saw the number of police-reported hate crimes increase by 37 per cent, or 718 more incidents, compared with the previous year. Between 2019 and 2020, the number of police-reported crimes motivated by hatred of a race or ethnicity increased 80 per cent, from 884 to 1,594. Much of this was a result of more hate crimes targeting the Black population (+318 incidents), East or Southeast Asian population (+202 incidents), the Indigenous population (+44 incidents), and the South Asian population (+38 incidents).

What do *you* think?

A sense of "entitlement" is the expectation that holding a particular set of statuses will guarantee a certain kind of success. But "entitlement" in the United States extends to the Second Amendment to the Constitution about the right of citizens to bear arms. To the writers of the Constitution, this permission applied to a common armoury to which the citizens had access if under enemy attack. How has that permission turned into a sense of entitlement to every citizen owning firearms? Can these definitions of "entitlement" explain the rise of white nationalism? How is Canada different from the United States in regard to racism and in regard to gun ownership? Why would members of the Canadian Armed Forces ally themselves with the Proud Boys? Why did the original Proud Boys group carry the name "Proud Boys Canada First?"

For a very brief time in 2016, this flyer could be found on telephone and hydro poles in Toronto. Canada has white nationalists and alt-right groups. Do you think the visibility of these groups is less than it is in the United States? What reasons can you give for this difference?

4.8 Social Roles

A role is a set of behaviours and attitudes associated with a particular status. Roles attached to a status may differ across cultures. For example, people holding the status of elder in traditional cultures of China and Africa and Indigenous communities of North America are expected to have acquired a certain level of wisdom. The same expectations seldom exist in mainstream Canadian culture, where the status of elder has few positive role expectations attached to it; the status is more "old person" than it is "elder." One reason that Western social scientists were slow to question the myth of Inuit elder abandonment—the idea that it was once common for Inuit communities to abandon their elders during food shortages and other tough times—is that Western culture lacked its own positively defined role of elder, making the myth much more credible in their eyes.

A given status may be associated with more than one role. Robert Merton (1949) developed the idea of the **role set**, which comprises all of the roles attached to a particular status. As professors, we have the role of teacher to our students, but we are also colleagues to our peers, employees to our schools, and trouble-making underlings to our administrators. Students have a peer role with classmates in addition to their student role with instructors. To the college or university, they are paying customers.

Role Strain

Role strain develops when conflict exists between roles within the role set of a particular status. For example, if a student complains to his professor about a teacher in another class, the professor is placed in a conflict between her roles as an educator, in which she has the student's best interests at heart, and as a colleague with a mutual responsibility to the faculty. Similarly, a student who catches a classmate cheating on an exam is at once a member of the academic community with a responsibility to report the offence and a member of the student body who would prefer not to pillory a peer. Role strain also can affect a single role. Consider the parent who feels more at ease with one of his children than with another but tries to balance his attention and shows of affection between them.

Role Conflict

Another useful concept for understanding social tensions is role conflict. **Role conflict** occurs when a person is forced to reconcile incompatible expectations generated from two or more statuses they hold. If you are both a mother and a student, then you know all about role conflict. Imagine: it's the night before the big exam and you need to study—part of the set of behaviour expectations attached to being a college or university student. However, your daughter needs help with her homework, your son is ill, and your husband plans to be out with friends watching the big game—he's been looking forward to it for weeks. You're on your own with the demands of conflicting statuses of mother and student.

Role Exit

Role exit is the process of disengaging from a role that has been central to one's identity, and attempting to establish a new role. **Helen Rose Fuchs Ebaugh** (an ex-nun turned sociologist) has studied role exit processes extensively. Her findings are summarized in *Becoming an EX: The Process of Role Exit* (1988). According to Ebaugh—who wrote about not just ex-nuns but also ex-priests, ex-convicts, and recovering alcoholics—role exit involves shifting your master status. If you were forced to retire having always defined yourself by what you did ("I am a nurse"), you might feel uncomfortable when asked, "What do you do?" If you are a stay-at-home mother and your children grow up and move away, you have lost a very important purpose in your day-to-day life that is not easily replaced (and a role as grandmother might

Quick Hits

Status and Role: What's the Difference?

A number of sociology students over the years have had problems distinguishing between status and role. This stems largely from the fact that both terms have somewhat different meanings outside sociology. Status in a non-sociological sense often refers to importance or prestige (CEO being high-status and cleaning staff being low-status). Role is commonly linked to the characters that actors play in a movie or TV show; a TV role is closer to what sociologists would call "status."

So here are essential differences between the two sociological concepts. A status is a position that is recognized in society. It can be a job, such as teacher, minister, banker, lawyer, accountant, or nurse. Status can also be a recognized position in a family: mother, uncle, grandmother, brother, daughter, and spouse. It can also include neighbour, citizen, student, driver, and pedestrian.

A role is a set of *socially shared expectations* about the behaviours and attitudes that belong to a given status. Take the roles associated with being a student. You may have received a document from your college or university outlining the expectations for students attending your school. These expectations include such things as attending classes regularly, completing homework and other assignments, maintaining academic integrity, and being diligent and responsible. These expectations reflect the role your school associates with the status of student. You and your friends or roommates may have other expectations that define the role you associate with being a student: studying late into the night or morning, being tired all the time, drinking late into the night or morning, having the freedom to live by your own set of house rules. Your parents, meanwhile, will have their own expectations about the role associated with your student status. They may be accommodating your need for time and space in a crowded home to study. They expect you to bring new subjects into the family conversations. They know that you will have less time to contribute to the family's distinctive goals and strategies and that you will be reaching out to a larger community that may reverberate with the family.

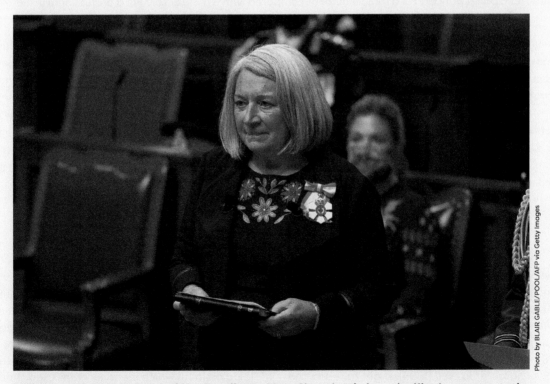

Photo by BLAIR GABLE/POOL/AFP via Getty Images

Indigenous Governor General Her Excellency Mary Simon's role is as the King's representative in Canada; her status is Governor General.

AP Photo/Matt Rourke

A tearful Allen Iverson announces his retirement from the National Basketball Association in October 2013, over two-and-a-half years after his last appearance in an NBA game. Do you think he struggled with role exit? Some roles and lines of work have early retirement expectations built into them. Do people in low-paying jobs in service industries experience role exit distress? What changes does retirement entail for a ballet dancer? For a female actor as compared with a male actor? For a professional athlete?

be far in the future). If you are a father and your parental role is reduced because your ex-spouse gains primary custody of the children, then becoming a part-time dad may feel like a role exit.

The role exit of married and common-law partners who become single through separation, divorce, or death of a spouse is difficult, as it entails shifting from "we" to "I." Previous relationships with friends and family change. In the case of divorce, some people take sides. Some people you've been close to might start avoiding you, treating your divorce like something contagious and you as a carrier of the "failed relationship" virus. On the other hand, others might begin to pay you more attention, and in ways you haven't been used to. As a "single," you may be expected to be "out there" meeting other eligible singles. Role exit does not apply only to marital roles; it is something we all experience during our lifetimes.

Wrap It Up

Summary

Everyone undergoes processes of socialization and resocialization. To see what human life without socialization would be like, check out the film *The Wild Child* (1970), based on the true story of a young boy who grew up entirely on his own in the wilds of France. Another "wild child" is Jody Foster's character in *Nell* (1994), a girl raised in the isolation of backwoods North Carolina who has never known people other than a twin sister, who died when young, and her handicapped mother, who also has died. The doctor who discovers her wants her to adjust gradually to life in her familiar surroundings while the psychologist working with him wants Nell to be protected in a psychiatric hospital. The story is based partly on a case of "idioglossia" in which identical twins used their invented language to communicate until they were about eight years old. These films illustrate how we cannot become the people we are without the agents of socialization we've grown up around—parents and family, educators, peer groups, culture, and the media. Sometimes these agents work together, but sometimes they send conflicting messages. How influential are these messages? What part does hearing play in socialization as compared with sight? To a cultural determinist, who you are depends almost entirely on the messages you receive from your social environment. Others, though, like Dennis Wrong, believe we have the power to choose which messages we hear and obey—or not.

Postsecondary educators (myself included) are heavily engaged in resocialization, in preparing students for careers, and in helping them think critically about how they have been and are being socialized. In fact, this chapter (like the ones that precede and follow it) has been written in an effort to resocialize you. How is it working?

Think Back

Questions for Critical Review

1. Explain, in your own words, what socialization is. When does it begin in humans? When does it end?
2. Under what circumstances can socialization be harmful? Give some examples.
3. Identify at least five different agents of socialization and outline their roles.
4. What is the difference between biological determinism and social determinism? Which one allows for a greater degree of agency?
5. Career, clothing, hobbies: Do you believe each of these is more socially or more biologically determined?
6. How do Mead's concepts of significant and generalized others relate to primary and secondary socialization?
7. What are some things you learned from your family that you unlearned from forces of secondary socialization, including friends, classmates, educators, and the media?
8. As an agent of socialization, what has been the impact of media—including television, video games, movies, and the internet—on your life?
9. Do organized sports represent a positive or a negative form of socialization? Consider the chapter's opening narrative and the views of Elkind and Postman discussed later in the chapter. Draw on your own experience as well.
10. If you were a parent of a boy and a girl, what could you do to ensure they had the best opportunity to succeed equally in STEM and non-STEM subjects?
11. Is the continued prevalence of hazing in spite of new laws to combat it a result of few socially approved and encouraged rites of passage from adolescence to adulthood in modern North American society?

Read On

Suggested Print and Online Resources

Ruth Benedict, *The Chrysanthemum and the Sword* (Boston: Houghton Mifflin, 1946); David Riesman, ***The Lonely Crowd: A Study of the Changing American Character*** (New Haven, CT: Yale University, 1950)
Classic examples of national character studies, perhaps most valuable for their flaws.

Cody Delistraty, "Untangling the Complicated, Controversial Legacy of Sigmund Freud," *The Cut*, September 5, 2017, https://www.thecut.com/2017/09/sigmud-freud-making-of-an-illusion-book.html
A valuable survey of Freud's outsized influence and misbegotten theories and clinical practices.

Randall De Trinis, "A Novice and His Master," 2010, https://mertonocso.wordpress.com/2010/06/26/a-novice-and-his-master-part-one-2/
A succinct, insightful account of monastic life, and about surviving and leaving its strictures, as told by a man whose spiritual director at the Trappist monastery of Our Lady of Gethsemani was the widely renowned and influential Catholic contemplative and mystic Thomas Merton.

Sigmund Freud, *On Sexuality: Three Essays on the Theory of Sexuality and Other Works* (New York: Penguin, 1953)
This collection features three of Freud's key articles on sexuality, ranging in scope from sexual abnormality to puberty.

Isabelle Knockwood, *Out of the Depths: The Experiences of Mi'kmaw Children at the Indian Residential Schools at Shubenacadie* (Lockeport, NS: Roseway, 1992)
Knockwood's work is an insightful ethnography on the residential school experience by one who survived the experience herself.

Laurie Kramer, "Siblings as Agents of Socialization: New Directions for Child and Adolescent Development," *New Directions for Child and Adolescent Development* 126 (Winter 2009)
A look at how brothers and sisters act as socializing agents in ways similar to and different from those of parents, and as differing in different cultures and classes.

National Longitudinal Survey of Children and Youth, www23.statcan.gc.ca:81/imdb/p2SV.pl?Function=getSurvey&SDDS=4450&lang=en&db=imdb&adm=8&dis=2
Launched in 1994 by Statistics Canada and Human Resources and Development Canada, the NLSCY is a 15-year study of Canadian children designed to follow their development and well-being from birth to early adulthood.

Patrick O'Sullivan with Gare Joyce, *Breaking Away: A Harrowing Story of Resilience, Courage, and Triumph* (Toronto: HarperCollins, 2015)
A former NHL player discusses growing up with an abusive hockey dad and how it affected his adolescence—a model of how not to socialize children.

Social Psychology Network, http://Huesmann.socialpsychology.org
Maintained by Wesleyan University professor Scott Plous, the Social Psychology Network is dedicated to psychological research and teaching. This page presents an overview of the work of Rowell Huesmann, with free access to some of his articles.

Shirley Steinberg & Joe L. Kincheloe, eds, *KinderCulture: The Corporate Construction of Childhood*, 3rd ed. (Boulder, CO: Westview Press, 2011)
An important look at how corporate marketing is socializing small children and teenagers.

The Hurried Child, www.youtube.com/watch?v=IOWbh8qqTGU
David Elkind, who pioneered the concept of hurried child syndrome, talks about the importance of play in this YouTube video.

5

Culture

Reading this chapter will help you to . . .

- Describe Canada's dominant culture.

- Explain what it means for culture to be contested.

- Recognize the difference between a subculture and a counterculture.

- Know how the concept of agency relates to popular culture and mass culture.

- Appreciate how cultural norms and sanctions constrain and define our behaviour.

- Understand how folkways, mores, and taboos differ.

- Explain how values and language contribute to culture.

- Define ethnocentrism and explain its significance with regard to culture.

For Starters

When Does Culture Need Protecting?

Someone once wrote that the difference between Americans and Canadians is that Americans don't care about the difference between Americans and Canadians.

It's true. Canadian media and scholars have been and continue to be very conscious of how we differ from Americans. The same can be said more broadly. When travelling, we bristle when someone mistakes us for American; we really bristle when we correct them and they say, "Same thing." (Although we love it when they then apologize and buy us a beer, which has happened to me in Scotland.)

We imagine ourselves having a rich cultural tradition that differs from that of the global elephant to the south. Yet we feel pride when one of our own achieves success on the American cultural scene, like Drake, the Weeknd, Alessia Cara, Ryan Gosling (or Reynolds—take your pick of the Ryans), or Margaret Atwood. And we tend to be very conscious of how our culture is viewed in America. The day after Sandra Oh hosted *Saturday Night Live* in March 2019, some mainstream Canadian news outlets reported on how many references to Canada she made. A month later, an episode of *The Simpsons* set in Canada made headlines in many Canadian media outlets both before and immediately after it aired, reflecting first anticipation at how our culture might be portrayed and then disappointment that it was largely reduced to simple cultural stereotypes.

Does it matter? Is it important to have and protect a distinct national culture (or national cultures)? It is important enough that our broadcast regulator, the CRTC, has rules requiring Canadian television and radio networks to air a specified amount of made-in-Canada programming during daytime hours; those requirements were extended to online streaming services via Bill C-11, which received royal assent in 2023. (Needless to say, American broadcasters do not face similar regulations.) Our CanCon quotas are designed to ensure that we see ourselves and hear our music and stories reflected in Canadian broadcasting. CanCon regulations helped homegrown bands like the Guess Who get a strong start in the smaller Canadian market. The same quotas undoubtedly contributed to the success of Nickelback, the Barenaked Ladies, Avril Lavigne, and many others in the time before streaming services diminished the influence of local radio stations.

We have Canadian content regulations to thank for folksy sitcoms such as *Corner Gas*, *Schitt's Creek*, *Letterkenny*, and *Kim's Convenience*. Perhaps, if you live in a small town as I do, you see yourself reflected in those shows, and many of us can relate to the ubiquitous Korean convenience store. But then we have the second-hand Canadian versions of shows like *American Idol* and the *Real Housewives*, which are of questionable value as products of Canadian culture and are questionable generally.

We really lose out in the movie category. The Canadian film industry is booming with American productions shot in Toronto, which stands in for New York or Chicago, and in Vancouver, the

Northwood Entertainment

A scene from *The Grizzlies* (2018), about a group of Inuit teens who come together to form a la-crosse team in an Arctic community scarred by the legacy of colonialism. Canada is home to award-winning directors (Denys Arcand, Deepa Mehta, for instance), and Canadians have made award-winning feature-length films set in the North (*Atanarjuat: The Fast Runner*, 2001) and Quebec (*The Barbarian Invasions*, 2003). But most products of our flourishing film industry are big-budget American movies. Why?

body double for Los Angeles or Seattle. We sel-dom see movies that reflect our own stories of World Wars I and II. And think about how many times you have seen an actor play the president of the United States in film, on TV, or in real life (i.e., Ronald Reagan), and then how many times you've seen an actor play the prime minister.

In short, Canadians fret a good deal about our Canadian culture—what it is, how it's pro-tected, whether it's different enough, if it's inclu-sive, if it's unique. Our American cousins have no such insecurities. Should they? Should we? Or is our culture doing just fine, despite the presence of the American elephant in the culture room?

5.1 Introduction: What We Mean by Culture and Why It's Contested

The word "culture" has a lot of different meanings. Some people equate it with a sophistication of manners and tastes, something you either have (if you enjoy, say, the opera, ballet, and fine dining)

or lack (if your idea of a good breakfast is cheap beer and leftover pizza). But that's just one kind of culture—*high culture*—which we'll get to a bit later on.

More broadly, **culture** is a system of behaviour, beliefs, knowledge, practices, values, and concrete materials, including buildings, tools, and sacred items. It is expressed through language and the things we make (artifacts). In this sense, everyone has culture. But although I've described culture as a system, I'm not suggesting there is total agreement concerning any one culture and its constituent parts. Those who belong to a particular society (the collective group) may disagree about what the culture of that society does or should include.

Let's talk hockey. Just about everybody would agree that hockey is part of Canadian culture—but that's where agreement ends. Does success by Canada's national teams in international competition mean we've succeeded as a culture? Not everyone would say so. Is fighting an integral part of the Canadian game? Does the sport's long history in this country make it more culturally important than soccer, even though the latter has higher youth participation rates and tends to be played by boys and girls in more equal numbers, representing a far broader range of ethnic and socioeconomic backgrounds? A 2012 study commissioned jointly by Hockey Canada and equipment company Bauer found that only 10 per cent of Canadian families have children playing hockey (Ralph, 2013)—a surprising finding if we assume that active

Popular among tourists, the town of Helen, Georgia, bills itself as a Bavarian alpine village—in the American Appalachians. The local business community, in an effort to revive the struggling town, turned it into a Bavarian-themed village in the 1960s as a way to attract tourism. Canadian cultural geographer William Norton (2006) comments: "Tourists to theme parks such as Epcot Center are aware that they are visiting simulations, but towns such as Helen implicitly suggest that the ethnic landscape has foundations in the settlement of the area" (p. 371). How does Helen represent MacCannell's concept of staged authenticity?

participation alone defines the centrality of hockey in our cultural fabric. Television viewership and, before that, radio, as well as attending games at all levels, challenge that assumption. Periodically, a brazen historian will offer evidence that—brace yourselves, hockey fans—the sport was not even invented here but traces its origins to some other nation (see Gidén, Houda, & Martel, 2014, for example). All of which goes to show that hockey as part of our national culture is **contested**.

In more serious cases, aspects of a culture may be contested when they become instruments of oppression. Anne McGillivray and Brenda Comaskey, in *Black Eyes All of the Time: Intimate Violence, Aboriginal Women and the Justice System*, argue that we should not assume that Indigenous women who have suffered spousal abuse "will view 'cultural' solutions in the same way as Aboriginal men" (McGillivray & Comaskey, 1999, p. 18). Indigenous justice typically calls for forgiving offenders and reintegrating them into the community. However, many of the women McGillivray and Comaskey interviewed said they would prefer that their male abusers spend time in jail to give the abused time to feel safe again. Thus, these aspects of Indigenous justice—forgiveness and keeping offenders in the community—become contested.

Culture often is contested over the question of **authenticity**. Culture involves traditions but is not confined by them. It is dynamic, changing over time. Authenticity carries the idea of being true to a particular time, place, or context, yet think of how broadly the word "authentic" can be applied and understood. For some, an "authentic Italian meal" may be something you can get from the pizzeria down the street; for others, it is something you would have to fly to Tuscany to experience. But even once you touch down in Pisa, your experience may be carefully stage-managed. You have bought a vacation package that places you in a district designed for tourists, where your "authentic Italian meal" isn't truly authentic but meant to please the visitor's palate. Urban sociologist Dean MacCannell ([1976]/1999), drawing on Canadian-born Erving Goffman's **dramaturgical approach** to the presentation of self, explains that tourists, in seeking out authenticity, are looking for the **back stage** of a cultural setting; what they often get is a sanitized version. MacCannell finds this *staged authenticity* in many settings, including the re-created period town, a city's historic district, and, yes, the restaurant promising authentic cuisine.

Authenticity becomes a problem when a colonial society studies a colonized culture and claims to know the secret of its authenticity. Edward Said, in *Orientalism*, criticized Western intellectuals for forming their impressions of the Middle East and Asia from accounts written by nineteenth- and twentieth-century Western scholars and adventurers. Once they had formed an idea of what "the Orient" was, these intellectuals negatively compared their rather romanticized (think *Aladdin*) notions of the Eastern world's traditions to their negative perceptions of its present. In effect, they said: "You are a corruption of what you used to be."

It is a common mistake to view one's own culture as being dynamic and complex, while holding a narrow view of other cultures as somehow simple and fixed. This leads to unhealthy cultural stereotypes—that all Americans are *jingoistic* (extremely nationalistic), warmongering bullies with guns in their homes, or that Irishmen are always drunk and fighting but make up for it by singing sweetly. It is important to appreciate that all cultures are contested and subject to change.

5.2 What Kinds of Cultures Are There?

There are different kinds of culture, apart from culture in the general sense just outlined. These can be seen in terms of two oppositions:

1. dominant culture versus subculture and counterculture
2. high culture versus popular culture and mass culture.

As we examine these oppositions, you will gain a better idea of why we say that culture is contested.

Dominant Culture versus Subculture and Counterculture

Subcultures and countercultures exist in opposition, or at least in contrast, to the dominant culture. So we will begin this discussion by outlining the characteristics of the dominant culture.

Defining Canada's Dominant Culture

Look around, and it isn't hard to see the signs of the dominant culture in Canada. The **dominant culture** is the one that, through its political and economic power, is able to impose its values, language, and ways of behaving and interpreting behaviour on a given society. The people most closely linked with the cultural mainstream are sometimes referred to as **dominants**. Although statistically their share of the overall population has dropped significantly in the last 20 years, it is fairly safe to say that Canada's dominants are white, English-speaking people of Christian and European stock. It is also fair to say that the dominant culture is middle-class.

We can narrow our picture of Canada's dominant culture by taking a regionalist perspective. People living in the Atlantic provinces have good reason to suspect the dominant culture lies in central or western Canada, where banks and multinational companies have their head offices, and where most of the national population is situated. But western Canada has several times produced political parties (the Social Credit, Reform, Wildrose, and, most recently, Alberta parties, for instance) to protest the West's exclusion from the dominant political culture and its unfair treatment at the hands of institutions dominated by and situated in central Canada (like the big banks and the agencies of the federal government). Power and wealth tend to be concentrated in large cities, and central Canada is home to the country's two largest metropolitan areas, Toronto and Montreal.

Feminists argue that Canada's dominant culture is male. In the federal election of September 2021, 103 females were elected to the House of Commons, comprising 30.5 per cent of Canadian MPs. This number has grown steadily in recent elections, and the percentage is now higher than a global average for elected democracies. This is up from 2014, when it was 25 per cent. On the other hand, there was a nine-month period in 2013 when women led six of Canada's provinces and territories (Nunavut, BC, Alberta, Ontario, Quebec, and Newfoundland and Labrador); as of 2022, only two women were provincial or territorial leaders—Heather Stefanson in Manitoba and Caroline Cochrane in the Northwest Territories—and two were Indigenous—Cochrane and P.J. Akeeagok in Nunavut. Notably,

Thunderbird TV

Television both reflects and contributes to our sense of culture. Pick a sitcom you're familiar with (it's probably American, unless, like me, you're a big fan of *Kim's Convenience*, depicted above). In your opinion, does it reflect the dominant culture we've just described? What are the principal attitudes, concerns, and occupations of its main characters? What sexualities and ethnic backgrounds do they represent (and represent positively, not just as the subject of jokes, which can be a form of marginalizing people)? How much are the main characters like you?

both Nunavut and the NWT have majority Indigenous populations. Eleven Indigenous MPs (3.3 per cent) were elected in the 2021 federal election, the highest number to date but still somewhat lower than Indigenous representation in the total Canadian population.

Adding age to the picture, we can say that those who are just starting or who have just ended their careers often feel peripheral to the dominant culture. Other factors to consider are sexual orientation, level of education, and overall health (since those with disabilities or chronic medical conditions often feel they are outside the dominant culture). To summarize, Canada has been and remains a settler society, and the dominant culture consists of white, English- and French-speaking, heterosexual, male university graduates of European background between the ages of 30 and 55, in good health. Many own homes in middle-class neighbourhoods of cities and suburbs in Ontario or Quebec, even as the costs of homeownership have skyrocketed. They may not be blamed for the inequities built into Canada's "cultural mosaic," but they do benefit from their privileged cultural, educational, gendered, and social positions.

Minority Cultures, Subcultures, and Countercultures

Minority cultures are those that fall outside the cultural mainstream. As a multicultural society, Canada is home to a diverse abundance of cultures defined by religion (Sikh culture), language (francophone culture), ethnicity (Latin American culture), and

Quick Hits

Are You Excluded from the Dominant Culture?

1. Are political leaders (your prime minister, premier, local federal or provincial representative, mayor, etc.) like you in sex, religion, clothing style, language, and ethnic background? ☐Yes ☐No
2. Do the homes portrayed in most television shows you watch look like yours? ☐Yes ☐No
3. Do the leading characters in movies live lives like yours? ☐Yes ☐No
4. If you work, is your boss of the same sex, ethnicity, race, and age as you? ☐Yes ☐No
5. Do the people who get arrested on reality-based police shows look like you and your neighbours? ☐Yes ☐No
6. Are people like you frequently made the subject of news stories for demonstrating or protesting something? ☐Yes ☐No
7. Are there a lot of derogatory slang terms that refer to people like you? ☐Yes ☐No
8. Are people like you described as a "special interest" group? ☐Yes ☐No
9. Are people like you often told they're "too sensitive" or "too pushy"? ☐Yes ☐No
10. Are you often asked, "Where do you come from?" ☐Yes ☐No

A "no" answer to questions 1–4 equals exclusion from the dominant culture; for questions 5–10, a "yes" answer equals exclusion from the dominant culture.

race (African Canadian culture). Canadian law protects cultural pluralism as a core political value and social good, meaning that these cultures are not expected to assimilate into the broader mainstream culture but are able (in fact, encouraged) to preserve the characteristics that make them stand out in the Canadian cultural mosaic. But although multiculturalism has been a federal government policy since 1971 and was enshrined in law in 1988 (Canadian Multiculturalism Act), in reality the cultures that sit outside the dominant culture are not treated equally, as John Porter described in *The Vertical Mosaic* (see Chapter 1). There is, according to Porter, a hierarchy according to which certain minority cultures, particularly those based on ethnic background, are favoured more than others.

Some minority cultures fall within one of two subcategories: countercultures and subcultures. **Countercultures**, such as peace and environmental activists or biker gangs, are minority cultures that feel the power of the dominant culture and exist in opposition to it. **Subcultures** are minority cultures that differ in some way from the dominant culture but don't directly oppose it. Subcultures may be organized around occupations or hobbies and typically exhibit a fairly neutral contrast to the mainstream: there is no significant opposition to the dominant culture. Examples include Bollywood fans, sociologists, and other biker groups, such as that of Canadian military veterans who bond through biking and other activities following their post-military service (Samuels, 2022).

The Point Is . . .

A Subculture Offers Its Members a Sense of Belonging

Furry fandom is a subculture of people who enjoy dressing up in animal costumes and meeting up with others who share their passion for "fursuits" and anthropomorphic animal role-play. If you are familiar at all with furry fandom, you may think it has to do with animal fetishes and sex. I'll remind you here that it is wrong to presume you have someone else's culture figured out based on stereotypes and a few things you've heard.

So who are furries, and why do they dress up? For answers, we turn to a report published by a team of American and Canadian social scientists at the University of Waterloo (Plante, Reysen, Roberts, & Gerbasi, 2016). Their International Anthropomorphic Research Project (IARP) involved a five-year study of furries in North America.

According to the report, the majority of furries—75 per cent of those studied—are adults in their early to mid-twenties. Older furries may be labelled "greymuzzles," a term considered either a sign of respect or an insult. Furries are predominantly white (83.2 per cent), and two-thirds of them are male. They tend to be well-educated, either having a degree or working toward one,

and 45 per cent of those studied were living with their parents (which is consistent with the non-furry population of 20- to 25-year-old postsecondary school students).

People involved in furry fandom adopt different "fursonas" and don their costumes for regular conferences and smaller meet-ups. Fursonas are usually large predator species, such as wolves, dogs, big cats, and dragons.

Why do people join this subculture and stay in it for years? The number one reason, according to the IARP report, is that furry fandom participants enjoy being part of a group and having a sense of belonging with other like-minded individuals, with whom they frequently form close friendships. The second biggest reason is that furry fandom offers a form of escapist entertainment. But what about the sex? It is exaggerated: of the group studied, 23 per cent said that it had little or nothing to do with their becoming involved with the furries, while 37 per cent said that it was a small part of their interest. The activities members identified as being most central to furry fandom are art and craft work (e.g., designing and crafting pictures and the clothes of their fursonas).

(Continued)

PETER STEFFEN/AFP/Getty Images

LARPers don elaborate costumes to engage in live-action role play, re-enacting battles from history or fantasy. Subculture or counterculture?

High Culture versus Popular Culture

High culture is the culture of the elite, a distinct minority. It is associated with theatre, opera, classical music and ballet, "serious" works of literary fiction and non-fiction, "artsy" films (note: *films*, not *movies*) that may be difficult to appreciate without having taken courses on the subject, and a "cultivated palate" for certain high-priced foods and alcoholic beverages. High culture is sometimes referred to as "elite culture," which Canadian sociologist Karen Anderson describes as

> produced for and appreciated by a limited number of people with specialized interests. It tends to be evaluated in terms of "universal" criteria of artistic merit and to be seen as a sign of prestige. Appreciation of elite culture usually entails a process of learning and the acquisition of specific tastes. (Anderson, 1996, p. 471)

French sociologist Pierre Bourdieu (1930–2002) coined the term **cultural capital** to refer to the knowledge and skills needed to acquire the sophisticated tastes that mark someone as a person of high culture. The more cultural capital you have, the "higher" your cultural class (Bourdieu, 1970).

Popular culture, on the other hand, is the culture of the majority, particularly of those who do not have power (the working class, the less educated, women, and racialized minorities). At the same time, there are no firm lines of demarcation between elite culture and popular culture; rather, they overlap and often borrow from one other. The Toronto Symphony Orchestra, for example, has done entire performances centred on music from popular movies, and cross-fertilization between high and popular culture in music has been common for many years, as exemplified by the late twentieth-century American hitmaker Billy Joel, whose "Uptown Girl" (1983) uses music from classical French composer Maurice Ravel's "Boléro" (1928), and, in a different direction, Gotye's hugely popular 2011 hit, "Somebody That I Used to Know," takes off from the nursery rhyme tune to "Twinkle, Twinkle, Little Star" and "Baa, Baa, Black Sheep." Similarly, folk music often has been central to the compositions of classical composers, such as the American Aaron Copland and the Hungarian Béla Bartók, and American composer George Gershwin was largely influenced by African American music. More recently, Jeremy Dutcher, a classically trained two-spirit Wuastukwiuk opera singer from New Brunswick, used the early twentieth-century wax cylinder field recordings of his people's traditional music to create an album that won the 2018 Polaris Music Prize. Much the same has been the case in theatre, where "classics" of the past such as Shakespearean plays are given new, edgy, and popular treatments. (And note that Shakespeare, in his own time, was a popular playwright, not a producer of high culture.)

Serious academic discussion of popular culture has grown with the rise of **cultural studies** courses and programs. Cultural studies draws on both the social sciences (primarily sociology) and the humanities (primarily literature and media studies) to cast light on the significance of, and meanings expressed in, popular culture, a topic previously neglected by most academics.

Popular Culture and Mass Culture

A crucial distinction exists between popular culture and mass culture. The two differ in terms of agency, the ability of "the people" to be creative or productive with materials given to them by a dominant culture. Sociologists disagree on how much agency people have. Those who believe that people take an active role in shaping the culture they consume (e.g., the clothing they buy, the music they listen to, the websites they visit and contribute to, the TV shows and movies they watch) use the term "popular culture" to describe the consumers and producers of culture outside the world of the cultural elite.

Those who believe people have little or no agency in the culture they consume and produce use the term **mass culture**. They tend to believe that multinational companies (such as Walmart, Disney, Google, and Apple) and powerful governments dictate what people buy, watch, wear, value, and believe. Mass culture is not benign. Critical theorists Theodor Adorno (1903–1969) and Max Horkheimer (1895–1973), who belonged to what is known as the Frankfurt school, called mass culture the output of the culture industry. In *Dialectic of Enlightenment* ([1944] 2002), a work they co-authored, they described how cultural products—particularly movies but also radio shows and magazines (1944 was pre-television)—are mass-produced to keep society happy and submissive. To them, mass culture stifles creative freedom and individuality while keeping people dependent on these products of capitalism.

The internet was once seen as a boon for popular culture, enabling users to have their stories, social commentaries, photos, and videos seen by an enormous audience without any intervention by large media companies. Today, however, these products of popular culture are mediated by dominant technology services like Facebook, Google, and YouTube, which control the results that appear at the top of your search while promoting the content most likely to generate clicks by consumers.

One feature of mass culture is what French sociologist **Jean Baudrillard** (1929–2007) called **simulacra**. Simulacra are stereotypical cultural images produced and reproduced like material goods or commodities by the media and sometimes by scholars. For example, Inuit are often represented by simulacra of described practices (e.g., rubbing noses, throat singing) and physical objects (e.g., igloos, kayaks). These images tend to distort contemporary Inuit "reality." Consider the way the inukshuk, the Inuit stone figure, has become a Canadian cultural symbol, with models of these stone figures sold in tourist shops across the country and inukshuks to be seen along highways at the edge of farmers' fields and swamp land in rural southern Canada. The inukshuk has such cultural currency it was incorporated into the logo for the 2010 Winter Olympics held in BC—a province with no Inuit community. Indigenous people are often represented by simulacra of described practices, such as shape-shifting and performing magic. These simulacra account for some of the strange questions my Native American Facebook friends receive, such as:

- Can you interpret my dreams?
- Do you talk to animals?
- Can you teach me to be a shaman?
- Are you a shape-shifter?

This image, which I call the "hyper-spiritual Native American" simulacrum, does not come from talking to and being with Indigenous people; instead, it comes from popular media, particularly novels and

The Point Is . . .

There Aren't a Lot of Goth Grandparents . . . Yet

What happens when a youth counterculture ages? Does it just disappear with the youth of its members? Or does it last as part of their lives into middle age?

Consider Goth counterculture, which is still in evidence today. You can probably summon up a rough image to fit the term: dyed black (or, less often, blue) hair, dark clothes, and white makeup that contrasts sharply with clothing and hair colour. You may associate Goths with their fascination with death and with art, especially music and film that reflect this fascination.

Goths tend to be young, white people from middle-class families. Their opposition to dominant culture is expressed most clearly in their dress and overall appearance, but it goes beyond the visual. Goths of the 1980s rejected the yuppie world of financial self-indulgence and conservative politics. They pursued a life concerned with less world-exploitive politics and with cultish small-market arts. Generally, they find beauty in things the mainstream culture finds repulsive, frightening, or ugly.

Some bloggers claim there are three generations of Goths, each not so aware of its predecessors or reincarnations. Because of this generation gap, the Goth lifestyle is invented and re-invented by the youth cohort of the time. So what happens to Goths when they grow up?

Sociologist Paul Hodkinson (2011, 2013) studied people who entered the Goth counterculture during the 1980s in their teens and early twenties. He followed them as they aged, using participant observation at Goth events, observing

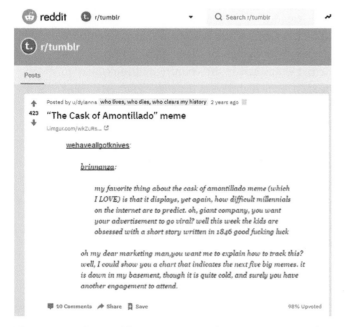

If you were born this century, you have grown up with the world's most powerful medium for creating, transmitting, and consuming cultural products. Do you consider what you engage with online to be popular culture or mass culture?

films such as *Little Big Man* (1970), *Dances with Wolves* (1990), and *Thunderheart* (1992).

Baudrillard (1983) describes simulacra as being "hyperreal"—that is, likely to be considered more real than what actually exists or existed. He illustrates the principle with an analogy of a map, but we will consider a GPS system instead. Imagine you are driving down a country road on a winter night. Your GPS system tells you to turn right onto a major road that will lead you straight home, yet all your eyes see is a narrow dirt road covered in snow. If you follow that road and get stuck at a dead end, the GPS system was hyperreal to you: you believed the information it was giving you was more real than what your eyes detected. This information is thus a simulacrum. When sociologists encourage their students to be critical of what the media present, they are hoping their students will be able to detect simulacra.

British sociologist John Fiske (2010) takes the popular culture position. He does not believe that people are brainless consumers of mass culture; rather, he believes that the political and cultural

Goth communication online, and doing in-depth interviews with 19 men and women aged 27 to 50. He noted that from the late 1990s,

> the previously very small number of older goths in the scene began to grow and, as a result of the coincidence of this with slower recruitment of youngsters, the average age of the scene rose, to the extent that some events now are thoroughly dominated by over-thirties. The goth scene therefore provides an example of a subculture dominated by "the same body of continuing participants" (Smith, 2009, p. 428), something which contrasts with the isolated older participants in otherwise adolescent cultures focused on in my other studies. (Hodkinson, 2013, p. 1077)

As they aged, the Goths followed dominant cultural practices by getting married and becoming parents (to "baby bats" or "gothlings"). Women were more likely than men to withdraw from the Goth scene as they settled into more conventional domestic arrangements. Aging Goths turned to monthly Goth festivals that included supervised children's activities. They subscribed to online countercultural magazines and blogs that included discussions of Goth-themed baby outfits and children's clothes. When they did go out at night, they spent less time preparing their appearance, drank less, and came home sooner—and with their spouses, not with someone they had just met. Nevertheless, it's clear that not all Goths grew out of the counterculture; instead, the counterculture has evolved to accommodate its aging members.

Philartphace/iStockphoto

Hodkinson's research suggests that most youths in a counterculture—Goths excepted—withdraw from the counterculture as they age. Why do you think this is so? Can you think of why Goths may differ in this regard?

institutions with the greatest influence on society merely supply people with resources that they resist, evade, or turn to their own ends. He recognizes agency and warns about the dangers of sociologists presenting people as mere dupes of mass media.

An important distinction between the two positions involves the contrast, identified by de Certeau (1984), between *decipherment* and *reading*. **Decipherment** involves looking in a text for the definitive interpretation, for the purpose (conscious or unconscious) the culture industry had in mind in creating the text. For sociologists who believe that mass culture predominates, decipherment is about looking for the message that mass media impose on consumers, who are left without the opportunity to challenge or reject it. Sociologists who believe that popular rather than mass culture predominates tend to use the term "reading." **Reading** is the process in which people treat what is provided by the culture industry as a resource, a text to be interpreted as they see fit, in ways not necessarily intended by the creators of the text.

5.3 Cultural Norms

Norms are rules or standards of behaviour that are expected of members of a group, society, or culture. There isn't always consensus concerning these standards: norms may be contested along the sociological lines of ethnicity, race, gender, and age. A quick illustration: a student of mine once told me he remembered being embarrassed, as a child, when his grandmother refused to "pick up" after her poodle. Although stoop-and-scoop laws weren't yet in effect, it had become common custom, as far as the boy was aware. Yet his grandmother was completely unselfconscious, even as the neighbours eyed her and her poodle with annoyance. Many years later, when the boy, now a young man, was engaged to be married, he was reprimanded by his grandmother for failing to write out the wedding invitations by hand. "It is bad form," she told him, "to send *printed* invitations unless you are inviting more than one hundred guests." Coming from different generations, the student and his grandmother recognized different norms of behaviour in these two instances.

Norms are expressed in a culture through various means, from ceremonies that reflect cultural and religious customs (a wedding, for example) to symbolic articles of dress (the white dress most commonly worn by the bride). In the following sections, we'll consider different ways in which norms are expressed and enforced.

Sanctions

People react to how others follow or do not follow norms. If the reaction is one that supports the behaviour, it is called a **positive sanction**. It is a reward for "doing the right thing." Positive sanctions range from small gestures like a smile, a high five, or a supportive comment, to larger material rewards like a bonus for hard work on the job. A hockey player who gets into a fight is positively sanctioned by teammates at the bench banging their sticks against the boards, or by the cheering crowd.

A **negative sanction** is a reaction designed to tell offenders they have violated a norm. It could be anything from a glare, an eye roll, or a sarcastic quip to a parking ticket or the fine you pay at the library for an overdue book. When someone around me says, "Hey, look—it's Santa Claus," I know that behind the apparent joke is a negative sanction about my well-proportioned frame and my bushy, grey beard. Both positive and negative sanctioning occurred during the COVID-19 pandemic: from the T-shirts of grocery clerks saying "Thank you for social distancing" to the dark looks and sharp words that at times greeted those who refused or were unable to wear masks in public settings and the vitriol spewed by sometimes organized anti-vaxxers and anti-maskers.

Folkways, Mores, and Taboos
Folkways

William Graham Sumner (1840–1910), the first person in North America to teach a course called "sociology," distinguished three kinds of norms based on how seriously they are respected and sanctioned. He used the term **folkways** for norms governing simple day-to-day matters. These are norms that you *should* not (as opposed to *must* not) violate. They are the least respected and most weakly sanctioned. The term "etiquette" can often be applied to folkways. George Costanza, on the TV show *Seinfeld*, continually violated folkways, for instance, by double-dipping chips at a party or by eating a chocolate pastry out of the garbage.

Mores

Mores (pronounced like the eels—*morays*) are taken much more seriously than folkways. You *must* not violate them. Some mores—against rape, killing, vandalism, and most forms of stealing, for example—are enshrined in the criminal code as laws. Violation of some mores, even if they are not laws, will meet with shock or severe disapproval. Booing the national anthem of the visiting team prior to a sporting event is likely to cause offence among supporters of the visitors and even anger or embarrassment among fans of the home side. Mores are complicated and may be contested. Mores of cleanliness, for instance, are in the cultural eye of the beholder. In Britain, dogs are allowed in pubs; in Canada, they are not. This does not mean that bars in Canada are more sanitary than those in Britain. Differences in mores of cleanliness can lead to serious problems when, for instance, an overdeveloped Western sense of what is hygienic jeopardizes the health of a hospital patient (see the discussion of Hmong refugees in Chapter 14, on medical sociology).

Like folkways, mores change over time. A young woman sporting a tattoo would once have been seen as violating the mores of acceptable behaviour for "a lady." Today, many women have tattoos and display them without arousing the kind of shock or condemnation generally produced when mores are violated.

Taboos

A **taboo** is a norm so deeply ingrained in our social consciousness that the mere thought or mention of it is enough to arouse disgust or revulsion. Cannibalism, incest, and child pornography immediately come to mind. Taboos affect our dietary habits. Eating dogs, cats, or other animals that might be considered family pets is taboo in North American culture. There are religious taboos surrounding the consumption of certain foods—pork by Jews and Muslims, beef by some Hindus. Some cultures recognize gender taboos, such as those surrounding women who interfere with or attempt to partake in typical male activities. Like folkways and mores, taboos differ from culture to culture.

You can think of folkways as unwritten rules of etiquette established through custom and enforced through social coercion. How might someone show their disapproval of the violation depicted above?

5.4 Culture Symbols

Symbols are cultural items that hold significance for a culture or subculture. They can be either tangible (i.e., physical) material objects (as illustrated later in this section in the narrative on culture symbols) or intangible, non-material objects, such as songs or even remembered events. Just as culture itself is contested, culture symbols are likely to be interpreted differently by people inside and outside of the culture they represent.

Symbols of nationality tend to take on tremendous cultural significance. Think of the maple leaf Canadian tourists stitch to the backpacks they wear when travelling in Europe. It's meant to stand not just for their country of origin but for a whole set of qualities that we like to think make up the Canadian cultural identity—courtesy, tolerance, knowledgeableness, peacefulness, and so on. To the European who sees and recognizes it as a symbol of Canadian cultural identity, the maple leaf might conjure up a very different set of qualities: our foot-dragging on climate change, our seal hunt, our historical treatment of Indigenous peoples, our wanting to have it both ways in global economics and politics. Some of these are recent developments, illustrating another point: the cultural significance of symbols can change over time.

The Point Is…

An Important Culture Symbol May Puzzle an Outsider

In the fall of 1989, I travelled through rural Virginia on a short lecture tour, having been invited by staff and students of Southwest Virginia Community College who had attended a lecture of mine during their spring break. I spent the first night of my stay at the home of the college president. It was elegant, finely furnished, with everything in its place. While there, I noticed something that surprised me. In a glass case—the kind normally used to hold curios and objets d'art, such as glass and china figurines—I saw two six-pointed objects, each one made of three nails. They reminded me of the jacks I had played with as a child, but bigger, and menacing. Why were these on display?

The next night I stayed with a coalminer's family. There I learned about the dynamics of a months-long coalminers' strike in the one-industry area. I was taken on a tour of the strike centre, where bunk beds were being built to accommodate the families of striking workers who had been thrown out of their homes for failing to pay the rent. The people I met there were friendly, but the long strike was crushing their spirit.

The mining company was owned by people from outside the area—foreigners, in the eyes of the locals. The company owners had circumvented the picket lines by trucking the coal out at night, but striking miners in camouflage had found ways to thwart their efforts.

The next day, at the college, I spoke to a sociology class about symbols. Near the end of the class, I asked students to name some local symbols. One student shouted out "jackrocks." When I asked what "jackrocks" were, I got a description of the six-pointed objects I had seen in the president's glass case, as well as a bag full of jackrocks handed to me by a student who went to his car to get them. I was told that one of the tactics used to keep the coal trucks from shipping out the coal was to toss these jackrocks underneath the tires. The jackrocks had become symbols of the miners' resistance. They appeared in store windows in the town nearest the mine, and I was given a pair of small, aluminum jackrock earrings. I then understood why the college president kept the two jackrocks in the glass case. He was from Florida, and therefore a "foreigner" to the area. By keeping the jackrocks in a place of honour, he was expressing solidarity with his students and their community.

The *Hijab* as a Symbol for Some Canadian Muslim Women

Few clothing symbols have a greater power to evoke emotions than the *niqab*, the veiled head covering worn by some Muslim women. To many in the West, it is a symbol of patriarchal domination by religious extremists, similar in effect to the full-length, screen-faced *burqa* that many Afghan women wear and to the *chador* that Iranian women are forced by law to wear. Even the *hijab*, which covers the head and hair but not the face, may be seen by non-Muslims as a symbol of religious oppression, especially following the terrorist attacks on the United States on 11 September 2001. In the lead-up to the 2015 federal election, Canadians debated whether the *niqab* aligned with our national cultural values. The issue came to the fore when a young woman, Zunera Ishaq, wanted to take her oath of Canadian citizenship while wearing the veil. The federal government under Conservative Prime Minister Stephen Harper denied her that right, claiming that most Canadians would find it offensive, but the Supreme Court overruled the government, upholding Ishaq's right to keep her face covered during the public ceremony. In October 2015, shortly before the election, she took her citizenship oath while wearing the *niqab*.

It is important to understand why women of various cultures—especially in Canada—choose to wear a *hijab* or *niqab*. For this information there can be no better source than the community of Canadian Muslim women who have considered the choice themselves. Some of them have provided the narratives that appear later in this section. What stands out as we read their views is that to some Muslim women in Canada, taking the veil is a matter of choice, not command.

Telling It Like It Is

Student Points of View

The *Hijab* as Worn by Young Canadian Muslim Women in Montreal

The Narrative of a 19-Year-Old Palestinian Canadian Woman

The veil has freed me from arguments and headaches. I always wanted to do many things that women normally do not do in my culture. I had thought living in Canada would give me that opportunity. But when I turned 14, my life changed. My parents started to limit my activities and even telephone conversations. My brothers were free to go and come as they pleased, but my sister and I were to be good Muslim girls. . . . Life became intolerable for me. The weekends were hell.

Then as a way out, I asked to go to Qur'anic classes on Saturdays. There I met with several veiled women of my age. . . . None of them seemed to face my problems. Some told me that since they took the veil, their parents know that

they are not going to do anything that goes against Muslim morality. The more I hung around with them, the more convinced I was that the veil is the answer to all Muslim girls' problems here in North America. Because parents seem to be relieved and assured that you are not going to do stupid things, and your community knows that you are acting like a Muslim woman, you are much freer (cited in Hoodfar, 2003, pp. 20–1).

The Narrative of a 17-Year-Old Pakistani Canadian Woman

Although we did not intermingle much with non-[South Asian] Canadians, I very much felt at home and part of the wider society. This, however, changed as I got older and clearly my life was different than many girls in my class. I did not talk about boyfriends and did not go out.

(Continued)

I did not participate in extracurricular activities. Gradually, I began feeling isolated. Then my cousin and I decided together to wear the veil and made a pact to ignore people's comments; no matter how much hardship we suffered at school, we would keep our veils on. . . .

At first it was difficult. At school people joked and asked stupid questions, but after three months they took us more seriously and there was even a little bit of respect. We even got a little more respect when we talked about Islam in our classes, while before our teacher dismissed what we said if it didn't agree with her casual perceptions (cited in Hoodfar, 2003, pp. 28–9).

The Narrative of Mona, an Egyptian Canadian Woman

I would never have taken up the veil if I lived in Egypt. Not that I disagree with that, but I see it as part of the male imposition of rules. . . . The double standard frustrates me. But since the Gulf War, seeing how my veiled friends were treated, I made a vow to wear the veil to make a point about my Muslimness and Arabness. I am delighted when people ask me about my veil and Islam, because it gives me a chance to point out their prejudices concerning Muslims (cited in Hoodfar, 2003, p. 30).

A Response to the Narratives by a Muslim Feminist

The following was written by a 19-year-old university student in Alberta, who describes herself as a Muslim feminist (not a contradiction in terms). After reading the above narratives in a previous edition of this textbook, she felt compelled to comment.

Hijab and the veil are religious decisions to be made between the person choosing to wear it and God. It is highly disrespectful to belittle the value of Hijab, making it to be something as simple as a political statement or a statement to your classmates or parents. If you're wearing Hijab simply so your parents can treat you the same as your brother, you are using a religious statement to combat culturally driven inequality (which, in fact, goes against Islam).

These responses made Hijab seem entirely misogynistic, when it is in fact the exact opposite. Compare it with the following. In almost any magazine, book, advertisement, or movie you encounter, women are overly sexualized. Women are used to sell products, and are constantly treated as no more than just eye candy. Magazines injected with unrealistic beauty standards tell you "How to Lose 10 Inches Off Your Waist!" and "How to Be the Sexiest Woman in the Room!"

In movies and TV shows, girls are constantly purchasing cosmetics and discussing weight loss, talking about boys, and competing with one another to impress boys. Everything about Western media values women according to appearance, sexualizing and exploiting us in every way possible, just to please the male-kind. From a young age, women are trained to prioritize our physical appearance so that we can "fit in" and be "normal."

When young women fail to meet these unfair beauty standards naturally, we see millions of dollars spent on cosmetics and cosmetic surgery. Money aside, we also find an increase in eating disorders (i.e., anorexia and bulimia) as well as mental disorders (i.e., depression and anxiety), resulting from a lack of self-worth and self-esteem, which can ultimately lead to drug abuse or suicide.

Now back to the topic about Hijab. I chose to wear Hijab to protect myself from all of that. Hijab and the veil create a barrier between the woman choosing to wear it and the rest of the world. It forces people to actually listen to what she has to say, rather than to pass judgments solely on her physical appearance. Hijab gives me the comfort and liberty of knowing that I'm being judged according to my intellect rather than my sexual appeal. I know that I can freely stroll down the street without feeling insecure because men are staring at my body or talking about it to others. Not that they should in the first place, but Hijab and the veil ensure that they don't have the opportunity.

The perspectives featured in the previous Telling it Like it Is box are part of a ground-breaking study carried out by Iranian Canadian anthropologist Homa Hoodfar (2003) in Quebec, where the right of public servants—from politicians to schoolteachers, bus drivers, and nurses—to wear symbols of religious faith continues to be a source of political debate. The voices Hoodfar recorded speak compellingly of their choice to wear the veil as a way of opposing restrictions placed on them (and not their brothers) as teenagers by parents concerned that their daughters would fall prey to the irreligious sex-, alcohol-, and drug-related behaviours of North American culture. Some of those interviewed saw the decision to wear the *hijab* as a step, together with Qur'anic study and banding together with Canadian Muslim women of different cultural backgrounds, down a path of opposition to some of the patriarchal mores of their specific cultures. In addition, taking the veil gave some women the opportunity to defend their faith against the ethnocentric ignorance of some of their fellow Canadians.

5.5 Values

Values are the standards used by a culture to describe abstract qualities such as goodness, beauty, and justice, and to assess the behaviour of others. Values have long been a topic of interest to sociologists. Max Weber's identification of the Protestant work ethic is one early example of a sociological study of values. Many others have followed. But in spite of these studies, values remain difficult to understand and to represent accurately. What makes the issue especially puzzling is that the values people claim to have are not always the ones they act upon. In other words, there is a discrepancy between the **ideal culture** that people believe in and the **actual culture** that really

exists. Do we recognize, then, the value professed or the value reflected in human action? Is the person who preaches a value but fails to honour it in everyday life necessarily a hypocrite?

Canadian and American Values

As I noted at the start of this chapter, Canadians sometimes wonder about where we fit in the North American cultural landscape, and whether Canadian culture really exists as something other than American culture + more snow, colourful banknotes, and the metric system. The exercise becomes more difficult when considering cultural *values*, which are not as easy to pinpoint as cultural *symbols*. This is why Canadians, finding themselves at a loss to summon up uniquely Canadian values, will sometimes define themselves in contrast to Americans, as in "Canadians are like unarmed Americans with better health coverage." That doesn't really say much for Canadian values, and even these differences, if one were to rely only on headline news, seem to be converging.

Michael Adams, of the Environics Research Group, has been conducting and publishing opinion polls since the early 1980s. During the 1990s, he measured and tracked 100 "social values" among Canadians and Americans, including such things as acceptance of violence, obedience to authority, penchant for risk, and sexual permissiveness. He published the results of his work in *Fire and Ice: The United States, Canada and the Myth of Converging Values* (2003). His thesis was that Canadians and Americans are becoming more different rather than more alike in their values. It certainly seemed so in 2003, when the American military was heading into Iraq and Canada was not, and when a modest majority of Canadians supported gay marriage and the liberalization of marijuana laws, which a majority opposed in the United States.

Adams based his findings on data from Environics polls conducted in the United States and Canada in 1992, 1996, and 2000. It's always important to look at the data critically. For instance, the polls invited respondents to "talk" about their values. But you will recall that there is often a difference between the values we profess and those we act upon. Another point: Is the time period—from 1992 to 2000—long enough to produce evidence of what he called "long-term shifts"? All of the data were gathered before the 11 September terrorist attacks, which occurred in 2001. Adams speculated that the events of 9/11 would only make the differences he had identified greater.

In the early first decade of the twenty-first century, Canada and the United States underwent some significant changes that caused Adams to revisit his thesis. During the period of his initial study, the United States had a conservative Republican administration led by George W. Bush, and Canada had a Liberal administration headed by Jean Chrétien. However, from 2006 until 2015, Canada had a prime minister, Stephen Harper, with very conservative values, on par with those of American Republicans; in contrast, in 2008 Americans elected a liberal Democrat, Barack Obama, as their first Black president. In a 2014 presentation at the Woodrow Wilson Center in Washington, DC, Adams asked whether Americans and Canadians were trading places. He then answered his own question with a resounding *no*.

Between January 2009, when Obama took office, and October 2015, when Harper's Conservatives were defeated in a federal election, political and social values—and differences between the two countries—remained relatively stable, as shown in Figure 5.1, which presents Adams's data on one factor related to patriarchy. In the United States, however, the trend had been upward, toward greater support for household patriarchy. Now in 2022, as I'm writing this book, Canada has a Liberal prime minister, Justin Trudeau, who succeeded Harper in late 2015. Trudeau's outlook on many social issues sets him in stark contrast to his Conservative predecessor. And the United States is led by a moderate Democrat, Joe Biden.

What occurred politically in the United States in the interim between Obama and Biden, as well as the global COVID-19 pandemic that was declared in early 2020, polarized the values of our neighbours to the south, and some of this began to spill over into Canada. The United States was governed by a controversial Republican demagogue, Donald Trump, who came to power thanks largely to his regressive anti-immigration, anti-free trade stance, his divisive "us versus them" rhetoric, and his platform as a reality TV star (*The Apprentice* and *Celebrity Apprentice*). Soon enough he was showing support for neo-Nazi protesters who fought against the removal of public statues of Confederate Civil War heroes, cozying up to dictators in Russia and around the world, tear-gassing peaceful protesters after police in Minnesota murdered a Black man named George

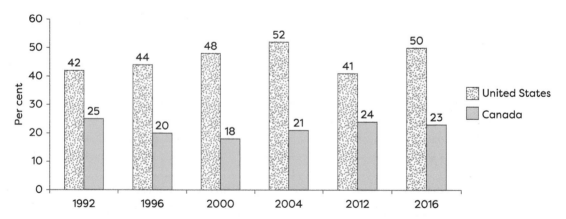

FIGURE 5.1 Percentage Agreeing with the Statement "The Father of the Family Must Be Master in His Own House," US and Canada, 1992–2016

Source: Adams (2017).

Floyd, telling right-wing militias to stand by until he called, and, ultimately, organizing and instigating a mob of followers to storm the US Capitol on 6 January 2021, to stop the peaceful transition of power after he had been soundly defeated in the US election. In this social and political climate, anti-vaxxers (those opposed to vaccinations) became radicalized, people fought over mask mandates intended to slow the spread of COVID, mass murders with high-powered assault weapons practically became normalized and gun sales rose, and the US Supreme Court struck down the long-standing right of women to access abortion. All in the name of "freedom."

In Canada, a convoy of trucks and other vehicles organized and descended on Ottawa, effectively taking over the centre of the nation's capital for a period in January and February of 2022, and others blockaded border crossings to the United States to protest mask mandates and vaccination requirements. Here, too, the cause for such protest was "freedom." What began as complaints from some cross-border truckers morphed into something larger and eerily similar to the values expressed by those on the far right and by their political followers in the United States.

Despite (or because of) the many legal cases, both civil and criminal, that Donald Trump faced from his time in office and from his private business dealings, he continued to make sounds of running for president again. And then, in November 2022, said he was. But Trumpism, a "freedom at all costs" view, has taken hold in a sizable segment of the American population, to the point that an NBC News poll in August 2022 placed threats to democracy as the top issue concerning Americans (Schonfeld, 2022). No directly comparable polling has been conducted to date in Canada, but then we have not had a prime minister who claimed an election was rigged even before the election, shouted about widespread voter fraud despite all proof to the contrary, and led an attempted coup that placed hundreds of his followers behind bars or on probation. It would seem that we polite Canadians consider the state of democracy more an issue of ongoing concern rather than a pants-on-fire existential threat, and we see democracy as a given value rather than contested terrain, despite some headline-grabbing actions and

some political leaders on the right having studied from the Donald Trump playbook.

5.6 Ethnocentrism

Ethnocentrism occurs when someone holds up a culture (usually one's own) as the standard by which all cultures are to be judged. It follows a simple formula: all cultures like the gold-standard culture are good, praiseworthy, beautiful, moral, and modern; those that are not are bad, ugly, immoral, and primitive. Ethnocentrism can manifest itself in many forms, but it often entails declaring that there is only one right way (the way of the cultural model) to run a business, handle finances, or manage social policy.

The term was coined by William Graham Sumner, the author of *Folkways* (discussed above). A staunch anti-imperialist, Sumner saw evidence of ethnocentrism in the arguments made by imperial governments to justify colonizing other, supposedly less-civilized nations. He was particularly critical of America's suppression of Philippine nationalism in the aftermath of the Spanish–American War (1898), when the United States gained control of the Philippine islands, previously a colony of Spain.

Generally, Sumner was of the opinion that "outsiders"—governments, imperial powers, or authority figures—should not meddle with or impose their values on the cultures of "insiders," such as the people of the Philippines, American citizens, or bankers and businessmen. Were he alive today we might call him a libertarian—a rare ideology for a sociologist—since he believed strongly in free-market capitalism, where businesses are free to operate without government restrictions. He was ordained as an Episcopal priest in 1869 but chose a career outside of the church, in part because he felt that ministers were expected to speak out against the rich, instructing them to do more to help the poor, who, he believed, should be doing more to help themselves.

Ethnocentrism is often the product of ignorance, something experienced by Hmong refugees who arrived in the United States from Southeast Asia during and after the Vietnam War. The Hmong were targeted in the United States in part because of their supposed practice of stealing, killing, and eating dogs. Lack of evidence or truth did not deter an ethnocentric public from spreading these stories about

The Point Is...

The Maple Leaf and the Stars and Stripes Carry Very Different Strings of Meaning

Culture symbols that are physical objects are sometimes called cultural artifacts. Like other culture symbols, artifacts have strings of meaning attached to them, giving them special significance to particular cultural groups. The more strings of meaning attached to an artifact, the more powerful it is as a symbol of the culture for which it has relevance.

Consider the flags of the United States and Canada as cultural artifacts. The American flag has more cultural value for Americans than the Canadian flag has for Canadians. This is because the Stars and Stripes has more cultural strings of meaning.

Let's start with the star-spangled banner. First, there is the apocryphal story of the flag's origins: that it was first sewn by a young Pennsylvania seamstress, Betsy Ross, at the request of George Washington, the future first president, during the American War of Independence. That the patriotically romanticized account has been disputed by some historians in no way diminishes the power of the flag's origin story.

The story of the flag's connection to America's revolutionary history is invoked whenever the US national anthem (which was inspired by events during the War of 1812) is played, reminding us that the flag was around at the dawn of American nationhood and making it a symbol of the country's successful fight for independence.

Third, the American flag has important visual symbols on it: 13 stripes for the 13 colonies that revolted against the British Crown, and 50 stars for 50 states, updated as necessary (there were just 48 stars when I was born). These symbols give the flag a universal significance: whether you live in Alamosa, Colorado, or Kittery Point, Maine, your place in the country is represented on the flag.

Fourth, the pledge of allegiance to the flag is a solemn exercise performed with right hand over heart at the start of the school day and the commencement of government meetings. Americans may take the pledge for granted, but this is a practice that America shares with very few other countries.

Fifth, there is the strong association between the flag and the military. This goes back to the flag's introduction during the American Revolution, but it was solidified by the classic picture of five US marines and one Navy corpsman raising the flag on the Pacific island of Iwo Jima during World War II. In both world wars, as well as in the Korean War and subsequent wars, the flag has been with the troops.

Sixth, laws and censures exist against any desecration of the flag. You may not decorate your ceiling with it, make it into an article of clothing, or fly it carelessly so that it touches land, water, or the floor. And you certainly may not burn it.

The Maple Leaf is internationally recognized as a symbol of Canadian identity, but Canada's flag carries far fewer strings of meaning than the Stars and Stripes does. When I used to ask my students when the Canadian flag was first used, hardly anyone could give me the correct answer without googling it on their phone. (It was February 1965, nearly 100 years after Canada became a country.) I couldn't imagine a student knowing that the man who designed the flag was historian Colonel George Stanley.

The flag was not the product of any revolution, although it was the subject of fierce debate in Parliament when the first suggestions that it replace the Union Jack were raised. I don't need to tell you we don't pledge allegiance to it, and we have no flag desecration laws in Canada.

The central symbol of the flag is the leaf of a tree that isn't native to much of Canada. Our national anthem does not include reference to the flag. In 1867, when Canada achieved its nationhood, the soldier and poet Alexander Muir wrote a rousing tune called "The Maple Leaf Forever," which did include some references to historic battles. It was an unofficial national anthem for a time, but it never made it officially because it was strongly rooted in British heritage and celebrated the defeat of Canada's French population at the hands of the British. The "Maple Leaf" in the song's title and chorus is an emblem on the national coat of arms. It is not a reference to the flag, which was created 60 years after Muir's death.

Canada's armed forces have served under various flags. Land forces in World War I most commonly used the Union Jack, but merchant seamen used numerous versions of the red ensign, a red flag with a Union Jack in the upper left-hand corner and a central shield with different emblems. Two versions of the red ensign are used today as the provincial flags of Manitoba and Ontario.

In 1996, the federal government established 15 February as National Flag of Canada Day, although it is not a holiday and I'll bet you were unaware of the occasion. By comparison, in the United States, Flag Day has been observed nationally since 1916, and it is a holiday in some parts of the country. Canadians may proudly wear a modest pin with the flag on it when they go to other countries, but the Maple Leaf still lacks the strong cultural meaning attached to the Stars and Stripes.

© Charla Sylvester

Titled "Home and Native Land," this photo was taken by Charla Sylvester, a 25-year-old student from the Beausoleil First Nation. As a culture symbol, what do you think the Maple Leaf means to her?

What do you think?

Could you argue that our flag has more cultural value for Canadians than the American flag has for Americans? How could you study this?

a "foreign" culture. The false stories followed particular themes, as Anne Fadiman explains in her book on Hmong Americans:

> [Rumoured] methods of [dog] procurement vary. Some are coaxed home by Hmong children. Some were adopted from animal shelters. . . . Others are strays. The most common accusation is theft, often from backyards, sometimes leaving the head and collar as mute testimony to Rover's passing. . . . The dog is usually an expensive one, often owned by a doctor. The theft is observed, the license plate number is marked down. When the police check, the dog is already in some Hmong family's pot.
>
> The supposed proof varies. That fixture in the urban legend, the garbage man, reports the presence of canine remains in Hmong garbage cans. Carcasses are seen hanging in the cellar by meter readers, salesmen, or whomever. Freezers are said to be full of frozen dogs. A bizarre touch is that the dogs are supposedly skinned alive to make them more tasty. (Fadiman, 1997, pp. 190–1)

On a larger scale, ethnocentrism has played a role in the colonizing efforts of powerful nations imposing their political, economic, and religious beliefs on the Indigenous populations of lands they "discovered."

Potlatch and Peyote: Ethnocentrism and Indigenous Cultures

The following case studies highlight how North American Indigenous communities were forced by ethnocentric governments to abandon traditional customs.

The Potlatch Act of 1884

The **potlatch** is a traditional ceremony of Northwest Coast Indigenous peoples living in the United States and Canada. It often involves the acquisition or affirmation of hereditary names. These hereditary names carry more than just symbolic significance: they are connected with rights to fish, hunt, or forage for plants in particular territories, and with the responsibility to conserve the living entities in those areas. Potlatches thus serve to maintain the strength and social unity of the group.

An important aspect of the potlatch is the giving away of gifts and possessions. Traditionally, a high-ranking man could prove he was worthy of his position by making gifts of the possessions he had acquired. The hierarchical nature of Northwest Coast culture made this competitive, as those holding or aspiring to high rank gave away a great deal. The level of competition rose after European contact, because of the sudden availability of European manufactured goods. The population of the Kwakwaka'wakw or speakers of Kwak'wala of Vancouver Island, for example, dropped from roughly 8,000 in 1835 to around 2,000 in 1885. When diseases decimated lineages entitled to important names, more distant relatives would vie for prestigious family names. In some cases, competition could become socially divisive, and there were even incidents in which property was destroyed as a show of wealth ("I am so rich, that this property means nothing to me"). Such incidents appear to have been rare but overreported in the literature.

This aspect of the potlatch gained the notice of government officials in Canada, who saw the ceremony as an impediment to assimilation. For one thing, the Europeans who had settled in North America viewed the drive to accumulate wealth as an important lever in their burgeoning capitalist economy (recall Weber's Protestant ethic). The notion of redistributing wealth among people who had not earned it through hard work was difficult to understand and potentially dangerous. In the nineteenth century, the peoples of the Northwest Coast were already comparatively wealthy, but the prevalence of the potlatch and the quantity of goods given away gave Europeans the impression that Indigenous people were poor and, perhaps worse, lazy because a good number of them were benefiting from handouts (Lutz, 2012, p. 306). Christian missionaries also disliked the potlatch, which did not fit within the model of religion they were attempting to establish among the Indigenous population.

In 1884, the Canadian government banned the potlatch, making participation in the ceremony a misdemeanour. In 1921, 45 of the highest-ranking Kwakiutl were arrested. Twenty-two were sentenced to prison terms of two to three months. The people lost many sacred potlatch items that were taken as a condition for the release of community members arrested but not charged. The items became the property of the minister of Indian Affairs, who distributed them to art collectors and museums.

In 1951, the potlatch ban was repealed. But it wasn't until 1975 that the National Museum in Ottawa declared it would return the sacred items—provided they would be kept in museums. The Royal Ontario Museum returned its items in 1988, and the National Museum of the American Indian in New York repatriated some of its holdings in 1993. Some items were never recovered.

Outlawing Peyote

When Spanish explorers arrived in Mexico in the sixteenth century, they encountered an Indigenous population that practised a *monotheistic* (literally "one god") religion they could relate to because of its similarity to their own Christian belief. It revolved around an omnipotent and omnipresent "Great Spirit" who had created the universe very much like the Christian God the Spanish believed in. There was an important difference, however. Central to the religious practice of some Indigenous groups was a small, spineless cactus known as the peyote. The people believed the Great Spirit had provided the peyote to help them cure disease, gain spiritual enlightenment, and communicate with the Great Spirit (James, 2009).

The edible buds of the peyote contain mescaline, a hallucinogenic substance. The Spaniards did not approve, and they attempted to ban the use of peyote among the native inhabitants. This merely pushed practitioners of the peyote-based religion into hiding and, eventually, over the border into what is now the United States. During the nineteenth century the peyote-based religion, combining traditional Indigenous practices with elements of Christianity, spread in the American Southwest. As a narcotic, peyote helped the many nations that had been dumped into Indian Territory (later to become Oklahoma) deal with the harsh realities of life confined to reservations (Fikes, 1996). Again, it met resistance from state authorities, who attempted to outlaw the substance beginning in the late 1800s. To gain an exemption from harsh state-level drug laws, the peyotists banded together to form the Native American Church, which was officially recognized as a religion in 1918, but they

continued to face persecution until the passing of the American Indian Religious Freedom Act in 1978. Card-carrying members were permitted to take peyote in ceremony. Similar legislation was passed in Canada in 1953.

This did not end the legal difficulties of the Native American Church. In 1990, a Supreme Court decision sided with the state of Oregon in the case of *Employment Division of Oregon v. Smith*. Two Native Americans had been fired from state jobs, and because it was a "drug firing," they were denied unemployment benefits. The response to this perceived threat to the First Amendment from both liberal and conservative groups resulted in the Religious Freedom Restoration Act, which was passed in Congress in 1993. The lack of effectiveness of the provisions of this Act concerning Native American religion resulted in the passing of the Religious Freedom Act Amendment of 1994.

Today the Native American Church has roughly 80 chapters coming from 70 nations in Mexico, the United States, and Canada, numbering around 250,000 members (Fikes, 1996).

Eurocentrism

Eurocentrism involves taking a broadly defined "European" (i.e., western and northern European, plus North American) position to address others, and assuming that the audience shares that position (or that it should). It can be seen in historical references to the "known world"—that is, the world as it was known by Europeans—and to Christopher Columbus "discovering," in 1492, continents that were already home to millions of people. It foregrounds discoveries and contributions that are Western, and backgrounds those that are not. Did you know that our standard numbering system is known (poorly) as the Hindu–Arabic system? Did you know that chocolate and vanilla, corn, squash and pumpkins, most beans, peppers, potatoes, tomatoes, and sunflowers were first grown by Indigenous people? The Eurocentric perspective of many textbooks used in the West tends to champion advances made by

Constantino Brumidi, Fresco, c. 1875, Senate wing, U.S. Capitol

Columbus and the Indian Maiden (c. 1875) is one of a series of frescoes adorning the vaulted ceiling of the US Capitol building in Washington, DC. It was painted by Italian-born American historical artist Constantino Brumidi (1805–1880). Works of art are important cultural artifacts that are used to tell the story of a culture. What story does this mural tell about Columbus and America? What culture is it intended for? And what do you mean you find it "creepy"?

people of European stock while downplaying or altogether ignoring important non-European developments such as these.

Cultural Globalization

Global studies expert **Manfred Steger** defines cultural globalization as "the intensification and expansion of cultural flows across the globe" (2003, p. 69). Our concern is with the one-way flow of culture from the West, or what we might call the "Americanization" of the world. Think of the factors. First of all, English has emerged as by far the most prominent language of science, of the internet, and of other powerful media. Second, American movies and television are seen in almost every country in the world. But to label this "American" culture is perhaps giving it too broad a scope. It is just a small number of transnational companies—AT&T, Verizon, Comcast, Viacom, and Disney in the United States, as well as

the European companies Bertelsmann and Vivendi, and Sony in Japan—that control most of the media. Not only do these companies reap enormous dividends by exporting their respective brands of Western culture to consumers across the globe, but as Steger points out, they draw audiences abroad away from the culture of their own countries into a global "gossip market" that revolves around the "vacuous details of the private lives of American celebrities like Britney Spears, Jennifer Lopez, Leonardo DiCaprio, and Kobe Bryant" (Steger, 2003, p. 77). We could update this list to include Rihanna, the Kardashians, Taylor Swift, Jay Z and his wife Beyoncé Knowles, Kanye West (who now fashions himself as "Ye"), and Canada's own Justin Bieber. Some other global stars, such as Toronto's Drake, have taken a more managed approach to their own publicity, for the sake of privacy and in the belief that not all publicity is good.

It's worth noting that interpretations of globalized items of Western culture are not necessarily the same abroad as they are in their countries of origin. The classic study of a cultural reading of a Western cultural item by a non-Western audience is described by American anthropologist Laura Bohannan in "Shakespeare in the Bush" (1966). In it she describes her experience of telling the story of *Hamlet* to the Tiv of West Africa, and the reading they put on it. The article concludes with the words of a Tiv elder. After admitting that he had enjoyed Bohannan's story, told "with very few mistakes," the elder said:

> Sometime . . . you must tell us some more stories of your country. We, who are elders, will instruct you in their true meaning, so that when you return to your own land your elders will see that you have not been sitting in the bush, but among those who know things and who have taught you wisdom. (Bohannan, 1966, p. 47)

5.7 Cultural Relativism

Cultural relativism is an approach to studying and understanding an aspect of another culture within its proper cultural context. Because of the *holistic* nature of culture—because a culture is a complex system in which everything is connected—no single cultural practice can be understood in isolation, outside of its social, historical, and environmental context. Just as you cannot understand a single part of a car without understanding the system of which it is a part, you cannot attempt to understand individual aspects of culture without looking at their cultural context.

Unlike what Spock used to say in the original *Star Trek* series, logic (as a pure entity) does *not* dictate. Logic is a cultural construct, and every society has its own cultural logic. Any explanation of a cultural practice or belief must in some way incorporate this logic. This is especially important in medicine. Western medicine is dominated by a kind of ethnocentric logic that states that nothing worth knowing comes from non-Western traditions. Yet in order to cure or to heal, it's important to respond to the way the patient envisions the healing process. This point comes across with striking clarity in Anne Fadiman's study of Hmong refugees in America (1997), mentioned

earlier in this chapter. The book describes the way American doctors and nurses failed to respect, among other things, the Hmong people's spiritual connections to medicine, the importance of encouraging their belief that a cure is available, and the role this belief plays in the curing process.

Cultural relativism is about not just how we *understand* cultural practices that are not our own but how we *judge* those practices. One prevailing viewpoint argues that individuals should not be judged by the practices of their culture. They have relatively little choice in what they do. After all, those living today no more invented those customs that you might find objectionable than you invented customs in Canadian culture that others may find strange. Consider the Maasai, an African people located in Kenya and northern Tanzania. Their strong warrior tradition includes a custom in which boys, at the onset of puberty, are circumcised. It is frightening and painful, but it is an important initiation ceremony: only once he has gone through the ceremony is a Maasai boy treated as a man and permitted to have sex with women. It is easy for Canadians to judge this custom negatively, to be critical of those who perpetuate what they consider a barbaric ritual. But is that right? The Maasai might identify as a sign of our cultural weakness the fact that most Canadian boys today are never ritually transformed into men.

Judging the Past by Present-Day Standards: Cultural Relativism versus Presentism

The doctrine of cultural relativism becomes problematic when studying historical practices and views that were once widespread but are now considered abhorrent and offensive. The city of Halifax recently had to consider the appropriateness of honouring its founder, Edward Cornwallis, who, as governor of Nova Scotia, endorsed the use of violence to eliminate the colony's Mi'kmaq population in what some have called an act of genocide. In 2010, a new statue of women's rights activist Nellie McClung in Winnipeg touched off similar debates. While McClung was instrumental in winning Canadian women the right to vote and hold public office, she was also a proponent of eugenics, the movement to improve the population by sterilizing people with mental and physical disabilities, as well as people of races deemed "inferior." Not even Canada's first prime

What do you think?
Is judging practices and attitudes of the past by the majority standards of today a form of ethnocentrism? Why or why not?

minister is safe: in 2016, the board of governors at Wilfrid Laurier University shelved a plan to erect on campus a statue of John A. Macdonald—and 21 other past prime ministers—after students and instructors protested, citing in particular Macdonald's racist policies toward Indigenous people. Another major Canadian university, Ryerson, became Toronto Metropolitan University in 2022 because of objections by some that the nineteenth-century educator Egerton Ryerson, after whom it was named, was among the architects of Canada's long-standing Indian residential schools policy. During protests in 2021, a statue of Ryerson on campus was toppled, beheaded, and thrown in Toronto harbour (and the head later appeared on a pike on the Six Nations Reserve west of Toronto). The university renaming was seen by those who supported it as a positive response to the "Calls to Action" in the 2015 report of the Truth and Reconciliation Commission of Canada.

The Go-Between, a 1971 movie based on a novel of the same name written by British writer L.P. Hartley, begins with the line, "The past is a foreign country: they do things differently there." That captures the spirit of the doctrine of cultural relativism, which suggests we should judge figures like Cornwallis, McClung, Sir John A., and Ryerson not by today's moral standards but by the standards of their own time; failing to do so is known as **presentism**. But can we really let bygones be bygones when assessing certain cultural practices that are so repugnant? And should we not acknowledge that even when majority social views were different than they are today, some or many progressives (not to mention those directly affected) outspokenly objected to the majoritarian views on such issues as slavery, eugenics, freedom of religion, and Indigenous education?

Cultural Relativism, Ethnocentrism, and Smell: Two Stories

Our senses—the way we perceive what is beautiful or ugly, pleasant or disgusting—are culturally conditioned. Think of media portrayals of idealized female beauty. For many North Americans, the image that comes to mind is that of a tall, rail-thin model sashaying down a fashion runway. Do you think this is true in other cultures?

What about our sense of smelling "good" or "bad"? Part of how we smell is determined by the food we eat (e.g., dairy products, meat, garlic, curry), but there is more to it than that. As a member of the Peace Corps, an organization of volunteers operating in developing countries, Tom Bissell observed how his colleagues working in the Central Asian country of Uzbekistan reacted to sharing space with local inhabitants who were overdressed for the weather and, understandably, hot and sweaty:

> When I was in the Peace Corps, one of my least favorite things was when my fellow volunteers complained about Central Asian body odor. . . . But Gandhi probably smelled bad. Surely Abraham Lincoln smelled. William Shakespeare was, in all likelihood, rank. . . . Most certainly Jesus and Julius Caesar and the Buddha all smelled terrible. People have been smelly for the vast majority of human history. By gooping up our pheromonal reactors with dyed laboratory gels, could it be that we in the West are to blame for our peculiar alienation? Might not the waft from another's armpit contain crucial bioerotic code? Could it be by obscuring such code we have confused otherwise very simple matters of attraction? (Bissell, 2003, p. 98)

In a very different setting, Emma LaRocque, a Métis writer, came to a similar conclusion:

> Several summers ago when I was intern-teaching on a northern reserve, one of the teachers told me how she "had to get used to" the smells of the children. She insisted it was not just stuffiness but a "peculiar odor." . . .
>
> Oddly enough, the "peculiar" smell was a redolent mixture of spruce, moosehide, and woodsmoke. All the while this teacher was complaining about the smell of the

children, the children reported a "strange" odor coming from the vicinity of some of the teachers and their chemical toilets. And it never seemed to occur to the teacher that she could be giving off odors.

More to the point, both the teacher and the children attached value judgments to the unfamiliar odors. As a friend of mine noted, "to a person whose culture evidently prefers Chanel No. 5 or pine-scented aerosol cans, moosehide and woodsmoke can seem foreign." The converse is true, I might add. (LaRocque, 1975, p. 37)

As we have seen, ethnocentrism and cultural relativism are opposing ways of looking at cultures, both our own and those of others. Ethnocentrism is laden with negative judgment, while cultural relativism is characterized by a greater appreciation for context in understanding and evaluating culture. This is not to say that everything is relative, or that there are no universal standards. Certain practices, such as killing, are not unique to one culture and may be widely rejected by many cultures. Practices such as female genital mutilation, the use of land mines and child soldiers, and the torture of political prisoners can be added to this list.

The point to take from this is that it's important to realize how easy it is to make an ethnocentric assessment of a different culture. It is important to try to understand why different cultures do what they do. And, while true appreciation of aspects of other cultures might not always be possible, it is worth the trip to take a few steps down that path.

5.8 Sociolinguistics

Sociolinguistics is the study of language as part of culture. Language exists at the centre of communication between individuals and groups. It is a source both of understanding and of misunderstanding. It is also the main vehicle for transmitting culture, and a culture cannot be understood without some sense of the language(s) it uses and the way those languages fit with other aspects of culture. Sociolinguistics thus looks at language in relation to such sociological factors as race, ethnicity, age, gender, and region.

Dialect as a Sociological Term

A **dialect** is a variety of a language, a version that is perhaps different from others in terms of pronunciation, vocabulary, and grammar. To the sociologist, the distinction between dialect and language is interesting because it can be as much a product of social factors as of linguistic ones. Dutch and German, for instance, are considered separate languages, although going strictly on linguistic criteria they could be called dialects of the same language. For some German speakers living near the Netherlands, Dutch is easier to understand than dialects of German spoken in Austria or Switzerland.

Dialects, unlike languages, are often evaluated according to whether they represent proper or improper, casual or formal, even funny or serious versions of a language. These judgments usually depend on the social status of the dialect's speakers. In Britain, the "King's English" is an upper-class dialect, more highly valued in formal communication than regional dialects like that of the city of Manchester. The latter is often used by characters on TV shows such as *Coronation Street*, where it signifies that the characters are "real people" rather than upper-class people with what are called BBC accents. A few years ago, a commercial for an SUV featured a voice-over spoken in a Newfoundland accent. The accent here was used to put the audience in a receptive mood by evoking the famed good nature and affability of the people of Newfoundland and Labrador. You might not hear that same accent extolling the marketable features of a Lexus.

Linguistic Determinism and Relativity

The relationship between language and culture is sometimes discussed in terms of the **Sapir–Whorf hypothesis**, which posits the existence of **linguistic determinism** (or **causation**). The principle of linguistic determinism suggests that the way we view and understand the world is shaped by the language we speak. Like theories of biological or social determinism, the Sapir–Whorf hypothesis can be cast either as strongly or weakly deterministic—that is, language can be seen to exert either a strong or a weak influence on a person's worldview. I tend to favour a weak determinism: I believe that linguistic differences are a valid form of cultural relativism, that exact translation from one language into another is impossible,

The Point Is . . .

Speakers of the Same Language Don't Always Share a Culture

I was enjoying a midday meal with colleagues in the Flemish city of Leuven, Belgium. My companions were three Belgian academics, two of them professors at the local Catholic university, the third a PhD candidate. We were studying an eighteenth-century grammar of Wendat (Huron) written by a Belgian Jesuit missionary, but took a break to enjoy the weather and a beer in a courtyard surrounded closely by several old buildings. It was all very "civilized."

Our quiet conversation was suddenly disturbed by a boisterous group of students, who passed so close to our table that they bumped us, without an apology or any sign they were aware of their rude intrusion upon our peaceful lunch. It took only an instant for one of my colleagues to identify them as Dutch. This was followed by a short lecture on the difference between the Dutch and the Flemish (the people of Flanders), who speak dialects of the same language but apparently share little else in terms of their culture. The Flemish were part of the United Kingdom of the Netherlands until the Belgian Revolution of 1830. They opposed the authoritarian rule of the Dutch King William I, and being Catholics, they were uneasy with the dominance of Protestants in the kingdom. Belgium became a country in 1839, but Flanders has maintained a connection with the Netherlands because of their shared border and language (elsewhere in Belgium, French and German dominate). The discussion of how the Flemish differ from the Dutch reminded me a lot of conversations I had been part of comparing Canadians with Americans and New Zealanders with Australians. In each pair, one group is considered loud and brash, the other quieter and more respectful.

---

and that knowing the language of a people is important to grasping the ideas of a people. This, after all, is why so many Indigenous groups and nations in Canada are deeply involved in recovering, preserving, and expanding the use of their native languages: their ideas, their views of the world, are interwoven with their languages. Though the elders of today will die, their teachings will not.

Noun Classes and Gender

Consider linguistic determinism in the context of the following statement: the different noun classes that exist in a language can reinforce the beliefs its speakers have within their culture. English speakers in Canada have some awareness of difference in noun classes through the presence of gender exhibited by the Romance languages to which they are exposed (e.g., French, Italian, Portuguese, Spanish, and other languages based on Latin, the language of the Romans). Students struggling through French classes may wonder why every French noun has to be masculine or feminine. Why are the words for "tree" (*arbre*) and tree species masculine, while the parts of trees—roots, leaves, branches, bark, blossoms—are feminine?

While it does not have noun classes labelled as "masculine" or "feminine," English does have a certain degree of grammatically mandated gender, with our use of *he*, *him*, *his*, and *she*, *her*, *hers*. Take the following two sentences: *One of my sisters is called Ann. She is younger than I am, and her hair used to be the same colour as mine.* In the second sentence, the words "she" and "her" are grammatically necessary but do not add any new information. Am I assuming that you have forgotten the gender of my sister? We already know from the nouns "sister" and "Ann" that the person spoken about is female. The **Indo-European** languages—the family of languages that includes almost all the languages of Europe plus Farsi (Iranian) and the languages of Pakistan and northern India—all impose gender grammatically in some way.

Algonquian languages, which together make up the largest Indigenous language family in Canada and the United States, have no grammatically mandated gender, in either the French or the English sense. They have no pronouns meaning "he" or "she." They are not alone in that respect. Almost every Indigenous language spoken in Canada does not recognize gender grammatically. Does this mean that Algonquian speakers were traditionally more flexible about gender roles than their European contemporaries, or that there was a greater degree of equality between the sexes? The latter was certainly true at the time of contact, but whether that can be related to the absence of grammatical gender in their language is difficult to determine.

There have been campaigns to bring gender-neutral pronouns to English. In 2014, the Vancouver School Board agreed that students should have the right to be referred to by the pronoun of their choice, including the gender-neutral options *xe*, *xem*, and *xyr* (Brean, 2014). The decision was made to accommodate transgender, gender-fluid, and gender–non-conforming students for whom neither *he/him* nor *she/her* was appropriate. When assessing the validity of the Sapir–Whorf hypothesis, consider how you might feel as a transgender person repeatedly referred to as "him" or "her": How would you feel about yourself knowing that neither option adequately described you?

A Final Thought

Sometimes the terms that a language *doesn't* have tells you something significant about the culture. I have worked with the Wendat (Huron) language for 40 years. I have noticed that it doesn't have terms for the following concepts:

- ☐ *guilt* or *innocence*
- ☐ *best* or *worst*
- ☐ *command* or *obey*.

What do you think might be the cultural implications of these "holes" in the Wendat language? What "holes" can you identify in the English language?

Wrap It Up

Summary

Not only do cultures differ, but cultures are viewed and lived differently by people who occupy different social locations, based on gender, sexuality, race, ethnicity, age, and so on. Similarly, although humans, as intensely social creatures, cannot live without culture, they can also feel oppressed by their culture, if their social location is not one of power and influence.

Remember, as well, that cultures are contested, that not everyone is in agreement concerning the rightness or goodness of every aspect of their mainstream culture. This is why there are minority versions that exist in contrast or opposition to the dominant culture. Subcultures tend to organize around preoccupations—we might call them hobbies or pastimes—not found within the dominant culture. Countercultures oppose the defining elements of the dominant culture, but there's something inherently attractive in a counterculture—people like to cast themselves as rebels—and so a counterculture sometimes must reinvent itself repeatedly to keep from becoming mainstream. Even high culture, which occupies a privileged position, is a minority culture, concerning itself with sophisticated pursuits that may be beyond the reaches of the masses. Which brings us to popular culture or mass culture: the label you use depends on whether or not you believe people create culture independent of the powerful and manipulative influence of large commercial interests.

Think Back

Questions for Critical Review

1. What does Canadian culture mean to you? What parts of your definition might be contested by other Canadians?
2. Beer producers, banks, and coffee shop chains are just some of the companies that tap into the theme of Canadian culture in their advertising. How does this benefit them? What is the impact of their advertising on people who belong to the kind of culture they describe? What is the impact on people excluded from their vision of Canadian culture?

3. Using your own examples (as opposed to those mentioned in the chapter), explain the difference between a subculture and a counterculture.

4. What are some norms associated with being online? How are these norms reinforced through positive and negative sanctions?

5. Use examples to explain the difference between a folkway, a more, and a taboo.

6. Imagine you wanted to study how Canadian values differ from province to province and territory. What questions could you ask in a survey? How else could you investigate value differences?

7. In 2015, students at Princeton University in New Jersey lobbied to have Woodrow Wilson's name stripped from the university's prestigious Woodrow Wilson School of Public and International Affairs, and in 2020 the university's Board of Trustees renamed it the Princeton School of Public and International Affairs. A residential college and a student award also bore Wilson's name. A Nobel Peace Prize winner, Wilson had been president of the university, arguably the most positively transformational president in the university's long history, before being elected president of the United States in 1912. While in office as the American president, he passed progressive legislative reforms that included voting rights for women and restrictions on child labour, and he was instrumental in the founding of the League of Nations. He was also a racist, having endorsed segregation and the Ku Klux Klan. What do you consider an appropriate response to a situation like this? Find out online what was determined in regard to the naming of the college and the student award.

8. Your friend Sam informs you that they have chosen the self-identifying pronouns "they" and "them." What is your reaction? What does this tell you about yourself? What does Sam's decision tell you about them?

Read On

Suggested Print and Online Resources

Introduction to Anishinaabemowin, www.ontarioparks.com/parksblog/introduction-to-anishinaabemowin/
This is an excellent introduction to the grammar and other key aspects of the Ojibwe language. Students can consider linguistic determinism as they enjoy an introduction to an Indigenous language.

Michael Bibby & Lauren M.E. Goodlad, eds, *Goth: Undead Subculture* (Durham, NC: Duke University Press, 2007)
This edited collection of scholarly essays covering all aspects of Goth subculture—from music and film to fashion and aesthetics—includes a study of individualism within the subculture by British sociologist Paul Hodkinson, an authority on youth subcultures.

Cannabis Culture, www.cannabisculture.com
This Vancouver-based online retailer and information site reflects the viewpoints of the marijuana counterculture, particularly in Canada. Students can consider the aspects that define it as a counterculture at a time when recreational marijuana use has become legal. Is it still a counterculture?

Jennifer Carlson, *Citizen-Protectors: The Everyday Politics of Guns in the Age of Decline* (New York: Oxford University Press, 2015)
The author of this ethnographic study bought a gun and took courses to become trained as an instructor for the National Rifle Association. Her interviews with 60 gun owners in Michigan helped her discover that many young Americans, especially young men, carry guns out of a sense of responsibility to help maintain civil order.

John Fiske, *Understanding Popular Culture*, 2nd ed. (London: Routledge, 2010)
A classic sociological study of popular culture.

Sajida Sultana Alvi, Homa Hoodfar, & Sheila McDonough, eds., *The Muslim Veil North America: Issues and Debates* (Toronto: Canadian Scholars' Press, 2003)
This insightful look into the cultural image of the *niqab* focuses especially on the North American (particularly Montreal) experience of the 1990s.

TED: Culture, www.ted.com/topics/culture
The non-profit organization dedicated to "ideas worth spreading" has a good collection of curated TED talks on cultural themes ranging from "Misconceptions of Islam and Muslim Life" to "Pop Culture Obsessions."

6

Deviance and Crime

Reading this chapter will help you to . . .

- Avoid some of the leading misunderstandings of the term "deviant."

- Distinguish between overt and covert characteristics of deviance.

- Discuss the reasons that deviance is sometimes associated with ethnicity, culture, race, gender, sexual orientation, disability, and class.

- Explain how deviance is socially constructed and contested.

- Define some of the leading theories of criminal deviance, including strain theory, subcultural theory, labelling theory, and social control theory.

- Discuss recent trends in Canada's crime rate.

For Starters

Greta Thunberg and Uncomfortable Deviance

Greta Thunberg is a deviant. She knowingly participated in demonstrably deviant behaviour. This is not to say that either she or her behaviour is good or bad. Simply, she did something different, acting in a way that fell outside the boundaries of what is considered normal behaviour.

And it made some people very uncomfortable. Peaceful protest can do that, and it can also lead to social change. Indeed, Durkheim believed that deviance is necessary because it can bring about progressive changes.

On Friday 20 August 2018, Greta Thunberg, then 15 years old, skipped school to sit outside the parliament building in the Swedish capital of Stockholm. There she handed out leaflets that read, "I am doing this because you adults are shitting on my future." Beside her where she sat was a large, hand-painted sign that read *Skolstrejk för klimatet,* which translates as "School strike for climate." She continued her strike for 20 days. In September, she started striking just on Fridays.

What made this deviant? First, it was different from what other schoolchildren were doing. Greta Thunberg was not acting on behalf of any group or organization, or because her parents wanted her to. Her actions were her own, and they deviated from what is considered normal behaviour for a person of her age and position in society. Of note, Greta was and is "deviant" in another important way—she was diagnosed at a young age as being on the autism spectrum, with obsessive-compulsive disorder and Asperger syndrome. She went through a period when she ate little and suffered depression, and her condition manifests in selective mutism, which means speaking only when it seems necessary and to the point. The condition, which she calls her "superpower," also has given her freedom to be extremely blunt and direct in talking to world leaders and in speaking at climate change rallies.

Second, her behaviour was subversive. In Chapter 4, I described the dominant culture as

Michael Campanella/The Guardian/Eyevine/Redux

middle-aged and male. Not only does Greta fall outside that culture, but in criticizing adults who were failing to act—and, by extension, adults in positions of power—she was acting in opposition to the mainstream culture. Her actions inspired thousands of teenage students in Europe and Australia to go on a similar strikes, and in May 2019 there was a nationwide Friday strike in Canada.

Following Greta Thunberg's initial protests came predictable attempts to discredit her. Deviance is hard to ignore, and because it makes people uncomfortable or suspicious, a common strategy within society is to push it further toward the margins. There were accusations that Greta was not acting independently but was part of a larger, carefully orchestrated campaign.

There were hints that she was receiving attention mainly because she is on the autism spectrum. But then, when attempts to diminish her failed, something interesting happened. She was invited in November of 2018 to give a TED Talk in Stockholm, and a month later to address the United Nations at a climate change conference. In January 2019, she travelled by train to Davos to speak at the World Economic Forum, and in February she was asked to address the European Union's Economic and Social Committee. Large political and economic organizations, such as the various European legislatures she addressed, made up of the very kinds of powerful adults that Greta was criticizing were now trying to align themselves with her.

6.1 Introduction: What Is Deviance?

Many people, when they hear the word "deviance," think of behaviour that is immoral, illegal, perverse, or just "wrong." But **deviance** is better thought of as a neutral term. It simply means "straying from what is normal," or what the majority in society believe to be normal. It does not mean that the deviant—the one engaging in deviance—is necessarily bad, criminal, perverted, "sick," or inferior in any way. The word is based on the Latin root *-via-*, meaning "path." To deviate is simply to go off the common path.

When looking at deviant behaviour it helps to distinguish between **overt characteristics** of deviance—the actions or qualities taken as explicitly violating the cultural norm—and **covert characteristics**, the unstated qualities that might make a particular group a target for sanctions. Covert characteristics can include age, ethnic background, race, sexual orientation, sex, and degree of physical and mental ability. In an example presented later in this section, the *overt* characteristics of the young people associated with "zoot suit" culture included their clothing, hairstyle, and taste in music—fashions that violated the cultural norm. The *covert* characteristics were age (they were mostly teens) and race (they were mostly Latino or African American).

What do *you* think?

The case of Greta Thunberg may remind you of the students of Marjory Stoneman Douglas High School in Parkland, Florida, after the shooting deaths of students there in 2018. They organized March for Our Lives, an activist group that continues to protest and lobby, with some success, for stricter gun control laws in the United States. How are the cases similar? Would you consider the actions of the Parkland students deviant?

Deviance, then, comes down to how we define "the norm." It is also about *who* defines the norm, and the power of those who share the norm to define it and treat others as inferior or dangerous. And we must recognize that just as the norm changes—over time and across cultures—so does deviance.

When we invoke "the norm," we are usually referring to what we defined in Chapter 5 as the dominant culture. As you read through the different sections of this chapter, keep in mind that the dominant culture in Canada is white, English-speaking, of European heritage, Christian, male, middle-class, middle-aged, urban, heteronormative, able-bodied, and without visible signs of mental disability. Remember that behaviour deviating from that of the dominant culture may be labelled deviant, but that doesn't make it wrong.

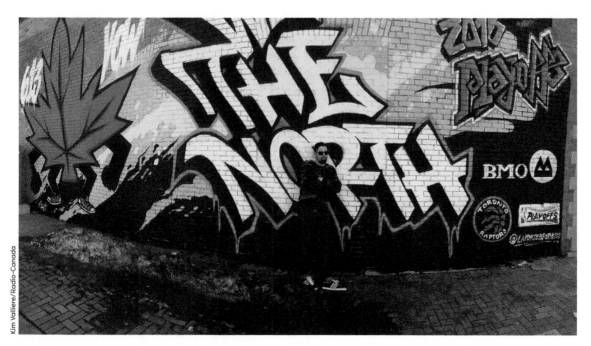

Kim Vallière/Radio-Canada

In 2016, the Toronto Raptors commissioned graffiti murals in six Canadian neighbourhoods, including the Glebe in Ottawa. Does graffiti lose some of its deviant cachet when it is commissioned and features sponsor logos?

Another term to revisit here is subculture. This is a group existing within a larger culture and possessing beliefs or interests at variance with those of the dominant culture. Subculture is the focal point of one of two early theories of deviance that we will examine later in detail.

6.2 Conflict Deviance

We might say that deviance is in the eye of the beholder: Behaviour considered deviant by one group may be considered acceptable or even standard by another. In this section, we will look at the ways in which deviance is contested among groups.

Deviance Is Contested across Cultures

What gets labelled deviant differs from culture to culture. Consider tattoos, for example. In mainstream Western culture, until recent years tattoos have been associated negatively with certain marginalized groups considered deviant. These groups include prisoners, sailors, sex workers, and performers in circus sideshows (sometimes called "freak shows"). But around the world, tattooing has been a long-standing practice among many cultural groups, including the Aborigines of Australia, the Austronesian peoples of the Pacific Islands, and Inuit in present-day Canada. Among some of these cultures

Quick Hits

Getting Deviance Straight

- Deviant just means *different from the norm, the usual.*
- Deviant *does not mean* bad, wrong, perverted, sick, or inferior in any way.

- Deviant is a category that *changes with time, place, and culture.*
- Definitions of deviance often *reflect power.*

the practice died out during generations of colonial oppression. Ashleigh Gaul (2014) describes how, in the North, tattooing the face of young women went from being "a widespread rite of passage and a source of Inuit pride to a mark of shamanism in a Christian-ized community." The practice has recently under-gone a revival in northern communities, sparked by young Indigenous people and cross-cultural contact with interested young people of dominant Western cultures. They view tattooing both as a link to the past and a way to display how "modern" they are.

Tattooing highlights three important aspects of deviance. First, deviance differs across cultures: what one culture defines as deviant may be consid-ered a venerable practice in another. Second, devi-ance changes over time. In the North, tattooing was a respectable practice for generations before becom-ing a cultural taboo. In mainstream Western culture, tattoos have now become so common that they are no longer widely seen as deviant. We may in fact have hit "peak tattoo": when your mom suggests getting matching mother–daughter tats, the practice loses some of the value it once held as an act of rebellion. Third, deviance is contested: whether something is or is not considered deviant can become a source of conflict among people within a community. This can have unfortunate social consequences when a dom-inant culture condemns as deviant the practices of a minority culture and, by extension, the minority culture itself.

Deviance Is Contested within Cultures

Definitions of deviance differ not only *across* but *within* cultures. It is true that the culture defines deviance—in other words, deviance is essentially a social or cultural construct—but it is important to remember that there is seldom total or even near total agreement within a culture as to what is devi-ant. Deviance, like other elements in a culture, can be contested.

When deviance is contested, we have a situa-tion known as **conflict deviance**. Conflict deviance is a disagreement among groups over whether or not something is deviant. It may be a sign that a prac-tice long condemned as deviant is gaining wider ac-ceptance in mainstream culture. Consider cannabis use, for example. In Canada, cannabis was made a prohibited substance in the 1920s. Those who flouted

Marjorie Tahbone, an Inupiaq woman from Alaska, chose to have three vertical lines inked onto her chin to signify her coming of age, re-viving an ancestral tradition that, she says, "a lot of the elders don't really know or understand because it's been asleep for so long" (Hanlon, 2015). Why do you think she decided to get this traditional tattoo when previous generations did not? Is this tattoo more or less deviant than the tattoo you might see on a Hell's Angels gang member? A mom at spin class? A Holocaust survivor?

the law were cast as deviant: they faced public con-demnation and arrests by police. During the late twentieth century, efforts to have possession and use decriminalized made cannabis a focal point of conflict deviance. In 2001, the government made it legal to possess small amounts of marijuana for me-dicinal purposes. In 2012, a Canadian Community Health Survey suggested that 3.4 million people aged 15 and older had used cannabis at least once in the previous year, a finding that went a long way toward changing public perceptions and normalizing the practice. Debates over whether possession of small amounts of cannabis for recreational use should be legalized entered the mainstream in 2015, when the Liberal Party of Canada successfully campaigned on a promise to legalize recreational use. It is now legal to buy and sell weed at brick-and-mortar cannabis retailers across Canada. This won't convince all Can-adians that consuming cannabis, whether smoking

The Point Is . . .

Mental Illness and Deviance: A Cross-Cultural View

The young Swedish climate activist Greta Thunberg spoke of her autism as being her "superpower," because it allows her to speak blunt truth to power. This points to the fact that different societies have understood and valued (or devalued) mental illness rather differently. Labelling has had much to do with this. While Judeo-Christian societies for millennia have labelled mentally unstable thoughts and behaviours as demon possession, insanity, schizophrenia, or simply mental illness, some North American Indigenous cultures, for example, have seen this as a gift of deviance to be supported or channelled (e.g., Herrera, 2015). Similarly, the vision quest practised among most Indigenous cultures in what is now Canada was and is an effort to achieve a special connection to and bond with the wider spiritual world—a culturally normalized deviance to gain spiritual power through physical deprivation and hallucination.

Perhaps the best-known example of Western treatment (or mistreatment) of the insane is Royal Bethlem Hospital (from whence comes the word "bedlam," meaning a place of chaos, madness, and insanity) in London, England, the administration of which was ceded to the city in 1547 by Henry VIII. The horrendous conditions of filth, starvation, degradation, and deprivation were repeated in countless other Western mental health asylums over the centuries, and Royal Bethlem in the seventeenth and eighteenth centuries became a popular tourist site, where for a small donation visitors could come to gawk at the "crazy" people—the deviants—all the while being aware that an unshackled inmate might hurl excrement at them. During the same period—and, one might argue, up to the present day—some other cultures sought to treat the mentally challenged or cognitively different in a more humane manner.

These cultural differences in how we understand, treat, and label mental illness are described in the following account of a Rwandan regarding severe posttraumatic stress disorder (PTSD) in the aftermath of the 1994 Rwanda genocide:

> We had a lot of trouble with western mental health workers who came here immediately after the genocide and we had to ask them to leave. They came and their practice did not involve being outside in the sun where you begin to feel better. There was no music or drumming to get your blood flowing again. There was no sense that everyone had taken the day off so that the entire community could come together to try to lift you up and bring you back to joy. There was no acknowledgement of the depression as something invasive and external that could be cast out again. Instead, they would take people . . . into these dingy little rooms and have them sit around for an hour or so and talk about bad things that had happened to them. (quoted in Davis, 2020)

Australian writer Jonathan Davis has said, "When face to face with a person experiencing involuntary states of non-ordinary consciousness, most of us—to put it bluntly—just want them away from us. . . . When I look at a person in such a crisis, I see a future potential mentor for others" (Davis, 2020). Greta Thunberg, I'm sure, would agree.

it or baking it in a brownie, is safe, responsible, or respectable. It remains a subject of conflict deviance, and possibly will remain so as long as research studies reveal deleterious effects from cannabis use, such as the relationship between early-age cannabis use and psychosis and the effects of cannabis potency on mental health (see, e.g., Cannabis & Psychosis, 2022; Petrilli et al., 2022).

Reefer Madness (1936) came out as a propaganda film at a time when exaggerated accounts of the drug's dangerous effects were causing panic among North American parents and lawmakers. It continued to be shown as an educational film in the 1940s and 1950s, in spite of its misinformation and low-budget production values. During the early 1970s it made a comeback among college students (personal experience) and became a cult classic thanks to its dated message, its lurid depiction of drug use, and its campy acting. It returned again on 20 April 2004, or 4/20: a date circled on the calendars of many pot users.

Social Constructionism versus Essentialism

One of the reasons deviance is contested has to do with the differing viewpoints of social constructionism and essentialism. **Social constructionism** is the idea that certain elements of social life—including deviance, but also gender, race, and other social

Fast-forward to October 2018, when a coalition of groups concerned about the health risks of marijuana voice their concerns in Vancouver on the very day recreational cannabis use became legal. What overt and covert aspects of deviance are raised in the poster?

What do you think?

Cannabis use in Canada, both its legal acceptance and increased social acceptance, has become a fait accompli. But has it? The weed you or your friends use is much more potent—fresher; less stem and leaf; more bud—than what was usually available to those labelled deviants in earlier generations. What once was a nice buzz might now lead to dangerous delusions, hallucinations, and schizophrenia. Do you think the cannabis "issue" is effectively solved in Canada, so that its production and sale are state-controlled like tobacco and alcohol? Or might government actions and social attitudes change in the future?

characteristics—are not natural but artificial, created by society or culture. **Essentialism**, on the other hand, reflects the view that there is something natural, true, universal, and therefore objectively determined about these characteristics.

When we look at certain social phenomena, we can see that each of these two viewpoints applies to some degree. Alcoholism, for instance, is a physical condition, so it has something of an essence or essential nature. However, whom we label an alcoholic and how we as a society perceive an alcoholic (i.e., as someone who is morally weak or as someone with a mental illness) is a social construct, one that will vary from society to society.

Quick Hits

How Canadians and Americans Differ on Issues of Conflict Deviance

In July 2016, American research company Gallup and Canadian research company Abacus surveyed North Americans to gauge their views on certain topics that, sociologically speaking, we might call matters of conflict deviance. Here are the percentages of Americans and Canadians who considered the listed behavio(u)rs morally right:

You can see that deviance is contested along national lines, but within Canada, deviance is also contested along age lines, with older Canadians being more approving or accepting of age-assisted dying and the use of animal furs in clothing but much less approving of pornography:

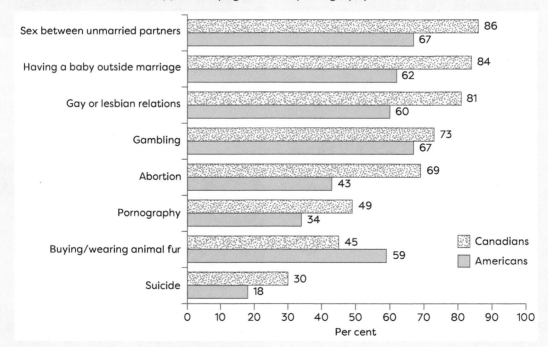

Source: Anderson & Coletto, 2016

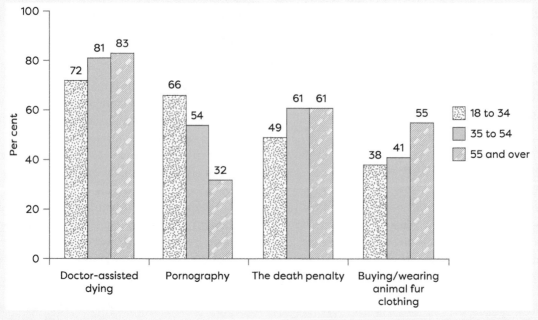

Source: Anderson & Coletto, 2016

The interplay between social constructionism and essentialism receives excellent treatment from Erving Goffman in his study of stigma and deviance (1963). A **stigma** is a human attribute that is seen to discredit an individual's social identity. It might be used to label the stigmatized individual or group as deviant. Goffman identified three types of *stigmata* (the plural of *stigma*):

- **bodily stigmata**
- **moral stigmata**
- **tribal stigmata**.

He defined them in the following way:

> First there are abominations of the body—the various physical deformities. Next there are blemishes of individual character perceived as weak will, domineering or unnatural passions, treacherous and rigid beliefs, and dishonesty, these being inferred from a known record of, for example, mental disorder, imprisonment, addiction, alcoholism, homosexuality, unemployment, suicidal attempts, and radical political behavior. Finally there are the tribal stigma of race, nation, and religion, these being stigma that can be transmitted through lineages and equally contaminate all members of a family. (Goffman, 1963, p. 4)

According to this definition, bodily stigmata exist physically, putting them within the essentialist framework. And yet how we define "blemished" is socially constructed: think of descriptions such as "too fat" or "too thin." People in a variety of societies "deform" their bodies to look beautiful according to social standards—for instance, by engaging in extreme dieting and exercising, by piercing their bodies, or, in certain cultures, by putting boards on their children's heads to give them a sloping forehead, all to achieve socially constructed standards of beauty and avoid certain bodily stigmata associated with deviance. Meanwhile, people who hear voices and see what is not physically present may be considered religious visionaries in some cultures, but they may be thought to require psychiatric treatment in others, where the tendency to experience visions is constructed as a moral stigma. Racializing groups based

What do *you* think?

How do you account for the difference in scores between Canadians and Americans on matters of conflict deviance? How much of the difference do you think has to do with the greater social and political influence of evangelical Christianity in the United States?

on their ethnicity or religion is another social process that gives rise to tribal stigmata: national identity is a social construct open to change over time, and a religion given privilege and respect in one society is very likely to be cast as deviant in another.

In this textbook, I take a view of deviance that is more social-constructionist than essentialist. Following Howard Becker's classic work *Outsiders* (1963), I do not see deviance as being inherently "bad," conformity to a norm being inherently "good." Instead, I generally follow the rule that, in Becker's words,

> social groups create deviance by making the rules, whose infraction constitutes deviance, and by applying those rules to particular people and labelling them as outsiders. . . . Deviance is *not a quality* of the act the person commits, but rather a consequence of the application by others of rules and sanctions to an "offender." (Becker, 1963, pp. 8–10)

The Other

An important concept in the sociological study of deviance is "the Other," or "Otherness." The **Other** is an image constructed by the dominant culture to characterize subcultures; it may also be used by a colonizing nation to describe the colonized. When the United States took over Haiti (between 1915 and 1934), Hollywood and the Catholic Church helped to make deviant the native religion of the Haitians by casting it as "other." Voodoo, which combines elements of Catholic ritual with traditional African magical and religious rites, became an example of how Haitians deviated from "civilized" norms. Along with sympathy and aid for Haiti following the January 2010 earthquake came criticism of Haitians, mostly in the conservative media, for their "fatalistic" or "superstitious" views and adherence to voodoo, which, some

The Point Is . . .

A Comic Strip Contributed to the Social Construction of a Deviant Group

An instructive case of deviance labelling and sanctioning surrounds the "Zoot Suit Riots" that occurred in June 1943 in Los Angeles, California. The targets were racialized groups—young African American and Latino men—who were convenient targets for wartime tension.

In the early 1940s, Los Angeles was undergoing rapid change. The city's population was growing, and its demographics were changing. Large numbers of Mexicans and African Americans were coming to the city. Teenagers made up a large share of the population, as older men and women had gone off to join the war effort. With a surplus of well-paying jobs left available by older brothers and sisters drafted into the military, the young people who remained made money that they were able to spend on music and clothes. These teens—black and Latino males in particular—adopted a unique style of dress, a distinctive haircut (the "duck tail," or "duck's ass"), and a musical style that were countercultural. The music was jazz, rooted in the African American experience and only slowly gaining general acceptance in the United States. The dancing (the jitterbug) was more sexual than dancing of the 1930s. The clothing was the zoot suit: a jacket with broad shoulders and narrow waist, balloooned pants with "reet pleats," "pegged cuffs," and striking designs. Participants in zoot-suit culture swaggered with a distinctive bold strut and posing stance and communicated with new slang words unknown to parents and other adults.

How did the zoot suit get labelled as deviant? The main media vehicle was the comic strip *Li'l Abner*, by Al Capp. In a time before television, comic strips were a major part of popular media. *Li'l Abner*, with maybe 50 million readers a day, was one of the most popular strips of the time. Its influence is difficult to overstate.

Al Capp identified the zoot suit as a target for his negative sanctioning humour. From 11 April to 23 May 1943, the strip presented the story of "Zoot-Suit Yokum," a character supposedly invented by US clothing manufacturers bent on taking over the country politically and economically. In Capp's strip, these industrialists had conspired to create a national folk hero, who would popularize their zoot suits by performing feats of bravery clad in this signature costume. The triumph of conservative clothiers was proclaimed in the third frame of the 19 May strip, which displayed the mock headline: "GOVERNOR ISSUES ORDER BANNING ZOOT-SUIT WEARERS!!" (Mazón, 1984, p. 35).

ENTIRE NATION GRIPPED BY ZOOT-SUIT MANIA!!

FROM MAINE TO CALIFORNIA A FANATICAL TYPE OF HERO WORSHIP HAS ENGULFED THIS ONCE CONSERVATIVE NATION. THE OBJECT OF ALL THIS ADULATION IS "ZOOT-SUIT YOKUM" WHO HAS, UPON INNUMERABLE OCCASIONS, RUSHED TO SCENES OF DISASTER ALL OVER THE COUNTRY—AND, WITH INCREDIBLE, FOOLHARDY COURAGE, PERFORMED AMAZING FEATS OF STRENGTH AND HEROISM. NATURALLY, "ZOOT-SUIT YOKUM" HAS BECOME THE IDOL OF ALL RED-BLOODED YOUNG AMERICANS—AND THIS IDOL-WORSHIP HAS LED MILLIONS OF MEN TO IMITATE HIS PECULIAR COSTUME, KNOWN AS THE "ZOOT SUIT." CLOTHING STORES REPORT THAT THERE HAS BEEN A MAD RUSH TO BUY "ZOOT SUITS"—WHILE THE REGULAR MEN'S CLOTHING MARKET HAS HIT ITS WORST SLUMP IN ONE HUNDRED YEARS.

ZOOT-SUIT YOKUM

A group of young men in their zoot suits detained by police on suspicion of being part of 1943 riots in Los Angeles. Do they look like troublemakers to you?

Beyond the pages of dailies carrying the *Li'l Abner* comic strip, hostility emerged between mainstream society and the zoot-suit counterculture. One LA newspaper ran a piece on how to "de-zoot" a zoot-suiter: "Grab a zooter. Take off his pants and frock coat and tear them up or burn them. Trim the 'Argentine ducktail' that goes with the screwy costume" (Mazón, 1984, p. 76). Whether it was intended with humour or not, instructions for the negative sanctioning of zoot-suiters were carried out by people opposed to the counterculture.

The conflict reached a climax in early June 1943, when thousands of young white men—soldiers, marines, and sailors on weekend leave from nearby military installations—launched a campaign to rid Los Angeles of zoot-suiters by capturing them, buzzing their hair down in a military style, and destroying their clothing. Historian Mauricio Mazón describes the extent of the riots and police intervention:

They were not about zoot-suiters rioting, and they were not, in any conventional sense of the word, "riots." No one was killed. No one sustained massive injuries. Property damage was slight. No major or minor judicial decisions stemmed from the riots. There was no pattern to arrests. Convictions were few and highly discretionary. (Mazón, 1984, p. 1)

The conflict lasted just under a week, and was brought to an end with two acts. First, the military reined in their troops. More significantly, on 9 June, Los Angeles City Council issued the following ban:

NOW, THEREFORE, BE IT RESOLVED, that the City Council by Resolution find that wearing of Zoot Suits constitutes a public nuisance and does hereby instruct the City Attorney to prepare an ordinance declaring same

(Continued)

a nuisance and prohibit the wearing of Zoot Suits with reet pleats within the city limits of Los Angeles. (Mazón, 1984, p. 75)

This, the culmination of a series of increasingly explicit and punitive sanctions, shows how humour with a social edge and a large audience can be used against a particular group.

What do *you* think?

1. Why do you think the zoot-suiters were targeted? What were the overt and covert aspects of their deviance?
2. Can you think of parallels between zoot-suiters of the 1940s and any group today?

Debra Wiseberg/iStockphoto

Canada's Mennonites are known for their belief in adult baptism, their commitment to non-violence, and the modest everyday fashion worn by the group's conservative members, all of which keep them outside of the cultural mainstream. Which of Goffman's three types of stigmata might be applied here? Would you consider it socially constructed or essentialist?

critics argued, made the people incapable of helping themselves. The "Other" label, once applied, can be extremely difficult to erase.

The Other can be depicted as mysterious, mystical, or mildly dangerous, but somehow it is ultimately cast as inferior. Edward Said, in his discussion of Orientalism (Said 1979), characterized the West's treatment of the Middle East as the creation of an Other. The dominant culture in Canada typically defines "Indigenous" as Other. In "slacker movies," such as *Animal House* (1978), *Cheech and Chong Up in Smoke* (1978), *Bill and Ted's Excellent Adventure* (1989), and *The Big Lebowski* (1998), written and directed by men and aimed at underachieving, socially inept, young white men, "woman" is constructed as an Other.

Deviant behaviour, once it has been associated with Otherness, is often subject to negative sanctions or punishment, as happened with the zoot-suiters. But should deviant behaviour be punished? Certain acts of deviance, those that fall under our criminal justice system, are considered illegal and have sanctions attached, ranging from a judge's warning to fines and jail time for more serious offences. But remember that deviance is not synonymous with criminality: it simply means anything outside the norm. Young people trying to establish their independence and individuality will often breach societal norms when it comes to fashion and style of dress. This can make them targets of the negative sanction of *bullying*—aggressive behaviour that includes shaming, ridiculing, physical attacks, and generally having unwanted attention drawn to their Otherness. Should this kind of deviance be punished?

Deviance and the Moral Panic

When Otherness is sensationalized in the media, it can become the source of a **moral panic**. A moral panic is a campaign designed to arouse concern over an issue or a group. The issue at the heart of a moral panic is typically something very small that has been exaggerated so that it seems like a significant threat to social order; in some cases, the issue has been fabricated entirely. To use a phrase I learned in my first sociology class, the moral panic is about a problem that is more apparent than real. It is also volatile: it rises and falls quickly in the public eye and consciousness.

A moral panic is spearheaded by a **moral entrepreneur**—someone who has something to gain from public fear around the issue. The term was coined by Becker (1963) to describe a person who tries to convince others of the need to take action around a social problem that they have defined. The moral entrepreneur could be a journalist sensationalizing an issue as clickbait, or an activist trying to draw supporters to a cause, or a politician hoping to advance a personal or policy agenda. Today, people from all sides of the political and social spectrum seek to become online influencers and instil moral indignation and panic through blogs, comments, and the spread of conspiracy theories. And there will be some or plenty of others ready to follow. When a man picked up on the QAnon-spread rumour that leading Democrats in the United States ran a secret pedophile ring in the basement of a Washington, DC, pizza parlour that feasted on the blood of children, he drove to Washington, heavily armed, to attack the pizzeria and save the children. Certainly, in the States, the leading moral entrepreneur in recent memory has been that country's least moral president in history, Donald Trump. His rhetoric about rigged elections, and about having won the 2020 election he clearly lost, led to the brutal storming of the US Capitol by his followers in January 2021. A number of people died (both police and insurrectionists), many lives were destroyed, and the very democracy of our southern neighbour teetered in the balance and may continue to for the foreseeable future. The moral entrepreneur often has a recommended course of action that is disproportionate to the actual threat, if any threat even exists at all. Al Capp could be considered a moral entrepreneur for his part in stoking moral panic around zoot-suiters.

A recent Canadian example of a moral panic, discussed in Chapter 5, concerns Zunera Ishaq, a Muslim woman who fought to wear her *niqab* while taking the oath of Canadian citizenship in 2015. In its efforts to uphold the ban on covering the face during citizenship ceremonies, the federal Conservative government created a moral panic, calling it "offensive" that anyone should want to "hide their identity at a time when they are committing to join the Canadian family" (Quan, 2015). In fact, Ishaq removed her *niqab* before an official, in private, prior to the ceremony to confirm her identity. In this case, the moral panic was socially constructed for political gain, although it would appear to have failed. An older Canadian example of a moral panic occurred in regard to the othering of Chinese Canadians, as described in the following The Point Is . . . box.

6.3 Race and Deviance: To Be Non-White Is Deviant

To racialize deviance is to link minority ethnic groups—particularly visible minorities—with certain forms of deviance, and to treat these groups differently because of that connection. We see this in movies and television shows that portray all Italians as being involved in organized crime, and in news reports that link young Black men with gangs and gun

The Point Is . . .

Drugs and Immigrants Are Common Features of Moral Panics

In the 1920s, Canada experienced a moral panic around racialized deviance and illegal drugs. The race was Chinese Canadians, and one of the people who gave fuel to the panic was Emily Murphy. Journalist, activist, and self-taught legal expert, born of a prominent and wealthy Ontario family, Murphy was a gender heroine of first-wave feminism. In 1916 she became the first woman magistrate in the British Empire. She would later play a role in the historic "Persons Case" (1928), which ended when the British Privy Council overturned a Supreme Court ruling that women were not "persons" eligible to hold public office.

In 1922, Murphy published *Black Candle*, a collection of her articles, many of which had originally appeared in *Maclean's* magazine. Murphy's four books of personal sketches, written under the pen name "Janey Canuck," were well known when she published *Black Candle* to expose the insidious details of the Canadian drug trade. The collection cast Chinese Canadians as the main villains in the trafficking of illegal drugs—particularly opium, heroin, and cocaine—although Blacks were also singled out for censure. The main theme was that Chinese men—those bachelors who, because of the restrictive head tax on Chinese immigrants, could neither be reunited with their wives nor find companionship among women "of their own race"—were corrupting white women through drug dealing, "ruining them" and making them accomplices in their dealing. The following excerpt from a chapter titled "Girls as Pedlars" is typical:

> Much has been said, of late, concerning the entrapping of girls by Chinamen in order to secure their services as pedlars of narcotics. The importance of the subject is one which warrants our closest scrutiny: also, it is one we dare not evade, however painful its consideration. (Murphy, [1922]/1973, p. 233)

Murphy believed that the "yellow races" would use the drug trade to take over the Anglo-Saxon world, and she warned North American readers to be wary of these "visitors":

> Still, it behooves the people in Canada and the United States, to consider the desirability of these visitors . . . and to say whether or not we shall be *"at home"* to them for the future. A visitor may be polite, patient, persevering . . . but if he carries poisoned lollypops in his pocket and feeds them to our children, it might seem wise to put him out.
>
> It is hardly credible that the average Chinese pedlar has any definite idea in his mind of bringing about the downfall of the white race, his swaying motive being probably that of greed, but in the hands of his superiors, he may become a powerful instrument to this very end. . . .
>
> Naturally, the aliens are silent on the subject, but an addict who died this year in British Columbia . . . used to relate how the Chinese pedlars taunted him with their superiority at being able to sell the dope without using it, and by telling him how the yellow race would rule the world. They were too wise, they urged, to attempt to win in battle but would win by wits; would strike at the white race through "dope" and when the time was ripe would command the world. (Murphy, [1922]/1973, pp. 187–9)

As a moral entrepreneur, Emily Murphy was a success. *Black Candle* had a huge impact on the perception of the drug trade and on drug legislation in Canada. Chapter XXIII, "Marahuana—A New Menace," was the first work in Canada to discuss cannabis use. It contained a lot of damning half-truths and anecdotes but nevertheless led to the enactment of laws governing the sale and use of marijuana in Canada.

violence. We see it when a person of Arab background is suspected of being a terrorist. Muslims who wear the *niqab* are seen as deviant for concealing their faces. Part of **racializing deviance** is making ethnic background a covert characteristic of deviance, as though all people of a particular ethnic group are involved in the same supposedly deviant behaviour.

Despite the public promotion in Canada of **multiculturalism** and its enshrinement in law—the set of policies designed to encourage respect for cultural differences—the pressure to **assimilate** (i.e., become culturally the same as the dominant culture) is persistent. Immigrants from some eastern European, Asian, and African source countries who have experienced the embarrassment of having anglophone Canadians stumble over their names may feel pressure to anglicize their names to make themselves more "Canadian," not least to improve their job opportunities or to help in regard to success in getting everything from a bank loan to a rental unit.

Racial profiling is one way in which deviance is racialized. Ontario's Human Rights Commission defines racial profiling as

> any action undertaken for reasons of safety, security or public protection that relies on stereotypes about race, colour, ethnicity, ancestry, religion, or place of origin rather than on reasonable suspicion, to single out an individual for greater scrutiny or different treatment. (OHRC, 2003, p. 6)

The report notes that racial profiling can arise from a combination of these factors, and that age and gender can also "influence the experience of profiling."

Racial profiling assumes that visible characteristics of an individual can be used to predict engagement in illegal activity. This is not the same as criminal profiling, which "relies on actual behaviour or on information about suspected activity by someone who meets the description of a specific individual." Racial profiling uses a person's otherness as grounds to single the individual out for different treatment, often involving some sort of sanction.

Racial profiling can occur in a variety of contexts involving various agents and individuals. Examples include incidents involving:

- law enforcement personnel, such as police and border control agents
- security personnel, such as private security guards
- employers, for example, in conducting security clearances of staff
- landlords, for example, when a property owner assumes that certain applicants or tenants will be involved in criminal activity
- service providers, for instance, an Uber driver who refuses to stop at night for certain people
- the criminal justice system, such as courts.

Racial profiling is commonly associated with *carding*, a police intelligence-gathering procedure in which officers stop, question, and document people when no offence is being committed. Individuals may be carded during police street checks or "community engagement" initiatives, carried out in neighbourhoods with high rates of crime. The practice has come under criticism from human rights groups, who argue that it disproportionately targets Black youths, Indigenous people, and other racialized groups. And it can provoke a response that becomes an excuse for arrest.

6.4 Gender and Deviance: To Be Female Is Deviant

Feminist sociologists teach us that in a patriarchal society (one dominated by men), what is "male" is treated as normal, while what is "female" is treated as Other and seen as inherently deviant. Male values and behaviours are **normalized** (i.e., made to seem normal, right, and good), through customs, laws, and culture production. Two related concepts are important here: misogyny and patriarchal construct. **Misogyny** means literally "hating women." In a patriarchal or male-dominated society, images of women are often constructed in ways that contain and reflect misogyny. **Patriarchal construct** refers to social conditions considered or structured in a way that favours men and boys over women and girls. Think, for example, of highly prized and well-paying jobs—corporate lawyer, investment banker, emergency room doctor—that have been constructed so that the job-holder is forced to place family in a distant second place to employment. This gives advantages to men, who in Canadian society are expected to fulfill fewer domestic and child-rearing duties than are women are.

Menstruating women in North America are cast as deviant. How so? You have probably never had to take your own toilet paper into a public washroom, or pay by the sheet for what is provided. Yet feminine hygiene products are not universally available in public washrooms; when they are, they are often sold from a vending machine. Women are essentially penalized for a naturally occurring bodily function. But this began to change when Scotland became the first country to make menstrual products free, a new law that was passed in late 2020 by the Scottish legislature and came into full effect in 2022 in an effort to stem "period poverty." It is likely that other countries will follow the Scottish lead (Guy, 2022). In Canada, some organizations, such as the Canadian Labour Congress, and some airports and libraries provide free feminine hygiene products, and federal taxes were lifted from these products in 2015.

Casting women as deviant is not new. Take the witch hunts waged in Europe and, later on, in colonial America from about the fourteenth to the seventeenth centuries. Women identified as witches were tried and, if found guilty, executed. Here we have a good example of moral panic surrounding deviance that was entirely fictitious. While some of those tried may have committed criminal acts, their alleged powers and connections with Satan were not real. Why were they believed to be involved in dark magic? The vast majority of those accused were women (the figure usually cited is 85 per cent). The word "witch" itself is closely associated with women, conjuring up negative images of pointed black hats, warty faces with pointed noses, and flying broomsticks: bad clothes, bad looks, and bad use of a female-associated cleaning implement. In a patriarchal society, this image of deviance is very much associated with femaleness, its opposite—normalcy—with maleness.

In the eighteenth and nineteenth centuries, European doctors and psychotherapists used a diagnosis of "female hysteria" to account for natural emotional states that, in women, were considered unacceptable or deviant (see Scull, 2009). Excessive emotionality, restlessness, and sexual desire were among the

This "women only" subway car in Tehran, Iran, exists with the officially declared purpose of protecting riders from sexual harassment. Is separating women—treating them as "Other"—the best way to crack down on groping and other sexual attacks?

symptoms of the supposed neurological disorders. Much like accusations of witchcraft (only with less severe punishment), the diagnosis of hysteria was used to account for and sanction behaviour that was considered deviant because it occurred in women.

"Fallen Women": Sexual Deviance as Gendered

The double standard that has long applied to male and female sexual activity is evidence that deviance can be gendered. The Magdalene asylums, which share certain traits with Canada's Indigenous residential schools, serve as a case in point.

Magdalene asylums existed in Ireland, Australia, and North America from the eighteenth to the late twentieth centuries. Their stated purpose was to house "fallen women": sex workers, unmarried women who were sexually active, and unwed mothers, but also women deemed by the Church to be at risk of being led astray. This includes very attractive and "feeble-minded" women who might be easily talked into unmarried sex. Moral purity was the Church-imposed standard for women, one that was to be preserved at all costs. Anything short of that standard constituted deviance. As a result, many women were incarcerated against their will and with no formal trial. They were stripped of their rights and their children. It seems hardly worth noting that men were not held to the same standard.

In Ireland, it is believed that up to 30,000 unmarried women were incarcerated because they either were or could become sexually active (Smith, 2007). They were held in institutions commonly known as **Magdalene laundries**, because the inmates were required to perform the hard physical labour of washing clothes (this was well before there were washing machines). The women laundered the uniforms of other prisoners, priests, and nuns, which enabled the institutions to be financially self-supporting. When not working, the women were forced to spend long periods of time praying, or at least remaining silent. They could not leave. The doors to the outside were locked, and there were iron gates, guarded by nuns.

Mari Steed was one of thousands of children born in Ireland and brought without permission to the United States, where she was put up for adoption. She now works for an organization seeking restitution for survivors of the Magdalene laundries. In an interview, she described the relationship between the nuns and the inmates this way:

[The nuns] may have started with the best of intentions, but by the very nature of Irish society and repression of women's sexuality, they began to see these women as less than human, and treat them that way. That's where we're seeing a lot of the abuse, and really torture, at the end of the day. (Matthews, 2014)

Referring to J.M. Smith's description of Ireland's "architecture of containment" for dealing with social deviants, she adds:

You had these industrial schools, the Magdalene laundries, the mother and baby homes, all with different remits, but the basic model was to contain and segregate anything that was deemed morally inferior by society, whether that's children, unwed mothers, the women in the Magdalenes, etc. (Matthews, 2014)

The last of Ireland's Magdalene laundries did not close until 1996. Irish popular singer Sinead O'Connor was an inmate of one of these institutions in the early 1980s.

Being Incorrigible: Gendered Deviance in Ontario

Canada has its own history of gendered deviance. From 1913 to 1964, thousands of women in Ontario were put into reformatories under the Female Refuge Act. Among the "offences" for which young women would be placed in these institutions was being sexually active outside of marriage. This kind of behaviour and the women guilty of it were branded "incorrigible."

In 1939, Velma Demerson, 18 years old and white, became sexually involved with a Chinese man. They intended to get married. When she became pregnant, her parents reported to the authorities that she was "incorrigible." Velma was arrested and sent to a "home" for young girls, then to the Andrew Mercer Reformatory for Women, Canada's first prison for women (ages 16 and over), which operated from 1872 to 1969. She was confined to a cell that was seven feet long and four feet wide, with one bare light bulb, a cot, a cold-water tap, and a basin. A covered enamel pail was provided for use as a toilet (Demerson, 2004, p. 5).

> **What do you think?**
> Why were the women taken to the Magdalene laundries perceived to be deviant?

6.5 Class and Deviance: To Be Poor Is Deviant

Poverty can be considered a covert characteristic of deviance. Marginally illicit activities like overindulgence in alcohol are more likely to be considered deviant in poor people than in middle-class or "rich" people. Jeffrey Reiman, in *The Rich Get Richer and the Poor Get Prison*, argues that the criminal justice system has a distinct class bias. This bias appears in the way we define what constitutes a crime, and in our processes of arrest, trial, and sentencing. Each step shows bias against the poor. As Reiman explains:

> The criminal justice system keeps before the public . . . the distorted image that crime is primarily the work of the poor. The value of this to those in positions of power is that it deflects the discontented and potential hostility of Middle America [the American middle class] away from the classes above them and toward the classes below them. . . . It not only explains our dismal failure to make a significant dent in crime but also explains why the criminal justice system functions in a way that is biased against the poor at every stage from arrest to conviction. Indeed, even at the earlier stage, when crimes are defined in law, the system primarily concentrates on the predatory acts of the poor and tends to exclude or deemphasize the equally or more dangerous predatory acts of those who are well off. (Reiman, 2007, p. 4)

This is how behaviours associated with poverty and criminality become synonymous with deviance, while criminal activity associated with wealth and

The Point Is . . .

White-Collar Crime Is a Serious Business

In a speech to the American Sociological Society in 1939, criminologist Edwin Sutherland (1883–1950) introduced the term white-collar crime. He defined it as "crime committed by a person of respectability and high social status in the course of his occupation" (1949, p. 9). His article "White Collar Criminality" was published the next year in the *American Sociological Review* (Sutherland, 1940). He later published a book on the subject (Sutherland, 1949).

Sutherland's work was a landmark in the sociological study of criminology. Previous work had focused on the crimes of the poor, creating a biased and very limited survey. But Sutherland's definition is not flawless. Associating certain kinds of criminal behaviour with a particular class reflects a class bias and a misleading view of the situation. After all, you don't have to be a person of "high social status" to commit identity theft, which tends to be classified as a white-collar crime. Sutherland's original definition implied that only people of the higher classes are capable of planning and carrying out crimes that are essentially non-violent. In this way it fails to recognize that industrial accidents caused by unsafe working conditions created by a negligent business owner are in a real sense crimes of violence.

More recent works have refined the definition of white-collar crime to remove the class bias associated with Sutherland's original definition. Clinard and Quinney (1973) went further, splitting white-collar crime into categories they named occupational crimes and corporate crimes. They defined the former as "offenses committed by individuals for themselves in the course of their occupations [and] offenses by employers against their employees" (1973, p. 188). Embezzlement and sexual harassment are examples. The latter include "offenses committed by corporate officials for their corporation and the offenses of the corporation itself" (1973, p. 188), including bribery, false advertising, and industrial accidents.

Embezzlement, "cooking the books" to indicate non-existent corporate profits, and tax evasion all have a long history in the corporate world. Well-known Canadian examples include Garth Drabinsky and Livent Entertainment; Harold Ballard, the former owner of the Toronto Maple Leafs and Maple Leaf Gardens; and Alan Eagleson, an NHL hockey player agent, founder and first executive director of the National Hockey League celebrity is often labelled "good business." Martha Stewart, media star and founder of a business empire aimed at aspiring home decorators and entertainers, was convicted of contempt of court for lying under oath during a probe into alleged insider trading, and yet she received a standing ovation from a mostly supportive public and press following a hearing at which she was sentenced to five months in prison.

Of course, Exhibit A in North America has been Donald Trump, who faced a potential snowball of civil and criminal legal actions after he left office, ranging from sexual assault and election tampering to theft and concealment of secret state documents. Years earlier he was forced to shut down his eponymous "university" as being a rip-off (and to pay a "paltry" $25 million in restitution), and his charity foundation was closed because of improper use of foundation money (among other things, he used it to buy framed pictures of himself). Indeed, as early as 1973 Trump and his father, as owners and managers of a New York real estate firm, were sued by the US Department of Justice for discriminatory rental practices against Black people (Rosenberg, 2016). Still, as of late 2022, many millions of followers hung on (and believed) his every word, and elected members of his own party avowed their support and dutifully "kissed the ring." He has yet to spend any time in jail.

From School to Prison: The Deviance of Students in Low-Income Neighbourhoods

Class bias is at the centre of what is known in the literature as the *schools-to-prison hypothesis*: the idea that in schools located in poorer, often racialized neighbourhoods, there is a biased application of practices such as "zero tolerance," which creates a

Players' Association, and organizer of the 1972 Summit Series between Canada and the Soviet Union. Drabinsky served about two years of a five-year prison sentence for making his theatre enterprise appear more successful than it was to encourage investment, and earned full parole in 2014. Ballard, convicted in 1972 of tax evasion and other charges related to misappropriation of company funds, spent three years of a nine-year sentence in penitentiary, most of that time in a minimum security facility, and later bragged that it was an easy life, like living in a motel with colour television and fine food and drink. Eagleson, charged with insurance fraud, taking extra money from players' contracts for himself, and skimming money off the top from financial dealings involving the Canada Cup international hockey tournaments he organized, spent six months of an 18-month sentence in an Ontario prison in 1998 and had to pay a large fine in the United States. Both Eagleson and Drabinsky were disbarred from practising law in Ontario and had their Order of Canada titles stripped from them.

If you notice a pattern here in regard to punishment, you are probably right. White-collar criminals generally receive shorter sentences, are incarcerated in minimum security facilities with more amenities, and get more time off for good behaviour than is the case for other felons.

However one chooses to classify white-collar crime, there are victims and there are consequences. White-collar criminals are not selfless Robin Hoods defrauding the rich to give to the poor. They defraud rich and poor alike, as in Ponzi schemes whereby people are convinced to invest large sums of money (sometimes, their life savings) in a non-existent enterprise because of the quick and handsome payout of returns to the first investors out of the money contributed by later investors. A simple and less sophisticated version of this is the chain letter, whereby the recipient is instructed to send a certain amount of money to the sender, add their own name at the bottom of the letter, and send it on to 10 other people, all of whom supposedly will in turn send them money. If you keep the chain going, you are promised good fortune and much greater; if you break the chain, bogus anecdotes tell of sudden death or worse. Variations on this hoax now populate the internet, often with the threat of dire consequences for anyone who breaks the chain or fails to provide sensitive information, and are used in phishing expeditions to steal personal data and passwords and to spread malware.

misleading perception of higher crime rates. Greater rates of suspension and expulsion, higher numbers of random locker and student searches, and tough anti-violence measures like the installation of metal detectors, the hiring of security guards, and even periodic police raids characterize the schools in these poorer neighbourhoods, but these measures are greatly out of proportion to the amount of violence and crime actually occurring at the schools.

Most of the literature relates to the American situation, which has changed significantly in recent years with the fear and reality of mass shootings at schools, but the schools-to-prison hypothesis applies in urban Canada as well. In a 2009 *Toronto Star* article, journalists Sandro Contenta and Jim Rankin reported that Ontario's Safe Schools Act, in force from 2001 to 2008, produced startlingly high numbers of suspensions and expulsions. The *Star*'s analysis, which examined school suspension rates for 2007–8 alongside sentences and postal code data for inmates in Ontario provincial jails, showed that the highest rates of suspension tended to be in those areas that also had the highest rates of incarceration. This is a positive correlation, which suggests that punishing youths from the city's poorest neighbourhoods with zero-tolerance measures reinforces the higher incarceration rate in those areas.

"But wait," I can hear you say, "isn't it possible that low-income neighbourhoods naturally produce crime, and that greater rates of true crime, not increased levels of scrutiny or harsher application of zero-tolerance policies, are responsible for higher incarceration rates corresponding to these neighbourhoods?"

Indeed, lower-class people are over-represented in the statistics on criminal convictions and admission to prison. That means that per population they are more often convicted and admitted to prison than are middle- and upper-class people, and this contributes to the idea that lower-class people are criminally deviant. However, a closer look at the statistics helps us see that statistics alone do not give us an accurate picture of the lower classes.

Crime in Low-Income Communities

"Lower class" is a designation often established by looking solely at recorded income, but it covers a broad and far from homogeneous set of individuals. Some are part of the working class, who labour for long hours with little financial reward. Others are on social assistance. These two subgroups of the lower class are probably not significantly more involved in criminal activity than are middle-class or upper-class people. In fact, it's a separate subgroup, representing a small minority of the lower class that is responsible for a high percentage of the crimes. These people are lumped together with the first two groups statistically because of their low reported income, giving a misleading forensic picture of the working poor.

Another reason for the over-representation of the lower class in crime statistics has to do with **social resources**. In this context, *social resources* refers to knowledge of the law and legal system, the ability to afford a good lawyer, influential social connections, and capacity to present oneself in a way that is deemed "respectable." Lower-class individuals generally have access to fewer social resources than middle- and upper-class people do, and this makes them more likely to be convicted of charges people from the wealthier classes might be able to avoid. Tepperman and Rosenberg explain the importance of social resources:

> Social resources help people avoid labelling and punishment by the police and courts. For example, in assault or property-damage cases, the police and courts try to interpret behaviour and assess blame before taking any action. They are less likely to label people with more resources as "criminal" or "delinquent" and more likely to label them "alcoholic" or "mentally ill" for having committed a criminal act. (Tepperman & Rosenberg, 1998, p. 118)

The authors make use of Goffman's concept of **impression management**, which they define as "the control of personal information flow to manipulate how other people see and treat you" (Tepperman & Rosenberg, 1998, p. 118). The upper classes are better at managing impressions than are people who belong to the lower class. Therefore, they conclude:

> Official rule-enforcers (including police and judges, but also social workers, psychiatrists and the whole correctional and treatment establishment) define as serious the deviant acts in which poor people engage. On the other hand, they tend to "define away" the deviant acts of rich people as signs of illness, not crime. They are more likely to consider those actions morally blameless. (Tepperman & Rosenberg, 1998, pp. 118–19)

6.6 Sexual Orientation and Deviance: To Be Gay Is Deviant

Homosexuality has long been socially constructed as deviant to varying degrees around the globe. Cultures differ in terms of how and what kind of social sanctions are applied. Homosexuality was not legalized in Canada until 1967, and prior to a US Supreme Court ruling in June 2003—only 20 years ago—sexual activity between consenting adult homosexuals was still against the law in 13 American states. Same-sex marriage was recognized nationwide in Canada in 2005 and 10 years later in the United States. Notably, the current composure of the US Supreme Court, with several relatively young and socially conservative justices, suggests that numerous laws and legal precedents protecting the rights of minorities could be overturned in the coming years. The Court's 2022 ruling in *Dobbs* removed women's abortion rights, which had stood for nearly 50 years as a result of the landmark 1973 ruling in *Roe v. Wade*.

Around the world, homosexuality remains illegal in over 60 countries, with penalties ranging from flogging and imprisonment to death (see Figure 9.5). The countries with the most severe penalties for homosexuality are Islamic countries of Africa and the Middle East, such as Somalia, Saudi Arabia, and Iran, as well as those countries like Nigeria where some lower-level jurisdictions follow Sharia law. In March 2019, the small Asian kingdom of Brunei joined the list of countries to make homosexuality punishable by death.

In countries where homosexuality is protected by law, it continues to be punished through informal social mechanisms. In Canada, young men especially continue to censure behaviour perceived as effeminate or weak with statements like "Don't be so gay" and by calling others "fags" or "faggots," and by various hazing practices on youth hockey teams and in university and private boys' schools. This homophobia is a way of pressuring individuals to behave according to gender role expectations.

AP Photo/Mindaugas Kulbis

Male homosexuality tends to be sanctioned more heavily than female homosexuality, and there are some countries (e.g., Jamaica, Uzbekistan) where only male homosexuality is illegal. Why do you think male homosexuality is viewed as more deviant than female homosexuality?

6.7 Disability and Deviance: To Be Disabled Is Deviant

Society, as we have seen, punishes deviance with negative sanctions, and offers positive sanctions to those who adjust their behaviour to conform to standards set by the mainstream. A negative sanction can be as simple as a rude hand gesture from a driver, but we also have an institutionalized criminal justice system that exists to identify and punish those whose behaviour is judged as deviant according to law. Legal penalties for deviant behaviour typically involve restriction of freedoms and measures to diminish the independence and self-respect of the person convicted.

A reasonable sociological question to ask is whether society punishes disabled people for their disability. For example, do the ways in which we design and build houses (with steps to the front porch and narrow interior stairways), public buildings (with revolving doors), sidewalks (without sloping edges to meet the road), public transport (cramped buses too small in which to manoeuvre a wheelchair), and shelving in grocery stores essentially punish—by limiting freedom, independence, and self-respect—those who cannot walk?

Lennard Davis and the Politics of the Disabled Body

Lennard J. Davis is a leading figure in the sociological study of disability. In his article "Constructing Normalcy," he writes:

> To understand the disabled body, one must return to the concept of the norm, the normal body. So much of writing about disability has focused on the disabled person as the object of study, just as the study of race has focused on the person of color. But as with recent scholarship on race, which has turned its attention to whiteness, I would like to focus not so much on the construction of disability as on the construction of normalcy. I do this because the "problem" of the disabled is not the person with disabilities; the problem is the way that normalcy is constructed to create the "problem" of the disabled person. (Davis, 2006, p. 3)

The politics of disability involves promoting respect for difference, as opposed to just respecting the "normal" and treating anything else as a problem to be solved. For example, proud and politically active members of the Deaf community have represented cochlear implants (surgically implanted electronic devices that assist the deaf in sensing sound) as an attempt to "normalize" people with hearing disabilities while disrespecting Deaf culture, with its long history of using sign language. Deafness, they argue, is merely a difference in ability and not a disadvantage to be corrected.

We all have different sets of mental and physical abilities; the world does not divide easily into those who are disabled and those who are not. Davis's point is that the social problem of disability is actually created by those people (typically able-bodied people) who view and treat those with a different set of abilities as "Other" rather than accepting their difference.

Henry Goddard and the Eugenics Movement

When it comes to "punishing" disability by failing to accommodate differences in physical ability, the sanction is often an act of omission. It is not that disabled people have been singled out; it's that they haven't been taken into account at all. But there are many cases in which people with disabilities have been targeted because of their difference. Consider the eugenics movement.

The **eugenics** ("good genes") movement was based on the mistaken beliefs (1) that intelligence can be measured easily, and (2) that it is inherited, transferred directly from one generation to the next. A popular philosophy during the first half of the twentieth century, it led to efforts to have the so-called feeble-minded sexually sterilized so that they could not reproduce.

A pioneer of the eugenics movement was American psychologist Henry H. Goddard, who promoted the idea that "feeble-mindedness" (then an accepted clinical term in psychology) was hereditary. In an article published in a 1911 issue of *American Breeders Magazine*, Goddard attempted to demonstrate the inheritance of feeble-mindedness among inmates in an institution for people suffering a range of poorly diagnosed mental health conditions. He was widely considered to be the "father" of intelligence testing, having earned the reputation at Ellis Island, where he screened thousands of prospective immigrants to the United States. His assessments

In what ways does society punish disability? Does the failure to better accommodate people with disabilities arise simply from carelessness, or can it be taken as a negative sanction of disability?

Telling It Like It Is

A Student Point of View

Mental Health and Deviance

As a child, I was labelled quiet, shy, and introverted. I was celebrated for these characteristics because family, teachers, and other adults saw me as sweet and polite. It took until adulthood for me to realize that I am actually talkative, outgoing, and extroverted. Undiagnosed mental health issues prevented me from expressing my personality, and my environment encouraged my introverted coping mechanisms. In 2018, at the age of 24, I was diagnosed with generalized anxiety disorder (GAD), obsessive-compulsive disorder (OCD), and symptoms of periodic depression.

As a millennial from a small town in southern Ontario, I was taught in elementary and secondary school about bullying and its effects but rarely about mental health as a whole. In rural communities, mental health is considered "new age" hippie urban thinking. It's abnormal to talk to a counsellor or therapist unless you have severe mental illnesses. Even in tragedy, you are expected to rely on your family and community for emotional support even though they are rarely certified to help you. In middle school, mental health education was taught through the effects of bullying. I was taught that suicide was a side effect of cyberbullying and could be prevented by blocking online harassment. But I was rarely bullied, and I contemplated suicide.

When I was diagnosed, my mother was shocked that I would have my mental health evaluated and expressed her fears for me: "What if a future employer finds out? You have a file now! You won't be hired if they know you have mental issues!" My mother, like others from the baby boomer generation, has an anxiety around the documentation of mental health. Once it's on paper, it's harder to hide. While I have confidence in the security of my medical files, I am also not ashamed of my diagnoses. For me, they are no different than a medical file documenting a flu I had years ago.

GAD, OCD, and depression have hindered 24 years of my life. I wish my culture had given me the tools and confidence to talk about my issues. I am a better and stronger person for my experiences, and for me I wouldn't change that. However, I worry about the generations following me who are increasingly absorbed in virtual reality and are losing touch with their bodies and minds. I worry that if our culture and our education system do not start normalizing mental health, then we will be facing a new adolescent epidemic.

What do *you* think?
1. How do the writer and her mother differ in their views of mental health and deviance?
2. How do you view mental illness: As something that is safe to discuss openly or as something that should be kept private? How do you think your attitudes are shaped by your age, your gender, your peers, and your community?

of institutionalized inmates were based on intelligence tests (flawed, even more than now, by cultural biases) and, I suspect, on "eyeballing" the inmates. The very fact of being in an institution or having been previously diagnosed could be enough for Goddard to conclude that an individual was a "moron" (a term he coined for clinical use, not for taunting classmates or heckling referees). He was strongly opposed to the notion that the social environment had any impact on a person's mental health, making him a biological determinist as we defined the term in Chapter 4.

Despite its now obvious flaws, Goddard's work on eugenics was very influential in the early twentieth century. We can see its influence in Alberta's Sexual Sterilization Act, which was in effect from 1928 until 1972. This legislation reflected the belief that controlled breeding could be used to improve the population by increasing the occurrence of favourable heritable characteristics and limiting the reproduction of unfavourable ones. Essentially, Alberta sought to make it impossible for people deemed "mentally inferior" to reproduce and also punished racial and ethnic deviants. Many of those targeted were Indigenous (see Karen Stote's *An Act of Genocide: Colonialism and the Sterilization of Aboriginal Women*, 2015) and eastern European, illustrating how racial

and cultural difference is often cast as deviance and punished. But the Act principally targeted people living with mental disabilities. The signal case in this regard is that of Leilani Muir.

In 1955, Leilani Muir was confined at what was then called the Red Deer Training School of Mental Defectives (later the Michener Institute). At the age of 14 she had taken an IQ test (one reflecting a number of biases concerning class, culture, and ways of evaluating intelligence) and had scored 64, earning her the official designation of "moron." ("Normal" intelligence is confirmed by any score around 100.) In 1989, Muir would take another test and score a "normal range" 87. By then it was too late. Following the earlier test she was informed that she would be taken into surgery to have her appendix removed; instead, at the age of 14, she was sterilized. This was the negative sanction for Leilani Muir's mental difference. In 1996, the Alberta government admitted she had been wrongfully sterilized and agreed to a court-appointed settlement of $740,280.

6.8 Criminal Deviance

Over the course of this chapter we have seen examples of how people in power have sanctioned deviant behaviour by making it illegal. Zoot-suiters, *niqab*-wearing Muslims, "fallen women," homosexuals, and the "feeble-minded" have all been persecuted under the law for deviant behaviour that places them outside of the mainstream.

Of course, while deviance and crime are not synonymous, deviance does encompass criminal behaviour. An important area within sociology is **criminology**, which focuses on the sociological (and psychological) study of crime in terms of such elements as causation, prevention, management or control, and the statistical patterns of crime. When I taught students in the Police Foundation program, I would open my first class by stating that I had much (perhaps most) of the sociological profile of a serial killer: I am male, white, middle-class, and highly intelligent, and I am deviant in a number of ways (I have a big beard, do not own a cellphone, and own eight parrots). The point is, criminology is about studying patterns in criminal behaviour to learn more about how crime can be predicted, prevented (or at least managed), and sanctioned.

Theories of Criminal Deviance

Beginning in the twentieth century, the study of criminal deviance became a specialized area of inquiry within sociology. Specifically, theorists sought to explain why certain people (typically young men) engaged in deviant behaviour.

Strain Theory: Robert Merton

Early sociological theorist **Robert Merton** developed **strain theory** (1938) to explain why, in his opinion, some individuals "chose" to be criminally deviant. The "strain" Merton identified was a disconnect between society's culturally defined goals and the unequal distribution of the means necessary to achieve those goals. Merton was describing a situation in which social reality—the real-life circumstances of many individuals—inhibits the attainment of "the **American dream**." The American dream is essentially success, however you choose to define it (e.g., fame, wealth, or social prestige), mythologized as an opportunity that any American citizen, regardless of background or circumstances, can seize provided they put in the hard work to get it.

Merton was aware that success was most available to those with upper- and middle-class resources (wealth, postsecondary education, and social connections). When those without these resources find themselves prevented from achieving society's culturally achieved goals, they experience a sense of social disconnection or exclusion that Durkheim called anomie (see Chapter 3). Merton's term for the realization that one lacks legitimate means to achieve success was *strain*, and people respond to it, he argued, in one of five ways:

1. They conform, striving against the odds to attain idealized goals through socially acceptable practices, such as upgrading their education and working hard for small promotions.
2. They lower their sights, showing the hard work that society expects but secretly setting less ambitious goals that are more within their means.
3. They give up on society's goals, and may wind up dropping out of school, engaging in very low-paid work, or living on the streets.
4. They reject and rebel against the established system of social goals, advancing new goals while attempting to subvert the prevailing social order.
5. They innovate, pursuing material success using improvised techniques that deviate from socially accepted, legitimate means.

It is the last of these groups that concerns us here. The rebels score high in intelligence and ambition, but without the means to attain success the "right" way, they turn to unconventional means, specifically crime. Consider, for example, computer hackers and identity theft.

Subcultural Theory: Albert Cohen

Albert Cohen developed **subcultural theory** to challenge and refine certain aspects of Merton's work. He was also building on foundations laid by Frederic Thrasher in his studies of gangs and by **E. Franklin Frazier** (1894–1962), who had carried out pioneering studies of African Americans in Chicago.

Cohen's study of teenage gangs (1955) presents a model of what he called the **delinquent subculture**, made up of young, lower-class males suffering from **status frustration**. Failing to succeed in middle-class institutions, especially school, they become socialized into an oppositional subculture that inverts the values of the school. For example, the youths he studied engaged in delinquent stealing that was primarily **non-utilitarian**—in other words, the objects weren't stolen because they were needed for survival but because the act of stealing was respected within the delinquent subculture.

Cohen stressed that becoming a member of the delinquent subculture is like becoming a member of any culture. It does not depend on the psychology of the individual, nor is the subculture invented or created by the individual. When members of the delinquent subculture grow up and leave the gang (to join adult gangs or mainstream society), the subculture persists. Cohen asserted "that a child need not be 'different' from other children, that he need not have any twists or defects of personality or intelligence in order to become a delinquent" (Cohen, 1955, pp. 11–12).

We can use Cohen's model to review other ideas presented earlier in the textbook. First, the norms of the delinquent subculture—the rules or expectations of behaviour—would be different, at least in part, from those of the dominant culture. The difference, according to Cohen, comes from the inverting of norms. In Cohen's words, "The delinquent's conduct is right, by the standards of his subculture, precisely *because* it is wrong by the norms of the larger culture" (Cohen, 1955, p. 28). Likewise, there is an inverting of the **sanctions**: the negative sanctions of non-gang members—the ways in which society shows its disapproval of the delinquent behaviour—are viewed as positive sanctions by members of the delinquent gang.

Labelling Theory: Howard Becker

One weakness of subcultural theory is that it stresses subcultural values as developed in opposition to mainstream society. The theory is only partially useful, and generally inadequate, to address social situations in which subcultural values, beliefs, and practices considered deviant by mainstream society in fact flow from the history and traditional culture of the people involved. Consider how Canada's Indigenous people are often cast as deviant. You could not argue that most of their cultural differences have been consciously shaped to oppose the culture of mainstream Canadian society. Certain aspects of their situation might be better explained by the **labelling theory** of Howard Becker.

Becker theorized that labels applied to individuals and groups outside the mainstream become internalized both by those cast as deviant and by the majority group. Take the image of the "Indian drunk." Cree playwright Tomson Highway described it as "our national image":

> That is the first and only way most white people see Indians. . . . In fact, the average white Canadian has seen that visual more frequently than they've seen a beaver. To my mind, you might as well put an Indian drunk on the Canadian nickel. (quoted in York, 1990, p. 191)

Yet when an image like this gets applied to an individual and becomes a master status, dominating all other statuses, it may eventually become internalized. This may have been the case when many Indigenous communities passed local by-laws banning the sale and consumption of alcohol after the federal Indian Act ban on consumption of alcohol was finally lifted in 1985, a prohibition that had been in place since 1884. Some Indigenous communities remain "dry" today (see, e.g., Gillis, 2012) or have recently created new restrictions.

A few facts should be presented here. One is that Indigenous people, in greater percentages than any other group in Canada other than Muslims, abstain entirely from alcohol: they do not drink. According to the 2012 Aboriginal Peoples Survey, 26 per cent of First Nations people aged 15 and over had not consumed alcohol in the previous 12 months, versus just 21 per cent of the total Canadian population (Rotenberg, 2016, p. 9). Second, Indigenous people who drink are more likely to be *binge drinkers* (i.e., people who have five or more drinks at a time). Third, there is no conclusive evidence that Indigenous people have lower tolerance of alcohol than other racialized groups. What effect do you think the image of the "Indian drunk" has on the first two statistics presented in this paragraph?

Another criticism of strain theory and subcultural theory is that while both have been used productively to address deviance in what can be termed "male culture," the research in this area falls short when applied to "female culture."

Social Control Theory: Travis Hirschi

Merton, Becker, and especially Cohen devoted much of their research to the question of why young people become delinquent. It is a complicated issue that involves such factors as *agency* (personal choice), family, religion, racism, and the extent to which social inequality denies young people the full range of choices, such as with regard to work.

For **Travis W. Hirschi** (1935–2017), a key factor was social bonding. He set out his argument in *Causes of Delinquency* (1969), in which he outlined his version of social control theory. A delinquent, or juvenile delinquent, is someone who is not yet an adult and becomes involved with acts considered deviant or anti-social—primarily, of course, breaking the law.

Hirschi was critical of strain theory for failing to account for why so many young delinquents grow up to become law-abiding adults, even when their position within the economic structure—the apparent source of their frustration—remains "relatively fixed" (Hirschi, 1969, p. 6). He also rejected—with italics—strain theory's tendency to link crime with the frustrations of people from the poorer socioeconomic class: "*Delinquency is not confined to the lower classes,*" he wrote (Hirschi, 1969, p. 7).

According to Hirschi, "Control theories assume that delinquent acts result when an individual's bond to society is weak or broken" (Hirschi, 1969, p. 16). That "bond" encompasses attachment, commitment, involvement, and belief. The theory went that if a child is bonded with such social institutions as

Photo by Martin Bazyl

Hosted by the University of Toronto in partnership with Toronto Community Housing, this Midnight Madness basketball league offers youths from high-risk communities the chance to learn drills and skills in a structured environment that also offers educational opportunities and life-skills workshops. In an ethnographic study of urban gang culture, self-described "rogue sociologist" Sudhir Venkatesh (2008) describes how community groups in Chicago used midnight basketball to keep at-risk kids on the hardcourt and off the streets. How does sport foster a positive bond with community?

family, religion, athletic teams, and school, then that child is unlikely to engage in delinquent activities. The child has accepted the positive social values of the institution and therefore will not commit anti-social acts.

This is a functionalist theory that fits comfortably with Émile Durkheim's idea of *anomie*, a lack of connection between citizens and their social institutions that Durkheim felt was a significant cause of both divorce and suicide. Even a casual reading of this textbook will tell you that I am primarily a conflict theorist, so I am critical of any theory that fails to look at how such factors as institutional racism and the exploitation of the poor by wealthy corporations contribute to delinquency.

This being said, I am a strong believer that kids should be involved with sports, for both physical and social reasons. I coached a baseball team that my youngest son was on and saw the positive effects of that bond to both his team and the sport. I was very happy to see both my boys become involved in organized baseball, hockey, and lacrosse. It was also a good opportunity for me, as a stepfather, to increase my stepsons' bonding to me and to our family.

Crime in Canada Today: Going Up or Going Down?

A 2017 report by the Canadian polling firm EKOS reveals that many Canadians believe the crime rate is rising, and that the increase is being driven by violent crime. The report was based on a survey conducted in 2015. On the question of whether crime had increased over the previous five years, 45 per cent of those surveyed said that it had, while 20 per cent thought that it had stayed the same. Only 31 per cent guessed—correctly—that crime had decreased over the previous five years (EKOS, 2017). When asked how many crimes out of 100 they believed to be violent, close to a quarter of the respondents put the figure anywhere between 60 and 80 per cent. The correct answer—that fewer than 20 per cent of reported crimes are violent—was given by just 18 per cent of those surveyed (see Figure 6.1).

Before we look at why Canadians tend to overestimate the rate of crime generally and of violent crime in particular, let's take a look at actual trends in the crime rate. Before we start, though, you should know that Statistics Canada relies on two rates of police-reported crime. The traditional crime rate is usually expressed as the number of crimes committed per 100,000 Canadians. The second rate is the crime severity index (CSI), which weighs serious crimes (like homicide) more heavily than less serious crimes (like jaywalking). The weight of the crime is based on the average prison sentence given for a conviction.

Figure 6.2 shows the police-reported crime rate in Canada from 1998 to 2017. Figure 6.3 tracks the crime severity index in Canada over the same period. Take a moment to look at these two graphs. Would

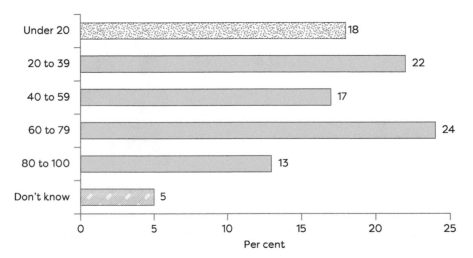

FIGURE 6.1 "Out of 100 crimes committed by adults and reported to the police, roughly what number do you think involve violence or the threat of violence?"

Source: EKOS Research Associates (2017), National Justice Survey: Canada's Criminal Justice System; http://publications.gc.ca/collections/collection_2018/jus/J4-52-2017-eng.pdf, p. 15.

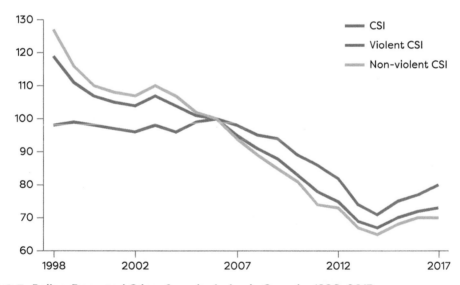

FIGURE 6.2 **Rate of Police-Reported Crime in Canada, per 100,000 Population, 1998–2017**

Source: Mary Allen (2018, July 23), Police-Reported Crime Statistics in Canada, 2017: https://www150.statcan.gc.ca/n1/en/pub/85-002-x/2018001/article/54974-eng.pdf?st=-5Rtky5_

FIGURE 6.3 **Police-Reported Crime Severity Index in Canada, 1998–2017**

Source: Mary Allen (2018, July 23), Police-Reported Crime Statistics in Canada, 2017: https://www150.statcan.gc.ca/n1/en/pub/85-002-x/2018001/article/54974-eng.pdf?st=-5Rtky5_

you say that crime in Canada is on the rise or on the decline?

If you answered "sort of," you would be right. The two graphs are consistent in showing an overall drop in the rate of crime since 1997—that's the good news. In fact, in the 10 years from 2007 to 2017, the crime rate dropped by 23 per cent and the crime severity index fell by 24 per cent. However, both graphs show an increase in crime since 2015—that's the bad news. Why the sudden increase? Part of the jump in serious crime has to do with a 13 per cent increase in reported

cases of sexual assault between 2016 and 2017. Sexual assault accounted for 6 per cent of all violent crimes in 2017 (Allen, 2018). We know that cases of sexual assault often go unreported, but 2017 saw the start of the #MeToo campaign to embolden victims of sexual assault to speak about and report these crimes. At the same time, police departments across the country committed to investigating sexual assault allegations more thoroughly than they had in the past. Taken together, these two factors likely contributed to the increase in reported cases of sexual assault.

In spite of the uptick in crime since 2015, there has been a significant overall drop in reported crime since the early 1990s. In 1991, the overall police-reported crime rate in Canada was 10,040 (per 100,000 population); in 2017, it was 5,334, representing a decrease of close to 47 per cent. The decrease was mirrored by a similar drop in the crime rate over the same period in the United States, meaning that this is not a uniquely Canadian phenomenon. So, how can we account for what one journalist and political commentator in the United States described as "one of the most stunning statistical and sociological mysteries of our time" (Hayes, 2017, p. 172)? No one explanation has emerged in the literature, although many factors have been considered (see Ford, 2016; Gramlich, 2017; Hayes, 2017; Zimring, 2007). Here are a few of them, some more credible than others.

All the Young Criminals Are Growing Up

Demographics is likely one of the larger factors in the declining crime rate. The huge bulge in the population created by the postwar baby boom of about 1946 to 1964 is in the past, with these people now seniors. Young men commit a disproportionately high number of crimes, and the percentage of adult men who are young has dropped drastically on both sides of the Canada–US border. Some support for this idea comes from the fact that other countries that experienced a baby boom in the wake of World War II have also seen lower crime rates.

The Criminals Are All in Jail

This proposed explanation applies particularly to the American situation, where mass incarceration is a factor. With such high numbers of people in prison, the criminal element outside of prison should be much smaller. The validity of this argument is called into question by the ever-growing incarceration rates of Indigenous people in Canada: in 2009 Indigenous people comprised 20.5 per cent of the prison population, but by 2019 this had climbed to 30.2 per cent (and Indigenous women made up a whopping 42 per cent of Canada's female prison population). The reverse was true for non-Indigenous Canadians, with a drop from 79.5 per cent in 2009 to 69.9 per cent 10 years later (Bell, 2020; see Figure 6.4).

The "Crack Years" Are Over

The mid-1980s are known in criminological circles as the "crack years." Crack cocaine entered big cities across North America at that time, and battles over territory and marketing led to increased crime rates. Once these battles were fairly settled, so the theory goes, the crime rate dropped. Similarly, changes in law, such as the legalization of cannabis in Canada, can mean that what was a crime no longer is.

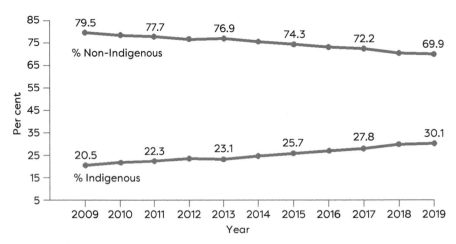

FIGURE 6.4 Federally Incarcerated Population Composition, Indigenous and Non-Indigenous, 2009–2019

Source: Bell, 2020.

The Number of Crimes Is Seriously Underreported

Survey data reveal several reasons why people do not report crimes, including shame or embarrassment, lack of faith in the justice system, and the feeling that a crime is too small to be of interest to the police. But these factors are nothing new, and according to Truman and Morgan (2016, p. 5), there has been no statistically significant change in the percentage of violent crimes and property crimes reported to police in the United States since 1993. For the under-reporting of crime to be considered a factor in the lowering of the crime rate, there would have to be another factor that caused reporting levels to fall—say, a demonstrated growth in the number of violent gangs responsible for crimes that victims are usually reluctant to report for fear of reprisal. But this does not appear to be the case.

The Police Have New Laws and New Methods to Fight Crime

What about policing practices and the institution of new laws? While police in some jurisdictions are using new and more sophisticated methods to track, predict, and prevent crime, the idea that these new methods are a leading cause in the declining crime rate is generally discounted by researchers. For one thing, the decline in crime is something we're seeing even in parts of the world where these new methods are not in use. In addition, the timing is wrong: many of these methods were introduced after the crime rate had already begun to fall.

Why Are Canadians More Afraid of Crime?

We can debate the reasons why Canada's crime rate is declining, but we cannot dispute the decline itself: the evidence shows that reported crime has declined steadily over the past 25 years. And yet a large number of Canadians believe crime has been increasing, violent crime in particular. As sociologists, we have to ask: What's going on?

One explanation is the rise of 24/7 news reporting. Media outlets are in fierce competition for viewers, readers, and clicks, and a story about a local stabbing or shooting tends to attract more eyeballs than an article about foreign policy initiatives or international trade. America's first cable news network, CNN, launched in 1980 but didn't become everyday viewing for Americans until 1991, when it came to

What do *you* think?

1. Of the factors discussed above, which do you think has had the greatest effect in the lowering of the crime rate?
2. Are there factors beyond those considered here that you believe have had an impact?

prominence with its coverage of the first Gulf War, notably through the on-the-ground reporting of Canadian journalist Arthur Kent, who became widely known as "the Scud Stud" for his live coverage of missile strikes. By that time, Canada's own all-news network, CBC Newsworld, was just two years old. Fox News launched in 1996. It is not unreasonable to see a connection between the rise of the cable news networks in the 1990s and the increasing fear of crime. The growth of the internet and social media platforms like Twitter and Facebook means there are more ways than ever for stories of crime to circulate and reach people.

The rise of international terrorism since the 11 September (2001) attacks has helped to make people more fearful of crime, as have numerous mass shootings and the rise of domestic terrorism in the States that inevitably creep into Canada. As media scholar Nikki Usher (2016) explains, terrorism succeeds in an environment where cable news networks and websites give events happening around the world an immediacy to viewers and readers at home.

Our fascination with crime has made us voracious consumers of crime entertainment. Whether it is the legion of procedural crime dramas on Netflix or the growing number of true-crime documentaries like *Making a Murderer* or CBC's *Somebody Knows Something* podcast, the menu of shows about killings and psychopaths seems to grow and grow. With their focus on the most gruesome of crimes, these shows not only exaggerate but distort the picture of crime in North America. Property crime far outweighs violent crime in both reported and unreported cases (Truman & Morgan, 2016, p. 7), and yet shows about serial killers outnumber shows about burglary and theft.

As media consumers, we should be able to distinguish between fictional crimes and real ones, and between distant events and those happening close to home. However, communications scholar George Gerbner (1919–2005) and others have argued that all of these media messages combine to make us believe the world is a frightening place. Gerbner coined the term "mean world syndrome" to describe this phenomenon: the more we hear about terrorist attacks in France or New Zealand or the United States, the more we come to see the world as a dangerous place.

It is no coincidence that the EKOS poll on Canadians' perceptions of crime (Swift, 2016) was conducted in the run-up to the 2015 federal election. There are politicians at all levels of government who will raise the spectre of criminal activity to support a law-and-order platform that comes with a promise to crack down on a crime epidemic that doesn't truly exist. Insurance agents, home-security companies, and gun shops are just some of the other groups that benefit when public fears around crime increase.

Wrap It Up

Summary

Deviance can be examined from one of two positions: essentialism and social constructionism. This chapter has taken a social-constructionist perspective, reflecting the belief that deviance is not natural but is socially constructed, artificial, and something that can vary from culture to culture and can change over time. What's more, the social construction of what is considered deviant is often contested or challenged within a culture. There is a power element found in deviance, with those who hold power in society getting to define what is deviant and what is "normal." The dominant culture's definition of deviance (in North America, a predominantly white, male, English-speaking, middle-aged, middle-class, and ableist definition) can override the definitions of deviance that come from people less powerful in the same society. People may be classified and treated as deviant not because of their behaviour but because of their ready identification as belonging to a group outside of what makes up the dominant culture. Once branded as deviant, these groups may find themselves the targets of social sanctions designed to punish members of minority cultures and people with "alternative" lifestyles.

Some deviant acts that do not meet standards of behaviour established by the dominant culture are relatively benign. Attending multiple comic book conventions dressed as your favourite superhero (when you are not paid to do so) isn't hurting anyone. However, some deviant acts, from begging and loitering to assault and homicide, have been socially constructed as criminal and are prohibited by law. Looking at criminal deviance in Canada presents us with a contradiction: the crime rate is dropping, and yet people fear crime more than ever. Neither trend has a simple explanation.

Think Back

Questions for Critical Review

1. Describe, with examples, what is meant by the term "deviant." Is deviance always bad for society?

2. Assess tattoos as a subject of conflict deviance. How do public perceptions of tattoo change over time and place, and depending on the situation?

3. From the moment they learned to draw, humans have been producing sexually erotic or explicit materials on cave walls, pottery, sketchpads, newsprint, film, and video. It will be no surprise to you that the internet has made all of this material much more widely accessible than ever before, though there is disagreement about the extent and the effects of North Americans' consumption of pornography. Is pornography strictly deviant, or are attitudes changing?

4. In sociology, what is meant by "the Other"? How is the concept of the Other related to deviance?

5. Outline how deviance can be associated with disability.

6. Find a recent example of a moral panic. What agenda does it serve? How is it spread? Who are the moral entrepreneurs behind it, and what do they stand to gain?

7. Those who study linguistics distinguish between marked and unmarked terms. The unmarked term is the usual one, while the marked term has a label added to distinguish it from the common term. "Field hockey," "light beer," "white chocolate," and "decaffeinated coffee" are all marked terms. What does the marked term "white-collar crime" suggest about the way crime is viewed in the mainstream?

8. Michel Foucault said that "the guilty person is only one of the targets of punishment. For punishment is directed above all at others, at all the potentially guilty." What do you think he meant by that?

9. The theories of criminal deviance discussed in this chapter were designed to explain primarily male gangs and behaviour around the mid-twentieth century. How well do these theories explain delinquent youth gangs—male and female—today?

Read On

Suggested Print and Online Resources

James William Coleman, *The Criminal Elite: Understanding White-Collar Crime*, 5th ed. (New York: Worth, 2002)
Coleman's work offers an in-depth analysis of how white-collar crime affects society, and an evaluation of the legal remedies.

critcrim.org: Critical Criminology Information and Resources, www.critcrim.org/index.php
Affiliated with the American Society of Criminology, this site provides a forum for organizations and individuals who are working to critically analyze, and change, the American justice system.

Velma Delmerson, *Incorrigible* (Waterloo, ON: Wilfrid Laurier University Press, 2004)
The autobiography of a white woman who was incarcerated for having a sexual relationship with a Chinese man.

Ava DuVernay, dir. *13th* (Kandoo Films, 2016)
Feature-length documentary available on Netflix that takes its title from the US 13th Amendment that abolished slavery. The film examines justice, race, and mass incarceration in the United States, much of which is applicable to Canada.

Dana Howse and Mandy Penney, "'When You Got a Disability You Get Good at Networking': An Interview about Work Mobility with a Disability and the Evolving 'Family' That Supports It," in *Families, Mobility, and Work*, ed. B. Neis, C. Murray, & N. Spinks, pp. 79–98 (St John's: Memorial University Press, 2022)
A good account of the barriers faced by someone with a physical disability and strategies for overcoming those barriers.

Michael Hviid Jacobsen, ed., *The Contemporary Goffman* (New York: Routledge, 2009)

This collection of readings by various authors imagines what kind of research Goffman might be involved in if he were living in the twenty-first century.

Claudia Malacrida, *A Special Hell: Institutional Life in Alberta's Eugenic Years* (Toronto: University of Toronto Press, 2015)
A powerfully written book about the Michener Institute, where people were imprisoned for being deemed "mental defectives."

Leilani Muir, *A Whisper Past: Childless after Eugenic Sterilization in Alberta* (Calgary: Friesen, 2014)
Leilani Muir describes in her own words the events that led to her incarceration in the Red Deer Training School for Mental Defectives and sterilization under Alberta's Sexual Sterilization Act.

Jeffrey Reiman, *The Rich Get Richer and the Poor Get Prison: Ideology, Class, and Criminal Justice*, 8th ed. (Boston: Allyn & Bacon, 2007)
Reiman's timeless work gives an excellent look at how class and deviance go hand in hand.

Kim Rossmo, "Place, Space and Police Investigations: Hunting Serial Violent Criminals," in *Crime and Place*, ed. D. Weisburd & J. E. Eck (New York: Criminal and Justice Theory, 1995)
Canadian criminologist Kim Rossmo developed methods of geographic profiling to map, predict, and prevent violent crime and pinpoint the home base of the offender.

Andrew Scull, *Hysteria: The Disturbing History* (Oxford: Oxford University Press, 2009)
A sometimes funny, always readable, and very instructive sociological history of the eighteenth- and nineteenth-century diagnosis of a "woman's emotional/mental disturbance."

SocioWeb: Criminality and Deviance, www.socioweb .com/directory/sociology-topics/criminology-and-social-deviance
The SocioWeb is a guide to sociology resources on the internet. This page gives links to websites covering topics in criminology and deviance.

John Steckley, *Learning from the Past: Five Cases of Aboriginal Justice* (Whitby, ON: De Sitter, 2011)

This short work outlines the deviance of being Indigenous in Canada through five notorious cases.

Sudhir Venkatesh, *Gang Leader for a Day: A Rogue Sociologist Takes to the Streets* (New York: Penguin, 2008)
A study of poverty, gangs, and drugs in Chicago, based on ethnographic research.

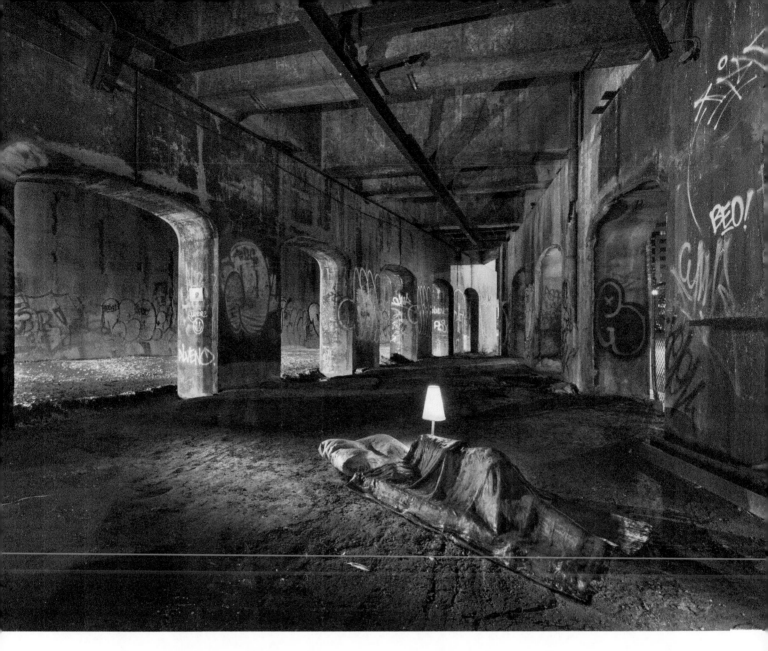

7 Social and Economic Inequality

Reading this chapter will help you to . . .

- Describe Marx's class structure and how it differs from Weber's.
- Differentiate between "class" and "stratum."
- Appreciate how wealth is distributed in Canada.
- Define ideology and give examples of a dominant ideology and a counter-ideology.
- Explain the difference between a minimum wage and a living wage.
- Discuss who uses food banks in Canada and what that information tells us about poverty.

For Starters

A Picture of Poverty in Canada's Backyard

Situated on the west coast of James Bay in Ontario's North, Attawapiskat First Nation gained international attention in October 2011, when its leaders declared a state of emergency, citing inadequate housing and poor sanitation. It was not the first time the Cree community had resorted to this measure. In May 2008, hundreds of residents had been evacuated from their tents, trailers, and shelters because of serious flood conditions. And yet in the fall of 2011, the media seized on stories of poverty and overcrowded, substandard housing as though they were new developments, while politicians claimed to have had no idea how bad the situation was.

How bad was it? You can read statistics about lack of housing, but to me, this account tells the story much more vividly:

In a one-room, tented shack where Lisa Kiokee-Linklater is watching television with her two toddlers, two mattresses lie on the floor. Each is a bed for three.

Mould is creeping across one mattress even though Ms Kiokee-Linklater just bought it last summer. It cost her $1,000.

There is no running water, no bathroom, and cold comes through the uninsulated floor. There is little room for her four children to play. The broiling cast-iron wood stove that takes up one corner of the room represents a burn hazard and eliminates the notion of the rambunctious play that is the norm for most young kids.

Moving into the tent was Ms Kiokee-Linklater's choice. It seemed a step up from her previous home next door, where she shared a single bathroom with 20 other people until it became too much for her and her growing family.

"It's kind of better, yeah," she said. . . . "But during the winter, it's hard. I cut back on the baths because it is so cold." (Scoffield, 2011)

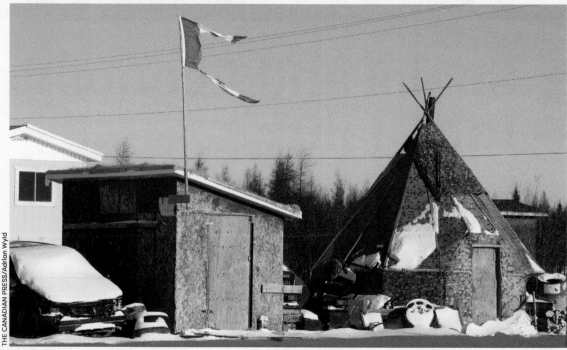

A situation like that doesn't just develop overnight. Nor is it quickly resolved. A year later, Attawapiskat chief Theresa Spence began a hunger strike to draw attention to the desperate circumstances of her own community and others across the country. The reaction in Ottawa and in the media focused on the alleged mishandling of funds in her community, a "red herring" that distracted the public from the real issue: the desperate state of Indigenous housing in Canada. Then in April 2016, Attawapiskat again declared a state of emergency, this time because of an eight-month-long epidemic of suicide attempts. In one month alone, 28 people in the community of 2,000 tried to kill themselves (Rutherford, 2016). The crisis was acute among young people suffering from bullying, sexual abuse, drug and alcohol addiction, and the dismal prospects they face in a town where jobs, housing, and even drinkable water are in short supply. Once again, politicians expressed shock at how grave the situation had become, as if it had happened overnight.

Attawapiskat had not always been a town in crisis. In 2003, anthropologist Bryan Cummins characterized Attawapiskat as a model of self-sustainability. His extensive fieldwork revealed how successfully the Attawapiskat Cree used their land for food, clothing, and building supplies. That was only 20 years ago. So what caused the community's fortunes to turn around?

In 2008, months after the town experienced disastrous spring flooding, a frequent occurrence for this beleaguered First Nations community, a wealthy neighbour took up residence less than 100 kilometres away. This was the international mining giant DeBeers, which opened up a diamond mine in the James Bay Lowlands. The operation was not good for local wetlands and wildlife, and it had a mixed effect on Attawapiskat's residents. Some locals recount that the mining development attracted a sudden influx of outsiders, who brought, acquired, and spent big money during their short stay in Cree country, creating short-term jobs for the locals and giving a tantalizing taste of what could be. But short-term wealth brings trouble, too—corruption, alcohol, drugs. In spring 2019, the mine closed for good, leaving a large open pit and questions about the community's future.

When it comes to poverty, neither causes nor solutions are easy to identify. Examining the situation from afar, politicians, newspaper columnists, and other citizens of the South, many of them well meaning, have mused that the community should simply resettle where there are schools, hospitals, and better economic prospects. This commentary ignores centuries of problems caused by "repeatedly hustling [Indigenous people] into new and unfamiliar environments," notes Tristin Hopper, adding that non-Indigenous Canadians, descended from immigrants, have a uniquely favourable view of leaving home in search of greener pastures (Hopper, 2016). Poverty is seldom simply a matter of setting; indeed, wherever it exists—in a northern Indigenous community, a drought-stricken farming region, a once prosperous Atlantic fishing village, a rundown urban neighbourhood—it is a complex problem. There is rarely one cause, never one solution.

7.1 Introduction: Is Social Inequality Inevitable?

For there will never cease to be poor in the land. Therefore I command you: You shall open wide your hand to your brother, to the needy and to the poor, in your land. (*English Standard Version Bible*, Deuteronomy 15:11)

The disposition to admire, and almost to worship, the rich and the powerful, and to despise, or at least, to neglect persons of poor and mean condition . . . is . . . the great and most universal cause of the corruption of our moral sentiments. (Adam Smith, *The Theory of Our Moral Sentiments*, [1759] 1976)

The study of social inequality has long been a part of the sociological tradition. You could argue that modern Western sociology evolved from the writings of eighteenth-century British economists such as **Adam Smith** (1723–1790) and Thomas Malthus (1766–1834). Smith, quoted above, was an early proponent of laissez-faire economics, the idea that governments should not try to manage or interfere in the so-called free market. To those who believe in laissez-fair economics, "interference" is anything that regulates or slows down how businesses operate. (It does not include the financial incentives, tax benefits, and bailout packages that governments sometimes offer to big businesses; that kind of interference is apparently okay.) To critics of laissez-faire economics, there is no such thing as a "free" market when it is dominated by multinational corporations with near-monopolistic power.

Smith was optimistic that a market free of government interference would raise standards of living for everyone, though he might have agreed with the idea that there will always be at least some "poor in the land." Malthus wasn't nearly as optimistic about the prospects for the poor. He predicted that dramatic population growth would inevitably lead to a scarcity of food and other resources. He warned that famine, disease, and war would "naturally" limit population growth unless other measures, including birth control and celibacy, were adopted.

Is poverty really inevitable? Is offering a handout to "the needy and the poor" really the best we can do? I like to think that most sociologists would say no to both questions. The political philosopher **Karl Marx** (1818–1883) certainly didn't see inequality as inevitable—and he was prepared to do something about it. Perhaps that is why he is often seen as one of the founders of sociology. But it would be wrong to suggest that all sociologists share his view. Indeed, few areas are more contentious in the sociological, economic, and political study of societies than the study of **social inequality**, the long-term existence of significant differences in access to material goods and opportunities among social groups.

Inevitable or not, social inequality is a function of many factors, only some of which we will cover in this chapter. Ethnicity, race, and gender are discussed in their own chapters, but they all have an impact on the economic well-being of an individual or family. This chapter will focus mainly on two related concepts, class and stratification, beginning with an introduction to the writings of Karl Marx.

7.2 Marx and Weber: Historical Approaches to the Study of Social Class

The main term used to talk about social inequality is "class," but its definition has been the subject of much debate since Karl Marx popularized the term. Near the beginning of *The Communist Manifesto* ([1848] 1967), Marx and his co-author, **Friedrich Engels** (1820–1895), give us some clues about their understanding of class:

> The history of all hitherto existing society is the history of class struggles. Freeman and slave, patrician and plebian, lord and serf, guild-master and journeyman, in a word, oppressor and oppressed, stood in constant opposition to one another, carried on an uninterrupted, now hidden, now open fight, a fight that each time ended, either in a revolutionary reconstitution of society at large, or in the common ruin of the contending classes. . . .
>
> The modern bourgeois society that has sprouted from the ruins of feudal society has not done away with class antagonisms. It has but established new classes, new conditions of oppression, new forms of struggle in place of the old ones.
>
> Our epoch, the epoch of the bourgeoisie, possesses, however, this distinct feature: it has simplified class antagonisms. Society as a whole is more and more splitting up into two great hostile camps, into two great classes directly facing each other—bourgeoisie and proletariat.

"Opposition," "fight," "antagonism," "hostile camps"—if you gleaned anything from these paragraphs, you will understand that Marx saw society as divided into two groups embroiled in a bitter rivalry. That sets the tone for much of what he says about the distribution of wealth in society.

Class, as Marx described it, is **relational**: it reflects the relationship of people to what he called the **means of production**—the resources needed to produce goods (and hence, wealth). In the pre-industrial Europe that Marx studied, the chief means of production was fertile land: wealth was produced by growing food crops and raising livestock. Once Europe began to become industrialized during the nineteenth century, when Marx and Engels lived, the means of production became capital, the money needed to build factories, purchase raw materials, and pay labourers to turn those raw materials into manufactured products. In spite of the fact he devoted an entire book (*Das Kapital*) to the topic, the precise meaning of Marx's term "capital" has been contested. For our purposes, we can understand it as the funds and properties necessary for large-scale manufacturing and trading.

For Marx, there were only two possible relationships to the means of production: either you owned them or you worked for those who did. In pre-industrial Europe, the owners were called **aristocrats** and the workers, **peasants**. Marx called the owners of capital in industrial-era Europe **capitalists**; he referred to the members of this class collectively as the **bourgeoisie**. The class of **workers**, which succeeded the peasant class of the pre-industrial era, made up the **proletariat**.

Marx identified various subclasses—the **petty** (or **petite**) **bourgeoisie**, made up of small-time owners with little capital, and the **lumpenproletariat**, the small-time criminals, beggars, and unemployed—but

Two centuries after his birth in 1818, an imposing statue of Marx is unveiled in his hometown of Trier, Germany. Marx looms large in the political discourse and popular imagination of the twenty-first century. Is it the vision of a classless society? The promise to topple the capitalist order? The big hair? What about Marx and his teachings resonates so much with academics, activists, and economic theorists today?

The Point Is . . .

Today's Working Class Is Precarious

In recent years a useful new term has entered the sociological literature: **precariat**. Coined by British economist Guy Standing (2011), it combines the word "precarious" (as in precarious employment) with Marx's term "proletariat". According to Standing (2014):

> One defining characteristic of the precariat is distinctive *relations of production*: so-called "flexible" labor contracts; temporary jobs; labor as casuals, part-timers, or intermittently for labor brokers or employment agencies. . . . More crucially, those in the precariat have no secure occupational identity; no occupational narrative they can give to their lives. And they find they have to do a lot of . . . work preparation that does not count as work and that is not remunerated. . . . They are exploited outside the workplace as well as in it, and outside paid hours as well as in them.

Standing (2014) points out that "this is also the first working class in history that, as a norm, is expected to have a level of education that is greater than the labor they are expected to perform or expect to obtain. . . . Few in the precariat use their full educational qualifications in the jobs they have." And, needless to say, they do not have the non-wage benefits, such as pensions and dental/health coverage, achieved over the course of the past century by unionized workers.

The precariat arose in the early days of the modern globalization movement, when large corporations and conservative governments started demanding greater "labour flexibility" from a previously secure and stable working class. The goal was competitiveness. Labour flexibility was achieved through a number of corporate and political strategies, including "downsizing" (the great euphemism for laying off workers), "outsourcing" (sending work to lower-paid labourers abroad), and, in the United States, "right to work" legislation (another euphemism, meaning the right to work without having to join a union).

As a business strategy, labour flexibility turned steady work into precarious employment and gave rise to the precariat, a vulnerable, unstable version of the Marxian working class. As Standing explains, Marx's proletariat came to signify

> a society consisting mostly of workers in long-term, stable, fixed-hour jobs with established routes of advancement, subject to unionisation and collective agreements, with job titles their fathers and mothers would have understood, facing local employers whose names and features they were familiar with. (Standing, 2011, p. 6)

Marx predicted that workers would eventually tire of being taken advantage of and would attempt to overthrow the capitalist system through revolution. In most capitalist countries, this didn't happen—partly, we could argue, because workers accepted their "bargain," as Standing puts it: the proletariat would submit to the capitalist class, giving their labour in exchange for stable, guaranteed employment and wages.

Today's precariat enjoys no such social contract or relationship of trust with either the state or the capitalist class. As a result, Standing argues, members of this new working class "are prone to listen to ugly voices, and to use their votes and money to give those voices a political platform of increasing influence" (Standing, 2011, p. 1). In other words, the success of populist demagogues like Donald Trump can be attributed directly to the spread of precarious employment, in Standing's view. I would add that the gig economy, characterized by disruptive innovation (for example, Airbnb, Uber, and Lyft), began as a more pragmatic, creative millennial response to precarious employment.

these terms do not have the significance of his two primary classes, the "two great hostile camps" referred to in the final sentence of the passage quoted above.

Marx's Historical Context

If you wonder at Marx's black-and-white view of society, remember the conditions he saw and the context in which he lived. Britain, where Marx lived from 1850 until his death in 1883, was operating according to those laissez-faire market practices advocated by Smith and others, in which business was supposed to take care of itself without any interference from government. The Factory Act of 1833, which targeted primarily the booming textile mills of Britain, was considered radical at the time. The mill-owning bourgeoisie claimed that the Act interfered with the "natural course" of business by "severely" limiting the hours that people were allowed to work. They complained that this legislation would ruin them financially, even drive them out of business. What limits did the Factory Act put on business? First, it stipulated that the working day was to start no earlier than 5:30 a.m. and end no later than 8:30 p.m. It also included these provisions:

- "No person under eighteen years of age shall [work] between half-past eight in the evening and half-past five in the morning, in any cotton, woollen, worsted, hemp, flax, tow, linen or silk mill."
- "No person under the age of eighteen shall be employed in any such mill . . . more than twelve hours in . . . one day, nor more than sixty-nine hours in . . . one week."
- "It shall not be lawful . . . to employ in any factory . . . except in mills for the manufacture of silk, any child who shall not have completed his or her ninth year."
- "It shall not be lawful for any person to employ . . . in any factory . . . for longer than forty-eight hours in one week, nor for longer than nine hours in one day, any child who shall not have completed his or her eleventh year."
- "Every child restricted to the performance of forty-eight hours of labour in any one week shall attend some school." (*Statutes of the Realm*, 3 & 4 William IV, c. 103)

These limits on the length of the working day and working week for people under 18 were the aspects of the Factory Act that mill owners thought would ruin them. We hear the same kind of concerns from business representatives today whenever someone proposes improving worker rights by raising the minimum wage or granting sick days to unsalaried employees.

Class as a Social Identity

Another characteristic of class in Marx's view is that it has a **corporate** (or **organic**) **identity** as a real social group. In other words, there is a shared sense of purpose among members of each class. A related term, **class consciousness**, means having an awareness of what is in the best interests of one's class. Marx believed that the owner class always possesses class consciousness, always knows what is in its best interests, and attempts to shape society in ways that promote those interests. Witness the **Highland Clearances** of the late eighteenth and early nineteenth centuries. Land-owning aristocrats in Scotland, aware of the rising value of wool to the rapidly industrializing textile industry, began evicting tenant farmers from their estates to make room for sheep. The clearances caused extreme hardship among the evicted "crofters," whose families had been on the land for generations. Many were forced to emigrate, notably to North America. The aristocrats knew that they would benefit in the long run from evicting the crofters.

The worker class does not always have such an awareness. On the contrary, it often has **false consciousness**, a belief that something is in its best interests when it is not. Marx believed that the proletariat's false consciousness kept them from waging open revolt against a system that was not working in their favour. Factors that could contribute to false consciousness include religion, which may be used to argue that poverty and wealth are parts of some divine plan; politics, which are often used to persuade low-income voters that pro-business policies will benefit everyone; and patriotism, which underlies protectionist policies that limit free trade between countries. More broadly, then, false consciousness entails the lower classes—through the education system, the media, political actions, and nationalistic rhetoric—taking as their own (and fully owning) the values and agenda espoused by the elite of society.

In what we might call "Universal Soldier" syndrome, for example, all war that involves *our* nation is just war.

Weber's Critique of Marx

Another early sociologist to look at inequality was Max Weber, whom we met in Chapter 1. Weber didn't quite agree with Marx's theory of class relations, and though the two men were not contemporaries (it is sometimes said that Weber engaged in theoretical discussions with Marx's ghost), their views on the subject are frequently compared. (Hint: the topic makes a good exam question.)

Like Marx, Weber ([1904] 1930, [1946] 1958, [1914] 1968) viewed society as divided into different economic classes, but he believed that Marx's materialist approach was too simplistic, that there was more to social inequality than just who owned the means of production. In particular, Weber stressed three elements—*wealth*, *prestige*, and *power*—as contributing to social inequality. For Weber, wealth, or material resources, includes not just factories and other property used to make money but also properties that are highly respected by members of the society in question: in Western society, the flashy car, the expensive house, the trophy spouse, the winning good looks you seem to find so often among Super Bowl quarterbacks. Prestige is the degree of respect with which individuals, their socially valued possessions, and their master statuses are viewed by the majority of people in a society. Prestige can be turned into various forms of social power, which is usually defined as the ability of individuals or groups to achieve their goals despite the opposition of others.

One example of a person embodying (literally!) wealth, prestige, and power is Arnold Schwarzenegger. As a young man, his good looks and muscular body were his wealth, earning him prestige as a bodybuilder (then his master status) and winner of the Mr Universe competition. The respect accorded him for his physical appearance enabled "the Ahnold" to change careers and become an actor, which brought him further prestige. This he turned into real social and political power, first by marrying Maria Shriver, a niece of the late President John F. Kennedy (the Kennedys being the closest thing to royalty the Americans have ever had), and then by being elected governor of California in 2004. He followed a course laid out by an earlier governor of California, Ronald Reagan, who had parlayed his own prestige as an actor into presidency of the United States. From a Weberian perspective, what is important is that Schwarzenegger's membership in the dominant social class was not about controlling the means of production in a Marxist sense.

This young man owns two gas-powered lawn-mowers and, with the help of his buddy Jake (whom he pays $18 an hour), operates his own small landscaping business. Assess his class position from both a Marxist and a Weberian perspective.

7.3 Using Class to Study Social Inequality Today

There are some problems with applying a traditional Marxist interpretation of class to contemporary societies in countries such as Canada. For one thing, many people, as employees of big businesses (bank presidents, corporate CEOs, business lawyers, hospital administrators, professional hockey players), would belong to Marx's class of "workers," even though their incomes put them in the top 1 per cent, on a par with the wealthiest of capitalists. Likewise, many farmers,

The Point Is . . .

The Gig Economy Is Nothing New

Those involved in the "gig economy" get by performing assorted part-time jobs, typically with hours flexible enough that a person can fit two or more kinds of work in around other commitments, such as going to school. To a musician, a gig is a one-night performance, and if you have ever known a working musician, you will know that it takes a lot of gigs to pay the rent and keep food on the table.

When we talk about the gig economy, we tend to think of ride-hailing services like Uber and other internet-mediated peer-to-peer services that connect people with underused assets (a spare bedroom, a cube van, a background in computer science) with people willing to pay for them. These arrangements are sometimes seen as disrupting the traditional economy, giving savvy millennials a way to undermine traditional capitalist structures. But stringing together part-time jobs is nothing new, and it isn't restricted to the generation that grew up with the internet on their iPhones. The gig economy is good for retired people like me. I retired from full-time work in 2015 but was hired to work part-time as the tribal linguist for the Wyandotte Nation of Oklahoma. I have a contract with Oxford University Press to update the textbook you're reading. Like a good number of baby boomers, I supplement my pension with the money earned from these gigs. This brings undeniable benefits: I set my own hours, and I work from home (sometimes, like now, with a parrot resting on my head), meaning I don't have to commute to work or attend staff meetings.

IAN KUCERAK / POSTMEDIA

While it's not quite the violent overthrow of capitalist machinery that Marx was hoping for, the growth of ride-hailing services like Uber does present a challenge to the traditional business models—or does it? Is it just another way for large multinational companies to exploit workers with low pay and no benefits? Or do you see a hint of Marxist revolution in the gig economy?

(Continued)

But the gig economy also means job insecurity, no medical benefits, and low income. Like many academics, I experienced that early in my career, before I had a regular teaching job. I did an 11-month contract for the Ontario Ministry of Natural Resources, developing wildlife programs for students in Grades 4 to 6. Before that I taught English part-time at a small private school while writing articles for newspapers and magazines and teaching a few courses at Humber College, where I was eventually hired full-time. I could not afford to have my teeth done, never went on vacation, and constantly worried whether I would ever have a "real career."

shop owners, and other small business operators have incomes more like those of workers. And unlike Marx, who was concerned with the binary opposition of the bourgeoisie and proletariat, we can argue for the existence of a very large middle group with a powerful sense of itself as a class.

Within the Canadian context, we can draw on the work of Curtis, Grabb, and Guppy (1999) to amend Marx's class paradigm by arguing that there are essentially three different classes in this country:

1. A **dominant capitalist class** "composed mainly of those who own or control large-scale production." This would include the presidents and CEOs of large businesses (including universities), who may not own their companies but who are paid handsomely for running them.
2. A **middle class** representing "a mixed . . . middle category of small-scale business people, educated professional-technical or administrative personnel, and various salaried employees or wage-earners possessing some certifiable credentials, training, or skills." This group includes small-business entrepreneurs, teachers and nurses, academic researchers, and those who have been able to translate a postsecondary degree into a modest but respectable job in an office or skilled trade.
3. A **working class** or proletariat, "made up of people who lack resources or capacities apart from their own labour power": people in construction or manufacturing, retail employees, and others in the service industry. (Curtis, Grabb, & Guppy, 1999, p. ix)

We will consider the middle class in greater detail later in this chapter.

Class Divisions and Popular Sport

There is a strong connection between class and sport at both the professional and recreational levels. The traditional association of sports like golf and tennis with the wealthy classes has been reinforced through the prohibitive cost of—and prestige surrounding—country club membership. Weber might recognize belonging to an exclusive Vancouver golf club as a form of wealth. Compare that with membership in a bowling league, where players enjoy a sport generally seen as having greater working-class appeal. Marketers and advertisers involved in professional sports often exploit these associations to attract a particular fan base to their sport, in spite of the fact that most professional athletes earn lucrative salaries that put them in the top 1 per cent.

Sports that offer people from poorer socio-economic backgrounds the chance to reap large financial rewards as professional athletes are called **mobility sports**. Any sport can be considered a mobility sport if it is cheap to play (with low costs for equipment and participation), if it offers people of all classes the chance to "be discovered," and if it provides middle- to upper-class incomes for the select few who "make it." Boxing is a sport with a tradition of providing young men raised in poor and sometimes violent circumstances an alternative to "the mean streets." Professional boxers rarely come from the middle class. The highest-paid athlete in 2018 was boxer Floyd Mayweather Jr, who grew up with poverty and abuse in New Jersey. He never completed high school but was wearing boxing gloves as soon as he could walk (Snowden, 2013). Boxing today has lost some of its popularity and prestige to mixed martial arts and its professional embodiment, UFC (the Ultimate Fighting Championship), which has developed a loyal and increasingly mainstream fan base rooted in lower- and middle-class North America. During the last 40 years, basketball in North America and

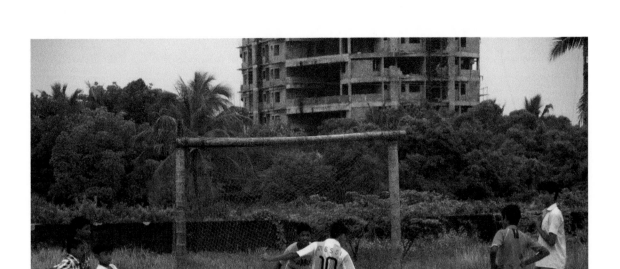

A youth in Cochin, India, wears the soccer jersey of Lionel Messi, ranked third on Forbes's list of wealthiest athletes in 2022 with an income of US$104 million (*Ecocnn, 2022*). How would you situate Messi within Marx's class framework? And what would it take for this youth to follow in his hero's footsteps? Is "the beautiful game" also the world's greatest mobility sport?

soccer globally have been mobility sports for racialized young people.

When a Mobility Sport Becomes an Elitist Sport

Canadian hockey lore is filled with stories of poor young men from farming communities in the West or mining towns in the East rising from poverty and humble beginnings to achieve celebrity playing in the NHL. Gordie Howe, who was born in 1928, was one of nine children raised on a failing farm in Depression-era Floral, Saskatchewan; he became a superstar with the Detroit Red Wings, arguably (among older fans) the greatest player ever. Born in 1935, Johnny Bucyk grew up in a rough neighbourhood of north Edmonton, the son of Ukrainian immigrants. In a memoir he recalls learning to play hockey with "road apples," without sticks, pads, or skates:

> In those days you couldn't afford to buy hockey sticks, nobody in our group could....

I played a lot of street hockey and we used brooms for sticks. We couldn't afford pucks either, so we'd follow the milk wagon which was pulled by a couple of horses, waiting until the horses did their job, dropping a good hunk of manure. Usually it would be a cold day, anytime between the start of October through the end of April, and we'd let it freeze up solid. We'd use it as a hockey puck. . . . I didn't get my first pair of skates until I was about 10 years old. It was a pair of my older brother Bill's, which he outgrew. (quoted in Lowe, Fischler, & Fischler, 1988, pp. 43–4)

Bucyk played in the National Hockey League from 1956 to 1978, most of that time with the Boston Bruins, and was inducted into the Hockey Hall of Fame in 1981.

Players like Howe and Bucyk earned decent livings playing hockey, though they came nowhere

Quick Hits

Minor Hockey, Major Cash

The cost of outfitting a child for hockey depends on what level the child is at, where you shop, and how much you're willing to pay. Below are two extremes based on the new equipment a 10-year-old might typically wear to play forward or defence (goalie equipment is even more expensive).

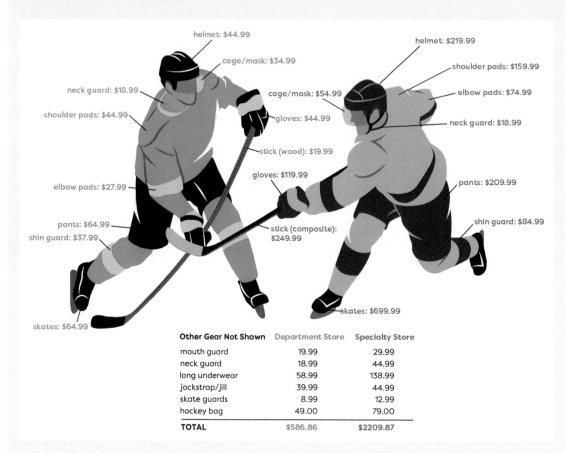

helmet: $44.99
cage/mask: $34.99
neck guard: $18.99
shoulder pads: $44.99
cage/mask: $54.99
gloves: $44.99
stick (wood): $19.99
elbow pads: $27.99
gloves: $119.99
pants: $64.99
shin guard: $37.99
stick (composite): $249.99
skates: $64.99

helmet: $219.99
shoulder pads: $159.99
elbow pads: $74.99
neck guard: $18.99
pants: $209.99
shin guard: $84.99
skates: $699.99

Other Gear Not Shown	Department Store	Specialty Store
mouth guard	19.99	29.99
neck guard	18.99	44.99
long underwear	58.99	138.99
jockstrap/jill	39.99	44.99
skate guards	8.99	12.99
hockey bag	49.00	79.00
TOTAL	**$586.86**	**$2209.87**

Other Basic Costs

- average registration for boys' or girls' house league: $700
- average registration for boys' or girls' competitive league: $3,000–$6,000
- ice time for extra practices
- power-skating lessons
- summer hockey schools
- gas, food, and accommodations for "away" games and out-of-town tournaments
- skate sharpening

Note: While the figures shown here and above are from more than a decade ago, more recent information indicates these costs have not risen significantly, with the cost of outfitting a beginner with new equipment ranging from $300 to $700. See New to Hockey (2018).

Sources: Ormsby (2007); Rutherford (2009).

What do *you* think?

Do you think that hockey in Canada can still be seen as a mobility sport, or has it become solely an elitist sport? What arguments can be made for each position? How could you test your hypothesis?

THE CANADIAN PRESS/Darryl Dyck

Fans packed Vancouver's Rogers Arena to watch teams compete for US$25 million in prize money during a week-long Dota 2 tournament in August 2018. The past decade has seen the rise of professional videogaming, which attracts large audiences live and online. Fans can wager on their favourite pro teams, like the Vancouver Titans, owned by the NHL's Vancouver Canucks. Some American colleges are offering scholarships to students recruited to their varsity esport teams, Ontario initiated a $1 million scholarship program in 2022 for students who want to become involved in development and marketing in the esports industry, and there's a push to add esports to the Olympics. Is online videogaming a mobility sport? Is it a sport at all?

near the earnings of professional athletes in North America today. They grew up at a time when the cost of playing organized sport was relatively low. Over the last 30 years, the costs associated with raising a potential professional hockey player have risen astronomically. Beyond the price tag for the latest equipment and league fees, a player who shows skill enough to play for a touring competitive team will incur travel costs and higher registration fees.

The rise in costs is a feature of the **professionalization** of elite minor hockey, which now depends heavily on professional coaches and trainers. The trend is evident not just in other sports but in activities such as music, drama, and dance. In some cases, it reflects the diminishing role of schools in delivering extracurricular activities. School boards facing tight budgets may be forced to cut dedicated gym and music teachers, leaving athletic and arts programs starving for staff and funding. It also reflects changing middle- and upper-class expectations concerning extracurricular activities, as parents indulge in the dream that, with sufficient funds, their children may one day become highly paid professionals. Many lower-class families cannot afford the same experience for their children, giving middle- and upper-class families a distinct advantage and making various sports—hockey in this case—much less of a mobility sport.

7.4 Social Stratification: Another View of Social Inequality

The class structure that Marx introduced remains a useful way to talk about social inequality, but it is imprecise. For example, many North Americans identify as middle-class, which makes sense: no matter how comfortable you are, there will always be others with more and less than what you have, and what you have never seems like enough; that puts you in the middle, right? Politicians exploit this when they pledge (if elected) to help the middle class: most voters see themselves as likely beneficiaries of those promises.

The trouble comes when we try to define what it means to be middle-class. Definitions vary so much that it can be hard to know who belongs. Does it have to do with what you own or what you earn? Is it more nuanced than that? A CBC article from 2015 quotes Scott Brison, then a federal Member of Parliament and finance critic for the Liberal Party, as saying the middle class includes "the broadest swath of Canadians whose working income gives them the capacity to provide decent housing, quality of life, and a good education for their families, while saving for retirement" (Blatchford, 2015). If that sounds vague to you, then you are thinking like a sociologist and not a politician. After all, shouldn't we be able to *quantify*, or measure, what it means to be middle-class?

This brings us to social stratification. When we talk about social stratification, we are borrowing a geological term to describe society as though it were divided into a series of layers. In geology, a stratum is a single level or layer of rock made up of tiny particles deposited together; if you look at a cross-section of sedimentary rock, you will be able to see the different strata and note the differences.

In sociology, a *stratum* is a group to which people belong depending on their level of income, education, or another social variable. **Strata** are used as units of analysis in stratified sampling, a research method in which equal samples are drawn from each stratum of the population instead of drawing one larger sample at random from the whole population. Stratified sampling produces a more representative sample to analyze.

Using Quintiles to Identify the Middle Class

Studies using stratified sampling to divide the population into even segments for analysis use quintiles, quartiles, or deciles. A **quintile** is a segment, or stratum, representing each of five equal groups into which the population is divided; each quintile

represents 20 per cent of the population. (Quartiles use four strata, deciles ten.)

Let's say that we wanted to divide the population into quintiles according to household (family) income. Using Statistics Canada's definition, a household is a person or group of people who occupy the same dwelling as their primary place of residence. Grattan (2003) offers a good explanation of how we would arrive at our quintiles:

> Imagine that all families are placed in a line, a family's place being determined by its income level. The poorest family is placed at the front of the line, followed by the next poorest, and so on, until the last family, with the highest income, is placed at the end. Next, the line is split into five equal groups. The first group, or quintile, is composed of the first 20 percent of the line. Obviously, this group will consist of the poorest people. The next group consists of the next 20 percent. A similar process occurs in selecting the third, fourth, and fifth groups. The fifth group, of course, comprises those families with the highest incomes. (Grattan, 2003, pp. 64–5)

Figure 7.1 shows what you would find if you conducted that procedure using Canadian families and their household incomes in a particular year. You can see that this gives us one basis for defining "middle class." We could define it narrowly as any family in the middle quintile—meaning the middle 20 per cent of Canadians—or more broadly as any family in the middle three quintiles, representing 60 per cent of Canadian families. Politicians prefer the latter of

Quintile	Household Income Range
Highest 20%	$125,010 and above
Upper-middle 20%	$88,075 to $125,009
Middle 20%	$61,929 to $88,074
Lower-middle 20%	$38,755 to $61,928
Lowest 20%	$0 to $38,754

FIGURE 7.1 Stratification of Canadian Households by Income, 2013

Source: Adapted from Hodges & Brown, 2015.

these two definitions, which gives them the largest group of "middle-class voters" to pitch their promises to. But consider this: is it realistic to treat the middle three quintiles as a single group when their household incomes range from a meagre $38,750 all the way to $125,000?

Assessing the Distribution of Household Wealth in Canada

Quintiles are useful for comparative purposes, both across time periods and across regions. Figure 7.2 repeats the exercise just described using total household wealth held by Canadian families over a four-year period. A family's total wealth, or net worth, is what it has left once the value of its liabilities (i.e., debt) has been deducted from the value of its assets (mostly real estate and savings). Using Grattan's method, imagine that we have placed all Canadian families in a line, beginning with families having the lowest total wealth and ending with the families having the highest total wealth. Then we divide the families into five equal groups and calculate the average household wealth for each group. Now imagine that we perform that exercise every year from 2014 to 2018: this is what Figure 7.2 represents.

Figure 7.2 shows us a couple of things very clearly. First, the average family in the highest quintile has nearly as much wealth as the families in the other four quintiles combined. Second, while overall household wealth in Canada rose between 2014 and 2018, the share of wealth held by families in each quintile remained more or less constant. Table 7.1 adds detail to this picture by showing how the distribution of total household wealth by quintile changed between 2010 and 2018. You can see that between 2010 and 2018, the share of wealth held by families in the top two quintiles dropped by 2 percentage points, while the share of wealth held by families in the middle and lower-middle quintiles rose by 1 percentage point each. The share of wealth held by families in the lowest quintile remained nearly constant over the eight-year period.

Keep in mind that if household wealth were distributed equally across Canada, then each of the five quintiles would have 20 per cent of the total. Because wealth is not distributed equally, the highest quintile will always have the largest share, well above 20 per cent; the lowest quintile will always have the smallest share of wealth, well below 20 per cent. The narrower the gap between the highest and lowest quintiles, the greater the equality. So, another way to assess income inequality is to find the ratio of wealth controlled by families in the highest and lowest quintiles. In 2018, Canada's top quintile held 48.7 per cent of all household wealth, while the bottom quintile held 5.5 per cent. The ratio is 48.7 to 5.5, or 8.85 to 1—an improvement over 2010, when the ratio was 10.27 to 1.

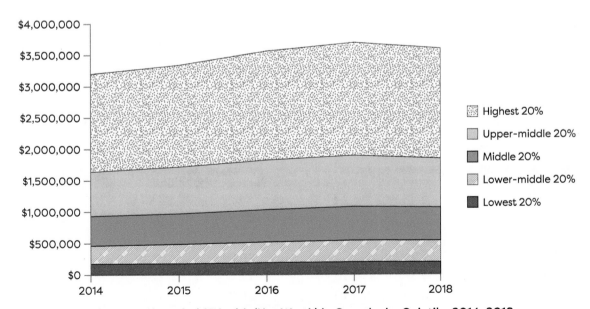

FIGURE 7.2 Average Household Wealth (Net Worth) in Canada, by Quintile, 2014–2018

Source: Statistics Canada Table 36-10-0587-01, Distributions of household economic accounts, income, consumption, and saving, by characteristic.

TABLE 7.1 Distribution of Household Wealth in Canada (%), by Quintile, 2010, 2014, and 2018

	2010	2012	2014	2016	2018
Highest 20%	50.4	49.3	48.7	48.7	48.7
Upper-middle 20%	22.0	22.0	22.0	22.2	21.7
Middle 20%	13.6	14.6	14.7	14.5	14.7
Lower-middle 20%	8.5	8.6	9.1	9.3	9.5
Lowest 20%	5.4	5.5	5.4	5.4	5.5

Source: Statistics Canada Table 36-10-0586-01, Distributions of household economic accounts, income, consumption, and saving, by characteristic.

Comparing the Distribution of Wealth across Regions

Table 7.1 gives us a picture of how household wealth is distributed across quintiles in Canada, but how does this national picture compare with the situation in different regions? For that view, we turn to Table 7.2, which shows the distribution of total household wealth in a single year (2018), again by quintile, for all of Canada and five different regions. Take a quick look at the table and see if you can predict, based on the data, which regions will have the greatest and least wealth equality. You can confirm your prediction by referring to Figure 7.3, which shows the high-to-low quintile ratios for Canada and the five regions profiled in Table 7.2, in order from greatest to least equality.

When looking at Figure 7.3, remember that the lower the score, the greater the degree of wealth equality. Here, only Quebec and Atlantic Canada have wealth equality scores below (i.e., better than) the national rate. As shown in Table 7.2, these are also the two regions with the greatest share of wealth held by families in the middle quintile. Meanwhile, in Ontario, BC, and the Prairies (Alberta specifically), where many wealthy multinational companies are headquartered, the wealth gap between the top and bottom quintiles is above the national score. Based on Table 7.2 and Figure 7.3, we can argue that when it comes to total household wealth among Canadian families, Quebec and Atlantic Canada have the lowest degree of inequality in Canada.

A Few Final Thoughts on Social Stratification

Let's return to our question about Canada's middle class with one last figure. Figure 7.4 shows the change in average household wealth from 2010 to 2018 for Canada's highest, middle, and lowest 20 per cent of families (the upper-middle and lower-middle quintiles have been omitted from this graph). In percentage terms, the middle quintile experienced greater growth than either the highest or the lowest quintile: over the eight-year period, wealth per household in the middle quintile rose by 54 per cent, compared with 38 per cent and 45 per cent, respectively, in the highest and lowest quintiles. This suggests the gap is narrowing slightly between the top and the middle, and to a lesser between the top and the bottom.

TABLE 7.2 Distribution of Household Wealth in Canada and Regions (%), by Quintile, 2018

	Lowest	Lower-Middle	Middle	Upper-Middle	Highest
Canada	5.5	9.5	14.7	21.7	48.7
British Columbia	5.6	9.0	11.2	20.4	53.8
Prairie Region	4.8	6.8	11.0	21.5	55.9
Ontario	5.3	8.6	14.0	21.8	50.2
Quebec	6.5	13.4	22.6	22.4	35.1
Atlantic Region	6.1	13.7	16.3	22.7	41.2

Source: Statistics Canada Table 36-10-0586-01, Distributions of household economic accounts, wealth, Canada, regions, and provinces.

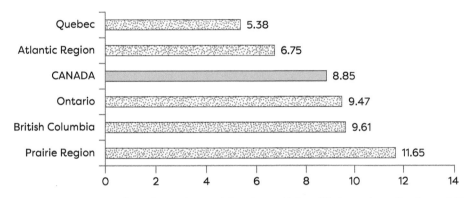

FIGURE 7.3 Income Inequality, Canada and Regions, Using High to Low Ratios of Household Wealth Quintiles

Source: Statistics Canada Table 36-10-0586-01, Distributions of household economic accounts, wealth, Canada, regions, and provinces.

Quick Hits

The Mean and the Median

The mean and the median can give very different impressions of the same set of figures. The *mean* (or *average*) is what you get when you add up a set of figures and divide the total by the number of figures in your set (2 + 2 + 4 + 10 + 12 = 30 ÷ 5 = **6**). The *median* is the figure in the middle of the ordered set (2, 2, **4**, 10, 12). If you've been waiting four-and-a-half chapters to demonstrate your mastery of the concept, here's your big chance. Have a look at the figure below, which compares the mean and median wealth for households in Canada and the five regions Statistics Canada uses for its analysis.

In Canada and each region, the median household wealth is less than 50 per cent of the mean household wealth. Why in each case are the mean and median values so different? What does that difference tell us? Which measure would you use if you belonged to a lobby group advocating for an increase to the minimum wage? Which measure would you use if you were a politician opposed to such a recommendation?

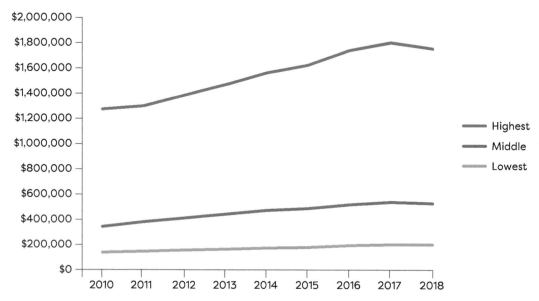

FIGURE 7.4 **Total Household Wealth in Canada, Lowest, Middle, and Highest Quintiles, 2010–2018**

Source: Statistics Canada Table 36-10-0586-01, Distributions of household economic accounts, wealth, Canada, regions, and provinces.

If that does not seem to match what you see in Figure 7.4, it's because the line graph charts the growth of each of the three quintiles in actual dollars. Families in the highest quintile saw their wealth per household rise by 38 percentage points but $480,516 in actual dollars. That is over two-and-a-half times the increase in net worth, in actual dollars, of families in the middle quintile ($185,450), and nearly eight times the dollar growth per household in the lowest quintile ($62,012). This serves as a reality check on the health of Canada's middle class relative to the country's highest income earners. It also makes us wonder if that 54 per cent increase for the middle quintile is significant.

Throughout this section we have been basing our analysis on household wealth, or net worth, because it is a variable that is easy to trace over time (thanks to the friendly agents at our federal statistics bureau). When considering economic disparities between the rich and the poor, many other quantitative factors could be considered. Household income is one; debt as a percentage of income is another. And when we consider poverty it is important to take regional differences into account: that toonie in your pocket will go further in Moncton than it does in Calgary. This is why some measures of middle class rely on *purchasing power*, which is the value of your wealth based on the cost of living in your city, town, village, or hamlet.

In short, there are many ways to define Canada's middle class, based not just on wealth or income but also on employment status, occupation, and education. Some even argue that when discussing Canada's middle class, *qualitative* variables must also be taken into account—that belonging to the middle class is about cultural values or state of mind. Perhaps a better question to ask is why politicians, the media, economists, and, yes, sociologists devote so much time to contemplating the middle when it's the families in the lowest stratum we should really be worried about.

7.5 Ideology: Explaining Social Inequality

When political economists write and speak about social inequality, their arguments and ideas are typically shaped by their ideology. An **ideology** is a set of beliefs about society and the people in it, usually forming the basis of a particular economic or political theory. In this section we will consider some of the ideologies that shape discussions of social inequality.

What do you think?
Studies have shown that people tend to view themselves as belonging to the middle class even when they clearly fall above or below the middle in terms of wealth. Why do you think people identify so strongly with the middle?

The Point Is . . .

How You Experience Poverty Depends on Your Social Location

I completed my master's degree in the mid-1970s at Memorial University in Newfoundland. During that time, I was statistically poor. My annual income consisted of a $2,500 fellowship combined with a $2,500 salary for my work as a research assistant. During my first year, I supported my wife and my dog on just that much money, paying monthly rent of $150 for a unit in a large apartment complex.

Although we were poor by pure statistical measures, there were unmeasurable factors that made life easier. We didn't pay for our furniture: we built our own, using planks I "liberated" from various undisclosed building locations. A neighbour who worked on the ferry that travelled between Newfoundland and the mainland regularly supplied us with free toilet paper. On Saturday and Sunday mornings I would walk the dog to places where teenagers drank beer so that I could collect empty bottles, worth five cents each. That can add up when you have a shopping cart full of empties. I learned which nearby fields had wild blueberries, raspberries, and partridgeberries (a Newfoundland favourite, related to cranberries). I had friends who hunted moose.

There were still things we had to pay for, but they were things you could get cheaply if you knew who to talk to or where to go. I bought fresh cod—then a staple of the Newfoundland diet—for 40 cents a pound from a guy who sold fish from the back of his pickup truck in the parking lot of a shopping plaza. In our second year we obtained, third-hand, a weather-beaten Ford pickup that needed a new starter motor. As I was under the truck removing the old one, I saw a pair of boots approach the vehicle. When I pulled myself out from under the truck, the person standing in the boots told me he could get me a new starter motor cheap, if I didn't care how it was obtained. I didn't. It cost me a bottle of screech.

It was not a glamorous life, but we were buoyed by the optimistic belief that living in poverty was but a short-term condition. I was a graduate student with prospects. I was expecting to become a college professor and move up into the middle class. The books on my homemade shelves reminded me of possibilities: the hope I would one day have a store-bought bookcase featuring books that I had written. It took a little more than 10 years and a lot of short-term contract work in a variety of jobs for me to realize that dream, but the dream always kept me from feeling poor.

What do *you* think?

1. Not everyone living in poverty can feel so optimistic about their future prospects. How might my outlook have differed if certain aspects of my social location—my gender, my race, my ability, for instance—had been different?
2. As a student, do you consider yourself poor? Why or why not? If you do, how long do you expect your state of poverty to last?

Dominant Ideology

A **dominant ideology** is the set of beliefs put forward by, and generally supportive of, society's dominant culture and/or classes. In Marxist terms, it reflects the class consciousness of the ruling capitalist class and is used to defend or justify the status quo.

An example of a dominant ideology in North America is **trickle-down theory**. The term refers to a view that if the wealthy are given the freedom to generate more wealth, others in society will benefit: new jobs will be created, more money will be spent on consumer goods, and a good part of the generated wealth will eventually find its way into the hands of members of the middle and lower classes. American author and historian William Blum describes it as "the principle that the poor, who must subsist on table scraps dropped by the rich, can best be served by giving the rich bigger meals" (Blum, 2003, p. 20). As a dominant ideology, trickle-down economic theory is used to justify policies that favour wealthy business owners. These policies include government subsidies for certain industries and low corporate taxes and other incentives for businesses that promise to "invest" in Canada by setting up offices and manufacturing plants here.

Neoliberal Ideology

Neoliberalism, or **neoliberal ideology**, is a dominant ideology that views the individual as a more or less independent player on the sociological scene. Drawing on classical economic liberalism of the eighteenth and nineteenth centuries (*neo-* means "new"), it reflects a belief in a great deal of social mobility—the ability of individuals to move (generally upward) from one class, or stratum, to another—and downplays concerns over social inequality. According to neoliberal ideology, when people are successful, it is because they have justly earned that success, not because they have benefited from the social privileges of race, ethnicity, class, or gender. The American dream—the belief that anyone can "make it" if they are willing to work really hard for it—reflects neoliberal ideology. Failure to achieve the American dream (resulting in the "American nightmare" of poverty) is likewise placed solely on the individual. **William Ryan** (1976) referred to this as **blaming the victim**, assigning individuals responsibility for events or circumstances that have broader social causes, such as the quality of a person's upbringing and education or a lack of the resources and social connections that help a person secure a well-paying job. Other examples of blaming the victim include the following arguments:

- People become alcoholics because they lack willpower; biological factors (genetic predisposition) and sociological factors (racial or ethnic stereotypes, systematic oppression) need not be considered.
- People receive social assistance because they don't have a strong work ethic, not because they come from poor families with the odds of success stacked against them.
- People convicted of crime offend and reoffend because they have a "criminal mind," not because they were raised in socioeconomically disadvantaged circumstances, or because they belong to a group disproportionately targeted by the criminal justice system, or because our prison system is based on punishment rather than on rehabilitation and healing.

Note that classical liberalism and neoliberalism derive their names from the core belief in the right of citizens to conduct their affairs free ("liberated") from government interference. Adam Smith, discussed briefly at the start of this chapter, was a classical liberal in this sense. Over the course of the twentieth century, the term "social liberalism" came to describe the movement to loosen laws around such practices as homosexuality and abortion. This makes things complicated because political parties that champion neoliberal economic policies tend to oppose socially liberal policies. In Canada, political parties most closely associated with a neoliberal ideology on financial matters tend to describe themselves as conservative (or Conservative). Political parties taking a liberal stance on social policy issues like same-sex marriage, cannabis legalization, and safe-injection sites for drug addicts may describe themselves as liberal (or Liberal), even though they tend not to be the strongest proponents of unregulated financial markets.

Counter-Ideology

Not everyone embraces the dominant ideology. Consider the critique of trickle-down theory presented by Linda McQuaig and Neil Brooks in *Billionaire's Ball: Gluttony and Hubris in an Age of Epic Inequality* (2012). She is a journalist; he is a college instructor in tax law and policy. They see "Reaganomics," a nickname for the economic policies adopted to help bring the United States out of a recession in the 1980s under President Ronald Reagan, as ushering in a period of uneven growth in income and wealth:

> Between 1980 and 2008, the incomes of the bottom 90 percent of the population grew by a meager 1 percent, or an average of just $303. Meanwhile, over those same years, the incomes of the top .01 percent of Americans grew by 403 percent, or an average of a massive $21.9 million. The richest 300,000 Americans now enjoy almost as much income as the bottom 150 million. (McQuaig & Brooks, 2012, p. 5)

The authors point out that this contrasts greatly with the pre-Reagan period, when, from 1950 to 1980, the bottom 90 per cent experienced "income growth of

75 percent, or an average of $13,222" (McQuaig & Brooks, 2012, p. 6).

A **counter-ideology**, then, is one that offers a critique of the dominant ideology, challenging its justice and its universal applicability to society. Today, with vast swaths of western North America being consumed by wildfires, Indigenous communities and rural settler farming communities facing changing environments and water crises, and unprecedented flooding in Pakistan and other countries, the environmental/climate change movement is front and centre as a counter-ideology to the basic assumptions of capitalism. People promoting a counter-ideology are typically looking to create significant socioeconomic and institutional change. Classical Marxism, which predicted the overthrow of the capitalist classes by the proletariat, is an obvious example of a counter-ideology. The Occupy movement began in 2011 in the United States in reaction to government bailouts to banks and other corporate giants following the 2008–9 economic meltdown. Its slogan, "We are the 99%," reflected that 99 per cent of the world's wealth is concentrated in the hands of 1 per cent of the world's population and must be subject to greater taxes in order to be distributed more equitably, and provided a sharp challenge to the dominant ideology of trickle-down economic theory.

Finally, among many other examples, a counter-ideology has been developing among contemporary Indigenous people in Canada, who are drawing on traditional values and who are critical of the capitalist/materialist society that has oppressed them. In 2012, the movement coalesced around Chief Theresa Spence of the Attawapiskat First Nation under the banner Idle No More, drawing attention to the federal government's elimination of environmental protections in order to fast-track pipeline construction and industrial development. This fight was taken up in 2018 by the Secwepemc (pronounced suh-wep-muh), a Salish people, in their resistance to

© Brian Jungen and Cartriona Jeffries Gallery

Prototype for New Understanding #23 (2005), by Dane-zaa artist Brian Jungen, who lives in Vancouver. What do you think the message of this artwork is? What ideology could it be critiquing?

the expansion of the Trans Mountain pipeline in the interior of British Columbia.

Hegemony

Antonio Gramsci (1891–1937) was a critic of the dominant ideology. The Italian-born political theorist and activist was a co-founder and leader of the Italian Communist party and an opponent of Fascist dictator Benito Mussolini. Jailed in November 1926, he remained a political prisoner for nearly 10 years. During that time he developed the concept of hegemony.

Gramsci (1992) used **hegemony** to mean non-coercive methods of maintaining power. He believed that the ruling classes relied on something more than their military and police forces to keep society running smoothly while quietly oppressing the masses. In her study of Gramsci, Kate Crehan defines hegemony as all the ways by which "the power relations underpinning various forms of inequality are produced and reproduced" (Crehan, 2002, p. 104).

Hegemony can take many forms. It is expressed in the reproduction and celebration of the idea that the path to prosperity is available to everyone equally, and that inequality exists not because of problems in "the system" but because some people are willing to work harder than others. It is also seen in the spread of cultural products, from the Disney empire of films and theme parks around the globe to the intrusion of southern Canadian television shows and values on TV sets in northern Indigenous communities.

Recalling the case of Attawapiskat described at the start of this chapter, we can consider the response of the federal government under then Prime Minister Stephen Harper as an instance of hegemony. In November 2011, Stephen Harper defended his government's handling of the crisis, arguing that they had spent $90 million on Attawapiskat since taking office and suggesting the funds had been mishandled by the community. In 2013, he sent an auditor to examine the community's finances, later ordering the First Nation to pay back $1.8 million it had been unable to account for. He thereby shifted blame *onto* the people and the handling of their money by the chief and council, and *off of* the inadequate measures taken by the federal and provincial governments and the exploitative practices of the powerful mining company, DeBeers, that employed Indigenous workers at the lowest levels of its workforce in Canada's North. That exercise of hegemony worked, as the government managed to avoid any serious backlash for failing to avert a crisis that had been building for years.

Even an introductory sociology textbook could become an instrument of hegemony. Say its author portrayed Canadian society as though there were no destructive social splits based on race, ethnicity, gender, ability, and class—in other words, as though there were none of the social divisions that create and sustain social inequality. In this sense, the textbook would be playing a part in maintaining the power of the ruling classes by suggesting that no problems of social inequality needed to be addressed.

7.6 Poverty and Excess: The Real Effects of Social Inequality

So far in this chapter we have looked at how social inequality is talked about by theorists, how it is measured by economists, and how it is sometimes explained or justified by policy makers. In the final section of this chapter we will look at some of the ways social inequality affects society. Since studying social inequality is often about looking at the extremes, we will start with the people using Canada's food banks and end with the country's top 1 per cent of earners and where they stand in relation to the average Canadian.

Food Banks
Changing Rates of Food Bank Use

One indicator of social inequality in Canada comes from statistics concerning the use of food banks. A **food bank**, as defined by Food Banks Canada, is a "central warehouse or clearing house, registered as a non-profit organization for the purpose of collecting, storing and distributing food, free of charge, directly or through front line agencies which may also provide meals to the hungry" (Food Banks Canada, 2004). Food Banks Canada is a national charitable organization that supports provincial agencies and community groups dedicated to fighting hunger. Each year the organization issues *HungerCount*, a report on national food bank use. *HungerCount* provides a good snapshot of food bank use that can be tracked from year to year, serving as an indicator of how some of Canada's neediest citizens are faring. *HungerCount* covers just one aspect of efforts to relieve hunger in

Canada: it does not include the efforts of other free food providers such as soup kitchens, shelters, and breakfast programs for schoolchildren.

When the COVID-19 pandemic struck Canada in the spring of 2020, the initial response was hopeful for poor families and individuals reliant on food banks. The Canada Employment Relief Benefit (CERB), which lasted from March to September of 2020, provided $500 per week in support to nearly nine million recipients whose employment and income were affected by COVID. Consequently, for a short period food bank use in Canada appeared to decrease, and this influx of assistance called attention to the desirability of a guaranteed annual income for all Canadians. In September 2020, CERB transitioned to a handful of more targeted relief programs for recovery, sickness, and caregiving, but these did not provide the broad protection that resulted from CERB. And quickly enough the food banks were offering stopgap support for more clients than they had been pre-pandemic, as inflation, stagnant income, and rising housing costs, along with ongoing unemployment and underemployment, took a bite out of people's ability to feed themselves. Indeed, March 2021 saw over 1.3 million food bank visits, a 20.3 per cent increase from 2019 (Food Banks Canada, 2021, p. 4). Table 7.3 gives a snapshot of food bank use

in March 2021, showing the percentage change by province/territories from 2019 to 2021 (the pandemic meant that Food Banks Canada was unable to conduct a thorough study for the year 2020).

Obviously, the number of food bank visitors in Canada varies from year to year and from province to province, and this can affected by other variables. In Saskatchewan, for example, with a sizable rural population and a relatively large Indigenous population, one might assume that informal neighbourly and community support and on-reserve assistance programs at the time of the COVID crisis helped to fill needs that might not be so readily met in urban environments. At the same time, it is a mistake to think that food bank users represent distinct geographic regions or a single homogeneous group: an unexpected job loss or an unprecedented environmental disaster can turn someone living in a stable financial position into a food bank user in the blink of an eye. Consider that in March 2014, 10 per cent of all food bank visitors were using a food bank for the first time. Many Canadians simply do not have the financial reserves to withstand a sudden change in circumstances.

Who Uses Food Banks?

So who do you think the typical food bank user is? Some of the details might surprise you. First, just

TABLE 7.3 Food Bank Use in Canada, 2019–2021, by Province and Territories

Region	Total Food Bank Visits, March 2021	% Change in Total Visits, 2019–2021	Total Meals and Snacks Provided
British Columbia	131,001	5.0	128,697
Alberta	116,396	29.6	523,019
Saskatchewan	32,827	–11.8	6,610
Manitoba*	65,100	–	256,485
Ontario	419,532	23.5	707,461
Quebec	474,002	38.1	1,415,652
New Brunswick	20,408	–8.3	81,085
Nova Scotia	26,090	1.8	83,093
Prince Edward Island	3,241	9.5	3,997
Newfoundland & Labrador	10,803	0.9	10,532
Territories**	4,597	24.8	–

*Comparison to previous year not available due to changes in provincial network structure and methodology.
**Not enough data for this variable.
Source: Food Banks Canada (2021, p. 10).

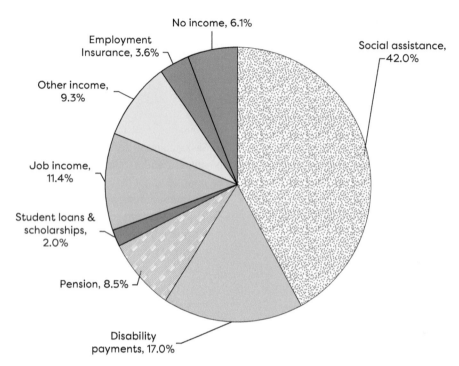

FIGURE 7.5 Household Primary Income Source among Food Bank Visitors, March 2018

Source: Food Banks Canada, 2019.

5 per cent of food bank users are homeless, a category that includes those living temporarily with family or friends. Roughly 67.9 per cent of food bank users pay market rent, while 15.7 per cent live in subsidized housing and 8.3 per cent own their own homes (Food Banks Canada, 2021, p. 9).

In March 2018, 45 per cent of all food bank visits were made by people living in single-person households. Another 19 per cent of visits were made by single parents with children. And yet only 6 per cent of visits were made by people reporting no income (Figure 7.5). Taken together, these findings point to the difficulty of living on a single source of income, whether that income comes in the form of a salary or government assistance.

In terms of age, 35 per cent of people served by food banks in March 2018 were children under the age of 18. People aged 45–64 made up the next largest group of food bank visitors (23 per cent), while over 6 per cent of those served by food banks were aged 65 and over (Figure 7.6).

Writing Food Insecurity

Food insecurity is a relatively new sociological term, although what it refers to is not: inadequate or unreliable access to food in terms of amount, variety, quality, and general desirability. It has a negative impact on both physical and mental health.

Food bank use, as we have seen above, can provide a good measure of social inequality, particularly regarding changes that are taking place. Besides the annual *HungerCount* from Food Banks Canada, other food banks gather useful sociological data about their clients. One example comes from the Daily Bread Food Bank and North York Harvest Food Bank in Toronto (*Who's Hungry 2021. From Crisis to Resilience: A City's Call to Action,* 2021).

When clients "check in" the food banks record **intake data**, that is, basic sociological characteristics about the clientele. The study for the period from 1 April 2020 to 31 March 2021 was particularly enlightening concerning the negative effects on social equality brought on by the COVID-19 pandemic. The 1,449,780 visits were the highest number they had ever had, and at 47 per cent it was the greatest year-over-year rise. For the first time in their relatively long recording history, new clients outnumbered previously existing clients, with a 61 per cent increase over the previous year (Daily Bread Food Bank and North York Harvest Food Bank, 2021, pp. 5, 13). In regard to stressors that caused people to seek assistance from these food banks, housing

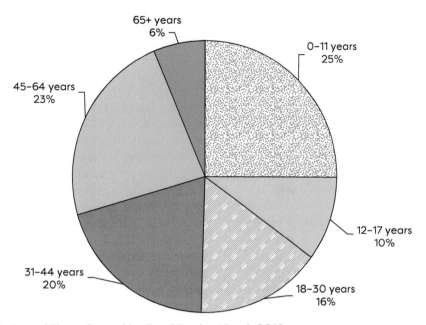

FIGURE 7.6 Age of Those Served by Food Banks, March 2018

Source: Food Banks Canada, 2019.

costs certainly stood out. In regard to housing, the researchers define **core need** as more than 30 per cent of a household's income and **deep core need** as more than 50 per cent of a household's income. The median month's income for those surveyed was $1,106 and the median of income spent on rent and utilities was 69 per cent, which is above both core need and deep core need. In terms of unaffordable or affordable, the statistics (Daily Bread Food Bank and North York Harvest Food Bank, 2021, p. 29) given for those surveyed were:

Deep core need	80 per cent
Core need	15 per cent
Affordable	5 per cent

Minimum Wage and Living Wage

In any jurisdiction, the minimum wage is the lowest hourly rate a person can be paid for their work. Setting the minimum wage is a provincial responsibility, and the rate varies widely across the country, from a low of $11.81 in Saskatchewan to a high of $16 in Nunavut (as of October 2022; see Table 7.4). Some provinces, such as BC, have plans to increase the minimum wage incrementally over the coming years, but a change of government can bring about a swift change to such plans. Witness Ontario, where in 2018 the newly elected Conservative government

made cancelling a planned minimum wage increase one of its first orders of business.

Minimum wage increases are often a source of fierce debate among labour and anti-poverty activists, on one hand, and business supporters on the other. Pro-business politicians argue that raising the minimum wage hurts workers by forcing small-business owners to lay off employees in order to offset the increase in labour costs. Keeping the minimum wage low, so the argument goes, allows businesses to flourish, preserving or even creating those precious (albeit low-paying) jobs. (If this sounds to you like something a champion of neoliberalism and free-market capitalism would argue, you are spot on and have clearly been paying attention.)

Social activists and sociologists who study poverty often argue about the need for what they call a **living wage**. It is a vague term, but it generally represents a target above the existing minimum wage,

> **What do you think?**
> 1. What reasons can you give for the large increases in food bank usage in 2021?
> 2. Do you think the terms "core need" and "deep core need" are accurate or useful?
> 3. Does your current housing situation fall into one of these categories?

The Point Is . . .

Are Students on Campus Hungry? You Bet They Are!

I remember the first time my research team learned that students on college campuses were going hungry. It was 2008, and we were conducting an evaluation of a financial aid program. Going out to talk to students across Wisconsin, we had one simple question [a very, very open-ended question]: "How's college going?" Most spoke of challenges paying for school, fitting in, or doing the academic work. But a few surprised us, speaking instead of difficulty finding food, even being distracted from class by persistent hunger. (Goldrick-Rab, 2016, p. 1)

This comes from the preface to *Hunger on Campus: The Challenge of Food Insecurity for College Students* (2016). For this study, the researchers interviewed 3,765 students using food banks and food pantries in 12 American states, at 34 colleges and universities. The researchers' revelations broke several stereotypes of the typical food bank user. For instance, of the students surveyed, roughly 75 per cent received some form of financial aid, and 43 per cent had some kind of meal plan. Still, they needed to rely on food banks. Another 56 per cent of the students using food banks had a paying job.

The authors define food insecurity as "the lack of reliable access to sufficient quantities of affordable, nutritious food" (Dubick, Mathews, & Cady, 2016, p. 6). It is usually associated with other indicators of poverty. For instance, roughly two-thirds of the students surveyed were also coping with housing insecurity: they faced frequent change of residence, couch surfing, and even periods of homelessness.

A similar Canadian study explored the same issues. In *Hungry for Knowledge: Assessing the Prevalence of Student Food Insecurity on Five Canadian Campuses* (Silverthorn, 2016), researchers considered the situation at Brock University, Dalhousie University, Lakehead University, Ryerson (now Toronto Metropolitan)

University of Alberta

University, and the University of Calgary through survey research involving approximately 4,000 self-selected respondents who replied to social media requests, on-campus flyers, and other means of recruitment. Among the findings: while 61 per cent were deemed to be food secure, fully 39 per cent experienced moderate or severe food insecurity. Principal reasons for food insecurity were cited as the cost of food (52.7 per cent), tuition fees (51.2 per cent), and increasing housing costs (47.5 per cent) (Silverthorn, 2016, p. 1).

Since this survey was undertaken, the impacts of the COVID-19 pandemic likely exacerbated the food insecurity of some students, as has the inflation that especially struck food prices in 2022. Although tuition costs in Canada remain lower for college as opposed to university, college students face the same challenges of food insecurity. For example, in 2018 a pay-what-you-can Soup Bar opened at Humber College in Toronto, accessing food destined for landfills from bakeries, restaurants, groceries, and food terminals.

What do you think?

1. Do you know if there's a food bank on your campus? (Hint: there probably is.) Do you know where to find it?
2. What do you think would be the best way of dealing with food insecurity among college students?
3. The voluntary nature of the Canadian study, *Hungry for Knowledge*, "means that food insecure students may have been more likely to respond" (Silverthorn, 2016, p. 14), and females comprised 77.3 per cent of respondents (Silverthorn, 2016, pp. 14, 13). Do you think these factors affect the reliability of the overall study? Would you want to change the methodology to correct for such over-reporting? How?
4. Three of the policy recommendations made in *Hungry for Knowledge* are for a periodic national food and housing security survey of university and college students in Canada; the potential inclusion of postsecondary students in a guaranteed annual income; and local programs and policies to provide postsecondary students with affordable housing (Silverthorn, 2016, p. 2). Which of these options would be the most useful? Why? What, if any, policy recommendations would you add to this list?

which is considered too low for the "working poor" to live on. People paid minimum wage often have to use food banks, especially if they can find only part-time work and if they are supporting or helping to support a family. You could safely say that anyone using a food bank is not paid a living wage.

As a sociologist in training, how would you calculate a living wage? The Vancouver-based Living Wage for Families Campaign uses the Market Basket Measure, which we examined in Chapter 3. As you will recall, the MBM is based on the cost of a standard set of goods required to support an individual or family, and it is adjusted to account for regional variations in the cost of housing, food, and other necessities. A visit to the organization's website (www.livingwageforfamilies.ca) provides living wages for 21 municipalities in southern BC and Vancouver Island. Vancouver and Victoria have

among the highest hourly living wages ($20.52/hr and $20.46/hr, respectively) because of the high cost of accommodation in BC's two largest metropolitan centres. However, at the top of the list is the small island community of Clayoquot Sound ($21.15), where the scarcity of affordable childcare makes the cost of living greater. As of October 2022 the minimum wage in BC was $15.65, the highest of any province in Canada. According to the Living Wage for Families Campaign, the lowest living wage in the province is $16.33, in Nanaimo on Vancouver Island.

The "Mincome": A Manitoba Town's Modernist Experiment

During the 1970s, the Manitoba town of Dauphin was home to a progressive social experiment

TABLE 7.4 Minimum Hourly Wage in Canada, Provinces, Territories, and Federal Government, 2022

Saskatchewan	$11.81
Manitoba	$11.95
Newfoundland & Labrador	$13.20
Prince Edward Island	$13.70
New Brunswick	$13.75
Nova Scotia	$13.75
Quebec	$14.25
Ontario	$15.00
Alberta	$15.00
Northwest Territories	$15.20
British Columbia	$15.65
Yukon	$15.70
Nunavut	$16.00
Federal government	$15.55

Source: Dodge (2022).

around a simple idea: What if every family in the town received a guaranteed, unconditional annual income? Would citizens become lazy, knowing their income was guaranteed no matter how hard they worked? Would they stop working altogether?

The pilot project was introduced in 1974 under the province's NDP government and the Liberal government of Canada. Under the plan, families were guaranteed a minimum income based on family size. The guaranteed minimum income (or "mincome," as it came to be known) would be reduced by 50 cents for each dollar the household earned.

During the four years the project lasted it was studied by anthropologists, sociologists, and economists. It was stopped in 1979 by Conservative governments that came to power at the provincial and federal levels. As Dutch historian Rutger Bregman explains in his book *Utopia for Realists* (2016), hardly any of the results were analyzed by staff overseeing the project. Boxes of paper files and questionnaires were left to rot in the archives.

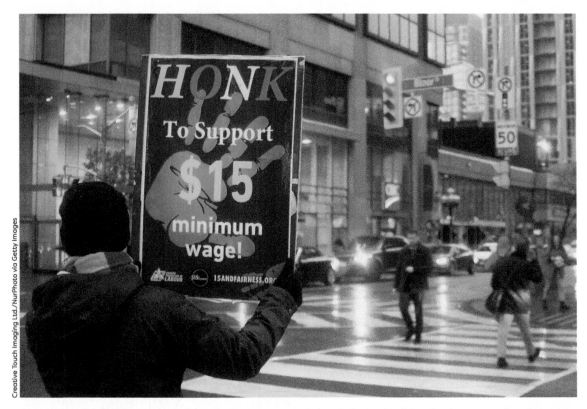

Creative Touch Imaging Ltd./NurPhoto via Getty Images

At a news conference announcing her government's intention to roll back plans to raise the province's minimum wage, Ontario's minister of labour, Laurie Scott, vowed to "reduce the regulatory burden for anyone willing to create jobs in Ontario" (*Bouw, 2018*). What kind of ideology does this statement reflect?

Twenty-five years later, University of Manitoba researcher Evelyn Forget unearthed the documents shortly before they were to be destroyed. She found that during the time of the study, the town recorded fewer work-related injuries, fewer mental-health visits, and an 8.5 per cent drop in hospital visits overall (Forget, 2011). There were only minor reductions in the number of hours worked by Dauphin residents, except among young adults, where the decrease was greater. However, the decrease in hours worked meant that young adults were more likely to complete their high school educations, and young families were likely to devote more time to the care of young children.

The argument in favour of providing a guaranteed minimum income is that it benefits people living in poverty, providing them with the stability and time to find employment (or more lucrative employment) or to upgrade their skills through education. At the same time, the cost of administering a guaranteed income is less that the cost of administering the many other government social assistance programs it would replace. The chief arguments against the policy are that it would diminish the incentive to work while being far too costly to implement.

In 2017, the Liberal government of Ontario announced its own plans to pilot a guaranteed basic income in three jurisdictions over a three-year period. The participants chosen for the study were all living on a low income, defined as less than $34,000 per year for single people or $48,000 per year for couples, with or without children. The participants would be given up to $16,989 less 50 per cent of earned income for single people, and up to $24,027 per year less 50 per cent of earned income for couples. Two years into the study, the newly elected Conservative government announced plans to end the pilot project, arguing that the cost was too great with benefits going to too few.

Canada's "1 Per Cent"

In the fall of 2011, protesters in cities around the world joined the Occupy movement to draw attention to the fact that 1 per cent of the world's population controlled 99 per cent of the world's wealth. Does the ratio apply in Canada?

On 3 January 2012, Canadians beginning their work year learned that by noon that day, each of the top 100 chief executive officers (CEOs) in Canada had already earned as much as the average Canadian would make in an entire year ("Canada's Top CEOs," 2012). The report, prepared by the non-profit Canadian Centre for Policy Alternatives, was based on figures from 2010, when the average Canadian was earning $44,300 per year, while the average annual salary for the top 100 CEOs was $8.4 million. These CEOs included the heads of well-known companies such as Canadian Tire, Rona, Air Canada, Loblaws, Rogers, Shaw, Telus, and Cineplex (no wonder the popcorn is so expensive) as well as a significant number of oil and mining companies and the "big six" banks.

Reports like this are meant to shock us by sensationalizing a situation we all know exists. Issued in the early days of the calendar year—a notoriously slow time for news—they play well in the media. As students of sociology, we have to look at the statistics critically. Here, then, is some context. The figure cited as the average salary of the top 100 Canadian CEOs in 2010—$8.4 million—represents an increase of 27 per cent over the previous year, while the average Canadian salary went up by 1.1 from 2009 to 2010 (Flavelle, 2012). Another way of looking at the situation: the highest salary of a Canadian CEO in 2010 was 189 times that of the average wage earner in 2010. Compare this with the situation in 1998, when the best-paid CEO made 105 times what the average Canadian earned, and in 1995, when the wealthiest CEO's salary was 85 times that of the average Canadian (Flavelle, 2012). This suggests that social inequality in Canada is growing, not diminishing.

More recent figures released in 2018 by Statistics Canada confirm this trend. They show that from 1982

What do you think?

1. Forget attributes the demise of the Dauphin project to "a change in the intellectual and economic climate" (Forget, 2011, p. 8). What do you think she means?

2. About 45 years after the Dauphin experiment ended, talk of implementing a guaranteed basic income has been picking up at both the federal and provincial levels (notably in Ontario and PEI). Why now? What is it about Canada's changing employment landscape that has politicians musing seriously about an idea once was dismissed as foolhardy and impractical?

Quick Hits

Who Are the Top 1 per cent of Earners in Canada?

In a 2015 study for the Institute for Research on Public Policy (IRPP), economists Thomas Lemieux and W. Craig Riddell developed a profile of the top 1 per cent of earners in Canada. Here's a snapshot of what they found.

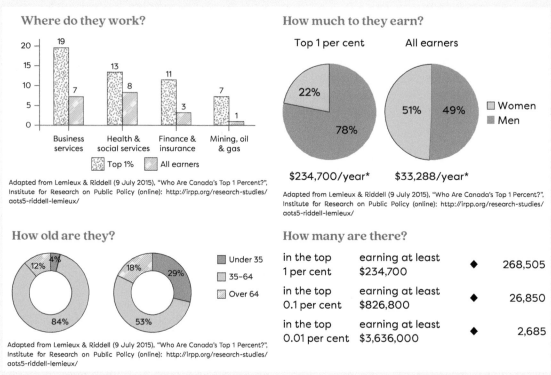

Where do they work?

Adapted from Lemieux & Riddell (9 July 2015), "Who Are Canada's Top 1 Percent?", Institute for Research on Public Policy (online): http://irpp.org/research-studies/aots5-riddell-lemieux/

How much to they earn?

Top 1 per cent — 22% Women, 78% Men — $234,700/year*

All earners — 51% Women, 49% Men — $33,288/year*

Adapted from Lemieux & Riddell (9 July 2015), "Who Are Canada's Top 1 Percent?", Institute for Research on Public Policy (online): http://irpp.org/research-studies/aots5-riddell-lemieux/

How old are they?

Under 35 / 35–64 / Over 64

12%, 4%, 84%   18%, 29%, 53%

Adapted from Lemieux & Riddell (9 July 2015), "Who Are Canada's Top 1 Percent?", Institute for Research on Public Policy (online): http://irpp.org/research-studies/aots5-riddell-lemieux/

How many are there?

in the top 1 per cent	earning at least $234,700	◆ 268,505
in the top 0.1 per cent	earning at least $826,800	◆ 26,850
in the top 0.01 per cent	earning at least $3,636,000	◆ 2,685

to 2014, the share of income earned by the bottom half of all earners fell by 28 per cent, while the share earned by the top half increased by 5 per cent. That increase might sound modest, but the biggest gains over the period were made by the top 1 per cent of earners, whose share of income rose by 53 per cent. The top 0.1 per cent saw their earnings rise by 90 per cent, and the earnings of the top 0.01 per cent rose by 133 per cent.

Wrap It Up

Summary

We began the chapter with a hefty question: Is social inequality inevitable? Karl Marx didn't think so. What was inevitable, he thought, was that society's poor workers would rise up against their wealthy masters in a revolution aimed at levelling the playing field. Things haven't played out quite as Marx imagined. There have been popular movements to challenge a system organized around class divisions—the Occupy movement and Idle No More, to name just two—but the ideology that prevails in the West perpetuates the idea that if a small percentage of the population is allowed to generate enormous wealth, everyone else will benefit.

Social inequality seems less unjust when there are good avenues for mobility, which might give someone from a lower class a decent chance to climb the socioeconomic ladder. Education is one: you may feel very poor now, but just think of the riches that await you once you complete your honours sociology degree. Alternatively, you might be spending the time you aren't in class playing Fortnite, hoping to join the esports circuit to make your fortune in one of the fastest-growing mobility sports. (It's a faint hope, I'm afraid.) Most people looking for a road out of poverty rely on social assistance: policies involving minimum wage, living wage, and guaranteed basic income are very real to them. Even with that social assistance, they may have to rely on food banks and other charitable organizations. Food bank user statistics give us a good idea of who is poor in Canada; they also suggest that social inequality isn't going away any time soon.

Think Back

Questions for Critical Review

1. Is social inequality in Canada inevitable? Explain your answer.
2. Explain why the class structure that Marx described does not fully apply to contemporary Canadian society.
3. Explain what is meant by the term "precariat," and describe its relationship to (a) populism and (b) the gig economy.
4. Identify what quintiles are and explain how they are used. What is the relationship between quintiles and class?
5. What goes into defining Canada's middle class? Is it something you can quantify, based on wealth or income alone? And does the middle class have class consciousness in the way that Marx defined the term?
6. Where would you find the greatest degree of economic equality in Canada? What factors might give one region greater equality than others?
7. Identify what neoliberal ideology is. Who supports it, and on what grounds? Who opposes it, and on what grounds?

8. Imagine that you have been asked to study trends in the use of food banks in Canada and put forward recommendations to help reduce Canadians' reliance on them. Which of the following policies would you recommend, and why?
   a. implement a "living wage" to replace the minimum wage
   b. increase the age of retirement
   c. increase family allowance cheques
   d. introduce a guaranteed basic income
   e. crack down on employment insurance fraud to ensure there is more money in the system for deserving families
   f. increase the availability of low-cost housing
   g. implement free or minimal-cost daycare
   h. subject EI recipients to drug testing and provide counselling services as necessary
   i. create incentives for businesses to hire and train unemployed people
   j. make postsecondary education free
   k. raise the tax rate on the top 1 per cent of earners.
   l. write your own:

   _____

Read On

Suggested Print and Online Resources

Patrizia Albanese, *Child Poverty in Canada* (Toronto: Oxford University Press, 2009)
An important work by a Canadian sociologist on theories of, and possible solutions to, child poverty in Canada.

Zygmunt Bauman, *Collateral Damage: Social Inequalities in a Global Age* (Malden, MA: Polity Press, 2011)
The author explores how contemporary society is producing an underclass of disposable people.

Bryan D. Cummins, *Only God Can Own the Land*, Canadian Ethnography Series Vol. 1. (Toronto: Pearson, 2003)

This book looks at how the life of the Attawapiskat Cree changed once diamond exploration and mining began in Ontario's North.

Food Banks Canada, www.foodbankscanada.ca
On its website Food Banks Canada documents the hunger problems of the poor in Canada and proposes policy solutions. Its annual report, *HungerCount*, gives details of the organization's activities and findings on a yearly basis.

Ed Grabb and Neil Guppy, eds, *Social Inequality in Canada*, 5th ed. (Toronto: Pearson, 2008)
An insightful collection of articles edited (and with some articles written) by two leading Canadian sociologists studying social inequality in Canada.

**Living Wage for Families Campaign, www
.livingwageforfamilies.ca**
Visit this website for more information on how the BC-
based organization calculates its living wage for different metropolitan centres and why a living wage is
important.

**Kristina Rutherford, "Is the Cost Keeping Kids
Out of Minor Hockey? Absolutely, Players and
Parents Say," 2009, www.cbc.ca/sports/hockey/
ourgame/story/2009/01/16/hockey-costs-too-
much.html**
This feature CBC article provides an informative look
at the high price of hockey in Canada, which may
be to blame for falling minor hockey registration
numbers.

**Michele Simon, "Walmart's Hunger Games:
How America's Largest Employer and Richest
Family Worsen the Hunger Crisis," 2014, www**

**.eatdrinkpolitics.com/wp-content/uploads/
Walmarts_Hunger_Games_Report.pdf**
Over a decade ago, Walmart drew some bad press over
its treatment of employees. This report argues that
Walmart "builds their wealth off of workers' inability to
afford food," by underpaying their employees and then
redeeming the food stamps their low-paid workers rely
on. The report is subtitled "A Call for Walmart's Owners
to Change," and you can research the company online
to see if, in the years since 2014, they have changed,
and if their practices differ in Canada.

**Micah M. White, *The End of Protest: A New Playbook
for Revolution* (Toronto: Knopf, 2016)**
A former editor with Vancouver-based Adbusters and
a co-founder of the Occupy Wall Street movement,
Micah White calls for a new approach to social activism
given that the disruptive tactics behind some of the
largest protests in history have failed to fundamentally
change society.

"Race" and Ethnicity

Reading this chapter will help you to . . .

- Define "race" and ethnicity, and explain why they are social, rather than biological, constructs.

- Understand how Indigenous people, Blacks, and Asians have been racialized in Canada.

- Gain some appreciation for the discrimination and racism directed toward Indigenous people in Canada.

- Apply different approaches to studying and understanding ethnicity.

- Appreciate the contributions of some pioneering Black sociologists in North America.

- Distinguish between different forms of racism, including systemic racism, friendly racism, and colourism.

- Demonstrate how Canadian immigration laws reflect institutional racism.

For Starters

On White Privilege and Being Invisible

Like a lot of white North Americans, I am, for all intents and purposes, invisible to others of European ancestry. I have an Anglo name.

I blend into the crowd at a concert or a ballgame. I pass through the security gate without anyone double- or triple-checking my bag; no one gives me a second glance.

Pedestrians don't cross the street to avoid me; passengers don't change cars when I get on the subway. No one becomes visibly agitated when I board their flight.

I can walk past a police officer without fear of being stopped and asked to empty my pockets or show my ID.

Strangers don't tell me they wish they had my hair, my fascinating complexion, or my innate talent for dancing or math.

I've never had to interrupt an awkward conversation with someone who has mistaken me for another white person who looks just like me.

Being white and invisible is like having a superpower that keeps me safe. We could call this superpower white privilege. It's something easily taken for granted.

I haven't always been invisible. In the 1960s, I chose to become visible for a time because of my long hair. With this new status (that of the countercultural hippie) I took a few baby steps down the long path of unmasked prejudice. Police, folks from small towns, and denizens of the big city's "greaser" neighbourhoods all made me highly aware of my visibility, causing me to feel vulnerable to the emotions of others. Once, waiting for a bus in northern Ontario, dark from a summer's work in forestry, straight hair hanging well below my shoulders, one of the people working at the bus depot thought I was Indigenous. I got a glimpse—very brief—of what it was like to be the object of racial disdain.

When I returned to southern Ontario I became invisible once again. I was home, and I felt safe. Many North Americans who do not enjoy white privilege as I do may never know what that feels like.

Paul Sampson / Concepts / Alamy Stock Photo

What do *you* think?

Think of a situation when your "race" or another social characteristic—your sex, your age, your accent—made you feel visible. What was it like to stand out? Did your visibility cause you to gain or to lose status?

8.1 Introduction to "Race": Why the Scare Quotes?

The word "race" came into the English language as a generalized term, meaning "sort" or "kind"—in the late sixteenth century. The term was first applied to groups of humans sharing similar skin colour during European colonial expansion. However, in the seventeenth and eighteenth centuries, through the political and philosophical writers who held beliefs about biological superiority and inferiority in the context of colonial power, the white "race" was elevated among the others, which became an excuse or a justification for domination of non-whites by whites.

When late-eighteenth century naturalists, such as Carolus Linnaeus, described these "newly discovered" humans, they at first thought in terms of three "races" in the original sense, which they termed Caucasian, Mongoloid, and Negroid, according to approximate skin colour and location. This loose distinction left out certain groups, such as the Ainu of Japan and the Aborigines of Australia. Differences *within* supposed "races" often outnumbered those *between* "races." For example, "Negroid" people have included among the tallest and shortest people in the world, and people of greatly varying skin colour and build.

Africans and their descendants during the first two or three generations in the American colonies had as much social flexibility as whites. The "ideology of inequality or inferiority" was absent, and Blacks were freed at the end of their tenure as indentured servants. Some became slave-owners themselves; many became businessmen, craftsmen, and farmers with full civil rights. However, in the late 1600s, the Virginia Assembly deliberately rearranged the social order by drawing poor whites into the protected category of the upper-class whites while Blacks, Indigenous peoples, and all others, whether rich or poor, were victimized into a socially racialized caste. The "engineered" social circumstances of those approximate distinctions in appearance soon became attached to each group: the white Europeans as conquerors, the subjugated Amerindians, and the Blacks who initially were imported to the colonies as slaves (Takezawa, Wade, & Smedley, 2020).

At that point, "race" no longer carried its former general meaning but an intensely political and specific social division of people according to their appearance and history. The English were not alone in having a long tradition of "othering" people they wanted to serve them. When the Irish proved resistant, the English turned to other shores and colonized as much of the world as they could, as did the French, Spanish, Dutch, Portuguese, and Russians, all of whom fought among themselves as well. In the late 1700s, those intent on using slave labour further developed the myth of inferiority regarding the groups—whether African, Indian, or North American—that it wanted to dominate. At the same time, a significant number of Christians were opposed to slavery and to the subjugating trends of the more powerful social groups. Their numbers grew in England, Canada, and in the northern states of the United States, gaining social and political strength until they formed the opposition to the Confederate States of America in the American Civil War.

During the 1700s and 1800s, people with political and economic interests in preserving slavery turned to emerging forms of science to support those interests. For example, Kant (German), Voltaire (French), Hume (Scottish), and Jefferson (American) expressed negative views on "race" based on their reading of works by explorers and other travellers. Some influential figures, such as a

A nineteenth-century artist's representation of five "human races": (*clockwise from top left*) American, Malayan, Mongolian, Ethiopian, and Caucasian. What role do you think politics and religion might have played in scientific efforts to prove the existence of different "races" during the eighteenth and nineteenth centuries?

Dr Charles White, engaged in a limited sort of pseudo-science that led him to claim humans were divided into different species. The Swedish botanist C. Linnaeus and the German physiologist J.F. Blumenbach derived categories and named separate species of humans, some based entirely on myths and some based on cultural characteristics that they conflated with physical features. A false aura of "science" grew up in the public mind around the notion of "race." For a hundred years, the partial or utterly false "sciences" of various writers exerted great influence on American political leaders and the public, especially in the Revolutionary War and again in the Civil War. One of the most influential theorists

was the anti-Semitic and Black demonizer Joseph-Arthur, compte de Gobineau, who constructed the myth of the "purity" of the Germanic "Aryan" white "race." Americans and Germans were his most avid followers.

The arrival of Franz Boas early in the twentieth century, and of other physical anthropologists and human biologists who had access to better information, showed their readers and students that physical characteristics, language, and culture were separate categories and not to be conflated.

Around 1900, with the renewed interest in Mendelian laws of inheritance, blood groups (ABO) were discovered. At first, it was assumed that these blood groups would prove racial categories; but exactly opposite findings quenched that false notion. Next, it was assumed that frequencies of genes or gene clusters would pertain to racial groups and confirm those distinctions. Again, the findings were precisely opposite. Most genetic differences are subtle and widely spread in terms of the geography formerly ascribed to particular "races." "The internal variations within races have proved to be greater than those between races. . . . physical, or phenotypic, features assumed to be determined by DNA are inherited independently of one another." By the mid-twentieth century, those sciences had established that there is only one human species—one physiological race—albeit one that displays variation among its members (Takezawa, Wade, & Smedley, 2020).

Throughout this chapter you will see "race" set in quotation marks. This is to remind you that there is just one human species, and that using the term "race" to define a group of humans who share a set of physical characteristics is intensely political.

8.2 "Race," Racialization, and Visible Minorities

While the idea that the world's human population can be separated, biologically, into different "races" has been disproven in science, "race" persists as a social concept, primarily in the form of racism. When we form judgments about others based solely on the colour of their skin—when we think we know something about a person we've never met simply because of the way they look—we are perpetuating the idea that people who share physical characteristics can be viewed as a social group. "Race" is a social construction of a set of behaviours assumed to be somehow related to skin colour and other features. But "race" is meaningless as a biological construction. "Race" is the mental product of social practices called **racialization**. Racialization is a social process in which individual humans are viewed as necessarily belonging to a group of (even vaguely) look-alikes, and who are assumed to be essentially inferior in terms of their intellect, morality, values, and innate worth because of those perceived similarities in physical appearance, language, dialect, or cultural heritage. Racialization is the basis for racism, which we'll consider later in the chapter.

"Race" is not just an informal social construct. Canada's population census collects information on how individuals perceive their own "race." While the questionnaire avoids the term "race" in favour of "population group," Statistics Canada states explicitly that the question is asked "to derive counts for the visible minority population," defining **visible minority** as "persons, other than Aboriginal peoples, who are non-Caucasian in race or non-white in colour" (Statistics Canada, 2017b). Here are the options available to non-Indigenous respondents in the 2016 census questionnaire:

- White
- South Asian
- Chinese
- Black
- Filipino
- Latin American
- Arab
- Southeast Asian
- West Asian
- Korean
- Japanese

There is a write-in option if none of these applies, and respondents are permitted to select more than one option. Note that many of the choices are equivalent to "country of origin." Why does the government collect information on "race"? The stated purpose is to create programs that promote equality in access to employment opportunities, health care, education, and other services.

What do you think?
"Visible minority" is a uniquely Canadian term that gained legitimacy when it was written into the 1986 Employment Equity Act. Critics argue that it's imprecise, lumping together non-white populations whose experiences are very different. Do you think we need a word for non-Caucasian, non-Indigenous Canadians?

Consider these two Canadians. For each one, would you describe their "race" as white, Black, or Indigenous?

8.3 The Racialization of Visible Minorities in Canada: A Brief History

When they say that history is written by the winners, that history is what Michel Foucault called the master narrative. A **master narrative** is the story a nation tells about itself to celebrate its past and present. It evolves over time, reproduced and refined in schoolbooks, museums, government publications, and popular culture. To a greater or lesser degree, depending on the honesty of the nation involved, the master narrative will often gloss over or omit altogether certain unpleasant events that complicate the national self-identity. Stories about the exploitation of Indigenous people or the repression of ethnic or religious minorities may be excluded, becoming what Foucault (1994) called "buried knowledge."

Canada's master narrative is the story of a harmonious multicultural society made prosperous by its open-arms acceptance of immigration and diversity. While there is much evidence to support this narrative—indeed, Canada aims to welcome 500,000 immigrants in 2025, up from 405,000 in 2021—it does not include some buried knowledge about the discrimination against various racialized groups. Canadians have recently been coming to terms with certain elements of buried knowledge, particularly around this historical mistreatment of Indigenous people, but there is still a lot to be unearthed. In the following sections, we will have a chance to dig up some of episodes that make up Canada's buried knowledge.

Indigenous People in Canada

When I was in school, the "official" version of early Canadian history presented in our textbooks described how First Nations people cooperated with Europeans to make the fur trade successful by obtaining the furs, teaching Europeans how to use canoes and snowshoes, and providing the Europeans with new foods, such as pemmican (buffalo jerky) and corn. Of course, this account overlooked the exploitation and social destruction that occurred when Europeans introduced alcohol into the fur trade, setting off a pattern of ruinous colonial intrusion into the lives and culture of Indigenous people. Canada has begun to address the buried knowledge surrounding the government's relationship with Indigenous people, issuing formal apologies to survivors of residential schools and the Sixties Scoop (see Chapter 11), but the recent Inquiry into Missing and Murdered Indigenous Women and Girls shows that we have a long way to go to address the racialization of Indigenous people in Canada.

The racialization of the Indigenous population of the Americas began in the sixteenth century in Europe, with a discussion of whether or not Indigenous people were human and had souls. To some western Europeans, Indigenous people were so different in terms of their way of life, their language, and their approach to religion (all considered unsophisticated by Europeans) that their humanity was questioned. Notwithstanding the "official" view, many of the first explorers, the coureurs de bois and the voyageurs, took Indigenous wives. The mingling of cultures was mutually beneficial. Racialization became a way to explain the whole set of differences, starting with physical appearance. It was used to justify colonial occupation of lands inhabited by this inferior "race" of darker-skinned people.

Indigenous people have been living in what is now Canada for at least 14,000 years. The first Europeans (the Norse or Viking explorers) did not arrive on Canada's eastern shores until about 1,000 years ago, and they left shortly thereafter. In fact, approximately 93 per cent of "Canadian history" is Indigenous alone. Yet as Métis writer Emma LaRocque explains, sociologically, Indigenous people have been studied most often not as founders but as problems:

> Several years ago in a sociology class on social problems, I recall wondering if anyone else was poor, because the professor repeatedly referred to Native people as statistical examples of poverty. . . . Not for one moment would I make light of the ugly effects of poverty. But if classroom groups must talk about Indians and poverty, then they must also point out the ways in which Native people are operating on this cancer. To be sure, the operations are always struggles and sometimes failures, but each new operation is faced with more experience, more skill, more confidence and more success. (1993, p. 212)

It does not help that the voices of Indigenous people have barely been heard in the sociological study of their people (Steckley, 2003). Indigenous people have only recently been able to take advantage of graduate-level work in Canadian universities, and Indigenous studies remains one of several research areas in sociology that continues to privilege outsiders.

Research and "Race" Neutrality

Clearly, complete objectivity in sociology is a myth. Sociologists bring into their research their subjectivities of gender, "race," class, ethnicity, age, and life experiences. These subjectivities can and do influence their research. The truth of this in terms of sociological research concerning Indigenous people is discussed in Shawn Wilson's *Research Is Ceremony: Indigenous Research Methods* (2008). A Cree from northern Manitoba, he currently teaches at Gnib College of Indigenous Australian Peoples at Southern Cross University in Australia. His work in Australia has enabled him to learn about how the Indigenous peoples of Australia and Canada have had similar experiences with respect to being the subjects of research engaged in by non-Indigenous scholars. He comments on some of the negative aspects of that research history: "At the very least the choice of research topic and methodology reflects researcher bias. . . . In addition, this approach focuses on problems, and often imposes outside solutions, rather than appreciating and expanding upon the resources available within Indigenous communities" (Wilson, 2008, p. 16).

Respect is a key word in Wilson's discussion of outsiders doing sociological research among Indigenous people. A good part of this involves respect for Indigenous cultural knowledge that has been passed down over generations orally, not just in writing (which he refers to as "empirical knowledge"). As he writes:

> The notion that empirical evidence is sounder than cultural knowledge permeates western thought but alienates many Indigenous scholars. Rather than their cultural knowledge being seen as extra intellectual, it is denigrated. It is the notion of the superiority of empirical knowledge that leads to the idea that written text supersedes oral tradition. For Indigenous scholars,

empirical knowledge is still crucial, yet it is not their only way of knowing the world around them. (Wilson, 2008, p. 58)

Respect is one of the three Rs mentioned by Wilson, which also include *reciprocity* (giving back to the community researched) and *relationality* (developing a meaningful relationship with the research subjects). These refer to having the Indigenous participants approve of the research and of the methods employed, and that they must feel and be safe (i.e., with respect to confidentiality and their relationship to the community).

This can be expressed in three of the "10 things to consider" of Dr Jesse N. Popp, an Anishinaabe scholar. Before reaching out to an Indigenous scholar (or an Indigenous subject or participant generally), she proposes, among other things, that you should:

> *Think about your intentions.* Do your interests genuinely support reconciliation and prioritize the rights, values and ways of knowing of Indigenous Peoples? . . .
>
> *Ensure your ideas include meaningful engagement.* We want to collaborate in meaningful ways. Never tokenize us.
>
> *Prioritize reciprocity.* Is what you have in mind of mutual benefit? Think about how we might be able to help each other. (Popp, 2021)

To a certain extent these Indigenous scholars are replicating the distinction Foucault (1994) made between a master narrative and buried knowledge. Where the master narrative celebrates a nation's past and present, it often glosses over or omits altogether certain unpleasant events and interpretations that complicate the national self-identity. **Buried knowledge** is an alternative view that comes from groups or individuals with less power and opportunity to speak. This knowledge can challenge the accepted views of the majority, making the latter look bad.

The Doctrine of Discovery

A relatively unconscious but still major support for the Canadian master narrative regarding Indigenous peoples in Canada is the **Doctrine of Discovery**. When, in the summer of 2022, Pope Francis came to apologize to Indigenous peoples for the harm that the Catholic Church did to them in residential schools for several generations, a number of Indigenous leaders called for the rescinding of the Doctrine of Discovery. It did not happen.

The Doctrine of Discovery, as it applied to the Indigenous peoples of the Americas, was declared in a Papal Bull by Pope Alexander VI in 1493. He was saying to the European explorers, soldiers, and traders who later made the trip across the Atlantic that with the authority of his position in the Catholic Church, and with the intent of converting the Indigenous peoples to Christianity, he could and did grant ownership and control of "New World" lands to the "discovering" European powers, notably Spain. Needless to say, the "discovered" Indigenous inhabitants of the Americas, who had lived on and used the lands for many thousands of years, were not consulted on the matter. They were simply objects to be Christianized and then swept aside.

Indigenous Status

Indigenous people in Canada are defined by a complex system of legal statuses that separates them from non-Indigenous people and from each other. The main designations, as defined in Canadian legislation, are:

- **registered Indian**
- Bill C-31 Indian
- band member
- reserve resident
- treaty Indian (a category with its own subdivisions, as each treaty is different)
- Métis
- Eskimo.

The legal differences come from the Indian Act, which was administered by the federal Department of Indian Affairs (now called Crown–Indigenous Relations and Northern Affairs Canada). Passed in 1876, the Indian Act enshrined a sexist definition of "Indian" as (1) any man of "Indian blood" reputed to belong to a particular band, (2) any child of such a man, or (3) any woman married to such a man. A man kept his status no matter whom he married, but a woman, if she married someone not legally an Indian, lost her status, and her children would share that fate. A non-Indian woman could gain Indian status by marrying an Indian man. This discriminatory law was in force until 1985, when Bill C-31 was passed, enabling people who had lost their Indian status through marriage or through the marriage of their mother to apply to be reinstated. (Incidentally, if "Indian" and "Eskimo" strike you as old-fashioned, they are. The terms are found in legislation written before the 1970s and should be used only in that context; the Quick Hits box that follows offers some guidelines on how to refer to Indigenous people.)

Inuit (from a word in their language meaning "people"; the singular is "Inuk") differ from "Indians," having been in Canada for a shorter time—somewhere between 5,000 and 10,000 years. It was not until 1939, when the federal government wanted to assert territorial claims in the Arctic, that Canada officially took responsibility for the Inuit. Each Inuk was given a metal disc with a number that was to be used as a token of their status. Today, about 60 per cent of Inuit have disc numbers. The lives of many Inuit changed on 1 April 1999, when the territory of Nunavut ("Our Land") came into being. Inuit make up nearly 85 per cent of the territory's 35,580 residents. They own 18 per cent of the land, have subsurface rights to oil, gas, and other minerals for about 2 per cent of Nunavut, and will receive royalties from the extraction of those minerals from the rest of the territory. They do not require a licence to hunt or fish to meet their basic needs. Nunavut is one of four regions that make up Inuit Nunangat, the Inuit homeland in Canada; the other three regions are Inuvialuit Nunangat (the Inuvialuit Settlement Region of the northern Northwest Territories), Nunavik (arctic Quebec), and Nunatsiavut (coastal northern Labrador).

The term **Métis** is used in two ways. It is commonly used, often with a lowercase *m*, to refer to anyone of mixed Indigenous and non-Indigenous heritage. With an uppercase *M* it usually refers to the descendants of (mostly) French fur traders and Cree women. Starting in the late eighteenth century, the Métis developed a culture that brought together European and First Nations elements. Over time, they achieved a sense of solidarity from their shared legal struggles with the Hudson's Bay Company (HBC) over the HBC's trade monopoly. The HBC owned most of the prairies and about half of present-day Canada, thanks to a 1670 charter granted by the English King Charles II, who knew little about the land. In 1867,

Quick Hits

Which Terms to Use and Avoid When Discussing Indigenous People

When sociologists talk about Indigenous people living in Canada, they are referring to the earliest inhabitants of this land and their descendants. The Canadian government recognizes three distinct groups of Indigenous people: First Nations, Métis, and Inuit.

While it is appropriate to speak of Indigenous people *in* Canada, you should try to avoid the expressions "Indigenous Canadians," since not all Indigenous people embrace Canadian citizenship, and "Canada's Indigenous people," which reinforces centuries of paternalistic treatment by Canadian governments. "People" is used when referring to a group of individuals or the entire Indigenous community; "peoples" is used only when referring to distinct groups (as in, *the Gitksan, Nisga'a, and other Indigenous peoples*). "Aboriginal," when used as an adjective, is an acceptable synonym for "Indigenous," but it has become less common since Canada officially adopted the UN's Declaration on the Rights of Indigenous Peoples in May 2016. Do not use "Aboriginal" as a noun (as in "Aboriginals living in Canada").

Although it is embedded in the Indian Act, the word "Indian" has gradually given way to "First Nations," just as "Eskimo" has been replaced by "Inuit" (plural) or "Inuk" (singular). Wherever possible, use the self-defined name of the community you are discussing instead of a more general term (e.g., *a Mi'kmaw woman*, instead of *a First Nations woman* or *an Indigenous woman*; and note, here, that "Mi'kmaw" is the singular and adjectival form of the plural "Mi'kmaq," which means "the people"). Keep in mind that most of the names that identify specific Indigenous peoples in history books are not the people's names for themselves, such as "Huron" rather than "Wendat."

An excellent resource for further information is *Elements of Indigenous Style*, by Gregory Younging (2018).

---

the HBC negotiated the sale of most of its lands to the federal government, which, with no regard for Métis land rights, set up a colony in Manitoba. In 1869, a college-educated 25-year-old, Louis Riel, led the Métis in a military takeover, setting up an independent government to negotiate with Ottawa. The Manitoba Act of 1870 established the province and recognized the rights of the Métis. The Métis were given *scrips*, certificates declaring that the bearer could receive payment in land, cash, or goods. But government officials and land speculators swindled the Métis out of their land, buying up the scrips for next to nothing. Most Métis moved west. In 1885, with western expansion again threatening their rights to the land, the Métis, led again by Louis Riel (who had been living a peaceful life in Montana before he was asked to lead his people), made a stand in Saskatchewan. Canadian forces attacked and defeated them. Riel was hanged for treason.

The Métis settled in a patchwork of rural prairie communities and nearly disappeared altogether. But during the 1930s, Alberta Métis pushed for the creation of communal settlements similar to First Nations reserves. In 1938, 11 Métis "colonies" were formed (eight remain). These colonies carry some political rights, making them like rural municipalities. However, they do not have rights to the royalties for oil and gas extracted from their land. Beyond these colonies, the Métis are represented by the Métis National Council and provincial organizations in Ontario and the western provinces.

Indigenous People in Canada: What the Census Tells Us

Indigenous people make up just under 5 per cent of the population of people living in Canada, but their population is growing at a rate over four times that of the non-Indigenous population (Figures 8.1 and 8.2). In the 10 years between the 2006 and 2016 censuses, the population of Indigenous people rose by 42.5 per cent, including a 51 per cent increase for Métis. The most likely reason for this increase is a heightened tendency to self-identify as Indigenous, but increased life expectancy and high fertility rates also

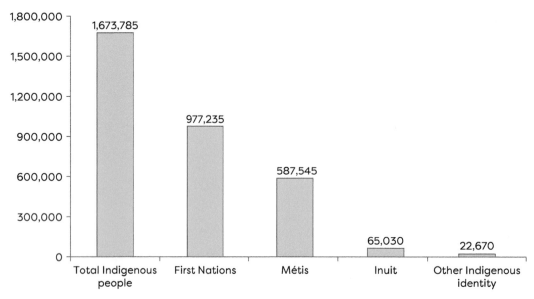

FIGURE 8.1 Indigenous Population in Canada by Identity Group, 2016

Sources: Statistics Canada (2015), p. 6, Chart 2; Statistics Canada (2018).

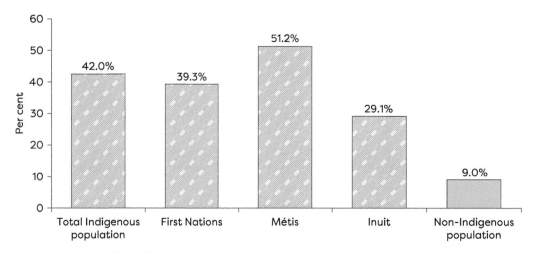

FIGURE 8.2 Increase in Indigenous and Non-Indigenous Populations in Canada by Identity Group, 2006–2016

Source: Statistics Canada (2017a).

play a role. The Indigenous population is young—the average age (32) is nine years younger than the average age of non-Indigenous Canadians—which means that their population growth will likely continue to outpace increases in the non-Indigenous population.

Colten Boushie and Helen Betty Osborne: The Racialization of Indigenous People in the Criminal Justice System

Imagine you are an Indigenous woman, a Cree mother whose 22-year-old son was killed by a white man. You are in the courtroom and you look around. The judge is white, the lawyers are white, in all probability the bailiff and other court officials are white, the witnesses called by the defence lawyer are white, and very significantly so are all of the members of the jury who will decide guilt or innocence of the white killer. How would you rate the chances that your son's killer will be found guilty?

In August 2016, Colten Boushie, from the Cree Red Pheasant First Nation in Saskatchewan, was killed by gunshots fired by Gerald Stanley, a white

No wonder the Métis population is on the rise: from the runway to the summer music festival, "going native" has become cool. For those seeking what Tuck and Yang (2012) describe as a "move to innocence," Métis ancestry is ripe for appropriation because it is perceived to be harder to disprove than First Nations official status. What is the difference between "appropriation" and being invited to join in a kinship celebration with an Indigenous group?

56-year-old farmer. Boushie and four of his friends were out in an SUV when it got a flat tire. They had been drinking. They drove up Stanley's driveway to where a number of vehicles were parked (Stanley worked part-time as a mechanic). The SUV collided with one of the vehicles, and one of Boushie's friends started an ATV that was parked nearby. Stanley became aware of the commotion and took action. Armed with a loaded semi-automatic pistol and accompanied by his 28-year-old son, he approached the youths and fired two warning shots. Boushie was sitting in the driver's seat of the SUV, asleep, when Stanley arrived at the vehicle. As Stanley reached in to turn off the ignition, his gun went off, firing two shots and killing Boushie. Stanley later claimed that it was hangfire, which occurs when a gun delays in firing.

Stanley was arrested and tried for second-degree murder. Jury selection involves assessing lists of potential candidates. In a practice known as *peremptory challenge*, a lawyer can have a jury candidate excluded. The reasons for the challenge do not have to be stated clearly. In the trial of Gerald Stanley, the defence lawyer exercised peremptory challenge for *all* of the Indigenous candidates; as a result, Stanley was tried before an all-white jury.

In February 2018, Stanley was acquitted by a jury of his peers.

This has happened before, notably in the case of Helen Betty Osborne. She was a Cree woman from Norway House, Manitoba, who was abducted and killed in 1971 by a group of young white men looking "to party" (see Steckley, 2013). She was raped repeatedly and burned. Her case remained unsolved until the late 1980s, when two of the four men implicated in her murder were charged. Notably, a lawyer for one of the accused men, defending his use of peremptory challenge, stated, "There was no deliberate campaign to keep the Natives off [the jury]. . . . But we didn't want these men to be convicted for all of the ills of society" (Priest, 1989, p. 143). In the end, one of the accused men was acquitted, while the other

What do *you* think?
1. Do you think that peremptory challenge is an instrument of institutional racism in Canada?
2. How do you think the case of Colten Boushie should have been handled?

was convicted and given a life sentence. He was released after serving 10 years. The Osborne case later became the subject of the Aboriginal Justice Inquiry, which recommended replacing peremptory challenge in such cases. The implementation of Bill-C 75 on 21 June 2019, removed the use of peremptory challenges in Canada.

Mexican Ethnicity

Most Canadians are not aware of it, but there is a well-established Mexican racialized ethnicity in Canada. It is oppressive on the people and difficult for them to escape. The federally established Seasonal Agricultural Worker Program (SAWP), part of the Temporary Foreign Worker Program (TFWP), began in 1966, when employers found that it was difficult to get sufficient numbers of Canadians to do the hard work involved for such low pay.

Between 50,000 and 60,000 migrant workers come into the country each year, and more are from Mexico than from other southern countries. Many do greenhouse work harvesting tomatoes. Work in Canada pays better than work in their home country. They can support their families, giving their children a chance to have a better life. Returning each year to do the work is important to most workers. Some have been migrant workers for 20 years or more. The program for migrant agricultural workers is not without problems, however.

The Closed Contract

The "closed contract" means the visas of the Mexican workers are tied to one particular employer with very few of the rights that Canadian workers have. This arrangement gives employers great power. If they are not satisfied with the work that the Mexicans do, or if the workers complain, the employer can fire them without "just cause," ending the visa and sending the workers back to their home country. In only a few cases have there been open contracts in which a worker can try to find work with another employer without losing his visa. Migrant workers typically keep silent about the way they are treated because their job has no security.

Furthermore, the "temporary" nature of their immigration status has also had a negative effect on these workers' access to benefits, rights, and services that citizens enjoy (Henao Castrillon, 2018, p. 49).

The Mexican Consulates and the Canadian Government

Workers' rights are given short shrift by both national governments. Where there are sufficient numbers of workers, a Mexican consulate is established in Canada. However, these consulates seem to be more concerned about the employment continuing, because it brings money to Mexico, than they are about the rights of their citizens. At the same time, the Canadian government has not defended their rights as workers in Canada. It has privatized some government responsibilities, handing them over to employer associations (e.g., the Ontario Fruit and Vegetable Growers Association), thus supporting the employers' view of and actions in situations of conflicting interests.

Working and Living Conditions

There are few health and safety checks by government inspectors on worksites. There have been problems with workers' use of hydrated lime (calcium hydroxide), a powder used in insecticides and to cure blossom-end rot in tomatoes, which can burn eyes, lungs, and skin. Workers have 10- to 12-hour shifts for up to six days a week and often complain of being verbally abused by employers and supervisors, something they see happening less often with Canadian workers. They are encouraged to compete with one another with respect to productivity, so it is difficult for them to speak as a group. Employers often note who is contributing the most, working the fastest, and those at the bottom of the list (which is sometimes posted for all to see) lose a few hours' or even a few days' pay.

If the Mexicans' working conditions are compromised, so, too, are the conditions under which they are housed. Workers often live in overcrowded bunkhouses with as many as 24 men to one dormitory. This resulted in the rapid spread of cases of COVID-19, with some dying. Even when they do not live on the job site, they sometimes live in crowded conditions in houses owned by their employers, so they are under constant surveillance.

On the Town

When the Mexican migrant workers go to town, to shop and relax after a long shift, they face "evidence of racism and racial attacks ... in stores, banks, restaurants, pubs, roads, streets, and other public spaces in the communities where they work" (Becerril, 2007, p. 134). That includes Leamington, Ontario, "the tomato capital of Canada." It could also be called the Mexican capital of Canada. In the 2016 census, the town had a population of 27,595 with 3,225 Mexican immigrants. That would not include *all* the migrant workers.

Ontario is not alone in being a difficult and unwelcoming locale for Mexican migrant workers. As Alexandra Henao Castrillon outlines in her 2018 doctoral dissertation, "A Critical Analysis of Mexican Migrant Farm Workers in British Columbia," workers in British Columbia have encountered similar workplace and community oppression and racialization.

What do you think?

1) Were you aware of the racialization of Mexican migrant workers in some parts of Canada?
2) How important are the following in reducing the racism directed against Mexican migrant workers? Score each out of 10.
   a) Providing easily accessible lessons in English.
   b) Making government services available in Spanish so that the workers will know their rights, and where they can go for help.
   c) Significantly reducing the number of "closed contracts" while increasing the number of "open contracts."
   d) Increasing health and safety inspections of both the work sites and the housing of migrant workers.
3) If you were mayor of a town or small city that had a large number of Mexican migrant workers, what would you do to try to reduce the potential for racialized contact between Canadians and Mexicans?

The Point Is ...

North American Team Sports, Racialization, and Racism

If you are a fan of North American football, you have watched this scene countless times: a white guy (the centre), flanked by four white guys (offensive guards and tackles), snaps the ball to another white guy (the quarterback), whom all five white guys try to protect. This white guy looks up, sees that there are several, mostly Black guys coming after him, and so hands the ball off to a Black guy (the running back, sometimes jokingly called the running *Black*), who gets tackled by the onrushing players. If the running back is stopped before advancing 10 yards, another white guy might come in to try to kick a field goal.

To be sure, these are generalizations. Black quarterbacks have won the Super Bowl, as have star white running backs, and in the National Football League today (November 2022) arguably the best quarterback—Patrick Mahomes of the Kansas City Chiefs—is of African American ancestry, and the best all-purpose running back—Christian McCaffrey of the San Francisco 49ers—is white. But the racialization of positions and of sports continues. In 2022, for example, for the first time since the colour bar was broken in Major League Baseball, not a single player for either team in the World Series was an African American (i.e., a Black born in the United States), although a number of players were Blacks from Caribbean and Latin American countries and the manager of the winning Houston Astros, Dusty Baker, is an African American.

From Canadian and American points of view, one of the least told but most telling stories is that of Johnny Bright. In 1951, Bright, a Black quarterback/running back (the two positions tended to be conflated at that time), was touted as the likely winner of major end-of-season awards in college football. But when his undefeated Drake University team played at Oklahoma A&M (now Oklahoma State) in October, a white defensive player for A&M targeted Bright well behind the play, after Bright had handed off, and smashed his jaw with a forearm. The photo sequence of what clearly was a racist attack won a Pulitzer

(Continued)

Drake University Archives & Special Collections

Prize for two *Des Moines Register* photographers; Bright had to wait till the team returned to Iowa to receive medical attention, including having his badly broken jaw wired shut, because no hospital in Oklahoma would treat a Black patient. One upside of the attack was that it led to mandated face masks and mouth guards for college football players. Another was that Johnny Bright ended up in Canada.

Johnny Bright was still named a first-team All-American that year, but because of his shortened season he missed out on other awards. And he chose to miss out on the National Football League. The first draft pick of the Philadelphia Eagles, he signed with the Calgary Stampeders of the Western Interprovincial Football Union (a precursor to the Canadian Football League)

rather than risk the racist taunts and targeting that would have awaited him in the NFL. After going from Calgary to the Edmonton Eskimos a couple of years later, Bright amassed Edmonton and CFL rushing records that stood for many years after his retirement in 1964. And, because Canadian professional football players especially held second jobs during the off-season (and sometimes during the season), Bright established himself as a leading educator in Edmonton, as a teacher, coach, and school principal, until his untimely death in 1983. Today, Johnny Bright School, a K–9 school in Edmonton, is named after a Black man from Drake University in Des Moines, Iowa, who chose Canada because of a racist attack on a football field in the United States (see, e.g., O'Leary, 2018; Freeborn, 2008).

Anti-Black Racism in Hockey

Hockey is the whitest professional sport in North America. The most often quoted figure is 97 per cent of the players for 2018 in the National Hockey League were white, 60 years after the first Black player in the league, Willie O'Ree, began his NHL career in 1958. It was the last major team sport in North America to have Black athletes:

> So, it should not be too surprising that there are anti-Black racist actions, sounds, and words that occur not just in the NHL, but in the minor leagues too. A recent publicized example of that occurred when five players of a PEI team hurled racist insults at Mark Connors, a Black goalie who played for Nova Scotia in a tournament held in the fall of 2021. Later that weekend in the hotel where some players were staying, Connors received more verbal abuse from PEI players, including that he should not play hockey because it is "a white man's sport." (Clow, 2022)

The players were suspended for 25 games, and they had to "complete an educational or learning experience to the satisfaction of the executive director of Hockey PEI." Significantly, this has to be more than a passive "general training session or online webinar where the player is merely present" (Clow 2022).

In the NHL in 2018 fans yelled "basketball, basketball, basketball" at Washington Capitals forward Devante Smith-Pelly as he sat in the penalty box. The "Hockey Is for Everyone" commercial begins with "Shouldn't he be playing basketball. Stick to basketball." In 2020, the NBA was about 74.2 per cent Black. It is unlikely that anyone yells "Stick to hockey" to a white player in that league.

In 2014, defenceman P.K. Subban scored a game-winning playoff goal, to which the response was racist posts on social media. In the "Hockey Is for Everyone" commercial, Subban is told by an anonymous voice, "Go back to where you belong." He replies, sitting down at a table, with a big microphone as would be used in an interview session: "This. This is where we belong." Then he pounds the table.

In January 2022, his brother Jordan was taunted in a minor league game by an opponent making monkey-like gestures. An articulate response to this is a YouTube video entitled "P.K. Subban discussed the racial act against his brother, Jordan Subban."

What do you think?

If you are a sports fan, explain to someone who does not follow sports why our understanding of sports is sociologically important. If you are not a sports fan, can you justify excluding sports from any serious analysis of society?

New Brunswick-born O'Ree was the first Black person to play in the NHL, as a winger for the Boston Bruins in the 1957–8 and 1960–1 seasons. He accomplished this despite the fact that he had no vision in his right eye due to being hit by a puck in 1955, a secret he had to hide. His family has been in Canada for more than 200 years. His escaped-slave ancestor Paris O'Ree (named after his owner's surname Horry) arrived in Canada in the eighteenth century. Paris's first child was born in New Brunswick in 1791.

After receiving a call to replace an injured player, Willie O'Ree played his first regular season game on 18 January 1958. He was interviewed on *Hockey Night in Canada* with no mention of his being Black. The *Globe and Mail* had a back-page article entitled "First Negro to Perform in the NHL, Willie O'Ree Thrilled, Nervous" (O'Ree & McKinley, 2020, p. 123).

He would experience verbal and physical abuse. In his autobiography, O'Ree states, "there wasn't a game in my first NHL season when an ugly racial remark wasn't directed at me" (O'Ree & McKinley, 2020, p. 144). He would face such abuse and get into racially provoked fights with players and opposing team fans.

He received recognition for the pioneering role he played for Black hockey players in the 1990s, culminating in his being voted into the Hockey Hall of Fame and working since 1998 as the NHL's Diversity Advisor, giving presentations at schools and conferences. Recognition also has come from those following his lead. Wayne Simmonds commented upon meeting O'Ree:

> I was meeting my hero. For every single kid who was ever told to "stick to basketball," Willie was like the first man on the moon. He wasn't just a hockey player. He was an astronaut. Without Willie, there would be no Jarome Iginla. There would be no Grant Fuhr, or P.K. Subban or Ray Emery or Dustin Byfuglien, or so many others who have had the honor of playing in this great league. There would definitely be no Wayne Simmonds. (O'Ree & McKinley, 2020, p. 229)

Blacks in Canada

Black Communities in Atlantic Canada

Black communities have existed in Nova Scotia since the British Proclamation of 1779 offered freedom to enslaved people who left their American masters to fight on the British side in the American Revolution. More came north in the first half of the nineteenth century. They were offered significantly less land and fewer opportunities than white immigrants, and they endured a litany of hardship, prejudice, and racism. Africville, originally (1835) on rural land near Halifax, is perhaps the most notorious of the enclaves that persisted despite such hardships. Yet to the rest of Canada, such communities were almost invisible. Despite their ancestors having located in Canada more than 200 years ago, Nova Scotian Blacks are treated as if they were recent immigrants when they travel west in Canada; "But where are you really from?" is a question they are often asked.

Tensions have long existed between Black and white communities in Nova Scotia, and so it is little surprise that the province was home to a Canadian civil rights hero who has only recently gained the national recognition she deserves for her role in opposing racial discrimination. Viola Desmond (1914–1965) grew up in Halifax, in a well-respected, middle-class Black and white family. Inspired by her father, a successful independent businessman, she aspired to open a beauty parlour in her hometown. However, she was unable to train as a beautician in Halifax, since very few of the city's schools accepted Black students. She pursued her education in Montreal and then in the United States. When she returned to Halifax she established a hair salon, a beauty school, and her own line of beauty products.

On a fall evening in 1946, as she was travelling on business to Sydney, her car broke down in the town of New Glasgow. Since she would have to wait several hours for repairs, she thought she would take in a movie at New Glasgow's Roseland Theatre. She bought a ticket and proceeded to a seat on the main floor. After taking her seat, she was advised that her ticket entitled her to sit in the balcony, not on the main floor, where seating was more expensive. She offered to pay the difference but was informed that she would not be permitted to sit on the main floor. She soon became aware that Blacks were expected to sit in the balcony, and that the main floor was reserved for whites. When she refused to surrender her seat, she was forcibly led from the theatre and held in jail overnight to await her trial the next day.

Desmond was charged with fraud for attempting to take a seat on the main floor without paying the one-cent tax charged for the more expensive seating. Even though she had offered to make up the difference and had been refused, she lost the case and was fined $26. The case was later appealed to the Supreme Court of Nova Scotia, where Desmond's conviction was upheld. She eventually left Nova Scotia for Montreal and, later, New York, where she died at the age of 50. Segregation in Nova Scotia was legally ended in 1954, and Desmond, long after her death, was issued an official apology and pardon by the government of her home province in 2010. She has been featured on Canada's $10 bill since 2018.

The Black One Thousand: Black Settlement in Alberta

In the late nineteenth century, many Black Americans living in the eastern United States migrated west to find a place where they would be free from prejudice and discrimination. In Oklahoma, they established all-Black communities, but many of these towns' Black residents, feeling crowded out and unwelcome, travelled north in search of a new frontier to settle. Western Canada was a promising destination. Harrison Sneed, a minister from an all-Black town called Clearview, went first to scout the land. The federal government granted him land far north in Alberta, where white settlers did not want to live and farm. And so, in 1909 Sneed returned to Alberta with a group of 194 men, women, and children. They carried more than just their hopes for the future: they brought 200 rail cars filled with their baggage, livestock, and other possessions. A group of 200 Black settlers followed shortly after, and in the years that followed, Black settlements spread across the countryside.

The white citizens of Edmonton responded predictably in 1911. They issued a petition to the federal government, signed by roughly one-quarter of the city's 24,000 residents. It began:

> We, the undersigned residents of the city of Edmonton, respectfully urge upon your attention and upon that of the Government of which you are the head, the serious menace to the future welfare of a large portion

of Western Canada, by reason of the alarming influx of negro settlers. . . . Last year several hundred negroes arrived in Edmonton and settled in surrounding territory. Already this season nearly three hundred have arrived; and the statement is made . . . [that] the advent of such negroes as are now here was most unfortunate for the country, and that further arrivals in large numbers would be disastrous. We cannot admit as any factors the argument that these people may be good farmers or good citizens. It is a matter of common knowledge that it has been proved in the United States that negroes and whites cannot live in proximity without the occurrence of revolting lawlessness and the development of bitter race hatred. (from the *Edmonton Capital*, 25 April 1911, as quoted in Cobb, 2017, p. 19)

Canadian Prime Minister Wilfrid Laurier (the guy on our $5 bill) accepted the petition that year, declaring a prohibition of "any immigrants belonging to the Negro race, which race is deemed unsuitable to the climate and requirements of Canada" (Cobb, 2017, p. 19). By 1914, the immigration that had resulted in the settlement of "The Black One Thousand," as they were known, had ceased.

The Black Population in Canada Today

The Black population of Canada has declined several times. In 1792, nearly 1,200 Black Loyalists left for the new African colony of Sierra Leone. Many more left Canada for the United States following the Civil War. Between 1871 and 1911, there was a slow decline in Canada's Black population, from 21,500 to 16,900, and a further drop (following a brief resurgence) from 22,200 to 18,000, between 1941 and 1951. It was not until the 1970s that the Black population

Once a thriving Black farming community, Amber Valley was large enough to have its own baseball team. Today, it is a ghost town. How is this story of Black settlement in Alberta at odds with the prevailing narrative of how western Canada was settled?

began to increase consistently, rising from 34,400 in 1971 to 239,500 by the end of the decade (Milan & Tran, 2004, p. 3).

According to the 2016 census, close to 1.2 million people who identified as Black were living in Canada, representing the third-largest visible minority population in the country (Figure 8.3). About 37 per cent of Black Canadians were living in Toronto, where they made up 7.5 per cent of the city's population (Statistics Canada, 2019). Montreal, where Blacks are the largest visible minority group, had the second-largest Black community in Canada, thanks to recent immigration from former French colonies such as Haiti, Rwanda, Chad, and Cameroon. In fact, the Black population in Quebec grew by 142 per cent from 1996 to 2016, and by 70 per cent from 2006 to 2016 (Table 8.1).

Asian Canadians

As of the 2016 census, two-thirds of visible minority Canadians were of Asian ancestry, with South Asians and Chinese Canadians making up the two largest visible minority populations in the country (see Figure 8.3). Asian Canadians do not always face the same barriers to success that other racialized minorities do, and so they are in some ways the heroes of the master narrative of Canada that I described earlier. But this ignores many pieces of buried knowledge, not least being the large increase in hate crimes targeting Chinese Canadians in the wake of the COVID-19 pandemic (discussed at the end of this chapter).

Chinese immigrants began to settle on Canada's west coast in the mid-nineteenth century, arriving first from American cities such as San Francisco, and then directly from China. They were driven

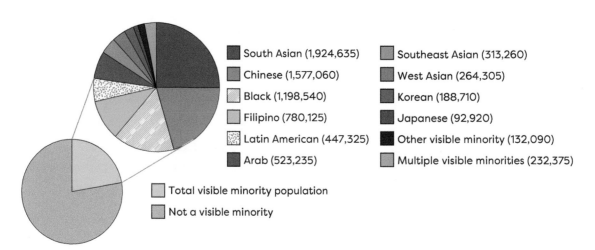

FIGURE 8.3 Visible Minority Populations in Canada, 2016

Source: Statistics Canada (2017b).

TABLE 8.1 Canada's Black Population by Region: Total, Percentage, and 10-Year Growth Rate, 2006–2016

Region	British Columbia	Prairie Provinces	Ontario	Quebec	Atlantic Provinces	Territories
Total Black population	43,505	174,655	627,710	319,230	32,080	1,350
Share of total population	1.0%	2.8%	4.7%	4.0%	1.4%	1.2%
Growth rate 2006–2016	+53.6%	+157.5%	+32.5%	+69.7%	+27.2%	+125.0%

Source: Statistics Canada (2019).

from China by poverty and political upheaval and drawn to British Columbia by opportunities to work. Thousands of Chinese labourers (estimates range from 7,000 to 15,000) helped to build the Canadian Pacific Railway, risking their lives for lower rates of pay than other workers and being tasked with the most dangerous jobs. Not only did their contributions go unrecognized, but in 1885—the same year the last spike of the CPR was driven at Craigellachie, BC—Chinese immigrants were targeted by Canada's first "head tax."

Head Taxes and an Act to Prevent the Employment of Female Labour

From the time they arrived in British Columbia, Chinese immigrants were viewed by the predominantly white European settler population with suspicion verging on disgust. To stall the influx of undesirable immigrants, the federal government, in 1885, imposed a $50 head tax on any Chinese migrant entering the country. There were similar policies in place in the United States, New Zealand, and Australia, but no other immigrant group in Canada was targeted with an entry fee. In 1900, when it was clear the policy was not stalling immigration enough to appease anxious British Columbians, the government doubled the head tax to $100 and then, under continued pressure from politicians and residents of the province, increased the tax to $500 in 1903. To put this in perspective, it has been estimated that the average Chinese labourer made around $300 a year (Chan, 2019).

The new tax had a dramatic effect on Chinese immigration, as it was meant to do. For the overwhelmingly male population of Chinese immigrants who had already settled in Canada, it meant the chances of marrying a Chinese woman were greatly reduced (the ratio of Chinese men to Chinese women in Canada in 1911 was roughly 28 to 1). While this limited population growth among Chinese Canadians, the gender imbalance became a new cause for panic among white Canadians, who worried that white women would be subjected to unwanted advances by desperate Chinese men, although as many white women might be as interested in interracial relationships as not. It was this kind of worry that led the government of Saskatchewan, in 1912, to create the Act to Prevent the Employment of Female Labour in Certain Capacities. It declared:

No person shall employ in any capacity any white woman or girl or permit any white woman or girl to reside or lodge in or to work in or, save as a *bona fide* customer in a public apartment thereof only, to frequent any restaurant, laundry or other place of business or amusement owned, kept or managed by any Japanese, Chinaman or other Oriental person. (quoted in Backhouse, 1999, p. 136)

Two months after the legislation was enacted, restaurant owner Quong Wing was convicted and fined for employing two white women. His appeals to the supreme courts of Saskatchewan and Canada failed. Twelve years later, in 1924, a Regina restaurateur, Yee Clun, challenged the law. He had strong support from members of the city's Chinese and non-Chinese communities. But local newspapers were spreading poorly researched stories of Chinese men bringing opium into Saskatchewan and turning white women into "drug fiends." Clun won the case in court but found his efforts foiled by the Saskatchewan legislature, which passed another statute authorizing any municipal council to revoke the court ruling. The Act was not repealed until 1969.

In 1923, amid renewed immigration from China, the Canadian government enacted its firmest anti-immigration measure to date. The Chinese Immigration Act, sometimes called the Chinese Exclusion Act, banned nearly all Chinese migrants from entering Canada. At the time, roughly 82,000 Chinese immigrants had come to Canada since 1885, paying around $23 million in taxes to do so. It would take 24 years for the Act to be repealed (it violated the Charter of the United Nations, which Canada signed in 1945) and 20 years after that for Chinese immigration to Canada resume.

Japanese Canadian Soldiers in World War I

During World War II, roughly 22,000 Japanese Canadians were placed in internment camps and dispossessed of their property because Canada was at war with their country of origin and designated them retroactively as "enemy aliens." It is a shameful but well-known episode in Canadian history. Less well known is the story of Japanese Canadian soldiers who volunteered to serve in the Canadian Expeditionary Force in World War I. At first they were turned away, just as many Indigenous volunteers were. But by 1916, year three of the war, at least 222 had been admitted. It is interesting that although the majority of them lived in British Columbia, only 28 enlisted in that province, while 169 enlisted in Alberta, where they believed their chances of being accepted in the army were better. Japanese Canadian soldiers tended to be grouped together in sections of the battalions to which they belonged. Some fought and died at Vimy Ridge, in a battle that has become an important part of Canada's national narrative.

Japanese people had been in Canada since the 1870s. Many came from Japanese fishing villages and, once in Canada, settled in fishing communities along the west coast. Their service in World War I earned them no favours from the federal government. In 1919, the year after the war ended, the federal Department of Marine and Fisheries responded to growing concern that Japanese Canadian gill net salmon fishers were "taking over" at the expense of white Canadian fishers. In the words of Port Alberni MP Major R.J. Burde, reported in the Victoria *Colonist* in May 1920, "they have become so arrogant in their feeling of security that many white settlers are reaching the limit of tolerance" (quoted in Adachi, 1976, p. 105). In response, the government drastically reduced the number of licences that Japanese Canadian fishers could obtain. The new law had a swift impact: in just three years, white fishers gained 493 licences (an increase of 33.5 per cent), while Japanese fishers lost 974 licences (a drop of 48.9 per cent).

In 1920, the same year a Japanese Canadian War Memorial was dedicated in Vancouver's Stanley Park, the Japanese Canadian veterans' association lobbied for the right to vote in provincial elections; this was not granted until 1931. Eleven years later, when Canada declared war on Japan, the perpetual light shining on the Japanese Canadian War Memorial was extinguished. A branch of the Canadian Legion that was home to many Japanese Canadian veterans was shut down and many of its members interned. Among them was the branch's head, Masumi Mitsui, who had been awarded the Military Medal for his leadership in World War I. In 1985, at the age of 98, Mitsui was part of a ceremony commemorating the relighting of the Japanese Canadian War Memorial (Dick, 2010).

Not Wanted on the Voyage: The *Komagata Maru*

Most of the first South Asians to come to Canada were Sikhs, who had been given special status by the British for their service as soldiers and police serving imperial purposes throughout the world. In 1904, they began to arrive in small numbers, many of them settling in Port Moody, east of Vancouver. By 1906, their numbers had increased considerably, with as many as 5,000 Sikhs entering the country between 1905 and 1908 (Johnston, 1989, p. 5; Burnet & Palmer, 1988, p. 31). They were young men, most of them single, though a good number had wives back in India. They arrived in British Columbia at a time when there was a shortage of labourers willing to work in the sawmills, on the roads, and in the bush, cutting wood and clearing land. Many settled in Vancouver, while Vancouver Island received some of the first communities of these immigrants. Some were greeted with a measure of respect because they were British army veterans, and they soon earned a reputation for their hard work. An October 1906 report in the Vancouver *Daily Province* quoted one employer as saying, "I would have White labourers of course if I can get them. . . . But I would rather give employment to these old soldiers who have helped fight for the British Empire than entire aliens."

BC's natural resources-based economy has long fluctuated between periods of success and recession. Slow times produce unemployment, and newcomers are accused of taking jobs from whites. It wasn't long before the initial acceptance of the hard-working Sikh immigrants was undermined by a growing unease over their rise in numbers. The local press fuelled the simmering discord with stories about the unfamiliar cultural practices of these "Hindus" (as South Asians collectively were called, regardless of their religion). "Hindus Cover Dead Bodies with Butter" announced a headline in the *Daily Province* in October 1906 (quoted in Johnston, 1989, p. 3).

Amid a growing moral panic, Vancouver police began taking Sikh immigrants directly from the immigration shed to the BC interior to keep them out of the city. In spite of the deplorable accommodations in which they were placed, the Sikhs showed tremendous resilience, as Johnston records:

Two thousand had arrived during the latter half of 1906. By the end of December, with the exception of some 300 who had taken steamers for Seattle and San Francisco, all but fifty or sixty had found employment in British Columbia, most of them in saw mills. The authorities would gladly have deported any convicted of vagrancy, but there were few such cases; those who were out of work were looked after by their companions, and . . . none became a public charge. (Johnston, 1989, p. 3)

Nevertheless, opposition to the immigrants broke into hostilities in anti-Asian riots in several cities down the Pacific coast in 1907.

Facing pressure from white British Columbians affronted by the influx of Sikh immigrants and from British government officials in India who wanted to curtail emigration, the Canadian government responded with insidious discrimination. They passed a law requiring that all Asian immigrants entering Canada possess at least $200—a large sum for people who typically earned about 10 to 20 cents a day and eight times the amount required of white immigrants. In what was known as "Continuous Journey" legislation, they also prohibited the landing of any immigrant arriving directly from any point outside of India—significant because most Sikhs were making the journey from Punjab province by way of Hong Kong—while pressuring steamship companies not to provide India-to-Canada service or to sell tickets to Canada from Indian ports. These measures brought Sikh immigration to a halt. Unable to bring their wives and families over, denied the right to vote or hold public office, and facing open discrimination, Canada's Sikh population became discouraged.

Opposition to Sikh immigration continued to grow. In December 1913, the *Daily Province* claimed that the "Hindu problem" had assumed "a most serious and menacing aspect" (Johnston, 1989, p. 22), even though only 39 Sikhs had entered the area that year. However, during the run-up to World War I, the Germans saw alliances with Indian plots as a way of undermining the British. In December 1912 an attempted assassination of the British Viceroy Hardinge was just one of many signs of unrest in India. In the United States, immigrant Indians, both workers and students, were involved in the support of Indian nationalism. San Francisco was the pivotal point for organizing the Ghadar coalition, which

Germany intended to foster. The following spring, the Japanese steamship *Komagata Maru* left Yokohama, Japan, for Hong Kong to pick up a contingent of immigrants headed for Canada. Rented by a 55-year-old Sikh, Gurdit Singh, a Singaporean businessman who supported the Ghadar (a Punjab–American–German conspiracy, which was one of three such violent, inter-related plots during World War I) efforts to overthrow the British Raj in India, the ship carried 376 passengers, including two women: 340 Sikhs, 24 Muslims, and 12 Hindus. Two dozen were Punjabis from the north of India, which was the hotbed of opposition to British rule. However, the entire load of passengers were being recruited to the Ghadar cause while en route to Canada. News of the ship's approach was announced in the newspapers with headlines such as "Boat Loads of Hindus on Way to Vancouver" And "Hindu Invasion of Canada." Why did these people come when they knew they were challenging an existing law? The year before, the law had been *successfully* challenged in a Vancouver court. Unfortunately for the revolutionaries, the Canadian government knew that some of the Indians on board intended to agitate in Canada for the overthrow of British rule in India because Gurdit Singh, the organizer of this challenge to Canadian law, was an outspoken Ghadar supporter. When the ship reached Vancouver in May 1914, the local South Asian community was ready with lawyers, funds, and food to assist the passengers, but local immigration officials, politicians, and vigilante groups also were ready. The passengers were not allowed to disembark. For about two months, government officials prevented anyone trying to aid the ship's passengers, so they were forced to endure severe shortages of food and water during the legal battle. Only 24 of the passengers were permitted to enter Canada. In July 1914, the passengers and the *Komagata Maru* were forced to leave. Two weeks later, World War I began. But the conspiracies and collaborations between the Punjabi dissidents, the Germans, and other anti-British groups, such as the Irish, continued to play out in India. Meanwhile, Canada had joined England and France against Germany.

Not surprisingly, immigration policies did not change quickly for South Asians after the end of the war in 1918. A few of the men were able to bring to Canada their long-absent wives and children, but most could not afford such an expense. By 1941,

Vancouver Public Library, Special Collections, Accession Number: 6231

Sikh passengers aboard the *Komagata Maru*. Despite the fact that Sikhs have been in Canada since 1904, their visibility still prompts the question, *Where are you from?*

there were no more than 1,500 South Asians in Canada. Most were men, many aged between 50 and 65. Only when India was granted its independence from British imperial control in 1947, laying to rest insurrectionist goals of Indians worldwide, were South Asians given the vote and full citizenship status.

When Immigrants Are Refugees

We have seen that East Asian immigrants arriving in large numbers are greeted with suspicion by Canadians. What if they are refugees?

A case to consider is that of Vietnamese Canadians. In 1954, the French regime in Vietnam was overthrown by a resistance force in the north, backed by China and led by Ho Chi Minh. The country was partitioned into two states, the northern one Communist, the southern one not. Eager to contain the spread of communism, the Americans aligned themselves with the government in the south and devoted massive amounts of soldiers, weapons, and money to a fight they could not win. In 1973, they withdrew from the war, which ended two years later with the reunification of the country under Communist rule.

Following the war, Vietnamese people from the south, fearing retaliation and oppression, began to leave their country, many in small boats barely capable of making the dangerous journey across the Pacific. With these "boat people" heading for Canadian shores, the federal government in 1976 passed new legislation that defined refugees as a separate class of immigrant. Refugees would not have to meet the admission criteria imposed on other immigrants.

In 1979–80, Canada received some 60,000 refugees from Vietnam and neighbouring Cambodia and Laos. The federal government promised to aid the refugees by matching funds raised by individual citizens, churches, and other private organizations. During that summer, while working at Sainte-Marie among the Hurons, I took part in two fundraisers: a positive contribution I could make after strongly opposing the American presence in Vietnam.

The striking thing about this episode is the empathy with which Canadians viewed the Vietnamese boat people. I wonder if Canadians today continue to regard Vietnamese people more positively than they do immigrants from other East Asian countries.

I also wonder if Canadians feel the same degree of acceptance toward refugees generally versus other immigrants. How would you research such a question?

8.4 Ethnicity

Ethnicity and "Race": What's the Difference?

Earlier in the chapter I commented on historical attempts to identify different human "races." These quasi-scientific efforts were based mostly on analyzing biological features, including skin, hair, and eye colour, facial profile, height, and even brain size. While we have established, scientifically, that there is but one human race, the legacy of those efforts is that we continue to lump people into different categories of "race" based primarily on visible characteristics.

"Race" is something you are socialized into. It has nothing to do with your nationality, the language(s) you speak, or your cultural practices. It is based on how you look to socialized others, and throughout your life you will be judged by it, favourably or unfavourably, by some people. It is also a category that may be supported or denied by the state and other social institutions. You did not choose your "race" and probably cannot opt into another one. I could not, for instance, stand in front of a room of students and claim to be Filipino, since it would be apparent to everyone that I am not.

Ethnicity is different. It refers to membership in a particular national or cultural group in the world. Ethnicity differs from "race" in several ways. First, most people identify with just one "race" but may have many ethnicities. Imagine you were born in Italy and moved to Canada with your family as a child. Your father is Italian; your mother is Canadian and Jewish. You may consider yourself mostly Canadian, since you grew up in Canada, but your sympathies may lie with Italy during soccer's World Cup. Though you are not religious, you may, because of your mother's heritage, feel a deeper connection to the suffering of Jews when your class is studying World War II. While you may look "white" to others, your ethnicity is multifaceted and not necessarily easy to see or to define.

Unlike "race," ethnicity is something you can opt into, as many people do when they cite a distant forebear from Ireland as a pretext to celebrate St Patrick's Day. This sleight of hand leads to another key difference between "race" and ethnicity: physical appearance seldom yields any clues to our ethnic affiliations. I *could* stand before a class and claim a whole range of ethnicities—Manx, Walloon, Abruzzi, Cajun—that would be difficult to contest.

Your ethnicity is not the same as your nationality, though it may be (if, for instance, your family has lived in Canada for so many generations that you feel no connection to the culture of your distant ancestors who came to this country from somewhere else). And ethnicity is no clue to your "race."

To understand the difference between nationality, ethnicity, and "race," imagine you were born in Canada to parents who immigrated to Quebec from Haiti. Your nationality is Canadian. That may also be your primary ethnic affiliation, though you may feel equal or greater connection to various other ethnicities, including Haitian (the nationality of your parents), Caribbean (reflecting the broader culture of the Caribbean islands), Québécois (emphasizing a strong cultural connection to the province), or francophone (signifying an affinity with the broader French-speaking community). Your race is "human," but your "race" is likely to be Black, reflecting the racializing view of people considering the predominant skin colour of the population of Haiti.

Approaches to the Study of Ethnicity

Everyone belongs to at least one ethnic group. Membership in an ethnic group can be a source of pride, but differences among ethnic groups living together can also be a source of conflict.

There are many ways to study ethnicity, but I will concentrate on five approaches that are particularly useful in understanding ethnic conflict. The first three—*social constructivism, instrumentalism,* and *essentialism*—are commonly used in political sociology. Canadian sociologist Wsevolod W. Isajiw (1933–2023), who specializes in ethnic studies, discusses the third of these, essentialism, in relation to the *epiphenomenal approach*, which is helpful to consider here as well. Finally, I will introduce a fifth approach, *postcolonialism*, because it is essential to understanding ethnicity in the context of the case study I am about to present.

One of the most destructive ethnic conflicts of recent times involved two rival tribes, the Hutu and the Tutsi, in the central African country of Rwanda.

Rwanda was a colony of Germany and then of Belgium from 1890 until 1962, when it gained independence. The period that followed was punctuated by uprisings by the disenfranchised Hutu majority against the ruling Tutsi elite, causing the deaths of hundreds of thousands of civilians in both groups. The violence peaked in the spring and summer of 1994, when Hutu military forces massacred between 500,000 and 1,000,000 of the Tutsi minority, sending more than a million destitute Hutu civilians, fearing reprisals from the surviving Tutsi population, fleeing to refugee camps in neighbouring Zaire (now the Democratic Republic of the Congo) and Tanzania.

What causes neighbouring ethnic groups to become so hostile toward one another? It is easy to put it all down to tribal violence, but the situation is more complicated. We can better understand it by looking through the lens of our five theories of ethnicity.

Telling It Like It Is

A Student's Point of View

My Silent Ukrainian Identity

I was an adult when I informally learned of the *Holodomor*. During the 1930s, [the Soviets, under Communist Party leader Joseph] Stalin systematically starved and killed millions of Ukrainians. That horrid history lesson was absent from the social studies classes I attended as a youth. My Ukrainian grandfather never spoke of the genocide, and I think I know why. In 1933, my grandfather was the tenth of 10 children born to Ukrainian immigrants. Had my great-grandparents decided to stay in the motherland instead of departing for Canada in 1907, the Ukrainian branch of my family tree may have never existed.

Our surname caused my grandfather grief. Throughout his later life, I heard my grandfather recount the attempts some made to discredit his ethnicity. His acquaintances would say that "Kondro" isn't a Ukrainian name. It doesn't end in "ski," they'd say. You don't have a proper Ukrainian name, they'd say. You're not Ukrainian, they'd say. Nonetheless, my grandfather always identified with his Ukrainian ethnicity; he appreciated the food and the ethnic sense of humour.

My Ukrainian family members have performed extensive genealogical work. We can now accurately trace our own ancestry back to the mid-eighteenth century. However, there was an emotional and ethnic existential cost for our ancestral knowledge. Our Ukrainian family has ties to Poland; an uncle to my grandfather has Polish birth records. My grandfather was deeply troubled when he learned that he *could* be Polish. I remember him saying, "I don't want to be Polish."

A young "Galician" immigrant in Saint John, NB, in May 1905. Canada's Ukrainian population is among the highest in the world outside of Ukraine and Russia, yet during World War I many Ukrainian Canadians were put in internment camps, since much of present-day Ukraine was then territory of the Austro-Hungarian Empire, with which Canada was at war. Was this a case of ethnic prejudice or a practical necessity in wartime?

What was more troubling was my grandfather's uncle was placed in an internment camp in Banff, Alberta, during World War I; he was deemed an enemy alien and forced to perform manual labour. Various documents show he escaped in exile, first to Saskatchewan and then to the United States. The uncle left for Russia in 1920. After 1937, he wasn't heard from again.

I wasn't sure how I should feel when I learned of the interned relative and the genocide. I never saw myself as a Ukrainian like my grandfather and his immediate family saw themselves. Though my white identity is not threatened with starvation or unjust internment, I silently identify with the Ukrainian portion of my ethnic genes. I was always the closest to my Ukrainian grandfather.

The horrid history lesson of the *Holodomor* gave my silent Ukrainian identity a new emotional identity. It was a bad time for Ukrainians, but my family was simply lucky. When some stayed, others took a chance on Canada. Their gamble is paying dividends to their descendants. The sadness I feel for my distant relatives is silent. My white privilege consciously mutes it.

Now that my grandfather is dead, I expend more thinking than I ever have before on his life and his immigrant parents' lives. I took for granted that my grandfather was uniquely Ukrainian and though he spoke sparingly of the attempts to discredit his ethnicity, I never recognized the full implications of his family's immigration to Canada.

—Jonah Kondro

Essentialism

Essentialism (sometimes called **primordialism**) is the view that every ethnic group is defined by a list of traits carried down from the past to the present with little or no change. So, for instance, we could look at the traits that differentiated the Tutsi and Hutu. The Tutsi were, on average, taller and thinner than the Hutu, with longer and thinner faces. One study (Chrétien, 1997) found that the Tutsi averaged 1.75 metres in height, while the Hutu measured 1.66 metres. The tribes also differed in terms of occupation: before colonialism, the Tutsi were mostly pastoralists who owned and herded cattle; the Hutu were agriculturalists, growing crops.

Essentialism presents a static view of ethnic culture, in which culture does not change without the influence of outside forces. Applied to our case study, it ignores the fact that the differences were not absolute: some Hutu herded cattle, some Tutsi grew crops, and intermarriage between the two groups was not uncommon. Adopting the essentialist view uncritically leads to believing that the ethnic conflicts in Rwanda have a deep history that existed long before colonialism, and that these conflicts reignited only after the "stabilizing influence" of the colonial power left. In this way, it absolves colonial powers of any blame. However, cultures are not static. They change and react to inside and outside influences, both natural (e.g., hurricanes, drought, earthquakes)

and human (e.g., neighbouring warfare, the rise of leaders, the transmission of disease). Colonization is only one of many other potential causes of cultural change.

Postcolonialism

Colonialism is the economic and political exploitation of a weaker country or people by a stronger one. Because the history of the modern world is often tied to European colonization, we often hear about the European states that dominated an African, Asian, or American people. We don't need to look far to see how European settlers and successive federal and provincial governments wielded colonial control over Indigenous peoples in Canada.

Postcolonialism (or **anti-colonialism**) is a framework that analyzes the destructive impact colonialism has on both the colonizer and the colonized. This viewpoint was first developed by writers such as **Frantz Fanon** (1925–1961) and **Albert Memmi** (1920–2020) to examine French colonies in North Africa and their fight for independence from France. Fanon, born in the French West Indian colony of Martinique, was radicalized by his work as a doctor and psychiatrist in Algeria during the fight for independence there. His influential works *Black Skin, White Masks* (1952) and *The Wretched of the Earth* (1961) address the psychological effects of colonization and have inspired considerable sociological study. Memmi was a Jew born in predominantly Muslim Tunisia, which gained its independence in 1956. In *The Colonizer and the Colonized* (1957), he demonstrates how the two groups negatively conditioned each other, and how no party could be "neutral" in the relationship between the two.

Postcolonial theory, as it applies to ethnicity, identifies colonialism as a factor in the conflict between ethnic groups. In the African context, it is usefully applied to study situations involving **indirect rule**, a governance policy in which a European nation uses the members of a tribe or ethnic group as its intermediaries in ruling African territory.

In Rwanda prior to the colonial period, a person's sense of identity was derived mainly from lineage and clan. Lineage heads were important figures, and a single clan could include members of both Hutu and Tutsi ethnic groups. Under colonialism, lineage heads lost power to chiefs appointed by colonial administrators. Drawing on the conclusions of European social scientists, these administrators saw the Tutsi as a superior conquering race, based on the physical differences noted earlier and the fact the Tutsi appeared to have come to Rwanda after the Hutu. As a result, when appointing chiefs, the colonial administrators overwhelmingly favoured Tutsi. The blurred lines of distinction between Tutsi and Hutu became solid, reinforced by the fact that Rwandan citizens now had to carry identification cards showing their ethnic group. This produced an ethnic-based class system with Tutsi at the top and Hutu at the bottom.

Ethnicity as Epiphenomenal

"Epiphenomenal" describes a secondary effect that arises from, but does not causally influence, a separate phenomenon. Marx first applied it in a sociological context. He believed that economic structure was the main causal factor in society, and everything else was epiphenomenal.

Epiphenomenal theory suggests that any ethnic conflict is just a by-product of the struggle between economic classes. Thus, the strife in Rwanda stems from a situation in which the country's wealthy elite (the Tutsi) were exploiting its poor (the Hutu and the poorer Tutsi). Ethnicity made it impossible for Hutu and poorer Tutsi with shared class interests to overcome their oppression by the Tutsi elite. This was because poorer Tutsi identified more with the wealthy Tutsi than they identified with the Hutu who were, like them, being exploited. There is a measure of truth in the epiphenomenal explanation, yet it fails to fully account for why the poor identified with the rich.

Instrumentalism

Traditionally presented as opposite to essentialism, and compatible with the epiphenomenal approach, is instrumentalism, which focuses on emerging ethnicity rather than on long-established ethnic characteristics. It acknowledges that elites can mobilize others who identify with them ethnically. In the words of political scientist Catharine Newbury, ethnic groups are created or transformed when they "gain self-awareness (become 'self-conscious communities') largely as the result of the activities of leaders who mobilize ethnic followings in order to compete more effectively" (1993, p. 15).

Elite members who mobilize ethnicity for personal gain are called **ethnic entrepreneurs**. The classic example of ethnic entrepreneurship is Adolf Hitler's construction and manipulation of the German "Aryan race." A more contemporary example is the manipulation of vulnerable sectors of American society with false statements by Donald Trump. In our case study, an instrumentalist approach better explains how frustrated Hutu leaders could invoke the injustice of Tutsi oppression to draw poorer Hutu into their political parties and their acts of revolution. It also explains why poorer Tutsi identified closely with the Tutsi elite.

Social Constructivism

Social constructivism is the view that ethnicity is "artificial," constructed by individuals to serve some agenda. Like instrumentalism, it explains how ethnicity is constructed by the elite. However, as a theory of ethnicity it suffers by overstating the influence of the elite. It generally fails to attribute to the non-elite members *any* agency, any power to act without being manipulated. A social constructivist theory of ethnicity would look to the motivations of the broader group.

The social constructivist approach makes sense of the Rwandan genocide. For most of the twentieth century, Rwanda was a very crowded land, where many people, particularly Hutu, experienced malnutrition because their farms were insufficient for their

AP Photo/Ben Curtis

Twenty-five years after the 1994 Rwandan genocide, children play in the streets of Mbyo, one of six "reconciliation villages," where convicted perpetrators who have been released from prison after publicly apologizing for their crimes live side by side with genocide survivors who have professed forgiveness. How do villages such as Mbyo undermine social agents for divisive ethnicity? What stumbling blocks might they encounter?

needs. People suffered through famines and cattle diseases even as the country's population rose, causing farm size to shrink. Social constructivism helps explain why the rural Hutu became so thoroughly engaged in driving off and killing local Tutsi.

Summary

What happened in Rwanda? We can say that, prior to colonialism, the experience of being a member of an ethnic group was not a major part of the day-to-day lives of most Rwandans. It did affect the people's sense of identity in the way lineage, clan, and chiefdom did. Under the Belgians, a dual colonialism developed in which Europeans and elite Tutsi collaborated to forge a rigid ethnic divide between Hutu and Tutsi. And when Belgian rule ended in 1962, the common oppression experienced by Hutu of all classes sparked a social revolution in which the majority Hutu overthrew their oppressors, only to set up an ethnic dictatorship of their own. Ethnic violence

was a predicable outcome, and easily fanned racial hatred, combined with a powerful need for land, led in 1994 to the massacre of the Tutsi and neutral Hutu.

8.5 Landmarks in the Sociological Study of "Race"

Standpoint theory argues that the perspective sociological researchers bring to their work is so strongly influenced by their social location, their perspective as it is shaped by gender, age, ethnicity, sexual orientation, and other social characteristics, that objectivity is not possible. This does not mean that sociologists should study only "their own people." But pioneers in the sociological study of specific groups—women, for instance, or Black people—are often those who belong to the group themselves. They bring unique and valuable insights to the study. In this section, we will look at some of the pioneers in the sociological study of "race" in North America.

W.E.B. Du Bois: The First Black Sociologist

W.E.B. Du Bois (1868–1963) was the first African American sociologist. He researched and wrote about the major problems concerning Africans, both those living in the United States and those living elsewhere. He was a "pan-Africanist," meaning he looked at the connection between the oppression or success of Africans and that of their descendants around the world.

Du Bois's sociology had an applied perspective to it. He was one of the founders of the National Association for the Advancement of Colored People (NAACP). He used his position as editor-in-chief of their magazine, *Crisis,* to advocate for causes such as opening up training schools for Black military officers and initiating legal action against white people who lynched African Americans. He was a prolific writer, producing several landmark studies, including *The Suppression of the African Slave Trade in America* (1896), *The Philadelphia Negro* (1896), *The Souls of Black Folks* (1903), *Black Reconstruction* (1935), and *Dusk of Dawn* (1940). The following excerpt captures his oratorical power and sense of justice:

It is the duty of Black men to judge the South discriminatingly. The present generation of Southerners are not responsible for the past, and they should not be blindly hated or blamed for it. . . . The South is not "solid"; it is a land in the ferment of social change, wherein forces of all kinds are fighting for supremacy; and to praise the ill the South is today perpetuating is just as wrong as to condemn the good. Discriminating and broad-minded criticism is what the South needs—needs it for the sake of her own white sons and daughters, and for the insurance of robust, healthy mental and moral development. (Du Bois, 1903)

Daniel G. Hill: The First Black Canadian Sociologist

Although he was not born in Canada, Daniel G. Hill (1923–2003) is considered the first Black Canadian sociologist. Born in Missouri, Hill moved to Canada in his late twenties to study sociology at the University of Toronto, receiving his MA in 1951 and his PhD

[*left*] In his work as director of the Ontario Human Rights Commission and, later, as ombudsman of Ontario, Daniel Hill reached out to Ontarians of all ethnic and cultural backgrounds. The pamphlet shown here testifies to the importance he placed on the accessibility of his position to all provincial citizens. [*top*] Daniel G. Hill, ombudsman of Ontario, circa 1985.

in 1960. His primary writings include "Negroes in Toronto: A Sociological Study of a Minority Group" (1960) and *The Freedom Seekers: Blacks in Early Canada* (1981). However, Hill is best known for his applied sociology work. He was a researcher for the Social Planning Council of Metropolitan Toronto (1955–8), executive secretary of the North York Social Planning Council (1958–60), and assistant director of the Alcoholism and Drug Addiction Research Foundation (1960). In 1962, Hill became the first full-time director of the Ontario Human Rights Commission, and 10 years later he became Ontario Human Rights Commissioner. He formed his own human rights consulting firm in 1973, working at various times for the Metropolitan Police Service, the Canadian Labour Congress, and the government of British Columbia. From 1984 to 1989, he served as Ontario's ombudsman, fielding complaints from citizens concerning their treatment by provincial government agencies. In 1999, he was made a Member of the Order of Canada.

Crenshaw, Collins, and Intersectionality Theory: Tracking "Race" and Gender

Intersectionality is an increasingly important concept in current sociological research. It refers to the way different social factors—"race" and ethnicity, gender, sexuality orientation, class, age, and disability—combine to shape the experience of a minoritized group. It recognizes that, for instance, the discrimination and prejudice experienced by a young Black woman is different from that experienced by a young white woman or a young Black man.

Intersectionality theory was first developed by Kimberlé Crenshaw, and then elaborated shortly thereafter by critical sociologist Patricia Hill Collins in *Black Feminist Thought: Knowledge, Consciousness and the Politics of Empowerment* (1990). Intersectionality theory argues against the notion, promoted by early white liberal feminists, that the experience of being "female" is basically the same for all women. It states that gender is experienced differently, with unique forms of oppression when combined with negatively valued social locations, such as certain minoritized ethnicities (e.g., African American, Hispanic, Indigenous, and South Asian). Gender-based stereotypes, when combined with racial prejudice, create an **interlocking matrix of domination**

> ### What do *you* think?
> Indigenous groups have organized to provide safe places, night transport, and counselling for vulnerable girls and women, many of whom have escaped violent situations at home only to find themselves homeless and without the means to secure stable housing in cities such as Vancouver, Toronto, and Winnipeg. What should federal, provincial, territorial, and municipal governments do to remedy the situation? How can other organizations help?

significantly more powerful and oppressive than gender alone.

In Canada, the interlocking matrix of domination has been experienced painfully by many Indigenous women. This led to the five-year National Inquiry into Missing and Murdered Indigenous Women and Girls, which heard testimony from 2,386 people, including 1,484 family members of victims. The release of the inquiry's final report, in June 2019, coincided with the publication of a book (Jolly, 2019) about Tina Fontaine, an Anishinaabe teen from the Sagkeeng First Nation in Manitoba, whose lifeless body was found in Winnipeg eight days after she was reported missing in August 2014. Her body had been wrapped in plastic and dumped into the Red River, weighted down with rocks. The publicity surrounding her case, in which the man charged with her murder was found not guilty, triggered the call for the national inquiry. Her case led social service agencies and volunteer groups to establish new programs to help at-risk Indigenous girls and women. The stories are told. It is time now for action to take place.

William Julius Wilson and the Culture of Poverty

How you explain racial inequality may depend on where you fall along the political spectrum. At one end of the spectrum are far-right conservatives who attribute high rates of poverty, incarceration, and substandard housing among Black people to two factors: the individuals and their culture. According to this view, which has been criticized as "laissez-faire racism," Black people are individually responsible for the situations they find themselves in, but through hard work they can find their way out of poverty. Government assistance fails because it keeps them from taking ownership of a situation they control.

At the left end of the spectrum are liberals who ascribe poverty among Blacks and other racial minorities to systemic, or institutional, racism that is built into the social structure. Liberals accuse conservatives of blaming the victim; conservatives accuse liberals of making excuses for people who have made bad choices. The best explanation is far more nuanced and lies somewhere between these oversimplified, polarized views.

An interesting explanation was proposed by American anthropologist Oscar Lewis (1914–1970), who studied poverty among villagers in Mexico, Puerto Rico, and northern India. In each of these cases, he observed what he called a "culture of poverty." Essentially, he saw among the poor he studied an entrenched set of attitudes that were handed from one generation to the next, keeping the people from aspiring to better circumstances. These attitudes include widespread feelings of powerlessness, inferiority, and "personal unworthiness" (Lewis, 1998).

Enter Black sociologist William Julius Wilson (b. 1935), with his important and controversial work *More Than Just Race: Being Black and Poor in the Inner City* (2009). Wilson argues that both structural and cultural forces are involved in the urban poverty of Black people. Structural forces include what he calls *social acts*—"stereotyping; stigmatization; discrimination in hiring, job promotions, housing, and admission to educational institutions," and so on—and *social processes*, which are "laws, policies, and institutional practices that exclude people on the basis of race or ethnicity" (Wilson, 2009, p. 5).

These structural forces that Wilson identifies as contributing to Black poverty are uncontroversial. Where his argument takes a more contentious turn is in his discussion of the cultural forces that keep Blacks from finding middle-class jobs and inclusion in the broader society. Wilson's cultural forces fall into two categories: national views and beliefs on "race," and cultural traits. National views come from the stereotypes perpetuated uncritically through news and entertainment media. These views are reinforced when white people experience Black people

in settings that confirm those stereotypes. White people may "see" *only* the homeless Black person pushing a shopping cart's worth of belongings into a downtown alleyway; they may not "see" the Black investment banker, lawyer, or schoolteacher.

Cultural traits, according to Wilson, may also "contribute to the perpetuation of poverty." He describes these as

> shared outlooks, modes of behavior, traditions, belief systems, worldviews, values, skills, preferences, styles of self-preservation, etiquette and linguistic patterns that emerge from patterns of intragroup interaction in settings created by discrimination and segregation and that reflect collective experiences within those settings. (2009, pp. 14–15)

Wilson argues that certain beliefs and behaviours prevalent among Black people can keep them from climbing out of poverty. As an example, he describes "street smarts," a set of behaviours adapted to get by in tough neighbourhoods:

> It is wise to avoid eye contact with strangers and keep to yourself. This mind-set may also lead someone to approach new situations with a certain level of skepticism or mistrust. Although such an approach is logical and smart in an unsafe neighborhood, the same behavior can be interpreted as antisocial in another setting. Moreover, this street-smart behavior may, in some cases, prevent individuals from performing well on job interviews, creating a perception that they are not desirable job candidates. (Wilson, 2009, pp. 17–18)

Another set of behaviours could be called the "code of shady dealing," to borrow a term coined by Wilson's student Sudhir Venkatesh in *Off the Books: The Underground Economy of the Urban Poor* (2006). The back-alley market for drugs, stolen goods, and other legal and illegal items exists as "a response to circumstances in inner-city ghetto neighborhoods, where joblessness is high and opportunities for advancement are severely limited" (Wilson, 2009, p. 19). The underground economy is not random or

What do you think?
By citing cultural factors that contribute to Black poverty, are Lewis and Wilson blaming the victims?

A clip from the TV show *Cops* shows a suspect being taken down in Fontana, California. The immensely popular reality show, which has been running since 1989, has generated controversy over its portrayal of poor and racialized minorities. How might Wilson view the role of shows like *Cops* in perpetuating Black poverty?

unregulated: it is governed by its own code of rules, and operating in this space requires a very particular set of skills.

8.6 Current Issues in the Study of "Race" and Ethnicity

Racism

Racism can be understood as the product of four linked elements. The first is *racialization*, the construction of certain groups of people as different and biologically superior or inferior. This fosters ideas of relative worth and quality, which leads to **prejudice**, the "pre-judgment" of others on the basis of their group membership. The third element is **discrimination**, which involves individuals being treated differently—rewarded or punished—based on their group membership. Finally, there is *power*, manifested when institutionalized advantages are regularly handed to one or more groups over others.

American psychologist and educator Beverly Daniel Tatum touches on the importance of power in this equation:

> People of color are not racist because they do not systematically benefit from racism. And equally important, there is no systematic cultural and institutional support or sanction for the racial bigotry of people of color. In my view, reserving the term *racist* only for behaviors committed by Whites in the context of a White-dominated society is a way of acknowledging the ever-present power differential afforded Whites by the culture and institutions that make up the system of advantage and continue to reinforce notions of White superiority. (Tatum, 2003, p. 10)

In other words, without power, non-white people can be prejudiced but not racist. They can perform discriminatory acts, but they cannot be racist without institutional, structural, ideological, and historical support.

This is certainly true of systemic racism, which by definition involves power. Recently, though, sociologists have been studying how racism exists even among people of the same ethnic or racial group. **Colourism**, sometimes called shadeism, refers to the unique experience of a racialized person based on how light or how dark their skin is. For instance, in a study of people living in Vancouver and Toronto, sociologist Gerry Veenstra found that darker-skinned Black people were more likely than lighter-skinned Black people to report poor mental and physical health, "indicating that colourism, processes of discrimination which privilege lighter-skinned people of colour over their darker-skinned counterparts, exists and has implications for well-being in Canada" (2011, p. 1152). Colourism is also evident in the preference for lighter skin shown by people outside but also within a particular racialized group, such as Blacks, Latin Americans, and South Asians. The likelihood is that the preferences of the dominant white culture in some aspect of life they want to inhabit has influenced their beauty standards and ideals, the way some Orientals choose to have eyelid folds created surgically to look more like Westerners.

There are different kinds of racism. **Racial bigotry** is the open, conscious expression of racist views by an individual. When racist practices, rules, and laws become institutionalized, then we have **systemic** (or **institutional**) **racism**. The Chinese Exclusion Act (1923–47), which prohibited the immigration of Chinese people from China and other countries, is an example of systemic racism. Canada's residential school system, aimed at suppressing Indigenous culture, is another example of racism.

What do you think?

1. Do you have racist feelings or ideas? How are they different from your views of different ethnicities? How are they different from your view of different religions?
2. Are you in some ways engaged in making Canada a post-racial society? Are you recognized for those efforts by people of different "races"?

Sometimes, racism can be subtle, hidden behind a smile or words that seem friendly to the person performing the gesture. This is called **friendly** (or **polite** or **smiling**) **racism**. Henry Martey Codjoe provides an example:

The realtor who showed our house to prospective buyers quietly hinted that if I wanted my house to sell quickly, I would have to remove all traces of anything that indicated that Blacks had lived in the house: no family pictures, no African art or crafts, everything Black or African must go, and we must be out of the house before he showed the house to prospective buyers. He would call and let us know. No matter what we were doing, we must leave. One time we were late in getting out and we ended up hiding in our minivan in the garage. When he showed the garage, we ducked. It was a shameful and degrading experience. The house sold, but my wife and I never did meet the family that bought it. (Codjoe, 2001, p. 286)

A common form of friendly racism is the *micro-aggression*, a casual remark or gesture that reflects racial prejudice and causes offence. In many cases, micro-aggressions aren't intended as insults; they may even be misguided compliments or attempts at conversation. Even so, they are offensive. Though the comments may be spoken without any intent to cause insult or self-consciousness, they are hurtful because they reflect the speaker's awareness of racial difference and preconceptions based solely on the visible racial characteristics of the person addressed. A good example of a micro-aggression is contained in the title of a book by Ojibwa writer Drew Hayden Taylor, who called his 1996 collection of essays, *Funny, You Don't Look Like One: Tales of a Blue-Eyed Ojibway*. Here are some remarks that are considered micro-aggressions:

- Where are you really from?
- What are you?
- I never think of you as Black.
- You're really pretty for a . . .
- But you sound white.

Moviestore collection Ltd / Alamy Stock Photo

"Fair skin has been in favour for, what, the past hundreds of years. But, now the pendulum has swung back. Black is in fashion!" Starring Daniel Kaluuya (shown here), Jordan Peele's 2017 horror comedy *Get Out* satirizes white liberal envy of Black people and culture. Is Peele's target systemic racism or friendly racism?

Quick Hits

Racism

Racism is the product of four linked elements:
- racialization
- prejudice
- discrimination
- power.

Different kinds of racism include
- racial bigotry
- systemic (institutional) racism
- friendly (polite/smiling) racism
- colourism.

Carding and Racial Profiling

Despite their long history in this country, particularly in Atlantic Canada and southern Ontario, Black people are often regarded as relative newcomers. Canadians are sometimes smug about our role in helping slaves escape the American South during the eighteenth and nineteenth centuries, but slavery was practised in pre-Confederation Canada, and many freed American slaves were treated with hostility and contempt upon their arrival here.

Black people today continue to be racialized by mainstream Canadian society. Blacks are greatly over-represented in our prisons: from 2005 to 2015, the Black inmate population grew by 69 per cent (versus 10 per cent for the inmate population overall), and the rate of incarceration for Black people is three times their rate of representation in society, according to Canada's correctional investigator, Howard Sapers (2015). There is evidence—difficult to obtain because Canada does not keep race-specific crime data—that while Blacks may be over-represented in some forms of violent crime, they also are victims of bias in policing and the administration of criminal justice (Owusu-Bempah & Wortley, 2014). Like Indigenous people, Blacks are often targets of racial profiling, a form of prejudice in which people are suspected of criminal activity based solely on racial characteristics and other aspects of their physical appearance, such as clothing. Racial profiling is often at play in the practice of carding, in which police stop, question, and document people when no offence has been committed, ostensibly as a way of gathering intelligence in crime-prone neighbourhoods. In the fall of 2018, the Nova Scotia Human Rights Commission hired Scot Wortley, a professor of criminology at the University of Toronto, to investigate the rate and manner in which Black people in Halifax were subjected to random street checks. His finding that Blacks were six times more likely than white people to be stopped led to calls for an end to carding in the city (Wortley, 2019). In November 2017 the Ontario Human Rights Commission announced an inquiry into racial profiling by the Toronto police (OHRC, 2017). The findings of the inquiry, as reflected in the second interim report, were hardly surprising: Black people in Toronto are much more likely to be arrested, to be charged and over-charged, and to be struck, shot, or killed by Toronto police than are any other demographic groups (OHRC, 2020).

Telling It Like It Is

A Black Canadian's Point of View

The Skin I'm In: Being Interrogated by Police—All Because I'm Black

When I was 22, I decided to move to Toronto. . . . In Toronto, I thought I could escape bigotry and profiling, and just blend into the crowd. By then, I had been stopped, questioned, and followed by the police so many times I began to expect it. In Toronto, I saw diversity in the streets, in shops, on public transit. The idea that I might be singled out because of my race seemed ludicrous. My illusions were shattered immediately. . . .

I was carded for the first time in 2007. I was walking my bike on the sidewalk on Bathurst Street just south of Queen. I was only steps from my apartment when a police officer exited his car and approached me. "It's illegal to ride your bike on the sidewalk," he informed me. "I know, officer, that's why I'm walking it," I replied edgily. Then, the cop asked me for ID. After sitting in front of the computer inside his car for a few minutes, the officer returned nonchalantly and said, "Okay, you're all set." I wanted to tell him off, but thought better of it and went home. I still don't know what he saw when he ran my name.

Over the next seven years, I was carded at least a dozen times. One summer evening in 2008, two friends and I were stopped while walking at night in a laneway just north of my apartment, only a few hundred metres from where I was carded the first time. Two officers approached in their cruiser, briefly turning on their siren to get our attention. Once they got out of the car, they asked us what we were doing. "We're just walking, bro," I said. The cops immediately asked all of us to produce identification. While one officer took our drivers' licences back to his car, the other got on his radio. I heard him say the word "supervisor," and my stomach turned. Within 60 seconds, a second cruiser, marked S2, arrived in the laneway, and the senior officer at the wheel got out to join his colleagues.

The officer who had radioed for backup returned and asked us to empty our pockets. As the supervisor watched, the radio officer approached us one at a time, took our change and wallets and inspected them. He was extremely calm, as if he was thoroughly accustomed to this routine. "I'm going to search each of you now to make sure you didn't miss anything," he explained. I knew it was my legal right to refuse, but I couldn't muster the courage to object. The search officer approached me first. "Before I search you, I want you to tell me if I'm going to find anything you shouldn't have," he said gravely. "I don't have anything," I replied, my legs trembling so violently I thought they'd give out from under me.

The officer patted down my pockets, my pant legs, my jacket, my underarms. He then repeated the search with my two friends, asking each of them before touching them if he would find anything. One of my friends spoke up: "I have a weed pipe in my back pocket, but there's nothing in it." The officer took the pipe and walked with the supervisor to the car with the officer who had taken our ID. As the policemen huddled for what felt like an hour, my friend apologized. "It's not your fault," I replied. I cursed myself for choosing that route rather than staying on Queen Street, where hundreds of people would have been walking. Here, we had no witnesses.

When the officers finally came back, they returned the pipe to my friend. "Are any of you currently wanted on an outstanding warrant?" asked the search officer. We all said no. "Okay, guys, have a good night," he said. I was still too scared to move, and apparently my friends were too; we just stood there and looked at the cops for a second. "You can go," the officer assured us. I made sure not to look back for fear they'd interpret some outstanding guilt on my part. I was certain that the police had just documented my name along with the names of my friends, one of whom was carrying a pipe for smoking an illegal substance. This information would be permanently on my record.

After years of being stopped by police, I've started to internalize their scrutiny. I've doubted myself, wondered if I've actually done something to provoke them. Once you're accused enough times, you begin to assume your own guilt, to stand in for your oppressor. It's exhausting to have to justify your freedoms in a supposedly free society. I don't talk about race for attention or personal gain. I would much rather write about sports or theatre or music than carding and incarceration. But I talk about race to survive. If I diminish the role my skin colour plays in my life, and in the lives of all racialized people, I can't change anything.

—Desmond Cole

What do *you* think?
What effect has carding had on the writer of this narrative? What effect do you think these interactions have on police?

Race-Based Hate Crime in Canada

A hate crime is an act of aggression or intimidation motivated by prejudice against an identifiable group defined by its race, religion, or sexual orientation, designed to harm or terrify not just the victim but the group to which the victim belongs. Hate crimes include advocating genocide, inciting or promoting hatred, or causing damage to property associated with an identifiable group (for instance, a place of religious worship).

In 2017, there were 2,073 reported hate crimes in Canada (Armstrong, 2019). While the total made up just 0.1 per cent of all police-reported crime, it represented a year-over-year increase of 47 per cent, with the largest increases occurring in Ontario and Quebec. The majority of those hate crimes—43 per cent—were motivated by hatred of race or ethnicity. Figure 8.4 shows the distribution of hate crimes by racial or ethnic group. The greater part of the criminal activity motivated by hatred of race (56 per cent) was non-violent, most of it falling under the heading "mischief," which can include, for example, graffiti painted in a public place. While the number of reported hate crime incidents is low, it is worth noting that as many as two-thirds of all hate crimes go unreported (Dauvergne & Brennan, 2011).

During 2020, the first year of the COVID-19 pandemic that originated in China, hate crimes targeting East and Southeast Asians increased by just over 300 per cent, with 269 police-reported hate crimes directed at this group, compared to 67 in 2019. This was a larger percentage increase than that for any other demographic group, although Blacks and Indigenous people continue to bear the brunt of Canadian hate crimes. As Statistics Canada summarized, "a total of 2,669 hate crimes were reported to the police in Canada in 2020" (Yun, 2022). Notable here is the phrase "reported to the police," as many more assaults and abuses will not have been reported, least of all by those from relatively small and scattered communities who fear additional attacks.

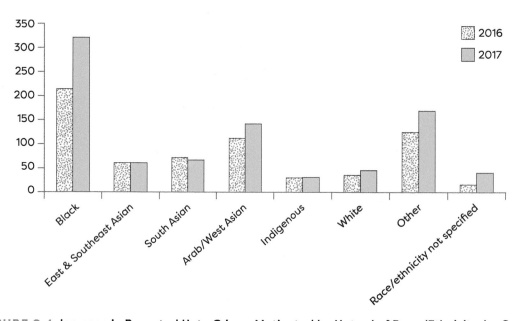

FIGURE 8.4 **Increase in Reported Hate Crimes Motivated by Hatred of Race/Ethnicity, by Group, 2016–2017**

Note: "Other/unspecified" includes motivations based on race or ethnicity not otherwise stated (e.g., Latin American, South American) as well as hate crimes that target more than one race or ethnic group (such as immigrants generally).

Source: Armstrong (2019, Chart 6).

Wrap It Up

Summary

There are no human "races." From a sociological standpoint, "race" (or, rather, racialization) is a social process that reflects the ways in which people of different ethnic background are treated, and have been treated over time, by institutions such as our provincial and federal justice systems, our legislative bodies, our schools, and the media. It's also about how we view one another. Racism or hatred of the Other applies to how Indian Hindus sometimes view Pakistani Muslims, not only in India but in Leicester, UK, in the weeks following a cricket match in the Asia Cup that India won (Firstpost, 2022). Racism is how Hutus view Tutsi and Twa in Rwanda. The mutual distrust of the Dutch-speaking Flemish and the French-speaking Walloons in Belgium has created social tensions and outbreaks of violence for over a hundred years. The Irish and British have made peace relatively recently, but only after centuries of violence, subjugation of the Irish by the British, and political executions. It is understandable that immigrants complain about racism when they settle in a new country, but the country they left is probably as full of racism and ethnic conflicts as the Canada they expect to be "different." It is tempting to turn the tables by accusing everyone of racism. Yet not all Canadians in our complex, diverse society are racist. No one should be held responsible for the racism of their ancestors. That will only make it more difficult for the younger generations to depart from that past.

However, racism is also a process, one that not only appears in personal biases and discrimination but becomes embedded in some of the social institutions we deal with every day. At the same time, racism certainly exists in some individuals. When their racism is supported by those social institutions, other individuals and political leaders can take steps to change those institutions so that racist individuals become and remain a small minority. Social support can be withdrawn from the features of institutions that maintain racism. For example, the police can be challenged and procedures changed. While the cessation of carding is not enough to alter systemic racism, it is a step forward.

Think Back

Questions for Critical Review

1. Explain what it means to say that "race" is a social construct rather than a biological one.

2. What is "white privilege"? What benefits belong to someone in Canada who is white? Are there any disadvantages to being white?

3. "Passing," in sociological terms, is the practice of downplaying or disowning an ascribed status by claiming another. Can a person ever pass for a "race" other than the "race" one was born into? Can a person pass for an ethnicity other than the ethnicity one was born into? Under what circumstances might *you* want to do so? What might the consequences be?

4. Are we in Canada getting closer to achieving a "post-racial society," in which "race" is not used as a way to categorize people and treat them differently? Is a post-racial society possible? Are there any post-racial societies in countries that you know of? How much do you think your answer depends on your own "race"? Do you know of any post-racial groups in your university?

5. According to the 2016 Census, 1 in 5 Canadians is a member of a visible minority. What characterizes a "visible minority"? The term is used in federal legislation. Why does the government distinguish between visible minorities and ethnic minorities?

6. Provide some examples of cases in which Canadian governments enacted new laws in response to moral panics around immigration. Who, in each case, were the moral entrepreneurs? What did they stand to gain?

7. What "races" are represented among those in Immigration Canada who make decisions about who can come into the country and how long they can stay? Have the "races" of people in those positions of authority had an influence on immigration policies over the past 50 years?

8. How is institutional, or systemic, racism different from other forms of discrimination?

9. What efforts are being made in Canada at present for people of different religions attached to ethnicities to communicate and find common ground?

Read On

Suggested Print and Online Resources

Adjusting to Canada: From ABCs to -40 Degrees, www.cbc.ca/archives/entry/ adjusting-to-canada-from-abcs-to-40-degrees
This 10-minute CBC interview from 1981 examines the experience of a Vietnamese refugee recently arrived in Canada.

Kay J. Anderson, *Vancouver's Chinatown: Racial Discourse in Canada, 1875–1980* (Montreal and Kingston: McGill-Queen's University Press, 1991)
A classic study of how "Chinese" and "Chinatown" have been expressed in the Vancouver area over a little more than a century.

Joanna Jolly, *Red River Girl: The Life and Death of Tina Fontaine* (New York: Viking, 2019)
Contains all that has been discovered to date about the circumstances concerning the violence that triggered the National Inquiry into Missing and Murdered Indigenous Women and Girls.

Ali Kazimi, director. *Continuous Journey.* Documentary film (2004)
This documentary deals with the *Komagata Maru* incident off the coast of Vancouver in 1914, placing it in the larger context of British imperialism, white supremacy in Canada, global anti-colonialism (i.e., the Ghadar Party), and contemporary measures against immigrants in this country.

Chris O'Leary, "In an Era of Systemic Racism, Bright Found Acceptance in Canada," 8 August 2018, https://www.cfl.ca/2018/08/08/era-systemic-racism-bright-found-acceptance-canada/
An account of Johnny Bright's impact in Canadian professional football and in the Edmonton community, told in large part from his daughter's point of view.

Ontario Human Rights Commission, "A Collective Impact: Interim Report on the Inquiry into Racial Profiling and Racial Discrimination of

Black Persons by the Toronto Police Service," November 2018, https://www.ohrc.on.ca/en/public-interest-inquiry-racial-profiling-and-discrimination-toronto-police-service/collective-impact-interim-report-inquiry-racial-profiling-and-racial-discrimination-black
This first interim report reveals "a lack of legal basis for police stopping or detaining Black civilians in the first place; inappropriate or unjustified searches during encounters; and unnecessary charges or arrests."

Lisa Priest, *Conspiracy of Silence: The Riveting Accounting of the The Pas Murder, Cover-up, and Inquiry* (Toronto: McClelland & Stewart, 1989)
Also made into a miniseries by the CBC (https://www.imdb.com/title/tt0101070/)

Reclaiming Power and Place: The Report of the National Inquiry into Missing and Murdered Indigenous Women and Girls, www.mmiwg-ffada.ca/final-report/
The product of the five-year inquiry into the causes and effects of the disappearance and killing of Indigenous women and girls in Canada.

Wanda Robson and Ronald Caplain, *Sister to Courage: Stories from the World of Viola Desmond, Canada's Rosa Parks* (Wreck Cove, NS: Breton Books, 2010)
Viola Desmond's sister, author and educator Wanda Robson, has done much to keep her sister's story alive since Viola's death at the age of 50. This is Wanda's account of Viola's story.

"Secret Alberta: The Former Life of Amber Valley," www.youtube.com/watch?v=OxXJubB2cPQ
This 15-minute video offers a look into the history of one of the larger Black farming settlements in Alberta, now deserted.

"Shades of Black: Colorism, Skin Color Discrimination," www.youtube.com/watch?time_continue=313&v=E3IzTyjhHLc
In this 7-minute documentary by Reginald James, people of different racial backgrounds discuss their experiences of colourism.

Tim Stelloh, "How *Cops* Became the Most Polarizing Reality TV Show in America: What One of TV's Longest-Running Reality Shows Says about Race and Our Relationship with the Police," January 2019. https://longreads.com/2018/01/22/how-cops-became-the-most-polarizing-reality-tv-show-in-america/
An examination of how reality TV has shaped North American understandings of "race."

"The Skin I'm In: I've Been Interrogated by Police More Than 50 Times—All Because I'm Black," http://torontolife.com/city/life/skin-im-ive-interrogated-police-50-times-im-black/
This is the full text of Desmond Cole's article, excerpted in the box "Telling It Like It Is: A Black Canadian's Point of View," which appeared in an April 2015 issue of *Toronto Life* magazine.

⑨ Gender, Sex, and Sexuality

Reading this chapter will help you to . . .

- Explain the difference between sex and gender.
- Describe what makes sex and gender social constructs.
- Cite some examples of the way in which society continues to be "gendered."
- Name some of the factors that explain why men or women may be over-represented in a particular kind of work or course of study.
- Explain what toxic masculinity is.
- Define sexuality and comment on how it relates to sex and gender.
- Talk about the stereotyping involved in the intersection of female gender and minoritized ethnicity/race.

For Starters

What It Takes to Be a "Real Man"

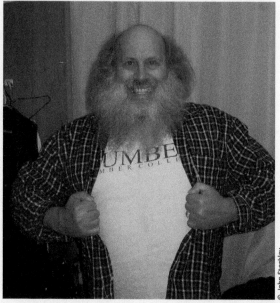

In 1982, American writer Bruce Feirstein published a short, tongue-in-cheek guide to male behaviour. It was called *Real Men Don't Eat Quiche*, and its memorable title quickly entered public discourse, even among those who hadn't read the book. It was a standard quip in conversations about what men do (or don't do), particularly when those conversations centred on activities viewed in mainstream North America as traditionally feminine—activities like baking, gardening, or figure skating. *No, I would not like to go to the quilting bee, and I don't eat quiche, either.*

But the title of Feirstein's satire on gender stereotypes was more than a punchline. In a decade when North American society was deeply suspicious of effeminate men and openly hostile toward homosexuals, "real men don't eat quiche" became a motto for the would-be "macho man," an idealized cisgender (socially aligned with his birth sexuality) heterosexual man embodying (supposedly) desirable male characteristics—good looks, sex appeal, strength, self-assertiveness. I had my own rules, many of them formed a decade or so before Feirstein's book was published.

Although I felt "secure in my masculinity," as we used to say, I would never . . .

- use an umbrella (in part because I lived in Newfoundland for a while, where "real men" were not afraid of getting wet)
- use a hair dryer (it seemed effeminate to blow my really long hair around like an actor in a shampoo commercial)
- use a snowblower instead of a shovel, or a leaf-blower instead of a rake (rakes are easy to operate: skinny end up, wide end down)
- shake hands in a "wimpy way"
- wear cologne or body spray (women *should* smell good; men should try not to smell bad)
- own more than three pairs of shoes (if I had to buy new shoes, I got rid of an old pair first)
- use the word "lovely"
- have a manicure or a pedicure.

I still use a shovel instead of a snowblower, by the way, and I try to meet a minimum standard of grip strength when shaking hands—evidence of how things we learn when we're young can become fixed in our sense of self and difficult to unlearn later.

As we will see in this chapter, "masculinity" is a social construct: like social concepts of "femininity," it is a set of attitudes—belonging to a particular time and place—about how men (or women) are expected to behave. Where do these ideas come from? There is nothing innately masculine about the traits I listed above. They were all learned—indirectly or, in some cases, directly—from role models I had growing up as a white, straight male in North America: from male family members, male characters I admired on TV (mostly cowboys), rockers I idolized, teachers I mostly hated, and friends in my peer group who, like me, had been socialized to believe there was such a thing as a "real man" as opposed to someone we might have called a wimp, a sissy, or a "homo," without having any real idea of what homosexuality entailed.

Feirstein's book is now close to 40 years old, but the old myth of the "real man" persists. It is the bedrock of toxic expressions of masculinity reflecting ideas about male superiority and how real men are supposed to defend their status, control women and children, and settle conflicts. We will also explore these ideas in this chapter.

> **What do you think?**
>
> How do you think the way you view masculinity and femininity differs from the attitudes of your parents and grandparents? Has what it means to be a man or a woman changed since your parents were your age? What socializing influences (family, friends, media, etc.) have conditioned your view of gender roles?

Quick Hits

The Contested Meaning of "Macho"

"Macho," from a Spanish word for a male animal, was a popular term in the late 1970s and 1980s for men showing aggressive pride in their masculinity. It became entrenched in mainstream North American discourse in 1978, when the Village People recorded their hit "Macho Man." Like their follow-up singles "Y.M.C.A." and "In the Navy," the song was a not-so-subtle tribute to gay male culture, but its double meanings were missed by listeners who thought it was simply a catchy disco homage to the heterosexual manliness believed to typify cowboys, police officers, leather-clad bikers, and construction workers—personas the band adopted. The moniker "Macho Man" was used by the actor/wrestler Randy Savage, a star of the wrestling circuit in the late 1970s and 1980s. Wearing flamboyantly "gay" costumes, his character, set up as an antagonist to more "heroic" characters, would routinely bully his manager, Miss Elizabeth (actually his wife) to jeers from the audience. Savage's campy performance was designed to entertain and rile up the audience, but many feminists of the time criticized the term as embodying patriarchal norms of masculine behaviour, including aggression and violence toward women.

9.1 Introduction: Sex, Gender, and Social Construction

Let's begin at the beginning—of life. Some babies are born with a combination of male and female sexual organs. These babies are "intersex." A Turkish study (Aydin et al., 2019) has found the percentage to be higher than previously thought. In an analysis of about 14,200 newborns, 18 had ambiguous genitalia. That's a rate of 1.3 in 1,000 births—much higher than the rate of one in 4,500 to 5,500 reported in previous studies. Fifteen of the newborns were diagnosed with 46,XY DSD, a condition in which a male infant can't use testosterone properly or testicles don't develop properly. Babies with the condition had lower birth weights, the investigators found. In addition, preeclampsia—a pregnancy complication character-ized by high blood pressure—was common in those pregnancies. As the Turkish researchers noted, "these findings support the hypothesis that early pla-cental dysfunction and androgen deficiency might be important in the etiology of male genital anomalies."

In other words, some proportion of such in utero developments might be prevented with proper pre-natal care of the mothers. Vitamin B with folic acid is a common supplement used by pregnant women to prevent other birth defects and might be helpful in preventing this form of intersex. An intersex person, Pidgeon/Jennifer Pagonis, who was raised as a female, explains the shock felt when a college teacher de-scribed Androgen Insensitivity Syndrome in class. "I was like, 'Oh. My. God! That's the thing the teacher was talking about' . . . And then I went into like a freefall" (Whitelocks, 2015). Experts today advocate against the sorts of surgeries that were common 35 years ago. Sometimes, those involved in the overall identifica-tion of the infant's genetic and physical profile make the wrong guess about gender, which is not discovered by the individual until puberty or later. If possible, it is advisable not to make permanent surgical changes until adulthood. Or not at all, as we shall see.

In the context of the sociology of medical re-search, perhaps in regard to gender, we might ask: Why have some lines of study not been pursued dil-igently? One concerns the concept of lateralization, which we know is active during fetal development because an extremely high proportion of infants are born with the language centres in the left cerebral hemisphere where they normally develop further during childhood, the heart develops asymmetri-cally toward the left side of the thoracic cavity, the appendix usually is on the right side of the colon (al-though anomalies appear fairly often), and so on.

A somewhat vague assertion among doctors, psychiatrists, and homosexuals exists that the con-dition of being gay or lesbian is not only gendered through social forces but fundamentally biological, although no one has put forth a clear theory. One prominent member of the gay community in San Francisco is a neurologist who has discussed the concept of sexual attraction in terms of laterality. Dr Jerome Goldstein (2008) states:

Qazi Rahman of Queen Mary University of London felt that handedness might have

something to do with being gay. [Of] 23,000 men and women in North America and Europe studied in the year 2000 [it was] found [that] being non-right handed . . . [carried] an increased chance of being gay in 34% [of] men and 90% [of] women. He concluded that his findings might have in-dicated a biological "error" where he more appropriately should have concluded that his findings were a biological "fact."

According to the French otolaryngologist Alfred Tomatis (2005), handedness develops not through a biological difference in the limbs or in the gonads but because the hearing apparatus normally is dom-inated by the right ear through (1) the number of nerves that disproportionately serve the opposite hemisphere of the brain (right ear to left-brain; left ear to right-brain) and (2) the mechanism of speech in the left-brain language centre that is neurolog-ically dominated by the right ear for the additional reason that the left-brain vagus nerve activating the larynx muscle has a shorter, more direct connection to the larynx than the right-brain's vagus nerve ac-tivating the larynx muscle; that is, the right branch of the vagus descends the neck into the chest, loops around the aorta to join the left, recurrent nerve that ascends the neck to the larynx.

From this point, the discoveries of the Indian American neurologist Vilayanur S. Ramachandran are helpful: the two halves of the brain normally are specialized to different functions: the left-brain to analytical and structured thinking, the right-brain to fluid or holistic and emotional awareness. (His stud-ies were of mentally normal amputees, so the inte-gration of these faculties was a given.) This normally asymmetrical arrangement in hearing and speaking that sorts the influences of the left, rational brain and the right, emotional brain into two separate streams with a time differential, which is then inte-grated by the left-brain's Wernicke's area and turned into speech by Broca's area, is interrupted if the right ear mechanism is not strong. Tomatis expressed this as "needing to learn to listen." But the mechanism per se may need repair. So-called will power cannot be exerted unless the left, rational brain is dominant, which depends on the strength and flexibility of the right ear. If not corrected, it can and does create a wide spectrum of handedness running from strong right-handedness through ambidexterity to a range of intensities of left-handedness. When weakness in the right ear interrupts the normal flow of sound energy through the nerves, abnormal neural pathways create abnormal learning; more specifically, greater influence by right-brain tendencies on how the left-brain can function. This discovery by Tomatis does not mean that all left-handed people are or could become gay, or dyslexic, or schizophrenic (or, generally, "loopy" like lefty Ned Flanders on *The Simpsons*!), or any of the other conditions that have been found to be associated with left lateralization. But it does offer biological evidence that gender preference has a set of biological correlates. To complete this neurological sketch, weakness in the left ear deprives the right-brain of the energy that elevates mood and, therefore, this can create a range of depression.

While the torture of "conversion therapy" has been outlawed in some countries and the celebration of gay and lesbian and other degrees of gender identification are better accepted in North America now than formerly, people with sexual and gender anomalies are in the minority and are often persecuted and marginalized by the straight majority. In some places in the world they are tortured, imprisoned, or killed. "Gender" is a highly contested area within sociology. Sociologists theorizing about gender and gender roles differ sharply, particularly on the degree to which gender is determined by either culture or biology. Popular culture still sometimes represents gender as an absolute duality (male–female), but there is widespread consensus among sociologists today that gender is not binary but represents a scale of roles and identities. Not surprisingly, the greatest part of the critical work on gender has been carried out by women, in particular by Black women and women of colour, reflecting the (now) obvious fact that before the women's movement of the 1960s and 1970s, sexuality and gender were considered the specialties of psychiatry and, to some extent, psychology. Freudian theory held sway. Anthropology was preoccupied with the different ways of expressing sex socially among "primitive" groups, and the writings of Margaret Mead and others were revising sociologists' notions of gender socializing (although Mead would much later recant some of her "discoveries"). White female sociologists still neglected to include women of colour in their scholarly and activist work in the 1960s.

What do you think?

How do you think these lines of research by biologists, neurologists, and medical researchers could affect LGBTQ2 individuals' concepts of how they perform gender?

Sex and Gender: What's the Difference?

Gender is distinguished from *sex*. **Sex** refers to the primary biological traits, including the sexual organs, that categorize people, usually as either male or female. **Gender** refers to the cultural meanings that societies attach to sex categories. Those two uses of the word are often conflated so that some people assume "gender" always means the behaviours that society considers "within the range of normal" or "appropriate" for a person of either sex. While the ancient cultures recognized not only the main sexes but a wide range of gendered expressions of those sexes—in their mythologies and in their social customs—the Western cultures were not lacking accommodations to a range of gendered manifestations of sexuality. Shakespeare's plays, for example, frequently entail characters masking their sex by dressing as the opposite gender, which also spins off the fact that males frequently played the female roles in Renaissance theatrical productions. Actors have tremendous opportunities for interpretations of those roles, just as people in real society can express their personal sense of gender in their own unique way.

British sociologist **Ann Oakley** (b. 1944) was among the first to formally distinguish sex from gender in sociological terms, characterizing "sex" as a biological "construction" and "gender" as a social "construction" (Oakley, 1972), although this constitutes a violation of meaning in the metalanguage of science where "biological" concepts are not considered to be "constructed" by the language but observed and described from nature translatable into any language. Candace West and Don Zimmerman (1987), in their influential article "Doing Gender," made an important contribution to the discussion when they distinguished between a person's *sex* and *sex category*. Sex, they agreed, was based on biology, specifically "a determination made through the application of socially agreed upon biological criteria" (West & Zimmerman, 1987, p. 127). However, they argued that a person could adopt a sex category that does not correspond to their assigned sex by taking on the manners and behaviours that society associates with that other sex category.

Of course, when we place others into sex categories, we are not performing DNA tests or asking about their genitals. Instead, we look for cues that, according to custom, signify membership in socially recognized sex categories. These cues include a wide range of displayed behaviours—the way a person dresses, walks, speaks, behaves, and interacts with others. The mental checklist we keep is much longer than that, and we continue to refer to it the more we get to know a person: what kind of work do they do, what their interests and hobbies are, and so on.

Some of this may remind you of the symbolic interactionists, particularly Erving Goffman, who observed people as though they were performing on a stage. In fact, West and Zimmerman drew on Goffman's work in describing gender as an exercise in impression management, "the activity of managing situated conduct in light of normative conceptions of attitudes and activities appropriate for one's sex category" (1987, p. 127). In other words, gender is how we behave to show that we identify as male, female, or something else. This is important because while our assigned sex and our sex category often align, they don't always. Even heterosexual people change their expected roles on occasion. Sometimes, the entire culture accepts "opposite gender" behaviour, clothing styles, occupations, sports, and so on into the main gender roles. Furthermore, a person assigned the sex of "male" at birth may identify with and choose to adopt the entire female sex category;

Touchstone/Kobal/Shutterstock

Played by actress and comedian Julia Sweeney, Pat was a recurring character on *Saturday Night Live* in the early 1990s. Sketches revolved around Pat's ambiguous gender and the frustration of other characters as they tried, in vain, to discover whether Pat was a man or a woman or androgynous. So popular was the running sketch that it spawned a feature-length film. Sweeney has commented on the role and its unexpected consequences (Itzkoff, 2019), and notes how other people have misused the character she created to other people's detriment. This situation raises profound questions about the nature of comedy, the healthy effects of laughter, the responsibilities (if any) of creative performers, and the sensibilities of people who are unconventional or disabled.

by performing the behaviours society expects a female person to engage in—by "doing gender," in West and Zimmerman's words—their gender performance gains them general social acceptance into the female sex category.

Sex Category and the Gender Role

This brings us to the concept of **gender role**, which is a set of attitudes and expectations concerning behaviour that relates to the sex we are assigned at birth. Think of a gender role like a movie role: it is the part that corresponds to the sex category we identify with, and how we play it reflects what we understand about what it means to act within a particular category. Like any movie role—say, the part of Spider-Man in the Marvel movie universe—different "actors" may interpret the part differently, but if they stray too far from a conventional portrayal of the character, their authenticity may be questioned.

Sociologists today recognize that sex as well as gender has a social construct aspect, a framework humans have devised to make sense of the world. In mainstream Western society, it is taken as a given that the biological sex of a child born with a penis and an XY chromosome pair is male, and that the biological sex of a child born with a vagina and an XX chromosome pair is female. In fact, not everyone fits these strict biological criteria. Consider a person born with a penis *and* ovaries, who menstruates, or a person with XY chromosomes *and* a vagina. As we saw at the outset of this chapter, we use the term **intersex** for anyone born with both "male" and "female" sexual characteristics. Intersex people may identify with either the male or the female sex category, or they may see themselves belonging to a unique sex category. They may use terms like *non-conforming* and *non-binary* to signify their resistance to pressure to conform to either of the categories that the prevalent society views as acceptable options.

On top of the biological variability, there is a strong neurological component to sex identity, meaning that someone who possesses "male" sexual characteristics may not feel male in the way society expects a male person to feel. We sometimes describe people who do not identify with their assigned sex as **transgender**, a term that reflects Western society's binary view of sex and gender (i.e., if you're not one, then you must be the other). We may use the term "gender–non-conforming" or "fluid"

What do *you* think?

In 2019, Brooke Lynn Hytes (shown in the photo at the start of the chapter) became the first Canadian to perform on *RuPaul's Drag Race*. When not in drag, Ms Hytes (a.k.a. Brock Hayhoe) identifies as male, though many drag queens and kings are transgender. How does dressing in drag exemplify the performance aspect of "doing gender"?

for people who identify as neither male nor female, or else as male one day and as female on another day; this term also perpetuates the use of the gender binary as a reference point, as though people who don't identify as exclusively male or exclusively female are in violation of a universal biological standard rather than a social construct. Other cultures recognize genders beyond male and female. For example, the fa'a fanine of Samoa represent a widely accepted third gender category, consisting of people who identify as neither male nor female but who display both male and female traits and behaviours. They would not view themselves as *trans*gender because there is an established gender category for them.

In this chapter, we will be looking at sex, gender, and human sexuality. Most of this chapter concerns the way society views gender categories and how we—with considerable variation—interpret and live out our roles as "men," "women," and "other" categories. The case studies that kick off the chapter show that gender is a powerful concept that can defy biology, socialization, and pressure to conform.

9.2 Case Studies in Sex and Gender

The following cases highlight some of the ways in which sex and gender intersect.

David Reimer: Assigning Gender

In May 2004, 38-year-old David Reimer of Winnipeg committed suicide. His decision to take his life was likely influenced by his separation from his wife, the loss of his job, and the suicide death of his twin brother two years earlier. But there is a deeper cause to examine. David was the victim of a childhood medical accident that was compounded by an unsuccessful social experiment in assigning gender.

Quick Hits

"Two-Spirit People" and "Manly-Hearted Women": Alternative Gender Roles among North American Indigenous People

Indigenous people in North America have traditionally had a more complex view of gender variability than the binary view adopted by settler-colonial cultures. Two-Spirit people is their umbrella term to describe those who identify with one of the many gender roles beyond male and female recognized by Indigenous groups across North America. The Navaho, for example, recognize four genders, using the terms *nadleehi* for male-bodied Two-Spirit people and *dilbaa* for female-bodied Two-Spirit people. Another example is the *Ninauposkitzipxpe*, or "manly-hearted women," found among the Piegan and described in the following passage by anthropologist Alice Kehoe:

> About a third of elderly (sixty years or older) North Piegan women in 1939, and a few younger women, were considered manly-hearted. . . . Such women owned property, were good managers and usually effective workers, were forthright and assertive in public, in their homes, and as sexual partners, and were active in religious rituals. They were called "manly-hearted" because boldness, aggressiveness, and a drive to amass property and social power are held to be ideal traits for

Photo by John H. Fouch, 1877. Courtesy of Dr. James Brust.

This stereoview photograph, taken in 1877, shows "Squaw Jim" (*left*), a Two-Spirit person of the Crow Nation. Do you think English lacks terms for genders beyond male and female?

men. . . . The manly-hearted woman is admired as well as feared by both men and women. (1995, p. 115)

As infants, David and his brother were circumcised electronically using an experimental method. During David's circumcision, too much electricity was applied, and his penis was damaged beyond repair. Desperate for a solution, David's parents consulted numerous specialists. Popular at the time was behaviourism, the psychological school of thought that emphasizes the power of socialization (nurture) over biology (nature). It was held in high regard by some feminist psychologists (both male and female) as it supported the notion that gender and gender roles were not "natural" but taught. In its extreme version, behaviourism advanced the theory that each of us starts out as a **tabula rasa**, or blank

slate, on which our social environment "writes" our gender. A proponent of this school, psychologist Dr John Money, was one of the specialists contacted by David's parents. He persuaded them to have David castrated and given female hormones; their child, renamed "Brenda," would be raised as a girl.

In articles that made the case famous, Money claimed that David was adapting successfully to his new gender, socially taught and hormonally enhanced. But his view of the situation was based more on wishes than on facts. In *As Nature Made Him*, an account of David Reimer's life, author and journalist John Colapinto (2000) shows that David's childhood was highly conflicted. He felt male, not female.

He didn't like wearing dresses, and he preferred roughhousing with boys to the company and play of girls his age. If he had been born female, you could say s/he was experiencing what doctors and sociologists today call *gender dysphoria*, where there is a disconnect between one's lived gender identity and the sex one was "assigned" at birth. But it was only later, after the circumcision surgical intervention maimed him that a "cover-up" gender intervention with further surgery was devised. That David suffered in this attempt to genderize him is proof that "gender dysphoria" cannot be faked. Moreover, it is proof that "gender" is not entirely a social construct even if some sociologists want it to be.

David wasn't told he had been born male until he was 13, when his parents, under pressure from Dr Money, approached him about allowing surgeons to create a vagina. David rebelled and several times attempted suicide. He abandoned his imposed female identity and sought out surgery to have his male sex restored. He later married and had stepchildren, but the effects of both the accident and the surgical and social experiment never left him.

What does the case of David Reimer tell us? David was born with traits that we categorize as male. He was forced to undergo surgery and hormone treatment to make him appear as if his biological sex (but not chromosomal sex) were female. He was raised to assume a female gender role. In spite of these efforts to change his biological sex characteristics and impose a female gender role, he continued to experience himself as belonging to the male sex category. This suggests, as research confirms (Kruijver et al., 2000), that gender has neurological components in addition to the biological genitals and hormones. Male and female brains differ. Male or female chromosomes affect all of the body's cells. The brain is an aspect of one's biological sex/gender. David's story also clearly demonstrates the dangers of allowing social theory to impose itself into premature assumptions in social practice.

Caster Semenya: Measuring Gender

Caster Semenya is a two-time Olympic medalist, having won the gold medal in the women's 800 metre race at the 2012 Summer Olympics in London and four years later at the Summer Games in Rio. But in 2009–10, she missed an entire year of competition while the International Association of Athletics

What do *you* think?
In what ways, if at all, have you experienced social pressure to conform to a particular gender role? Have you ever resisted gender socialization?

Federations (IAAF), track and field's official governing body, investigated claims that Semenya's body produced testosterone in levels 25 times greater than those found in most women. Results of the highly invasive "gender verification test" were leaked to the media, which sensationalized her condition and turned a situation that had been kept private into a source of controversy and criticism. "World athletics is in crisis over the gender of Caster Semenya after tests revealed the South African world champion has male sex organs and no womb or ovaries," read one article in London's *Daily Telegraph* (Hurst, 2009).

Semenya was cleared to compete in her lived identity—that is, as a woman—but in April 2011 the IAAF took up the case again. "She is a woman, but maybe not 100 per cent," said IAAF general secretary Pierre Weiss, shortly before the federation announced new gender verification guidelines based on a maximum level of testosterone an athlete may possess in order to compete as a woman. The limit, which was in place for the 2012 Summer Olympics, forced some intersex athletes to take treatments to reduce their testosterone levels to allowable standards. The rule was put on hold in 2015, but in November 2018 new rules came into effect for athletes with hyperandrogenism, the medical condition in which women have elevated levels of hormones responsible for the growth and maintenance of male traits and reproductive organs. The IAAF had identified seven events in which elevated testosterone might impact performance, but the new guidelines applied only to middle-distance races of 400 to 1,500 metres—events that are typically dominated by Black athletes from the global South. In a May 2019 ruling, the Court of Arbitration for Sport called the latest guidelines discriminatory but argued that "such discrimination is a necessary, reasonable, and proportionate means of achieving the legitimate objective of ensuring fair competition in female athletics" (York & Waldie, 2019).

In June 2022, FINA, the Federation Internationale de Natation (International Swimming Federation)

What do *you* think?

1. Many world-class athletes have physical characteristics that give them a competitive advantage, including long legs and greater-than-normal lung capacity. Why do you think the IAAF and FINA view hormone levels differently?

2. Is using hormone levels an appropriate way to "measure sex" in a competitive athlete? What other measures might be used? How should we determine whether an intersex athlete is permitted to compete in their lived identity?

voted to accept a "Policy on Eligibility for the Men's and Women's Competition Categories." FINA sets eligibility criteria for events leading to Olympic-level competitions. The 24-page document establishes limits on hormonal supplements for biological men transitioning to female gender within certain age limits and time frames related to puberty. At puberty, males develop 25 times the level of testosterone as females, which causes extensive biological changes that in strength, size, and other ways disadvantage females. As the goals of the organization are to provide safe opportunities for women, as well as men, to excel at sport safely, certain limitations on males, including those transitioning to females, must be made to ensure those goals of access, safety, and fairness. FINA also is planning to create separate events in which less regulation allows the organization to study the effects of treatments on "open" (to women and to transwomen) sports events with fewer restrictions.

Raising the Profile of Transgender People

In 2015, Caitlyn Jenner brought the experience of gender conflict to public awareness. An American track and field hero, gold medallist at the 1976 Montreal Summer Olympics, and member of the extended Kardashian clan, Bruce Jenner announced in a television interview that, though biologically male, she identified as female. She was featured on the cover of *Vanity Fair* two months later, and her transition was documented in an eight-episode miniseries. She underwent sex-reassignment surgery, completing the biological transition from male to female in January 2017.

Jenner may have become the world's most publicized transgender woman, but she is not the first

public figure to raise awareness around the rights of transgender people. Jenna Talackova, a Vancouver-born transgender woman and model, fought for and won the right to compete in the 2012 Miss Universe Canada pageant after initially being disqualified because she was born male. Thomas Beatie, a transgender man legally married to a woman, made headlines in 2007 when he became pregnant through artificial insemination—his female reproductive organs had not then been removed. Six years later, his male identity was challenged by an Arizona judge presiding over his divorce proceedings, who ruled that because Beatie was able to carry and bear children, he could not, in the eyes of the court, be considered a man. This rendered his marriage invalid in a state that did not then recognize same-sex marriage. The ruling was overturned by the Arizona Appeals Court in 2014.

While stories such as these have helped shine a light on a community that has long been misunderstood, the cases of Jenner and Talackova in particular have glamorized an experience that has caused discrimination, social exclusion, and depression among others who lack the same degree of private money and public support. A 2015 study by researchers at the University of Western Ontario reports that as many as 43 per cent of transgender people in North America and Europe have attempted suicide (Bauer, Scheim, Pyne, Tavers, & Hammond, 2015). The team found that the risk of suicide drops with increased social and parental support, reductions in transphobia, and greater access to transition treatments and surgeries, which are not available in all provinces and which can be costly in provinces where only some surgeries are covered by health insurance.

Trans people make up a minority of the LGBTQ2 population. They may experience discrimination within the medical system, where they face reluctance by doctors to make the necessary referral for surgery and reluctance by surgeons to operate (Ubelacker, 2015). In May 2016, Canada's only surgery clinic exclusively for trans people, located in Montreal, was targeted in an arson attack carried out by a man armed with a machete. The attack caused extensive damage and forced the clinic to close temporarily, putting off several scheduled surgeries. As Brightwell (2016) reports, the incident was underreported in the mainstream media and did not receive extensive coverage on social media, even among the LGBTQ2 community. Later the same

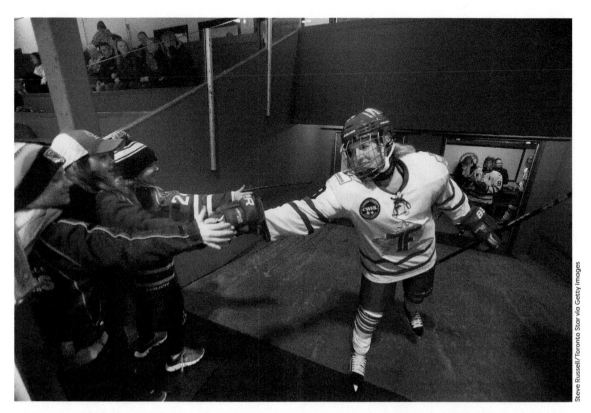

Steve Russell/Toronto Star via Getty Images

In January 2018, Jessica Platt, a forward with the Toronto Furies of the Canadian Women's Hockey League, came out as transgender, becoming the CWHL's first openly trans player. Three months later, Harrison Browne, openly a transman, retired from the rival National Women's Hockey League in order to begin hormone replacement therapy as part of his transition.

month, the federal government introduced legislation to extend the rights of transgender Canadians by adding gender identity and gender expression to existing laws against discrimination and hate speech. The legislation would make it easier to prosecute attacks such as the one on the Centre Métropolitain de Chirurgerie as hate crimes.

9.3 Feminism and Gender Theory: Four Categories

Much of the critical work on gender theory has been carried out by feminist sociologists. Some scholars have traced the evolution of feminism through a series of "waves," each distinguished by a different set of objectives. That is one way of viewing a dynamic movement and theoretical framework that has exerted tremendous influence on the growth of sociology. In this section we take a different approach,

looking at four strains of feminist theory and how they approach the study of gender. **Beatrice Kachuck** (2003) divides the diverse range of feminist theories into the following four categories.

Liberal Feminism

Liberal feminism, as Kachuck explains, is about securing equal rights for women in all phases of public life, including access to education, jobs, and pay. It is associated with the fight for **pay equity**, the guarantee that women in female-dominated industries (nursing, childcare, library science, for instance) receive salaries similar to those of people working in comparable (in terms of educational qualifications required, hours worked, and social value) professions typically dominated by men. Why do we pay so little to those in primary and early childhood education (ECE)? Liberal feminism is credited with securing benefits for women on maternity leave, including the

Quick Hits

Sex and Gender: A Recap

- Sex is a socially constructed set of categories (or identities) based on biological factors (genitals, chromosomes, hormones) as well as neurological ones.
- **Biological sex**, as it has been constructed socially in most cultures in the world, is binary, consisting of male and female sex categories assigned at birth on the individual's sex organs. However, the existence of intersex people, who are born with both male and female organs, shows that categories beyond male and female must be recognized. Sex undergoes certain changes over time, particularly at puberty and at menopause. Some cultures assign three sexualities based on sex organs: male, female, and intersex.
- Not everyone identifies with their assigned sex. A **transsexual** is someone with the physical characteristics of one sex category and a persistent desire to belong to another. Transsexuals feel they have been born into the wrong body and may pursue sex reassignment therapy or surgery to change their physical features despite their biological (chromosomal) sex. Several cultures assign identities based on degrees of transsexuality. North American Indigenous peoples recognize Two-spirited individuals like the Māhū of Hawaii; historically, the Japanese (Frank, 2017) recognized "wakashu" or "beautiful youths" as bisexual prostitutes; "Muxes" of Oaxaca, Mexico, are seen as binary males; "Bissu" is a fifth gender identified in Indonesia where dual genders (parallel to "lesbian" and "gay") additionally are assigned to some individuals; "Khawaja

Sira" in Pakistan (Azhar, 2017) are recognized traditionally but are under duress socially; "Xanith" homosexuals in Oman, who take the submissive role in homosexual relationships and dress like women, have legal status (Wiley Online Library 2015); "Hijra" (eunuchs, intersex, or transgender) in India (Khaleeli, 2014) recently has been reinstated legally as a third gender; "Kathoey" (typically transgender women) are recognized in Thailand (Ilada & Mount, 2015).
- Gender, as used in sociology, is a socially constructed set of expectations about the roles and behaviours associated with different sex categories. It need not be binary, as many cultures recognize genders additional to male and female. Gender role describes the actions people perform, naturally or consciously, to demonstrate affinity with a particular sex category.
- Not everyone identifies with the gender role corresponding to their biological sex. A transgender person is someone whose lived identity does not conform to the gender role associated with their assigned sex. Intersex people often fall under the umbrella of "transgender."
- A male-body person who feels a greater connection to the gender role associated with being a woman is a **transgender woman** (or a **transwoman**); a female-body person who identifies as a man is a **transgender man**, or **transman**.
- A **cisgender** person is someone who feels affinity with both the biological sex assigned at birth and with the socially constructed sex category of either male or female.

rights to claim employment insurance and to return to the same or an equivalent job in the same company after a fixed period of time (up to a year in Canada).

Critics of liberal feminism argue that it universalizes the position of white, middle-class, heterosexual, cisgender Western women, who have benefited in ways that other women have not. Liberal feminism has been far less successful in promoting

the interests of women who differ in class, race, ethnicity, sexual orientation, and nationality.

Essentialist Feminism

Liberal feminism argues that gender is an artificial social construct that assigns men and women different roles, rights, and opportunities based on perceived differences in intellect. It argues that men and women possess the *same* intellectual capabilities and, like all people (*inclusive* of gender, race, physical ability, etc.), should be treated equally. **Essentialist feminism** differs by arguing that women and men are essentially *different* in the way they think. Men, for example, see the world in terms of competition and opposition to others, and they have created a social order based on "paradigms of dominance and subordination" (Kachuck, 2003); women, in contrast, view the world in terms of unities. Women's "maternal thinking" (Ruddick, 1989) naturally gives women social norms and a sense of morality that (most) men do not possess. This morality is negatively valued in a *patriarchal* society (i.e., one dominated by and favouring male roles, views, and ideas).

Kachuck identifies three main criticisms of essentialist feminism:

- it universalizes women, assuming erroneously that all women experience gender alike;
- it confuses natural instincts with strategies that women have devised for coping with the demands of a patriarchal society; and
- it encourages us to see women "as social housekeepers in worlds that men build" (Kachuck, 2003, p. 66).

Thus, while essentialist feminism speaks constructively about valuing women's differences from men, it falls into the trap of generalizing sexualized concepts of gender that seem to uphold gender inequality, especially in the workplace.

Socialist Feminism

Kachuck explains that **socialist feminists** "revise their Marxism so as to account for gender, something that Marx ignored. They want sexuality and gender relations included in analyses of society" (2003, p. 67). According to this school of thought, insight is gained from looking at the intersections of oppression between class and gender. The struggles faced by, and resources available to, working-class women can be different from those of middle- and upper-class women, and feminist socialism is useful in identifying these distinctions. For example, when women are fulfilling a role as paid workers, many if not most also participate in the unpaid labour of reproduction and housework. Still, there is the danger that race, ethnicity, ableism, and sexual orientation get overlooked in the focus on class. Black women in North America face racism and stereotyping regardless of whether they come from the upper, middle, or lower classes.

Postmodernist Feminism

Postmodernist feminism takes a strong social-constructionist position, making it almost diametrically opposed to essentialist feminism. Social constructionism is the idea that there is no natural basis for identities attached to gender, ethnicity, race, and so on. Some postmodernists, for their purposes, dispute the existence of biological sex categories. Their notion is that identities are constructed by individuals or groups for different social purposes. From this perspective, it is impossible to form scientific, universally, or even generally, relevant accounts of what it means to be male or female. For this reason, postmodernist feminists see women as subjects rather than objects of sociological study. To clarify these terms in sociological research, a subject of study could be recent advances in agricultural practice and the objects studied would be 10 local farms. Postmodern feminism might be interested in women's work and would select 10 urban, 10 suburban, and 10 rural women to contribute their perspectives on the work they do, thus allowing the perspective of the women studied to guide their research. Standpoint theory is an important product of postmodernist feminism.

Another methodology that fits within the broad-ranging perspective of postmodernist feminism is **queer theory**, notably articulated in the book *Gender Trouble* (1990) by **Judith Butler**. Queer theory rejects the idea that male and female genders are natural binary opposites. It also disputes the idea that gender identity is connected to some biological "essence," arguing instead that gender identity is related to the dramatic effect of a gender performance. Gender is seen not as one of two categories—male and female—but as a continuum with male and female at the extremes; individuals act, or perform, more one way or another along the continuum at different times and in different situations.

Kachuck's main criticism of feminist postmodernism is that it leads to no conclusions. It merely problematizes other people's conclusions and generates no solid criteria for judging better or worse positions, but satisfies itself with "constructing a 'feminine' space where intellectuals aggressively play out tentative ideas" (Kachuck, 2003, p. 81).

9.4 Applying the Gender Lens to Life

An aging white man steps to the lectern and explains gender to an auditorium full of late teens and early twentysomethings. Yes, I see the irony in that. After all, I grew up at a time when a boy who preferred reading to football was likely to be branded a "sissy," and a girl who climbed trees and wouldn't wear dresses was considered a "tomboy." Both would be treated as slightly "deviant" for defying *gender norms*, society's expectations about what it means to be male or female.

In contrast, young people growing up in Canada today have, by and large, a remarkably sophisticated and nuanced understanding of sex and gender. That is not to say that gender discrimination no longer exists. But people today, and younger people especially,

are defying social expectations around gender in unprecedented ways, and are slowly succeeding in changing social attitudes around what "boys" and "girls" are allowed to do.

The Feminization of Work

The **feminization** of an occupational sphere occurs when a particular job, profession, or industry comes to be dominated by or predominantly associated with women. Since the start of World War I, when women began to work outside the home in greater numbers, many occupations have become feminized, including bank teller and secretary (now financial services adviser and administrative assistant, respectively), but job feminization was occurring well before that, as the first of the two examples below describes. Typically, the feminization of an industry works to the disadvantage of those involved in it, who earn lower salaries with less job protection and fewer benefits than those enjoyed by workers outside the feminized occupational sphere.

Women's Work during the Eighteenth-Century "Gin Craze" in London

Beginning around 1720 there was a sudden rise in the sale and consumption of gin in London, England, that lasted until the middle of the century. The liquor was sold not just in bars but in the streets, from

---

What do *you* think?

Some people, including author J.K. Rowling, have objected to the admission of transwomen (male to female) into places the majority of women regard as safe places from male predators. Such places include public washrooms, lounges, and areas designated for children accompanied by a parent. Do you think straight women are entitled to privacy from transwomen?

Telling It Like It Is

A Student Point of View

What It Means to Walk Home Alone as a Female Student

I was studying in the library with some classmates when my friend James suggested we grab a bite to eat afterward. I said sure, but since my phone had died, I asked if I could borrow his to text my roommate that I'd be home later than expected.

"Do your housemates really need to know where you are at all times?" he asked.

My friend Amy and I exchanged glances. "Uh, yeah, that way they know to worry when I'm not home on time," I explained. "And they know where I was last, and who I was with."

James looked surprised. "But it's like a 10-minute walk, and it's not even dark out." At that

point, Amy jumped in to explain all the precautions we take when walking on campus: that we try to stick to well-lit routes and avoid walking alone. That we'll cross the street to avoid someone we don't know. That we use the campus buddy system if we have to. And if we are alone, we carry our phone in one hand and our keys in the other. No headphones, no distractions, eyes out for any sign of trouble.

"What do you do if you're coming home late at night?" I asked him.

He took a few seconds to respond. "I just . . . walk home."

—Zoe S., McMaster University

wheelbarrows and baskets, in alleyway stalls, in shady one-room gin shops, and from boats floating on the Thames River.

Anyone selling gin without a licence was operating illegally. This was the case for the majority of the thousands of women involved in the gin trade, who couldn't afford the expensive licence. They operated at great risk, and were primary targets of the Gin Acts, which were passed chiefly to restrict the selling of gin to bars owned predominantly by middle-class men. Women were more likely than men to be arrested, and were more likely to be put in prison if convicted.

Why take the chance? At the time, thousands of young women were immigrating to London from Scotland, Ireland, and rural England, looking for jobs and for husbands. The quality and availability of both were greatly lacking. So why sell gin? Historian Jessica Warner gives three reasons:

> It required little or no capital; it did not require membership in a professional organization; and it was one of the few occupations from which women were not effectively or explicitly excluded. It was, in other words, a means of economic survival. (2002, p. 51)

The Gin Acts often pitted women against women. Enforcement depended heavily on the accusations of paid informants, half of whom were women. Warner describes the harsh economics involved:

> Consider the options of a young woman newly arrived in London in 1737 or 1738. She could work for a year as a maid and earn £5 in addition to receiving room and board, or she could inform against one gin-seller, and upon securing a conviction collect a reward of £5. There were two ways to make money, one hard, the other easy, and many people naturally chose the latter. Most did so only once, collecting their reward and then attempting to hide as best they could. (2002, p. 137)

Women's Clerical Work in Canada, 1891–1971

The early twentieth century saw a spectacular increase in the number of clerical workers in the Canadian labour force. It also saw the feminization of the position,

> **What do you think?**
> Did the feminization of the gin trade in eighteenth-century London benefit women or harm them? What alternatives might have been available to female immigrants to London who chose not to get involved in selling gin illegally?

along with the degradation of the role, as measured in terms of wages, skill level, and opportunity for promotion. How all three trends—growth, feminization, and degradation—mesh together is a story that gives insight on both the past and the present.

Clerical work historically was a man's job. The male bookkeeper's varied duties required a lot of what we now call multitasking. As companies grew in size, there was much more clerical work that needed to be done, and businesses moved toward a more "rationalized" and "efficient" approach to task management, according to the principles of **scientific management** (or **Taylorism**, discussed in Chapter 10). The result was a kind of assembly-line office work, in which several clerical workers were engaged in the rapid performance of repeated simple tasks, with little variety and few opportunities to move up in the company. The growing belief (based on assumptions about women's limited capabilities) that this was ideal work for women, who were supposed to be wives and mothers first and labourers second, was reinforced by discrimination that offered them few alternatives. The thinking of the time is illustrated in the following passage from a book called *Office Management: Principles and Practice*, published in 1925 by William Henry Leffingwell, a proponent of applying scientific management to the office:

> A woman is to be preferred for the secretarial position for she is not averse to doing minor tasks, work involving the handling of petty details, which would irk and irritate ambitious young men, who usually feel that the work they are doing is of no importance if it can be performed by some person with a lower salary. Most such men are also anxious to get ahead and to be promoted from position to position, and consequently if there is much work of a detail character to be done, and they are expected to perform it, they will

TABLE 9.1 The Feminization of Clerical Workers in Canada, 1891–1971

Year	Total Clerical Workers	Women Clerical Workers	
		Number	Percentage
1891	133,017	4,710	14.3
1901	57,231	12,660	22.1
1911	103,543	33,723	32.6
1921	216,691	90,577	41.8
1931	260,674	117,637	45.1
1941	303,655	152,216	50.1
1951	563,093	319,183	56.7
1961	818,912	503,660	61.5
1971	1,310,910	903,395	68.9

Source: Lowe (1980).

not remain satisfied and will probably seek a position elsewhere. (1925, p. 116)

This job transformation got a big push during World War I (1914–18), when women entered the workforce to replace men who had gone overseas to serve. During this time, the number of clerical workers in Canada jumped by 113,148—around half of them women. At the Bank of Nova Scotia's regional offices in Ontario, the percentage of clerks who were women jumped from 8.5 per cent in 1911 to 40.7 per cent in 1916. Although, overall, the number of women clerical workers in Canada fell slightly when the men returned from the war, the figure remained high and steadily grew, as Table 9.1 shows.

Gendered Work Today and the Pay Gap

Certain jobs, as well as the college and university programs preparing people to work in those jobs, continue to be gendered. That means, first, that one sex

will be over-represented among the people engaged in certain kinds of work or a particular program of study. Second, as Paul Sargent (2005) puts it, "the work itself is typically imbued with gendered meanings and defined in gendered terms." For example, the gendered profession of nursing is described with words like "caring" and "nurturing" typically associated with women; nursing, and other kinds of "care work" (such as childcare, teaching, elder care, and social work), is thus characterized as a natural offshoot of the mother role. In contrast, the job of police officer (still sometimes called "policeman") is described in terms of "toughness" and the "brotherhood" of officers.

Twenty years ago, in 2000, men outnumbered women by a ratio of at least 2 to 1 in the following occupations categorized by Statistics Canada:

- the primary industries of forestry, fishing, mining, and oil and gas
- manufacturing
- construction
- agriculture (Uppal & LaRochelle-Côté, 2014).

These industries are all part of the goods-producing sector, where men made up over 75 per cent of the total labour force. The gender split was much more equal in the services-producing sector, where women made up 53 per cent of the workforce and outnumbered men by at least 15 per cent in the following categories:

- finance and insurance
- educational services

What do you think?

1. Where in Canada can you see evidence of the feminization of work today? What effect do you think the feminization of these workplaces has on the employees working there?
2. Is there any evidence of a reverse trend that we might call the "masculinization" of work, in which a particular type of employment dominated by men acquires greater prestige and, of course, greater pay?

- accommodation and food services
- health care and social assistance (Uppal & LaRochelle-Côté, 2014).

In the last of these categories, the dominance was more than 4 to 1.

Data from Statistics Canada's 2018 Labour Force Survey (LFS) show that little has changed. Men made up 78 per cent of the labour force in the goods-producing sector, while women occupied 78 per cent of jobs in the services-producing sector (Figure 9.1a). Figure 9.1b provides a breakdown of the eight industries cited above and shows that women are still under-represented in manufacturing, construction, agriculture, and primary industries, while dominating professions in educational services, health care, and social assistance. In fact, since 1991, the top three jobs for young Canadian women with a university degree have consistently been (1) elementary school or kindergarten teacher, (2) registered nurse, and (3) secondary schoolteacher. According to the 2016 census, 19 per cent of 25- to 34-year-old women with university degrees were employed in one of these three jobs (Statistics Canada, 2016).

Figure 9.2 shows the top 10 jobs for people aged 25 to 34 who have recently graduated with a certificate, diploma, or degree from a college or university. While there are some occupations that appear in the top 10

for both women and men, the list of jobs held by men shows a greater share of roles associated with computer technology, trades, and engineering (mechanical engineer and civil engineer fall just outside of the top 10 for 25- to 34-year-old men). In contrast, the list of jobs held by women is dominated by occupations that involve care work, including nursing, education and childcare, social assistance, and food services. In 2015, 41 per cent of working Canadian women were involved in these industries, compared with just 13 per cent of working Canadian men. As Statistics Canada analyst Melissa Moyser (2017, p. 22) observes, women's employment "often parallels their traditional gender roles of homemaking and caregiving."

Another common feature of many of the most common jobs for women is what American sociologist Arlie Hochschild called *emotional labour*. Emotional labour describes the effort required to manage our emotions and the emotions of others "in accordance with organizationally defined rules and guidelines" (Hochschild, 1983, p. 147). Imagine you're working at a coffee shop, and the patron you have just served begins berating you for using whole milk instead of 2 per cent in the foam of his cinnamon dolce latte. Rather than confronting him with the fact he didn't specify 2 per cent milk in his order, you apologize with servility because "the customer is always right." It has cost you a fair bit of emotional

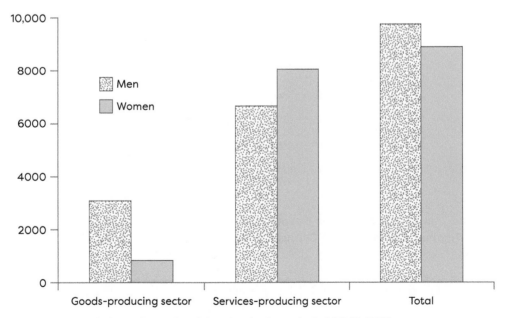

FIGURE 9.1a Labour Force Participation in Canada (× 1,000), 2018

Source: Statistics Canada (2018b).

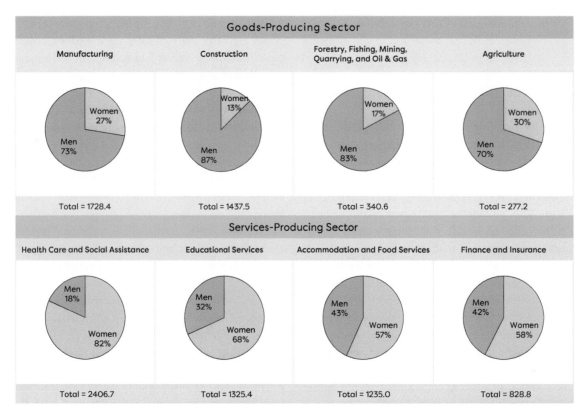

FIGURE 9.1b Labour Force Participation in Canada by Sex (× 1,000), Select Industries, 2018

Source: Statistics Canada (2018a).

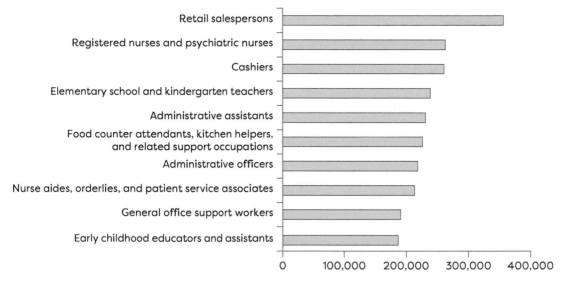

FIGURE 9.2a Top 10 Occupations for Canadian Women Aged 25–34 Holding a Postsecondary Certificate, Degree, or Diploma (2016 Census)

Source: Statistics Canada (2016).

labour to allow the customer to leave satisfied that he has taught you a lesson.

Emotional labour involves manipulating the emotions of others through our own display of

emotion. A flight attendant puts on an air of calm to put nervous airline passengers at ease; a store clerk fawns as she tries to make a customer fall in love with one of the store's dresses. Hochschild made

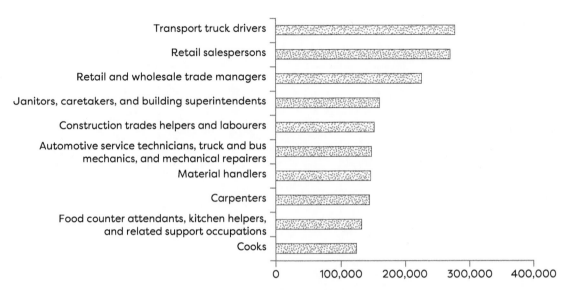

FIGURE 9.2b **Top 10 Occupations for Canadian Men Aged 25–34 Holding a Postsecondary Certificate, Degree, or Diploma (2016 Census)**

Source: Statistics Canada (2016).

two key observations about emotional labour. First, it is used to bring about feelings of satisfaction and well-being in others, which is a role traditionally associated with women more than with men. Second, it requires us to make a false display of emotion while concealing what we are actually feeling, and in this way emotional labour can lead to alienation and burnout over time.

It is worth noting that care work and emotional labour are hallmarks of the largest occupation not on this list: the unpaid work of raising and caring for children, which falls disproportionately on the shoulders of mothers.

So are men's jobs better? Figure 9.2 shows that apart from retail positions, the most common jobs for men fall outside of the service industry, where emotional labour is a prerequisite, and none would be considered care work. In fact, a list of "men's jobs" is dominated by those that require minimal interaction with others, such as trucking, construction, carpentry, and electrical work. Jobs in these fields can be alienating in their own right, not to mention dangerous.

Sociology students need to look at what might cause these gender specializations to occur. A place to start would be postsecondary education, where men and women typically take different routes. We'll consider education shortly.

Being a Gender Minority in a Gendered Occupation

When people find themselves in gendered jobs where they belong to the minority sex, it can affect their gender performance. Sargent (2005) discusses the phenomenon among men in early childhood education. Sargent incorporates Raewyn Connell's (1995) four performances of masculinity—essentially, four ways of acting out male gender roles:

1. **hegemonic masculinity**
2. **subordinate masculinity**
3. **marginalized masculinity**
4. **complicit masculinity.**

Sargent explains them this way:

> Hegemonic masculine practices are those that serve to normalize and naturalize men's dominance and women's subordination.

What do you think?
Michael and Michelle graduated from university together and were hired by the same advertising company. Five years later, Michael is earning 15 per cent more than Michelle. How could you account for the wage gap in this context?

Zety Akhzar/Shutterstock

In 2019, Barbie celebrated her sixtieth anniversary with an inspiring campaign teaching girls that they can be anything—as long as they have long hair and less than 20 per cent body fat. (The message was surely not lost on many boys, parents, and nostalgic adults also.) Does the campaign promote a healthy or unhealthy message about gender and work?

The Point Is . . .

Women's Work in Canada Is Devalued

The gap between what men and women earn in Canada has narrowed since the 1980s, though as Figure 9.3 shows, women still earn just 87 cents for every dollar a man earns. Why?

In large part it is because of the different kinds of work that men and women do. Women are over-represented in low-paying professions in health care, education, and social services. This kind of work is devalued compared with high-paying and male-dominated professions in fields like engineering, architecture, and natural resources (Moyser, 2017, p. 28).

It isn't because "men's work" requires more education or expertise. The National Occupational Classification is a tool used by the federal government to organize jobs by the amount of skill and training they require. For example, paraprofessional work in legal, social, and education services falls within the same classification as work in industrial, electrical, and construction trades: both require college education or apprenticeship training. The average rate of pay for the former is $22.57; for the latter, it is $29.76 (Moyser, 2017, Table 10). Needless

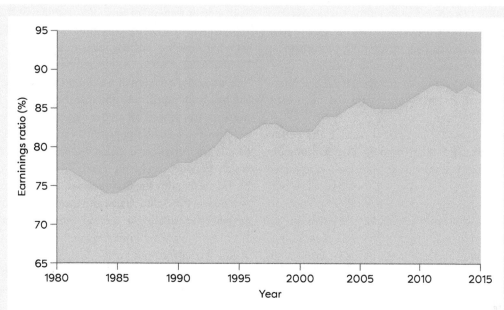

FIGURE 9.3 **Total Women's Earnings as a Percentage of Men's Earnings, 1980–2015**

Source: Moyser (2017, Chart 17).

to say, women predominate in former, men in the latter.

It is also the case that men and women are paid differently for doing the exact same work. Even in the "female" occupations such as nursing and teaching, men out-earn women. Moyser, in her excellent report for Statistics Canada, summarizes the possible explanations for the wage gap:

> One interpretation is that women experience wage discrimination on the basis of their gender. In this case, a woman is paid less than her male colleague for doing the exact same job. An alternative . . . interpretation is that, within occupational groups, women choose the less demanding and/or more flexible positions in order to accommodate their caregiving responsibilities. Women may also be less adept at negotiating their pay or less interested in competing, as these attributes are deemed "masculine" in the context of gender socialization. (2017, p. 30)

Subordinate masculinities are those behaviours and presentations of self that could threaten the legitimacy of hegemonic masculinity. Gay men, effeminate men, and men who eschew competition or traditional definitions of success are examples frequently cited. . . . These men are vulnerable to being abused and ridiculed by others. Marginalized masculinities represent the adaptation of masculinities to such issues as race and class. For example, a Black man may enjoy certain privileges that stem from success as a small business owner, yet still find himself unable to hail a cab. . . . Finally, complicit masculinities are those that do not embody hegemonic processes *per se*, but benefit from the ways in which hegemonic masculinities construct the gender order and local gender regimes. (Sargent, 2005)

Sargent argues that men working in early childhood education are caught in a conflict between performing a subordinate masculinity (for example, by being "nurturing") and engaging in more stereotypical masculinity performances. Men in early childhood education often have to suppress tendencies toward subordinate masculinity to avoid being associated by others with the popularly reproduced image of the homosexual–pedophile, which mistakenly conflates two very different sexualities. This is why male ECEs are not allowed the caring physical contact that female teachers are encouraged to have and are reduced to less threatening performances of complicit masculinity, which include "high fives" and handshakes rather than hugs. This is a compromise that can be demoralizing for the male early childhood educator.

Another gender image that restricts the performance of male gender roles in the ECE environment is the "man as disciplinarian." Because it is assumed that men more naturally perform discipline, they may be assigned greater responsibility for monitoring the behaviour of "problem kids." Classrooms occupied by male teachers then become seen as sites of discipline. No matter what the male ECE's natural classroom approach may be, he may be forced to conform to a masculinity performance that reinforces male authoritarian stereotypes.

In Chapter 14, we look at the first women and the first Black women and Black men who entered medical practice. But one woman is an exceptional example of her sex. She was born in Ireland around 1789 and named Margaret Anne Bulkley. After her parents' grocery business went bankrupt, her father went to debtors' prison, leaving his wife and children destitute. But three years later, her mother's brother James Barry died. He had been a professor of painting at London's Royal Academy and left Margaret's family little except his circle of friends. When she wanted to become a doctor, they plotted to help her to do so, disguised as a man. So in 1808, taking on the name of her uncle, James Barry, and the groups' collaborating on papers saying that she was his nephew, s/he gained admission at the Edinburgh School of Medicine, graduating in 1812. In Moses Orina's version of the story (2011), during medical school Barry's voice and size led to the supposition that he was prepubescent. Upon graduation, his secret was revealed and he was offered the opportunity to reclaim his previous gender. Instead, he became a military surgeon in the British Army, enjoying a long, successful career. He was posted in Canada in 1857

as Inspector General of Hospitals. He died on 25 July 1865, with orders not to be examined. Nevertheless, a servant preparing the body for burial discovered that Dr James Barry was a female and had stretch marks indicating the carrying of a child. Research suggests she had been raped at 13 and that the child she bore perhaps was passed off as her sister. The story was published in a Dublin paper on 14 August 1865. The details are intriguing from several standpoints from which "gender" can be regarded. Dr Barry was notable for performing the first successful Caesarean section delivery in South Africa and the fourth recorded anywhere in which both mother and child survived. He was known for a kind and gentle demeanour as well as for advocating for the poor. To balance that performance, a note from Emily Knell's blog (2017) suggests he may have overplayed the role:

> Those values make her sound like a soft caring human being, but when Florence Nightingale met Dr. Barry, she said, "He behaved like a brute. [He was] the most hardened creature I ever met throughout the army." Dr. Barry fought two duels, swore like a sailor, and flirted with married women.

The Gendered Pay Gap among Physicians

In 2021, the Ontario Medical Association published a study of the pay gap between male and female doctors in the province, as recorded in 2017–18, with 31,481 reporting (Table 9.2). Two measures of the pay gap were made: daily and annual. The daily gap was a 13.5 per cent difference. Much of this figure could be explained through the greater percentage of specialists, particularly in fields such as neurosurgery, cardiology, and vascular surgery.

Another issue is the difference in payment type, with a greater difference when there is a fee for every service, as opposed to a fixed payment per patient. More males appear to be taking the higher-paying fee-for-service model. In this instance, the annual

TABLE 9.2 The Gendered Pay Gap among Doctors

Year	Specialists		Family Doctors		Overall	
	Male	Female	Male	Female	Male	Female
2017	63.8%	36.2%	54.5%	45.5%	59%	41%

difference was greater, with a pay gap of 32.8 per cent. An important factor here is that the female physicians worked fewer days a year than the male physicians did. Reasons given involved female physicians taking maternity leave, and that they are more likely to have family responsibilities of parenting and of being caregivers to older relatives that require their presence.

Gender and Education: What Keeps Women from Taking Math and Engineering?

Earlier we looked at how different kinds of work are gendered: how the "care work" fields of nursing and early childhood education are dominated by women, while skilled trades such as carpentry, electrical engineering, and computer programming are dominated by men. It is reasonable to expect we will find similar patterns in the postsecondary courses that women and men in Canada are taking. Let's see if that is borne out by the evidence.

In 2016, Canadian colleges and universities awarded 230,274 undergraduate degrees. Women took home close to 60 per cent of those degrees—135,000 in total (Statistics Canada, 2018c). Women received more degrees than men did in nearly every one of Statistics Canada's 13 program categories, from education and performing arts to business and public administration. The two exceptions were engineering and architecture, and math and computer science. Those programs represent the "E" and the "M" in STEM, the set of science- and technology-related courses that receives considerable attention because they offer good career prospects and because their enrolment typically has been dominated by men.

Figure 9.4 shows the distribution of undergraduate degrees awarded in STEM fields and other program types. You can see that when it comes to STEM programs, women received a greater share (58 per cent) of degrees in physical and life sciences but a much lower share of degrees in math and computer science (26 per cent) and engineering (21 per cent). This helps to account for why computer programmer, interactive media designer, and systems analyst are in the top 10 jobs for men but not for women in Figure 9.2. However, this is only part of the story.

In a study of Canadian STEM graduates, Statistics Canada's Darcy Hango found that while the unemployment rates for young men and women graduating with non-STEM degrees were about the same (5.5 per cent and 5.7 per cent, respectively), the unemployment rate for male STEM graduates was over two points lower than the unemployment rate for women with STEM degrees (4.7 per cent versus 7.0 per cent) (Hango, 2013, p. 3). That's not all. Hango then looked at the rate of "employment mismatch." Sometimes called the **underemployment** rate, the **mismatch** rate represents the percentage of university graduates in jobs requiring a high school diploma or less—jobs, in other words, for which that expensive university education really isn't required. Overall, women STEM graduates had a much higher employment mismatch rate than their male counterparts (18.3 per cent vs 11.8 per cent). Women with degrees in mathematics and computer engineering had a mismatch rate of 22.4 per cent, compared with just 10.1 per cent for men. The only STEM field in which women had the lower mismatch rate was technology (20.5 per cent vs 23.5 per cent for men); that happens to be the STEM field associated with the lowest average pay. Incidentally, the mismatch rate among those with non-STEM degrees was lower for women than for men (18.5 per cent vs 22.2 per cent).

Do these findings help us understand why women are under-represented in STEM programs at Canadian colleges and universities? It may be part of the story, but it's not the whole story. In an American study aimed at finding out why women drop out of computer science programs at a disproportionately high rate, sociologist Joanne Cohoon (2006) found that attrition rates were lower in departments where the proportion of female students was higher. The presence of more female students offers more opportunities for same-sex peer support and helps to combat the notion that women do not belong in computer science (Cohoon, 2006). That finding may extend as well to engineering programs (although employment opportunities factor in), and it suggests we cannot simply conclude that young women are not interested in these programs, but that significant barriers, once removed, possibly will open these programs and their many career paths to more women.

Before we leave the topic of gendered education, have a look at Part C of Figure 9.4. Health and related fields are somehow not part of STEM, despite the fact that quite a lot of science is required

A. Undergraduate Degrees Awarded in STEM Fields

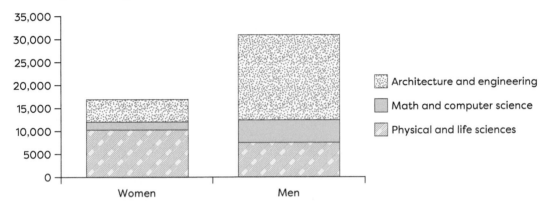

B. Undergraduate Degrees Awarded in Social Science and Humanities

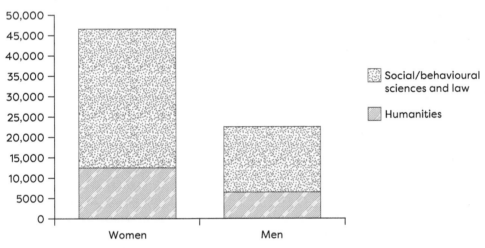

C. Undergraduate Degrees Awarded in Health and Related Fields

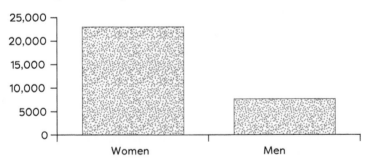

FIGURE 9.4 Undergraduate Degrees Awarded in Canada by Program Type and Sex, 2016

Source: Statistics Canada (2018c).

by those preparing for careers in nursing, human and veterinary medicine, dentistry, and pharmacy. If we are asking what keeps young women in Canada from taking math and engineering, should we also be asking why men are under-represented in undergraduate pre-health programs? Is it a problem that needs to be addressed with the same urgency?

© Christina Dun

Toronto Metropolitan University came under flak when it was reported that its engineering students were dragged through slush in their underwear as part of a hazing ritual. How do social expectations of women conflict with this controversial rite of passage? If you are a woman, would it make you think twice about applying to one of the country's engineering schools?

9.5 Race and Gender: Intersecting Oppression

The following cases highlight ways in which race and gender intersect.

Violence against Indigenous Women

Women and girls experience violence differently than do men and boys. This is primarily the case with sexual violence and murder that begins with sexual violence. Among no population is this truer than with Indigenous women. This extends to two forms of institutionalized sexual violence involving the reproduction rights of these women: sexual sterilization and abortions without consent (informed or otherwise). Reliable statistics—that is, "official" statistics that do not under-represent the problem—are hard to come by. I will use one reasonably representative figure that comes from Karen Stote's *An Act of Genocide: Colonialism and the Sterilization of Aboriginal Women* (2015). From 1971 to 1974, 580 Indigenous women were sexually sterilized in Medical Services Hospitals (run by the federal Department of Indian Affairs, as it was then called) in mostly northern parts of Alberta, Saskatchewan, Manitoba, and Ontario, as well as what are now the three territories of Yukon, Northwest Territories, and Nunavut (Stote, 2015, p. 79).

Several books have been written about Indigenous women murdered by white men. One is Lisa Priest's *Conspiracy of Silence*, about the sexually initiated killing of Helen Betty Osborne in northern Manitoba in 1971 (Priest, 1989; see also Steckley, 2013, ch. 2). W.D. Goulding's *Just Another Indian: A Serial Killer and Canada's Indifference* (2001) is about the serial killer John Martin Crawford, who killed at least four Indigenous women. S. Cameron's *On the Farm: Robert William Pickton and the Tragic Story of Vancouver's Missing Women* (2010) is about the man who became the most notorious of known serial killers of Indigenous women.

Among federal commissions, the most recent is the high-profile Inquiry into Missing and Murdered Indigenous Women and Girls, which published its final report in 2019. Its recommendations are too fresh to have been implemented, and too late to spare so many Indigenous families so much agony over their stolen sisters.

What do _you_ think?
1. Why are Indigenous women and girls targeted in this way?
2. What is necessary for the situation to change?
3. Do you think that the situation will change significantly?

Gender and Immigration

As is common in most countries in the world, Canada has permitted or encouraged to immigrate only the men or the women of a particular national or ethnic group. We saw in Chapter 8 that Chinese and South Asian women were effectively blocked from entering Canada early in the twentieth century. Later in the century, women from the Philippines were encouraged to immigrate to fill labour shortages in certain feminized occupations. However, their immigration was subject to strict conditions.

Immigration to Canada from the Philippines is distinctive for allowing women to become the "pioneers." They made the journey before their husbands and other male family members. They endure hardships in order to send most of their earnings, together with care packages of bargain-hunted goods, back to their families in the Philippines. They sponsor relatives into Canada and provide them with a place to stay in their own homes. During two periods of Filipina immigration to Canada, the first wave brought nurses, mostly women, while the second brought nannies, also women, who suffered more from the intersectionality of gender and race than did the earlier generation of Filipina immigrants.

In 1981, the Canadian government instituted its Foreign Domestic Movement Program (FDMP) to address the growing need for in-house childcare that was created as more women began working outside the home. In 1992, the FDMP was replaced by the more restrictive Live-In Caregiver Program, which required selected immigrants to commit to 24 months of domestic work within a three-year period, during which time they were also required to "live in" with the family. Nannies came mainly from the Philippines, Jamaica, and Britain. The percentage of domestics coming from the Philippines rose from 10.6 per cent in 1982 to 50.5 per cent in 1990. This trend occurred not just in Canada but in Hong Kong, Singapore, Saudi Arabia, Britain, and the United States. The political and economic unrest that surrounded the fall of the corrupt Marcos government made the Philippines a place many wanted to leave.

The women of the second wave were older than their compatriots who had migrated earlier: those aged 30–34 predominated, with those aged 25–29 and 35–39 forming smaller but roughly equal groups, and those aged 20–24 and 50–54 sharing about the same low percentage. It was more difficult for this second wave of Filipina immigrants. They were better educated than immigrating British and Jamaican nannies. Among those receiving authorization for temporary employment as nannies between 1982 and 1990, 8 per cent held bachelor's degrees, 7 per cent had at least some university education, 17 per cent had some trade and technology training, and 12 per cent had other non-university training. Working as nannies made these women grossly underemployed, as sociologist Anita Beltran Chen (1998) argues. Yet only domestic work could bring them into Canada.

In 2015, Christina Gonzales published an award-winning article on Toronto's Filipina caregivers, which shed considerable light on the work, hopes, and lives of five of these women. In her words, "The sales pitch was hard to resist: help raise our children for two years, and we'll reunite you with yours and give everyone a shot at permanent residency" (Gonzales, 2015).

She noted that because of that, from 1992 to 2015 some 75,000 of these women had become permanent residents of Canada through the caregiver program, but for many, even after two years of employment, the approval could take years, owing in part to a bureaucratic backlog. And this would mean that their children would be growing up without them: "And with rock-bottom wages in the Philippines, going back isn't a viable option" (Gonzales, 2015).

Concerning that last statement, one of the caregivers, when she left the Philippines in 2012, was making $100 a month working for a "lending institution." Another was making $300 a month as a teacher.

Much of the money the Filipina nannies earn, like that of the Chinese railroad workers before them, is sent to the family back home.

The numbers for the five women in this article are as follows:

Earnings per Month	Money Sent Home per Month	Per cent of Earnings
$1,720	$570	33%
$1,400	$600	43%
$2,000	$800	40%
$2,200	$1,400	64%*
$2,000	$800	40%

*This woman was unemployed during the time of the interview, as her employer replaced her with daycare.

One woman was 39 in 2015. At the time of the interview, she was working for a female lawyer:

> I look after her three kids, aged three, five and seven, and I cook, tidy up the house and do the laundry. I haven't considered what I'll do if my application [for permanent residence] is rejected—I prefer not to think about it. . . . My sons are 14 and 15 now. They live with my father back home. I visited them this past March and they followed me everywhere I went. When I had to leave, my elder son took it the hardest. He cried as he hugged me goodbye and escaped to his room before I left. I miss them both so much. (Gonzales, 2015)

Another stated:

> I haven't been home to see my kids in almost 10 years. When I left, my younger daughter hung a photo of me inside the mosquito net that surrounds her bed. She would talk to my picture before she went to sleep. I try to keep myself busy so I don't think about how much I miss them. . . . My daughters are studying hotel and restaurant management. They tell me that when they arrive here, they'll find work, and I'll finally be able to rest.

As women, as visible minorities, and as temporary and poorly paid employees subject to few industrial controls, the women were vulnerable to exploitation and physical, emotional, and sexual abuse. Those who had been trained in a specific field, such as nursing, also had to fight losing their skills through disuse. Between 15 and 20 per cent were married and had to endure separation from their husbands and, often, children. Those who were single returned a large portion (estimates vary around 75 per cent) of their income to their family back home, holding onto little money to look after themselves. They are restricted by the stereotypes of race and gender that treat Asian women as caregivers, overlooking skills that might make them productive in other areas of Western society.

Misogynoir

In 2010, as a graduate student—she is an associate professor in the Department of Communication Studies at Northwestern University—Black gay feminist Moya Bailey introduced the term "misogynoir." It refers to the combination of racism ("noir") and sexism ("misogyny") experienced by Black women. It was first used in reference to the way Black women have been presented in hip hop, and generally in American visual and popular culture. Black feminist women writers assert that it is not confined to non-Black people. As Jamilah Lemieux wrote in her foreword to Michele Wallace's *Black Macho and the Myth of the Superwoman*, "it can come even from those who are black, who were raised by black women and profess to value black people" (Lemieux, 2015).

Kesiena Boom is a radical, Black feminist, lesbian, sociologist, and writer based in Manchester, England. In 2015 she wrote "4 Tired Tropes Perfectly Explain What Misogynoir Is and How You Can Stop It." A trope is an image or characterization that is cliché, stereotypical, often false, and can be harmful to those depicted. In her article, she described two examples of misogynoir that occurred when she was walking through the "city's queer district" with two white women. A white woman came up to her, said "You're hot," and grabbed one of her breasts. It wasn't the first time that something like that happened. A few minutes later a white man came up to her, snapped his fingers, and said "Damn, girrrrlfriend! Work it! You *look fierce*."

She contrasted her appearance with that of her two white friends:

> On this particular day, I was makeup free, clad in my omnipresent black Doc Martens

boots, and dressed in baggy overalls that make me look like a plumber who just got off shift. There was nothing fierce about it. My two non-Black female friends who stood next to me, however, *did* look fierce—dressed and made up to the nines and resplendent in high heels. Yet, they went on unnoticed. If these accounts seem gross—but totally unfamiliar—to you then my guess is that you might be white. (Boom, 2015)

The four tropes that Boom describes are: (1) the *Sassy Black Woman*, "a common stereotype that portrays us as one-dimensional sasspots who click our fingers and roll our necks and shout 'Mmhmm!' at any given moment. . . . The SBW stereotype dehumanizes us by presenting us as cardboard cut-outs with no depth of feeling or emotion." (2) The *Hypersexual Jezebel* depicts Black women as "sluts, whores, and hoes. . . . Blackness added to womanhood creates the expectation of rampant sexuality. Presenting Black women's bodies as the antithesis of the 'innocence' of white womanhood marks Black womanhood as a signifier of guilt. . . . We are relegated to animalistic and primitive by suggesting that we're unable to exercise self-control." (3) The *Angry Black Woman* trope plays on the idea that "any discomfort expressed by a Black woman is unreasonable . . . seen as something that can be ignored. . . . I have often been told that I'm 'too aggressive' in my activism, especially by white feminists, even when I'm being decidedly placid and reasonable. It's a tactic used in order to belittle our valid anger by portraying it as an inherent character flaw, rather than a justified reaction to circumstances." Finally, (4) the *Strong Black Woman* is "a cultural narrative that positions Black women as able to withstand any and all emotional difficulty we face without any support. . . . It's been preferable for people to see us as able to deal with anything and everything, because then we can be treated in deplorable ways. This trope also contributes to many Black women's unwillingness to seek help for mental health issues *and* for us to be less likely believed when we do try and get help or discuss it."

Then there is *transmisogynoir*, the negative treatment and attitude toward Black people who are born assigned the gender of male but identify with the female gender. This triple combination is literally deadly. One study found that between October 2013 and September 2014, 226 transgender people were murdered worldwide, most of them transwomen of colour (O'Hara, 2014).

Gender Abroad: *Boyat* and Deviant Gender Performance in the Arab World

In Arab countries such as Qatar and the United Arab Emirates, an emerging pattern of deviant behaviour cuts across gender and ethnic lines. It involves young women who adopt a masculine style of dress, including baggy jeans or military pants, aviator shades, heavy watches and other jewellery, combat boots or running shoes, and so on; many of the women keep their hair cut short. A woman dressed this way wouldn't look out of place in North America, but in many parts of the Arab world women in public customarily wear a *burqa* or *abaya*, a full-length, loose-fitting robe that covers the whole body from the shoulders down, or at least a veil, or *niqab*.

The women are known as *boyat* (singular *boyah*), an Arabic word akin to "tomboy" and sometimes translated as "transsexual." But the behaviour is not sexual. It is more a deviant way of acting out and exploring gender. The conventionally masculine style of dress is liberating: *boyat* are able to talk and act more aggressively and independently than they could if they were dressed as women. But their gender performance goes beyond the "costume." The women involved consider their behaviour a way of life, and they find an important kind of solidarity with other women engaged in the same behaviour (see *Globe and Mail*, 2009; Naidoo, 2010, 2011).

What are the factors influencing the *boyat* phenomenon? Globalization has played a role, by exposing women and girls in Middle Eastern countries to images of women acting more independently than women in the Arab world are traditionally permitted to do. Social media allow *boyat* to communicate with one another anonymously and get together online without being seen. There are also links between the *boyat* phenomenon and higher education. A college or university education prolongs the period of unmarried youth for young women. Like-minded *boyat* gathering together in women's colleges and campuses like those of the UAE's Higher Colleges of Technology are less likely to arouse suspicion with their behaviour. In such settings, their increasing number makes them the majority, putting them in a position to poke fun at and even bully their more conservative female peers.

In most settings, *boyat* remain a minority, and deviant behaviour is met with negative sanctions. Some opponents of the *boyat* phenomenon have attempted to medicalize the "problem" by proposing rehabilitation therapy and medicine. In some jurisdictions, cross-dressing has been made illegal.

Compare this relatively tolerant behaviour with the death on 17 September 2022 in prison of 22-year-old Iranian woman Mahsa Amini, who was arrested for not wearing her *hijab* tied tightly enough. "Witnesses accused police of beating Amini inside a van as she was led to a detention center. The young woman died at a hospital Friday after three days in a coma" (Steinbuch, 2022). As of this writing (December 2022), protests in Iran that began with Amini's death continue to challenge the status quo conservatism that restricts women's education and work, and forces compliance with strict social rules.

Masculinity, Race, and Toxic Masculinity

Not all masculinities are the same, even within one society. Some of them can be considered "toxic," meaning not healthy either for the males involved or for the society of which they are a part. Race is a persistent factor in the production and reproduction of toxic masculinities like the ones described below.

Jamil Jivani (2018) provides three good illustrations of how ideas about masculinity are intertwined with race. Jivani's father came from Kenya to Toronto, where Jivani was born. As a Black youth, Jivani experienced deep prejudice from early on, moving always within the gaze of a suspicious mainstream society that watched him carefully once he became an adolescent:

> As I grew up, I was also frequently stopped or followed by cops and security guards on my way to and from school. It's hard to feel you belong when your mere presence on the street, at the mall, and at the bus stop draws the suspicion of people who are supposed to keep our community safe. (Jivani, 2018, p. 3)

Jivani's father, who had been abandoned by his biological parents and whose adoptive parents died when he was 14, did not play a positive role in demonstrating masculinity to his son. The masculine role models that Jivani fashioned himself after were what he calls Hollywood gangster rappers. He sees correlation and argues for causation between the degree to which the people he hung out with watched and listened to gangster rap and the way they spoke, what they talked about, and how they acted:

> We adopted aspects of gang culture, including bandannas and rapper-inspired nicknames. We even gave gang names to our friend groups. . . . Some of us began smoking [marijuana] and talking about getting it from drug dealers. We would hang out and loiter, with nothing to do but share gangster fairy tales. It became normal to speak about women in disrespectful language and to pursue sexual relationships with our female classmates as sport. For kids who didn't have much money, we became oddly obsessed with expensive clothes, particularly the kind you'd see on rappers and basketball players. (Jivani, 2018, pp. 27–8)

Jivani himself cultivated a tough-guy "gangsta" image and reputation:

> In my backpack, I carried a police-style baton and a hunting knife so I could protect myself in fights and also intimidate people older and bigger than I was. I also kept an old Louisville Slugger wooden baseball bat in my locker. If I suspect a fight might break out at school, I would hide the baseball bat in the baggiest pair of jeans I owned and walk around with a limp. All these things made me feel cool. My friends and the older guys we knew seemed impressed by this behaviour, so I kept it up. (Jivani, 2018, p. 34)

At the point where he was planning to get himself a gun, he started down a different path. He graduated from high school and took a college program that would get him into university. At that time, he became one of my students. The person I saw at that time was not a gangster rapper type (we had a number of those in class, so I knew what they looked like), but an intelligent, soft-spoken young man who wanted to learn from me about his tribal heritage as a Kikuyu from Kenya.

Jivani went on to university, first in Toronto, then into a law program at Yale, where campus security guards directed a careful gaze on a student who did not look like the typical Ivy League student. He became an advocate for groups that supported young Black men, both in Canada and the United States.

When a Moroccan terror cell in Belgium connected to ISIS attacked Paris in 2015, Jivani decided he needed to learn about the circumstances of these young Black men. He travelled to Europe and soon found patterns in a community in Brussels, Belgium's capital city, that were similar to those he had experienced growing up Black in North America. The race, religion, and immigrant status of these young men restricted their opportunities, and their capacity to identify themselves as Belgian. The opposition culture they were vulnerable to was that of Muslim terrorism. It was a way of "being a man" that garnered them a kind of respect, a kind of redemption for criminal activities and lack of financial success, a way of opposing the Western system that oppressed their people.

Insightfully, Jivani then turned his analytical eye to another racialized-based group of young men, this time white nationalists, the alt-right supporters of Donald Trump, who, like the young Black men of his own time and place, and like the Moroccan Belgians he studied in Europe, are alienated from mainstream culture and express their alienation through a racialized, "toxic" masculinity. The common insult used by this group is "cuckservative," or "cuck" for short. A blend of "cuckold," an archaic term for a man whose wife has cheated on him, and "conservative," it is used with disdain to describe someone who, out of a need for acceptance, approval, and affection, has debased his masculinity by adopting liberal, especially feminist, values. To the alt-right, these men have sold out not just their masculinity but their culture and race:

> The alt-right attempts to emasculate young white men who don't identify with them and refers to them as weak beta males. The young men who gravitate to the alt-right feel disconnected from their country much as ISIS recruits do, but what's distinct is a feeling of decline. In their worldview, the West used to be theirs but is no longer because "cucks" have allowed Europe and North America to be overtaken by various minority groups. (Jivani, 2018, p. 188)

Jivani's main answer to these toxic masculinities, especially with males who have not experienced positive role modelling from their fathers, is with youth groups for young men that are run by older men who help them cope with careers, racism, and identity, in large part through role-modelling a positive masculinity.

9.6 Sexuality

In 2018 Canada had about one million people who are LGBTQ2+, which accounts for 4 per cent of the total population aged 15 and older. To recapitulate a distinction we made early in this chapter, *gender* is distinguished from *sex*. Sex refers to the primary biological traits, including the sexual organs, that categorize people as either male or female. Gender refers to the cultural meanings that societies attach to sex categories and greatly extends the range of sexualized behaviours. Much of our discussion in this chapter has been about that 4 per cent of the population. The 96 per cent of the population identifying as male or female both biologically and in terms of gender role choose to make those designations on census and other forms. In sociological terms, when that large a proportion of a population self-describes in a particular way, that description constitutes a "norm." Part of my assumption is that those 25 million people who meet that norm need to stop making certain assumptions about the other 4 per cent (if they do). Beyond the 4 per cent who identify as LGBTQ2+ are other people about whom gendered assumptions are made.

People sometimes assume that a person's sexuality can be accurately deduced from their gender performance—that a woman who adopts some masculine gender behaviours must be sexually attracted to women, or that a man who dresses as a woman must be attracted to other men. Neither of these assumptions is *necessarily* correct. It is also not safe to assume that a person assigned the male sex at birth who identifies as female is sexually attracted to men. A transgender person may be sexually attracted to people of the same or the opposite sex, or both, or neither. Of course, it would be just as wrong to assume that someone attracted to people of the same sex must secretly wish to change sexes. All of this is

The Point Is . . .

Yes, Toxic Femininity Is Also a Thing

After learning about toxic masculinity, many of the men in your class, and some of the women, are asking whether toxic femininity exists as well.

There are a growing number of non-academic blog posts and magazine articles on the subject, many of them written more in humour than in serious analysis (but they are funny). Perhaps we should begin by dispelling some false impressions of what toxic femininity is. Keri Mangis provides a helpful list in her 2017 contribution to The Good Man Project. Toxic femininity does *not* describe the behaviour of a woman who:

- expresses her anger or outrage at legitimate offences
- attends rallies, protests, or marches to fight for equality
- wears clothing not traditionally associated with femininity
- expresses a contrary or dissenting opinion
- refuses a man's advances
- rejects prescribed gender roles
- expresses feminist views
- isn't sexually attracted to, or only to, men.

Lync Dalton (2017) offers a description of what she believes toxic femininity involves. She presents the following list of social beliefs or myths about femininity that she considers toxic:

- An acceptable woman presents as morally pure but accommodating, refined, and nurturing. She doesn't exert direct power over others.
- An acceptable woman's power comes from her ability to charm and influence the people—particularly the men—around her to bring their own powers to bear toward her purposes.
- A woman's worth is principally determined by men's sexual desire for her.
- Women must appear to appreciate and support one another, but they're actually constantly and secretly in competition over beauty, male attention, and other things that define their worth.
- An acceptable woman's mission is to competently and quietly fulfill the emotional, nutritional, domestic, and sometimes sexual needs of the people around her. The most worthy women are the most selfless women.

The combined effect of all these myths is toxic femininity, which

teaches us to centre our looks in most matters, and hold our bodies to impossibly high beauty standards. It teaches us that if we wish to control a situation, we must do so covertly, by manipulating the people involved. It also teaches us that men are conduits to self-worth and power as much as they're individual human beings with their own sets of needs, all while overlooking our own intrinsic power and worth.

And . . . men absorb these messages too, and it shapes what they see in—and expect from—the women in their lives, in obvious to subtle ways. (Dalton, 2017)

to say that we should not make assumptions about a person's sexual preferences based on their gender expression or sex identity, or vice versa. How can we consider sexuality apart from sex and gender?

Sexuality refers to feelings of sexual desire and attraction and how these are expressed. Sexuality constitutes a spectrum and often changes over time. Nevertheless, views of sexuality in North America have traditionally been shaped by two ideas. The first is that all people are defined sexually by whether the person is attracted to people of the same sex or to people of the opposite sex, based on a binary (male–female) understanding of sexes. According to this framework:

- A **heterosexual** or "straight" person is sexually attracted to people of the opposite sex (women to men, men to women). Generally speaking, about the 96 per cent, that may be true. Sexual attraction to people of the opposite sex is called heteronormative and it is not a pathological condition. However, **heteronormativity** becomes a problem when it creates social exclusion for the rest of the citizenry.

Further assumptions are less likely to be accurate:

- A **homosexual** is sexually attracted to people of the same sex (**gay** and **queer** are accepted synonyms).
- A **lesbian** is a woman who is sexually attracted to other women.
- A **bisexual** is sexually attracted (equally or unequally) to both males and females.

Psychiatry believed until the late twentieth century that bisexuality—genuine attraction to both men and women—did not exist, but that people claiming to be bisexual were really gays and lesbians who were in denial because of social pressure (see Rosario, Scrimshaw, Hunter, & Braun, 2006, for a discussion of this myth). Of course, some people can be attracted to both men and women. Others can also be attracted to transmen and transwomen, adding a nuance not adequately covered by the binary terms *homosexual* and *heterosexual*. Today it is widely understood that gay, straight, and bi are but three shades of the sexuality spectrum, and a growing list of terms are gaining currency to describe other hues of sexual preference. These include "asexual" (no sexual attraction), "demisexual" (sexual attraction only once an emotional bond is formed), "pansexual" (attraction to those of all sexes and genders), and "sapiosexual" (attraction to people of high intelligence).

In the 72 countries of the world where homosexuality continues to be criminalized (see Figure 9.5), a range of forms of opposition exist. In 2013, Russia, where homosexuality is not in itself illegal, passed a federal law prohibiting anyone from producing or distributing "propaganda of non-traditional sexual relations" among minors in a move that essentially made it illegal to equate gay and straight relationships (Elder, 2013). If you are fortunate to live in a country where such draconian measures are not in place, you can still find commercial targeting of the largest potential market: lots of evidence where heterosexual couples with children are emblematic

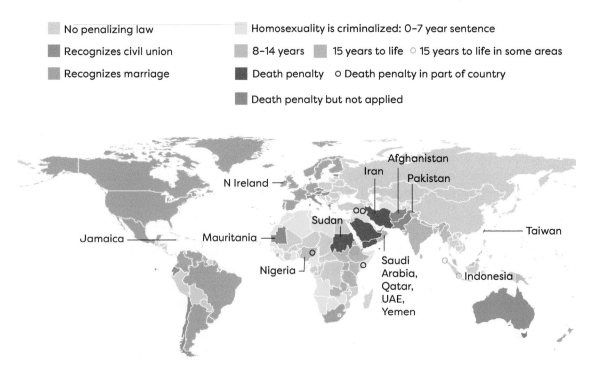

FIGURE 9.5 **The Legal Status of Homosexuality around the World**

Telling It Like It Is

A Student's Point of View

Gender Roles and Being Lesbian

People in my life in the past have tended to believe that because I am a lesbian, I automatically have more male-specific interests, and that I do not enjoy typical girl-oriented activities. Shortly after I told my brother, he invited me to a football game, stating, "You like football now, don't you?" Although he was joking at the time, this is a typical comment often made to me. Although I may enjoy fixing things around the house, my partner is a sports fanatic, and while I like to sew and knit, she enjoys cooking and romantic comedies. The gender stereotyping, which is exactly what this comes down to, even goes so far as to include the style of clothes I wear. I remember one time that I went into work wearing a baseball cap, although I usually do not wear a hat to work, as I find it unprofessional. This particular day I was coming from school and in a rush. Immediately after entering work, I began to hear comments and mutters from my co-workers. It seemed that in their eyes because I was wearing a hat, I was portraying a male characteristic. They assumed that being a lesbian is the closest thing to being a male.

There is a significant difference between sexual orientation and gender identity. All of the gay people that I know, including myself, are very happy with their sex. They just happen to be attracted to the same sex as well. I am proud to be a woman. I enjoy it and would not want to change it.

Hero Images Inc. / Alamy Stock Photo

Do you think this couple spends a lot of time worrying which of them is "being the man" at any given moment?

(Continued)

For one reason or another people with little understanding of the gay population seem to need definite clarification of "who's the man and who's the woman," a question that I have been asked on too many occasions to count. In many gay relationships there are no specific roles, and each individual's identity is not masculine or feminine, but it slides on a continuum. It is ridiculous to assume that there is a male and female figure in the relationship. If I wanted a male–female partnership, I wouldn't be gay.

Many people believe that gay people, male or female, are involved in a sexual scene full of promiscuity, voyeurism, and *ménages à trois*. This is evidenced by the number of people that have made suggestive comments to me about non-committed casual sexual encounters. Although these beliefs are positive in one aspect as they break down the very untrue opinion that women cannot have the high sex drive that men are more known for, it also reflects a larger belief that being in a gay relationship is all about the sex. This leads people to believe that gay people do not commit and take part in stable, settled relationships. I remember talking with my father once about the relationship I was in and he responded, "It's alright if that's what you want, but it's unfortunate because those relationships don't last; they just don't settle." Ironically, I must say that gay relationships in fact have very little to do with sex. As a heterosexual relationship has many dimensions, so does the homosexual one, encompassing all one's needs such as emotional support, companionship, the sharing of values and spirituality, and of course, physical attraction does play its role as well. I once saw an advertisement that mocked this expectation of such extravagant sex lives. The poster was in a bookstore located in a gay community. The caption read, "What do lesbians do in bed?" and the picture had two women in bed wearing flannel pyjamas, one watching television and the other reading a book. I saw this as an accurate portrayal and a clever way to challenge this opinion.

What do *you* think?
What examples of heteronormativity has the author of this narrative encountered?

of wholesome family values that companies would like their products—cars, breakfast cereal, furniture, you name it—to be associated with. And, unfortunately, you can find plenty of examples of targeting and discrimination against those in the LGBTQ2+ community. Look no further than the United States, where animosity toward (and one might say fear of) homosexuals has a sordid history, especially in recent years since the rise of social media–fuelled hate and the rise of Trumpism: the Pulse shooting in Orlando, Florida, in June 2016 that killed 49 people at a gay nightclub; the shooting at Club Q in Colorado Springs, Colorado, in November 2022 that killed 5 and physically wounded about 20 other people; threats and abusive protests from right-wing militia groups at drag queen shows on an almost daily basis.

In this chapter and throughout the book I have used the initials LGBTQ2 (lesbian, gay, bisexual, transgender, queer/questioning, Two-Spirit) as an all-encompassing term to refer to people who do not identify as heterosexual and cisgender. An "A" is sometimes added to denote asexual, and an "I" is sometimes added for intersex. Note that some Indigenous activists reject the "2" (or "2S") addition to the initials because they consider Two-Spirit people to fall outside mainstream Western ideas of transgender. LGBTQ2 encompasses gender identities as well as sexualities, and so it is not a perfect analogue of "heterosexual," which refers specifically to sexuality. It is a term that comprises disparate categories that have been grouped ideologically because they represent a shared experience of discrimination and the fight for equality and recognition. Neither is it an acronym for other groups experiencing discrimination and the fight for equality and recognition, notably the Black, brown, and Asian communities that sometimes object to an equivalency being drawn between their ethnic causes and the complaints of LGBTQ2 communities.

Wrap It Up

Summary

We have seen that gender and sex are different. You are born with a sex: typically male or female, although intersex people may be born with both male and female sexual organs. Your gender is socially constructed to a significant extent. It may not fit neatly into the binary categories "male" and "female" but may sit somewhere between these two points. The social construction of gender applies not just in obvious areas such as clothing and colours, but in occupations as well. You need be neither a woman nor a feminist to recognize that the feminization of an occupation—making it unrewarding in terms of pay, power, and social status—helps to create inequality between men and women. This inequality, reflected in pay ratio and in the greater likelihood of women working part-time, is changing very little. As sociologists, we need to investigate why this is so, and look for ways to address the inequity. We also must ask ourselves whether the separate paths that men and women take in postsecondary education lead to social inequality or just difference, an issue we considered in Chapter 4, on socialization.

Think Back

Questions for Critical Review

1. Explain, in your own words, the difference between biological sex, sexual identity, and gender.
2. What do the cases of David Reimer and Caster Semenya tell you about the relationship between biological sex and a person's lived sexual identity?
3. What does it mean to say that sex and gender are socially constructed to a significant extent?
4. The "pink tax" is a phenomenon where a product used by both sexes has a version that is marketed and sold to women or girls at a higher price. The classic example is the woman's razor, which may be identical to a man's razor except in colour and cost. Explain why razors are gendered.
5. Summarize the gender differences in Canadian postsecondary education and how they relate to the most common jobs for women and men. What do these differences suggest about the different career paths that young women and men pursue?
6. Do you think there are still common stereotypes in North America surrounding those who transgress gendered work roles (e.g., the male nurse, the woman construction worker)? If so, do you think they can be changed? What would it take?
7. Describe how gender and ethnicity intersect to create stereotypes about women of different ethnic backgrounds.
8. How do you think gender-based immigration (i.e., with immigrants of one sex entering the country in much greater numbers than the other) affects the settling experiences of different groups, such as Filipinos?
9. Describe how the myth of the "real man" relates to toxic masculinity.

Read On

Suggested Print and Online Resources

Laura Bell, "Working Out Is a Minefield When You're Non-Binary," *Vice*, 13 September 2018, www.vice.com/en_ca/article/yw4gpx/working-out-is-a-minefield-when-youre-non-binary In this article, Laura Bell explains why working out at the gym is a challenge for non-binary people.

Judith Butler, *Gender Trouble: Feminism and the Subversion of Identity* (New York: Routledge, 1990) Butler's pioneering work launched the study of queer theory.

Canadian Press, "Canadian Medical Journal Acknowledges Its Role in Perpetuating Anti-Black Racism in Health Care," 24 October

2022, https://www.cbc.ca/news/health/cmaj-anti-racism-1.6627312

Dr Omi Soore Dryden, co-lead of the national Black Health Education Collaborative, says, "In some ways, Canada very much is a welcoming place. However, that can act as a barrier in understanding how racism manifests—it's not just the racial slur. It's not just the racist targeting. But it is in the very systems of continuing to practice race-based medicine."

Soraya Chemaly, *Rage Becomes Her: The Power of Women's Anger* (New York: Atria Books, 2018); Chemaly, "The Power of Women's Anger," TED Talk (2018, November), www.ted.com/talks/soraya_chemaly_the_power_of_women_s_anger?language=en

In her book and in her TED Talk, Soraya Chemaly looks at how anger is gendered in such a way that anger "confirms masculinity and confounds femininity."

John Colapinto, *As Nature Made Him* (New York: Harper, 2000)

Colapinto provides the definitive account of David Reimer's life and tragic death.

Jamil Jivani, *Why Young Men: Rage, Race, and the Crisis of Identity* (Toronto: HarperCollins, 2018); Daemon Fairless, *Mad Blood Stirring: The Inner Lives of Violent Men* (Toronto: Random House, 2018); Rachel Giese, *Boys: What It Means to Become a Man* (Toronto: HarperCollins, 2018)

Read together, these books give excellent insight into male violence and toxic masculinity. Jivani begins with a look at what draws young Black men to violence and sees parallels with white nationalists and Islamic terrorists. Fairless interviews convicted criminals and fighters to see if the violent impulses that drive them exist near the surface in all men. Giese looks at why, at a time when gender expectations for girls are broadening, social expectations about masculinity remain as narrow as ever.

Melissa Moyser, *Women in Canada: A Gender-Based Statistical Report*, Statistics Canada, cat. no. 89-503-X (Ottawa: Minister of Industry, 2017)

In her report for Statistics Canada, Melissa Moyser offers many insights into what defines women's work in Canada today.

Amelia Naidoo, "Cross about Cross-Dressing: Is It a Wicked Western Habit That Should Be Stopped?" 28 January 2010, *The Economist*, www.economist.com/node/154403091; and "Shedding Light on the 'Boyat' Phenomenon: Conference Separates Fact from Fiction on the Issue," 21 April 2011, http://gulfnews.com/news/gulf/uae/general/shedding-light-on-the-boyat-phenomenon-1.796816

The author provides an account of the "debate about fashion in Qatar" and looks at both sides of the issue of cross-dressing and *boyat* in the Middle East.

Ontario Equal Pay Coalition, *Economic Equality Insights: An Omnibus Survey with Ontario Residents*, 4 April 2022

This survey, conducted with Environics Research, shows how Ontarians view the male–female pay gap and its effect on livelihoods.

P.J. Raval, director, *Call Her Ganda*, 2018 documentary film, https://www.callherganda.com/

Film that examines the brutal murder of a Filipina transwoman, Jennifer Laude, by a US marine, and the efforts of three women—an activist attorney, a transgender journalist, and Jennifer's mother—in pursuing justice and confronting the long history of US imperialism.

Toronto Star, "The 'Genderless Baby' Who Caused a Storm of Controversy," www.thestar.com/news/article/1105515—the-genderless-baby-who-caused-a-storm-of-controversy-in-2011; "Remember Storm? We Check in on the Baby Being Raised Gender Neutral," www.thestar.com/life/parent/2013/11/15/remember_storm_we_check_in_on_the_baby_being_raised_genderneutral.html; "Baby Storm Five Years Later: Preschooler on Top of the World," www.thestar.com/news/gta/2016/07/11/baby-storm-five-years-later-preschooler-on-top-of-the-world.html

These *Toronto Star* articles look at the life of Baby Storm from the eve of the infant's first birthday to the start of preschool.

Sadie Whitelocks, "I Exist in the Gray: 29-Year-Old Who Looks Like a Woman but Has Male Genitalia Speaks Out about Rare Intersex Condition," *Daily Mail*, 17 April 2015, updated 29 April 2015, https://www.dailymail.co.uk/news/article-3043767/I-exist-gray-29-year-old-looks-like-woman-male-genitalia-speaks-rare-intersex-condition.html

Pidgeon/Jennifer Pagonis describes a childhood in which she was raised as a girl, then discovered she was born intersex and subjected to "mysterious" (to her) surgeries.

Social Organization and the Sociology of Religion

Reading this chapter will help you to . . .

- Learn about different kinds of social organizations and understand how they affect our lives.
- Appreciate the values of social organization and its dysfunctions.
- Locate yourself in the larger society and recognize how your gender and your personal experiences continue to shape your attitudes and beliefs.
- Identify the principal elements of religion.
- Understand how new religious movements differ from established religious traditions.
- Outline Émile Durkheim's sociological approach to religion.
- Analyze the relationship between organized religion and family.
- Discuss the relationship between organized religion and gender roles.

For Starters

My Experience with the Baha'i Faith: The Social Support of a Religious Community

The year 1987 was a bad one for me. My second marriage was breaking up; within the year, I would be divorced. I was lonely and disheartened, believing this was my last chance at a serious relationship. Then, you might say, I got religion.

A cousin of mine and his wife were Baha'i. He had been born into a Christian household, and she was raised Jewish, but as adults they sought out a religious community that respected both faiths. Baha'i began as an offshoot of Islam, although it is generally considered a religion unto itself today. It was started by an Iranian prophet of the nineteenth century, who spoke of the truth of the prophets of all religions and of the equality of religions. The Baha'i have been persecuted in Iran and other Muslim countries, where the faith is viewed as a renunciation of Islam. Dozens of Baha'i were executed during the last two decades of the twentieth century, including Mona Mahmudnizhad, a 16-year-old who was sentenced to death and hanged in 1983 for "misleading children and youth and for being a Zionist." Canadians who grew up watching the early days of MuchMusic in the mid-1980s learned of her case in the song and video "Mona with the Children," written and recorded by a Canadian musician, Doug Cameron (you can find it on YouTube).

My cousin and his wife intervened because they knew the state I was in. They also knew that I loved playing sports, and so they told me about Friday-night volleyball at a school not far from where I lived. Most the participants were Baha'i. It soon became the highlight of my week: volleyball followed by Pizza Hut (no alcohol; they don't drink). It later extended to Saturday-afternoon baseball . . . and Pizza Hut.

I developed some strong friendships with the people, both North American and Iranian. I was welcomed into people's homes and invited to ceremonies, which I readily attended and enjoyed. I felt a very strong sense of belonging. At no point was I pressured to make any kind of commitment to joining, although they made sure that I learned about the faith. I was referred to as a "friend of the faith," which I definitely was and still am. They helped me rebuild my confidence, and I owe a huge debt of thanks to this religious community for that.

What do *you* think?

This story about the kindness of people toward an unhappy sociologist is a story about social interactions around the sometimes-unwelcome subject of faith. Three identified faiths are mentioned. In what ways do the friends represent the tenets of the faiths they were raised in? In what ways are their expressions of kindness identifiable as characteristically Baha'i? How would you describe the characteristics of the small group's interactions? Would they be expressed in the same way in a workplace? In an educational institution? In what culture might those interactions be prohibited or limited?

10.1 Introduction: Studying Social Interaction in Small Groups

As we saw in Chapter 4, status and role are important concepts in understanding the individual's identity formation. The statuses we hold are elements of how we see ourselves. They also lay the groundwork for interaction with others. A woman walks into the intensive care unit. Her status as the cardiologist and final arbiter of the treatment for three of the patients in the ICU establishes certain expectations around the interactions she will have with the nurses delivering her instructions and prescriptions to the patients. Before anyone says a word, we can predict how each one might act based on the statuses that

Quick Hits

Pecking Order

In the 1920s, Norwegian zoologist and comparative psychologist Thorleif Schjelderup-Ebbe introduced a term that, when translated into English, became "pecking order." It originally applied to chickens (hens in particular), with reference to which ones can get away with pecking others. The hen no other chicken pecks is at the top of the flock's social hierarchy, or pecking order. The eight parrots I live with have a tail-pulling order. Gus, a cockatiel and the smallest of our birds, has had his tail pulled by all seven of the others, demonstrating that he occupies the lowest position on our parrots' social hierarchy.

each one holds in that situation. Statuses related to seniority, and whether the doctor has been practising in that hospital for weeks or for years will also have an effect. The seniority and experience of the nurses also come into play. To the extent that the patient is aware of his surroundings and the people in charge of his care—and the care of a woman patient in the patient bay on one side and of a surprisingly young man on life support in the patient bay on the other side—also will influence the patient relying on his knowledge of those statuses.

In small-group settings, statuses can be a valuable way to establish the **pecking order**, or who is in charge. You have grown up through a school system where principal, vice-principal, teachers, teacher's assistants, guidance counsellors, custodial and other staff created your day-to-day learning environment. To build and operate that environment, their hierarchy of statuses, each with its own set of roles or expected behaviours, helped that environment to be consistent, energetic, organized, and beneficial to the students. The same social structure was designed to be beneficial to those responsible for it. An aspect of its smooth operation was the reporting structure: From whom does the vice-principal take orders, and who answers to them? What further authorities function in this public education system?

Small-Group Studies and the Definition of the Situation

The study of small-group interaction came early to sociology with the pioneering work of German sociologist Georg Simmel (1858–1918), who was among the first to narrow his focus to the daily, one-on-one social interactions of individuals. As a microsociologist

> ### What do *you* think?
> What kinds of behaviour do humans coexisting in small groups use to establish a pecking order? Consider (a) students in a college dormitory, (b) the staff of a busy doughnut shop restaurant, and (c) a faith group that you have been part of or that you have studied.

he was a forerunner of the symbolic interactionists we have encountered earlier:

> Society and the social structures that comprise it are, in actuality, only the sum of the individual interactions. The appropriate locus of sociology, then, shifts away from the macro structures, such as economy and class, to the study of the processes underlying the interaction of individuals. (Simmel, 1971)

Others working in this tradition around the turn of the twentieth century include Charles Cooley (1864–1929), whose concept of the looking-glass self we discussed in Chapter 4, and **Frederic Thrasher** (1892–1962), whose classic study of gangs in Chicago (Thrasher, 1927) represents a study of group interaction rooted in fieldwork. He saw the gangs as small clusters of intense interaction separated from the larger social world:

> An immigrant colony . . . is itself an isolated social world. . . . The gang boy moves only in his own universe and other regions are clothed in . . . mystery. . . . He knows little of the outside world. (Thrasher, 1927)

Thrasher's ethnographic research on gangs and small-group interaction was carried on in William Whyte's *Street-Corner Society* (1955), which we considered in Chapter 3. The social interactions of North American gang worlds continues to be an area of study for sociologists, including Humber College criminologist Mark Totten, author of *Nasty, Brutish and Short: The Lives of Gang Members in Canada* (2012) and *Gang Life: 10 of the Toughest Tell Their Stories* (2014).

Another important contribution to the study of small-group interaction—and another study of European immigrants entering North America during the first two decades of the twentieth century—came from the symbolic interactionist William I. Thomas, whose monumental work with Polish sociologist Florian Znaniecki, *The Polish Peasant in Europe and America* ([1918–20] 1996), illustrated the important part narratives play in defining social situations. Dorothy Swaine Thomas, his wife, was a sociologist in her own right and contributed significantly to the concept of personal narratives. The foundational concept here is that individuals are consciously or unconsciously interpreting their own behaviour as the story of their life. The Thomases show that the way people interpret their own lives is a sociological element worth studying because the "situations we define as real become real in their consequences" (Thomas, 1966, p. 301). This idea, which came to be known as the **Thomas theorem**, influenced other developments in symbolic interactionism, including a concept known as the **definition of the situation**. The term refers to the difference in perspective on a social situation of two or more people, based on their subjective personal narrative about their experiences. For this reason, understanding how an individual defines a situation is crucial to understanding the individual's actions and responses to it. The researcher should not assume that people passing through similar circumstances will have experienced those circumstances the same way. Similarly, in understanding personal interactions, the different perspectives of the individuals should be acknowledged.

A classic case of how different ways of defining a situation can lead to misunderstanding and mistrust surrounds the practice that Europeans referred to as "Indian giving." In traditional Indigenous culture, people would give gifts as statements that they wanted to strengthen the bonds between them. In the Wendat (Huron) language of the trading people, the verb meaning "to trade" translates literally as "to give *to each other*." Accepting a gift was an important gesture: it was the first step in acknowledging and accepting the wish to strengthen bonds. Returning the favour was the second, equally important step: it confirmed the desire to establish friendly terms. From the European perspective, when an Indigenous gift-giver expressed a desire for a gift in return, that gift-giver was judged as demanding and selfish. You can see how different the personal narratives are in such situations.

Interaction Process Analysis

During the 1950s, a Harvard research team headed by social psychologist **Robert F. Bales** (1916–2004) brought the study of small-group interaction to the laboratory. Bales and his colleagues developed a system of coding for social interaction in small groups, called **interaction process analysis (IPA)**. It dealt initially with ways of determining whether groups and their members were task-oriented or relationship-oriented. The researchers later developed the methodology to identify patterns of behaviour such as dominant/submissive, friendly/unfriendly, and accepting of authority/non-accepting of authority. For several reasons, IPA has lost followers.

First, studying small-group interaction was the product of a structural-functionalist perspective, which has become a minority perspective today. Second, small-group studies at the time when they were popular seemed to lack consideration for distinctive social roles: gender, race, ethnicity, and other sociological factors that matter to those individuals and now are considered essential to any rigorous inquiry.

What do you think?

1. Five female nursing students are engaged in a group project on doctor–nurse interaction in a hospital. How might the addition of one male nursing student affect the dynamics of the group?
2. Five male students from the police foundation program are engaged in a group project on handling domestic disputes. How might the addition of one female student affect the dynamics of the group?
3. How would IPA approach each of these small group interactions?

Imagine how the dynamics of a group of women change when a man is part of the group. Imagine how the opportunities and strategies for leadership differ in a small group of women as compared with a small group of men. How do those dynamics change when race is brought into the discussion? Third, many contemporary sociologists view the study of small groups—especially in a lab setting—as "artificial."

10.2 Studying Social Interaction in Large Groups

So far in this chapter we've looked at how status and role serve to structure one-on-one and small-group interactions. Whenever we look at individuals and small groups, we're taking a microsociological approach. We are now shifting to macro as we look at social organization from a bird's eye view that grasps the larger scale of group interactions.

When we think of the term "social organization," we might think of the way a society and its institutions—the family, organized religion, the legal system, the government, and so on—are organized. What we seldom consider is that the basis for social organization, whether imagined or real, rests on a particular set of principles.

In the sociological literature, "social organization" is rarely defined, and when it is, it's often *conflated* (i.e., confused by mixing) with the terms "social structure" or "social institution," as though they were all synonymous. They are not. "Government" is a social institution; the democratically elected House of Commons and the appointed Senate that comprise the bicameral legislature are social structures of the Canadian government. The social organization of Canada's government is a constitutional monarchy: the figurehead English monarch represented by the Governor General and the elected Parliament headed by the prime minister, the leader of the political party that won in the democratic election process. While social institutions *are* social structures and *are* socially organized, social structures and social organization are subordinate concepts to the social institutions. So, what is social organization?

We can think of **social organization** as the social and cultural *principles* around which people and things are structured, ordered, and categorized. In this way, we are able to speak about the social organization of cultures, of social institutions, or of corporations. Social organizations are formed to protect people and to advance certain causes. For example, a community may be socially organized around the principle of **egalitarianism**, a social organization that views its members as equals, such as a teachers' union. Or, the community could be organized on the principle of hierarchy, a social organization based on clear, well-defined ranks or levels, such as many churches. On a larger scale, the Hindu caste system mentioned in Chapter 4 reflects this hierarchical model of social organization. Governments almost always are hierarchical.

Organizational Structure

Under the old European system of feudalism, which was a particular kind of social organization, a serf owed allegiance to—in order—God, the king, the feudal lord, and the king's territory or lands. What factors following the fall of the Roman Empire created that European feudal system? The collapse of a central ruling force made way for inroads of other factions, such as the northern Teutonic tribes and local groups that reasserted their independence: the Gauls, the Celts, the Angles, and the Saxons. Agricultural people gathered around the fortress-castle of a wealthy family for protection from that warfare. Since those centuries are "dark" to us in the sense of a lack of dependable recorded information, we try to piece together the social structures from what remains of those relatively few documents, artifacts, and architecture. We continue to learn about human behaviour so that we can apply that learning back into history as well as forward into the future.

Over centuries, feudal social organization was replaced, as European and other societies moved from being states organized around a prevalent religion (Christian **theocracies**) centred primarily on Rome, to **secular** states maintained by much wider commerce, and from kingdoms or monarchies to national democracies whose alliances with one another crumble and coalesce. The religions did not disappear. The religious commitments of citizens still informed their choices of governors. But the governments generally were separate from the religious institutions. The tendency of people to hold different beliefs operates even at the level of governments and has led to social organizations that permit people to join others of like beliefs in "political parties." They contest who will join the structure of government to represent those factions. You are already familiar with the tensions that come into play when people disagree passionately about who can represent their personal point of view in an organization that must have a unified purpose to function.

When the new social organization known as **democracy** spread, the nation-state or country claimed allegiance and loyalty from its citizens. Consider this: when we go to war, we fight for our country because our religion and our other social attachments may be protected under its aegis and lost if the power of that country is overwhelmed. We do not fight for a particular leader because leadership can change while the fight goes on. We fight for the social groups that reside on our shared territory. And yet in spite of the emotions—pride, loyalty, sentiment—that are aroused when we sing the national anthem or win an Olympic gold medal, Canada is an imagined and intellectually constructed geopolitical space. It is a vast geographical territory (most of which is uninhabitable) with a diverse population that is signified through symbols such as the anthem and the flag, and unified through our loyalty to our Constitution with its statements of organizational and ethical principles. Canada is not a "natural" social form. It is, like any country, a socially organized invention based on certain collectively shared principles. Its organizing principles are upheld by shared *cultural* beliefs, for example, in the law that limits the role of the monarch—starting with Magna Carta in 1215—and maintained through a network of social relations such as the structures of federal, provincial, and municipal governments. If you find this a challenging idea to wrap your head around, it might help you to think of it this way: for the vast majority of human history, there were no countries at all, just contested territories. The idea of "countries" was largely an invention of the eighteenth, nineteenth, and twentieth centuries.

At the heart of organizational structures are principles about the ways the culture produces knowledge about the world. These principles constitute a particular **cosmology**. A cosmology is an account of the origin and ruling principles of the universe, especially the role of humans in relationship to non-humans (living and non-living). Cosmologies and corresponding myths are often regarded as a high form of truth, for example, the European notion of the "divine right of kings" that cast the role of the monarchy in terms of divine predestination and made rebellion against the monarchy not just an affront to power but a sin against God.

Indigenous cosmologies are rooted in the belief that all matter, both inanimate and animate, is interdependent: everything is connected. They emphasize the interdependence of humans and nature. Judeo-Christian and Islamic cosmology emphasize human dominion over nature as decreed by God, but what sort of stewardship that dominion entails is debated. With the emergence of modern science, that cosmology has been co-opted to justify "control over nature" as an organizing principle of Western culture. The flaws in this argument are the prevailing agnosticism of science, the greed of extraction industries, and the word "responsible" missing ahead of the word "control." Whether or not science is connected to Judeo-Christian or Islamic cosmology is an individual matter; some would say, a class matter. Consider the fact that both sides of the climate change debate in some senses believe that humans *can* control the environment. Those who deny that climate change is a problem believe that humans can easily minimize the effects of carbon emissions and manufacturing waste, whereas those who are concerned about global warming think that we are not organizing our societies well enough to combat these effects fast enough to preserve human life on the planet. Where do you place your hope or faith in the future? Why?

The Study of Organizations

To recap: organizational principles are based on our knowledge or understanding of the world, which is informed by our cosmology. These principles determine not just how our culture and society are organized but how other social bodies are organized, whether we're talking about social institutions like the family and education, or bureaucracies and corporations, or community-based organizations. It is important in the study of organizations to distinguish both the level of organization and the level of analysis.

Max Weber considered society to be organized along three principles: social class, status, and power. Within those social orders were obvious conflicts. His belief was that "rationalism"—the human capacity and drive for logical thought—was operative in resolving those conflicts. In this belief, he differed

What principles make up the social organization of your college or university—democracy or hierarchy (e.g., in administration–faculty and faculty–student interaction)? Freedom versus restrictions on discussion and debate? Commercialism? Elitism versus access? If you are not sure, how could you detect or demonstrate the presence and influence of these factors?

from Karl Marx, who thought that the class struggle was driven by economics and could only be solved through warfare. While Weber's focus was on social groups, he emphasized that individual "social action" was a force for changing the nature of those social groups (Weber, [1914, 1922] 1978). Interest in the sociological study of organizations picked up after Weber conducted his detailed work on bureaucracy (late 1800s) and when the study of organizations filtered into the business sector (post–World War I) so that commerce degree programs more often were offered at colleges and universities. The study of organizations shifted during the 1980s with the wide availability of Weber's *Economy and Society*, especially the chapter on bureaucracy, from the examination of social institutions to the examination of business corporations as a way to uncover more effective and efficient management practices. The result was an explosion of studies in the fields of **organizational theory** and **organizational behaviour** (see Mills & Simmons, 1995).

During the last 25 years, the study of organizational behaviour has expanded by integrating approaches from other disciplines. Anthropology, for instance, has contributed to the study of organizations through its understanding of corporations as communities in which an **organizational culture**, with "organizational rituals" and "symbolic acts," is an aspect of organizational dynamics. An *organizational ritual*, as defined by Islam and Zyphur (2009, p. 116), is "a form of social action in which a group's values and identity are publicly demonstrated or enacted in a stylized manner, within the context of a specific occasion or event." TV shows such as *The Office* and *Parks and Recreation* and the comic strip *Dilbert* make fun of such organizational rituals as the employee-of-the-month awards, the local sports team sponsorship, and the charity golf tournament—events intended to project a specific identity the organization wants to convey. A sociologist may also study the informal organization of a company to determine how decisions are made or how information actually flows from person to person in that structure—processes that may not quite follow the mandated, formal structure of the organization and that may be inefficient and counter-productive, depending on the company's goals regarding "branding," for example.

With the spread of globalization came increased study of cross-cultural organizations—such as the publisher of this book and automobile manufacturers—that have divisions in more than one country. These studies are of particular interest to international businesses and to those who study organizational behaviour. In the 1980s, organizational structures based on models derived from the productive corporate culture of Japan were implemented in North America. They failed, in part because they did not account for the organizational principles of Japanese culture, which are more *collectivist* than the *individualist* organizational principles favoured in Canada and the United States. Organizational structures based on a *collective* model, in which employees work in teams toward common goals and share the glory of success, did not work as well when applied to the competitive individualism found generally in North American business culture and in the larger society.

Much of the increase in organizational studies has been fuelled by Western capital, invested by companies in an effort to find ways to increase profits by managing employee behaviour and practices more efficiently. This effort has led to questions about the ethics of controlling worker behaviour, not to mention the inherent ethnocentric and capitalist assumptions in organizational theory in the context of global cultures. These critiques have fostered the growth of **critical management studies**, which challenge traditional theories of management. Mills and Simmons (1995), for example, have challenged the assumptions of mainstream accounts of organization. They point out that there is little in the literature of organizational theory and behaviour that deals with race, ethnicity, class, or gender, despite the high participation rates of women and visible minorities in the labour force. They also note that too little attention is given to the impact organizations have on the social and psychic life of individuals and groups affected by organizations, a concern that animated Weber. Despite the demonstrated link between typical organizational structures and employees with a lack of self-esteem, a sense of powerlessness, segregated work lives, stress, physical injuries, pay inequality, sexual harassment, and racism, standard organizational theory and behaviour studies continue to ignore these issues (Mills & Simmons, 1995).

Social Organization Meets COVID-19

The coronavirus pandemic created the sorts of crises in health care, in workplaces, in most of the major social institutions in most of the nations on the Earth that we usually associate with warfare and catastrophic natural disasters. The US military acronym for a *Volatile, Uncertain, Complex, and Ambiguous* situation, VUCA, applied almost everywhere. In "Responding to Covid-19: Lessons from Management Research" (Nembhard, Burns, & Shortell, 2020), the advice is to put people first, manage operations creatively, attend to teamwork and communication, create outside partnerships, and embrace clear and humble leadership. Did you notice people in your community following the advice that these management researchers offer here?

Years into the pandemic, massive shifts have relocated some workers to their homes; other workers have extended their workloads to or past the breaking point, physically and mentally. Many have quit their employment. Do *you* notice whether some of the problem areas have (1) abated or (2) become more serious in terms of a sense of powerlessness, segregated work life, stress, physical injury, pay inequality, sexual harassment, or racism?

Organizational Structure and Gender

In October 2017, a single tweet encouraged women to share their stories of workplace sexual harassment under the hashtag #MeToo. As the movement went viral, it exposed the prevalence of gendered sexual violence in patriarchal organizations ranging from corporate boardrooms and movie studios to political offices and churches. The issue brought calls to advance women to positions of power within organizations as one way to limit the ability of men in positions of authority to prey on female employees. And yet as of 2018, there were fewer women in powerful executive positions within Canada's largest companies than there had been five years earlier. An analysis of companies on the TSX 60 index revealed that not one of Canada's 60 largest publicly traded companies had a woman as chief executive officer, and just three had a woman listed as its chief financial officer. Those figures were down from one and eight, respectively, in a similar study conducted in 2012 (Ligaya & Deschamps, 2018).

Photo by FOX Image Collection via Getty Images

Television's favourite NYPD detectives get into the holiday spirit in a classic episode of *Brooklyn Nine-Nine*. Dressing up for Hallowe'en is a plotline staple of office-based sitcoms. Can you think of other rituals, events, or symbolic acts that reflect the organizational culture where you have worked or where you go to school? What message do these organizational rituals communicate to or about the organization?

Why is this the case? It isn't that women are ineffective leaders. A summary of relevant research by the American Psychological Association found that women and men are equally effective as leaders (APA, 2006), despite the differences in their leadership styles. Male leaders are more likely to adopt what the APA describes as a "command-and-control" approach, which emphasizes strong, central leadership that extends from the top of a hierarchy down through the ranks. Female leaders, in contrast, tend to adopt a transformational style of management, a more collaborative approach that revolves around coaching, mentorship, and shared decision-making (APA, 2006). Coincidentally, or not, the research showed that male leaders were more effective than female leaders in male-dominated organizations, while women were more effective when leading female-dominated organizations, such as institutions of education. We can surmise from this a female organizational structure that differs from

traditional male organizational structures. However, that "surmise," which leads to an assumption that the female is more "democratic" and involves a greater distribution of power and responsibility while the male is more "autocratic" and hierarchical, has not been established. And part of the reason it cannot be is that too few women have been in such positions for sufficient periods of time to have been adequately studied. We have information about outstanding women in leadership, government, and corporate positions but they can still be considered anomalies. Where some sources of information provide data, we must examine their data sources and their corporate affiliations very carefully.

Corporate structures are considered to be pragmatic divisions of labour with the greatest power and the least financial risk invested in the leadership. Where might we see female social organization at play? In her study of *feminist* organizations, Carol Mueller (1995) identified three models that typify the kind of organizational structure that has developed in contrast to traditional, male forms:

1. **formal social movement organizations,** which are professional, bureaucratic, and inclusive, and which make few demands of their members (examples include organizations dedicated to basic women's rights)
2. **small groups or collectives,** which are organized informally, and which require large commitments of time, loyalty, and material resources from its members (examples include publishing companies dedicated to promoting women authors)
3. **service-provider organizations,** which combine elements of both formal and small-group organizations (examples include organizations dedicated to specific women's rights, such as providing counselling services and protection to victims of domestic abuse).

Mueller found that these organizational forms *varied* in the degree to which they practised "typical feminist" organizational principles, such as inclusivity and democratic participation. She also found these forms combined in a variety of structural configurations ranging from coalitions to complex social movement communities.

What do you think?

1. Why do you think inclusivity and shared decision-making would be qualities favoured by feminist organizations? Do you think these qualities are entirely absent from traditional organizations dominated by men?
2. Do you think that Indigenous forms of organization provide similar challenges? What are the gender differences between chiefs?
3. Imagine yourself planning a sociological study of some local medium-sized businesses' organizational structures. Your budget covers 10 people: a designer assistant to work with you; two staff co-ordinators, and six data collectors who will double as data processors. How would you staff a team for your study, ensuring that it is an equal-opportunity project for males and females?

In Chapter 4, we noted the differences between the way grey matter and white matter in the male and female brains is used.

> Male brains utilize nearly 7 times more *gray matter* for activity while female brains utilize nearly 10 times more *white matter*. . . . Gray matter areas of the brain are localized. They are information- and action-processing centers in specific splotches in a specific area of the brain. . . . White matter is the networking grid that connects the brain's gray matter and other processing centers with one another. (Jantz, 2014)

Without delving into other chemical differences, we can say that females have certain cognitive advantages over males, generally. They can transition between tasks faster than males, which leads to their capacity for multitasking. They excel at social networking. They are cerebrally integrated for using the specialized abilities of each half of the brain synchronously. For these reasons, they choose more varied work; therefore, more such work has been expected of them, including continuing the care of home and family while working outside the home. More work may be expected of them on the job, too. But the males who already have senior positions are the least able to delegate more *authority* to them because they tend to feel threatened. Their hierarchy incites competition for the place at the top, wherever they happen to be on a rung of the ladder.

For their part, males have a cerebral structure better suited to focusing intensely on individual projects. Those projects can be many and quite complex, of course. Can we assume that the hierarchical organization we see in government, business, medical institutions, educational organizations, the military, and in other places relate to males' cognitive abilities and are best suited in those aspects of society? If so, what type of social organization would lead to more egalitarian organizations without withdrawing from the male half of the population the kinds of work they do best?

It appears at this point in the COVID-19 pandemic that some of the women who were forced to work from home were not entirely displeased with the arrangement. We do not yet have reliable statistics on how many workers in government and

Photo by Jane Hynes

The Terra Nova Chapters is one of five book clubs active in the small town of Glovertown, Newfoundland and Labrador. According to sociologist Elizabeth Long (2003), women use reading clubs to openly discuss their own experiences in the context of the books they're reading, and in this way consider the place of women in society. What makes the book club a typically female organization? And why aren't there more book clubs for men?

business are being allowed to choose to remain workers-from-home, so we also do not know the gender split.

10.3 Bureaucracy

The Origins of Bureaucracy

As Israeli American sociologist Amitai Etzioni pointed out over 50 years ago, "organizations [and bureaucracies] are not a modern invention" (1964, p. 1). In fact, we can trace the origins of the bureaucracy back nearly 5,000 years, to a time when organized states and writing systems were just coming into existence.

As empires emerged and grew, administrative bureaucracies expanded at a pace to match imperial expansion. In Han Dynasty China (fifth century BCE), the bureaucratic system developed out of Confucius's concern for creating social stability, which required a system of administrators to ensure good governance. Administrators were appointed based on merit examinations (i.e., written tests). What became known as the imperial examination system continued in China until the early twentieth century.

The term "bureaucracy" originated in eighteenth-century France and comes from the word "bureau," meaning "writing desk"—in other words, the place where officials work. The cumbersome processes of bureaucracies are sometimes referred to as "red tape," which dates back to nineteenth-century Britain, when government officials used red ribbon to tie up official documents until they were needed. Red tape, then, refers to the slow procedures associated with acquiring and dispensing bureaucratic information. Most of us have encountered bureaucratic red tape in our federal, provincial, or municipal agencies—when applying to replace a lost passport or driver's licence, for instance—but such tedious routines are not confined to government agencies.

Many private companies, including banks, the cable company, your internet provider, perhaps even your college or university admissions office, entail "red tape." As we will see, despite their inefficiencies and the difficulties in changing bureaucratic organization to meet individual and societal needs, bureaucracies are necessary for the successful functioning of complex societies.

Bureaucracy and Formal Rationalization

Max Weber's extensive work on bureaucracy is still frequently cited today. It was part of his larger study of the process of rationalization, specifically, his examination of **formal rationalization** (or **rationality**). "Rationalization" is a term frequently used in business reports, where it serves as a euphemism for firing workers and cutting jobs in an effort to reduce costs and become more efficient. Formal rationalization, according to Weber, has four basic elements:

- efficiency
- quantification
- predictability
- control.

We will look at the implications of these terms shortly, in the section on McDonaldization.

Formal rationalization, with its emphasis on forms, differs from other models of rationalization, such as **substantive rationalization**, which involves the "substance" of values and ethical norms. Organizations governed by substantive rationalization are constantly asking themselves, *are we reflecting our values?* By contrast, organizations governed by formal rationalization tend to ask, *have we instituted the most efficient or predictable forms in our organization?* Governments are run by formal rationalization. Consider Indigenous organizations. Democracy, spirituality, and respect for elders are important values among Indigenous people. Forms that reflect those values are open meetings, where anyone can speak and be listened to, and prayers spoken by elders. How do you think Indigenous organizations and government organizations for Indigenous people, each at opposite ends of the substantive rationalization–formal rationalization spectrum, would interact?

Weber was critical of both formal rationalization and bureaucracy, arguing that the former led to the "irrationality of rationality" and that the latter was dehumanizing by nature. Workers within the rational, bureaucratic organization of various companies and political bodies came to be viewed as "cogs in the wheel," reminded frequently that they could always be replaced. You may feel similar effects even when you're not part of the bureaucracy but are confronted by the impersonal nature of its public face. When you're told, "Your call is important to us," you know that it isn't (see Laura Penny's *Your Call Is Important to Us: The Truth about Bullshit*, 2005). These examples speak to the dehumanizing feelings we experience daily through our interactions with bureaucratic organizations.

The "irrationality of rationality" involves the "disenchantment of the world," an important concept in Weber's writing. Weber believed that with the increase in formal rationalization, the West was becoming increasingly **disenchanted**—lacking in magic, fantasy, and mystery—which could only lead to further alienation on the part of individuals. Enchantment is a quality that cannot be efficient, quantified, predicted, or controlled. Disney's "Magic Kingdom," for instance, is anything but magical: it is a rationalized system of pre-packaged enchantment commodities—there *must* be no surprises. Weber worried and warned about the oncoming danger of the "iron cage of rationality," meaning a world in which every aspect of life is controlled by the formal rationalization of bureaucracy, a world dehumanized and over-controlled.

The Evolution of Formal Rationalization

The Industrial Revolution, in the late eighteenth and early nineteenth centuries, was the starting point for the development of formal "rationalization" of the characteristics of social organization. **Francis Galton** (1822–1911), considered the father of modern statistical analysis, was a pioneer in developing methods to measure the capabilities and productivity of individuals who make up groups. He had a natural love of numbers and made formal rationalization a part of his everyday life. For example, he spent many hours getting the quantities (temperature, volume, etc.) just right for the "perfect" pot of tea.

Along these same lines, **Frederick W. Taylor** (1856–1915) developed scientific management. Based on "time-and-motion" studies, scientific management (later known as **Taylorism**) was intended to discover the *one best way* of doing any given job. Taylor and his team of "efficiency experts" studied the time, methods, and tools required for a proficient worker to do a particular job. His objective was to eliminate wasteful or "inefficient" (i.e., slow, non-productive) motions or movements. Frank Gilbreth, a follower of Taylor, undertook an intensive study of a bricklayer's job and reputedly reduced the number of motions involved in laying a brick from 18 to just 5. He and his wife and co-worker Lillian Moller Gilbreth carried this approach into their family of 12 children, prompting two of their children, Frank Jr. and Ernestine, to write about their experiences in *Cheaper by the Dozen* (1948). Assembly line work also used Taylor's methods to the maximum efficiency, though Henry Ford is credited with making the assembly line an industry standard.

One of the weaknesses of Taylorism/scientific management of social institutions is that it didn't allow the individual worker to develop a broad set of skills, because he or she was asked to perform a single set of actions over and over again. Workers often became alienated from their work, with little sense that they had anything to do with the overall manufactured product. They had fewer means of moving up in the organization.

Taylorism, slightly modified, was still practised in North America during the 1980s and 1990s. Then, the success of Japanese auto manufacturing prompted North American businesses to implement "non-Tayloristic" Japanese business practices in their training sessions. Among these practices was the **team approach**, which incorporated worker input and fostered the idea that workers could be involved in several stages of the manufacturing process, generating a greater sense of "product ownership"—an instance of substantive rationalization. This approach was first adopted by car manufacturer Saturn, which, until the downturn in the automotive

Do you think you would be happier performing one task in the assembly of 20 vehicles or several tasks in the assembly of five? The first approach reflects formal rationalization principles such as maintaining quotas. The second reflects the substantive rationalization principle of worker ownership of the work and the product. Why do you think some instructors feel as though their college or university endorses the first of these two approaches to education?

sector in 2008, was very successful, in large part because it managed to reduce the sense of alienation among its workers.

The McDonaldization of the World

George Ritzer, in *The McDonaldization of Society* (2004), draws on Weber's concept of formal rationalization in his conception of **McDonaldization**. McDonaldization is similar to "Disneyfication," "Walmartitis," and "Microsoftening"—in Ritzer's words, "the process by which the [rationalizing] principles of the fast-food restaurant are coming to dominate more and more sectors of American society as well as the rest of the world" (2004, p. 1).

Ritzer applies the four fundamental elements of Weber's formal rationalization—**efficiency**, **quantification**, **predictability**, and **control**—to his examination of contemporary fast-food restaurants. To see how McDonaldization is affecting other areas of everyday life, let's apply his theory to the world of postsecondary education.

Efficiency relates to the streamlined movement in time and effort of people and things. This efficiency is achieved mainly by breaking up larger organizational tasks into smaller, repeated tasks performed by individuals who are separated from each other by a division of labour. Later, smaller tasks are often performed by machines rather than by people. It should be noted that efficiency has different meanings in the different layers of a social organization. What is efficient for a college administrator might not be efficient for a college professor. Speaking from personal experience, while the former finds "efficiency" in the networking of printers, the professor would prefer to have his own little printer and not wait in line when print requests are heavy in the department.

Being efficient in terms of money costs is not necessarily the same as being *effective* in terms of teaching, although it's possible for a teaching process involving the printing of student materials to be both efficient and effective. Think of the potential differences between being an efficient teacher—one who teaches quickly and articulates a great number of concepts—and an effective teacher—one who successfully communicates to students all or almost all that is in the course. A teacher can be one or the other, both, or none of the above. At college and university, the multiple-choice test is a classic example of bureaucratic efficiency: often, questions are

provided by the textbook's publisher, and they can be marked quickly or, if they're delivered online, graded automatically. But are they the most effective means of promoting and testing learning? Would you be surprised to learn that the author of this textbook never uses multiple-choice questions?

One of the offshoots of academic "efficiency" are platforms such as the Turnitin internet-based plagiarism detection company that sells its detection services to universities and other educational institutions. While the concept of plagiarism may need to be taught to students, especially those from countries where individual learning is expected to involve collaboration, bringing in technology to detect it has ethical problems. The detection company is based financially on the labour of students whose copyrights are being infringed and whose intellectual property is being harvested, which contravenes one of their human rights. The student is positioned as untrustworthy, which undermines a collegial relationship between teacher and student.

Quantification in formal rationalization in bureaucracy involves the *measurement* of as many elements as possible. The efficiency, or "success," of the process is the completion of a maximum number of quantifiable tasks. For instance, the success of call centres is primarily measured by how many calls are handled rather than by how many clients actually are satisfied. When educational administrators pressure instructors to quantify the type and exact percentage of tests on a course syllabus the assumption of their formal rationalization is that if courses are equally quantified, then students are equally served. With bureaucratic education, administrators and instructors can quantify the number and length of interactions between students and professors through computer platforms that monitor such things as the number of emails and the number and length of "chats." In the classroom, instructors can monitor students by having them use electronic clickers to respond to questions, which is an attempt to counteract the impersonal nature of large, "efficient" lectures with increased (quantifiable) electronic interaction. One type of impersonal interaction is substituted by another only slightly less impersonal. What costs would be involved in giving professors and students greater opportunities for personal communication?

Predictability means that administrators, workers, and clients all know what to expect from employees, underlings, colleagues, and companies, which is accomplished by the "uniformity of rules." A Big Mac in Moscow (that is, until McDonald's departed Russia under pressure following that country's invasion of Ukraine in 2022) is the same as a Big Mac in Calgary. You can wake up in a Holiday Inn anywhere in the world and not know where you are until you look out the window. Hollywood, too, is all about predictability—if you've seen one Will Ferrell movie, you've seen them all—and if you liked the last one, you'll be more likely to see the next one. With the advent of rationalized, bureaucratic education, teachers become replaceable in the delivery of predictable, pre-packaged courses, and creative, innovative input shrinks. Students who have already taken a course can tell others almost exactly what to expect and what will be taught. Pre-packaged online courses cut down on the time spent by teachers planning lessons, thus making class prep more "efficient," leading to what might be called the "silicon cage" of rationalization. However, in a recent lecture, culture critic Henry Giroux (currently the McMaster University Chair for Scholarship in the Public Interest in the English and Cultural Studies Department and the Paulo Freire Distinguished Scholar in Critical Pedagogy) noted that the *indeterminate* in education—the unpredictable and free-flowing, "don't know where this is going" instructor–class discussion—creates an inspiring, memorable classroom experience. This creative process is lost through formal rationalization and the imposition of predictability.

Control, for Ritzer, is always hierarchical. He characterizes the hierarchical division of labour in the following passage:

> Bureaucracies emphasize control over people through the replacement of human judgment with the dictates of rules, regulations, and structures. Employees are controlled by the division of labor, which allocates to each office a limited number of well-defined tasks. Incumbents must do the tasks, and no others, in the manner prescribed by the organization. They may not, in most cases, devise idiosyncratic ways of doing those tasks. Furthermore, by making few, if any, judgments, people begin to resemble human robots or computers. (2004, p. 27)

This control is exercised over both workers and clients. People who work at McDonald's are taught exactly what they have to do, while customers have their selection controlled by the menu board. Even the uncomfortable seating is part of the process, helping to control how long customers stay in the restaurant. We can see the formally rationalized, bureaucratic package at its most extreme in the following overview of material from a 1958 copy of the McDonald's operations manual, cited in John F. Love's *McDonald's: Behind the Arches* (1995):

> It told operations *exactly* how to draw milk shakes, grill hamburgers, and fry potatoes. It specified *precise* cooking times for all products and temperature settings for all equipment. It fixed *standard* portions on every food item, down to the *quarter ounce* of onions placed on each hamburger patty and the *thirty-two slices per pound* of cheese. It specified that French fries be cut at *nine thirty-seconds of an inch* thick. And it defined quality *controls* that were unique to food service, including the disposal of meat and potato products that were held more than *ten minutes* in a serving bin. (quoted in Ritzer, 2004, p. 38)

As with people who have only ever eaten French fries from McDonald's, never "real chips" cut and prepared on site, students experiencing today's increasingly bureaucratized education will become less able to judge the quality of the instruction they are receiving. Furthermore, the value of the personal experiences the instructor may bring to her or his teaching, which provide a much more nuanced passing on of culture, is lost or diminished. A teacher inspired by a love for the discipline and who can bring great enthusiasm to a student audience is more likely to fill lecture halls and to generate interest in the discipline than an automaton hurrying through a syllabus.

Formal Rationalization in the Digital Age

In their wildest dreams, Francis Galton and Frederick Taylor could not have imagined a world where a hungry customer could, from their home,

Telling It Like It Is

An Author Point of View

Little Boxes: Mass-Produced Suburban Communities

After the end of World War II, which marked the start of North America's "baby boom," there was a fairly severe housing shortage in both Canada and the United States. One response was the development of mass-produced suburban communities. The first and standard-setting effort in this regard was the series of "Levittowns" built in the eastern US. Between 1947 and 1951, Levitt and Sons built 17,447 houses on Long Island, New York, creating an instant community of about 75,000 people. This model would soon be reproduced in Pennsylvania and then New Jersey. The company began by building warehouses for their supplies, their own workshops for wood and plumbing manufacture, and gravel and cement plants. Ritzer describes the rationalization of the house-building process in the following excerpt:

> The actual construction of each house followed a series of rigidly defined and rationalized steps. For example, in constructing the wall framework, the workers did no measuring or cutting; each piece had been cut to fit. The siding for a wall consisted of 73 large sheets of Colorbestos, replacing the former requirement of 570 small shingles. All houses were painted under high pressure, using the same two-tone scheme—green on ivory. . . . The result, of course, was a large number of nearly identical houses produced quickly at low cost. (Ritzer, 2004, p. 36)

The owners of the construction company knew that their employees did not enjoy many of the intrinsic rewards experienced by skilled independent tradespeople, but they felt that the extrinsic rewards of money would make up for that:

> The same man does the same thing every day, despite the psychologists. It is boring; it is bad; but the reward of the green stuff seems to alleviate the boredom of the work. (A. Levitt, 1952, quoted in Ritzer, 2004, pp. 35–6)

This kind of rationalized uniformity can come at the cost of oppression of minoritized people. In the case of Levittown, the covenants (agreements signed by homeowners with the developer) included racial segregation. Blacks were not allowed. The story of how one family "conspired" to bring a Black family into Levittown, and how it was resisted, sometimes violently, by neighbours and social organizations illustrates this (see Kushner, 2009). This leads to the question: Does extreme rationalization of organization lead automatically to social oppression?

In Canada, the neighbourhood of Don Mills, constructed during the early 1950s, became known as Toronto's "first planned community." I grew up there beginning in 1956. It had the city's first shopping centre, the first Country Style doughnut shop, and the first Shopper's Drug Mart. As a teenager, I was a "plaza boy"—a term for someone who spent his leisure hours hanging around the mall. Famous Canadians from this community include comedian Rick Green (of *The Red Green Show*), "Martha" of the 1980s band Martha and the Muffins, and singer and song writer Dan Hill. It also produced an outstanding Canadian sociologist: Neil Guppy, now retired from the University of British Columbia. And yours truly, of course.

Did I feel alienated by the rationalism of my planned community? I definitely grew up to be a rebel, pushing back against anything I thought confined me. I grew my hair long (which it still is, although on top it is long gone), and the bands that I was in were blues bands whose lyrics reflected the trials of life in the south side of Chicago more than the suburbs of Toronto. I generally disliked conformity in its many forms, and that is still true. Of course, I may have been a product of the 1960s as much as I was a product of a particular suburb embedded in one of the safest big cities in modern times. That both were significant contributors to my socialization is undeniable.

What do *you* think?

Think of a suburb you're familiar with. What aspects of it do you think reflect formal rationalization or "McDonaldization"? Do you think these qualities are beneficial or not?

place an order for food, without having to speak to anyone, and have it delivered within 30 minutes by an independent contractor on wheels or on foot. The internet allows for an enormous degree of formal rationalization. In spite of Weber's warnings about the "iron cage of rationality," we welcome it into our lives. We shop online in growing numbers, reducing the need to make time-consuming trips to the mall. We can leverage the reach of the internet to crowdsource start-up companies or raise funds for the needy, as concerned global citizens did for the families of the victims of the Humboldt Broncos bus crash. We are nearing a time when we may never again need to set foot in a grocery store, because our provider of groceries and other household products, tracking our daily consumption, will replenish our stocks automatically, via drone.

I plan to be the last holdout against this trend, because I like going to stores, handling the wares, speaking with the sales staff. Although, there is a small family-run business in the town where I live, whose owner, nearing retirement age, will eventually pass the business on to his son, a poor manager and lazy worker who does not seem particularly interested in extending his father's legacy. The business's better employees have no incentive to overachieve because, not being part of the family, they can never rise to the top of the small corporate hierarchy. Could a measure of formal rationalization save it as our purchasing moves increasing online?

Social Order through Social Organization

Social organization and social stability are fundamental aspects of the human condition. We couldn't dispense with all social organization without chaos ensuing. However, the foundational principles and forms of organization themselves can have a profound effect on society and on individuals, and so they deserve to be critically examined.

As we have seen, social organization impacts everything from the environment (through our relationship with nature) to the places where we work, study, and live, where the dehumanizing effects of formal rationalization sometimes prevail. Large, bureaucratized organizations, instead of serving the

Smartphone: check. Fitbit: check. Were he alive today, what would Weber say about rationalizing technologies that keep us connected, on time, and on pace at all times?

needs and interests of individuals, often dictate our values and interactions. Think of your most recent shopping experience at a mall or big box store as compared with a set of shops that specialize in particular products. If we use Ritzer's work on McDonaldization as an indicator, the perils of bureaucracy and formal rationalization that Weber warned of long ago have only become worse. The inefficiency of efficiency seems to dominate organizations from the military and businesses to hospitals and postsecondary institutions. Red tape, long lineups, quantity over quality, apathy, and even violent reactions (going "postal," road rage, fighting with the registrar's office or school board, assailing and assaulting politicians) have become the norm both within and outside of organizations and bureaucracies. In short, we need the **social order** that organizational structures promote, but there is evidence that bureaucracy has lost sight of the "greater good" of a greater number and a broader world. Through a perversion of means and ends, in which the means become ends in and of themselves, organizational bureaucracies become increasingly self-serving, behaving as though they were self-sustaining communities with no meaningful positive social connections to the citizens they are intended to serve.

10.4 Religion: A Particular Kind of Social Organization

Religion is a particular kind of social organization that we will consider in the remainder of this chapter. What is religion? This complex question is something people tend to think they understand until they are asked to define it. How does a religion start? What purposes does it serve? What distinguishes a religion from a cult? Or for that matter, from that really dedicated workout group that meets in my local park at the same time every week and is always trying to get me to join?

Psychologists, philosophers, theologians, and sociologists provide different answers to that question, which reflect the qualities of religion most relevant to their respective disciplines. As a sociologist, I look at religion primarily as a social organization and institution. Thus, I see religion as having ritualized social practices that members can engage in alone or, more often, in small or large groups, in a way that fosters a sense of shared experience and of belonging. Belonging, or inclusion, usually implies exclusion, and so religion is a powerful engine of ingroup/outgroup dynamics. People attached to a religious association (their ingroup) may regard those outside the group (the outgroup) as threatening or inferior. Religions often are structured hierarchically and can be divided along the usual social fault lines of race, ethnicity, class, and especially gender, reflected in persistent beliefs about appropriate roles for men and women, such as the "complementarian" churches in Christianity. Notable, then, are the religions or sects that are egalitarian. Which churches support which view?

In general, denominations [within North American Christianity] that tend to lean complementarian include Southern Baptist, Roman Catholic, some Lutheran, some Mennonite, some Presbyterian, and Reformed.

Denominations that tend to lean egalitarian include Assembly of God, Nazarene, Episcopalian [Anglican], some Evangelical Lutheran, Free Methodist, Friends [Quakers], some Mennonite, some Presbyterian, United Methodist, and Wesleyan. (Roat, 2019)

Most religions promote a code of moral values that identifies right and wrong behaviour to help guide the social interaction of their members. Religious beliefs typically involve a reality that is beyond the purely physical, one in which there are

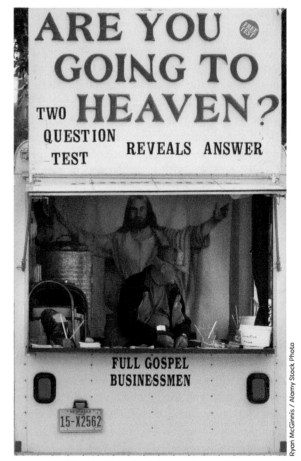

Ryan McGinnis / Alamy Stock Photo

At a state fair in Lincoln, Nebraska, a man promises to reveal the likelihood of your salvation with a free two-question test. Can you guess what two questions might determine whether or not you are destined to go to Heaven? Can you imagine a booth like this being found at a fall fair in Canada?

"spiritual" or "supernatural" beings. These beings are part of the social world of religious members, and the relationship between human and spiritual beings may mirror the social dynamics of people on Earth with sanctions, norms, deviations from norms, and so on. If you live in a hierarchical society, then your relationship to spiritual beings likely also will be hierarchical.

In sum, religion, defined sociologically, is a particular form of social organization with ritualistic practices, value-driven behaviour, and a belief in non-human entities.

What Is a Cult?

Many cults are spinoffs from established religions, from which they may selectively borrow certain elements that they combine with secular practices into new religious forms. One way to describe a cult is as a religion that deviates in its beliefs and/or practices. "Deviant" is not necessarily a moral judgment of good or bad. Applied to cults, "deviant" means differing from or offering an alternative to older, established religions such as Islam, Judaism, and Christianity.

Cults tend to be newly arrived on the religious scene, as the followers of Jesus of Nazareth were to the Jews of the first century after his birth. Although cults of various kinds have existed for centuries, they came to prominence during the 1960s and 1970s, when, thanks to a few notorious (but not especially typical) cases, they became associated with the larger counterculture movement of that era. The charismatic movement that brought Pentecostal practices into mainline churches was regarded by some conservative Christians as a cult. No doubt some of the outgrowths of that vast movement deserved the term "cult" although most did not, and a great many functioned within the existing churches.

The murder-suicide of 914 followers of the American cult Peoples Temple in Jonestown, Guyana, in 1978 exemplifies a cult with a leader who became so anti-social that he required the deaths of the membership. In March 1997, 39 members of Heaven's Gate cult in California committed suicide, as they believed, to join a spaceship following in the wake of the anticipated Comet Hale–Bopp's perihelion appearance in Earth's sky on 1 April 1997. The Canadian sociologist Lorne Dawson, who has done extensive research on the topic, prefers the term "new religious movement" (or NRM), which does not carry the sinister overtones hanging over the word "cult." He identifies four types of new religious movement (Dawson, 1998, p. 14):

1. NRMs associated with Asian philosophy, meditation, and magic (e.g., the International Society for Krishna Consciousness, or ISKCON, whose beliefs are based on Hindu scripture)
2. NRMs drawing on pop psychology's "human potential movement" (the Church of Scientology fits here)
3. NRMs associated with occult revival (e.g., Wicca)
4. NRMs seeking spiritual salvation through contact with extraterrestrial beings (e.g., Heaven's Gate).

Cults may develop around a single charismatic leader or a small group of people, but don't mistake "cult" in this sense from the related term "cult of personality," which is an excessive admiration for someone who has a prominent public role. Donald Trump is the focal point of a cult of personality, but his supporters are not a cult in the sense described above (even though there is a Christian element among some of his most devoted followers). A cult can develop over time to become a full-fledged religion with a general acceptability in society. Or it can die off with the passing away of the leader or leaders, or in some cases, such as the non-marrying or breeding Shakers, the membership.

Durkheim and the Elementary Forms of Religious Life

Although he was not particularly religious, **Émile Durkheim** (1858–1917) had a profound effect on how sociologists view religion. His father and grandfather were rabbis, yet he himself felt no religious calling. His great work on religion, *Les formes élémentaires de la vie religieuse* (1912), was published in English in 1915 as *The Elementary Forms of the Religious Life*.

Durkheim took sociology into areas where it did not seem to belong, including suicide (surely, the realm of psychology) and religion (certainly, the realm of theology). His contemporaries viewed suicide and religion as firmly rooted in the individual, not in the group or society. Strong resistance to his ideas came from people studying psychology and religion.

Durkheim's aim was to identify the basic elements of religion. He believed he could do this most effectively by studying the religion of the most basic society: the Aborigines of Australia, who were being studied by other social scientists. Through this study he hoped to develop a sociological model applicable to all religions.

Durkheim's Definition of Religion

Here is how Durkheim defined religion:

> A religion is a unified system of beliefs and practices relative to sacred things, that is to say, things set apart and forbidden—beliefs and practices which unite into one single moral community called a Church, all those who adhere to them. (Durkheim, [1912] 1995, p. 44)

In using the term **moral community**, Durkheim was recognizing that religious groups are "made up of individuals who have mutually recognized and recognizable identities that set them, cognitively and normatively, on shared human terrain" (Fields, 1995, p. xxxiv). It is clear from this how dramatically Durkheim deviated from his contemporaries, who considered religion something experienced by the individual rather than corporately (by the larger community).

Three Key Elements of Religion

There are three key elements in Durkheim's analysis of religion. The first is the equation *god = society*. Durkheim formulated this idea in the context of the totems of the Australian Aborigines.

Totem is a word that came into English in the late eighteenth century from the language of the Anishinaabe or Ojibwa people. It comes from the word *ndotem*, meaning "my clan" in Ojibwa. When Anishinaabe people introduce themselves in formal situations, they often follow the statement of their name by saying something such as *waawaashkeshndotem*, meaning "deer is my clan." In this way, they are telling something about their identity and who they are.

Anishinaabe elder Edward Benton-Banai, a leading figure in the tradition-based Three Fires Midewiwin Lodge and the author of *The Mishomis Book: The Voice of the Ojibway*, identified seven original clans

of the Anishinaabe (Benton-Banai, 1988, pp. 75–7). Traditionally, he explains, each clan was associated with a specific function and certain ideal characteristics of clan members. These characteristics connect with the clan's totem animal (see Table 10.1).

In regard to Durkheim's explanation of the *god = society* equation, a totem is a symbolic representation both of a god and of the society that reveres it. Another way of looking at it is that societies fashion deities represented as having characteristics like the people themselves. These characteristics are then projected back onto both the culture and the individuals. The god and the people are one and the same.

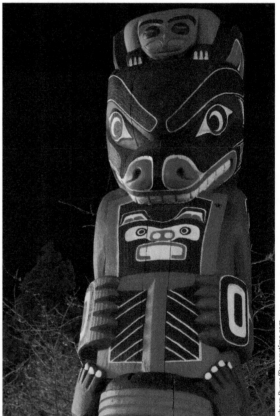

Barbara Burns/Dreamstime.com

The images in this totem pole are culturally stylized versions of the totem animals of clans of the artist's First Nation. What impression do you think these totem poles made on the Christian missionaries arriving in villages on the Pacific coast? What impression do they make on you? Are there objects in other religions that have totemic quality?

TABLE 10.1 Clans and Totems of the Anishinaabe

Clan/Totem	Associated Characteristics
Crane Clan Loon Clan	leadership, chieftainship
Fish Clan	mediation, settling disputes; philosophy
Bear Clan	protecting the community; medicinal plants
Marten Clan	warfare and war strategy
Deer Clan	poetry
Bird Clan	spiritual leadership

Collective Consciousness and the Sacred and Profane

Durkheim focused primarily on the group experiences and rituals of people belonging to a particular religion. These sacred experiences foster what Durkheim called a **collective consciousness**. In Muslim countries, the cry of the muezzin over the loudspeaker calling the faithful to prayer five times a day, followed by the collective deep bowing of the people, is a compelling example of collective religious experience.

Durkheim distinguishes between experiences, acts, and objects that are *sacred* and those that are *profane*. **Sacred** objects and acts are set apart from more ordinary (**profane**) ones as being positively regarded, holy, and therefore deserving of reverence or respect. Sacred objects include prayer beads, crosses, flags, and items in the medicine bundle of

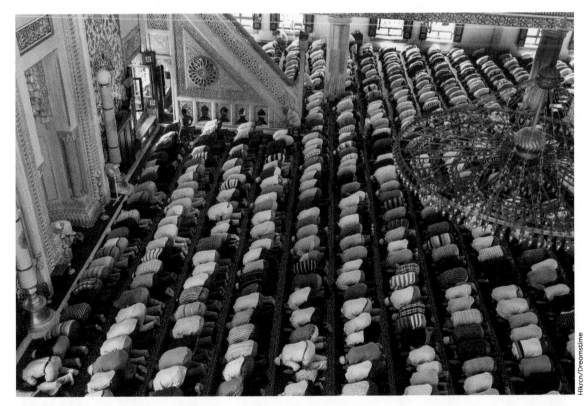

Muslims pray at a mosque in Turkey. How do you think this kind of communal prayer generates a sense of collective consciousness?

The Kandariya Mahadeva temple, a Hindu holy site at Khajuraho, in Madhya Pradesh, India. Close inspection reveals its erotic reliefs. Sacred or profane?

an Aboriginal shaman; sacred acts include prayer, some Aboriginal dances, and keeping kosher. But Durkheim used the term "sacred" also for that which is forbidden or taboo. The Arabic term used in Islam, **haram**, applies here. Canadian writer **Haroon Siddiqui**, in *Being Muslim*, lists the following prohibited objects and practices:

> Haram Foods: Pork and its by-products, carnivorous animals (those that tear their food apart with claws, such as lions), almost all reptiles and insects, animals that died before being properly slaughtered, blood, and all alcoholic or intoxicating drinks.
>
> Haram Lifestyle: Gambling, including lotteries; all drugs that cause intoxication, alter sensory perception (hallucinogens), or affect one's ability to reason and make sound judgments; and paying and accepting interest. (Siddiqui, 2006, p. 80)

Durkheim argues that objects were not sacred by nature but acquired their sacred status socially.

10.5 Religion and the Family

Religion is often applauded for promoting strong families with a moral compass. Usually, it does. Viewed in the light of Robert Merton's three kinds of function—manifest, latent, and latent dysfunction (Merton, [1949] 1968)—we could reasonably identify "strengthening the family" as a manifest (i.e., intended and recognized) or latent (largely unintended and unrecognized) function of religion. Yet there have been times when family and religion have stood in opposition, particularly when a certain kind of family situation has been negatively valued by state officials armed with religion.

In nineteenth-century Ireland, the Catholic Church established institutions to "rehabilitate" sex workers and unwed mothers. They were called "Magdalene asylums" (referencing Mary Magdalene, the classic "fallen woman" of the Bible) or sometimes "Magdalene laundries," since the women were often forced into hard labour laundering clothes to earn money for the institution. Many unwed mothers had their children taken away and put up for adoption. Magdalene asylums were established throughout Ireland and Britain, and Canada, some surviving until the late twentieth century (see Smith, 2007).

In Canada, thousands of Indigenous children were sent to church-run residential schools for about 100 years (1867–1998); they were closing rapidly after 1970. Consider the conditions:

> Children were taken from their parents and extended families for periods of time that often lasted the entire school year, even when the residential schools were located in the students' own communities. Parental visits, when they were permitted, were typically closely monitored in a special "visiting room." Brothers and sisters were often kept apart in strict sexual separation, meaning that siblings in many cases could communicate with each other only by waving from one building to another or through secretly arranged meetings. (Steckley & Cummins, 2008, p. 194)

Residential schools had a strong detrimental effect on parenting skills in First Nations communities. Raised under the strict and often abusive authority of underpaid, underqualified, and poorly screened teachers and administrators, described by historian J.R. Miller as the "devoted and the deviant" (1996, p. 321), about five generations of Indigenous parents had only these harsh role models on which to base their own parenting.

Imports from Britain

In *Empty Cradles*, British social worker **Margaret Humphreys** describes how thousands of British children—the vast majority born to parents who were either poor or socially marginalized as single parents—were shipped to Australia to live in church-run orphanages. Certainly, some of these children benefited from their change in circumstances. Yet as Humphreys relates, many of the children were told that their parents were dead, and were subjected to the same hard labour and abuse that Indigenous children experienced in Canadian residential schools. The following questions come from a woman who was shipped out to Australia when she was eight:

> Do you think I've got any family? Cousins, anybody. I'm not fussy. Anybody. They told me that my parents were dead. Do you think

that's true? . . . I don't know anything about myself. Until I married, I didn't even have a birth certificate. I felt ashamed. . . . Can you find out why they sent me? What did I do wrong? (Humphreys, 1995, p. 14)

Humphreys collected a story of a five-year-old girl who had long, curly, blonde hair when she entered the Catholic orphanage named Goodwood:

After being at Goodwood a few days, she packed all her possessions in a bag and ran down the drive in her nightie. The nuns followed her and dragged her back. The next morning, all the girls were made to line up in the yard and watch her being punished. . . . Two of the nuns held the little girl down, while another started cutting off her hair with garden shears. . . .

When they had finished, there was just an inch or two of hair left on her head. "God wants her punished more than that," one of the nuns said, and she produced a pair of secateurs [small pruning shears]. She started cutting again and didn't stop until the young girl's hair was gone completely and her scalp was bloody with cuts. (Humphreys, 1995, p. 125)

In looking at the treatment of British and Irish orphans and Canadian Indigenous children, we can see common themes that characterize this conflict between religion and family:

- the marginalized (in terms of race, class, and sexual behaviour) backgrounds of the families from which the children were taken
- the statistically deviant choice made by religious workers such as missionaries, priests, and nuns to opt for "religious life" over "normal" family life in their own society
- the strict hierarchical nature of religion operating in institutions such as religious orders, residential schools, and church-run orphanages
- the strict codes of discipline associated with religious-based institutions

- the ease with which religious concepts such as "sin" can be associated with negative judgment and used to justify harsh punishment.

Hutterites: Religion and Family

The preceding sections illustrate situations in which religion and family come into conflict, with damaging results. In contrast is the strong positive connection between religion and family found in Canada's Hutterite communities. In 2001, the last year for which we have such detailed census data, the Hutterites were the Canadian religious group with the youngest median age (22.2). Children aged 0–14 made up 37 per cent of their population, while young people aged 0–24 made up 54 per cent—well over half—of their total population. The Hutterites' fertility rate, despite declining somewhat in recent decades, approaches the maximum fertility rate possible for a single community and is famous in the sociological literature (see Nonaka, Miura, & Peter, 1993). The high fertility rate is attributed to several sociological factors, including:

- cultural/religious norms opposing contraception
- farming as the main industry, requiring a large population of strong, young farmhands
- the practice of communal living, which ensures that childcare, a shared responsibility, is always available.

The Hutterites are named after Jacob Hutter, the leader of a radical Christian movement started during the 1520s and 1530s in Tyrol, Austria. Along with Mennonites, they were part of the Anabaptist religious movement, which advocated that baptism should be administered only to believing adults. What made them radicals? They opposed the class linkages between the established church, the state, and the rich. They also were pacifists, adhering strictly to the commandment *Thou shalt not kill*. Their belief that people should be baptized as adults, when they're old enough to make a mature choice, ran counter to the rules of the Catholic Church and the law in Austria. Hutter was tortured and killed for his ideas. His followers moved several times, notably to Ukraine, before their diminished numbers moved to the northwest in America and the southwest in Canada.

Telling It Like It Is

A Historian's Point of View

The Minister's Role in a Hutterite Community

The following passage comes from a study of the Hutterite community of Pincher Creek, Alberta, published by historian David Flint (1975).

> [The] minister . . . is the single most important member of the community. Not only does he attend to the spiritual needs of the colony, but his advice is often asked on everything from when the pigs should be marketed to the price that should be charged for eggs. He is the colony leader, and his election is the most vital decision the colony makes in affecting its future nature. . . .
>
> Hutterites expect the minister . . . to set standards and demand conformity, and to guard the traditions and values of their religion, and they readily obey him. If the minister is easy-going about slight deviations in dress, the colony will reflect his attitude. On one new colony there was not yet a minister in residence. Dress became sloppy—women went around in summer without kerchiefs and shoes and socks. When asked about this, one embarrassed man replied, "When the cat's away, the mice will play." He admitted that there was laxity and confessed that this would change when the minister arrived. . . .
>
> In the week-by-week, year-by-year operation of the colony, group consensus and Sunday-evening meetings play a vital role in maintaining solidarity and discipline. It is an accepted practice to bring pressure to bear on those adults who do not conform to the will of the community. It is considered ethical and necessary to report an individual's misdoings to the colony meeting, and this is accepted for the common good and in recognition of the weakness of human nature. Usually the minister will first caution any person who is stretching the colony regulations too far—for instance by showing too much interest in photographs or pictures (considered to be vain), by being overly concerned with one's flower garden (over-watering taxes the limited water supply), or by frequent outbursts of anger. If change is not evident in the person's behaviour, then the preacher and the elders will decide on a punishment. The commonly accepted practice is to have the guilty party stand during church service, or kneel in front of the entire congregation and confess guilt, or sit with the children. . . . In cases of minor transgressions against colony rules, the minister, as the elected official responsible for maintaining colony discipline, needs deep human understanding to know when and where to draw the line.

The Hutterites were driven from one European country after another until they immigrated to the United States during the 1870s. In 1889, the Canadian government, wanting sturdy farmers to exploit the agricultural potential of the Prairies, offered them exemption from military service if they moved to Canada. During World War I, many Hutterite communities, fearing persecution in the United States, moved to Canada.

The social organization of the Canadian Hutterites involves three communal groups (called "Leuts," meaning "people"): Lehrerleut, Dariusleut, and Schmiedeleut. Each forms a moral community in Durkheim's sense. The Lehrerleut and Dariusleut are found mainly in Alberta, Saskatchewan, and BC, while the Schmiedeleut are in Manitoba. The differences between them are slight, a measure of how conservative or liberal each is.

The three groups exist among roughly 300 farming colonies in Canada, each comprising 60 to 150 people who share a "community of goods," except for small personal possessions. They have frequently

Independent Picture Service / Alamy Stock Photo

Hutterite children sit on the front porch of their home in a colony near Moose Jaw, Saskatchewan. More than a third of Canadian Hutterites are below the age of 15. Do you think this means their population is on the rise?

encountered opposition to their communal farming practices from other farmers and, in the past, also from provincial governments. The Hutterite system gave them several advantages over single-family farms. By pooling their resources, they could amass greater funds for equipment and supplies, and secure large contracts for their agricultural products, supplied by a large, well-trained, and comparatively cheap workforce.

10.6 Religion and Gender

Organized world religions are generally characterized by patriarchal power structures. Women tend to have subordinate roles that marginalize their participation in the power hierarchy, which is not the same thing as being marginalized. During the second wave of feminism in the 1960s and early 1970s, some women in North America and Western Europe became increasingly critical of Christian practices. They viewed Christianity's embedded patriarchy as an influential cultural factor in the reproduction

of gender inequality. Consider, they said, just a few examples from the Bible:

- "Man" was created in God's image, while "woman" was created from a rib, we are told, to be his companion.
- The first woman, Eve, is blamed for having all humans banished from the paradise Eden after she succumbed to temptation by eating an apple supplied to her by the devil.
- The most memorable female characters in the Bible are associated with sin and destruction; among them are Mary Magdalene, who is commonly identified as a prostitute; Delilah, who brought about Samson's downfall; and Jezebel, who was denounced for introducing the worship of rival gods into Israel, and whose name is synonymous with immorality.

Add to these points the Christian tradition of a wife's obedience, subservience, and even belonging to her husband, and you have some powerful examples that inform, transmit, and reproduce patriarchal structures of inequality, including **androcentrism** (from *andro* meaning "man") and sexism. This same patriarchal inequality is blamed for numerous instances of women's oppression in society, from the denial of voting privileges and work opportunities to sexual objectification and male violence. In this sense, Christianity—in fact, all **Abrahamic religions** (including Islam and Judaism)—has much to answer for, from a feminist perspective.

To be fair to the larger body of women who came to identify with feminism, this view of the Judeo-Christian scriptures is oddly biased. The two Biblical Creation myths are viewed as symbolic of different aspects of human nature, male and female, and both in relation to God; "Adam" was punished as severely as "Eve"; and the scriptures are full of examples of strong, independent women of faith, as well as a remarkable roster of female "outsiders" to the Jewish faith who are showcased as essential contributors to the ancestry of Jesus. These women include Rahab the harlot, who helped the spies of Joshua to escape from Jericho; Ruth, who returned with Naomi as an alien to become the wife of Boaz; Esther the Queen, who saved her people with a formidable combination of beauty, faith, and wits; Bathsheba, who was widowed by David's treachery to her husband so he could take her as a wife; Jesus's mother Mary, who would have been disgraced and possibly killed except for Joseph's fidelity to their contracted marriage, and who clearly was the source of much of Jesus's teaching as well as the principal informant for Luke's gospel (some scholars [see Zolfagharifard, 2014] think she actually authored it). Also, recall Judith, the woman who decapitated Holofernes with his own sword. Biblical "patriarchy" is matched and sometimes outstripped by strong women.

Women Priests in the Anglican Church

The Church of England, known as the Anglican Church (in Canada) or the Episcopal Church (in the United States), is the largest Protestant denomination in the world, with an estimated membership of between 76 and 84 million. Over the past half-century, the battle for women to take on the orders of deacons, priests, and bishops has been long, hard, and accompanied by very emotional dialogue that has at times seriously divided the Church. Of the 38 individual provinces that make up the Anglican Church,

the first two to be permitted to ordain female priests were the United States and Canada. In Canada, on 30 November 1976, six women were ordained almost simultaneously (so that no one would be considered the first), in four different dioceses.

The situation in the United States is not as clear. While the General Convention passed a resolution stating that "no one shall be denied access" to ordination into the three orders (deacons, priests, bishops) on the basis of their sex, another resolution protects bishops who oppose women priests in their dioceses. As late as 2004, there were still three (of 100) dioceses whose bishops would not allow the ordination of women. After 1998, when the Japanese province voted to ordain women priests, most Anglican provinces accepted female clergy. The "mother church" in England began permitting ordination of women only in 1993, four years after the first female bishop was ordained in the United States. The first female Anglican bishop in Canada, Victoria Matthews, was consecrated in 1994; at the time Canada was only the third Anglican province to have a woman bishop. As of 2019, Canada and the United States have had more women bishops (eight) than any other province. England itself did not have a woman bishop until 2015, and presently just half of the Anglican provinces allow the consecration of women bishops.

The resistance to women holding positions of authority within the Church is not restricted to Anglicans. It remains the official position of the Roman Catholic Church and of some fundamentalist Christian groups in Canada and the United States (e.g., the Southern Baptists) that women should not be ordained.

Why is there such opposition? Much of it comes back to Christianity's embedded patriarchy, which is extremely difficult to overcome in an institution that derives much of its meaning from its history and traditions. Many Church leaders still justify their opposition to the ordination of women on the grounds that Jesus had no female disciples. Of course, in the patriarchal culture in which Jesus lived, there would have been strong social opposition to his having female disciples.

He was revolutionary enough in his respectful treatment of women. And he had women followers who dedicated their lives to learning from him, with his approval (see his attitude toward Mary, sister of Martha, in Luke 10: 38–42). The negative attitude of the disciple Paul, as expressed in his letters to the Corinthians, reflects the Jewish attitude toward women at that time (although the Greeks and Romans were not "liberated" either, except in their mythologies):

> As in all the churches of the saints, the women should keep silence in the churches. For they are not permitted to speak, but should be subordinate, as even the law says. If there is anything they desire to know, let them ask their husbands at home. For it is shameful for a woman to speak in church. (1 Cor. 14: 33–35)

What do you think?

1. Do you think that Paul's statements were "culturally conditioned"?
2. Why do you think that the "innovations" of female priests and bishops came not from the centre of the Anglican Church in England, where the Head of the Church, Elizabeth, the Queen of England, lived, and where the Archbishop of Canterbury lives, but from the merely 250-year-old branches of the Church in New Zealand, Africa, and North America?

In July 2018, Jane Kryzanowski, of Regina, became the Canadian bishop for the Roman Catholic Womenpriests (RCWP). The international organization asserts a connection to the Roman Catholic Church, even though it is not recognized by the Catholic Church, which bars the ordination of women. Can a religion that bars women from positions of priestly authority accommodate all of its members equitably?

A similar attitude is expressed in Paul's correspondence with Timothy:

> Let a woman learn in silence with all submissiveness. I permit no woman to teach or to have authority over men; she is to keep silent. For Adam was formed first, then Eve; and Adam was not deceived, but the woman was deceived and became a transgressor. Yet woman will be saved through bearing children, if she continues in faith and love and holiness, with modesty. (1 Tim. 2: 11–15)

Paul's historical role was to take the ideas of Jesus and organize them into a structure. That the role itself was patriarchal reflects the culture of his upbringing and experience. Paul certainly was not Jesus.

Strong women rose into leadership during medieval times as heads of convents, often paired with monasteries headed by abbots. Many powerful women administered the castles, properties, and serfs when their consorts left for the Crusades.

Banning Burkini, Headscarves, and Other Conspicuous Religious Symbols

In 1905 the government of France passed a law separating church and state. It stated that the government would not officially recognize or fund any religion. The law was invoked in the 1980s, during debates about French children wearing signs of their religion: Christian students wearing crosses, Jewish boys wearing yarmulkes (kippahs), Sikh boys wearing turbans or carrying kirpans (ceremonial swords), and Muslim girls wearing headscarves. The debate centred on two competing principles: freedom of expression and *laïcité*, or secularism of the French state. The same debate has played out numerous times, in France and elsewhere, pitting secularists on one side against defenders of religious freedom on the other. Those who oppose any ban on veils, yarmulkes, and turbans insist that these symbols are indispensable elements of their religious observance and should be protected in societies that value freedom of expression and of religion. Proponents of laïcité claim to find the public display of "conspicuous" religious symbols offensive and inappropriate in a secular society. Of all the religious symbols that secularists find objectionable, it is the Muslim headscarf that seems to make them most uncomfortable.

In 2016, controversy erupted when several towns on the French Riviera imposed bans on the "burkini," a body-covering swimsuit that allows beach-going Muslim women to comply with Islamic code regarding modesty of appearance. The mayor of Cannes, the first town to pass the ban, characterized the burkini as "a symbol of Islamist extremism" (Poirier, 2016). A French court that upheld the ban adopted a similar view. Later that year, a higher French court overturned the ban.

The dark underbelly of Islamic dress codes for women was seen when a 22-year-old Iranian woman, Mahsa Amini, was arrested by Iranian authorities in September 2022 for improper wearing of the *hijab* and was reportedly beaten to death while in custody of the radically conservative Islamic state. This led to nationwide protests for women's rights and secularization in Iran that continued into 2023, in which upward of 500 protesters were killed and at least two protesters were publicly executed.

Canada has had other debates around the display of conspicuous religious symbols. Sikh officers in the Royal Canadian Mounted Police were prohibited from wearing turbans on duty until 1990, and Sikhs have frequently gone to court to defend their right to carry the kirpan, in schools, in government buildings, and on flights. However, the Muslim headscarf remains the flashpoint in debates. In 2007, a nine-year-old girl was kicked out of a soccer tournament in Quebec for wearing a headscarf. The soccer association cited FIFA, the Fédération Internationale de Football Association, in defending its decision. In December 2011, the federal government banned the wearing of the face-covering *niqab* for new citizens taking the oath of Canadian citizenship; the law was eventually overturned, but not before sparking bitter debates about the right to religious freedom versus the expectation that newcomers to Canada should renounce the traditions of their homeland if they clash with Canadian mainstream cultural values such as a woman's right to reveal her face in public.

In 2013, Quebec's Parti Québécois government proposed a law to ban the wearing of all conspicuous religious symbols in public-sector workplaces, including not just government offices but hospitals, government-run daycares, and public schools. The bill failed to pass before the PQ was defeated by the Liberals in the 2014 provincial election. Five years later, in June 2019, the ruling Coalition Avenir Québec (CAQ) passed Bill 21, which prohibits the province's public-sector employees (e.g., teachers, police officers, Crown prosecutors, and judges) from wearing religious symbols while carrying out their civic duties. While the law applies to all visible religious symbols, including Christian crosses and Jewish kippot (singular kippah), it will disproportionately affect *hijab*-wearing Muslim teachers.

Why has this happened in Quebec? In part it is a legacy of the Quiet Revolution that began in the 1960s. Quebec nationalism is another factor. The CAQ was born out of the ashes of the Parti Québécois (PQ), the party that campaigned persistently for Quebec to separate from Canada. Quebec's premier, François Legault, was first elected to the National Assembly as a member of the PQ before becoming a co-founder of the CAQ.

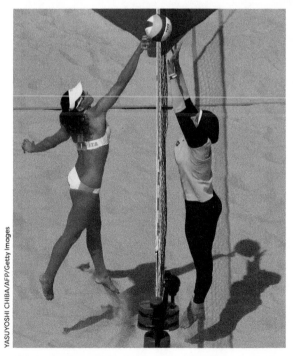

YASUYOSHI CHIBA/AFP/Getty Images

During the beach volleyball competition at the 2016 Summer Olympics in Rio de Janeiro some Muslim women donned body-covering burkinis, challenging the norms of a sport where women are expected to put their bodies on full display. Are both of these athletes conforming to the patriarchal gender expectations of their respective cultures? Is either one really free to dress as she pleases?

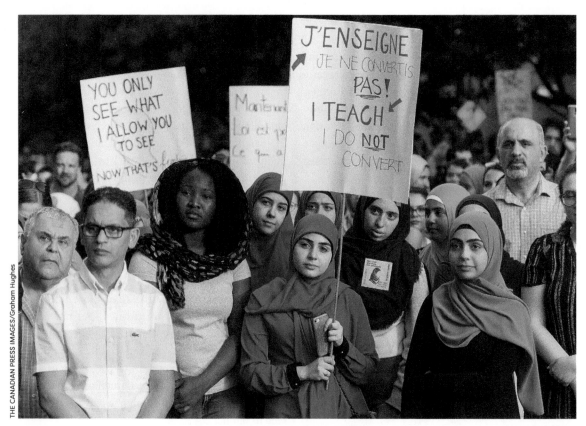

"Conspicuous symbols of religion" include turbans and yarmulkes—head coverings for men—and yet the debate always seems to centre on clothing worn by Muslim women. Why do you think that is the case?

What do you think?

1. What is your position on Bill 21? Where should we draw the line between defending the freedom of religious expression and promoting secularism, or the separation of church and state?
2. Do you expect other provinces to follow Quebec's lead in passing legislation like Bill 21?

Nationalism often comes with a dark side. The French term *pure laine* (literally "pure wool") is used in Quebec to denote a kind of French racial purity going back to the seventeenth century. This concept is ironic in consideration of the fact that the francophone population includes a high percentage of Indigenous genes. Quebec nationalism may have taken its darkest turn in January 2017, when a young white nationalist murdered six people at a mosque in Quebec City. The killer's name was one of several inscribed on the rifle used to kill 51 Muslims in Christchurch, New Zealand, in March 2019, testifying to the domino effect in acts of extremism.

Quick Hits

The Myth about Islam and Women

While it can be argued that there is a tendency for women to be oppressed in all countries where organized religion is strong, the countries of the Middle East, where Islam is the dominant religion, have been singled out as especially oppressive and misogynistic. The British-Turkish novelist Elif Shafak examines those tendencies cross-culturally through women who go to Oxford University in England to study and return to their homelands at their peril. She has had to stay away from her homeland of Turkey to remain safe. On the other hand, some women (including non-Muslims) *seek* Salafism, an extreme cult of Islamic Sunni fundamentalism, because, they say, they *want* to be told how to live their lives (Inge, 2016). When examining Islam and the rights of women, it is important to separate those anti-female practices that are specifically Muslim from those practices that happen to occur in Muslim countries but are not supported by the arbiters of the faith. The following list draws on Haroon Siddiqui's book *Being Muslim* (2006):

- The practice of honour killings (killing female relatives for alleged sexual misconduct that brings dishonour upon the family)

in countries such as Pakistan, Turkey, and Jordan is *not* an Islamic tradition.
- The practice of female genital cutting (FGC) in North and Central Africa is *not* condoned by Islam. At the First Islamic Ministerial Conference on The Child, held in Morocco in 2005, FGC was condemned as un-Islamic.
- The number of cases of polygyny (one man having more than one wife) in Muslim families in Western and Muslim countries may be legal but is greatly exaggerated. Most Muslim marriages are a male-plus-female couple. The cost of supporting more than one wife is a strong mitigating factor.
- Most Muslim women around the world do not wear a *hijab* or head-covering (Siddiqui, 2006, pp. 96–125).

Wrap It Up

Summary

We all deal with large organizations—banks, service providers, the local motor vehicle office—that often frustrate us with their lack of flexibility and human contact. Studying organizational behaviour, as we have done in this chapter, should, hopefully, enable you to see these personal frustrations through the lens of the sociological imagination. Don't take it personally—it's not just your call that isn't important to them, but everybody's.

Religions touch the spiritual and address human needs that are universal. These aspects of religion are, for the most part, outside the critical eye of sociology. However, religions have social organizations and practices that are well within the domain of the sociologist. They are intimately linked with other aspects of society—hierarchy, gender roles, and colonialism, to name just a few—that sociologists consider their purview.

Think Back

Questions for Critical Review

1. Are you or have you been a member of social organizations? Make a list of these organizations.
2. Would you say your view of society and your place in it tends toward complementarian or egalitarian? Give examples from your personal relations and experiences.
3. Has your experience to this point in your postsecondary education been one of McDonaldization, or do you as a student feel more than merely a student in a large, impersonal institution?

4. Can you identify ways in which your gender shapes your views on organizational structures and religion?
5. How would you—in your own words—define religion? What characteristics do the largest established religious traditions (e.g., Judaism, Christianity, Islam) share?
6. Could the workout group in my local park that often asks me to join them be considered a cult? What features would it need to be considered a new religious movement?

7. On balance, would you say that religion is a force for good in Canada today?
8. What is the relationship between religion and colonialism?

9. Would you say that in your own life, religion plays a large, small, or negligible role? Why do you think that is? What would make religion more relevant to you?

Read On

Suggested Print and Online Resources

Casefile, Case 60: Jonestown, https:// casefilepodcast.com/case-60-jonestown-part-1/
This three-part podcast examines one of the cults that gave new religious movements a bad name, the Peoples Temple Agricultural Project, otherwise known as Jonestown. The series traces the movement from the childhood of its charismatic leader, Jim Jones, all the way to the group's mass suicide in 1978 and offers insights into Jones's motivations and his appeal to those who followed him.

Timothy J. Gianotti Jr, *In the Light of a Blessed Tree: Illuminations of Islamic Belief, Practice, and History* (Eugene, OR: Wipf & Stock, 2011)
This is an excellent, readable work explaining the basic beliefs and practices of Islam.

Margaret Humphreys, *Empty Cradles: A Shameful Secret, a Miscarriage of Justice, and a Woman Who Wouldn't Give Up* (London: Corgi Books, 1995)
This book introduces the reader to the story of over 150,000 English children from marginalized families who were deported to Australian orphanages and similar institutions.

Isabelle Knockwood, *Out of the Depths: The Experiences of Mi'kmaw Children at the Indian Residential School in Shubenacadie, Nova Scotia* (Halifax: Fernwood Publishing, 2001)
This classic work by a First Nations writer examines life at a residential school for Mi'kmaw children.

Daniel Markovitz, "How McKinsey Destroyed the Middle Class," *The Atlantic*, 23 February 2020,

https://www.theatlantic.com/ideas/archive/2020/02/how-mckinsey-destroyed-middle-class/605878/
Milton Friedman's 1970 dictum that a company's chief responsibility is to the shareholders, not to its employees or to those who purchase the end products, was embraced by a management company whose reputation is becoming synonymous with social destruction.

Marx, Weber, and Durkheim on Religion, www .jeramyt.org/papers/sociology-of-religion.html
Jeramy Townsley's very useful (and often plagiarized) article compares the three main sociological theorists of religion.

Haroon Siddiqui, *Being Muslim* (Toronto: Groundwood Books, 2006)
This well-written work is designed to inform non-Muslim readers on what Islam is and is not about.

The Immanent Frame: Secularism, Religion, and the Public Sphere, http://tif.ssrc.org
Founded in conjunction with the Social Science Research Council's program on religion and the public sphere, this site provides intelligently written blogs and useful articles on the sociology of religion, contributed by specialists representing a range of disciplines.

The Sociological Study of Religion, http://hirr .hartsem.edu/sociology/about_the_field.html
Maintained by the Hartford Institute for Religion Research, this site presents a good overview of topics and current researchers in the sociological study of religion.

Family

Reading this chapter will help you to . . .

- Appreciate the diversity of the Canadian family.
- Learn some of the ways in which the family in Quebec has differed from family in the rest of Canada.
- Discuss nine major changes that have affected the makeup of families in Canada over the past 50 years.
- Understand the different forms that conjugal roles can take, and how these roles are changing in Canada.
- Describe the varying impacts of endogamy on different racial and ethnic groups in Canada.
- Outline and comment on the argument that Indigenous families were "under attack" during the twentieth century in Canada.

For Starters

Lisa F. Young/Shutterstock

You probably know someone who blames their family for all of their problems—the inability to find meaningful relationships, financial success, a fulfilling career, and so on. Blaming the family is a common theme among stand-up comics and sitcom writers, who have mined the "dysfunctional family" as a source of humorous material. And venting has become a therapy prescribed by psychoanalysts who draw on Freud's notion that we all harbour a volatile mix of love and anger toward our parents that we need to bring into consciousness. Rooted in mainstream psychology of the late twentieth century, this idea gave a veneer of legitimacy to a certain breed of pop psychologists who turned blaming the family into a daytime and late-night television phenomenon known as the tabloid talk show. This variety of confessional television flourished under hosts such as Jerry Springer and Maury Povich, who encouraged guests to confront their family members in episodes that often ended in onstage fistfights and chair-throwing. While these shows may have mocked conventional family dynamics in a setting contrived to create drama, the raw emotion at the heart of many episodes was real.

Family-blaming is not restricted to trash TV and online psychology forums. Consider the anger of the following lines written by acclaimed British poet Philip Larkin (1922–1985) in the poem "This Be the Verse" (1974):

> They fuck you up, your mum and dad.
>   They may not mean to, but they do.
> They fill you with the faults they had
>   And add some extra, just for you.
>
> But they were fucked up in their turn
>   By fools in old-style hats and coats,
> Who half the time were soppy-stern
>   And half at one another's throats.

Man hands on misery to man.
    It deepens like a coastal shelf.
Get out as early as you can,
    And don't have any kids yourself.

Of course, "getting out" is one thing; escaping your upbringing is quite another. We can see Larkin's poem as a very cynical take on socialization, the process of learning the values and standards of behaviour required to become members of the society to which we belong. As we saw in Chapter 4, socialization comes first through interactions with one's closest family members, and it leaves an impression that can last a lifetime.

Incidentally, this is a short poem I wrote in response to Larkin:

Larkin never married,
    But he did know how to rhyme.
He maintained non-committal relations
    With three women at one time.

He fed his family misery
    To readers down the years;

I'm glad he didn't have any kids
    To inherit all his fears.

As much as we may at times want to blame our families, we have to recognize the value that families bring in shaping responsible citizens of a society that functions harmoniously and advances over time.

Ultimately, you cannot run away from your family. You're better off understanding how your family made you who you are and how the family as an institution gives shape to society. By the end of this chapter, you should have some ideas.

What do you think?
1. What negative aspects of family was Larkin describing? In what ways is his poem a cynical interpretation of the process of primary socialization?
2. Are you optimistic or pessimistic about your future family life as a life partner or parent? Why, sociologically, do you think that is?
3. Do you have married uncles and aunts who have chosen not to have children? If so, why do you think they didn't?

11.1 Introduction: Family Is Diverse

The opening line of Russian novelist Leo Tolstoy's tragic romantic novel *Anna Karenina* reads: "Happy families are all alike; every unhappy family is unhappy in its own way." I disagree. Happy families, functional families, and good families exist in many forms, and are alike only in their success at serving basic purposes, such as providing emotional support for family members, taking care of elders, and raising the next generation. In most other respects, happy families are diverse. But Tolstoy and even Larkin were right in one regard: there are many ways to screw up family.

It would be misleading to say that one family form is demonstrably better than any other for its members. And yet conservative media are filled with judgmental remarks about contemporary family forms. Even traditional sociology is not free from this bias. If you were presented with the terms **nuclear family** (which includes a parent or parents and children) and **extended family** (which might include, in addition, grandparents, aunts, uncles, and cousins), you might be led to believe that the former is "normal" and the other some kind of deviation from the regular model. This is not the case. For some cultures, historical and current, using the word "family" to mean parents and children alone would be as odd as using the term "body" to refer just to the heart.

The Wendat (Huron) language of the seventeenth century had no terms for "nuclear" or "extended" family. The common way for the Wendat to refer to family was through the noun root *-hwatsir-*, meaning "matrilineage," or the verb root *-yentio-*, meaning "to belong to a matrilineal clan." Matrilineage is the line of descendants that follows the mother's line. A woman, her mother, and her sisters and brothers would belong to the same matrilineage. The longhouses that the people lived in would usually be dominated by one matrilineage, with married sisters and their husbands and children forming the nucleus of the people living in one house. Thus, the most common term for "family" in Wendat referred to what we would probably describe as an "extended family."

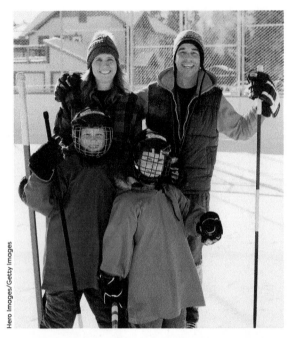

Hero Images/Getty Images

Would you call this a typical Canadian family? How many families do you know that look like this? Does yours?

More useful than "nuclear family" and "extended family" are terms proposed by Frances Goldscheider and Regina Bures in their study of intergenerational living arrangements in the United States. They favour the terms "simple household" and "complex household." A **simple household** consists of unrelated (by blood) adults with or without children. Conversely, a **complex household** includes "two or more adults who are related but not married to each other and hence could reasonably be expected to live separately" (Goldscheider & Bures, 2003). A simple household tends to consist of a single adult or married adults living with or without children. Probably the most common form of complex household in Canada today is one in which adult children live at home with a parent or parents. For a few years my household was complex: my wife and I lived on the main floor, with our youngest son and his wife living in the furnished basement. They moved out, and now we're simple.

When sociologists talk of a family's diversity, they may mean one of two things. Some mean

Quick Hits

What Is a Census Family?

For the purpose of collecting census data, Statistics Canada defines a family as:

- a same-sex or opposite-sex couple, married or common-law, living together in the same dwelling, with or without the child or children, if any, of either or both spouses;
- a lone parent (single, separated, married, or divorced) living together in the same dwelling with at least one child.

The first of these is considered a *couple family*. A situation in which a child or children live with their grandparents but not their parents is also considered a census family.

A couple family in which at least one child is the biological or adopted child of one parent only is a *stepfamily*. In a *simple stepfamily*, all of the children are the biological or adopted children of one parent only. In *a complex stepfamily*:

- there is at least one child of both parents and at least one child of only one parent;
- there is at least one child of each parent; or

- there is at least one child of both parents and at least one child of each parent.

These configurations can be lumped together under the term "blended families." Blended families, in effect, are stepfamilies: one or both of the cohabiting or married couple, by reason of the relationship, are also step-parents. The iconic *Brady Bunch* TV show that ran for five years on network television in the late 1960s and early 1970s, and which led to three short-lived spin-off series and no less than five made-for-TV movies, helped to normalize the blended family in the North American imaginary. If all of this seems somewhat convoluted and confusing, welcome to the complex problem of grappling with what a "family" is and counting how many of what kinds of family there are in Canada. And there's a good chance the terminology and the operational definitions will change in the years to come, as researchers seek new (or more efficient) ways to describe the lived experience of small groups of people in one household.

Hoxton/Sam Edwards/Getty Images

Compare this photo with the previous one. Is this family any less typical of the families you know? What factors in our culture might lead us to view one family as more conventional than another?

"diversity" in the sense that there are different family structures: dual-earner, single-earner/two-parent, lone-parent. I use "diversity" here and throughout this text in a broader sense that includes not just differences in structure but also cultural differences in the roles performed by each member. The discussion of the family in Quebec later in this chapter highlights this broader sense of diversity.

11.2 Nine Changes in the Canadian Family

The makeup and behaviour of Canadian families has changed dramatically over the past 40 years. I can, and in the sections that follow will, present several statistics to back up this claim, but one piece of evidence is especially revealing: Statistics Canada, our national data intelligence bureau, no longer keeps track of marriages and divorces.

For 90 years, from 1921 until 2011, Statistics Canada published annual marriage rates for the country; beginning in 1972, the agency began publishing annual statistics on divorces as well. These data enabled sociologists and other social scientists, economists, and policy makers to track not just how many Canadians were marrying but at what age, how often, and for how long. Combined with rates of cohabitation—common-law unions that have not been solemnized in a city court or place of worship—marriage rates tell us about how Canadians are coming together in social groups for mutual comfort, care, and support. Examined against the backdrop of economic recessions and other tumultuous events, divorce rates give us a clue to the stressors that cause marriages to break down.

So why did Statistics Canada decide to stop collecting data on marriage and divorce rates? One explanation is that it was a cost-savings measure necessitated by budget cuts made by the Conservative government of Stephen Harper, who fought some very public battles with the federal agency and its chief statistician, Munir Sheikh. That may have played a role, but I don't think it was the main factor. What happened, I think, is that marriage and divorce became difficult to define. With the traditional church wedding on the decline, an increasing number of couples have entered into conjugal unions that resemble marriage but may or may not be recognized as such in the province where they live. In Ontario, for instance, a couple needs to be living together continuously for three years to receive some of the rights and benefits of married couples; in other provinces, the period is shorter. Not all provinces recognize "common-law marriage," though they might recognize "marriage-like relationships." In BC, people living in marriage-like relationships are considered "unmarried spouses." Then consider that two people may live together for the purpose of raising a child but may not (or no longer) be intimately involved and may have romantic partners outside of that parenting union; are they "married"? What about roommates who have been sharing a dwelling because they cannot afford to live singly: they may be occasional sexual partners but would not consider themselves married, even in a common-law sense. And then, while ending a marriage involves a sequence of legal steps, a marriage-like union can be dissolved without any formal procedure other than walking out the door.

The point is that while many people still aspire to a formal church wedding, Canadians are increasingly coming together in unions that resemble traditional marriage in some ways—shared costs and mutual financial support; co-parenting of a child; a sexual relationship; intimate friendship—but not in others. People in these arrangements may not consider themselves married and may even bristle at the word "couple." And this reflects one of the ways in which the family in Canada is changing. The following are some other trends worth noting.

The Marriage Rate Is Decreasing While the Cohabitation Rate Is Rising

Let's dig into the 90 years' worth of marriage rates we do have to see what trends they reveal. We can then look at the changing percentages of married people since 2008, the last year for which Statistics Canada calculated a marriage rate.

The **crude marriage rate** is the number of marriages that occur in a given year per 1,000 people in a population. "Crude" refers to the fact that no statistical wizardry has been used to "refine" the rate (to use an oil analogy); it's not a social comment on

marriage itself. Since the population rises over time, the crude marriage rate gives a better indication of trends than the overall number of marriages taken alone. (If the number of marriages were the same for 2002 and 2012, the actual rate of marriage would be decreasing, since the population overall is rising; a sociologist would conclude that fewer people were getting married.)

The crude marriage rate has fluctuated over the years. In 1920, it was relatively low at 6.1 per 1,000 people. Many young Canadian men (married and single, totalling more than 60,000 in service) had died during World War I, and the Spanish flu epidemic of 1918–19 killed about 55,000 Canadians, most of whom were young adults. When I think of that statistic, I think of two of my great aunts who were young then—Aunt Nell the nurse, Aunt Margaret the teacher. They were gifted, intelligent women adored by the children and grandchildren of their married brothers. Neither of them ever married.

The marriage rate rose to a peak of 11.2 marriages per 1,000 people in 1946, representing a post–World War II marriage boom that would precede (and contribute to) the postwar baby boom (Statistics Canada, 2011, Chart 6). After dropping a little in the years that followed, the marriage rate remained fairly high over the next three decades, peaking at 9.0 in 1972 and hovering around 8.0 for the rest of the decade (Statistics Canada, 2011, Chart 6). But by 2008, Canada's crude marriage rate was at 4.4 per 1,000 population, having fallen below 4.5 for the first time in history. The highest provincial rate was 6.8 in PEI, the lowest was Quebec, with 2.9. Quebec, in fact, was the only province under the national rate, accompanied only by the three territories.

Fewer *marriages* does not mean fewer *couples*. The number of **common-law** (or **cohabiting**) unions has been rising since the 1980s. There never was a "crude common-law marriage rate," comparable to the crude marriage rate, since society doesn't ritually mark the beginning of common-law relationships the way it records marriages. However, Statistics Canada does produce estimates of the population by marital status, indicating how many Canadians at any one time are single, married, living common-law, and so on. As Table 11.1 shows,

TABLE 11.1 Marital Status of Canadians Aged 15 and Over (%), 1998–2018

	1998	2008	2018
Single	27.8	29.0	29.1
Married	49.5	46.1	44.7
Living common-law	8.6	10.8	11.8
Separated	2.8	2.7	2.7
Divorced	5.3	5.9	6.1
Widowed	6.1	5.6	5.6

Note: The categories in this table and in Figure 11.1 are considered mutually exclusive of one another. So, while a person who is widowed or separated from their spouse may be single, "single" means never married.

Source: Statistics Canada (2019).

the proportion of Canadian adults in common-law unions grew by over 3 percentage points between 1998 and 2018, while the percentage of married Canadians fell by nearly 5 points. Figure 11.1 provides a snapshot of Canadians aged 15 and over by marital status. Note that the categories used in Table 11.1 and Figure 11.1 are considered mutually exclusive of one another: here, only one status can apply per person. So "single" is reserved for people who have never married, and a person who was once married but is no longer in a committed relationship must be separated, divorced, or widowed. I have been divorced twice, but in the eyes of Statistics Canada I am married, reflecting not my past but my present status.

The increasing share of common-law relationships raises a number of questions. First, is cohabitation replacing marriage? So far, the answer is a tentative no: despite the increase in the percentage of common-law couples since 1998, and the accompanying decline in traditional marriage, married couples still make up the predominant family structure in Canada by a wide margin, as Table 11.1 shows. Does the shifting balance signify that people today lack commitment? Or does it reflect the fact that an expensive church wedding is not a priority for younger people who are increasingly secular and leaving university with unprecedented levels of student debt? And does cohabitation benefit men more than women? It depends on how you look at it, and possibly on your sex. As Figure 11.2 shows, the numbers of men and women who are living in common-law relationships are pretty close: among Canadians aged 15 and over, 12.0 per cent of men and 11.5 per cent of women

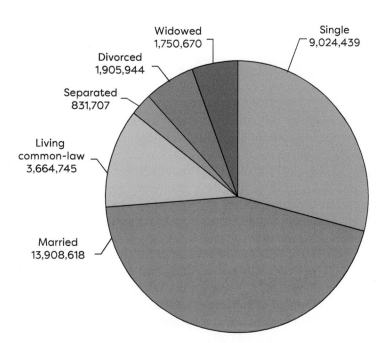

FIGURE 11.1 Marital Status of Canadians Aged 15 and Over, 2018

Source: Statistics Canada (2019).

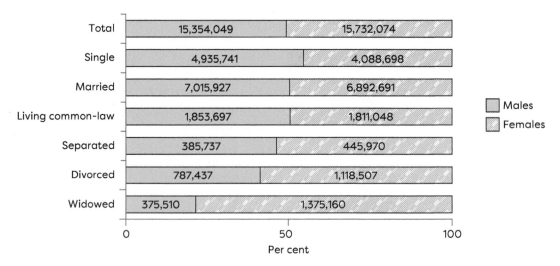

FIGURE 11.2 **Marital Status of Canadians by Sex, 2018**

Source: Statistics Canada (2019).

are living common-law. The marriage numbers are also close: in 2018, 45.7 per cent of men and 43.8 per cent of women were married. More men than women are single (never married), but more women than men are separated, divorced, or widowed. Finally, how does cohabitation, compared with marriage, affect children? These are questions sociologists today are asking.

The Age of First Marriage Is Rising

The average age of first marriage in Canada has risen steadily since the early 1970s, but as Figure 11.4 shows, it wasn't until the 1990s that the figures really began to climb.

Again, because Statistics Canada stopped tracking marriage rates in 2011, we have no first-marriage

Quick Hits

How Quebec Skews the Marriage Data

In a number of areas where change in the Canadian family is occurring, families in Quebec are leading the way. This is not to say that they are "further ahead" in some kind of modernist progressive model, but that they offer the clearest evidence of certain general trends.

The cohabitation rate in the United States has traditionally been much lower than the rate in Canada. For instance, in 2001 the American cohabitation rate of 8.2 per cent was barely half the Canadian rate of 16.0 for the same year. We could propose a number of explanations to account for this difference, including a greater attachment to religion and traditional family values in America. However, the Quebec factor looms large in the analysis. In 2018,

11.8 per cent of all Canadians aged 15 and over were living in common-law relationships; in Quebec, the figure was nearly 10 percentage points higher, at 21.5 per cent. Figure 11.3 shows the ratio of cohabiting to married adults by province. In most provinces, cohabiting adults make up somewhere between 15 per cent and 19 per cent of the sample; in Quebec, the figure is 38.7 per cent! Quebec, in fact, is the only province with a cohabitation rate higher than the national average, which means that it is pulling the national average above the rates of all other provinces. This is why when we consider trends in the Canadian family, we have to look at Quebec to see how it aligns with the rest of the country.

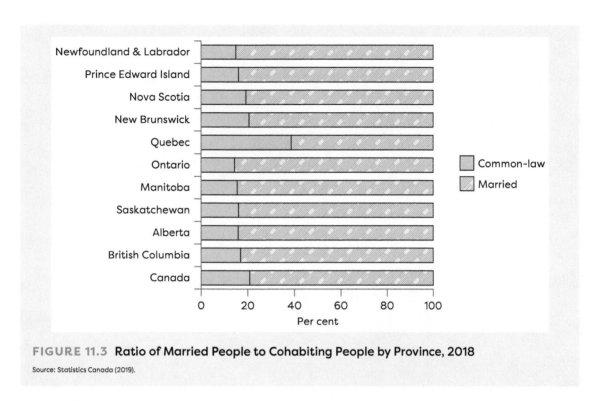

FIGURE 11.3 Ratio of Married People to Cohabiting People by Province, 2018

Source: Statistics Canada (2019).

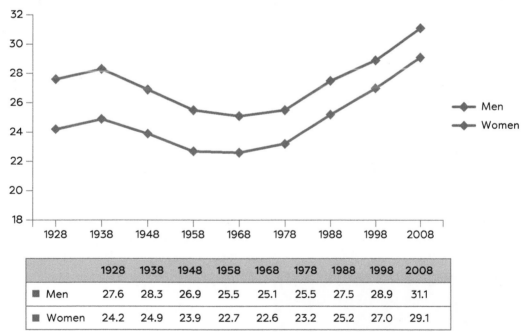

	1928	1938	1948	1958	1968	1978	1988	1998	2008
■ Men	27.6	28.3	26.9	25.5	25.1	25.5	27.5	28.9	31.1
■ Women	24.2	24.9	23.9	22.7	22.6	23.2	25.2	27.0	29.1

FIGURE 11.4 Average Age at First Marriage by Sex, Canada, 1928–2008

Source: Human Resources and Skills Development Canada (2014).

rates for the years since 2008. However, we do know that the percentage of Canadians under 30 who have never married or lived common-law rose from 77.3 per cent in 2008 to 78.9 per cent in 2018 (Statistics Canada, 2019). It's not a large climb, but it is a steady climb. Provincial percentages range from a low of 74.1 per cent in Alberta to a high of 82.2 per cent in Ontario (in this case, Quebec is not an outlier).

Dmitry Rukhlenko/iStockphoto

Shows like *Say Yes to the Dress* and *My Big Fat Gypsy Wedding* celebrate the commercial and secular aspects of the modern wedding ceremony. But even stripped of its religious significance, the wedding remains for many people an important rite of passage that distinguishes marriage from living together in an important way. To you, how important is the institution of marriage? In what ways does it differ from living together? How much do you think your answer is influenced by factors such as your age, your sex, your sexual orientation, your ethnicity, and your family background and religious upbringing?

Questions arise. Will young people continue to defer marriage, or has this trend peaked? What is the cause for the high percentage of people under 30 who have never married or lived in a common-law relationship? How does this trend relate to the decline in the marriage rate noted in the last section?

What do *you* think?

Having paid a small fortune for our son's wedding, I am left wondering—sociologically, not parentally—why it is that "middle-class" weddings have become increasingly expensive over the last decade or so. Is it the influence of the shows noted in the caption to the photo above? Is it related to the decline in the religious aspect of weddings? Does it have to do with the need to put on a big show in order to make it worthwhile for family members attending from far away? What do you think?

There Are More Divorces Overall, But the Rate Is Falling

Analyzing divorce statistics can be complicated. If you ask a group of people whether they think the divorce rate is rising or falling, they would probably say that it's going up. This is not the case. The rate has jumped on several occasions over brief periods of time, but we can account for these, in part, by looking at changes to the legislation surrounding divorce.

In 1961, there were 6,563 divorces in Canada, producing a divorce rate of 36.0 per 100,000 population. In 1968, the grounds for divorce were expanded in most of Canada: no longer was adultery the sole grounds for divorce. From 1968 to 1969, the divorce rate shot up from 54.8 per 100,000 to 124.5 (Figure 11.5). Remember that the average age of first marriage was at an all-time low in the 1960s. This is

The Point Is ...

Child Marriage Is More Common Than You Probably Think It Is

As you read the title, you may have imagined that I was going to focus on Muslim couples in South Asia or the Middle East. If you did, you were wrong. Instead, let's turn our attention to the United States, where the majority of child marriages take place between Christians.

Almost every provincial, territorial, and state jurisdiction in North America follows the principle that once you reach the age of 18, you can legally marry without parental consent; if you are 16 or 17, you need the consent of one of your parents. But almost half of the states in the United States have no minimum age for marriage, provided a judge approves the union. Remember, of course, that most judges are older men.

While accurate statistics are hard to obtain, a report published in the *New York Times* (Reiss, 2015) sheds some light on the situation in one state, New Jersey, between 1995 and 2012. During that period, the state licensed marriages involving 3,481 people under the age of 18. Of that total, 163 of the people were aged 13, 14, or 15. Very rarely, these marriages may have involved two people under 18 marrying each other. However, 91 per cent of the under-18-year-olds were married to adults (18 and over), and 90 per cent of these minors were girls. According to the report, these cases involved "age differences that could have triggered statutory-rape charges, not a marriage license" (Reiss, 2015). We can speculate that a good number of these marriages were arranged by parents, and that the underage parties were forced to marry against their will. Complicating the matter is the fact that no one under 18 can legally apply for divorce.

A more recent report in the British newspaper *The Independent* (Baynes, 2017) claimed that in the United States between 2000 and 2015, a total of 207,468 marriages took place in which at least one of the partners (girls in 87 per cent of the cases) was a minor. Tennessee led the shock parade with three 10-year-old girls marrying partners who were 24, 25, and 31. In a strange exception to the trend, an 11-year-old boy married a 27-year-old woman in the same state.

It is worth noting that the statistics in both reports came from Unchained at Last, a New Jersey-based group campaigning to abolish child marriage. At the same time, the reported figures may actually understate the real number of child marriages in the United States, since statistics on the subject are not always well managed and some states provided no statistics at all on the subject.

What do *you* think?

1. What sociological factors might contribute to child marriage in the United States? Income? Religion? What about teen pregnancy and family reputation and "respectability"?
2. If you were in a position to draft policy on child marriage, what laws would you propose?

significant as there is an inverse correlation between age at marriage and the likelihood of divorce (i.e., the younger the couple, the greater the chance the marriage will end in divorce).

By 1982, the number of divorces had peaked at a rate of roughly 280 per 100,000 population. Then in 1985, the Divorce Act was changed again to permit divorce on the grounds of "marital breakdown." By 1987, the numbers had peaked again, this time producing a rate of 363.75 divorces per 100,000. By 2002, the numbers were back down to mid-1970s levels: a total of 70,155 divorces for a rate of 223.7.

As with other marriage data, Statistics Canada stopped collecting regular information on divorces in 2011. However, Mary Bess Kelly, for a 2012 Statistics Canada *Juristat* article, collected data on the number of divorce cases initiated in a sample of six provinces and territories (Ontario, Nova Scotia, BC, Nunavut, Yukon, and Northwest

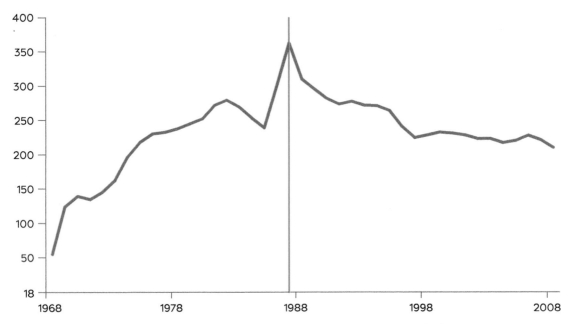

FIGURE 11.5 Crude Divorce Rate in Canada, 1968–2008, per 1,000 population

Source: Statistics Canada, CANSIM Table 053-0002.

Territories). She reported that the number of cases fell by 8 per cent between 2006 and 2011, decreasing each year (Kelly, 2012). That's good news for marriage, right?

Not necessarily. It is possible that some married couples are staying together longer, particularly if we look at falling divorce rates in the context of what else we have learned in this chapter—specifically, that people are marrying later and marrying less. It suggests that people today are being more selective in their marriage choices, perhaps leading to greater levels of commitment. However, it could also be that divorce rates have fallen because a greater proportion of couples are living common-law, meaning that fewer couples require formal divorces when their relationships end. Finally, consider this: we know that the average age of first marriage in 2008 was roughly 30. Those people would have been nine years old in 1987, when divorce was at an all-time high in Canada. What effect do you think it might have on your commitment to marriage if you grew up in a household that experienced marital discord and breakup? Is it possible you might be more likely to stay in a less-than-perfect marriage to avoid putting your own children through the kind of situation you went through growing up?

More Women Are Having Children in Their Thirties

In 2010, the average age of a woman giving birth in Canada surpassed 30, a figure not seen since the 1930s (Statistics Canada, 2016, Chart 1). This signifies that the number of women in their thirties giving birth is increasing. Not only that: the number of women in their thirties giving birth *for the first time* is also increasing. In 1987, 4 per cent of women who gave birth for the first time were aged 35 and older; by 2011, the percentage had tripled to 12 per cent. Over the same period, the percentage of first-time mothers who were over 30 increased from 15 per cent to 28 per cent.

Another way of looking at this is by considering what proportion of all births were to women aged 30 and older (Figure 11.6). As the table below shows, just under one-fifth of all births in 1975 were to women over 30; by 2015, well over half (56.4 per cent) of all births were to women over 30.

Year	Percentage of All Births by Women over 30					Change
	1975	1985	1995	2005	2015	
Percentage	19.2	27.8	42.5	48.9	56.4	+37.2%

Source: Statistics Canada, CANSIM Table 102-4503, Table 13-10-0416-01.

	1992	1997	2002	2007	2012	2017
■ Under 20	6.1	5.8	4.7	4.1	3.4	2.1
▨ 20–29	56.0	49.8	47.9	46.4	43.6	39.6
▥ 30–39	36.7	42.6	44.7	46.5	49.6	54.4
☐ 40 and over	1.1	1.9	2.6	2.9	3.5	3.9

FIGURE 11.6 **Percentage of Live Births in Canada by Age of Mother, 1992–2017 (select years)**

Source: Statistics Canada (2018), Table 13-10-0416-01, Live births by age of mother.

At the other end of the scale, we see a sharply contrasting profile in births to mothers in their teens. From 1995 to 2015, the proportion of births to young women under 20 decreased to just 2.5 per cent. While not the sole reason for the decrease, improved access to abortion since 1988, when the Supreme Court struck down Canada's anti-abortion laws, has certainly played a role in the decrease in births to teen mothers.

	Percentage of All Births by Teens					Change
Year	1995	2000	2005	2010	2015	
Percentage	6.3	5.3	4.1	3.9	2.5	–3.8%

Source: Statistics Canada, CANSIM Table 102-4503, Table 13-10-0416-01.

There are significant regional differences in teen pregnancy today. In 2017, Quebec, British Columbia, and Ontario had the lowest percentages of births to mothers in their teens, at 1.4 per cent, 1.5 per cent, and 1.6 per cent respectively (Statistics Canada, Table 13-10-0416-01). The provinces with the highest percentages of births to young women under 20 were Saskatchewan and Manitoba (4.7 per cent). Nunavut was an extreme outlier with a rate of 17.7 per cent. The provincial/territorial differences roughly correlate with differences among urban and rural populations. Canadian regions with the highest percentages of rural residents have the greatest number of teenage mothers. Is this coincidence, or do you think that living in a rural community is a causal factor in teen pregnancy? What other factors might be involved?

An interesting set of statistics related to this is the average age of mother at the birth of her first child, which has a different profile:

	Average Age of Mother at Birth of First Child							
Year	1945	1955	1965	1975	1985	1995	2005	2015
Age	25.2	24.1	23.5	24.3	25.5	26.3	28.0	29.2

Sources: Statistics Canada (2016, Chart 1); Provencher, Milan, Hallman, & D'Aoust (2018, Table 4).

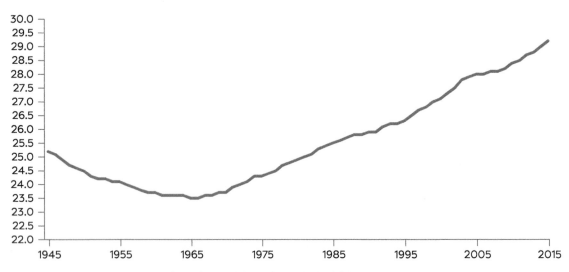

FIGURE 11.7 Average Age of Mother at First Birth, 1945–2015

Source: Statistics Canada (2016, Chart 1); Provencher, Milan, Hallman, & D'Aoust (2018, Table 4).

Plotting the average age of the first-time mother in Canada shows a steady drop from the mid-1940s to the mid-1960s, followed by a gradual climb that hasn't yet stopped (Figure 11.7). It's no coincidence that the shape of this graph is nearly identical to the line in Figure 11.4, depicting the average age at first marriage. Following a decade of economic depression, World War II (1939–45) caused young people to delay marriage and childbearing until soldiers returned home in the mid-1940s. The age of first marriage and first birth fell from that time until the 1960s, when the women began to pursue higher education and participate in the workforce in greater numbers. At the same time, the sexual revolution changed social attitudes that had frowned upon sex before marriage and the use of contraception. World War II had caused families to delay marriage and childbearing out of necessity; the sixties, especially with the introduction of the female birth control pill in 1960, brought new freedoms that enabled couples to delay marriage and childbearing by choice, and "the Pill" was instrumental in the shifting sexual mores at that time.

In 2014, the age-specific fertility rate for women in their early forties (10.9 births per 1,000 women) surpassed the rate for women in their late teens (10.2). You may see those two figures as being so close that they are nearly identical, but don't discount the significance of this landmark. After all, just 15 years earlier, the fertility rate for women in their early forties was barely one-quarter that rate of women

in their late teens. Historically, the age-specific fertility rate for young women aged 15 to 19 was high throughout the late 1940s all the way to the 1960s. In 1959—the peak of the baby boom—it was 59.7 births per 1,000 women, nearly six times the 2014 rate for this age group! In general, the period throughout the 1980s to the present has seen the lowest fertility rates for young women in the data observed since 1926. Meanwhile, since 2014, the fertility rate for women in Canada aged 40–44 has continued to climb, and as of 2020 had reached 11.6 births per 1,000 women.

An important factor to consider when looking at delays in childbearing is **fecundity**, the physical ability to conceive. This ability changes during a woman's fourth decade. Estimates are that 91 per cent of women at the age of 30 are physically able to become pregnant. This drops to 77 per cent for women aged 35 and just 53 per cent of women at 40 (Rajulton, Balakrishnan, & Ravanera, 1990). It could be that the fact that more women are waiting longer to have their first child is having a lowering effect on the total fertility rate, the subject of the next section.

The Number of Children per Family Has Dropped Below the Replacement Rate

The **total fertility rate** is an estimate of the average number of children that a cohort of women between the ages of 15 and 49 will have in their lifetime if

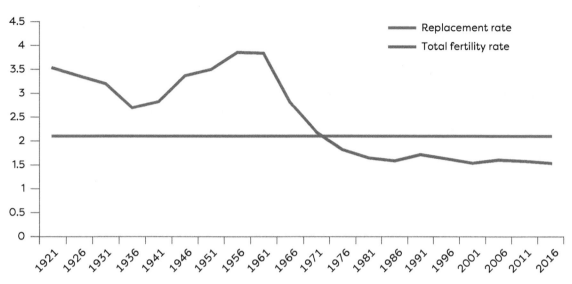

FIGURE 11.8 Canada's Total Fertility Rate since 1921

Source: Statistics Canada, Canadian Vital Statistics, Birth Database, Survey 3231, and Demography Division, Population Estimates Program.

current factors remain constant during their reproductive years. It's a projection, in other words, based on current fertility rates, even though we know that these actual rates will change.

Figure 11.8 shows the trending total fertility rate from 1921 to 2016. In 2002 the total fertility rate in Canada bottomed out at 1.51; after a short recovery, it fell again beginning in 2009, and as of 2016 it was at 1.54, just a hair above that low-water mark reached in 2002. How does this compare with the rate for other countries? Rates for the 100 most populous countries in the world in 2014 ranged from 2.22 to 6.89, with 9 of the top 10 fertility rates being in Africa. Those countries with fertility rates below Canada's include eastern European countries, such as the Czech Republic (1.43); some Mediterranean countries, including Italy (1.42), Greece (1.41), and Portugal (1.52); and several East Asian countries—Singapore (0.80), Hong Kong (1.17), Japan (1.40), South Korea (1.25), and Taiwan (1.11). In each of these countries, the population is expected to fall. Why do you think their fertility rates are so low? Is it just economics (national and family), or is some pessimistic sense of the future involved as well?

Consider the following. Of women born between 1927 and 1931, 31.0 per cent had five or more children. Compare that with women born between 1952 and 1956, of whom just 1.3 per cent had five or more children. Among the latter group, 38.3 per cent

had just two children, and 33.7 per cent had one child or no children, meaning that a total of 72.0 per cent of women born in 1952–6 had two children or fewer, compared with 42.7 per cent of women born in 1927–31.

Figure 11.8 also shows the **replacement rate**, the number of children that the average woman must bear if the overall population is to continue at the same level. The replacement rate is 2.1, meaning that 2.1 children must be born for every woman in a population aged 15–49 in order for the population to hold constant. As Figure 11.8 shows, it's been almost 50 years since Canada had a total fertility rate above the replacement rate.

So what does a country do when its national fertility rate is below the replacement rate? Canada makes up for its low fertility rate with high levels of immigration. Take note, however, that immigrants from countries with higher fertility rates soon begin to reproduce at a rate consistent with the fertility rate in this country.

Are there ways to boost the fertility rate? Would government incentives—a "baby bonus"—help to offset the cost of having and raising children? Would a system of universal, publicly funded daycare change things significantly? Both of those mechanisms are used in Quebec, where the fertility rate has been falling and stood just a little above the national average at 1.59 as of 2016. (The highest provincial rate was

Saskatchewan's, at 1.93—still below replacement; the lowest rate belonged to BC: 1.40.) Recent studies in the United States suggest that women are willing to have more children when their husbands are willing to take a greater share of responsibility for childcare and general housework.

There Are Nearly as Many Couples Without Children as With

Related to the decline in the total fertility rate, the proportion of couples living *with* children has been surpassed by the proportion of couples living *without* children. In 2001, couples with children made up 43.6 per cent of all census families, while couples

without children accounted for 40.3 per cent. By 2011, childless couples comprised 44.5 per cent of all census families compared to 39.2 per cent for couples with children.

We have to be careful not to jump to hasty conclusions. This is just a 10-year trend, which is pretty short by demographers' standards. The 2016 census shows a modest reversal, with the ratio of couples with children to couples without at 51.1 to 48.9. (Note that here the base is *couples*, as opposed to *census families*.) Still, it's worth asking: Are these figures explained by the fact that women are waiting longer to have their first child? Or do they have more to do with the fact that Canada's overall population

The Point Is ...

The "Typical" Family Has Changed a Lot in 70 Years

Between 1948 and 1953, sociologists John Seeley, Alexander Sim, and Elizabeth Loosley studied a white, upper-middle-class neighbourhood in North Toronto, which they nicknamed "Crestwood Heights." The following is a brief introduction to their chapter on the family:

> The family of Crestwood Heights . . . consists of father, mother, and two (rarely more) children. The children are healthy, physically well developed, attractively dressed, and poised as to outward behavior. The mother, assured in manner, is as like an illustration from *Vogue* or *Harper's Bazaar* as financial means and physical appearance will allow. The father, well tailored, more or less successful in radiating an impression of prosperity and power, rounds out the family group.
>
> This small family unit is both lone and love-based. It is, more often than not, formed by the marriage of two persons from unrelated and often unacquainted families . . . who are assumed to have chosen each other because they are "in love." Other reasons for the choice (perpetuation of property within one family, the linking of business or professional interest, an unadorned urge to upward social mobility and so on), even

if influential, could not reputably be admitted as grounds for marriage.

> This family unit is not embedded in any extended kinship system. The newly formed family is frequently isolated geographically and often socially from the parental families. It is expected that the bride and groom will maintain a separate dwelling removed by varying degrees of distance from that of each set of parents. . . . The isolation of each family acts to decrease the ability of the family to transmit traditional patterns of behavior, which might otherwise be absorbed from close contact with, for instance, grandparents. The absence of kinship bonds also tends to concentrate the emotional life of the family upon a few individuals. (Seeley, Sim, & Loosely, 1956, pp. 159–60)

What do *you* think?
Identify a middle-class neighbourhood in the city or town where you live and go to school. Give it a fictitious name, and then write a brief description of the "typical" family that lives there today. How much (or how little!) does your family sketch differ from this description of the Crestwood Heights family?

is aging, which means there are more older couples whose grown-up children have left home? If you're thinking the latter, consider the following.

Children Are Leaving Home at a Later Age

The term **cluttered nest** is sometimes used to describe the phenomenon in which adult children continue to live at home with their parents (the opposite, **empty nest**, describes a household in which children have moved out to live on their own). In 1981, 33.6 per cent of women aged 20–24 and 51.4 per cent of men of the same age were living with a parent or parents; by 1996, those figures had risen to 50.4 per cent and 64.3 per cent, respectively (Beaujot, 2000, p. 98). The rates have levelled off somewhat since then: as of the 2016 census, 57.6 per cent of women aged 20–24 and 65.7 per cent of men aged 20–24 were living at home (Figure 11.9). Note that if you are a student away at university but you return to the home of your parents or grandparents for the summer, you are still considered to be living at home, despite the independence you probably feel from September to April.

Causation is easy to establish. For a start, it takes more time and education nowadays to establish a career. Some adults living with parents are "boomerang kids," who have returned home after going away to college or university, prior to setting up on their own. In addition, earlier generations didn't face the current higher cost of living, including rising housing prices, as well as a number of other costs, such as an internet connection and cellphone service. Among Canadian cities, Toronto topped the list, with 47.4 per cent of young adults of ages 20–34 living with parents (Statistics Canada, 2017b); in fact, Ontario in 2016 was home to the top seven cities in Canada. Also, with couples marrying later and later in life, it takes that much longer to set up a dual-earner household, the only model that is financially viable for some people who want to move out of their parents' home.

Culture or ethnicity is another factor that affects young adults living at home. Some cultures, such as South Asian and Chinese Canadians, are more open to young adults living with one or both parents. As a 28-year-old Pakistani Canadian woman explained, "In our community, there's no stigma attached to coming back and staying with your parents, so you don't feel that pressure to be independent as other communities do" (Ansari, 2019). Clearly, the situations of some young adults make it sensible for them to live at home while they become more able to strike out on their own. Both of our boys, at different times in their late twenties/early thirties, lived with us in the home where they grew up when they were working early in their careers and living with the women who would later become their wives. We live a little north of Toronto and wanted them to be able to save the money required to buy a house. Both eventually did.

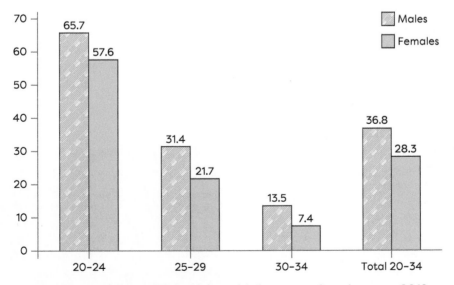

FIGURE 11.9 Percentage of Young Adults Living with Parents or Grandparents, 2016

Source: Statistics Canada, 2016 Census of Population, Statistics Canada Catalogue no. 98-400-X2016028.

Jeremy Richards/iStockphoto

Does it surprise you that young men (20–34) are more likely than young women to be living at home with their parents? Why do you think this is the case?

There Are More Lone-Parent Families

The number of lone-parent families in Canada has been increasing since 1966 (which followed a 35-year period of decrease from 13.6 per cent during the Depression year of 1931). In 1966, 8.2 per cent of all families were lone-parent families; since then, the figure has risen steadily to 12.7 per cent in 1986, 14.5 per cent in 1996, and 15.9 in 2006 (Statistics Canada, 2012, p. 5). Since then the number dropped to 14.2 as of 2016 (Statistics Canada, Table 11-10-0017-01).

People often speculate about the negative effects on children of living in lone-parent households, particularly with regard to school dropout rates and criminal activity. The critics need to be cautious here, though, as most lone-parent households began as two-parent households. It is hard to determine whether unfavourable conditions existing in the pre-divorce or pre-separation family—an abusive parent perhaps, or parental fighting—could have

been the real cause of a child's crime or truancy. You can't just blame the lone-parent situation.

Another trend that must be considered, though it is difficult to document, is the planned lone-parent household, which has not resulted from the breakup of a marriage or common-law relationship. Adoption as well as advances in fertility technology give individuals today various avenues to parenthood without having to be in a traditional heterosexual union.

What do *you* think?

Roughly 80 per cent of lone-parent families have a female family head, although that percentage is down since the early 1990s, when lone-mother families made up 88 per cent of all lone-parent households. Do you think the gap between lone-mother and lone-father families will continue to shrink? Is it likely to be erased in your lifetime?

There Are More People Living Alone

In 1996, Beaujot (2000, p. 117) reported, 12 per cent of the entire Canadian population aged 15 and over were living alone; the rate was highest for those over 85 (48 per cent), and lowest for those younger than 55 (10 per cent). By 2016, the overall percentage of Canadians living alone had climbed to 13.9 per cent (Statistics Canada, 2017a). The percentage of adult women living alone is greater than the percentage of adult men living alone (14.5 per cent versus 13.1 per cent); the fact that women tend to outlive men contributes significantly to this difference, as Figure 11.10 shows.

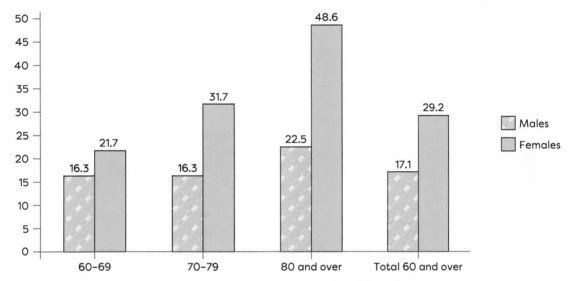

FIGURE 11.10 **Percentage of Canadian Males and Females Living Alone over Age 60, 2016**

Source: Statistics Canada, 2016 Census of Population, Statistics Canada Catalogue no. 98-400-X2016028

Quick Hits

Delayed Life Transitions

In "Delayed Life Transitions: Trends and Implications" (2004), University of Western Ontario demographer Roderic Beaujot linked together some of the trends discussed in this section as part of a phenomenon he calls delayed life transitions.

We go through a number of major transitions in our lifetime—getting a full-time job, moving out to live on our own, getting married, having children, retiring, and so on. During the prosperous socioeconomic times of the 1950s, 1960s, and early 1970s, people went through what we could call "sped-up life transitions," making these major life changes at a relatively young age. The situation has changed considerably, as Beaujot observes, and people today are making these transitions later and later in life.

Which brings us to some questions. First, to what extent is our current speed of life transition "delayed," and to what extent is it simply "normal"? It may seem normal to you to live at home with your parents until your late twenties, when you've settled into a career and have paid off some of your student debt, but to be living at home would have seemed abnormal for a typical North American 30-year-old of your parents' generation. What are the implications for today's college and university students of having parents who went through life transitions at a much more advanced speed, perhaps at a rate that was "less normal" than now? And which version of "normal" is better, anyway?

11.3 Family in Quebec

By just about every statistical measure, the family in Quebec is sociologically distinct from the family in other parts of Canada. For example, consider that Quebec has been the province with:

- *the highest cohabitation rate*: 38.7 per cent of all couples, almost twice the national average (20.9 per cent) (see Figure 11.3)
- *the lowest marriage rate*: 2.9 per 100,000, significantly lower than the next lowest rate (Ontario and Manitoba, tied at 4.9, based on 2008 data)
- *the highest divorce rate*: 69.2 per 100 marriages, far ahead of Ontario's rate of 46.7 (again, based on the latest data we have, from 2008)
- *the highest number of divorces* among couples married less than 30 years, with 61.0 per 100 marriages (Ontario's rate of 43.1 was the next highest).

In 2011, Quebec was the province with the greatest number of total births by single (never married) women. By percentage (58.5 per cent), the province trailed only Nunavut (New Brunswick was the next closest province at 47.5 per cent). At the start of the century Quebec also had the greatest percentage of births to women who were divorced (2.1 per cent in 2002), but has since dropped to sixth place (1.2 per cent in 2011). Why might this one ranking have changed?

Another feature unique to Quebec is the province-wide support for same-sex marriage well ahead of its legalization (see Table 11.2). In a poll conducted among 10,015 Canadian adults in August 2003, residents of Quebec showed the greatest support for changing the legal definition of marriage.

In March 2004, it became the third province (following Ontario and BC) to legally recognize same-sex marriage.

In social statistician Reginald Bibby's 1995 Project Canada survey, Quebec had the highest rate of approval for premarital and extramarital sex (Bibby, 1995, p. 76), with 88 per cent supporting the former (compared with 82 per cent, the next highest, in BC) and 24 per cent supporting the latter (compared with 14 per cent, the next highest, in the Prairies).

Quebec residents have also shown a difference when it comes to parenting, as indicated by a *Globe and Mail*/CTV poll of 648 Canadian parents conducted by Ipsos-Reid and published in the *Globe and Mail* on 10 April 2004. The poll noted the following results:

Percentage of parents who said they spanked their children for disciplinary reasons:	
Alberta	60%
British Columbia	52%
Saskatchewan/Manitoba	46%
Ontario	45%
Atlantic Provinces	42%
Quebec	22%
Percentage of parents who agreed that using flashcards at an early age makes kids smarter:	
British Columbia	71%
Saskatchewan/Manitoba	67%
Alberta	63%
Ontario	60%
Atlantic Provinces	57%
Quebec	25%

TABLE 11.2 Support for Changing the Definition of Marriage to Include Same-Sex Unions, by Region, 2003

	Agree somewhat (%)	Agree strongly (%)	Total (%)
Quebec	36	25	61
British Columbia	26	25	51
Atlantic Provinces	19	26	45
Ontario	19	23	42
Prairies	16	17	33

Source: TNS Canadian Facts, www.tns-cf.com/news/03.09.05-samesex-charts.pdf, 2003. The study was conducted by TNS Canadian Facts (formerly NFOCF group), one of Canada's leading full-service marketing, opinion, and social research organizations.

In case you're wondering, section 43 of Canada's Criminal Code, since it was first enacted in 1892, has permitted teachers, parents, and "persons standing in the place of a parent" to use reasonable force to discipline a pupil or child under their care, provided "the force does not exceed what is reasonable under the circumstances" (Revised Statutes of Canada, c. C-34, s. 43, n.d.).

What should we make of these differences between Quebec and the rest of the provinces? First, it is noteworthy that a number of statistical indicators show a major change from the situation in Quebec prior to the **Quiet Revolution** of the 1960s, when the province underwent significant social and economic reforms and increased secularization. Take divorce. Prior to 1968, if you were living in Quebec and you wanted a divorce, you had to seek it through the federal Parliament. A growing separation from the Catholic Church since the 1960s has been cited as a possible explanation for the rising divorce rate. Yet in the 2011 National Household Survey—the last national survey that gathered information on Canadians' religious affiliation—Quebec had the second-lowest percentage of residents declaring they had "no religious affiliation" (12.1 per cent, ahead of only Newfoundland and Labrador and well below the national average of 23.9 per cent). Of course, being affiliated with the Church and being influenced by it can be two different matters. The Catholic Church considers abortion a sin, but in 2005—the last year Statistics Canada provided this information— Quebec, the most Catholic province, led all provinces with an abortion rate of 7.6 per 1,000 women, or 372.5 per 1,000 live births (trailing only Northwest Territories in the latter statistic).

Can we say that family life is falling apart in Quebec? After all, since 1981, Quebec has had the highest growth in the number of citizens living alone, and in 2016 led all other provinces with 17.7 per cent of the population living alone. Three Quebec cities—Trois-Rivières, Sherbrook, and Quebec City—had the highest rates of living alone in Canada. Could this be attributed to a greater percentage of elderly people in Quebec living on their own? It's a good guess, but it's wrong. Among people 85 and over, Quebec has a relatively low rate of living alone, thanks to a higher-than-average rate of older people living together in retirement homes (Tang, Galbraith, & Truong, 2019, p. 13). Statistics Canada proposes that "many of the sociocultural and economic developments that occurred in Quebec . . . [during] the Quiet Revolution included an evolution towards a more individualistic orientation that may have led to more persons living alone by choice" (Tang, Galbraith, & Truong, 2019, p. 13).

A more likely interpretation for Quebec's dissimilarity from the rest of Canada is that the province went through more rapid modernization and outright change during the last 40 years than any other province. The falling away of old structures does not mean the falling apart of the institutions. Québécois are perhaps best seen as reinventing family as they are reinventing other institutions—political, religious, and educational.

11.4 Same-Sex Couples and Marriage

Since same-sex marriage was legalized in 2005, a better understanding has begun to form regarding the importance of formalizing same-sex relations. Table 11.3 provides data on the status of these couples from 2001 to 2016, while Table 11.4 shows marital status for Canadian couples by sex and sexual orientation.

TABLE 11.3 **Marital Status of Same-Sex Couples, 2001–2016**

Year	Common Law	Married	Total
2001	34,205	0	34,205
2005	same-sex marriage becomes legal		
2006	37,885	7,465	45,350
2011	43,560	21,015	64,575
2016	48,510	24,370*	72,880**

*33.4% of all same-sex couples
**0.9% of all couples in Canada

Source: Statistics Canada (2017c).

TABLE 11.4 Marital Status of Those Aged 25–64, by Sexual Orientation and Sex, 2015–2018

Heterosexual	Male	Female
Married	56.1%	55.4%
Common law	16.0%	15.0%
Divorced/separated/widowed	7.4%	12.3%
Single (never married or living common-law)	20.5%	17.3%
Lesbian/Gay	Male	Female
Married	12.5%	25.3%
Common law	31.6%	29.3%
Divorced/separated/widowed	5.7%	9.0%
Single (never married or living common-law)	50.2%	36.4%
Bisexual*		
Married	22.5%	23.3%
Common law	24.3%	22.0%
Divorced/separated/widowed	6.3%	12.1%
Single (never married or living common-law)	46.9%	42.6%

*Bisexual is here defined as feeling a sexual and/or romantic attraction to both males and females.

Source: Statistics Canada (2021).

What do *you* think?

According to the statistics in Table 11.4, lesbians are much more inclined to marry than are gay men and gay men are more likely to live single. How do you explain this?

Telling It Like It Is

A Student's Point of View

Telling Your Family You're Gay

Growing up in the small town of Whitby, Ontario, I never felt the negative effects of discrimination. I am an English-speaking, Caucasian female and had never been a part of a minority group, in any sense of the word. At the age of 21, this changed, and I became aware of how easily people are judged. I am a lesbian, and from the moment I became open about my sexual preferences, I felt first-hand what it feels like to be viewed based solely on one aspect of your life, and not as an entire person. When meeting someone new in my life it was as though I was wearing a sign on my forehead reading, "I am gay," and it was perceived as "I am gay . . . that is everything you need to know about me." Once I divulge this information, almost instantly people form opinions on who I am as a person and who I should be. They develop expectations that quite often are illogical and unrealistic. By writing a paper such as this one, I am being given the opportunity to address a few of these numerous stereotypes and prejudiced beliefs. Hopefully, I can educate some to stop these beliefs from spreading.

From my experience, the original thought that people tend to have when finding out that I am gay is that it is simply a phase I am going through, a time of experimentation and rebellious behaviour. My brother's reaction was as such. He believed that it was just a phase and that it would pass. He continued to express this for an entire year after I had told him. He realizes otherwise now. . . . When telling my mother . . .

I was shocked to hear her initial reaction to what I had told her. After a moment or two of silence, she . . . said, "But I thought you wanted to get married and have kids one day." The thought of these dreams possibly fading away is what seemed to unsettle her the most. I found two things wrong and rather presumptuous about this statement. To begin with, the idea that a woman must want/need a husband and children to live a fulfilling life is old-fashioned and a step backward from the times we live in today. I figure, why can't a woman who is independent and who has a satisfying career be considered to lead a successful, happy life, despite the fact that she has no family to raise. Furthermore, my mother was correct in assuming that I did want a family, but it was not the family that she had in mind. Marriage and children are a large part of my future plans, and, with adoption, and artificial insemination, this is a very feasible option for lesbian couples. Simply because a woman falls in love with another woman, it does not mean that she didn't grow up with the same desire for nurturing children and caring for a home and family that a lot of heterosexual girls do.

What do *you* think?

1. What are your future plans in regard to family, or are you taking it a day at a time?
2. In what ways, if at all, is your view for the future shaped by your experiences growing up?

11.5 Conjugal Roles

Conjugal (or marital) roles are the distinctive roles of the husband and wife that result from the division of labour within the family. The first important sociological study done on this subject was a 1957 work called *Family and Social Networks*, by Canadian/British social scientist Elizabeth Bott. Bott characterized conjugal roles as being either segregated—in which tasks, interests, and activities are clearly different—or joint, in which many tasks, interests, and activities are shared. These ideas came to be known as the Bott hypothesis. Her study was set against a backdrop in which men were primarily responsible for the financial support of the family, while women were primarily responsible for the housework and childcare. This was 1957, remember—how much do you think that situation has changed?

Earning and Caring: Changes in Conjugal Roles

In 2000, Roderic Beaujot published *Earning and Caring in Canadian Families*. He wanted to study how conjugal roles were changing from a situation in which they were more or less *complementary* to one in which they were *companionate*. **Complementary roles** (like Bott's model of *segregated roles*) cast men primarily as earners or breadwinners, doing paid work, with women involved primarily in the unpaid work of childcare and housework. In **companionate** relationships (like Bott's *joint* relationship) the roles overlap.

Beaujot recognized that the shift from complementary/segregated conjugal roles to companionate/joint roles is far from complete. But he also stated that complete overlap was not necessarily possible, nor even desirable. Gender roles are different to a significant extent because men and women are different biologically. There is, however, a point at which we may be able to say that a basic fairness or justice has been reached. We are far from that point. As Beaujot documents, married women do more total work per day than married men do, even though married women are more likely to do part-time paid work. Married women, especially the mothers of small children, do much more *unpaid* work than married men do. And while women have caught up to men in their participation in the workforce, men have not gone as far in taking on new roles at home. This has created an imbalance in conjugal roles, where women take on what some sociologists have called a **double burden** or **second shift** (Hochschild & Machung, 1989). Canadian sociologists Pat Armstrong and Hugh Armstrong ([1978]/2010) used the term **double ghetto** to describe the marginalization working women experience in the workplace and in the home. The difficulty of correcting this imbalance in households with small children has led some women to conclude, pessimistically, that "childlessness is the easiest route to equality" (Beaujot, 2002).

In 1995, sociologist M. Reza Nakhaie published "Housework in Canada: The National Picture," a summary of his study demonstrating that gender was a greater factor than either relative income or amount of available time in determining how much housework an individual did. The author's most striking discovery concerned the relationship between gender, hours of paid work, and share of the housework. Nakhaie found an inverse relationship between the hours of paid work a man does and the size of his share of the housework: the more paid hours he has, the smaller his share of the housework. However, the same is not true for women. A direct relationship seems to exist over a particular number of hours of work: an increase over 30 in a woman's hours of paid work per week correlated to an *increase* in her contribution to housework.

A more recent study, by Houle, Turcotte, and Wendt (2017), appears to confirm these findings. The researchers found that mothers do more household work than fathers regardless of how much time they spend on paid work: on a typical workday, 86 per cent of Canadian mothers who worked eight or more paid hours would spend additional time on household work, compared with 65 per cent of fathers who had worked eight or more paid hours and 87 per cent

Fuse/Getty Images

What does your reaction to this image tell you about our perception of the gender roles handed down by society?

of fathers who had participated in no paid work (Figure 11.11b). The same study found that between 1986 and 2015, the percentage of fathers who participated in household work had increased by 25 points, from 51 per cent to 76 per cent, but the percentage of mothers who performed household work did not change over the same period and was much higher (93 per cent; Figure 11.11a).

The key to correcting the gender imbalance is to recognize that gender roles are not carved in stone. Rather, they are products of what Arlie Hochschild terms a **gender strategy**, which is "a plan of action through which a person tries to solve problems at hand, given the cultural notions of gender at play" (Hochschild & Machung, 1989, p. 15). These "problems at hand" include the fact that small children have to be taken care of. From the studies that Beaujot cites, it is clear that the typical strategy for infant care is for the mother to take time off, then to work part-time as the infant matures toward school age, eventually to try to go back to full-time work.

The responsibility for care of children is the main reason that married women are much more likely to work part-time than are married/unmarried men or unmarried women. It is also the cause of what Beaujot calls the **occupational segregation** of men and women. Women choose occupations in fields such as education and health care, which have the greatest flexibility in terms of care-related **work interruptions** (which include staying home to care for a sick child or taking a longer-term leave to care for a newborn). Beaujot presents something of a chicken-and-egg scenario: women seek out jobs in employment areas that offer greater flexibility, but part of the reason these jobs offer greater flexibility is that they are dominated by women. Do you think that as women enter traditionally male-dominated occupations in larger numbers, a similar flexibility will develop?

The Ethnic Factor in Conjugal Roles

One weakness of Beaujot's work is that he ignores ethnocultural factors in the gendered division of household labour. A classic study of conjugal roles among North American immigrant groups is Sathi Dasgupta's "Conjugal Roles and Social Network in Indian Immigrant Families" (1992). Although the article was written over 30 years ago about South Asian

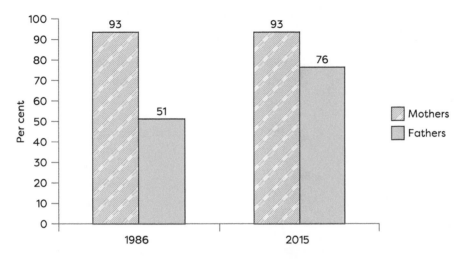

(a) Percentage of Mothers and Fathers Spending Time on Unpaid Household Work, 1986 and 2015

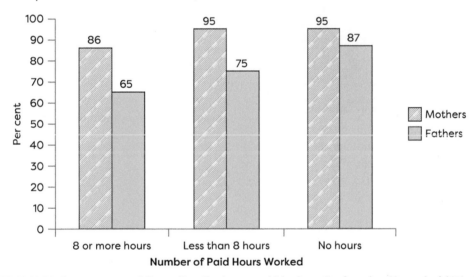

(b) Percentage of Canadian Fathers and Mothers Who Performed Household Work, by Number of Paid Hours Worked, 2015

FIGURE 11.11 **Percentage of Canadian Fathers and Mothers Performing Household Work**

Source: Houle, Turcotte, & Wendt (2017, Table 2).

immigrants in the United States, its findings have relevance to the situation in Canada today.

Dasgupta studied 25 couples and found that *segregated* conjugal roles dominated. The men were invariably the primary breadwinners and made virtually all major decisions affecting the household, while the women, with few exceptions, were full-time homemakers and primary caretakers of the children. Interestingly, however, there were aspects of joint conjugal roles among the immigrant families that would not be nearly as well accepted back in India. These include joint discussion of the children's

education and of the couple's social life (with joint leisure activities the norm).

Change will come, as immigrants to North America adopt a more "Western" approach to dividing conjugal roles, but the ethnic factor still must be considered in any study of gender roles in the Canadian family.

Division of Domestic Labour and Gender

In 2021, using the 2011, 2016, and 2017 versions of the General Social Survey, with sample sizes of 12,787, 19,596 and 11,272 male-female couples respectively,

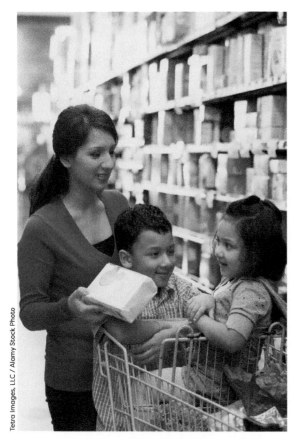

Tetra Images, LLC / Alamy Stock Photo

Do you think Dasgupta's findings on the separation of conjugal roles among immigrant families are applicable in Canada today? To what extent is this "ethnic factor" still at play?

Statistics Canada researchers Kristyn Frank and Marc Frenette examined the apportionment of household and childcare tasks as perceived by couples in various socio-demographic groups (Frank & Frenette, 2021). The couples were either married or living common-law. For both kinds of tasks, the estimated percentage mostly done by women was significantly higher than that mostly done by men, except in "gardening" and "outside work (repairs)." The household tasks in which it was estimated that the highest percentages were done equally by both sexes were doing the dishes, grocery shopping, and gardening (see Table 11.5). All of the childcare activities had the highest percentages for being done equally by females and males, but the "mostly women" percentages were much higher than those for "mostly men" (Table 11.6).

Responses Concerning Household Tasks by Gender of Respondent

One limitation of this study is that it doesn't account for same-sex marriages, a demographic variable that does not always receive the full attention of those who collect the data and those who analyze it. In this study, however, as might be expected, both women and men gave higher estimations of the amount of work they do than did the opposite sex. In regard to the various tasks required to maintain a household, the greatest difference between the two was with the "mostly female" estimates of the grocery shopping,

Telling It Like It Is

A Student's Point of View

Italian Families and Conjugal Roles: Four Generations

When I think of the topic of gender in an Italian family, I laugh. The struggles between what it means to be male and what it means to be female arise so very often in my family, at every dinner and almost every conversation. The discussions are always split between the three generations because my grandmother lives with my parents and she never misses an opportunity to include her views. The eldest generation undeniably believes that the female's role in life is to be a complement to her husband; everything she does is based on his needs and his demands.

All domestic duties and child-rearing except for punishment are her responsibility. Working outside the home is secondary to household work. The husband makes all decisions, although she can make suggestions. It is the male's responsibility to take care of the family financially.

My parents (second generation) feel similarly, the main difference being that the father should be very involved with the children, not solely in areas concerning punishment. Where my grandmother would discourage my father from helping around the house, my mother would welcome the help though not demand or expect it. In this generation, family decisions are made together; however, household duties are still very divided, even with my mother working full-time outside the home. For the female, postsecondary education and career are second to marriage and family. The main female role in life is keeping a clean house, cooking good homemade food, and keeping everyone happy and healthy. The main male role is to keep the food on the table by providing the family with its main source of income.

The third generation around the dinner table changed things a little. This generation in my family consists of my husband and me, the middle brother and his wife, and the "baby brother." Most of us are in agreement that gender roles in the new Italian family have changed. No longer is the female solely responsible for all household duties. Husbands cook, clean, and change diapers, something my father had never done even with having three children! The females have postsecondary education and careers and are not a complement to their husbands, but an equal.

I also grew up with a huge double standard that affected me immensely in all areas of my life. It goes something like this: "This is what boys can do and this is what girls cannot do" (my father's infamous words). Boys can play all day and not help their mothers (girls can't), boys can fight and play rough (girls can't), boys have to do well in school (girls don't have to), boys can go out whenever they want (girls can't), boys have to play sports (girls don't have to), boys can stay out late (girls have to come home early).

"This is what girls must do and this is what boys do not have to do." Girls must cook and clean (boys do not), girls must learn the traditions (boys do not), girls must be good always (boys do not), girls must stay home to take care of the family (boys do not), girls must not be left alone with their boyfriends (boys can live with their girlfriends). I fought with my younger brothers fairly consistently growing up. The words "that is not fair" were spoken often. I disliked one of my brothers for years. It was not until he got a family of his own that we began to grow closer together. We even talked about the jealousy we felt for one another over different family issues and how the double standards we grew up with had a great deal to do with it.

My family's views on gender have had a great impact on my life. It has carved me into the woman I am today. Much to my parents' chagrin, I cannot cook. I hate housecleaning, run away from tradition whenever I can. I am constantly in school working on a career, and even though I am married, I frequently go out with my friends and stay out late! Being married has been difficult at times also. I always have an intense instinct to run from the gender roles that surround me, and yet I realize that in many circumstances they are needed to preserve peace in a family. I now have many concerns for my daughter. I know she will not be faced with an obvious double standard, as I do not have any sons, and I am fully aware that being completely opposite of the Martha Stewart-like woman is not anything to be proud of. Something in the middle would be nice. Since little girls are greatly influenced by their mothers, I know I must be really careful to set a positive female role in our family. I truly hope the difference for my daughter will be the ability for her to choose the woman she wants to be instead of madly running away from what I demand her to become.

—Alina Mucci

where 64.7 per cent of women perceived this as a "mostly female" job while only 30.6 per cent of men saw this as "mostly female." To a lesser extent this was true across the range of household tasks—meal preparation, housework, cleaning dishes, laundry, gardening, outside work and repairs, and organizing social activities—with each sex estimating their contributions as greater than did their partners.

In this regard, the researchers asked about the satisfaction or dissatisfaction of couples' share of the household tasks. *Spoiler alert!* The men were more satisfied than the women were (Table 11.7).

What do you think?

1. What kind of narrative do you think the writer's brothers would write about conjugal roles, based on their upbringing?
2. Do you foresee any gender role conflict concerning the writer and her daughter?

TABLE 11.5 Couples' Collective Estimate of the Division of Household Activities, 2017

	Mostly Women	Equally	Mostly Men
Preparing daily meals	56.4%	32.7%	10.8%
Doing housework	46.2%	45.2%	8.6%
Doing the dishes	32.6%	51.5%	15.9%
Laundry	61.1%	31.2%	7.7%
Grocery shopping	35.8%	48.9%	15.3%
Gardening	28.3%	36.3%	35.4%
Outside work (repairs)	3.3%	13.8%	82.9%
Organizing social life	45.4%	50.2%	4.4%

Source: Frank & Frenette (2021).

TABLE 11.6 Couples' Division of Childcare Activities, 2016

	Mostly Women	Equally	Mostly Men
Supervising	38.5%	58.8%	3.0%
Taking to activities	33.3%	55.2%	11.5%
Bedtime activities	39.0%	55.8%	5.2%
Helping with homework	42.1%	48.0%	10.0%

Source: Frank & Frenette (2021).

TABLE 11.7 Satisfaction with the Division of Household Labour

	Satisfied or Very Satisfied	Neither Satisfied nor Dissatisfied	Dissatisfied or Very Dissatisfied
Female	76.3%	14.0%	9.7%
Male	88.4%	9.1%	2.6%

Source: Frank & Frenette (2021).

Some Factors in Dissatisfaction

A number of factors related to dissatisfaction were identified by the researchers. Women in older couples (both 45+) were more dissatisfied with the division of labour within the family than were women in couples where both partners were under 45 years old. These older women also estimated, in general, the highest burden of household tasks. In addition, women who had children younger than 15 were more likely to be dissatisfied than those who did not.

Postsecondary education, place of birth, and women's employment status also were found to be differentiating factors. Men in couples in which both partners had postsecondary education were more likely to be dissatisfied than men without postsecondary education whose partners had postsecondary education. At the same time, women with postsecondary education but whose partners did not were more likely to be dissatisfied than women in which both had postsecondary education. Country of origin also played a role in dissatisfaction. Women in relationships in which both partners were Canadian-born were more likely to be dissatisfied than immigrant women whose partners also had immigrated to Canada, and Canadian-born women with immigrant partners were more likely to be dissatisfied than immigrant women whose partners had immigrated to Canada from abroad. Finally, and perhaps of special note, women with full-time paying work were more likely to be dissatisfied than women who were not engaged in paid work.

Marrying "In" and Marrying "Out"

Endogamy is an anthropological term that means "marrying within." It refers to marrying someone of the same ethnic, religious, or cultural group as oneself. The opposite of endogamy, marrying *outside* of one's group, is **exogamy**.

Support for exogamy, once quite low in Canada, has increased, according to findings published by Bibby (see Table 11.8). However, I believe that this set of statistics gives a picture that is more positive than it is real. It seems more an expression of an ideal and decidedly Eurocentric culture than an indication of

probable practice. After all, according to data from the 2011 National Household Survey, only 4.6 per cent of all married and common-law couples in Canada were mixed unions (Statistics Canada, 2014, p. 4). Table 11.9 shows which visible minority groups in Canada are most likely to form mixed unions.

For all of the visible minority groups shown in Table 11.9, only people of Japanese ancestry are more likely to form a mixed union; the majority of people in all other groups—including the two largest visible minority groups in Canada, South Asians and Chinese—marry or cohabit within their own group.

Bear in mind that this survey includes people born outside of Canada, who might have been married when they immigrated. Couples made up of people born in the same country overwhelmingly form non-mixed unions, and this is particularly the case for people born in the same country outside of Canada: 94 per cent of those couples were non-mixed. By comparison, 75 per cent of couples where both people were born in Canada were non-mixed (Statistics Canada, 2014, p. 5). Figure 11.12 illustrates the composition of all unions and mixed unions according to whether one or both of a couple were born abroad or in Canada.

Remember, too, that at different times in its history Canada has weighted the immigration of certain groups in favour of one sex (consider the pattern of early immigration among Filipino women, discussed in Chapter 9). What influence could factors like these have on the data?

TABLE 11.8 Canadians' Approval of Intergroup Marriage (%), 1975–2015

	1975	1980	1985	1990	1995	2000	2005	2015
Whites and Indigenous people	75	80	83	84	84	91	93	95
Whites and Asians	66	75	78	82	83	90	93	95
Whites and East Indians	58	66	72	77	80	87	91	92
Whites and Blacks	57	64	72	79	81	88	92	94
Any other kinds of racial or cultural mixed unions	–	–	–	–	–	–	–	93
Protestants and Catholics	86	88	89	90	92	93	95	–
Protestants and Jews	80	84	84	86	90	91	93	–
Roman Catholics and Jews	78	81	82	85	89	91	92	–
Christians and people of other world faiths	–	–	–	–	–	90	90	89

Source: Bibby (2016).

TABLE 11.9 Mixed Couples by Visible Minority Group, 2011

Visible Minority Group	Number of Couples	Mixed Unions (%)		Non-mixed Unions (%)
South Asian	407,510	13.0		87.0
Chinese	351,640	19.4		80.6
Black	167,950	40.2		59.8
Filipino	155,700	29.8		70.2
Latin American	112,265	48.2		51.8
Arab	94,315	25.4		74.6
Southeast Asian	74,560	21.9		78.1
West Asian	51,300	19.5		80.5
Korean	41,370	22.5		77.5
Japanese	32,820	78.8		21.3
Multiple visible minorities	40,415	65.9		35.1
Other visible minority	27,215	52.4		47.6
All visible minorities	**1,557,060**	**27.0**		**73.0**

Note: A mixed couple is any common-law or marital relationship comprising one spouse or partner who is a member of a visible minority group and one who is not, as well as couples comprising two members of different visible minority groups.

Source: Statistics Canada (2014).

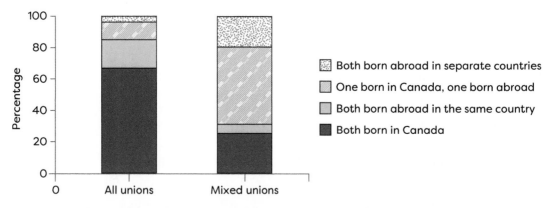

FIGURE 11.12 Composition of Canadian Unions and Canadian Mixed Unions, 2011

Source: Statistics Canada (2014, p. 4).

What do *you* think?

1. Consider Table 11.6. Do you think that Canadians' attitudes toward exogamy are different from what they were 10 years ago?
2. Have you ever been involved in a relationship with someone from a different ethnic or cultural group? If so, what kinds of challenges did you face? If not, could you imagine yourself in such a relationship?

zorann/iStockphoto

Based on findings from the 2006 census, Milan, Maheux, and Chui (2010) report that people in mixed unions "were younger, did better socio-economically, and were more likely to live in large CMAS [census metropolitan areas]" than non-mixed couples. How could you account for these facts?

Telling It Like It Is

A Woman's Point of View

The Religious Factor in Conjugal Roles: Polygamy and the Case of Bountiful, BC

In the aptly named commune village of Bountiful, British Columbia, there is a long history of **polygamy** (many marriages) or **polygyny** (many wives) practised by the leaders of the Fundamentalist Church of Latter Day Saints, an offshoot of the Mormon Church. The commune has attracted attention and criticism, stemming mainly from reports of forced and underage marriage and the abuse of women and children. Beginning in the 1990s, the community was the focus of police investigations and attempts to enforce Canada's anti-polygamy laws on the commune.

The following quotations are taken from the testimony of a woman in her forties, given in a BC Supreme Court case examining the constitutionality of Canada's laws against plural marriages. The mother of nine children married one of the leaders when she was 16; her husband was already married to her older sister. She herself has nearly 30 siblings; her father had five wives. The woman is well educated, with six years of postsecondary training in nursing, elder care, and midwifery.

I did not know him well; I knew he was in good standing in the church. . . .

He (my father) told me, "You do not have to marry him if you don't want to." I felt good about him, and I married him. My sister wife and I have lived at times

(Continued)

in the same home, we've lived in different homes. I feel that we are both very committed in having a good relationship with each other. . . .

I feel my husband really supported me through my years of education and he really has been a life-long friend to me, as well as watched my children when I went to school. . . .

I believe that there's so many people in mainstream society that make so many assumptions about us that we are treated with bias and prejudice, and that affects my everyday life. If I wanted to go anywhere and get any sort of counselling in mainstream society, I feel like I would not be accepted. . . .

My beliefs are that living plural marriage isn't for everyone. (*CTV News*, 2011)

In November 2011, the chief justice of the Supreme Court in BC ruled that the ban against polygamy was constitutional, even though it violated the religious freedom of this group. Protecting the rights of the women and the children, he ruled, was of greater importance than protecting the religious freedom of the commune's residents. This paved the way for the trial of two former religious leaders of the Bountiful community on charges of practising polygamy; both men were found guilty in July 2017 and later sentenced to house arrest and community service. These were the third and fourth polygamy convictions in Canada's history; the previous two occurred in 1899 and 1906.

YASUYOSHI CHIBA/AFP/Getty Images

Students play an afternoon game of basketball at Bountiful Elementary-Secondary School. What relationship between these young women does the photo appear to convey?

What do *you* think?

If you had been a government lawyer, what kinds of questions would you have asked the witness quoted in the narrative above? What concerns would you have voiced about plural marriage?

11.6 Family and Ethnicity

As we saw in Chapter 8, on "race" and ethnicity, Canada has a history of federal government policies designed to deprive racialized minorities of family. The prohibitively expensive head tax levied on immigrants from China and South Asia in the late nineteenth and early twentieth centuries made it impossible in many cases for married couples or their families to reunite in Canada. Canadian sociologists Nancy Mandell and Ann Duffy, in *Canadian Families: Diversity, Conflict and Change* (1995), noted a similar connection between government immigration policy and the denial of family for Black women, calling it

> a policy of the government not to encourage the possibility of developing families among women of colour who came as domestic workers. Thus, their status as "single" and as "temporary" is deliberately organized by immigration policies. (Mandell & Duffy, 1995, p. 157)

The policy they refer to was initiated in 1910–11, during one of the country's greatest periods of immigration. About 100 Black women from the Caribbean islands of Guadeloupe came to Canada to work as domestic servants, but when authorities discovered that many of the women were not as "unattached" as they had claimed to be—many had children they had been forced to leave behind—the women were sent back.

Between 1955 and 1967, a number of women from the Caribbean—primarily Jamaica—were allowed to come to Canada to work as domestics. They had to be young, of "good character," and single (in other words, not married or cohabiting). They were given the status of landed immigrants, but they could not seek other work until they had served at least a year of domestic duty. Roughly 300 Caribbean women came to Canada each year between 1955 and 1960, the number rising to about 1,000 a year during the 1960s (Bolaria & Li, 1985, p. 178). Many of them agreed to work as domestics, even though they were trained as teachers or secretaries. Many, in order to be "single," left family behind, all because it was the only way they could enter the country.

Naturally, those immigrants who had left husbands and children in the Caribbean wanted to sponsor their families to join them in Canada, but their efforts were blocked by immigration officials. In 1976, seven Jamaican women applied to sponsor their children to come to Canada. They were ordered to be deported for having failed to report their children on their applications to come to Canada (Leah & Morgan, 1979). After an intense legal struggle, the seven women won their appeals and were allowed to stay in Canada.

Attacks on the Indigenous Family

Immigrant families are not the only ones affected by restrictive Canadian legislation. The Indigenous family has long been a target of federal policy. The following passage describes how, during the early twentieth century, an "Indian agent" (the federal government official from Indian Affairs who oversaw policy and government programs in a region or on a specific reserve) used the Blackfoot community's need for food rations as a tool to ensure the people remained monogamous:

> In my last report, I expressed thankfulness that there had been no plural marriages during the preceding year. That report was barely out of my hand when I learned that three members of the band were dissatisfied with one wife each and had taken another. I immediately directed that the rations of these families be withheld until such time as they saw fit to obey the rules in this respect. One family missed one ration, and then decided that it was better to abide by the rules. The other two families held out for several rations, and then they succumbed and put away wife No. 2. (Dosman, 1972, pp. 52–3)

This incident, in which food rations were withheld to control marriage (and other) choices, is not atypical of the kind of treatment Indigenous families suffered at the hands of government agents.

It's important to note that actions like this were often products of well-meaning agencies and their representatives. With the benefit of modern perspective, we can see just how misguided and racist these policies were. The following section looks closely at three policies aimed at controlling Indigenous families. In some cases, as we will see, the same strategies have targeted other groups that governments have felt they needed to manage, including certain cultural and ethnic groups as well as people with physical or mental disabilities.

Residential Schools

Among the institutionalized instruments of control devised to manage the lives of Canada's Indigenous populations, the system of residential schools tops the list for the devastating effects it has had on Indigenous families. As early as the seventeenth century Catholic missionaries in New France established some non-mandatory residential boarding schools with the principal aims of Christianizing the young people and providing schooling and care. By 1831 the more formally organized Mohawk Institute in what is today Brantford, Ontario, began to provide boarding for some students, most of whom came from the Six Nations reserve. The real push for an organized residential school system began with the Indian Act of 1876, which mandated that Indigenous people were the responsibility of the federal government, and by the early 1880s residential schools began to take children from their homes and native cultures in an effort to assimilate them into the lower rungs of mainstream Canadian society, in effect, as was often said, to "take the Indian out of the child." At the same time, the government sought through the schools to help Indigenous peoples to become economically self-sufficient—and thereby ease its constitutional requirement to provide for them. As settlers took over their lands, the old semi-nomadic lifestyle of many of the land's first human inhabitants became increasingly untenable.

The industrial and boarding schools that comprised the patchwork **residential schools** program were created with the almost explicit objective of keeping Indigenous children away from the supposedly harmful influences of their parents and their home communities. Families were ripped apart as parents reluctantly signed over legal guardianship of their children to school principals, then watched their children leave for the state- and church-run boarding schools, where they would live for most, if not all, of the year. Parents were discouraged from visiting. Those who did were closely monitored. Brothers and sisters were kept apart, sometimes not seeing each other for months on end. Many families were never reunited. Ultimately, this colonial experiment in social engineering was doomed to fail, and many children were stuck between two worlds: they were deprived of their cultures and native languages, yet they were not assimilated to become productive (and upwardly mobile) participants in the larger Eurocentric society. After all, many Indigenous people had been relegated to remote reserves on marginally productive land.

Historian J.R. Miller tells the story of a Cree woman who went to a residential school that was 19 kilometres from her reserve. For hours on end, she would stand at the corner of a fence that surrounded the school property:

> She would put her hand through the fence, because that meant she was closer to her home and family by the length of her arm and watch for her parents. She would say to herself, "the next black horse that comes along" will be drawing her parents' wagon on a visit. Disappointment only led to repetitions of the childlike incantation, a wish and a prayer that never seemed to come true. (Miller, 1996, pp. 338–9)

Physical, emotional, and sexual abuse by some residential school employees demoralized the students. And as those who have been abused so often become abusers, many Indigenous children grew up to bring the abuse they learned at school to their home communities. In recent years, Canada's Truth and Reconciliation Commission (TRC) has detailed the many harms and the societal damage the residential schools brought to many Indigenous individuals and groups. Chaired by Justice (later, Senator) Murray Sinclair, the first Indigenous judge in Manitoba, the TRC put forth 94 "Calls to Action" indicating what the governments and people of Canada must do to repair the harms and provide closure for the individuals and groups affected by the residential schools. In effect, as the TRC presented in its voluminous final report, the residential schools visited a cultural genocide on the Indigenous peoples of Canada, most especially in the North and the Prairie provinces.

Sexual Sterilization

In its definition of **genocide**, the United Nations includes attempts to destroy a people by imposing measures designed to prevent births within the group. This describes certain policies aimed at Canada's Indigenous population during much of the twentieth century. For instance, in 1928, the government of Alberta passed the Sexual Sterilization Act, with the intent of sterilizing "mental defectives" so that their "bad genes" would not be passed on. The Act reflects the early twentieth-century belief in eugenics, the flawed notion that a single gene responsible for intelligence was absent in "stupid people," who would be capable of having only "stupid children"—in other words, children inheriting their parents' genetically defective intellect. We know now that there is a complex relationship between genetics and the various aptitudes that make up the biological potential known as intelligence. It is more accurate to say that we have **intelligences** of various kinds and levels (e.g., I have a talent for writing, but I am inept in drawing). This complexity makes the degree to which intelligence is inherited uncertain. We just don't know.

Eugenics has rightly been called **scientific racism**, as it was used to justify prejudices based on the supposed genetic inferiority or "feeble-mindedness" of certain immigrant groups to North America—particularly those from eastern Europe—as well as of Black people and Indigenous people. Since it was used to support prejudice against the poor, it is also an instrument of **scientific classism**. The traditional yardstick for measuring intelligence is the intelligence quotient (IQ) test. This test has been rightfully criticized for its bias against people representing certain language and culture groups. The test also perpetuates the myth that we have a **general intelligence** to which a single number can be assigned.

During the history of Alberta's Sexual Sterilization Act, which lasted from 1928 to 1972, 2,832 people were sterilized, most of them women. Sterilizations of Métis and First Nations people account for a disproportionately high number of the total, an estimated 25 per cent (roughly 10 times their percentage of the total population). Eastern European immigrants (Ukrainians, Russians, etc.)—people whose English-language skills and cultural capital were low—were also represented in high numbers in the sterilized group.

British Columbia passed legislation similar to Alberta's Sexual Sterilization Act in 1933, the same year that the notorious Law for the Prevention of Genetically Diseased Offspring was passed in Nazi Germany. Recently there have been accusations that, following both racial and religious prejudice, hundreds of non-Christian Indigenous people were sterilized by a United Church missionary doctor in a church-run hospital in the BC coastal community of Bella Bella, and that a good number of young Indigenous women made pregnant by residential school staff, clergy, and visiting officials were coerced into having abortions (see Truth Commission, 2001, pp. 12–13).

The Sixties Scoop

The United Nations definition of genocide also includes attempts to destroy a people by forcibly transferring children of the group to another group. This characterizes what has been referred to as the **Sixties Scoop**, a program, beginning in the 1960s, of separating large numbers of Indigenous children from their families and home communities. Children could be removed by government-affiliated agencies for a variety of reasons: some were children of parents judged to be alcoholics; some were newborns needing hospital care taken to the nearest city (and in many cases never returned); some were living in homes considered crowded or substandard. In 1964, the number of children of all backgrounds removed from their families was 4,228; roughly 34 per cent of those (1,446) were Indigenous children.

Between 1971 and 1981 in Manitoba, where Indigenous families were hardest hit, over 3,400 Indigenous children were removed from their homes. Many were taken from the province, and more than 1,000 of them were sent to the United States, where American child welfare agencies could get as much as $4,000 for each child placed. The province later launched an investigation into the practice, led by Justice Edwin Kimelman. In his summary of the investigation, *No Quiet Place* (1985), he stated:

> Cultural genocide has been taking place in a systematic routine manner. One gets an image of children stacked in foster homes as used cars are stacked on corner lots, just waiting for the right "buyer" to stroll by. (cited in Fournier & Crey, 1997, p. 88)

But statistics and judges' reports do not give a real sense of the suffering caused. The following statement comes from a research report on the emotional return of children to their families, communities, and people:

> I was sixteen years old when my daughter was taken from me. My partner at the time was drinking and at eighteen he went to prison. I had no way of looking after her and felt very alone. The social worker told me that my daughter would be better off with a "nice, normal family." I thought that I would at least be able to visit her sometimes, but she was placed in Pennsylvania and we did not meet her again until she was 20 years old. I took a bus to Windsor and that is where we met. I was alone and scared. She looked just like me when I was twenty, but with a very different attitude. She had suffered sexual abuse in her adopted home and she blamed it on me. She had a little girl of her own, but she would not let me meet her. I wish there was someone who could help us get past this pain. (Budgell, 1999, p. 6)

The removal of disproportionate numbers of Indigenous children into foster care continues to the present.

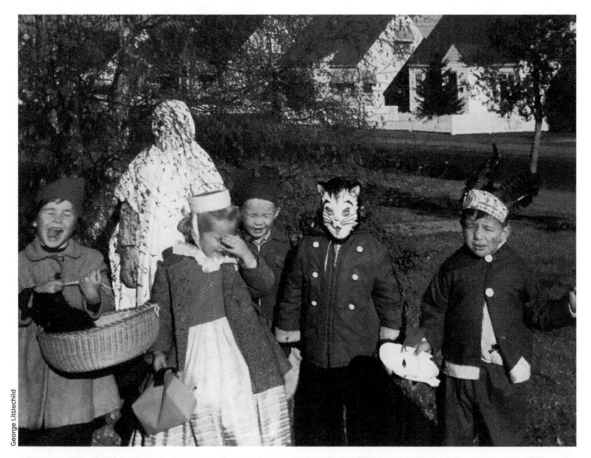

George Littlechild

Little Indian Foster Boy #4 is part of a multimedia art installation by George Littlechild, who was four when he was removed from his family and placed in the first of a series of foster homes. He is the child to the right of the group in this photo, trick-or-treating in Edmonton in the 1960s. In March 2018, a federal judge approved an $875 million settlement to be paid to victims of the Sixties Scoop, for their loss of identity, language, and culture, and for the abuse many suffered in foster care.

Wrap It Up

Summary

When we talk about the family in Canada, we are talking about a model of social organization that is diverse and complex, and has long been so. This diversity expresses itself in family size and structure, in age of marriage and of having children, in qualifications for family membership, in who is and is not considered eligible for marriage into the family, in the expectations and practices of gender roles, and in the relationship between children (of all ages) and their parents. And this diversity works—the "good" family takes many forms. This is why we find such diversity in the Canadian family of the past, the present, and no doubt, the future: the family adapts, evolving to fit changing social circumstances.

Think Back

Questions for Critical Review

1. Describe the diversity of the Canadian family, both historically and today.
2. What do you think has contributed to the perception that the nuclear family is the "normal" model? Do you think this perception is changing? If so, why?
3. Describe how family in Quebec is different from family in the rest of Canada. Give some examples and some possible explanations. What is the significance of Quebec's difference when it comes to family?
4. We looked at nine different trends in Canadian families. Of those, which two or three do you think are most likely to continue, and why? Are there any trends you think might level off or reverse?
5. Identify the different forms that conjugal roles can take. How are these roles changing? Are they changing quickly enough?
6. Setting aside the church ceremony or the trip to city hall, what characteristics do you think must be present for a relationship to be considered a marriage?
7. Do you think Canada's low birth rate is a cause for concern? Why or why not? Should Canadians be encouraged to have more children? How would you do that?
8. Sociologists like to throw around fancy words like "exogamy" and "endogamy," but does it really matter whether or not people are marrying outside of their ethnic or religious group? What does this information tell us about Canadian society?
9. Outline the measures used to place Canadian Indigenous families "under attack" during the twentieth century.

Read On

Suggested Print and Online Resources

Roderic Beaujot, *Earning and Caring in Canadian Families* (Peterborough, ON: Broadview Press, 2000)
One of this country's preeminent social demographers, Rod Beaujot, draws sociological conclusions about the Canadian family based on an analysis of statistical data.

Elizabeth Bott, *Family and Social Networks: Roles, Norms, and External Relationships in Ordinary Urban Families* (London: Tavistock, 1957)
This classic work introduced and developed much of the terminology and ideas used by social scientists studying the sociology of the family today.

Marguerita Cheng, "Grey Divorce: Its Reasons & Its Implications," *Forbes Magazine*, 26 February 2019, www.forbes.com/sites/margueritacheng/2019/02/26/grey-divorce-its-reasons-its-implications/#3530d1234acd
Baby boomers like to shake things up, and as this generation has grown older, we have seen an increase in divorce in couples 50 years old and over. This article looks at some of the causes of "grey divorce" and its social impact, including the affect it has on adult children.

Wayne Hower, *Does a Disabled Child = a Disabled Family?* (Authorhouse, 2006)

This self-published work combines the author's personal experience raising a disabled child with an academic and professional approach.

Nancy Mandell & Ann Duffy, *Canadian Families: Diversity, Conflict, and Change*, 3rd ed. (Toronto: Thompson Nelson, 2011)
This edited collection features articles that outline a number of ways in which family operates in Canada.

Barbara Neis, Christina Murray, & Nora Spinks, eds., *Families, Mobility, and Work* (St John's: Memorial University Press, 2022)
This lengthy collection includes first-person accounts, sociological analyses, and photo essays on the difficulties and rewards encountered by families and individuals who are part of an increasingly mobile Canadian workforce.

"Stolen Children," www.youtube.com/watch?v=vdR9HcmiXLA
This CBC story features interviews with survivors of Canada's residential school system.

Karen Stote, *Sterilization of Indigenous Women: An Act of Genocide* (Black Point, NS: Fernwood, 2015)
This book delves into the hidden history of the forced sexual sterilization of Indigenous women in Canada.

Vanier Institute of the Family, www.vifamily.ca
This Ottawa-based organization researches and publishes on issues affecting the Canadian family. You can read their recent publications on such topics as family vacations, the changing role of fathers, and young people who become responsible for the care of older family members.

Media and Society

Reading this chapter will help you to . . .

- Understand the origins of the media and public sphere.
- Recognize the role media has played in Canada's nation-building project.
- Explain the importance of Canadian content regulations.
- Understand how technological shifts in media have impacted how we understand the world around us.
- Recognize the importance of gatekeeping as it relates to social hierarchies.
- Understand how the algorithms impact social inequality.
- Explain the aspects of social media that affect our understanding of reality.
- Explain how social media affects construction of the self.
- Recognize how identity and society impact one another through social media.

For Starters

Do We Shape Our Tools—or Do Our Tools Shape Us?

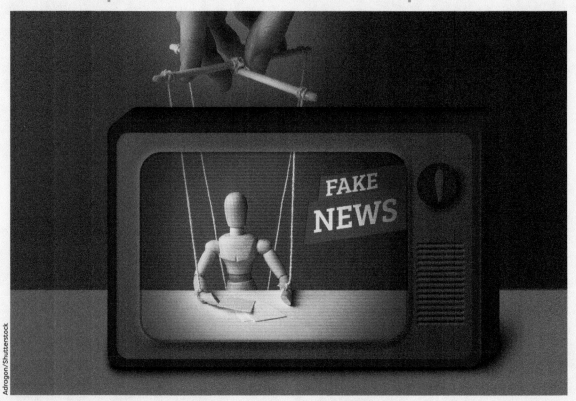

Adragon/Shutterstock

At the time of writing this, we are in the midst of one of the most tumultuous eras in recent history. The world has always been in a state of change and upheaval, but it's likely safe to say that we are contending with multiple and simultaneous potentially world-altering events. We have just emerged from a three-year global pandemic that caused over six million deaths worldwide; triggered a stock market crash; slowed the global economy into near recession; buckled global supply chains; strained global health systems to near collapse; deepened socioeconomic divides; and reignited civil unrest and conflict around the world. During the same time we witnessed an insurrection on the American capital; the withdrawal of American troops from Afghanistan triggering the overthrow of the Afghanistan government by the Taliban; the unprovoked invasion of Ukraine by Russia; the overturning in the United States of *Roe v. Wade*; Canada's own Freedom Convoy protest and occupation of Ottawa; environmental catastrophes around the world from wildfires to floods; the billionaire space race; the

most mass shootings in history complicated by a resistance to calls for gun control policies; and the unearthing of the bodies of Indigenous children's remains at Canadian residential schools. This is by no means an exhaustive list.

The one thing that all of these events have in common is the polarized views people around the world have about them—and the way in which we have come to learn about to-day's world and the people we share it with. The media, in all its forms, have come under intense scrutiny for several years as a cause, or at least a trigger, for many of the problems we're seeing today. That clearly cannot be the case. Media are merely technology. In and of themselves, they are inert. Media, and the algorithms that run them, are designed and used by humans. How we use media amplifies and propagates most of our social ailments. It is humans who create misinformation and disinformation and it is humans who design algorithms that force other humans into filter bubbles and polarized views of one another. Keep this in mind.

12.1 Introduction: The Media at Large

In this textbook, we have discussed race and ethnicity, gender and sexuality, culture, education, health, the environment, and socialization and identity. How many times as you were reading one of those chapters did you think to yourself or say to a friend, "I've heard about this" or "I saw a documentary [or movie or TV series] about this"? There are many ways we come to learn about and believe every aspect of our daily lives: our families and friends, our places of worship and schools, and the media—the news, social media, TV series, movies, books, and advertising. We are inundated with information and ideas every minute we're awake. Recently, I logged the time I spent in front of various media over a random 48-hour period. On average, I spent 15 of my awake hours reading in front of a screen of some type (e-books, online magazines, or news); working, attending classes; watching a movie, program, or YouTube video; playing an online game; scanning social media; and texting or emailing. This is an exercise worth doing not only to understand the amount of time you spend in front of a screen (too much, if you're anything like me), but also to understand how we come to know our lives amid the world around us. Another worthwhile exercise is to think about each of the topics of this textbook and identify where you first learned or heard about it prior to this course. Was it tweeted by someone you follow who heard it from someone else? Was it a meme on Instagram or TikTok? Was it a news segment on a mainstream Canadian station? Was it in a podcast produced by an American news media outlet? Was there any mention of where the information had originated? The answer to your question might be "I don't know, I just know I know it." If this is your response, then hegemony, ideology, and worldview are at work. These are terms that indicate the presence and influence of prevailing (or countervailing) ideas about the world that we come to know and believe because "society" has made them so. The media institutions mentioned above play a significant role in shaping our understanding of the world. In this chapter, we'll discuss the role the social and mass media play in shaping our ideas, worldviews, and, ultimately, our realities.

What do you think?

Imagine how different the COVID-19 pandemic would be without social and mass media. How long would it have taken us in Canada to learn about the outbreak? How would we come to understand and implement public health protocols? How would we communicate the need for lockdowns to protect society? How would we then have communicated with friends and family; attended work or school? Would anti-vaccination and anti-masking protests have ignited to the extent that they have? Would there be as much fear and division? Would we know the extent to which public health crises affect different segments of the population?

12.2 A Brief Historical Evolution of the Media

From earliest recorded times, individuals in social groups stood out for criticizing the behaviour of other individuals and of the group in general. Those who spoke eloquently about behaviour that might be affirmed were recognized as storytellers. People gathered around them to listen. Their stories were about what had been and about what was happening closer at hand. Those who dared to speak about behaviour that might be changed and what should be were called "prophets." They tended to be focused more on the present and on the future. Some of them could predict future events. These ways of telling about the past, present, and future were preserved, first, in oral traditions that formed religious beliefs and practices. Later, those oral traditions were recorded in various forms and held sacred by the societies that created them. Individuals who could hold up a mirror to the group to think more clearly about behaviour co-opted others into their storytelling, and theatre was born. Theatre in ancient Greece was storytelling that tried to preserve the important give-and-take of discussions around the night fires or of debates under the shade trees. Then, theatre brought those various voices of the "audience" onto the stage in designated individuals or groups called "the chorus." Theatrical stories tended toward three forms: drama that ended tragically in the death of the central character in the story; comedy that made its points about human behaviour and interactions that allowed the characters to go on living; and satire that held up certain kinds of behaviour to ridicule. The creators of theatrical presentations learned to mix and match those elements to keep the attention of their audiences.

Still, people sought for more powerful ways of protecting themselves and understanding the world around them. Civilizations in other parts of the world were following similar trajectories, formulating stories about the past and present, designating particular individuals as storytellers and dramatists, dealing with power struggles and forms of government, and developing religions that answered essential human questions in similar ways. We live in a time when the confluence of those human efforts to understand human behaviour individually and in the aggregate of societies has become widely available to everyone on the planet. The means of availability are various communication mediums, known collectively as "the media."

What are "the media"? This may seem like a straightforward question to answer. The media (for the purposes of this chapter) are essentially all of the forms of broadcast and interactive communication available to the public that are used to entertain and inform us. They shape society and culture and, in doing so, their responsibility is immense. Their presence, however, hasn't always been as profuse or as overwhelming as it is today.

The Public Sphere

In the Western tradition, starting with the Jews, Christians, and Muslims, a common ancestry in belief was "the religion of Abraham." During the fall of the Roman Empire, those factions became set against one another, ironically, in the name of Jesus, whose purpose was to create peace. That fracture started to heal during the Renaissance. The rediscovery of ancient learning and the new discoveries of science and technologies brought the Age of Enlightenment, when the idea that people were subject to the will of God and could only learn about the world through the teachings of priests, monarchies, and scholars was challenged by the idea that all people (or most of them) were rational, had free will to determine their actions, and could choose their own fates. This shift in thinking coincided with the invention of the Gutenberg printing press in 1450 and the invention of glass as a magnifier (probably in Muslim society)

that spread the use of small magnifiers in "spectacles" (eyeglasses) in the 1300s, which started in Italy, moved to the Netherlands, and soon stretched across Europe. The ability to print Bibles, books, political pamphlets, and newspapers en masse—and the ability of a much broader public to read them—began to create the social revolution of universal literacy, allowing ideas and news to be shared and interpreted quickly and widely. The tumultuous spread of ideas ushered in the Renaissance, the Reformation, the Age of Enlightenment, and the scientific revolution.

By the 1700s, the mass dissemination of these sources of information—newspapers, in particular—gathered people into town squares or the salons of the upper classes to discuss, debate, and develop their ideas about government and politics, religion, arts and culture, and society in general. The French salons were quite egalitarian as to the status of women, although the social stratum was elite. Remember that heads of states and contenders for those positions frequently were women, and not only as consorts, although many such wives of monarchs held tremendous power and influence. This sharing of ideas among men publicly and with women perhaps more privately was pivotal to the development of changes in religious belief, modern democracy, and innovative political thought. As the main source of political, economic, and cultural information, newspapers—for the rising middle class—became the fundamental medium and guide of public opinion and discourse (Habermas, 1996, p. 55).

During the eighteenth century, when democracy began to take shape, journalism became referred to as the "Fourth Estate" with a social responsibility of advocacy and an implicit ability to frame political issues. The first three estates, dating from the Middle Ages, were the Church (clergy), the Nobility (knight-warriors), and Commoners (peasants) *and* the parallel womanly estates of wives, widows, and nuns. The term "Fourth Estate," which existed conceptually in the late Middle Ages, was attributed by the British essayist Thomas Carlyle to the Irish-British parliamentarian, economist, and philosopher Edmund Burke in a debate in 1787 on the opening of the House of Commons to press reporters. Carlyle himself uses the term 50 years later to describe the press in his book *French Revolution* (1837). Although other authors used the term for different applications, the one that has persisted today is for press reporters. Since so much reporting has become digital, those internet-based media sometimes are distinguished as "The Fifth Estate."

As forms of government became more democratic, citizens needed unbiased and accurate information to inform their opinions about political, economic, and personal matters. Of course, this objective persists. Journalists became responsible not only for informing the public of relevant events—war, economics, local issues, politics, health, and culture—but for ensuring that their reporting was free from personal biases and, more importantly, the biases of those who owned the newspaper presses or who provided information and expert opinion.

Until the late 1900s, fewer sources of news and information made debates more likely to be two-sided, specific, and less confusing than what we experience from today's multiple media. Our news media remain bound to the objectives of the Fourth Estate but find it increasingly difficult (if not impossible) to maintain them in a time when media are converging. Previously independent media companies are being purchased to create larger, more powerful, competing media entities with complex ownership structures.

Media, Nation-Building, and Collective Consciousness

Governments, institutions, and private interest groups have used various media to shape the consciousness and identities of nations and society. Media are used by governing bodies to inform public opinion about important issues in ways that meet national objectives of identity, security, population health, and economic growth. For example, in much the same way that John A. Macdonald used the transcontinental railway to stitch Canada together as one economic nation from east to west in the 1880s, broadcast radio has been used in Canada to further the nation-building project by stitching together the ideologies of our vast and diverse country through the airwaves. If you think about it, sending individuals across a country the size of Canada to deliver cohesive narratives on national issues, as we do during federal political campaigns, is more time-consuming and expensive than a country of this size can afford to do often. The vast majority of Canadians live within about 300 kilometres of the Canada–US border, which makes travel fairly efficient. However, broadcasts reach every corner and outpost of settlement, uniting even the distant places where Canadians live.

In the 1930s, radio broadcasts began to forge a common Canadian consciousness to the country's population. In creating a common source of news and information for all Canadians regardless of their location, prime ministers William Lyon Mackenzie King (1921–26, 1926–30, and 1935–48) and R.B. Bennett (1930–35) believed that radio broadcast would help to unify Canadians and protect the blossoming national identity from the influences of our American neighbours. This objective remains a Canadian broadcast policy to this day.

Canadian Content

The means of influence of American ideas on Canadians isn't difficult to spot. While we're separated by the world's longest land border, we share a common language, landscapes, and industries. It's not difficult for Canadians to pick up American radio and TV broadcasts due to our close proximity and to the internet. What we don't share is a comparable population size—332,403,650 in the United States to Canada's 38,654,738 means we have 11.6 per cent of the US population's size. Our population distribution also is radically different because of the location of arable land. Ninety per cent of Canadians live within 160 kilometres of the US border. This distribution ratio of population to geography means that American media production companies spend much less to distribute their productions than Canada does as it tries to reach the 50 per cent of Canadians living north of the corridor of the major urban centres. Essentially, the cost of production and distribution divided by the number of outlets that distribute those productions is lower for American producers than Canadians because there are more outlets to share the burden of the costs. Such situations are known as *economies of scale*. Canadian producers must carry a higher burden of distribution cost so it is less expensive if they carry American productions than Canadian ones. Thus, for decades, Canadians have been exposed to more American than Canadian media content, which the Canadian government believes erodes our national identity and jeopardizes Canadian creative and production industries. As a result, Canadian content (CanCon) regulations and policies were put in place to protect the Canadian national identity and to ensure a market for Canadian creative and production industries.

There are two ways of analyzing Canadian content as it relates to radio, television, and film. One way is to look at the nationalities of those people involved in the production. This information is fairly straightforward to determine and is controlled by regulatory bodies. The other way is to decide whether or not the content reflects Canadian culture, and this can be difficult to pin down as Canada's immigrant population has grown exponentially.

Canadian Content in Radio and Television Production

The Canadian Radio-television and Telecommunications Commission (CRTC) is the federal organization that, among other functions, is responsible for regulating the amount of "Canadian content" on radio and on television. Although it is a federal organization, it acts "at arm's length" from the government, that is, independently from whichever federal political party is in power. Canadian content is determined by the roles played by Canadians in the production of the shows.

Radio

Canadian content in radio is determined by what is called the MAPL system: M = music, A = artist, P = performance (recorded or live), L = lyrics. In 1971, Canadian content rules were first established, at 25 per cent of airplay. This was raised to 30 per cent in the 1980s and to 35 per cent in 1999.

Some Canadian radio stations developed a strategy that involved technically following the rules, while significantly lowering the number of people who would be listening to Canadian music. It involved putting the Canadian content music into what came to be called the "beaver bin" of songs, to be played after midnight until the early morning. This practice has ended. Canadian content rules in radio have been highly successful over the years in showcasing Canadian musicians, songwriters, and producers in all of the music genres from classical, opera, and avant garde to country, rock, jazz, "oldies," and ethnic, regional, and Indigenous. Canadian storytellers, comedians, children's programmers, and religious programs also have lightened the days of listeners and kept them in touch with their fellow Canadians.

Television

Canadian content in television has been a bit more difficult to monitor and manage. Current Canadian content percentages are as follows: radio airplay is 40 per cent (with partial exceptions for some specialty formats such as classical), and broadcast television is 55 per cent yearly or 50 per cent daily (CBC has a 60 per cent CanCon quota; some specialty or multicultural formats have lower percentages). At least 50 per cent of programming aired daily in "prime time," that is, from six o'clock in the evening until midnight, must be Canadian content. The public network CBC devotes the vast majority of its prime-time broadcasting to Canadian content. One way that the private networks, CTV, Global, and CityTV have reached this quota is by relying on news (twice nightly) and on information programs that are considered to be Canadian. They have been rightly criticized for their low investment in the Canadian entertainment industry. Canadian versions of unscripted shows, such as game shows, reality shows, and baking shows, are another way of making a low investment in Canadian content.

Canadian television had a major triumph with *Schitt's Creek* (2015–20). In its last year, it swept all seven of the Emmy Awards for a comedy series: best series, best actor (Eugene Levy), best actress (Catherine O'Hara), best supporting actor (Dan Levy), best supporting actress (Annie Murphy), best writing (Eugene Levy), and best directing (Eugene Levy and Andrew Cividino). It is the first series, Canadian or American, to have achieved that status. While CBC gave the show its start, getting a Netflix contract boosted its capacity to rise to huge popularity.

Canadian Movies

The federal body for funding and promoting Canadian films is called Telefilm Canada. In 2015, they published a report on Canadian movies based on surveys conducted in 2013, 2014, and 2015, with anglophone and francophone participants aged 13 and over. The survey participants ranged in number from 1,800 to 3,087, a typical population sample for Canadian surveys. Two main points were made. The first related to being able to recognize that a movie is Canadian:

> English-speaking Canadians continue to struggle to recognize Canadian-made films, owing to a lack of clear markers that signify the country of origin of films. (Telefilm Canada, 2015, p. 2)

Another point was a low rating for the quality of the films: "Only 35% of Anglophones agree that the Canadian film industry has started making better films over the last few years" (Telefilm Canada, 2015, p. 17). There was a suggestion that this was related to the difficulties identifying which films were Canadian. The report concluded:

> Finally, working together to build recognition for the Canadian industry becomes a priority for all stakeholders involved in the production of Canadian content. Ensuring Canadians recognize homegrown talent and can discover homemade content is

essential for the future of Canadian media content. (Telefilm Canada, 2015, p. 22)

Statista, an organization that acquires and publishes statistics concerning Canadians, used figures concerning how much revenue (calculated in terms of millions of Canadian dollars) was generated by films shown in theatres in Canada. Three categories of where the films were produced were sorted in this way: American, Other Country, Canadian. Table 12.1 shows the results of this 2021 Statista study. It is rather depressing for Canadians in the movie business, and for those who want more Canadian content in movies, to see that over the 2007–19 period, box office revenues for Canadian films comprised a mere 1.7 per cent to 3.4 per cent of total box office revenues.

What do you think?

1. Do you think that it is hard to identify Canadian movies? If so, how could that be changed?
2. Do you think that Canadians generally have a low opinion of Canadian-made movies? If so, why do you think that exists?

TABLE 12.1 Theatre Box Office Revenue in Canada by Country of Production ($, millions)

	2007	2008	2009	2010	2011	2012	2013	2014	2015	2016	2017	2018	2019
United States	763	815	889	954	864	902	923	820	923	871	891	927	923
Other	67	80	84	42	109	165	95	97	71	104	70	67	71
Canada	28	26	34	32	32	28	27	24	28	18	32	20	17
Canadian percentage	3.1%	2.8%	3.4%	3.1%	3.2%	2.6%	2.6%	2.5%	2.6%	1.9%	3.2%	1.9%	1.7%

Source: Statista (2022).

For a comparison with another English-speaking country, we have the following figures for Australia (Table 12.2).

While there doesn't appear to be much improvement over the years for the homegrown film industry in Canada, there are a few positive stories. For example, Canadian film festivals show a number of Canadian films, some exclusively Canadian, and a few movie-based premium TV services such as Crave, Super Channel, Hollywood Suite, and Écran follow Canadian content regulations.

What Is Canadian Content in Terms of Story Themes?

One of the best ways of learning about the origins of contemporary media is to attend "legit" (for "legitimate") theatre where live actors perform in real time to a real audience, as has been happening around the world and in various ways for millennia.

TABLE 12.2 Country and Continent Percentage of Movies Released in Australian Cinemas, 2020

Country or Continent of Origin	Percentage
Asia	40%
United States	24%
Britain	11%
Australia	10%
Rest of Europe	7%
France	4%
Other	2%
New Zealand	1%
Canada	1%

Source: Cinema Industry: Number of Australian and Overseas Films Released in Australian Cinemas, 1984–2020. https://www.screenaustralia.gov.au/fact-finders/cinema/industry-trends/films-screened

The differences between the "real" and the "performance" become clearer. The purposes of playwrights, designers, actors, and production staff are written in your own responses to what you see and hear when you are physically present with the production. Becoming conversant with the theatrical techniques that elicit your responses makes you more aware of sham and performance outside the theatre. Regular exposure to direct, live performance where that one-on-one communication between actors and audiences takes place has become more rare. It is important, however, because it allows you to notice some of the realities that are hidden in other forms of media. The "hiding" may be as obvious as greasepaint on the actors' faces and costumes masking their actual body shapes and sizes; airbrushing of photographs in magazines and lighting and camera angles in film-making that create "beauty" or "ugliness" make us aware of the fundamental truths and lies when ideas are staged and voiced through actors. The obedience of actors to their roles is one of the ways ideas are made popular and attractive. Of course, the same may be said of religious ceremonies and those who perform them and of the rituals that surround other institutions, such as government and the military. A certain amount of illusion and delusion may be involved. Staying in touch with live performances can keep you grounded, which means being analytical and aware about the real meanings behind the messages of the performance. Canada has kept its people in touch with live theatre in many ways since colonial times.

We have seen that Canadian content is fairly well-defined in terms of Canadian involvement in the making or production of music, a television show, or a movie. The other side to Canadian content is the telling of a "Canadian story," one that reflects Canadian history, identifiable places, culture, values, its diversity, and so on. The comedian, television personality, political satirist, and author Rick Mercer (*This Hour Has 22 Minutes, Made in Canada,* and *The Rick Mercer Report*) and radio journalist, documentarian, author, humourist, and storyteller Stuart McLean of *The Vinyl Café* have exemplified personalities who have single-handedly mirrored Canadians to themselves by criss-crossing the country to research them and to perform for them.

In 2003, I bemoaned the lack of Canadian content in media storytelling regarding such elements as clearly placing locations in Canada, particularly cities, in songs, shows, and movies. I asked readers to recall all the times they had seen on TV or in movies someone play the part of the president of the United States, and contrast that with their never having seen someone play the part of the prime minister of Canada. I ended that part of the discussion by stating, "No wonder so many children believe that the leader of our country is a president" (Steckley, 2003, p. 278). Since then, Kiefer Sutherland, a member of Canada's royal family of actors (father Donald Sutherland, mother Shirley Douglas, stepmother Francine Racette, brothers Angus, Rossif, and Roeg, and sister Rachel), has played the American president brilliantly in the television hit *Designated Survivor.*

While Canadian settings frequently stand in for American locations in films, less frequently do Canadian locations become "the third character" in the plot. However, we have seen some notable exceptions. In 1965, Lucy Maude Montgomery's beloved orphan and gifted redhead Anne Shirley, from the fictional "Avonlea" in the entirely real Prince Edward Island, took to the main stage in the Charlottetown Confederation Centre of the Arts in the musical version of *Anne of Green Gables* and performed every summer until COVID-19 shut down the 2021 production. In its 49th season in 2014, it was touted in *Guinness World Records* as the "longest-running annual musical theatre production" in the world. While Canadian musical theatre has rarely been able to mount as lavish extravaganzas as the American Broadway musical, Vancouver's Theatre Under the Stars (est. 1940), Toronto's Melody Fair (which had a short existence in the early 1950s), and Winnipeg's Rainbow Stage (which continues to produce Broadway musicals) were able to give Canadians a taste of those stylish productions.

The journalist Tom Patterson founded the Stratford Shakespeare Festival in Stratford, Ontario, in 1953. As a world-class theatrical centre in a small Ontario town, it became a standard-setter that inspired the founding of other theatres in Winnipeg and Halifax. Soon, the relevance of Shakespeare's insights about human character and critiques of human institutions became much more common knowledge. The sober and sometimes tedious classroom study sprang to life at Stratford. The festival atmosphere and summer schedule soon attracted music ensembles. Other stages were opened in Stratford under the Festival's aegis. Young people's programs brought high school students by train to see the plays and learn more about the backstage activities that mounted legendary productions and brought great actors, directors, and designers to Canada, some for very long sojourns.

In 1967, *The Ecstasy of Rita Joe* by George Ryga brought a drama with music to a story important for its national and sociological implications. Rita is a Canadian Indigenous girl with hopes of achieving a better life in the city, who encounters instead racism, rape, and death. Although it opened in Vancouver, any of Canada's big cities suitably fit the play's location.

Much more common theatrical presentations were the less costly but politically pertinent "reviews" and "variety shows," starting notably with "The Dumbells" during World War I. The parallel (army, navy, air force) military road shows of World War II brought strong musical and theatrical talent into politically aware peacetime theatre. The dancing Lunds, Alan and Blanche, and director Mavor Moore, and the comedians Johnny Wayne and Frank Shuster and their fellow actors, writers, dancers, and choreographers, and musicians became the mainstays of various long-term theatrical enterprises: "Spring Thaw" in Toronto, The Straw Hat Players summer theatre at Port Carling, The Red Barn (summer) Theatre at Jackson's Point on Lake Simcoe, and in PEI the Charlottetown Summer Festival.

More recently, *Come From Away* was birthed in Toronto at Sheridan College and eventually set a Canadian Broadway record and played in the United States, Britain, and Ireland. It is the story with music of the people in the airport town of Gander, Newfoundland, and their 7,000 unexpected guests, who were stranded there by the terrorist attacks on the Twin Towers in New York on 11 September 2001.

Hockey as Canadian Content

There has been a lack of portrayal of Canadian hockey in film, our "national sport," unlike the frequent theme of football and baseball in American movies. *Slapshot* (1977) was a very Canadian story "about a one-industry town and its hockey team" with some French Canadian players, but it took place in an American town. The star of the film was Paul Newman, but the American–Canadian actor split was about 50–50, with four French Canadian hockey players acting their own ethnicity. A portrayal of "Charles Screaming Buffalo Swamptown," who wore a wig of long, black hair to appear Indigenous and whose character was violent, was *satirically* "racist." He bore a righteous grudge, calling his hockey stick "the Big Tomahawk" and the opposing players "the little scalps." The part was played by a white American actor, a minor league hockey player who had set the record for the most penalties in his league.

The Mighty Ducks franchise (1992, 1994, and 1996) had a few Canadian actors, including Canadian former NHL player Cam Neely, but the location of the team was Minnesota, and the films were little more than a Disney promotion of a Disney-owned team (from 1993–2005), until new ownership changed their name simply to "Ducks."

The hockey song "Big League" (1988), by Tom Cochrane and Red Rider, struck a chord with Canadians. It peaked at #4 on a Canadian chart. To my knowledge, there has been one hockey movie, *The Rocket* (2005 and 2006), that can be called a Canadian story with Canadian content. It is about Maurice "the Rocket" Richard, who was a scoring leader for the Montreal Canadiens from 1942 to 1960. He was the first player to score 50 goals in 50 games (1945). The film was marketed by Telefilm Canada in Denmark, Finland, Iceland, Norway, and Sweden, and it was picked up in the United States by Disney, among others. Its Canadian content includes the racial prejudice he faced as a French Canadian playing in a league that was, at the time, almost all English.

> ### What do you think?
> Have Canada's content regulations helped to protect our industry and our national identity? Do you think Canadians want more Canadian content? Why or why not?

War as Canadian Content

I grew up watching movies about how the Americans "won" World War II. As my Canadian father and two uncles were involved in that war, I dearly wanted to see a movie about Canadian soldiers and the major role they have played in both world wars and in subsequent conflicts. Since then, two war movies focused on Canadian troops have been produced by Paul Gross (who starred in the TV series *Due South*). *Passchendaele* (2008) tells the story of a pivotal battle in the fall of 1917, involving 100,000 Canadian troops. *Hyena Road* (2015) is about Canadians building a road in war-torn Afghanistan.

Diversity as Canadian Content

Diversity is definitely an aspect of Canadian culture. We have seen it in *The Beachcombers*, set on the BC coast and starring Italian Canadian actor Bruno Gerussi as Greek Canadian Nick Adonidas—with Indigenous actor Pat John playing Jesse Jim in 217 episodes. Robert Clothier, a former RCAF decorated veteran who was severely injured in an accident after World War II, recovered to play opposite Gerussi as his nemesis "Relic" Phillips in every episode. One of the longest-running Canadian shows, it aired 374 episodes from 1 October 1972 to 12 December 1990, with two Beachcomber-themed made-for-TV movies in 2002 and 2004. Chief Dan George, who was chief of the Tsleil-Waututh Nation in North Vancouver for a number of years and was nominated for an Academy Award for his portrayal of Old Lodge Skins in *Little Big Man* (1970), played Chief Moses Charlie in eight episodes of *The Beachcombers*. Other prominent Canadians who made special appearances included Gordon Pinsent, Ryan Styles, David Suzuki, and Bruce Greenwood.

Another popular CBC show, *Kim's Convenience* (2016–21), based on a play by Korean Canadian Ins Choi, who became a script writer for the TV show, was located identifiably in Toronto, where it also was filmed. *Little Mosque on the Prairie* (2007–12) centred on the Muslim community in the fictional prairie town of Mercy, Saskatchewan. The inspiration for at least some of the shows came from experiences that Muslim actress Zarqa Nawaz had with her family and friends.

Indigenous Content

The next Canadian TV show with significant Indigenous content was *North of 60*, which aired on the CBC as a television series from 1992 to 1997, followed by five made-for-TV movies (1999–2005). It took place in the sub-Arctic (north of 60 latitude) in the fictional Dene community of Lynx River and starred Indigenous actors Tina Keeper, Tom Jackson, Gordon Tootoosis, and Jimmy Herman. The writers/directors Barbara Samuels and Wayne Grisby were non-Indigenous. Since *North of 60*, the addition of Indigenous content to Canadian airwaves has made significant strides—but there is still room for improvement in telling these Canadian stories.

Aboriginal Peoples Television Network (APTN)

In 1991, TVNC (Television Northern Canada) started delivering shows to communities in Canada's North. APTN began broadcasting on 21 January 1999, developed from that former platform. It was the first network in the world dedicated to a country's Indigenous people and is a founding member of the World Indigenous Television Network. It is not largely government-funded, but is a non-profit charity organization. Its funds come from subscribers, commercials, and various partnerships. Its 85 per cent Canadian content is broadcast in English (56 per cent), in French (16 per cent), and in Indigenous languages (28 per cent), the latter being heard only on this network, not any other Canadian channels. This Indigenous mix includes languages of people in relatively high numbers: such as Inuktitut (east Arctic), Inuvialuit (west Arctic), Cree (including, as of 5 March 2022, *Hockey Night in Canada*), Innu (Quebec and Newfoundland and Labrador), Halkomelem (a Salish language of Vancouver Island and mainland BC), Anishinaabemowin (Ojibwa), and Mi'maw. Telefilm Canada contributed $1 million in funding for such shows (APTN.com).

Mohawk Girls

Tracey Deer is a documentary writer/producer who created the television show *Mohawk Girls*. She is Mohawk (Kanienkehaka, "people of the flint"), born on the reserve of Kahnawake in Quebec. When she was growing up, she seldom saw herself or people like her in the shows she saw on television. Although Deer also refers to it as "Sex and the City for the Native Set" (Hays, 2013), the series contains drama as well as comedy and is true to life, based on aspects of events in Deer's life. Many of the plotlines were based on her 2005 documentary of the same name,

for which she spent two years chronicling the lives of three teenage girls in Kahnawake (Wong, 2014). Three of the four actresses are Indigenous, two being Mohawk. The series ran from 2014 to 2017, picked up first by Omni, which deals with multicultural shows, and by APTN. It is currently streamed on CBC and was picked up by the NBC streaming service in 2021.

Trickster

The television series *Trickster* had its origin in the novel *Son of a Trickster* published by award-winning Haisla/Heiltsuk author Eden Robinson. It is described as a "darkly humorous coming-of-age story," in which an Indigenous teen, Jared, who is struggling to keep his family together and strong, begins to experience the supernatural. It premiered in 2020 on CBC, with initial plans to have more seasons. At first, Michelle Latimer appeared to be having a boom year. She directed *Trickster* and the documentary *An Inconvenient Indian*, which is an adaptation of the successful Thomas King non-fiction book of the same name. However, a highly publicized cancellation of the TV series and the withdrawal of the film from circulation by December 2020 followed as a result of controversy surrounding Latimer's heritage claims (Dowling, 2021).

Based on her family's oral history, Latimer had claimed Indigenous ancestry, a connection on her mother's side with the Algonquin of KitiganZibi, and the Métis. People in the community said that they had no knowledge of such a connection. The CBC and Latimer each hired researchers, who suggested that she may have a Quebec Métis connection going back to the seventeenth century. The legal status of such a group has yet to be established, and those who belong to recognized Indigenous communities are leery about its existence (Barrera, 2021).

Such pretensions as Latimer's are the subject of a recent documentary, *Pretendians*, by the

> **What do you think?**
> 1. What do you think are the appropriate roles for non-Indigenous people in the creation of Indigenous content on television and in films?
> 2. Do you think Latimer would have been given the chance to make *Trickster* if she hadn't claimed an Indigenous identity?

award-winning playwright, author, and journalist Drew Hayden Taylor, a resident of the Curve Lake Nation, an Ojibwe community in Peterborough County, Ontario (Taylor, 2022).

Is the Medium the Message?

In the 1930s, the power of radio to bring news and information from across the country and around the world into institutions, businesses, and people's homes in nearly real time impacted society and consciousness-building projects globally. News of the economy, war, and arts and culture travelled instantaneously. Through their home radios, people everywhere learned about the economic fallout of the Great Depression; the end of Prohibition; Mahatma Gandhi and his followers marching 200 miles to the salt beds of Jalalpur; the deaths of Bonnie and Clyde; the disappearance of Amelia Earhart; and the beginning of World War II. They also heard the broadcast of Orson Welles's radio adaptation of *The War of the Worlds*. Before radio broadcasting many of these types of events wouldn't be known for weeks or months, if at all.

In the 1950s, television became widely available in homes across Canada, adding pictures to the kinds of stories people had been listening to on their radios, allowing them to see events happening almost as soon as they unfolded. In 1952, Canadians first watched *Hockey Night in Canada, The Wayne and Shuster Show,* and *CBC News Magazine.* The ability to not only hear about but to see events happening around the world deepened people's experience of and interest in the world, transforming how they understood their place in it.

Radio and television brought distant places and people closer together by speeding the transmission of news, information, and communication. In doing so, people became aware of events, information, and ideas from outside their hometowns and countries, shaping not only national consciousness but individual and global consciousness as well.

The proliferation and innovation of media technology around the world has created what Canadian communications theorist Marshall McLuhan (1911–1980) called the *global village.* While we can interpret this in a utopian way to mean that the sharing of information globally through technological innovation would transform the disconnected world into one that would be connected through shared ideas, McLuhan was concerned about the impact this would have on the well-being of future societies:

> The world has become a computer, an electronic brain, exactly as an infantile piece of science fiction. And as our senses have gone outside us, Big Brother [the over-controlling government of Orwell's *1984*] goes inside. So, unless aware of this dynamic, we shall at once move into a phase of panic terrors, exactly befitting a small world of tribal drums, total interdependence, and superimposed co-existence. . . . Terror is the normal state of any oral society, for in it everything affects everything all the time. . . . In our long striving to recover for the Western world a unity of sensibility and of thought and feeling, we have no more been prepared to accept the tribal consequences of such unity than we were ready for the fragmentation of the human psyche by print culture. (McLuhan, 1962, p. 32)

We would be hard-pressed to argue against this prediction as we find ourselves facing global crises brought about by globalization that challenge the protective walls that nation-building projects have sought to construct. The problems we have to solve today, including climate change and the environment, food insecurity, global population health, war and social conflict, and the global economy cannot be solved by individual nations. One could agree with McLuhan that we are in a phase of panic leading us into a state of "interdependence and a superimposed co-existence."

Marshall McLuhan remains one of the best-known critics and theorists of modern media. McLuhan has been described by some as a media "prophet" and as a technological determinist, that is, someone who believes that technology can determine how humans act and think. McLuhan believed that technology has the power to determine social structures. While he was not a proponent of the idea that a *particular* technology would allow some groups to rise to power at the expense of others, we may wish to revisit that idea now that marginalized groups find themselves further oppressed by algorithms and the AI (artificial intelligence) projects of technology giants such as Meta, Amazon, and Google. We'll discuss algorithms later in this chapter.

Historic Collection / Alamy Stock Photo

Marshall McLuhan

One of McLuhan's most famous claims concerning the media is that "the medium is the message" (McLuhan, 1964, p. 23). By this, he meant that the medium—whether television, radio, print, tweets, memes, TikTok videos, whiteboards, or performance art—has a causative effect on the way human groups think, act, and organize socially. The importance of any medium is how it affects the way people interpret its messages, behave as a result of them, and how it "shapes and controls the scale and form of human association and action," beyond the specifics of its content (McLuhan, 1962). We can see modern examples of this in how former President Donald Trump was eager to take to Twitter in order to communicate directly with the public. He knew his message would be more readily and quickly taken up in this way than if it was filtered through the traditional press and news outlets, and the language and media formats they used. His use of Twitter messages in his punchy, emotional language struck quickly to the hearts of his followers, gaining traction and momentum as they spread. Indeed, the Twitter medium produced his message in a way no

What do you think?
Is the medium the message? Can you think of an example that demonstrates how technological advancements have changed how we understand the world through the media?

other could, shaping and controlling the scale and form of human associations and actions—and, arguably, regardless of the actual content of his tweets.

The Internet and Social Media

The current era of a dominant medium—the internet—is unique. In *The Power Elite* (1956), C. Wright Mills identified two main sociological characteristics of mass media: (1) a very few people control the communication of a great number of people and (2) the audience has no truly effective way to communicate back to those in control (Mills, 1956, p. 338). Wright argued that the mass media, as they were constructed back in the 1950s, were inherently undemocratic (Mills, 1956, p. 338). Governments, media outlets, and large corporations historically have been able to dominate the public consciousness with greater broadcast powers than smaller groups and individuals possessed. Traditionally, there was no effective way people could speak back to power and there was no easily accessible way to access volumes of information such as legal texts, medical texts, government documents, or academic research that were kept under lock and key by their gatekeepers— those in positions of power who control production and access to knowledge in society. It was with this in mind that **Tim Berners-Lee**, a British computer scientist and professor of computer science at Oxford University and Massachusetts Institute of Technology, set about researching and developing what would become the modern World Wide Web, or the internet. In 1989, his intention was to create a global information-sharing platform that would *democratize information*—that would give people at all levels of society around the world a tool to freely access, share, and benefit from all forms of knowledge and information, including those traditionally controlled by institutions of power. This vision largely has come to pass with the creation of content sharing and storage sites such as Wikipedia, JStor, and WikiLeaks; 1990s music-sharing platforms such as Napster; personal blogging sites such as Tumblr and Medium; personal website platforms such as WordPress; social media platforms such as Facebook, Instagram, and TikTok; and the move of news media to online platforms with public comment sections. All of these sources were made accessible by global search engines dating back to the early 1990s, including Netscape, Ask Jeeves, AOL, Yahoo!, Internet Explorer, and, more recently, Google and Bing. Sharing all of this information between individuals was made possible by the creation of electronic mail systems, such as Hotmail, Gmail, and AOL, and news aggregators known as RSS (really simple syndication) feeds. All of this became the messaging services we know today. With all of these tools to access information, what remained was a way to not only interact personally over the internet but to publicly share and discuss information and ideas, and to speak back to power in a forum that would allow for interaction, discussion, and debate. The true democratization of information and debate would take the form of a modern public sphere that could be accessed by everyone, everywhere—a form of media that would be broadly social.

The first social media site launched in 1997 when SixDegrees.com invited users to create profile pages, contact lists, and send messages within the network. SixDegrees was followed by Friendster in 2002, MySpace in 2003, Facebook in 2004, and then a wave of social media sites in 2005 and 2006 including LinkedIn, Flickr, YouTube, Twitter, and the blogging platforms WordPress and Tumbler. These mega programs set the stage for the proliferation of social media sites we see today, including TikTok, Instagram, Weibo, Reddit, and (unfortunately) 4Chan. We also saw the emergence of social games like FarmVille and CandyCrush and online dating services such as LavaLife, Match, eHarmony, JDate, okcupid, Tindr, Ashley Madison, and Grindr.

The introduction of information sharing and social media sites that provided global platforms for people to learn, communicate, meet, make friends (and enemies), find jobs, find partners, entertain themselves and one another, and create and share ideas changed society in ways Tim Berners-Lee could not have anticipated when he set out to democratize information. Not only were individuals joining these platforms by the hundreds of thousands and millions, so were news media outlets, corporations, associations, politicians, and private interest groups. Social media platforms have given all of these institutions a way to communicate instantaneously with the public. They have also provided a means for the people to publicly answer back and debate the issues at hand—to feel engaged with society and to influence the democratic process. However, gateways and other filtering methods have been devised. The appearance of democratic exchange on social platforms is beset with robotic sensors. Personal information is collected secretly for unknown purposes.

AI and Algorithms: The Dangers of Convenience

Social media platforms and search engines, driven by algorithms and artificial intelligence, have also been co-opted by government and private institutions to monitor, measure, categorize, predict, and change the behaviour of the people who use them (O'Neil, 2016; Zuboff, 2019). In monitoring and capturing the (what should be private) online behavioural data of their users, social media platforms and search engines categorize and predict the behaviour of their users. Then, they sell access to these data to institutions, corporations, and private interest groups who capitalize on those insights to create targeted advertising and communications for groups of people. In effect, they are able to deliver only ads and messages that are (or may be) of interest to those users and filter out content that is not. Social media platforms also use behavioural algorithms to make sure your streams and timelines continue to feed you more of the content you have previously watched, which they assume you continue to wish to watch. Do you click, share, or pause on cute cat videos? They'll give them to you all day long. Prefer right-leaning politics to left? You've got it. Have you recently searched for "Ugg winter boots Toronto," "Ted Lasso Season 3," "how to cut hair at home," or "best guitar pedals" on Google? Facebook will be more than happy to make sure you see ads from local clothing stores, video tutorials for hair styling techniques, and the latest Netflix series. Advertisers have co-opted our behavioural data that should be private through search engines and social media platforms to encourage us to spend more money—to be consumers in an aggressively capitalist economy (Zuboff, 2019). Political organizations have co-opted our behavioural data that should be private to entrench our existing political beliefs and values, whatever they may be (Zuboff, 2019). Private institutions such as insurance companies and loan financers have co-opted our behavioural data that should be private along with our personal information to determine what coverage and rates we are entitled to (O'Neil, 2016). In breaching our privacy, these institutions not only know our behaviours, they use that knowledge to attempt to inform the decisions we make, the opportunities available to us, and to influence the decisions we make about what we buy, where we live, where we go to school, how we regard our health, how we see ourselves and the people around us, what we believe, and, ultimately, our actions and relationships in and with society (O'Neil, 2016).

Media are far more than sources of information and entertainment. They have become essential to the creation and maintenance of social, political, and cultural institutions not only in the west but in Russia, China, and other countries with an agenda for increasing their power. They have become tools of modern capitalism and can be seen as part of a social apparatus that challenges democratic processes and further oppresses already marginalized groups of people (O'Neil,2016). Tracing the historical roots of media helps us understand how today's media are not only products of shifts in technology and communication, but how they produce dramatic shifts in how people have come to know the world around them and their relationship to it.

12.3 Media and the Social Construction of Reality

Earlier, we considered C. Wright Mills's argument that the main sociological characteristics of the first forms of mass media are that a very few people can communicate to a great number of people; that the audience has no truly effective way to communicate back; and that they were inherently undemocratic (Mills, 1956). Mills also believed that gatekeeping is the heart of media's power, claiming that those who are in charge of the media are in charge of ideas. There are a few things in this statement to unpack. First are the entwined ideas of gatekeeping and power as they relate to information and knowledge. Second is the idea of being "in charge"—for example, who owns (or funds) the media, and who has access to it as an instrument of communication. Third is how this power shapes what people know and believe about the world around them, essentially constructing their

> **What do you think?**
> Social media have been blamed for the erosion of democracy and critical thought. Many sociologists believe that social media merely amplify existing problems, sentiments, and behaviours in society. Do you think that in the absence of social media, we would be experiencing the political polarization that exists in North America today?

reality. Superior knowledge is integral to achieving and maintaining authority (Strange, 1994), and gatekeeping, as a tool of power and authority, is the act of deciding who is allowed access to knowledge and in what ways—and who is not. This matrix is put into effect through four key elements:

1. Production and ownership. Who has the means and funds to produce the content?
2. Language. Is the content in plain language everyone can understand rather than complex, verbose, academic, or technical language?
3. Access. Is it easily accessed by the public or is it kept behind paywalls, subscriptions, or other controls?
4. Dissemination. How widely is the information shared with the public?

The power associated with gatekeeping is that of ownership over the production of ideas in and about society. In the context of the media, gatekeeping is established through ownership, language, access, and dissemination. In other words, those who control production also control the narratives that inform the public on the issues that shape what we know and believe about the world. In Canada, more than 80 per cent of the media are controlled by five corporations: Bell Media, Rogers Media, Postmedia, Corus, and Torstar (Statista, 2022). These corporations own the dozens of smaller online, print, television, and radio companies that exist in Canada. As a result of competition arising from the growth of online media and the popularity of citizen journalists—along with rising labour, production, and distribution costs—smaller media outlets have struggled to survive for decades, gradually succumbing to ownership buyouts by large corporations. This convergence of media companies has dramatically reduced the diversity of voices and perspectives in Canadian media. Ownership of local media outlets by large corporations means that the news is rarely, if ever, produced at a local level by independent journalists. Rather, it is mostly produced on a regional or national level and pumped out by local online, print, television, and radio outlets with some local human-interest stories tacked on. In sum, five privately owned corporations dictate the national narratives about all of the issues that affect the lives of millions of very diverse Canadians. This is *not* to say that an invisible hand is manufacturing the news. But it is important to remember Mills's argument that those who control the media control the ideas. Even the earliest newspapers in Canada relied heavily on funding from governments and political parties (Yarhi, 2017), which inherently threatened their integrity and ability to report without bias. For example, the *Globe* (1844) was a personal platform of its publisher, the Reform politician George Brown, while the *Toronto Mail* (1872), was a platform for Conservative Prime Minister Sir John A. Macdonald (Yarhi, 2017). Much like today's news media landscape, these newspapers offered opposing perspectives on the same current issues. Today, mainstream media continue to be funded by entities with known or suspected ties to political parties, and the main sources for news and expert opinion come from these same organizations.

This social interaction raises the question of whether corporate interests and their relationships with political parties are informing the decisions made in newsrooms. There is no evidence that the CEOs of Bell or Rogers actively participate in editorial decisions of their respective news outlets, but a culture of political and economic posture has been nurtured over time that locates news outlets firmly in the camps of the political and corporate leanings of their owners. This bias has been clearly pronounced in American politics and news media where we see the overt alignment of Fox News with the Republican Party agenda and CNN with the Democratic Party agenda. In Canada, this type of alignment is seen, for example, with the *Toronto Star* supporting Liberal agendas and the *Globe and Mail* approving Conservative agendas.

What this type of ownership convergence translates into is politicized and polarized (or extreme and oppositional, sometimes confrontational) camps of population with strong beliefs about important social issues. Their beliefs have been shaped by the agendas of specific people in very powerful positions, who have the resources to distribute their ideas on a massive scale through news and public relations firms, drowning out the voices of smaller interest groups.

Filter Bubbles

People have always been polarized by their political and social views and the media have always been major contributors to that polarization. In Chapter 4 we discussed *primary socialization*. During this early period of our lives, our families and communities instil in us certain beliefs about the world and the people around us. For the most part, as we mature, we seek information and other people to confirm and uphold those beliefs. This perspective is known as *confirmation bias*. Such a predisposition leads us to associate with people who hold similar beliefs, to read, view, and listen to news media that support those beliefs, and to participate in activities and groups that support those beliefs. It also leads us to refute, ignore, or reject perspectives that conflict with these beliefs. These philosophical (and sometimes physical) spaces we create for ourselves that preserve our belief systems are known as *filter bubbles*—and they existed long before the age of social media. For the most part, people have surrounded themselves only with people who are alike and have always sought information and entertainment that confirms or reaffirms those belief systems.

The internet, and social media in particular, has amplified our tendencies to entrench ourselves in

What do you think?

During the COVID-19 pandemic, many people in North America believed that the health crisis was a hoax perpetrated by foreign forces to control society and the economy, and to take away our civil rights and liberties. Many of these theories were shared in online communities supported by what appeared to be legitimate news sources and experts. Do you think these beliefs were exacerbated by the filter bubble effect created by algorithms and social media? Imagining the absence of social media and filter bubbles, do you think more people would have been more likely to wear masks and get vaccinated, likely shortening the severity of the pandemic?

the comfort zone of our filter bubbles. Prior to the social media era, however, people were exposed to opposing views even if they didn't buy into them. Today, social media and its algorithms allow us to almost completely block out views that don't align with our own, robbing us of new and different perspectives that provide nuance and a broader understanding of the world and people around us. Being isolated in our filter bubbles means that we are unable to relate to or to communicate with people who don't share our perspectives. In some instances, we are left unaware of events and of important information, and we are unable to empathize with people who are different from us. We believe our view is the only one, and when confronted by something different we are alarmed, perhaps confrontational, and are unwilling to listen to or to accept a new point of view. Society becomes increasingly polarized as a result of the entrenchment of our filter bubbles.

The Attention Economy and News as Spectacle

Media in Canada are funded by two main income streams: subscriptions and advertising. The proliferation of online news media has severely compromised the subscription revenue model for both print and television media outlets, pushing them to produce more content online (much of it at no cost to the public) and to rely on advertising models for much-needed funding. The reliance on online advertising revenue means that content producers are in fierce competition for attention in an overcrowded, highly competitive online media landscape, which has changed the nature of news production around the world. Before the era of online media, news outlets had relatively captive audiences. There were fewer places to get the news and people had subscriptions or tuned in to their favourite sources. Revenue was secured through this model and advertising supplemented that revenue. Now, with their reliance on advertising revenue, media outlets need to find ways to get—and keep—eyes on their content. This demand has increased the sensationalized and rapid-fire style of news reporting. Headlines and their stories must be dramatic and catchy. They must appeal to an audience looking for quick, visual hits they can scan and share to their networks before their friends. The need to publish *first* (instead of factually) has decreased the integrity of much news reporting.

News events get into the public sphere before details are confirmed. This means that falsehoods or incomplete stories spread before they can be corrected and by the time they've spread, the correction doesn't matter (Lewis & Cushion, 2009, p. 313). The news media also compete with more entities than simply other news outlets. The rise of citizen journalism and rampant public opinion on social media mean that media outlets compete for attention with everyone on the internet (Argila, 2017, p. 32). Not only are journalists reporting live news events, so too are everyday people—and they are often on the scene posting photographs and video. The 2020 murder of George Floyd by police in Minneapolis very possibly never would have been fully known, or prosecuted, nor would the massive protests that followed have occurred, were it not for a young woman with a cellphone camera. Journalists are under intense pressure to "tweet it raw but tweet it now" (Argila, 2017, p. 15)—and to be ready to tweet it 24/7.

In their efforts to capture attention, news media now design their stories to compete with all of the other content people are inundated with in their feeds all day every day. The news now looks like advertising and advertising now looks like the news. Bold, pithy headlines accompanied by dramatic photos and videos all are meant to capture attention and **commodify** the news, social media platforms, and those who use them. The content of the *24-hour news cycle* has become fractured by commodification and the demands of the attention economy to such an extent that people are becoming unable to distinguish news from entertainment and from advertising. What does it mean for society when our ability to make this distinction has been compromised?

You recall from earlier in the chapter that journalism is meant to be the public's eyes on institutions of power and a trusted source of information about the world around us. What we understand through the news about politics, the people who lead us, and world issues is foundational to our ability to maintain a fully functioning democratic society. When this is turned into a *spectacle*, our access to the truth and our ability to see the truth become destabilized—and so, too, does democracy.

Theorists such as Guy Debord have argued for decades that society has become a spectacle that distracts us from the important issues that inform democracy (Briziarelli & Armano, 2017, p. 82).

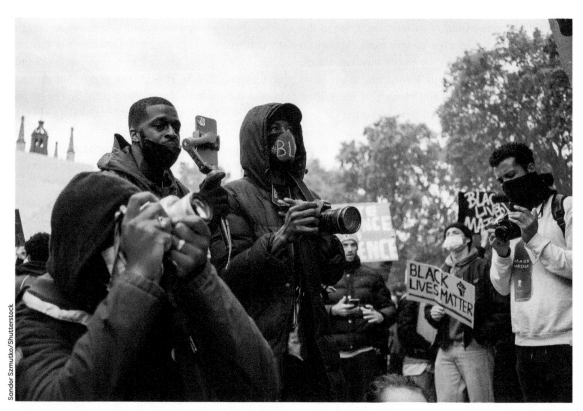

Sandor Szmutko/Shutterstock

Black Lives Matter protest during COVID lockdown in London

A spectacle, according to Debord, is the "detachment of images from every aspect of life fused in a common stream . . . rendering the pseudo-world . . . an object of mere contemplation" (Debord, 1967, p. 2). We can take this to mean that, in turning everyday life and important societal issues into a spectacle on social media, reality is made surreal or unreal, which threatens our ability to perceive reality or to understand the issues facing us. Essentially, in a world where more than 75 per cent of people access their news online, including through social media (Newman et al., 2020, p. 62), most of us are bombarded with news headlines and images conflated with trivial news stories, satire, entertainment, opinion, and advertising. For example, in any half-hour period, you might see various news stories on Twitter, Facebook, YouTube, Instagram, and Tik-Tok. Each of these services delivers content to you based on your previous online habits and the most popular and recent content on the platform without distinguishing between entertainment, advertising, or news. While we are hyper-exposed to streams of images, words, memes, and ideas curated for us by

opaque algorithms, we miss detail, context, and relevance. Details, context, and relevance are the tools that provide us with the ability to truly understand the world around us and the people we share it with; to make decisions about our place in it; and to have an educated point of view about what is just and fair. "Opaque" algorithms are *invisible* to users of social media and the internet-at-large. We cannot see them; do not know who creates them or for what purpose; have no ability to control how, when, or where they are used; and are not made privy to the data collected by them. Complicating this problem of "the spectacle" is that a lot of the content we're exposed to isn't even real. Whether intentional or otherwise, we are exposed to falsehoods and half-truths every day.

Fake News: Who Can You Trust?

Much like filter bubbles, polarization, and ownership biases, fake news also did not arrive with the internet and social media. There are plenty of examples throughout history, the most familiar dating from the eras of the Enlightenment, the colonial period, and Nazi Germany's Center for Information Technology

The *New York Sun*'s "Great Moon Hoax" of 1835 claimed that there is an alien civilization on the moon, and established the Sun as a leading, profitable newspaper.

and Society. Sensational headlines have always sold newspapers. Dramatic teasers and news clips have always coaxed viewers to tune into TV news shows. State and private actors have always conspired to smear the reputations of political opponents. Today, sensational headlines, dramatic photos, and absurd stories are clickbait that achieve those same ends while also increasing hits, rankings, and advertising dollars for their publishers.

What has changed since the *New York Sun*'s "Great Moon Hoax" of 1835 is the mass amplification of the effects of fake news. According to the Cybersecurity & Infrastructure Security Agency (CISA, n.d.), there are two main types of fake news.

- **Misinformation** is false, but is not created or shared with the intention of causing harm. For example, early in the COVID-19 pandemic, it was believed that taking ibuprofen (Advil or Motrin) could cause severe complications if taken to treat symptoms of COVID-19. Well-meaning people spread the news quickly and widely via social media without evidence of its factual (or non-factual) nature. Another important example of misinformation is the absence or erasure of information from the news cycle. When a news story disappears from the whirlwind of the 24-hour news cycle, we tend to forget about its existence even if it hasn't been resolved. Local stories most easily are forgotten or overrun by larger, more dramatic events.

- **Disinformation** is deliberately created to mislead, harm, or manipulate a person, social group, organization, or country. For example, in 2016, a lone, armed gunman burst into a busy Washington, DC, pizza restaurant and began shooting. Fortunately, no one was hurt. The gunman believed that the restaurant was a cover for a pedophile sex ring

The Point Is . . .

There Isn't a Blanket Answer to the Question, "Who Can You Trust?"

1. It requires that we pause before contributing to the ongoing infodemic and the spread of misinformation and disinformation. Here are some important steps you can take.

2. Stop! Don't just repost something because it looks cool, crazy, or because you're the first to see it. A healthy dose of skepticism can go a long way to protecting the truth. A headline that looks too good, too wild, or too suspicious to be true probably is—even in the midst of today's extremes of behaviour.

3. Pay attention to the source of the article or social media post. Is the source one that is recognized and reputable? Who grants that level of value to the source? Who pays their costs? Is it an old and trusted journalistic or academic source? Is its purpose satirical? Is the article an opinion piece, that is, the opinion of a particular person or representative of a group of people? What makes it credible to you?

4. Are other credible sources publishing the same information? If not, what is the consensus about this information among credible sources?

5. If an "expert" is being quoted, is the issue at hand part of that person's expertise? If not, don't assume their claim is accurate. A person expert at singing or acting may not be the most reliable source of news. A physicist is not necessarily knowledgeable about medical practice. Some fields of "expertise" really do not know what people assume they know, but they will not admit that openly.

6. If you're not sure about the quality of the information, don't share it—not even to say you're not sure it's real. People are less likely to read your opinion and are more likely to continue sharing the post.

---

led by Hillary Clinton and members of her campaign. The claims, which were by all accounts false, were fabricated and posted to anonymous online chatrooms by nefarious individuals with the sole intent of sowing division and causing legal problems for the Clinton campaign. Another important example of disinformation is the claim of disinformation with respect to facts. For example, the claim by a politician or expert that a factor in a story is untrue when, in reality, it is true causes confusion and dissention among the listeners. The politician's or expert's position of power—to many minds—gives them the benefit of the doubt, leading many to believe their false claim.

Both types of fake news sow confusion and create polarization between groups of people in society. This not only sows discord among families and friends but affects democratic processes, public health initiatives, climate policy, and civil rights movements.

12.4 The Technology of Social Media and Its Effects on Society

On the surface, social media seem quite harmless to the many people who use them to stay in touch with friends and family, share their recent adventures and life updates, find out what to watch, read, or listen to next, and search for new jobs, homes, products, and services. These acts, however, are precisely the behaviours that corporations and institutions use to understand and predict your interests in order

What do *you* think?

What are your media consumption habits? Do you enjoy being the first to share a breaking news story or hot take on a recent event? On what do you base your decisions when you do post?

Has the information about media in this chapter influenced you to do anything differently when you post or read something on social media?

to serve you content they think you need or want. The private corporations that own platforms such as Facebook, Instagram, TikTok, YouTube, and Google only survive because of advertising revenue. Their highly lucrative advertising models are built on data collection and algorithms that analyze those data. Social media platforms harvest the data related to your personal online behaviour and create profiles (or identities) and categories for every one of their users. They also build algorithms that compile and cross-reference all of your online behaviour along with others like you to make assumptions about who you are and predict all of the things you might be interested in. Then, they sell access to this information to product manufacturers, service providers, and content producers who want to promote their products, services, and ideas to you. The end result is the targeted ads you see on YouTube for the shoes you just searched for on Google, the suggestion to watch more videos about parrots because you watched one on Instagram, or the suggestion to join an activist group on Facebook because you watched a video by one of their spokespeople on TikTok. Again, this may seem harmless on its surface. Remember, however, that knowledge is integral to achieving and maintaining authority (Strange, 1994). The act of collecting data related to your personal online behaviour by institutions that are invisible to you, for reasons that are unknown to you, is an act of producing knowledge about you. And because you do not have access to it, it is an act of secretive gatekeeping and a powerful tool of power and authority. These same algorithms build filter bubbles feeding you more of what they think you want and less of what they think you don't want. In using algorithms to determine the best content for you, social media constructs your reality. It determines what is important to you, what you believe, what you like, and what you want in your life. On the other hand, even if you are hyper-aware of those "feeds," the algorithms are cutting you off from other sorts of information and possibilities that you might prefer. In ways subtle and not so subtle, they also determine what is possible and what your life outcomes might be.

Algorithms and Social Inequality

In producing knowledge about you, corporations and institutions use online behavioural data and algorithms to determine not only which products and services you might be interested in, but which opportunities are made available to you and what information is served to you, ultimately playing a role in shaping your life. Your online behaviour leaves a breadcrumb trail of data behind you that is used to compile a profile of who you are. Assuming you are most active online at home, your internet service provider (ISP) contains your postal code, which carries with it statistics about your neighbourhood including average income, crime rates, age, housing conditions, education, home rental versus ownership, debt, employment, and family size. Additionally, Google collects every search you've ever conducted and every link you've ever clicked—even using incognito browsers doesn't protect you entirely. The cookies present on every website you visit collect your clicks, time spent on a page, purchases, and shares to social media. Social media platforms collect what you view, click, like, share, join, and say on their sites. All of this data combined creates a profile of who you are and is used by corporations and institutions to play a role in determining your life chances.

Consider the case of Maria, a single mom renting a small home in a low-income neighbourhood trying to find a way to make a better life for herself and her kids. Like many of her neighbours she is a first-generation immigrant with a foreign college diploma and professional accreditation. She has a decent job as an administrative assistant at a local factory; she has a minor traffic infraction; and she has accumulated credit card debt to pay for her growing kids' needs. Her car is on its last legs, so she's been searching used car websites for deals. She has been searching for night school programs so she can improve her chances for a better-paying job. She has been searching online for a financial advisor to help manage her debt. This single mom trying to make a better life for her family is a target for ads from expensive, sketchy private colleges; same-day loan sharks; and less-than-reputable home and auto insurance providers. She is not a target for ads from certified postsecondary institutions or reputable insurance and banking institutions because their target profiles include people from higher socioeconomic backgrounds. Furthermore, because she clicks on the ads served to her by Google she is served more of the same information and ads in search results and on social media. Her opportunities, as far as she can see, are limited to the information presented to her online.

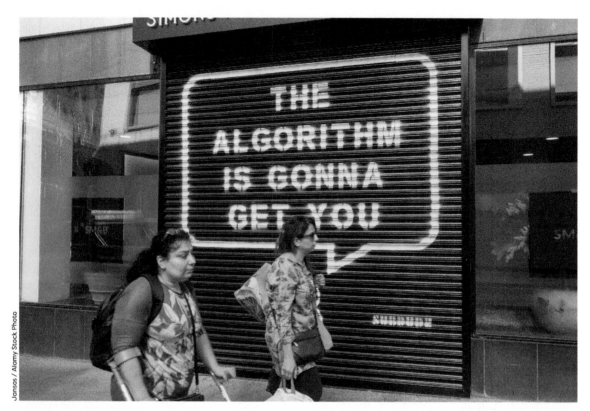

Jansos / Alamy Stock Photo

People walking past the Algorithm Is Gonna Get You by Subdude, across from Facebook's Rathbone Square HQ in London.

Furthermore, when Maria applies online for insurance, a loan, night school, or a new job, those institutions have access to the same data and algorithms and use them to determine her chances for acceptance. The decisions she makes based on this information trap her in a feedback loop that keeps her where she is—like many others like her—creating an environment that justifies the assumptions made by society and institutions about who people are, how they should be treated, and, ultimately, what opportunities and life experiences they will have (O'Neil, 2016, p. 29). At the opposite end of the spectrum are those who live in postal codes with higher average income, education, and housing prices. They are less likely to have encounters with law enforcement, less likely to need immediate debt management services, and more likely to have better life opportunities overall (O'Neil, 2016, p. 29). While they are still targets of ads and content generated by algorithms, they are more likely to be served content that helps them remain upwardly mobile (O'Neil, 2016, p. 81). By deciding who people are and what social categories they

"belong" to, the companies and institutions that use algorithms decide what options are available to people, ultimately constructing their reality.

Social Media and Democratic Society

In 2018, the world learned that the 2016 American election that made former President Donald Trump the 45th president of the United States had been influenced by foreign actors using Facebook's algorithms. The issue of surveillance by media that constitutes an invasion of the privacy of citizens has profound effects not merely on commerce but on the outcome of elections, national stability, and international conflicts (Zuboff, 2019). Major newspapers—the *New York Times*, the *Observer*, and the *Guardian*—received documents from a whistleblower inside European-based data firm Cambridge Analytica providing evidence that the firm improperly acquired the private Facebook data of as many as 87 million mainly American users. The intent was to build psychological profiles and targeted content on behalf of the Republican political campaign, thereby influencing the

The Point Is . . .

There's Always a Human in the Loop

While data and algorithms take a lot of blame for some types of social stratification, it's important to remember that algorithms do not create or analyze and use themselves. Much in the way that we can't blame the internet-at-large for other social problems like political polarization, we have to remember that the objectives of data and algorithms are established by humans with certain predilections and biases. Data-produced algorithms are analyzed and interpreted by humans who decide what is important and how it will be used. All of these purportedly neutral or objective processes are filtered through the biases (known or unknown) of naturally flawed (or nefarious) human intentions (O'Neil, 2016, p. 21).

decision-making of voters in the 2016 election (Confessore, 2018). Former Trump aide Steve Bannon was a board member of Cambridge Analytica; the firm had recently received a $15 million investment from a wealthy Republican donor (Rosenberg et al., 2018). Later the *New York Times* learned that Trump's security advisor, John Bolton, also had financial ties to the firm. The *Times* also learned that Cambridge Analytica had been in contact with a Russian-linked oil company that was interested in ways Facebook profile data were used to target American voters. These claims have been denied by the oil company (Confessore, 2018). Fallout from this massive breach of personal privacy resulted in the firing of Cambridge Analytica's chief executive. Facebook was called before the Federal Trade Commission, which was investigating whether Facebook had violated user privacy agreements. Many users deleted their Facebook profiles in protest. Facebook's Mark Zuckerberg met the issue with extended silence (Confessore, 2018). The *Times* and the *Observer* also reported that Britain's 2016 Brexit ("British exit," i.e., the United Kingdom's vote to leave the European Union in 2016) campaign used Cambridge Analytica to help swing the results in their favour, implicating advisors to then British Prime Minister Theresa May (Confessore, 2018).

You might wonder how so many users' data was harvested and used to build profiles that would be used to target them with content that would inform their voting decisions. While many have assumed that this was done using a simple Facebook quiz or game, it actually was done through an online psychology questionnaire hosted by a global online survey provider. In order to complete the survey and get their results, users were required to grant access to their Facebook profiles. This access opened the door to the company's access to all of the information in their profiles—and in their friends' profiles (Confessore, 2018). Using this information, Cambridge Analytica built psychological profiles and categories of users who would be sympathetic to the Republican political agenda and began serving them content that would encourage their support and their turnout on election day. Zuboff (quoted in Kavenna, 2019) points out: "The age of surveillance capitalism is a titanic struggle between capital and each one of us. It is a direct intervention into free will, an assault on human autonomy." It is the capture of our intimate personal details, even of our faces. "They have no right to my face, to take it when I walk down the street."

This example is not the only instance of Facebook and other social media being used by political actors to manipulate the decisions and actions of its users. Rohingya Muslims in Myanmar sued Facebook claiming that their negligence allowed the platform's algorithms to amplify the hate speech that contributed to acts of genocide (Milmo, 2021). In an attempt to subvert disinformation during the 2022 Philippine election, Facebook deleted hundreds of fake pages and profiles that were being used to influence voters. Twitter also has been identified as an important tool in the success of 2011's Arab Spring. On this point it's important to note that social media often are used as a tool to bring people together for meaningful political and social causes. The same algorithms and our inclination to gather with people like us also lead to charitable projects and beneficial social changes.

We mentioned *filter bubbles* and the *biases* of social media users and the creators of their platforms and algorithms. These concepts are important to

The Point Is . . .

Social Media Amplifies Polarization

There are groups of people who staunchly support political and social ideologies and act according to those beliefs. When groups of people become entrenched in those ideas, they tend to become politically and socially "poles apart" (like the Earth's north and south poles) with people in other camps—they are "polarized." This polarization creates tension in communities, families, and workplaces, and with governing bodies and institutions. It places us in opposing teams—winning teams and losing teams. It makes us dig in our heels when we are presented with evidence showing that those ideas might be incorrect. It makes us look for the alternate facts that prove our case. It makes us question expertise and authority. While healthy skepticism and the voice of dissent are important tools of the democratic process they must be rooted in credible evidence. When dissent is manufactured and amplified, it acts to destabilize democracy and our social fabric. The results of such dissent are events like the 6 January 2020 insurrection in Washington, DC; the February 2022 "Freedom Convoy" occupation of Ottawa; and anti-vaxxer movements that compromise individual and population health.

understanding how social media affect the democratic processes of society. They have been identified as critical factors in the increased polarization of populations. If you recall, one of the concepts behind filter bubbles is the idea that people like to associate with people who are like them. The sociological term for this is *homophily*. In this context, homophily works with algorithms to reinforce filter bubbles based on worldviews and political preferences, thus narrowing our fields of vision (Vaidhyanathan, 2021, p. 91). In other words, what we choose to look at on social media and search engines and how those platforms choose to give us content feed on one another (Vaidhyanathan, 2021, p. 91). Facebook profiles tend to be strong indicators of our likes, dislikes, beliefs, and opinions as well as which groups we belong to and which politicians and celebrities we follow. When political actors have access to the data found in user profiles, they have the ability target people who are likely to support their cause with content those people not only are likely to click and "like," but also share with their networks—activating the algorithms to provide more of the same content to those who consume it. By influencing what we believe about the world and our place in it, social media, through the intentions of various actors, algorithms, targeted content, and filter bubbles, construct our realities. They construct what we are willing to fight for, who we are willing to believe, what we believe is just, and how people should be treated.

12.5 The Effects of Social Media on the Individual

In earlier chapters, we have examined how our identities are socially constructed and negotiated. We discussed primary socialization, the social construction of the self, race, and gender, and how culture interacts with society and individuals to influence who we are and how we see ourselves—and others—in the world. We also discussed American psychologist and symbolic interactionist George Herbert Mead, who believed that we develop our sense of self by internalizing the values and behaviours of the "significant" and "generalized" others in our lives. For the purposes of this chapter, we have focused on the *generalized* other—the composite of all the people who make up a group such as a team, a local community, society writ large, and the people we're connected with on social media. Like other media, social media influence what we think of ourselves and how we want to be seen by the world around us. Social media comprise a 24/7, on-demand platform feeding us images, videos, and ideas that shape what we think about everything around us. On Instagram, TikTok, Facebook, and Twitter we see ads, videos, celebrity posts, and friends' posts of idealized bodies, "perfect" faces, luxurious vacations, fabulous jobs, sumptuous parties, and marvellous dishes from dozens of delicious cuisines. All of these offerings tend to shape our understanding of the ideal world, ideal

Damir Khabirov/Shutterstock

people, and our ideal self. What arises from this constant stream of unattainable perfection is constant tension—a gap between the place where we *are* and the place where we *think we could or should be*. Even when we know that photos are altered, that celebrities spend millions on their appearances, and that average people only post the best moments of their lives (not the worst—or even mediocre), regular social media users experience increased anxiety and depression as a result of unrealistic expectations about who they are in the real world versus how they portray themselves online.

In addition to informing how we construct ourselves, social media also provide us with a way to perform as who we want to be for others and how to negotiate how society views us. When we think about social media and the generalized other in this way, our focus shifts away from those who shape us to how we shape and present ourselves for others. **Erving Goffman**, who we discussed earlier in this book, would consider each social media platform to be one of the *stages* on which we perform ourselves, each representing a different context (where we are) and audience (who we're with). (Marwick, 2013, p. 356). Anthony Giddens (1991) is a British sociologist who considered identity to be a "project" that we work on throughout our lives, building our identities and setting ourselves apart from others through the media we consume, the clothes we wear, and how we manage the appearance of our bodies through exercise, diet, cosmetics, and surgery. On social media, we continue this project by sharing images and video

of ourselves that are composite expressions of all of those things (Marwick, 2013, p. 356). Charles Cooley would consider social media to be the *looking glass* through which we see ourselves in the eyes of our *imagined audience*. The imagined audience is who we think we're communicating with or performing for in a space where we don't know for sure, whether in public places or on social media venues.

The imagined audience has always played a significant role in helping us to decide what to think, say, and do in the various situations we might find ourselves in. On social media, though, who is our audience and how does that shape who we are online? In most real-life situations only one of our audiences would be present at a time and we perform differently for each of them. For example, we speak, behave, and even dress differently for our friends or colleagues than for our parents or for our employers. On the stages of Instagram, Facebook, Twitter, or LinkedIn you might have a mix of all of those people—plus other people you don't really know that well, like friends of friends or extended family, classmates, and colleagues. How do we manage to construct a performance meant to appeal to a certain group in a certain context when we aren't really sure who the audience is at any given moment for any given post or share? When our multiple and varied audiences are present with different expectations in our singular online world, this is known as *context collapse*—creating conflict when the norms associated with different groups conflict (Marwick & Boyd, 2011, pp. 114–33).

The Point Is . . .

Context Collapse Is More Than Fodder for Sitcoms

The repercussions of context collapse can have serious implications in our lives. For example, if you've called in sick from work to go to the beach with friends on a hot, sunny day and one of those friends tags you in a photo playing volleyball by the lake on Facebook, and your supervisor is one of your Facebook friends, you could be reprimanded or lose your job.

Managing the prevention of context collapse can be exhausting as we manoeuvre through our online worlds. We've learned various strategies to do it including segregated friends lists, limiting social media posts to neutral or impersonal content, or creating separate accounts used to share different content with different audiences.

What do *you* think?

As you find yourself transitioning from a time in your life where most of your social media followers are friends to a time when you might start to see potential colleagues and employers show up in your feeds, what strategies do you find yourself employing to manage how you perform and are perceived by these different audiences?

The Self and Society

Some scholars were hopeful that the internet and its varied outlets for constructing and negotiating our selves for the world would free society from the problems of race, gender, and even class (Marwick, 2013, p. 357). Radical theorists imagine a post-*human* world where cyberspace liberates people from their bodies, creating virtual versions of themselves with higher consciousnesses (Marwick, 2013, p. 357). What we've learned, though, is that people don't create online personas that are all that different from the real-world versions of themselves (Baym, 2010, p. 106). While some people create alternate or secret profiles to protect their private lives, the profile we share with the largest audience is the one that most closely resembles our real-world persona. And here I stress *for the most part*. Many people can only be their true selves in their limited, alternate online

worlds because they're afraid of judgment, ridicule, or persecution as a result of who they believe their true self is. People struggling to come to terms with their gender identity or sexuality, for example, use alternate profiles to explore their self-performance, understand better who they are, and find support in communities of people who are like them. Some eventually integrate their online worlds and real-life worlds, while many never do.

We also know that social problems such as racism, sexism, and homophobia are systemic and find their way into the online world as easily as they do in the real world (Marwick, 2013, p. 357). Social media are powerful tools for connecting people for social good, but they also sow division and further oppression (Marwick, 2013, p. 360). Despite the fact that social media provide people with tools to create and perform their desired identities, they continue to reproduce ideas of what society deems to be "normal" or "idealized," specifically, accomplished, attractive, fit, and educated (Marwick, 2013, p. 362). In these ways, social media further construct reality. They construct what we believe to be normal or acceptable in society, how we fit into those ideals, and how we perceive ourselves. They are tools we use to construct how others perceive us. In multiple and complex ways, social media construct our identities and the realities associated with them.

Wrap It Up

Summary

In this chapter I've tried to give you a sense of the varied and conflicting roles media play in constructing reality, society, and our identities. We've looked at aspects of what you've learned in other chapters about race and ethnicity, gender and

sexuality, culture, and socialization and identity because they are influenced by, and actively influence, media in a number of ways.

You've learned a bit about the evolution of media, including how it has been used as a nation-building tool in Canada and what measures have been put in place to protect that project. You've been introduced to some important concepts about media technology as well as some theories that help us understand the impact media have on society and individuals. We've also looked at how the pace and spectacle of information in the media are changing and how we consume content of all types, but particularly the news. In analyzing these shifts in media and technology, you have also been introduced to how media and media consumption are impacting important sociological foundations, such as our democratic processes, how we understand ourselves, and how we engage with the world around us.

Think Back

Questions for Critical Review

1. What was the importance of the public sphere and why does it still matter today?
2. How have media been used in Canada's nation-building project?
3. Why were Canadian content regulations created, and do you think they're still important in today's media-saturated environment?
4. What did McLuhan mean when he said "The medium is the message"? Do you think he was right? Why or why not?
5. How does gatekeeping reinforce social hierarchies? Can you explain an instance of gatekeeping that you feel has affected you?
6. How do the algorithms used in search engines and social media reinforce social inequality? Can you explain an aspect of your life that you feel has been positively or negatively affected by these types of algorithms?
7. How do filter bubbles affect our understanding of reality?
8. Do you feel that your sense of self is shaped by your social media activity? If so, in what ways and what do you think of that impact?

Read On

Suggested Print and Online Resources

Ground News, https://ground.news/
This Canadian-based news aggregator makes it easy to compare news sources, read between the lines of media bias, and break free from algorithms. It identifies the source, location, and time of a news item along with its bias (left, right, or centre). It will also determine which bias you lean toward and identify blind spots in your news consumption habits.

Joanna Kavenna, "Surveillance Capitalism Is an Assault on Human Autonomy," *The Guardian*, 4 October 2019
This interview with Shoshana Zuboff explains the importance of personal privacy and how the loss of it on social media and on the internet more generally is compromising our democracies.

Cathy O'Neil, *Weapons of Math Destruction: How Big Data Increases Inequality and Threatens Democracy* (New York: Penguin Random House, 2016)
O'Neil discusses the societal impact of algorithms and how big-data algorithms are increasingly used in ways that reinforce pre-existing social inequalities.

Karim Amir and Jehane Noujaim (directors), *The Great Hack*, documentary film, 2019
This Netflix documentary explores how Cambridge Analytica came to symbolize the dark side of social media in the wake of the 2016 US presidential election.

Siva Vaidhyanathan, *Anti-Social Media: How Facebook Disconnects Us and Undermines Democracy* (New York: Oxford University Press, 2021)
Vaidhyanathan details the ways in which social media interfere with democratic society.

13 Education

Reading this chapter will help you to . . .

- Discuss the history of public education in Canada from the mid-nineteenth century to the present.

- Explain how Foucault's concept of the docile body applies to education.

- Look critically at education through the lens of cultural reproduction theory.

- Outline the advantages and disadvantages of "streaming" (or "tracking") in elementary and secondary education.

- Discuss the positive and negative effects on postsecondary education of becoming reliant on (a) adjunct instructors, (b) online education, and (c) corporate sponsorship of research and infrastructure.

- State your view, from a sociologist's standpoint, of plagiarism occurring today in postsecondary institutions.

- Assess the social value of having schools run by and for marginalized groups such as Indigenous and African Canadian students.

Photograph by Della Rollins

For Starters

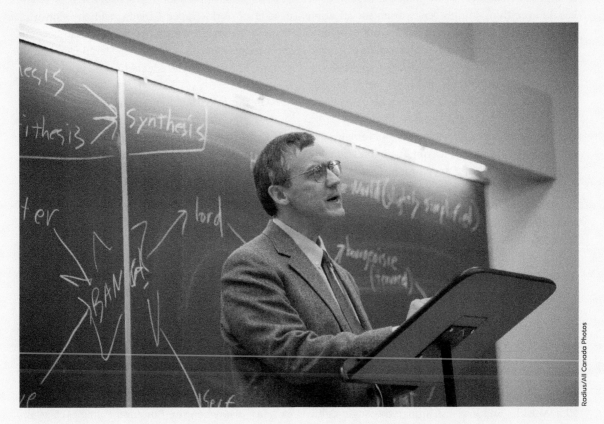

Radius/All Canada Photos

Take a good look at your sociology professor or TA—right now, while they're not looking. Are they relatively young? Do they always seem to be running late, to be hurrying in or out, to be distracted before and after class? Does your prof also teach at another school? Does the department secretary know who you're speaking about when you say your instructor's name?

If your instructor is teaching an intro sociology course, chances are they've been hired only for a session, a semester, or a year. They probably aren't a full-time, tenured member of the department. They likely fall into the category of "contract faculty" or "sessional staff." Or maybe they're an "adjunct professor," which sounds a bit loftier but still means that they're teaching courses and students—particularly intro courses—that permanent staff members don't want to teach. My *Canadian Oxford Dictionary* defines

adjunct as "an assistant or a subordinate person, esp. one with a temporary appointment only."

In other words, the person teaching you may be fully qualified but an academic nomad, part of a growing postsecondary underclass that gets paid less for teaching you than full-timers do. Their growing presence is an important change taking place in education today. In this chapter we'll look at what else is changing, and why—and, most importantly, how it's affecting students and society today.

What do *you* think?

Do you think you can tell the difference between a full-time professor and an adjunct? Do you know what percentage of your instructors fill the latter category?

13.1 Introduction: Education as a Social Institution

To a sociologist, the social institution of education is important because of the multiple influences it has on everything in the society, from socialization and status formation to social order and economic productivity. When we refer to the *institution* of education, we're referring to a set of ideas about education that is both enduring and historically evolving and how the goals of the nation can be fused to accomplish goals that are deemed important to an international society. Education is an extremely powerful tool for promoting ideas among impressionable young people. Children spend more time at school than they do with their parents.

Education has a significant impact on the socialization of children and young adults. At school, behaviours are modified, skills for future employment are taught, social interaction and conflict are negotiated, and notions of social reality are defined. How well children do in school plays a large role in determining their potential social acceptability and mobility.

Prior to World War II, Canada was comprised of two principal populations: Anglo-Celtic Protestant and Franco-Catholic, which were ethnocentric as regards immigrants who were Buddhist, Shinto, Sikh, Muslim, and Jewish. Through the Anglo-Celtic Protestant missions to China and India, less ethnocentric influences were being infused into the mix of classes who supported those missions through their churches. "Race" was not considered a barrier to faith. The emphasis in its immigration policy was to build Canada through its agriculture and mineral extraction and to build its infrastructure, especially the railroads joining east to west.

13.2 The Rise of Public Education in Canada

Before the Industrial Revolution in Europe and North America there was little interest in educating the masses. But beginning with the rise of industrial capitalism, companies started to demand more from their labour force. Specifically, as industry became more complex, it required a more disciplined, trainable, and literate workforce in order to be more economically productive. Industrialization and public education, then, became interdependent in the same way that labour is dependent on capital and capital on labour.

Egerton Ryerson, the son of a Loyalist, at the age of 23 began to oppose John Strachan, Anglican Archdeacon of York, Upper Canada, and the powerful "Family Compact." Within five years he had become the strongest voice in defence of Methodism and in support of better public education:

> On the importance of education generally we may remark, it is as necessary as the light—it should be as common as water and as free as air. Education among the people is the best security of a good government and constitutional liberty; it yields a steady, unbending support to the former, and effectually protects the latter. . . . The first object of a wise government should be the education of the people. . . . Partial knowledge is better than total ignorance. If total ignorance be a bad and dangerous thing, every degree of knowledge lessens both the evil and the danger. (*Christian Guardian*, 1831, quoted in Putman, 2019)

In Canada, education was seen as an important means of achieving economic modernization as early as 1846 when the Common School Act established the structure of the education system. Ryerson travelled in the United States and noticed aspects of the organization of public education that he published in his "Report on a System of Public Elementary Instruction in Upper Canada." It was so well received that it became the basis for the revision to the Common School Act in 1850. Ryerson became the president of Upper Canada Academy in 1841 when it was renamed Victoria College, the first of the original three church-affiliated liberal arts schools within the University of Toronto.

According to Canadian sociologist **Stephen Schecter** (1977), Ryerson's public education model was not just a method of producing social *order*: it was also a way to ensure social *control* by subverting potential conflict among immigrants, particularly the incoming Irish labourers forced to leave their country during the potato famine of the 1840s. Two waves of settlers were accommodated. However, in 1846–7, 100,000 immigrants arrived sick with typhus,

70 per cent of them Irish, and about 10,000 of them died in the ships or soon after they landed. The Irish were poor, and their reputation for rowdy hooliganism preceded them to North America. Speaking of the unskilled Catholic migrants, Ryerson warned: "The physical disease and death which have accompanied their influx among us may be the precursor of the worst pestilence of social insubordination and disorder" (Schecter, 1977, p. 373). Could education avert the threat of discontent from these "disorderly" labourers by assimilating them into the dominant Protestant culture?

To encourage social order, Ryerson brought a number of principles to his ideas for educational reform:

- Secularization that would keep any one church from dominating the educational system.
- Standardizing textbooks so that all students were receiving the best available vehicles for learning.
- Ensuring Canadian authors of textbooks so that students were receiving relevant teaching materials in terms of their own culture.
- Training teachers in the principles of pedagogy and ensuring that they had sufficient riches of education to pass on to their students (raising the levels of pedagogy through teachers' colleges called at first "normal schools" because they set "norms" not only for students but for the quality of teaching they would receive).
- Planning schools with school libraries as healthy, well-lit, and well-provided learning environments.
- Ensuring that education is free to all students, whatever their family incomes or social class. "Proving his point that education was a necessity, he was able to show, for example, in Toronto alone, less than half of the 4,450 children in the city were regular school attendees" (Putman, 2019).

The Common School Act of 1871 made education free and compulsory to the age of 12. Municipalities were required to provide the funding needs asked by their local school boards. It also permitted schools to be paid for entirely through provincial and municipal funds. Thus, school boards could eliminate school fees but were not compelled to. The Act also permitted the founding of separate schools, which would eventuate in provincially funded Roman Catholic schools and racially segregated schools.

As Methodism was not in the iconoclastic stream of Protestantism that haunted the Anabaptist sects, Ryerson initiated collections of art for the edification of student teachers in the teachers' college that were open to the public as well. This initiative fostered an appreciation and expectation for other such cultural institutions, such as the Ontario College of Art and Design, formed in 1876, and the Royal Ontario Museum, founded in 1914.

Schecter (1977) argues that compulsory, state-run education legitimized and acted to support social inequality, as it was premised on centralization and uniformity—instruments of social control to be used on the emerging working class. Schools, especially in rural areas, often were staffed from the "graduating" class of Grade 8 young people. To ensure more uniform standards of quality in education—from textbooks to teachers—provincial boards were established to act as executive bodies to set up and maintain provincial "normal schools." School boards were able to enforce codes of discipline and enact hierarchical authority relations that placed students and parents in positions subordinate to school officials, including the teachers. Such practices served to a significant extent to subordinate all social classes in attendance in the public schools and to punish those who could not meet the "norms" (i.e., "deviants").

For students with disabilities, compulsory education could be used as an instrument of crushing social subordination. Consider the way education was used to rank and sort children in ways that sometimes were extremely destructive to those deemed "inferior." University of Lethbridge sociology professor Claudia Malacrida studied Alberta's Michener Institute, where many children were forcibly detained after being labelled "feeble-minded," a technical term based on the questionable science of the time. In her study *A Special Hell: Institutional Life in Alberta's Eugenic Years* (2015), she identifies three ways in which children of different intellectual abilities were sorted out of the mainstream:

1. through truancy laws punishing those who did not come to class;

2. through tests and curriculums that standardized expectations of educational success; and

3. through "health" testing conducted via medical and psychological examinations (Malacrida, 2015, pp. 11–12).

Once sorted out of the regular system, these children were institutionalized in places such as the Michener Institute. There, most of their freedoms or rights (including their reproductive rights) were taken away. Their education (deemed "vocational") consisted mainly of forced labour that often served the financial needs of the institutions, a situation very similar to that of the residential schools that housed Indigenous children.

On the other hand, the School Act of 1891 provided for levels of education that represented a very great improvement in the status of the poor as more of them became workers with incomes that provided for smaller families. It provided better opportunities for the girls of the lower classes by raising the ceiling to 14 years of age. These were the students who would create the Canadian middle and upper classes as the society stood at the time of World War I. While the private schools still functioned as a hothouse for privileged boys (the one private school for girls at that time was Bishop Strachan School, 1867), the vast majority of students who would go on to become leaders in industry, government, medicine, education, law, and business rose through the public school system.

While state-run school systems legitimize the social order, the Canadian social order was aimed at peace, order, and good government. Ryerson's lack of imagination concerning Indigenous people and the residential schools had particularly dreadful effects because he underestimated their ability to meet the same norms as the rest of the population and he had no plan for carrying education into the reserves. However, he certainly did not expect his views to be picked up years later, and after his death, to be appended to a revised education act. He has been pilloried because he was well-enough known to provide a convenient political scapegoat. He had far more altruistic goals than a fear of uprising by the unschooled impoverished. He aimed to lift them out of destitution into self-respecting, working citizens and, for the most part, he succeeded admirably.

Postwar Expansion and the Human Capital Thesis

The Canadian economy after World War II required a workforce that was better educated than before, fuelling an expansion of colleges and universities across Canada to match the economic boom that peaked during the 1960s. Government officials may have loudly championed the expansion of postsecondary institutions as increasing access to education to all classes, but historians Newson and Buchbinder (1988) have argued that economic considerations were the driving force. One of the economic realities at that point in history was the huge wave of immigrants, most of them refugees from a ravaged Europe.

The perceived relationship between the expansion of education and economic growth is part of the **human capital thesis**, which asserts that just as industrial societies invest in factories and equipment to attain a higher standard of living, so they invest in schools to enhance the knowledge and skills of their workers. The human capital thesis argues that marginalized groups earn less money than dominant groups because they possess less human capital in the form of education, skill, and experience. Returning military people were offered exceptional opportunities at colleges and universities, which allowed many to train as teachers or for business in the burgeoning economy. But in the schools leading to postsecondary education, the Roman Catholic system struggled for four decades to be as fully and adequately funded as the public high schools. The public schools, meanwhile, were dealing with the increasingly diverse ethnicities of new Canadians by becoming less Protestant and more secularized. The privately funded Jewish schools remained sidelined as the much larger and more powerful Roman Catholic population finally received full funding to Grade 13 for all separate school boards in the province of Ontario with Bill Davis's Bill 30 on 12 June 1984.

Models of Public Education in Canada

The Assimilation Model

Education in Canada during its early history was based on a monocultural model that emphasized assimilation into the dominant culture. John Strachan and the Family Compact were intent on making Anglicanism the state and schools' religion before

The Point Is . . .

Corporate Sponsorship Poses a Double Threat to Academic Research

Universities and colleges facing government funding challenges (in other words, all universities and colleges) often seek out corporate sponsorships, particularly in the area of research. While, under the best circumstances, these relationships can bring benefits both to the corporate donor and to the postsecondary institution, they can bring a double threat to the credibility of research. The first threat is infringement on the academic freedom of academic researchers. The second is a conflict of interest on the part of senior academic administrators who may be on the payroll of the corporate sponsor, typically in a position on the board of directors.

Both of these threats arose in the case of the University of Calgary and the Enbridge Centre for Corporate Sustainability (ECCS), established 2011–12 and sponsored (not surprisingly) by Enbridge, the Alberta-based multinational fuel distributor. The situation has been well documented in a report commissioned by the Canadian Association of University Teachers (CAUT) in 2017 (Hearn & Van Harten, 2017), an "explainer" in the investigative journalism magazine *The Narwhal* (Wilt, 2017), and in a 2018 article in the *Canadian Journal of Sociology*, examining the sharp difference in corporate and non-corporate media coverage of the report (McCartney & Gray, 2018).

Under the sponsorship agreement, Enbridge was to give $225,000 per year for 10 years to the University of Calgary to fund a research institute within the university's school of business. The trouble was that the president of the university at the time held a position on a corporate board at Enbridge, a part-time job for which she was compensated $130,500 annually, a little more than one-third of her salary with the university (Wilt, 2017). This arrangement might not have been a problem had the president kept out of any business involving the proposed ECCS. However, the CAUT found evidence that she not only involved herself in the sponsorship negotiations but invoked her position on the Enbridge board to pressure university colleagues to support the deal.

Once the Enbridge sponsorship was in place, the university appointed a faculty member to head up the newly minted ECCS. He was subsequently removed from the position after publicly opposing the Enbridge Northern Gateway Pipeline. The individual later spoke of having received pressure from university administrators to toe the Enbridge line. To his thinking, he was being asked to step out of his role as an independent, objective researcher to publicly defend the corporate interests of Enbridge. The CAUT report concludes that the faculty member's academic freedom was compromised, "due to a desire on the part of senior U of C leadership to please a significant donor" (Hearn & Van Harten, 2017, p. 4).

One of the recommendations of the CAUT report was that senior university administrators should not hold corporate board positions outside of the university, as doing so might compromise the academic freedom of the university. At the very least, the president of the university should have recused herself from the sponsorship negotiations, refusing to participate because of her conflict of interest.

Egerton Ryerson jumped into the ring as the champion of greater freedom of religion in education and defused that monocultural model. Waves of immigration have brought particular challenges to further expand the parameters of that system. Catholics were allowed to have their own school system. Jewish people also were allowed to have their own schools. If people wanted to stay in their own ethnic circles and build their own ethnic churches and schools, they could and did. While Canada never proposed the sort of assimilation model practised in the United States, the relative power of the established school systems made the Canadian mosaic somewhat "vertical."

The flaw in the American assimilation model is that it failed to recognize that racial bias and discrimination—both inside and outside the school system—make the level playing field on which the

What do you think?

Since the early 1970s, decreases in the taxes charged to corporations (but not to individuals) have contributed to cuts in governmental funding for postsecondary institutions. This shift in the burden of taxation has allowed the corporate sector to form stronger ties with cash-hungry colleges and universities.

1. Should colleges and universities court and accept corporate sponsorship? (Remember, those sponsorships help to pay for new buildings and equipment you might benefit from.) If you say, "No," then what other avenues should academic institutions pursue to make up the shortfall in funding? If you say, "Yes," then what ground rules should be in place to govern these kinds of relationships?
2. Should university faculty be allowed to hold positions on corporate boards? If so, under what circumstances?
3. Shouldn't everyone be allowed to earn a little extra on the side? What happens to your fiduciary relationship to your students and to the university that hired you when you negotiate your academic freedom with a commercial firm that owes its loyalty only to the stockholders?

assimilation model is premised virtually impossible. According to Henry and Tator (2006, p. 213), the emphasis on monoculturalism (the promotion of just one culture) as opposed to multiculturalism formed a pervasive ideology that "influenced the training of educators, the practices of teaching, the content and context of learning, the hiring and promotion practices of boards, and the cultural values and norms underpinning all areas of school life." At first, students were expected to simply leave their cultural, religious, and ethnic identities at the door. Their first step in acculturation would be to learn English (or French). Gradually, classes teaching English as a Second Language (ESL) became available in many communities, which allowed young adults to prepare for further schooling or for jobs. Having a better command of English, or of French in Quebec, gave newcomers greater social mobility. The 1950s and 1960s saw family reunification immigration, mostly to the cities of Ontario. Toronto had the largest urban population of Italians outside of Rome. The Caribbean population

grew. More people came from the Philippines. In the next decade, immigration speeded up from Asia.

The 1990s brought more new Canadians from Africa but from different countries in Africa, which does not lead to a collective sense of the immigration experience or to mutual assistance programs. One study of the African diaspora in Vancouver indicates that these immigrants consistently experienced downward social mobility because their education and skills often are not recognized or valued in Canada. Many are drawn from professional and semi-professional careers in Africa only to find that they must pursue very low-status and vulnerable jobs. Immigrants are no longer necessarily victims of war or persecution. Many are making a move they consider strategic. For that reason, they may arrive in Toronto but also target for their destination a less dense urban centre, such as Halifax (Nourpanah & Barber, 2022). In 1997, the British handover of Hong Kong to its citizens prompted a huge exodus of its wealthy citizens as well as many of the very rich from the People's Republic of China. They were Chinese but had little in common with the Chinese Canadians long established in Chinatowns and suburbs of the big cities. They pushed up housing prices in Vancouver, Richmond, Surrey, Toronto, and Ottawa.

In less than a century, Toronto, the capital of Ontario, had metamorphized from a Victorian culture, 75 per cent British Anglo-Protestant and 25 per cent mixed European Roman Catholic, especially Irish, with small minorities of Jewish and other ethnicities, to a highly diverse population in which those of British heritage are in the minority. The suburbs expanded and with them the need for more schools. In the 1950s, boards of education doubled the number of public elementary schools. Secondary schools reorganized in the 1960s and provided more options for students to reduce the dropout rates. By the 1970s, the Metropolitan Separate (i.e., Roman Catholic) School Board had become the largest in Canada, with the largest educational research department. Many larger cities' school boards also had research departments studying options in school and classroom designs, running academic assessment tests, co-ordinating with academic superintendents, and tracking demographic changes throughout their jurisdictions. Heritage language classes were instituted in the 1970s.

Such rapid changes in the city's demographics, which were replicated in smaller cities and to some extent even in rural areas where high school children were bussed to district schools, created social conflicts among the older, established immigrants and newer ones that were passed down to their children. In *Towards Race Equity in Education* (2017), Carl James, in a study focused on Black students, provides an overview of the strategies undertaken by the provincial government to address the disadvantages experienced by Black children in Ontario: a provincial advisory committee working paper on race and ethnocultural relations (1988); the Stephen Lewis Report commissioned by Premier Bob Rae (June 1992).

> First, what we are dealing with, at root, and fundamentally, is anti-Black racism. While it is obviously true that every visible minority community experiences the indignities and wounds of systemic discrimination throughout Southern Ontario, it is the Black community which is the focus. It is Blacks who are being shot, it is Black youth that is unemployed in excessive numbers, it is Black students who are being inappropriately streamed in schools, it is Black kids who are disproportionately dropping-out, it is housing communities with large concentrations of Black residents where the sense of vulnerability and disadvantage is most acute, it is Black employees, professional and non-professional, on whom the doors of upward equity slam shut. Just as the soothing balm of "multiculturalism" cannot mask racism, so racism cannot mask its primary target. (James, 2017, p. 7, quoting Lewis, 1992, p. 2)

In 1992, the Bob Rae NDP government used the reports it had received to institute sweeping changes to the Education Act in Ontario to make education more equitable for Black and other visible minority students. The election in 1995 of a Mike Harris Progressive Conservative government ended this effort to reduce streaming, high drop-out rates, the Eurocentric curriculum, and a lack of visible minority teachers. In its place came a zero tolerance policy for misbehaviour, greater disciplinary authority for school officials, and the gutting of ethnocultural equity and anti-racism policies and programs. The Harris government also stopped the collection of data

that would have revealed quickly the effects of its draconian disciplinary strategy, the same sort of strategy that Stephen Harper would enact as prime minister in 2010 by cancelling the long-form census, thereby thwarting the data collection needed by sociologists and everyone else interested in social institutions.

Children of white ethnicities and multigenerational Canadian identities were caught in the same net of uncaring or ignorance and of intolerance that forced them out of school and into the streets and jails. Rural children who were economically disadvantaged or physically disabled were as likely to be damaged by these disciplinary policies as urban children. The rural teens were more likely to have British, Irish, Scandinavian, European, or Indigenous ancestry but they were as vulnerable as their urban peers who were Caribbean or African Blacks or Muslims from Iran or from Pakistan. Children with physical problems, such as auditory processing difficulties, uncorrected vision problems, and more severe disabilities such as spina bifida, dyslexia, or autism were met in their struggles with harsh methods and devastating consequences. One should not confuse Conservative provincial politics with the British or English influence on Canadian culture; the Harris government's policies in Ontario were equal-opportunity strategies for tragedy.

Multicultural Education

Canada's federal government implemented its official policy of multiculturalism in 1971 to preserve and promote cultural diversity, while removing the

> **What do you think?**
> 1. One of the assets of a Canadian education in English is that English has become the international language of commerce, diplomacy, digital communication, sport, entertainment, and (to some extent) education. To what extent is it important for people learning English also to learn about the heritage of British and American literature, history and politics, and the arts?
> 2. What would you say are the biggest obstacles (e.g., gaps in teacher training, lack of source materials, lack of political will) to designing and implementing a public school curriculum that reflects the diversity of Canadian students while tackling racism in a meaningful way? How might these obstacles be overcome?

Randy Risling/Toronto Star via Getty Images

Toronto's Africentric school opened in September 2009 to students of all ethnic backgrounds, but with a curriculum highlighting the perspectives and experiences of people of African descent. The only school of its kind in Canada has seen enrolment decline slightly over its 10-year history, despite producing decent student outcomes. Is it realistic to expect schools to cover all cultures in equal depth, or are schools centred on race and ethnicity the only answer for students who feel left out of the mainstream curriculum?

barriers that had denied certain groups full participation within Canadian society. With a new objective of creating a learning environment that would respect all learners, school boards launched initiatives to study and celebrate the lifestyles, traditions, and histories of diverse cultures (Henry & Tator, 2006). These initiatives were based on three fundamental assumptions drawn from a study of multicultural education in six countries:

1. Learning about one's culture would improve educational achievement.
2. Learning about one's culture would promote quality of opportunity.
3. Learning about other cultures would reduce prejudice and discrimination.

Problems developed. Teachers often had little knowledge of the cultures they were asked to

present. Classroom focus tended to develop a museum approach that overlooked the complexity and vitality of these different cultures (Dei, 1996). Educators would focus on historical material and the "exotic" aspects of different cultures—food, festivals, and folklore. They would omit the values and beliefs that were fundamental to shaping a particular cultural identity (Dei, 1996). They were not equipped to deal with the grim realities many Indigenous people face today.

Anti-Racism and Anti-Oppression Education

Henry and Tator (2006, pp. 213–14) argue that a glaring weakness of multicultural education is its failure to acknowledge that racism is systemic in Canadian society. While the superficial aspects of "other" cultures were being studied, the problems of racism and racial inequality were being ignored.

Anti-racism and anti-oppression education is meant to eliminate institutional and individual barriers to equity. It is intended to create a classroom environment where

- stereotypes and racist ideas can be exposed;
- sources of information can be critically examined;
- alternative and missing information can be provided;
- students can become equipped to look critically at the accuracy of the information they receive; and
- the reasons for the continued unequal social status of different group can be explored.

The aim of this model is to change institutional policies and practices, as well as individual attitudes and behaviours that reproduce social inequality.

Anti-racism and anti-oppression education first appeared in Canada in the 1980s, when some school boards introduced new policies including changes to teacher education, new criteria for reviewing and evaluating the practices of educators, greater analysis of teacher placement procedures, employment equity strategies, and resource and curriculum development (Henry & Tator, 2006). The policy has seen gains and setbacks. As Henry and Tator explain:

> While lip service is paid to . . . ensure equality of opportunity for all students in the classroom, in reality, individuals, organizations, and institutions are far more committed to maintaining the status quo, that is, the cultural hegemony of the dominant culture with which most educators identify. (Henry & Tator, 2006, p. 223)

Susan G. Enberg/Shutterstock

How do images like this support the "noble savage" version of Indigenous history? Who is left out of this image? How do Indigenous people want to be personified?

Telling It Like It Is

A Sociologist's Point of View

Eurocentric Curriculum and the University

Despite Canada's multicultural character and state-legislated multicultural policy, a Eurocentric curriculum still dominates our institutions of "higher learning." Such a curriculum offers a narrow view of the world even though there is a wealth of literature about non-European cultures by non-European academics. These works are not inferior to those of Europeans. They are integral to the attainment of a fuller, more encompassing education in which knowledge and ideas are derived from a wider, culturally diverse range of sources and perspectives. They are particularly useful in dispelling the racist assumptions and myths placed upon "others" by Western society.

In their inadequate attempts to be more inclusive, many of the professors I have encountered take a "just add and stir" approach to the inclusion of Native [*sic*] people, women, and "otherized" groups, which simply does not work. Just as they are treated as asides or special interest groups in society at large, women, Native people, and ethnic groups are often merely added on to Week 13 readings—if they are included at all. It was not until I experienced a course taught by a progressive, culturally sensitive anthropology professor who incorporated a multitude of perspectives that I became aware of the partial and limited view of the world to which I had previously been subjected. Those who perpetuate the mainstream academic curriculum seem to have fallen into a state of historical amnesia, whereby the contributions and, indeed, the very presence of non-Europeans have been omitted from Canadian history. Though Chinese, Japanese, and Indian immigrants arrived in Canada at the same time as most European immigrants, one could pass through the entire school system from kindergarten to university without being aware of the fact. Many students emerge from the school system rightfully well versed in the works of Shakespeare, Plato, and Marx, but how many learned about the cultural genocide of Native peoples, or slavery in Canada?

I am concerned that the exclusion from postsecondary curricula of minority groups, their perspectives, and their writings perpetuates a view of the world taken through a Eurocentric lens. This exclusion is also dangerous because it may lead some students to believe that since little is studied from "other" cultures, then perhaps those cultures have nothing of benefit to offer, or else they are inferior to European thought.

The courses I found the most valuable and educational were those that, though not designated as courses specifically about multiculturalism, or Native people, still managed to incorporate a variety of cultural perspectives into the readings, films, and seminars. A culturally diverse curriculum and alternative critical forms of pedagogy can also have a positive effect on the academic achievement of minority students, whose experiences and interests are not validated but are typically marginalized or excluded from the existing curriculum.

—A.R. Aujla, 1996

What do *you* think?

This narrative was written in 1996. In your experience, how much has changed?

13.3 Topics in the Sociology of Education

The Hidden Curriculum

The **hidden curriculum** is a hot topic in the sociology of education, though its definition varies depending on the issue being discussed and the vantage point of the sociologist doing the discussing. Essentially, the hidden curriculum consists of the unstated or unofficial goals of the education system. We can look at the hidden curriculum in terms of Robert Merton's concepts of **latent functions** and **latent dysfunctions**. A sociologist adopting a structural-functionalist view might say that the hidden curriculum performs a latent function (i.e., a largely unintended and unrecognized positive consequence of a social process or institution) by teaching the norms of society—the value of work, or the need to respect authority and to use one's time efficiently. A conflict sociologist might argue that the hidden curriculum reproduces the class system, hindering class mobility and therefore performing a latent *dys*function; in other words, the latent dysfunction is the unintended negative consequence of a social process or institution.

Discipline, Punishment, and Evaluation

Discipline is a key part of the hidden curriculum. Discipline here refers to controlled behaviour, not to the punishment administered for, say, speaking out of turn or passing notes in class. In primary school, discipline is focused on the body, restricting movement, impeding interaction, and normalizing confinement. Children are encouraged to use their "inside voices," to raise their hands before they speak or ask permission to go to the bathroom, to sit quietly in their seats, to keep their hands to themselves, to line up, and to be punctual. Secondary school continues to encourage physical discipline, while stressing a discipline of the mind.

Common at all levels of education is the external and internal "routinization" of the individual. Punishment is enacted if the rules are not followed: a "time out," a trip to the principal's office, a detention, or a poor mark on a report card. Grades are sanctions, designed to either negatively or positively reinforce norms.

While discipline can be enabling as well as inhibiting—many young students require and indeed thrive on a formalized structure of rules and routines—much of the discipline within the public school system can be considered repressive. This involves the mind as well as body. Children are naturally curious. Curiosity is the basis for asking questions, which is essential in the process of learning. Educators may learn at teachers' college that there are no "stupid questions," but when they have to stick to a strict schedule and a mandated curriculum, and when they are under pressure to see their students succeed on province-wide standardized tests used to measure the achievements of individual schools and teachers, they may respond negatively to student questions that deviate from the prescribed lesson plan. By the time students

reach college and university, many of them have lost much of their curiosity.

In many respects, public education creates what Michel Foucault termed the **docile body**, a group of individuals that has been conditioned, through a specific set of procedures and practices, to behave precisely the way administrators want it to (Foucault, 1977). Docile bodies are conditioned through three forms of disciplinary control:

1. hierarchical observation
2. normalizing judgment
3. the examination.

With **hierarchical observation** people are controlled through observation and surveillance. While Foucault used prisons as an example, the principle applies as well to schools and offices—places where our movements and activities are under constant surveillance within a setting based on hierarchical configurations. Educational institutions are based on a hierarchical structure in which authority figures observe and scrutinize the behaviour of students. For Foucault, hierarchical observation works on the psychology of observed individuals as much as it governs their specific movements. When people feel that they are always being watched, it induces in them an awareness of their permanent visibility, enhancing the power of the authority (Foucault, 1977, p. 172).

Normalizing judgment is another instrument of disciplinary control producing docile bodies. Individuals are judged not on the intrinsic rightness or wrongness of their actions but on how their actions rank when compared with the performance of others. Children are ranked at school, schools are ranked against one another, provincial education is ranked, and the level of education among countries is ranked. Ranking is a cultural artifact that we in Western society take for granted. Normalizing judgment is a pervasive means of control because regardless of how one succeeds, a higher level of achievement is always deemed possible.

The **examination** combines hierarchical observation with normalizing judgment. Foucault described it as "a normalizing gaze [that] establishes over individuals a visibility through which one differentiates them and judges them" (1977, p. 184). For Foucault, the normalizing gaze is the locus of power and knowledge, because it combines both "the deployment of force and the establishment of truth" (1977, p. 184). Test scores are documented and recorded, and provide detailed information about the individuals examined. Based on these records, various categories, averages, and norms are formulated by those in control, and these become the basis of knowledge. Power remains invisible, while those constructed as deviant become highly visible: those students with the thickest files are scrutinized by scores of anonymous, invisible functionaries (Foucault, 1977, p. 189). Deviance reflects difference from the norm. Both Lisa and Bart Simpson have the thickest files at school, for different reasons, but through normalizing they both are considered "deviant."

Cultural Reproduction Theory

The idea that the education system reproduces and reinforces the inequality of the surrounding society has been examined by a number of sociologists. In this section we focus on two of those researchers: Jeannie Oakes and Jean Anyon.

Jeannie Oakes and the Hidden Curriculum of Tracking

Does the education system, as part of its hidden curriculum, simply reproduce class divisions, as our conflict sociologist might argue? Jeannie Oakes (2005) put this idea, known as **cultural reproduction theory**, to the test in an influential study of tracking (or "streaming") in junior and senior high schools in the United States. Oakes defined tracking as "the process whereby students are divided into categories so that they can be assigned in groups to various kinds of classes" (Oakes, 2005, p. 3). Both classes and students are ranked according to different levels of aptitude and projected outcomes, such as whether or not students are expected to pursue a postsecondary degree. Oakes studied 297 classrooms in 25 schools in the late 1970s and early 1980s. Her work demonstrated that perceived ability is reflected through a lens of class, race, and ethnicity. She also showed that lower tracks often offer a lower quality of education than the higher tracks do. As a consequence, the American tracking system reproduces inequality.

Oakes argued that the disproportionate representation of lower-class and non-white students in the lower track reflects the cultural biases of testing and the prejudices of counsellors and teachers. The inferior quality of lower-track education came partly from the reduced expectations for students in the lower track. Lower-track English courses emphasized basic punctuation and form-filling as opposed to creative writing and studying great works of literature. Lower-track math courses emphasized basic computational skills rather than problem-solving, critical thinking, and abstract logic. Lower-track vocational courses focused on clerical skills, not the managerial and financial skills taught in the higher-track courses.

From a cultural reproduction standpoint, it is also important to examine differences in the relationships among students, between students and teachers, and between students and the institution generally. Samuel Bowles and Harold Gintis point to the "close correspondence between the social relationships which govern personal interaction in the workplace and the social relationships of the educational system" (1976, p. 12). In other words, the education system fosters social relationships that train students in the lower track to become lower-class workers.

Oakes found that teachers were more punitive in lower-track classes, while higher-track classes cultivated more trusting teacher–student relationships. She wrote, "trust, cooperation, and even good will among students were far less characteristic of low-track classes than of high. More student time and energy were spent in hostile and disruptive interchanges in these classes" (2005, p. 132).

Key to cultural reproduction theory is the **legitimization of inequality**. If students accept the notion that their differential tracking placement is fair, they believe the inequality reproduced by the education system is legitimate. Oakes found that "students in low-track classes tended to be saying that school's all right, but I'm not so good. In contrast, students in high-track classes were feeling pretty good about both their schools *and* themselves" (2005, pp. 143–4).

Overall, Oakes demonstrates that with the deep class, ethnic, and racial distinctions existing in mainstream American society, a tracking system can only reproduce inequality. She argues for a common curriculum shared by all students, and for more mixing of students of different ability levels.

Jean Anyon: Cultural Reproduction Theory in Five New Jersey Schools

An important aspect of cultural reproduction theory is the idea that the education system, as well as other social institutions, helps to reproduce the prevailing social structure. In other words, schools help upper-class children grow up to become upper-class adults, middle-class children to become middle-class adults, and so on. A landmark study of this theory is Jean Anyon's "Social Class and the Hidden Curriculum of Work" (1980), based on an ethnographic study of five elementary schools in New Jersey she carried out in 1978–9. Two of the schools she studied could be described as predominantly working-class. Here, most of the fathers had semi-skilled or unskilled jobs (assembly line work, auto repair or assembly, maintenance work); 15 per cent of the fathers were unemployed, and less than 30 per cent of the mothers worked. According to Anyon, schoolwork in these schools consisted of

> following the steps of a procedure. The procedure is usually mechanical, involving rote behavior [i.e., drilled memorization] and very little decision making or choice. The teachers rarely explain why the work is being assigned, how it might connect to other assignments, or what the idea is that lies behind the procedure or gives it coherence and perhaps meaning or significance. . . . Most of the rules regarding work are

designations of what the children are to do; the rules are steps to follow. . . . The children are usually told to copy the steps as notes. These notes are to be studied. Work is often evaluated not according to whether it is right or wrong but according to whether the children followed the right steps. (Anyon, 1980)

Students at a third school, which Anyon identified as middle-class, had parents working in skilled, well-paid trades (such as carpentry, plumbing, or electrical work), working as professionals (firefighting, teaching, accounting, etc.), or owning small

What do you think?

1. The strongest opposition to de-tracking comes from those involved with education of the "gifted." Why do you think they are more opposed to de-tracking than those involved with low-track education?

2. Imagine that you're the principal of a high school that is considering a tracking or streaming program. Come up with a list of pros and cons. How might your list change, depending on such social factors as the class, ethnicity, and overall demographics of your school?

Quick Hits

Student Examples from Oakes's Study

What is the most important thing you have learned or done so far in the class (in terms of subject matter)?

Answers from the High Track

- "We've talked about stocks/bonds and the stock market and about business in the USA."—student in junior high vocational education
- "Learned to analyze famous writings by famous people, and we have learned to understand people's different viewpoints on general ideas."—student in junior high English
- "The most important thing is the way other countries and places govern themselves economically, socially, and politically. Also, different philosophers and their theories on government and man and how their theories relate to us and now."—student in junior high social studies

Answers from the Low Track

- "Learns to fill out checks and other banking business."—student in junior high English
- "To spell words you don't know, to fill out things where you get a job."—student in junior high English
- "I learned that English is boring."—student in senior high school English

Source: Oakes (2005, pp. 68–71).

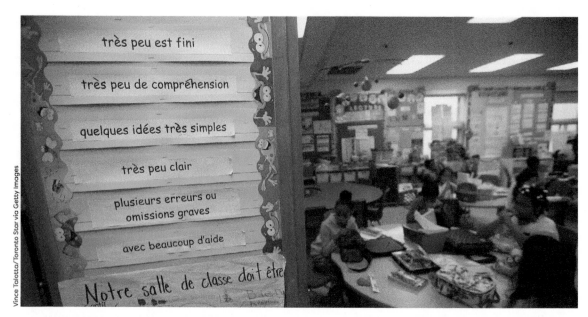

très peu est fini

très peu de compréhension

quelques idées très simples

très peu clair

plusieurs erreurs ou
omissions graves

avec beaucoup d'aide

Notre salle de classe doit être

Vince Talotta/Toronto Star via Getty Images

School boards across Canada have seen rising registration for public school French immersion programs. In some jurisdictions, competition has parents lining up overnight to claim spots for their children. French language instruction is part of the curriculum for all English-speaking students in Canada—so what do you think is the appeal of immersion programs? Is it all about learning French? A potential ticket to a job in government? Or is it just another high track available within the public school system?

businesses. Schoolwork here focused on "getting the right answer":

> One must follow the directions in order to get the right answers, but the directions often call for some figuring, some choice, some decision making. For example, the children must figure out by themselves what the directions ask them to do and how to get the answer: what do you do first, second, and perhaps third? Answers are usually found in books or by listening to the teacher. Answers are usually words, sentences, numbers, or facts and dates; one writes them on paper, and one should be neat. Answers must be given in the right order, and one cannot make them up. (Anyon, 1980)

A fourth school, identified as "affluent professional," had students whose parents were employed as corporate lawyers, engineers, and advertising executives. At this school, the work involved

> creative activity carried out independently. The students are continually asked to express and apply ideas and concepts. Work involves individual thought and expressiveness, expansion and illustration of ideas, and choice of appropriate method and material. . . . The products of work in this class are often written stories, editorials, and essays, or representations of ideas in mural, graph, or craft form. The products of work should not be like anybody else's and should show individuality. . . . One's product is usually evaluated for the quality of its expression and for the appropriateness of its conception to the task. (Anyon, 1980)

The fifth school Anyon called "executive elite," as most of the students' fathers held positions as presidents and vice-presidents of major corporations (it was 1979, so many mothers would not have been working). In this school, work involved

> developing one's analytical intellectual powers. Children are continually asked to reason through a problem, to produce intellectual products that are both logically sound and of top academic quality. A primary goal of thought is to conceptualize rules by which elements may fit together in systems and then to apply these rules in solving a problem. (Anyon, 1980)

If there were a sociology class offered at this school level, daily activities in each category might look like this:

working-class school	copying and memorizing the instructor's notes from the board
middle-class school	reading the textbook and finding the right answer
affluent professional school	finding information on an assigned topic and writing it up in one's own words
executive elite school	analyzing social systems and looking for strengths and weaknesses

Homework and Its Sociological Effects

Sociologists study homework to gauge the extent to which homework helps to reproduce class structure. Children raised by educated middle- and upper-middle-class parents have a number of advantages with respect to homework. Their parents typically are better able to understand teacher instructions and so are in a better position to help their children (sometimes doing the entire project themselves for their children). Parents who work in an office setting are more likely to have the software skills needed to support children whose teachers expect them to turn in polished assignments prepared in the latest presentation, image, and design editing software than children of parents who lack those computer skills. The children of better-off parents tend to live in larger homes, where they have a quiet, dedicated space for doing homework, high-speed internet access and a newer computer, a colour printer, and other aids to completing their work. As a result, the more a course depends on homework as opposed to class work, the more it favours children from middle- and upper-middle-class households.

The amount of homework a child receives can have a profound effect on family life. In 2008, Linda Cameron and Lee Bartel published the findings of a study on the impact of homework on Canadian households.

Quick Hits

Social Mobility: Meritocracy versus Cultural Reproduction

During the 1960s, John Porter wrote:

> No society in the modern period can afford to ignore the ability which lies in the lower social strata. Whatever may be said about average intelligence and social class, the fact remains that in absolute numbers there is more of the highly intelligent in lower classes than in the higher. If the principles of efficiency and equality are to be upheld, Canada must be prepared to put a great deal more money into education and educational research than it has. . . . Without such policies, intergenerational continuity of class will remain [and] mobility deprivation will continue. (quoted in Helmes-Hayes, 2010, pp. 137–8)

There are two fundamentally opposing positions concerning education and social mobility. One is that education is **meritocratic**: academic performance reflects natural ability (i.e., merit), and the system provides mobility for those lower-class and minoritized students who work hard to succeed. Cultural reproduction theory, by contrast, argues that the education system reproduces and reinforces the inequality of the surrounding society. Which one do you think presents the more accurate statement about education in Canada as you have experienced it?

Their research was based on an online questionnaire completed by over 1,000 parents, the vast majority of them in Ontario. Of the 10 main conclusions drawn from the qualitative part of the questionnaire, two related to family life. The first was that homework "reduces family time": "parents often expressed feelings of resentment toward homework and the effect it has on family balance" (Cameron & Bartel, 2008, p. 53).

The second finding related to family life was that homework "affects family relationships." According to the authors, homework was found to be "a primary source of arguments, power struggles, and disruptive to building a strong family." In the words of one respondent cited by the report's authors, "Fights over homework with my children are common and very upsetting" (Cameron & Bartel, 2008, p. 54). Education administrators have taken steps to limit the homework burden, but in an environment of increasing competition for the good grades required to gain admission to the most coveted universities and postsecondary programs, putting in the time outside of normal working hours is the surest way to get ahead—a lesson students will take with them into their professional lives.

Issues in Indigenous Education

The Politics of Representation in Textbooks

Textbooks, whether online or in print, form an important and influential part of education, and yet they remain an under-studied topic in the sociology of education. For my doctoral dissertation, I examined the representation of Indigenous people in 77 Canadian introductory sociology textbooks. What I discovered was a serious and progressive lack of Indigenous voice. Indigenous writers were not represented as a significant source of information on their own people. In Michel Foucault's terminology, theirs were *disqualified knowledges*—"knowledges that have been disqualified as inadequate to their task" (Foucault, 1980, p. 82). Yet their viewpoints offer a legitimate alternative to standard sociology knowledge.

Early Canadian introductory sociology textbooks contained collections of readings. As

sociologists were rarely studying Indigenous people then (that field of study belonged to anthropologists), contributions written about Indigenous people typically were authored by people who were not professional sociologists, including Inuit leader Abraham Okpik, Ojibwa author Wilfred Pelletier, and Cree politician and scholar Harold Cardinal (although he studied sociology for a while at Carleton University). When sociologists began to study Indigenous people in urban settings in the early 1970s, the Indigenous voice was lost from sociology textbooks: the only coverage of Indigenous people came from non-Indigenous sociology writers. It is coming back, but slowly.

Credentialism

Credentialism often blocks Indigenous people's attempts to improve education. "Credentialism" is the practice of valuing degrees, diplomas, and certificates over people's actual knowledge and ability in the hiring and promotion of employees. In many Indigenous communities, elders are deeply involved in educating children and young adults. However, elders do not typically carry paper credentials. Their qualification comes primarily from community recognition and valuing of their knowledge. Elders are recognized in Indigenous communities as being experts in traditional knowledge, such as hunting, fishing, spirituality, healing, childcare, and crafts. Most teachers coming from non-Indigenous communities are not familiar with elders because the role of elder is not assigned significant status in mainstream Canadian society.

Assessing Indigenous Education in Canada

Jo-ann Archibald is eminently qualified to speak of the past, present, and future of Indigenous education in Canada. A member of the Stó:lō people of British Columbia (known formerly as Salish), she has a doctorate in education and taught for 45 years, first at the elementary school level and later at the postsecondary level, where she specialized in training Indigenous teachers. Her book *Indigenous Storywork: Educating the Heart, Mind, Body and Spirit* (2008) is a classic in explaining Indigenous modes of education for non-Indigenous readers.

In a recent opinion piece in *The Tyee* (Archibald, 2019) she assesses enduring problems and also advances made in Indigenous education (which covers education of both Indigenous and non-Indigenous students). One of the main

> **What do *you* think?**
> If you were the principal of an elementary school, what reasons might you give for "banning homework"? What reasons would you give for taking the opposite position?

problems she identifies is what she calls "the racism of low expectations":

> Some teachers will say, "I can't do anything about the Indigenous kids; they come from poor homes," and feel hopeless. I would hope this feeling shifts to excitement and confidence in working with Indigenous students and parents, rather than feeling it's a dismal situation. (Archibald, 2019)

Archibald remains optimistic. She is especially encouraged by the increasing number of Indigenous people serving as resource educators in the school system. Still, she hopes for a much higher number of Indigenous full-time classroom teachers. Including Indigenous modes of teaching and learning, not just in courses in Indigenous studies but in all subject areas, is beginning to happen in the school system in British Columbia, necessarily so, in her view. It must be more, she says, than just a thoughtful "trip in the woods" but learning experiences that are connected to elders and their stories.

Archibald also expresses her hope that non-Indigenous teachers will begin to feel "confident" in teaching an Indigenous curriculum. The lack of confidence is a problem that exists at all levels of education. I have seen it directly. I once wrote a piece on the Haudenosaunee (Iroquois) Great Law of Peace, which, among other things, is a traditional story of Haudenosaunee political philosophy. I wrote it for what we were then calling the Humanities course, a compulsory elective at the college where I taught. As the article itself was not compulsory reading, many teachers did not discuss it, and those who did often communicated to me their discomfort in teaching it based on their lack of knowledge on the subject. Non-Indigenous teachers at all levels of education are generally ignorant of Indigenous language, culture, and history, because they have been trained in an environment that did not prioritize this knowledge. That is beginning to change, as it must if our education system is to reflect the true history and diversity of this country.

If there were 10 points that everyone in the Canadian education system should learn about Indigenous people, what would they be? Examples could include the fact that more than 95 per cent of the human history of the land that is now Canada is Indigenous history alone. Another point could be the source language and meaning of such place names as Canada, Quebec, Ontario, Manitoba, Saskatchewan, Yukon, Nunavut, Ottawa, Toronto, Winnipeg, Saskatoon, and Kootenay. What else?

Best Practices in British Columbia

Sociological discussions of Indigenous people's education tend to focus on the horrific stories of the residential schools and the poor academic performance of Indigenous students since then. An alternative perspective comes from a report published by the C.D. Howe Institute (Richards, Hove, & Afolabi, 2008). Summarizing the results of a study that examined Aboriginal student performance in non-Aboriginal public schools, the authors identified five "best practices" that are key to the success of Indigenous students:

1. collaboration between school district personnel at all levels and local Indigenous communities
2. commitment by administrators and teachers to incorporating Aboriginal content into the curriculum
3. creation of influential positions (such as full-time teachers and school trustees) dedicated to Indigenous education
4. relationship-building between Indigenous and non-Indigenous communities in the district
5. willingness of school district authorities to share responsibility for making decisions with Indigenous communities.

Interviews revealed that non-Indigenous teachers often presented obstacles to Indigenous involvement in their classrooms. While it is easy to say that personal racism is involved, sociologists look primarily for institutional barriers. The Canadian education system teaches very little about Indigenous people. Most Canadian teachers are ill prepared to work with an Indigenous curriculum—they are poorly acquainted with Indigenous history, language, and culture generally because they are products of a school system that has failed to adequately cover these subjects. For example, a 2015 report by the advocacy group People for Education found that only 29 per cent of elementary schools in Ontario and 47 per cent of the province's secondary schools offered training on Indigenous issues to teachers (Casey, 2015). The result is a self-perpetuating form of **institutional racism**.

> **What do *you* think?**
> What obstacles might there be to adopting the best practices referred to in this study?

Quick Hits

Gay–Straight Alliances: The Politics of the Schoolhouse

In 2015, the Progressive Conservative government of Alberta passed a law making it illegal for school boards or administrators to prevent students from setting up **gay-straight alliances** (GSAs) on school property. The move was applauded by anti-bullying activists and students, who had, prior to the law, been forced to hold GSA meetings outside of their schools. A recent study of Grade 8–12 students in British Columbia suggests that GSAs help reduce "suicidal ideation" (i.e., thinking about suicide) and suicide attempts, as well as the experience of discrimination not only among sexual minority youth but among heterosexual youth who do not conform to normative gender-based behaviour (Saewyc, Konishi, Rose, & Homma, 2014). Nevertheless, the legislation faced stiff opposition from some parents and administrators of faith-based schools, particularly officials in the publicly funded Catholic school system who believe GSAs are too political and promote a lifestyle that is inconsistent with Catholic teachings. After the NDP government in BC updated the legislation in 2017, a group of 24 private religious schools, eight parents, and two non-profit groups launched a constitutional challenge of a part of the law protecting the privacy of students joining GSAs in the province. In 2019, the province's United Conservative Party replaced the legislation with a new Act that removed the privacy protections for students, permitting school staff to inform parents of children joining a GSA. The new law also erased a provision compelling a school to set up a gay–straight alliance "immediately" if students request one, meaning that schools could agree to set up a GSA but delay doing so.

The debate in some ways mirrored the controversy sparked when Ontario's provincial government introduced its new sex education curriculum in 2015. Designed to teach students about diversity in sexual orientation and gender expression at an earlier age, the curriculum was initially opposed by some Catholic school educators who believed that parts of the curriculum did not align with Catholic values. In 2018, the incoming Conservative government put the curriculum on hold, having campaigned on a pledge to do so.

Catholic schools in Alberta and Ontario are part of the separate school system that exists in some provinces to protect religious minorities from discrimination by allowing them to direct their taxes to supporting faith-based elementary and secondary schools.

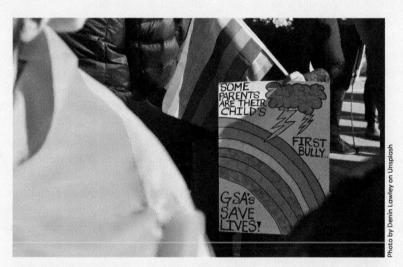

Should school staff have the right, under exceptional circumstances, to inform parents that their child belongs to the school's gay-straight alliance? What is the concept of "in loco parentis," and does it apply in all school boards?

What do *you* think?

1. Should a denominational school be forced to allow its students to set up a gay-straight alliance on school property when opposition to homosexuality is a key tenet of that denomination's teaching?

2. What role can sociologists play in a controversy such as the one described here?

13.4 Issues in Postsecondary Education

This section looks at some of the issues particular to postsecondary education. As a college or university student, you're probably keeping your own list of "issues"; it may be interesting to see how they compare with the topics we'll consider here.

Long-Term Adjunct Instructors: An Educational Underclass

The growing ranks of long-term adjunct instructors in postsecondary institutions is the product of several economic and social factors, including the increasing number of postsecondary students, the reduction of government investment in postsecondary education, the increasing levels of private corporate funding, and the rising influence of a corporate culture that regards education just like any other business. The trend of turning full-time teaching positions into long-term adjunct posts is not unlike contracting out skilled jobs to avoid having to grant the benefits or long-term commitment that come with full-time work.

Names for this class of education workers differ. They commonly are referred to as **adjunct professors**, but they may also be called "sessionals," "contract staff," or "part-time instructors" (a misleading term, since many put in more hours than full-time instructors do). In Canada, the term "adjunct" is used to refer specifically to an experienced instructor who, because of seniority, is the first in line to take the courses full-timer instructors can't or don't want to take on. Contract teaching used to be a first step on the path toward a full-time job or a tenure-track position. Now, that path is narrower and longer.

Ghosts in the Classroom, edited by Michael Dubson, is a collection of narratives written by adjunct professors at American colleges and universities. Almost all of the contributors are English instructors—not surprising, given that many of them teach writing for a living, and English departments are large, with lots of temporary work for adjuncts. There is a lot of competition for jobs in this area, illustrated in the writers' frequent use of the phrase "dime a dozen" to refer to their competitive position. One of the topics raised repeatedly is the low pay, which is especially tough to swallow given that salaries for full-time staff are well over double what adjunct instructors are paid. One of the collection's contributors speaks eloquently of the sense of **relative deprivation** felt by many adjuncts:

> If I teach eight courses in an academic year, I make approximately $16,000. They [full-time instructors] teach eight to ten courses during an academic year and make, on the average, $40,000. I must horde my money and pinch my pennies for I must live on it during the semester breaks. Full-time teachers get paid all year long, whether they work or not.

> Because the pay is so poor, . . . I must string together collections of adjunct course assignments from several different schools. I have taught six, seven, eight classes a semester at three or four different schools. . . . I have worked other jobs and taught on the side. I have split my time between teaching four or five courses, a full-time load, and another job. (M. Theodore Swift, cited in Dubson, 2001, pp. 2–3)

Many contributors to the collection comment on their working conditions, which might involve sharing a desk (or not even having a desk) and having restricted use of facilities and equipment such as the departmental photocopiers. Jody Lannen Brady's description is typical:

> I shared a dingy office with twenty other instructors, and some semesters I was lucky to find a chair to perch on during my office hours. I often met with students in the hallway because it was quieter than the office. I had one file cabinet drawer I could call my own, but I hauled all my papers and books back and forth from home to office and back each day because I couldn't work in the office, never knowing how many times I would have to jump up and answer the phone, and if I would have a desk to sit at. (cited in Dubson, 2001, p. 147)

What might surprise full-time professors is the extent to which the adjunct instructors feel they are engaged in a "class war" with full-timers. Two excerpts illustrate the point:

> At one college, I share office space one day a week with one of the full-time instructors. He put a sign with my name by the door as a sort of welcoming gesture. The next week, the secretary of the English Department wrote me a note. Two of the full-time teachers were in a fury at the arrogance of my putting up a nameplate. (Gale, in Dubson, 2001, p. 13)

> Once, in a heated personal discussion with a full-time colleague, she blurted out, "Who the hell do you think you are? You're only an adjunct here!" (Werner, in Dubson, 2001, p. 37)

Strained relations with colleagues are compounded by trying relationships with the students. Student evaluations are more important to the employment status of adjuncts than they are to the positions of full-time staff members. A poor evaluation won't get a full-timer fired, but it could cause an adjunct not to be hired back once the contract has ended. One writer explains:

> If I have poor course evaluations, I will be out. . . . If my students complain about me, legitimately or otherwise, I will be out. If a full-time faculty member faces any of this, he or she will be supported, worked with, helped. Full-time tenured faculty may not even be evaluated, and . . . if their students complain about them, nothing affecting their employment or job security will be done. (Swift, in Dubson, 2001, p. 3)

It should not be surprising that adjunct professors have been organizing. The kinds of conditions described above were a flashpoint in the strike by graduate student teaching assistants at York University in 2018.

Online Teaching: A Critical Sociological Approach

During the late 1990s and early 2000s, there was a push throughout North American colleges and universities to offer dramatically more online courses, even to the point of offering online diplomas and degrees, in some cases through "virtual" colleges based entirely online. This was driven by technological improvements, certainly, and by a desire to make education more accessible. But it was also spurred by cuts to postsecondary education funding. The online movement was hyped with the allure of "change as progress," and played well to the susceptibility of educators to changes in intellectual fashion. It also was driven by private organizations specializing in delivering educational packages over the internet, who coined or co-opted tantalizing terms like "advanced learning" and "open learning," in spite of their yet unproven ability to provide education that is either more advanced or more open. They invest heavily in hosting or attending "educational" conferences (popular perks among postsecondary instructors), where they offer product demonstrations, aided by their "pet" instructors.

The financial success of online education providers has come at a time when many colleges and universities, feeling the financial pinch, have turned to the private sector as a partial solution to an underfunded public system. The boosters of online education are more often administrators and education companies looking for the government

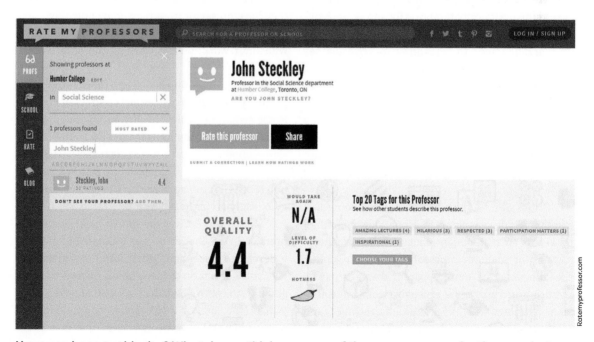

Have you been to this site? What do you think are some of the consequences of rating your instructors online? How are these consequences different for adjuncts and full-time professors?

dollars that flow to public institutions rather than actual instructors, though the latter group does include believers. Student demand for these courses is more unsupported myth than documented fact. The motivation is political and financial without any regard to quality in education. Ontario Premier Doug Ford's introduction of the idea of mandatory online high school courses in 2018 is a case in point.

In postsecondary education, a magic word is "access." Online courses promise access to education for those who would find it difficult to attend college or university otherwise, the so-called non-traditional students (a group that supposedly includes working parents, who traditionally have made good use of night-school courses). As we have seen, **access without mobility** can readily reproduce the class system, while seeming to improve the lot of the more marginalized social groups.

From a sociological standpoint, how do online courses differ from in-class courses? Before addressing this question, it's worth noting that another flawed feature of many a North American university is the large lecture hall, which shares some weaknesses with online courses. The teacher–student relationship that is possible in smaller classes is replaced by a student's relationship with a teaching assistant (or TA), who may be at the university only temporarily and is paid significantly less than a full-time, tenured lecturer. This arrangement that features massive classes supported by smaller tutorials is, like the online movement, driven by the perceived economics of postsecondary education. When I talk in this chapter about in-class teaching, I am referring to classes held in a classroom setting that makes interpersonal communication manageable, not the lecture hall or theatre that seats hundreds of students.

Critics of the online movement (including me) fear that it is driven mainly by economics rather than by access to high-quality education. Interestingly, though, the savings supposedly achieved by online education may be more apparent than real, since acquiring and upgrading expensive technical equipment combined with hiring additional technical and administrative staff can drastically reduce the profit margin.

When boosting revenue becomes the main objective, it leads to the **commodification** of education. Noble (2002) describes this as

the disintegration and distillation of the educational experience into discrete, reified, and ultimately saleable things or packages of things. In the first step toward commodification, attention is shifted from the experience of the people involved in the educational process to the production and inventorying of an assortment of "course materials"; syllabi, lectures, lessons, exams. . . . These common instruments of instruction barely reflect what actually takes place in the educational experience, and lend an illusion of order and predictability to what is, at its best, an essentially unscripted and undetermined process. Second, these fragments are removed or "alienated" from their original context, the actual educational process itself, and from their producers, the teachers. (Noble, 2002, p. 3)

Applicable here is the Marxist concept of **alienation**, the separation between people and the work that they are paid to do. People working on assembly lines are "disconnected" from what they do because they have no say in what they do or how they do it. Chefs with "signature dishes" are closely connected with their work; people working the chip fryer at McDonald's are not. In a similar way, instructors can become disconnected from their **intellectual property** when it is used as part of an online course. Noble elaborates: "Once faculty put their course material online . . . the knowledge and course design skill embodied in that material is taken out of their possession. . . . The administration is now in a position to hire . . . cheaper workers to deliver the technologically prepackaged course" (Noble, 1998).

Alienation involves the hierarchical *control* of a product, in which the boss has ultimate say in how it is developed, used, and distributed. The similarity to Foucault's objection to hierarchical observation that amounts to control over the person observed is clear. With online courses, the potential for administrative monitoring and control increases. Instructors can be more closely supervised through the educational

The Point Is . . .

Online Education Is a New Spin on an Old Idea

Historian David Noble (2002) reminds us that a movement similar to the online education movement happened from the 1880s to the 1930s, when correspondence courses, which enabled students to receive lessons and submit their work by mail (yes, mail!), became popular. The movement began with independent, privately run schools, before the universities, fearing competition and eager to benefit from a relatively easy source of profit, got involved. People marketing the correspondence courses used a language familiar to educators today. They promoted the ability to reach "non-traditional students" with the promise of "working on your own time." However, post-secondary administrators saw correspondence courses primarily as a good source of profit with relatively low overhead costs. Tuition was paid up front and was non-refundable, yet the drop-out rate was high, the majority of students never completing their courses. Noble refers to this as "drop-out money." At the same time, the faculty involved were underpaid, receiving between 25 and 35 cents a lesson. By the 1930s, the institutions involved were sharply criticized for being "diploma mills" that served up an inferior education.

The factors that sparked the establishment of correspondence courses in the late nineteenth century are similar to the ones that have created a favourable environment for the growth of online education today:

- the rise of *credentialism* (setting value on credentials such as certificates and diplomas)
- funding cuts, which prompt universities and colleges to seek out new sources of revenue
- the development of private training companies
- the rapid development of information technology (then, of course, advances in mail delivery services).

Noble sees online courses as suffering from the same flaws that plagued correspondence courses: profit considered over education, poorly paid staff with very little job security, and, on average, an inferior education when measured against its in-class equivalent.

products they have supplied for the course's website. Online courses also allow administrators to measure instructor interactions with students. How often are instructors logging on? How responsive are they to students' online questions? This kind of supervision is also possible with course components offered by means of packaged Web products such as Blackboard Learn.

The online delivery of education depends, like many exploitative systems, on getting workers to do more than they are paid for, relying on dedicated teachers who improve a bad situation with their talent and their labour. But some teachers "work to rule," calculating exactly how much work they have to do to get paid and then do no more.

So what about the students? These courses suffer from significant dropout rates. Students who succeed are typically highly motivated, disciplined people, who get through despite the flaws inherent in the method of delivery. Their good marks represent triumphs of individuals over systems.

Online education lends itself more to **instrumental education**, where courses are narrowly directed to a limited set of tasks, than to **critical education**, which involves analysis of ideas and, ideally, classroom discussion. With online courses, as the information flow is more one-directional than in the classroom, more controlled by the curriculum than by student–teacher interaction, students have less input into how the course proceeds. Their instructors have less input as well, since they usually are part-timers, vulnerable to administrative control. All of these shortcomings of online learning, at all educational levels, were readily apparent during the COVID-19 pandemic, when students were tied to computer screens with little if any direct contact with instructors or other students (that is, if they didn't drop out).

Some worry that a two-tiered, two-class system will develop through online education, with the middle and upper classes attending in-class institutions ("bricks and mortar" universities), preparing for jobs that will maintain their family's class standing, while those "attending" the digital institutions ("click universities") will be lower-class students and others for whom regular college or university attendance is financially impossible (including, for instance, single mothers and other working parents). They will receive lower-cost virtual vocational training that will lead them to lower-level, lower-paying service jobs. These are the people most likely to suffer, academically as well as socially, from the isolation that comes with online courses, the ones who would most benefit from in-class discussions. The system would then reproduce rather than challenge the class system.

Do You Want Fries with That Degree?

Students joke about the McJob—the low-paying, unskilled service job—they might get with their degree once they've graduated. The term refers to *underemployment*, which can have two meanings relevant to this discussion:

- involuntary part-time work for people seeking full-time employment
- low-wage, low-skill employment for people with valuable skills, experience, or academic credentials.

> **What do you think?**
> 1. What arguments would supporters of online education mount to combat the arguments given here?
> 2. Why might a sociology instructor be more critical of online education than an instructor from another discipline (business, for example)?
> 3. How could you do research that would test the effectiveness or ineffectiveness of online education? If you are using online education, how do you do in-depth research?

Statistics Canada defines "underemployed" as "seeking full-time work but finding only part-time work." The category does not include those who have been unable to work full-time for health or other personal reasons, nor does it acknowledge the problem of an over-skilled workforce. Underemployment is the result of several factors:

- the rate of unemployment
- regional disparity (lack of employment opportunities and resources like training and childcare in economically depressed communities)
- discrimination based on ethnicity, gender, disability, or lack of "appropriate" credentials.

How does this apply to postsecondary students? Those who hold high-quality skills and academic credentials become underemployed when there is low marketplace demand. The demographic bulge caused by the baby boomers means that access to employment is cut off for those newly entering the workforce, many of whom may be better qualified than their predecessors. For example, I received my college job with an MA. When I retired, my replacement was required to hold a PhD.

During the 1990s, universities in Canada produced 1.2 million graduates, but only 600,000 jobs requiring university-level credentials were created during that same period. Currently, there are about one million students in the postsecondary system. If job creation remains the same as it did in the 1990s, then several hundred thousand graduates each year will be pursuing fewer than 100,000 job openings. This could effectively increase the structural underemployment rate from the 50 per cent level found in the 1980s and 1990s to 75 per cent.

In a 2017 study of labour demand and supply, researcher Marie Drolet (Drolet, 2017) looked at the relationship between job vacancies and unemployment data for 2015 and 2016. She found that during that two-year period, there were 3.4 unemployed people for every job vacancy in Canada, and roughly half (49 per cent) of all unemployed people had at least some college or university education. However, a disproportionately high number of the job vacancies (37 per cent) were positions in sales

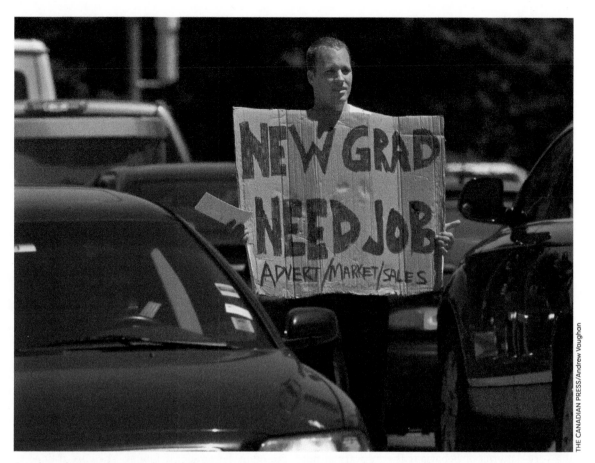

A university graduate takes his job search to the streets of Halifax. Should governments be allowed to cap enrolment in disciplines with low labour market demand? Or is it up to the student to find the educational path most likely to lead to meaningful employment? What's your plan to avoid underemployment after graduation?

and services, and overall, approximately two-thirds of the job vacancies required no more than a high school education. In other words, the population of unemployed Canadians was largely overqualified for the job vacancies.

In the case of new college and university graduates, underemployment can result from a lack of practical experience, even for those who have technical training in a specific field. As a result, recent graduates may be forced to work in low-paying or part-time jobs until they find work in their field. Canadian studies conducted between 1982 and 2004 suggest that while postsecondary education attainment has increased for various occupational classes, so has the underemployment rate for those same occupational classes. The same research also shows that the rate of underemployment is greater than the

under-qualified rate. In 2004, 45 per cent of those aged 18–24 saw themselves as being over-qualified for their jobs as opposed to 22 per cent of those 40 and over (Livingstone, 2004).

Among the solutions proposed to reduce underemployment are government-imposed restrictions on enrolment in postsecondary courses and programs with low labour market demand, although they often produce people who could make a significant contribution to the economy of the country. However, the university system would be unable to support such a proposal, as it would reduce student enrolment and, therefore, revenues.

The Sociology of Plagiarism

Ask any professor about the problems of teaching at a postsecondary institution, and **plagiarism** will be mentioned. This is particularly true of instructors teaching courses in the social sciences and the humanities—courses with a grade component heavily based on essay writing.

Plagiarism is the act of copying another person's work or of piecing together work from several sources into an academic pastiche. Basically, it involves passing off someone else's ideas or work as your own. The ideas and words aren't yours, and the sources of those ideas and words aren't properly identified or even mentioned. In pre-internet times, plagiarism was difficult to do by accident: you had to copy, in long hand, from a print source, such as a journal article or book that you found in the library. Today, you can plagiarize with the click of a mouse, and once a piece of information has been copied into your working document, it can be all too easy to forget where it came from. Students will sometimes copy and paste from anonymous websites, believing these are fair game because there is no attributed author. Make no mistake: it is still plagiarism.

Carol Thompson (2006) adopts a sociological approach to address why plagiarism has become such a common phenomenon. She emphasizes the influence of **role models**, asserting that students have the very patterns of behaviour they're warned not to fall into modelled for them by professors, school administrators, famous writers and academics, and politicians. More influential could be parents, who have often helped students in writing and assembling their projects in high school, and who may get involved in their children's postsecondary work as well. The idea that the work submitted does not have to have been prepared entirely on one's own could stem from that experience of having received help from parents.

In addition, international students may have a culturally different definition of plagiarism. Arif Abu, former co-ordinator of International Student Services for Ryerson University (now Toronto Metropolitan University), has said: "In some cultures, knowledge is public property and you often don't have to do proper citation—and in a friendship, you share your homework, so a lot of international students struggle with this at first" (Singer, 2019). For the importance of avoiding plagiarism, help for international students is offered by Smart Student Canada (Jadhav, 2022).

I experienced international student "plagiarism" as a teacher. I can think of one class in particular, in which there were more than 10 international students. Their weekly assignments were often too similar to have been done by one student alone without help from fellow students or from written work not cited. I gave them low marks for doing that, as I would have for Canadian students. What I should have done as a sociology professor was at least include in my early handouts (I didn't ever use computer platforms) or have as part of my first lecture a discussion of plagiarism standards in Canadian schools.

Plagiarism has spawned two booming industries. One is the essay industry, selling students ready-composed or, for a higher fee, customized papers. These companies are not engaged in anything that is technically against the law, although the means they sometimes use to obtain papers do involve theft of academic property. Copyright laws are fuzzy about academic work. The fact that numerous companies of this kind are out there, set up to accept your credit card number or payment via PayPal, might make the practice seem legitimate.

The industry can benefit graduate students, who are often desperate for money. They are trained to write academic papers. By selling their services to web-based essay providers, they are capitalizing on their hard-earned skills in an industry in which these skills are valued.

Another group that profits from plagiarism consists of businesses such as Turnitin and iThenticate, which sell their services to colleges and universities with the claim that they can catch the plagiarizers. They expand their database with every postsecondary institution that pays for their services. You have to wonder how many people working on this side of the business once worked on the other side, like hackers who become computer security specialists.

A potential social factor in the willingness to plagiarize is **social distance**. If you know your instructors and they recognize you by name or by sight, then you are less likely to submit a plagiarized essay, since it would be like cheating a friend. However, if your professor is just a blurry face at the front of a crowded lecture theatre, or an even more anonymous presence online, the social distance is far greater. Plagiarism might feel to some students to be like stealing from a large corporation. It appears to be a "victimless crime," since there is no easily identifiable injured party and the injured corporation has a huge financial cushion. However, the other injured party is the plagiarizer, who has compromised a learning process that is built from legitimate experiences. Furthermore, the institution in which the student is learning depends for its reputation on the truthfulness of its academics, even the junior ones. Plagiarism and all the other forms of academic dishonesty (see, e.g., St Petersburg College Learning Resources, n.d.) are self-defeating and corrupt the academy.

Cultures of Education

Plagiarism must also be viewed in terms of cultures of education. In mainstream Western culture the tendency is to emphasize the individual's competition with others. This emphasis is made stronger when, for instance, a large first-year course is known to allow a fixed number of students to receive A's, or is marked on a bell curve. This makes these precious marks more valuable by artificially putting them in limited supply. Other cultures put a greater emphasis on the group. Indigenous students, for example, have traditionally not wanted to be singled out in class. They whisper answers to peers who have been asked to reply to teacher questions, so that there will be no embarrassment for a classmate who doesn't know the answer. Research has shown that they are typically more likely to share answers on tests, the same way they would help their family members and friends. The cultural value of sharing is much higher than in mainstream Canadian culture.

The Western culture of education emphasizes putting ideas "in your own words." There are cultural traditions in the Middle East, Asia, and Indigenous societies in which "repeating the words of the master" or "the behaviours of the Elder" is more valued than personalizing an answer. When international students come to Canada, they are unlikely to have been told about how education in Canada follows a model that may differ from the model used in their culture of origin.

Another influential aspect of the Western culture of education is the increasingly corporate nature of postsecondary institutions, where students are viewed as customers (or "stakeholders").

Students may feel that it is their right as consumers to appeal grades or to sue teachers over disappointing marks. As long as school administrators feel that their institutions are competing for students, they may be reluctant to cultivate an unfavourable reputation by aggressively pursuing plagiarizers, risking bad publicity. And with the increased level of credentialism—the emphasis on "getting the piece of paper" rather than on learning—students may act more like customers than like learners.

The corporate culture of the postsecondary institution is also expressed and experienced internally, within the institution, and can have an influence on how plagiarism is treated and judged. Departments where students write a lot of essays (sociology, anthropology, history, literature, philosophy, English and other literatures, and so on) are more involved in providing electives to students who are studying in different programs than in training majors in their fields of study. Pressure can be brought to bear on a department's administrator by administrators of the students' programs to "just let my student pass," rather than doggedly pursuing cases of plagiarism. The competition for students goes on within colleges and universities, as different departments attempt to draw students to take their electives. A popular course gains status for the department and can be used to justify new hires and a higher budget. A course with a high rate of catching plagiarism offenders is not popular. The increased use of temporary, sessional, or adjunct professors, who "don't want to rock the boat," also weakens the impulse to take a firm stand against plagiarism. They want to be seen as "team players" so that they will get rehired. Finally, as Thompson (2006) notes, when it comes to plagiarism, word gets around. Those schools with a clear policy of dealing strictly with plagiarism have fewer instances of the offence. Where people often "get away" with it, student culture might simply become supportive of plagiarism.

What do you think?
1. Why is plagiarism on the rise at postsecondary institutions in Canada?
2. Do you accept the idea that students should always be encouraged to put things "in their own words"?

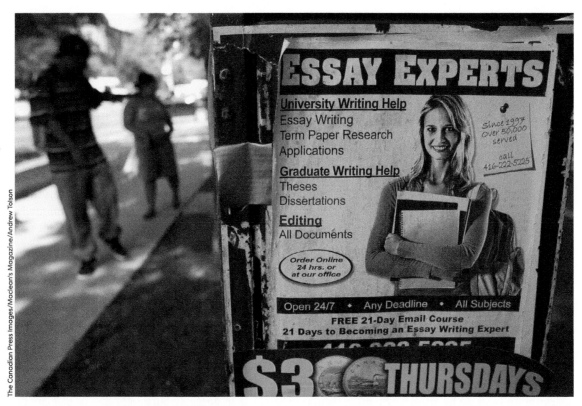

Ever been tempted by an ad like this? What about the advertising makes the service seem morally legitimate and socially acceptable?

International Students

Over the last decade or so, international students have been appearing in ever-increasing numbers in the classrooms (virtual and physical), lecture halls, and residences of universities and colleges in Canada. In an article published in March 2022, the number given was approximately 450,000 new students (El-Assal, 2022). Table 13.1 shows the top 10 source countries, by number of study permit holders on 31 December 2021. Of these, students from Asian countries comprised an overwhelming 85 per cent of all new foreign students.

Why do so many international students come to our colleges and universities? There are two primary reasons. One is the attraction to the students of Canada being mainly an English-speaking country with an education system that is generally respected. Second is the attraction of having high-paying students in Canadian postsecondary institutions that are decreasingly funded by provincial governments. As one study found, "In early 2020, more than 640,000 international postsecondary students studying in Canada were contributing $22 billion annually to the economy and supporting ~170,000 jobs" (Hanbasasa et al., 2021, p. 35).

Canada is certainly not alone in reaching out to international students. In 2019, it was reported that some 4.5 million students worldwide were receiving their postsecondary education in a foreign country. At that time, Canada drew roughly 5 per cent of such students, as compared to the United States with 17 per cent, the United Kingdom with 16 per cent, and Australia with 6 per cent (Singer, 2019).

Still, our numbers keep increasing. The level of average increase in the short period of time from 2017–18 to 2021–2 is shown in Table 13.2.

International Students Are Not All Rich

From these figures, some might characterize international students as rich and accustomed to luxury. A study that presents the point of view of international students at the University of Alberta (Hanbasasa et al., 2021) looks at the causes of their food insecurity. These involved the typical factors faced by students, such as lack of time, lack of family

TABLE 13.1 Canadian International Study Permit Holders, 2021

Ranking	Country	Continent	Number
1.	India	Asia	217,410
2.	China	Asia	105,265
3.	France	Europe	26,630
4.	Iran	Asia	16,900
5.	Vietnam	Asia	16,285
6.	South Korea	Asia	15,805
7.	The Philippines	Asia	15,545
8.	United States	North America	14,325
9.	Nigeria	Africa	13,745
10.	Mexico	North America	11,550
Total			453,460

TABLE 13.2 Increase in International Student Tuition Fees, Degree Programs

	2017–18	2021–2	Increase	Percentage Increase
Canada				
Canadian student	$6,618	$6,693	$75	1.1
International student	$25,549	$33,623	$8,074	30
Ontario (highest)				
Canadian student	$8,519	$7,938	-$581	-7 (decrease)
International student	$32,380	$42,185	$9,805	30.5
Newfoundland and Labrador (lowest)				
Canadian student	$2,821	$3,078	$257	9
International student	$9,241	$12,037	$2,796	30

Source: Statistics Canada (2021).

support, limited information about services and resources, as well as unemployment and under-employment (working for too little pay). But a cultural component was involved as well: the unavailability of culturally familiar food. Such foods were inaccessible or unaffordable, and in some instances non-cultural foods were abhorrent for religious or ethical reasons. The issue for Jews and for Muslims is whether or not the animals for meat have been slaughtered according to traditions considered cruel by Canadian standards. Their food insecurity was such that they were unable to concentrate, missed classes and exams, and suffered negative physical, mental, and social effects.

In Ontario, as in most other provinces, international students have no access to provincial health insurance, that is, to the Ontario Healthcare Insurance Plan (OHIP). They can enroll in the University Health Insurance Plan (UHIP), which in the academic year 2021–2 cost $756. If a student has dependants, the same amount has to be paid for each of them.

13.5 Social Inequality and Education

In most Canadian jurisdictions education is not just a right but a requirement for students between the ages of 5 and 18. Once you've graduated from high school, you suddenly face stern barriers to access if you wish to continue. This section will look at those barriers and how they affect people differently.

Participation Rates

Postsecondary education can be a major avenue of social mobility, offering people from lower-class families the opportunity to secure jobs paying middle- or upper-class salaries. But if postsecondary education becomes so expensive that low-income students either cannot attend college or university or leave because of crippling student debt, then this avenue for mobility is blocked.

Figure 13.1 shows the results of a recent study of the postsecondary enrolment rate of 19-year-old Canadians (Frenette, 2017). Students in this sample are separated into quintiles (five equal groups), based on the after-tax income of their parents. You can see that 19-year-olds in the highest income quintile have the highest rate of college and university enrolment at close to 80 per cent. This is over 30 per cent higher than the enrolment rate of 19-year-olds in the lowest quintile: only 47 per cent of 19-year-olds in the lowest income quintile attended college or university in 2014. The encouraging news is that while there is a clear correlation between parents' income and the likelihood that their children will attend college or university, the enrolment rate grew for each quintile, but grew *most* among 19-year-olds in the *lowest* income groups. Do you think that tuition became

more affordable over that 10-year-period? If not, how do you account for the fact that the percentage of 19-year-olds in college and university rose by 7.65 per cent during that period?

In Canada, college tuition costs less, which means that a college education is more accessible than a university education. Do you think the data in Figure 13.2 point to a class system in postsecondary education? Now compare Figure 13.3, which shows the median income of Canadians who graduated from college or university between 2010 and 2014. Together, Figures 13.1, 13.2, and 13.3 show a correlation between the amount of money your parents earn, the likelihood you will participate in postsecondary education, the type of credential you are most likely to earn, and the amount of money you will garner with that credential.

Tuition Fees and University Education

Tuition fees for university education rose significantly during the 1990s, and have continued to climb, albeit less dramatically, since the start of the twenty-first century. Consider that the average undergraduate tuition fee in Canada rose from $4,400 in the 2006–7 academic year to $6,838 in 2018–19, an

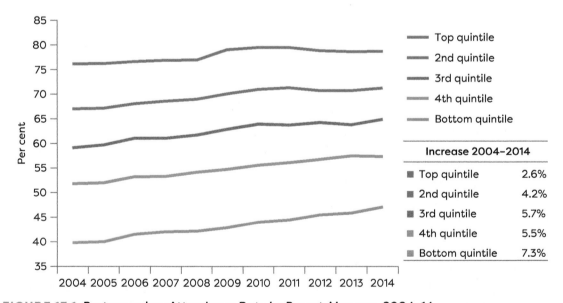

FIGURE 13.1 Postsecondary Attendance Rate by Parents' Income, 2004–14

Source: Frenette (2017, Chart 1).

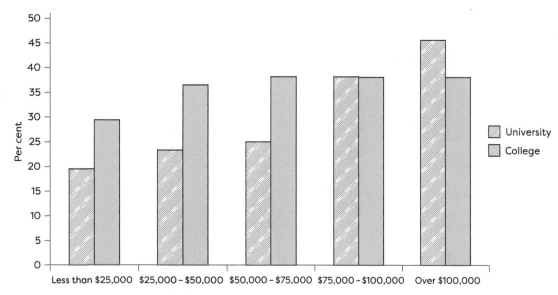

FIGURE 13.2 University and College Participation among 18- to 24-Year-Olds in Canada, by Parents' Income, 2001

Source: Drolet (2005).

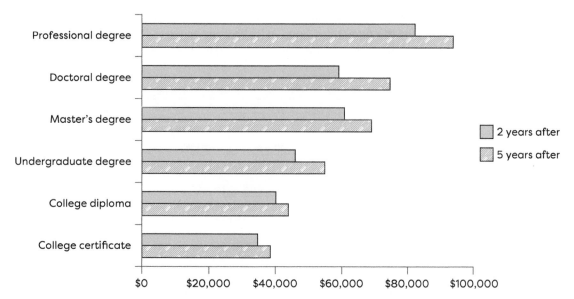

FIGURE 13.3 Median Employment Income of Postsecondary Graduates 2 and 5 Years after Graduation, by Educational Qualification, 2011 Longitudinal Cohort

Source: Statistics Canada (2018).

increase of 55 per cent (Statistics Canada, 2019a). Students in Ontario (71.4 per cent), Saskatchewan (57.6 per cent), and Quebec (53.2 per cent) have faced the steepest tuition increases over that period, although Quebec's tuitions remain among the lowest in Canada. A drop in federal and provincial funding for

postsecondary education has been a major factor contributing to the increase.

There are significant regional differences in tuition costs for both undergraduate and graduate students (see Figure 13.4). Ontario has the highest average tuition costs, at $8,838 for undergraduate

In March 2019, US federal prosecutors laid charges in connection with a scheme that enabled students to gain admission to American colleges through bribes and fraudulently inflated entrance exam scores. Could the same thing happen (or be happening) in Canada?

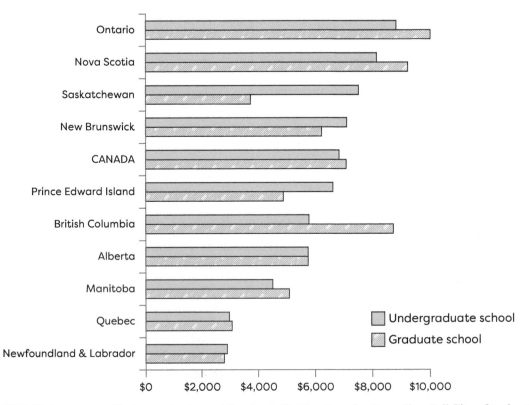

FIGURE 13.4 Average Undergraduate and Graduate Tuition Fees for Canadian Full-Time Students, by Province, 2018–19

Source: Statistics Canada (2019a).

students and $10,028 for graduate students. This should not be surprising as Ontario's provincial government spends less per postsecondary student than any other province. Nova Scotia, Saskatchewan, and New Brunswick are other provinces with undergraduate tuition fees above the Canadian average, while higher-than-average graduate fees are charged in Nova Scotia and British Columbia. The lowest tuitions, for both graduate and undergraduate students, are found in Newfoundland and Labrador and in Quebec, where the fees are below the average by several thousand dollars (see Figure 13.4).

Of course, what you pay depends on not just *where* you're studying but *what* you're studying. The so-called professional schools of dentistry, medicine, law, and pharmacy had the highest average fees across the country, at $23,474, $14,780, $13,332, and $10,746 respectively in 2018–19 (Statistics Canada, 2019b). Needless to say, this has affected who goes to the professional schools. The situation at professional schools changed dramatically after 1997, when tuition fees were deregulated (i.e., government controls on what the universities could charge were withdrawn). A study undertaken in 2004 by the five law schools in Ontario (where the

tuition is highest) looked at how the demographics of their students changed in the years following deregulation (King, Warren, & Miklas, 2004). The researchers found that between 1997 and 2004, there was a 4.7 per cent increase in students from families in the top 40 per cent in terms of total household income, and a decrease in the proportion of students whose parents earn incomes in the middle 20 per cent of the distribution (King, Warren, & Miklas, 2004).

As with postsecondary tuition fees generally, there is a regional disparity in the cost of attending a professional school. Table 13.3 shows the average cost of undergraduate programs in dentistry, medicine, law, and pharmacy in the nine provinces where these programs were available in 2018–19, presented in order of most to least expensive.

We can see that postsecondary education and economic class (that is, parental income) relate to one another, particularly when it comes to university and especially with the professional schools. The province in which the student lives is a factor, again, especially with the professional schools, with Ontario being the most expensive and Quebec the least expensive province for university education.

TABLE 13.3 Average Tuition Fees for Full-Time Canadian Students in Dentistry, Medicine, Law, and Pharmacy, 2018–2019

	Dentistry	Medicine	Law	Pharmacy
Ontario	$40,463	$26,838	$21,614	$19,927
Saskatchewan	$34,628	$17,474	$13,653	$10,025
Nova Scotia	$24,850	$20,067	$15,045	$11,479
Alberta	$20,184	$13,300	$11,025	$10,611
Manitoba	$21,673	$8,834	$10,359	$8,488
BC	$28,770	$18,110	$13,152	$12,751
New Brunswick	N/A	N/A	$9,366	N/A
Newfoundland and Labrador	N/A	$10,250	N/A	$2,805
Quebec	$3,962	$3,265	$2,881	$2,620
Canada	**$23,474**	**$14,780**	**$13,332**	**$10,746**

Note: The averages presented for Quebec and Nova Scotia take into account the different fees charged in these provinces to "in-province" and "out-of-province" Canadian students.

Source: Statistics Canada (2019b).

ROGERIO BARBOSA/AFP/GettyImages

In 2012, Quebec, the province with one of the lowest average tuitions (by a large margin), saw massive student unrest concerning a proposed tuition increase, yet the province with the highest tuition, Ontario, had no student response to this strike. How do you explain these different social responses?

Wrap It Up

Summary

We live in a time of important choices to make concerning the future of our education system. The sociology of education can help make those choices informed and democratic. The most important issue is whether the Canadian education system—from primary school all the way through our postsecondary institutions—is fundamentally meritocratic or whether it serves more to reproduce the class system and cultural privileges of the economically dominant. At the elementary and secondary levels, we need to ensure the suitability of the curriculum so that marginalized peoples get to read and hear about people like themselves who are succeeding within the system. The effects of "streaming" (or "tracking") must be carefully studied. At the postsecondary level, we need to look critically at such practices as the increasing dependence on adjuncts, corporate sponsorship, and online education to uncover the potential harm as well as the benefits they may bring.

Think Back

Questions for Critical Review

1. The foundations of Western postsecondary education were in the liberal arts, and the purpose of a liberal education was to broaden and deepen one's awareness of the wider world and to teach the student to think critically. How does this differ from education focused on labour markets and concerns about plagiarism? What has been lost in this paradigm shift? What has been gained?

2. What was public education designed to accomplish when it was first established in Canada in the mid-nineteenth century? How have the goals of public education changed since then?

3. How well does Foucault's concept of the docile body apply to the education you have received so far? In the time you have spent at school, have you experienced hierarchical observation, normalizing judgment, and examination? What are the pros and cons of those influences?

4. Is education—primary, secondary, postsecondary—an avenue for social mobility? Or does education reinforce existing social differences? Define cultural reproduction theory and explain how much you think it applies to education in the twenty-first century.

5. What evidence of corporate sponsorship exists on your college or university campus? What buildings are named after recognizable companies? What businesses have been granted the right to set up shop on the premises? What do you think are the drawbacks to corporate sponsorship of postsecondary education (including research grants)? Do they outweigh the benefits, including lower tuition costs?

6. Summarize the factors that contribute to the growing problem of plagiarism. Which factors make plagiarism possible? Which ones encourage it? Are there any factors that legitimize it? Is it really the problem we think it is? If so, how would you address it? Consider factors outside of education, such as online music sharing and music sampling. Do we live in a society where originality and authorship are less valued than they once were?

7. What do you see as the connection between the rise of online education and the growing reliance on adjunct professors? Are they both symptoms of the same factors? Which ones?

8. Have you experienced being "overqualified" for a job? Was it possible for you to "take the job seriously," as a less qualified worker might be able to do?

9. Postsecondary education offers many things: training for a future career, intellectual stimulation, an avenue to well-paying employment, a chance to break free from parental controls, social networking within your peer group, and numerous opportunities for personal growth. In what three or four ways do you hope to benefit from your postsecondary education? Do you think these benefits fall within the stated goals of your college or university? Is your college or university set up to help you achieve the things that are most important to you?

Read On

Suggested Print and Online Resources

Jo-ann Archibald, *Indigenous Storywork: Educating the Heart, Mind, Body and Spirit* (Vancouver: University of British Columbia Press, 2008)
Archibald's exploration of Indigenous storytelling explains, for a non-Indigenous audience, the value of Indigenous modes of education.

Jamie Brownlee, *Academia Inc: How Corporatization Is Transforming Canadian Universities* (Black Point, NS: Fernwood Publishing, 2015)

This is the first comprehensive look at corporatization as it affects Canadian universities.

James Côté & Anton Allahar, *Lowering Higher Education: The Rise of Corporate Universities and the Fall of Liberal Education* (Toronto: University of Toronto, 2011)
This work, from two University of Western Ontario sociologists, looks at the effects on education of universities forming closer ties with large corporations.

George Dei & Agnes Calliste, *Power, Knowledge and Anti-Racism Education: A Critical Reader* (Halifax: Fernwood Publishing, 2000)
An informative collection of readings on what anti-racism education entails.

Michael Dubson, ed., *Ghosts in the Classroom: Stories of College Adjunct Faculty—and the Price We All Pay* (Boston: Camel's Back Books, 2001)
This book uses the first-hand accounts of adjunct professors to present the experiences and perspectives of the educational underclass.

C.E. James, *Towards Race Equity in Education: The Schooling of Black Students in the Greater Toronto Area* (Toronto: York University, 2017), https://edu .yorku.ca/files/2017/04/Towards-Race-Equity-in-Education-April-2017.pdf
This study examines the issues facing Black community members, parents, students, and educators, but its findings and conclusions can be extended to other minority groups.

Jeannie Oakes, *Keeping Track: How Schools Structure Inequality,* 2nd ed. (New Haven, CT: Yale University Press, 2005)
A classic critique of the cultural reproduction function of tracking or streaming students.

People for Education, https://peopleforeducation.ca
This parent-led and parent-focused guide to educational issues in Ontario offers news and views, as well as research reports and survey findings. It includes a separate tab devoted to Indigenous education.

John Richards, Jennifer Hove, & Kemi Afolabi, *Understanding the Aboriginal/Non-Aboriginal Gap in Student Performance: Lessons from British Columbia* (Toronto: C.D. Howe Institute, 2008)
A useful guide to strategies used to improve Indigenous education.

Nicole Smith, "In Defense of the Traditional Classroom: An Argument against the Move to Online Classes," www.articlemyriad.com/ argument-traditional-classroom-online/
This online article defends the value of the traditional classroom. To better understand the other side of the argument, have a look at university Web pages defending the move to Coursera, like the following from UBC: http://ctlt.ubc.ca/2012/09/27/ ubc-to-offer-free-online-courses-through-coursera/

14 Health and Ability

Reading this chapter will help you to . . .

- Explain how health and ability are socially constructed.
- Define the terms "sick role" and "social course of disease."
- Outline the principles of biomedicine and contrast them with alternative medical practices.
- Discuss how the process of medicalization takes place in women and in men.
- Talk about the relationship between medicine and social factors such as race, gender, age, and class.
- Explain the difference between impairment and disability.
- Differentiate between medical models, economic models, and social constructionist models of disability.
- Discuss issues of public health and what we have learned from COVID-19.

For Starters

Gordon Dias, 1985–2001

When a person gets sick, we look for causes. Did you wash your hands? Maybe it wasn't such a good idea to use that gas station washroom. Could you have caught it from Gene? I had a feeling that sushi might have been off—I mean, it's been in the fridge since Friday. We don't imagine the illness originated with the individual: we look for contributing factors outside the person.

In Canada, we are coming to view mental sickness the same way we view other kinds of more obviously physical illness. However, there is still a tendency to look for its causes within the individual while ignoring the external factors that played a role. As you read the following story, think about what may have been happening outside the individual and how it contributed to what turned out to be a fatal illness.

It has been almost 20 years since my nephew Gordon Dias died by suicide. He was 16.

He hanged himself from a tree in front of a local high school. As a sociologist, and as his uncle, I struggle to understand why he did this. I believe the causes are social.

Gordon was a young, single man. This made him part of the social group most prone to suicide. He was on the margins of society in several ways. He was the youngest of three children, a child whose brother and sister demanded attention with their achievements. His older brother was the first-born grandchild and nephew on both sides of the family, a position that brought ready attention. His older sister is simply brilliant, a very hard act to follow. Both now have graduate degrees. In my earliest memory of Gordon talking, he is straining to be heard above his siblings.

He was a person of colour, the product of a mixed South Asian and Caucasian marriage, living in the very white city of London, Ontario. He was very close to his South Asian grandmother—so much so that when he left home for a while, he moved in with her. It could not have been easy in that city to have made that choice.

Gordon was artistic. It is not easy for a young man to express himself artistically in our culture, not without presenting some counterbalancing signs of macho behaviour. Perhaps that's one reason why he sought the social company

he did. According to my sister and brother-in-law, he had been spending time with guys who regularly got into trouble. This eventually got him suspended from school. Zero-tolerance policies aren't very forgiving of even temporary allegiances with groups of kids who act out. At some level, zero tolerance is simply intolerance. For Gordon, I guess, that was the final piece of the puzzle. The picture he was left with led him to suicide.

14.1 Introduction: Is There a Sociologist in the House?

Sociology students new to the discipline are sometimes surprised when they arrive for the lecture on **medical sociology**. Medicine? Sociology? Where's the connection? After all, when the restaurant diner starts choking on a fishbone, no one yells, *Is there a sociologist in the house?*

Medical practices and beliefs affect people directly: they are intensely social. Like other topics we have considered in earlier chapters—deviance, for example—health and ability are socially constructed. How they are defined and viewed varies from culture to culture and changes over time.

Consider dyslexia. Sometimes called "reading disorder," it is a general term for difficulties in spelling, learning to read or to read quickly, and being able to understand and sound out words that are written as well as those spoken. While humans may always have been affected by dyslexia, it shows up more clearly as a disability in a literate culture. However, since we all live in literate cultures, this disability is severe in its social implications. Those suffering from it feel like aliens because they are not understood and are, therefore, marginalized even when they are appreciated (Madaule, 1987). Dyslexia is mistaken for a lack of intelligence because the person is unable to process sound normally. Such people are not stupid or—to use an archaic term—"feeble-minded." In fact, they usually have some exceptional abilities, such as long-term memories, as well as compensatory skills they develop. However, dyslexic syndrome has been treated with a very high level of success (Bérard & Brockett, 2011, p. 101) in France as well as in private clinics in Canada and other

places in the world and could be approached that way globally within educational systems.

To take a different kind of example, there is a condition unique to Chinese and South Asian cultures called *koro*, which is a profound belief that one's external genitals or nipples are shrinking (Welsch & Vivanco, 2019, p. 283). Symptoms include acute panic attacks that can last from hours to days. Sociology can help us to understand why this very real psychological disorder exists in some cultures but not in others.

A large part of medical sociology involves **policy sociology**, which is about generating sociological data to help governments and health professionals develop the policies that drive health care in this country. Thus, we can say that one of the principal aims of medical sociology is to improve the delivery of health services through sociologically informed research. **Critical sociology** contributes significantly as well, especially when the focus shifts to the social aspects of the training of doctors, nurses, and other professionals; the practices of multinational pharmaceutical companies; the structure of medical schools, hospitals, and privately run, for-profit clinics and hospitals; and the various schools of thought in healing systems both inside and outside of those other social institutions and structures.

Healing is achieved through social interaction, so it's natural that sociology has a lot to contribute to our understanding of the field of medicine. Race, gender, ethnicity, age, and class—all social factors—can greatly affect an individual's experience of the medical professions. How? Let's say you are Anne M., a middle-aged teacher living in a rural area within driving distance of a small town that has a hospital. You are suffering from intensely painful feet. Your family doctor died last year, and you have had great difficulty trying to find a new one. You go to your local emergency room where, after a long wait, you are examined by a doctor, Aarvi N., who was born in Sri Lanka and educated in Britain, having qualified to practise in Canada just five years ago. She suspects a serious cause for your ailment, so she recommends an osteopathic surgeon. Specialists only practise in large hospitals, usually associated with a university. Which specialist she recommends also will depend on her professional social network, the circle of people she knows and trusts. This network depends on such social factors as where she did a residency, the location of her practice (she drives an hour from her suburban practice outside of Toronto three times a week to this small hospital to work in the emergency department for 12-hour shifts), and the status she has as a doctor (possibly determined by how long she has been practising and the degree to which she has been politically active in medical associations). Religion is not a factor in this case, but certain hospitals are governed by specific religious groups.

Compare this scenario with that of David W., a successful businessperson living in North York, with a prominent Jewish male doctor, Jerome G., who has hospital privileges at Mount Sinai Hospital in Toronto. This doctor has been the vice-chair on the Board of Directors of the provincial medical association and is often asked to present papers at medical conferences. Imagine how his professional social network might differ from that of young Dr Aarvi N., and how your treatment might differ as a result.

This illustration about medical social networks and patient social networks is just one reason why sociology cannot be ignored when it comes to health.

14.2 The Sick Role

American sociologist **Talcott Parsons** (1902–1979) came up with perhaps the first medical sociology term when, in *The Social System* (1951), he developed the concept of the **sick role** (or **patient role**). Like other sociological roles, he argued, being sick comes with certain expectations—four, in his thinking. Two relate to what the sick person can expect from society, and two to what society expects of the sick person:

1. The person engaged in the sick role should expect to be granted "exemption from normal social responsibilities." In other words, patients should be excused from regular duties, either at home or in the workplace, while they recover.
2. Patients should expect to be "taken care of" rather than having to take care of themselves.
3. Patients are socially obligated to try to "get well" rather than remain in the undesirable state of being ill. This expectation applies even to people with terminal illnesses.
4. The sick person is socially obligated to "seek technically competent help," in other words, the help of an approved health professional. The distinction between "approved" and "qualified" is a contested field.

The sick role, according to Parsons, gives the individual licence to be temporarily "deviant" with regards to the first two expectations, provided they act in accordance with the second two.

Parsons was a structural-functionalist. Structural functionalism presumes a social uniformity of experience that conflict or critical sociologists would challenge. Ask yourself this: Is the sick role the same for everybody? The first challenge to the uniformity of the structural-functionalist model came quickly. In 1954, Earl Koos wrote *The Health of Regionville: What the People Thought and Did about It*. It was based on research he had carried out between 1946 and 1950 on differences in what people thought and did about their health depending on their *class*. He learned that people in higher-class occupational groups were better able to afford to play the sick role, a privilege less available to those of lower occupational groups. Think about what happened in Toronto during the period of COVID-19 before antiviral treatments became widely available. The levels of illness in working-class neighbourhoods were dramatically greater, with more deaths than in wealthier neighbourhoods, a consequence of people in these neighbourhoods living in crowded conditions and, as essential workers, being unable to work from home and having to ride daily on crowded public transport (Taylor, 2021).

Similar arguments against the uniformity of the sick role can be made in regard to gender, race, and age. Society has different expectations for a mother than for a father. When children are sick, typically the mother is expected to take time off work to look after them. And who is *least* likely to be allowed to

BartCo/iStockphoto

This worker has just been injured on the job. According to the sick role, what actions is he expected to perform? Now assume he has a family dependent on his income, and his job is part-time (meaning he is paid only for the hours he works). Why might he opt out of the social contract that goes along with the sick role? What happened to "essential workers" during the height of the COVID-19 pandemic?

play the sick role if the whole family gets sick? Generally speaking, the mother. We can ask about people with chronic illnesses or disabilities: Are they to be considered permanently "deviant" according to Parsons's model?

It is hard to defend the universal applicability of Parsons's model of the sick role. In part, this is because the model changes over time. At the turn of the twenty-first century, Ivan Emke (2002) proposed five new expectations for Canadians in the sick role. Two of these are central. First, "patients in the new economy are responsible for their own illnesses." Emke's point is that instead of looking at social and environmental causes of sickness (pollution, unsafe working and living conditions, stress through overwork, economic insecurity, and social disruption), we've become inclined to blame individual "choices" (smoking, drinking, not belonging to a health club, not making time for exercise, eating the wrong foods). Emke notes that the bulk of cancer information then provided in ads and public health materials focused on *individual*

risk factors rather than those presented by *society*, such as polluting industries and weak anti-pollution laws. This division of blame lowers society's sense that everyone is equally entitled to free health care. Do we feel less sympathy for smokers with lung cancer? A person who has COPD (chronic obstructive pulmonary disorder) from having been exposed to asbestos in childhood receives the social criticism targeted to smokers. You can see how those who buy into this expectation might use the underlying argument to justify charging user fees for some medical services.

The second of Emke's new expectations is really a conflation of two: "the patient in the new economy is instructed to tread lightly on the system," and "patients in the new economy are not to be trusted." We could recast it, a little less subtly, as "patients are assumed to be abusing the system." Emke raises this belief in connection with a public education campaign to encourage people to use as few medical services as they can. He cites a 1994 pilot project by the Progressive Conservative Ontario government designed to encourage residents of London to stop going to their family doctor for relatively minor complaints. No research had been done to see whether people were actually "abusing" the system. The *assumption* underlying the project was that escalating healthcare costs can be attributed to too many "unnecessary" visits to family doctors. Perhaps rising costs are more the result of building huge technology-intensive hospitals that are less cost-effective than having a greater number of small-town and community-based medical centres. Perhaps nurses, who make less than doctors do, should be permitted to perform basic medical procedures (stitching wounds, for example) that doctors are normally responsible for, so that the same work can be done at lower cost.

What do you think?

1. How do you think factors such as sex and ethnicity affect the universality of Parsons's sick role concept?
2. Who do you think abuses our healthcare system most? Patients? Doctors? Hospital administrators? Governments? Pharmaceutical companies? Industries that cause pollution?

KatarzynaBialasiewicz/iStockphoto

Do you believe that people who smoke are fully entitled to free health care? What about people who eat "junk" food? People who engage in dangerous recreational activities? People who play video games all day? What about bad politicians, criminals, and people who can't afford to pay taxes?

14.3 The Social Course of Disease

A medical breakthrough of the nineteenth century was the realization that every disease has a natural course, a kind of lifespan during which you catch the disease, suffer through it, and gradually get well (or sicker, in some cases, and expire). The course of a disease depends on the virus or bacterium, and the way the individual human body reacts to it. For example, as of this writing, doctors can prescribe medicine to help alleviate the symptoms and speed up recovery of the common cold, but they can't fundamentally change the natural course of a cold. About 20 per cent of colds are caused by a coronavirus; about 33 per cent by one or more of the 200 rhinoviruses; adenoviruses and enteroviruses account for others; and many have not been identified.

Likewise, we can speak of the **social course** that diseases and disorders go through, a course affected by sociological factors such as the ethnic background, culture, class, age, and sex of the people affected. The following example traces the social course of an injury and illustrates how that course is affected by class.

I once injured myself while running when I should have walked, and I ruptured my Achilles tendon. During my initial visit to the hospital, my left leg was put in a cast, so that I could move only with the use of crutches. I was billed for both the fibreglass cast and the crutches, but because I was then a full-time salaried employee with benefits, my workplace health insurance covered the cost of both. My middle-class job did not require heavy lifting or great physical exertion, so I continued to work, despite having to hobble around the college on crutches for nine weeks. I could have decided not to work during that period, and a good disability allowance would have ensured that I lost no significant income. The injury caused a potentially deadly blood clot to develop, so my doctor prescribed a blood thinner. Fortunately, my drug plan covered most of the cost of this expensive drug.

My wife suffers from a disability that makes it very difficult for her to work full-time. Because I was well paid, we could afford to live on one income. My wife was able to be at home to take care of me during my recovery period. It would have been much worse for my emotional state and physical health if she had not been so diligent in helping me.

Once the cast was removed, I began physiotherapy. The cost was covered almost completely by my insurance plan at work. It helped immeasurably. My recovery proceeded much more quickly than I had expected.

I dread to think what the social course of my healing would have been if I had been an unskilled worker in a factory or warehouse. Other sociological factors that influenced the social course of my recovery include my marital status and the fact that I lived and worked near a large urban centre with abundant medical resources and facilities. What would the social course of my recovery have been if I lived alone, or in a rural area without access to transportation? What other factors might have changed the social course of recovery?

The Point Is . . .

Ethnicity Affects the Social Course of Tuberculosis among Inuit

Ethnicity is a sociological factor that can affect the social course of disease. Consider the treatment of Inuit with tuberculosis. By 1949, new antibiotics, combined with improved sanitation, screening, and treatment, had helped reduce the tuberculosis rate in Canada from about 165 deaths per 100,000 in 1908 down to 33. But at the same time, the tuberculosis rate among Inuit in Canada was rising dramatically, peaking in 1952 at 569 per 100,000 (the highest rate among any international population). In that year, there were 54 deaths in an Inuit population of approximately 10,000.

The high rate had a number of causes. First, the severe cold of the Arctic—although not cold enough to kill the *tuberculosis bacillus*—made the Inuit especially susceptible to respiratory problems. The intimate closeness of Inuit families living in snow houses and sod houses facilitated the spread of the bacteria. More consequential was the increasing contact with people from southern Canada:

> As the Inuit adapted to accommodate the desires of the newcomers, trapping to exchange furs for store goods or working for the RCMP or on military construction sites for cash, their highly nutritious fresh meat or fish diet and their warm caribou-skin clothing were gradually exchanged for a diet largely of white flour, lard, tea, jam, and canned goods, and for much less warm southern clothing. When the caribou declined or the pattern of migration changed . . . malnutrition occurred. (Grygier, 1994, p. 55)

Inuit tuberculosis patients were treated differently from other Canadians. At the time, TB patients would be confined for six months to two years in a hospital or sanatorium. These were not built in the Arctic, so Inuit TB patients were brought (forcibly, in many cases) to southern Canada. Grygier describes what happened after health professionals brought north by ship had conducted their patient examinations:

> When the doctors had made their final decision on whether an individual should go to hospital for treatment or stay in

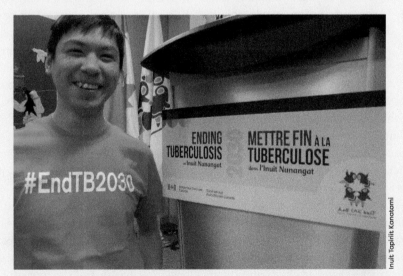

Inuit Tapiriit Kanatami

Tuberculosis is still a problem among Canada's Inuit. The federal government recently unveiled a plan to eliminate tuberculosis in the North by 2030. Why do you think ethnicity has, for so long, been a factor in the social course of this disease?

(Continued)

the North, the evacuees were sent down to the Inuit quarters in the prow of the ship and the rest were sent ashore. The evacuees were not allowed to go ashore to collect belongings, to say goodbye, or to make arrangements for their families or goods. If a mother was judged sick but her children were not infected, the children (sometimes including unweaned babies) were given to an Inuk woman going ashore. Fathers had no chance to arrange for someone to hunt for food for their families or to look after their dogs and equipment. Mothers had no chance to arrange for someone to care for their children or to sew and process the skins needed to keep the family warm. . . . Those needing hospital treatment were kept on board, the rest sent ashore, and on sailed the ship to the next settlement. (Grygier, 1994, p. 96)

The tuberculosis rate among the Inuit dropped during the 1950s to a low of 53 per 100,000 in 1959, but the effects of the separation lasted. Many families were never reunited, often because of death but even in cases where the TB-suffering family member recovered.

14.4 Biomedicine

Biomedicine is the application or use of Western scientific principles in the diagnosis and treatment of illness and disease. It uses physical tests to find defined, purely physical entities (such as bacteria, viruses, and trauma) and then applies purely physical medicines and therapies to counteract them. It has become the dominant practice in Western society.

Let's say you suffer from migraine headaches. You visit your family doctor, who prescribes medication to reduce the severity of your symptoms. That is biomedicine. If you grew up in Canada, this is probably what you expected when you booked your appointment.

Alternative (or **complementary**) **medicine** is the term for approaches to treatment that fall outside of conventional biomedical practice. For instance, your doctor might have recommended acupuncture for your migraines, or massage therapy or yoga to reduce the stress contributing to your headaches. Your doctor might even have tried to discover environmental causes of your condition—bright lights in the area where you read or study, for example. These would be considered "alternative" approaches.

A good example of divergent biomedical and alternative approaches to health is childbirth. Most North American women choose to give birth to their infants in a hospital, under the care of a team of medical professionals including an obstetrician, an anaesthesiologist, and several nurses. Increasingly, however, women are choosing to stay at home to give birth under the care of a midwife or doula. There are good reasons to recommend the latter approach. Many people find hospitals uncomfortable. Some women do not want to be separated from their families, especially if they have other young children. Knowing they will remain at home reduces stress once contractions begin. Unlike most obstetricians, a midwife or doula is available to provide continuous care before and after, as well as during, the delivery. And, it's important to point out, for thousands of years and in many parts of the world today, giving birth at home was and is the only option. Of course, there are many advantages to having a hospital birth, including ready access to doctors and medical equipment in the event that either the mother or the infant requires immediate care for life-threatening complications. Some women choose to combine these approaches by having a hospital birth attended by the midwife who has guided them through their pregnancy. In cases such as this, the term "complementary medicine" is really more apt: biomedicine and alternative medicine do not need to be mutually exclusive.

Biomedicine remains the norm in North America, but it is increasingly called into question by those who endorse a more holistic approach to diagnosis and treatment. Biomedicine has been criticized for looking at health from a **reductionist** perspective that attributes medical conditions to single factors treatable with single remedies. It may fail to take into account the broader set of circumstances surrounding a person's health or illness. Those involved in biomedicine are sometimes accused of being **absolutist**, in not recognizing that just as there are different cultures in business, policing, or fashion, there are **cultures of medicine**, each with a unique approach to interpreting health and sickness. Some critics argue that every patient should be treated in the context of their culture. No single treatment should be applied universally across all cultures.

In Chapter 5, I noted Anne Fadiman's study of the Hmong people living in the United States (Fadiman, 1997). Originally from China, the Hmong were forced to flee their homeland after opposing the Chinese government during the 1960s and 1970s. Fadiman shows how Western biomedical practices were at odds with Hmong cultural beliefs. She cites, as just one example among the Hmong, the perception of soul loss. Hmong adults, children, and even infants wear neckrings and cotton-string spirit bracelets to combat their fear of soul loss. But Hmong patients arriving at a refugee camp in Thailand had their spirit strings cut by American health workers, who claimed the rings were unsanitary. Which do you think posed a greater threat to the physical and mental health of the Hmong: the spirit strings or the fear of losing their soul?

14.5 Medicalization

An offshoot of biomedicine is a practice known as **medicalization**, defined by sociologists Chang and Christakis (2002, p. 152) as

> the process by which certain behaviours or conditions are defined as medical problems (rather than, for example, as moral or legal problems), and medical intervention becomes the focus of remedy and social control.

Medicalization has been criticized as a form of reductionism that reduces complex medical conditions to biomedical causes without examining possible sociocultural or political factors. Or, by turning a natural process such as childbirth into a medically supervised procedure. A related criticism is that Western health professionals are too quick to situate a problem exclusively or primarily in the individual human body, and in a very specific part of the body, rather than, say, in an oppressive social or political system. Medicalization, by ascribing conditions like alcoholism to genetic factors, excuses the sufferer by removing individual blame, but at the same time it portrays the sufferer as a genetic "victim" who can be saved only by an intervention engineered by the medical profession. It takes away the individual's ability to make empowering choices that could affect the outcome of the condition.

Medicalization leads to a further criticism: that it promotes the commodification of health care by identifying certain normal conditions as diseases that may be treated with "commodity cures" (e.g., drugs or procedures). In sociological terms, this makes the normal seem deviant. Examples, for the aging male, include obesity, male pattern baldness, increasingly frequent nighttime trips to the bathroom, and erectile dysfunction. These are not diseases. They are relatively normal aspects of the aging process that need not be medicalized.

This rationalization for "treatment" extends to cosmetic surgery and certain "corrective" surgeries. At what point is a person's dissatisfaction with the social "norms" an ethical reason for cutting, dismembering, drugging, injecting with dangerous substances (e.g., Botox, hormones), shaping, and otherwise altering the fundamentally healthy body?

Government agencies sometimes medicalize disorders traceable more to social or environmental factors than to purely medical ones. Medical journalist Lynn Payer offers an example in *Disease-Mongers: How Doctors, Drug Companies, and Insurers Are Making You Feel Sick* (1992):

> When . . . a child died of lead poisoning in Michigan, there was a call for screening for lead poisoning. But when you read the circumstances, you found that the child was homeless, living in an abandoned building. Calling for blood testing was obviously easier than calling for a policy of providing safe and low-cost shelter for the poor. (Payer, 1992, p. 39)

What do *you* think?

1. Do you think the medicalization of body shape and weight affects females more than males? If so, why?
2. Do you think the medicalization of women's bodies has been initiated primarily by male doctors?

The Point Is . . .

The Causes of Obesity: Take Your Pick

The concept of "obesity," even at younger ages, is contentious. And the focus of our society on obesity is astounding. Turn on the television and listen to some ads: nutritional weight-loss programs that sell you pre-packaged meals are legion; pharmaceutical commercials for drugs to treat quite different conditions often trumpet the fact that—bonus!—taking this drug also will lead to some weight loss. The assumption in our society is that if you aren't shaped like a Barbie doll or proportioned like a Ken doll, then you have a problem and must dramatically change your diet, hop on that exercise bike, and then waddle to the nearest gym to sheath yourself in self-shame and sweat. By that criterion, I most certainly have a problem! Apart from the conventional notions that obesity is the result of too much food (for supposed psychological and socialized or acculturated reasons) and/or of too little exercise, obesity may be caused by any one or a combination of these (or of other) factors:

(1) It is caused by a virus (adeno 37), according to researchers at the University of Wisconsin (http://www.eurekalert.org/pub_releases/2006-01/aps-coi012506.php##).

(2) It may be caused by hormonally triggered chemical changes in the gut that affect the brain's appestat (Bewick, 2012).

(3) It may be caused by genetics (CDC, 2013).

(4) It may be caused by faulty in-utero nutrition as well as by endocrine disruptors (*Toxicological Sciences* 76 [2003], pp. 247–9).

(5) It may be caused by sexual abuse of the child that alters hormone balances (Gustafson and Sarwer, 2004), and such female children also often menstruate early (Noll et al., 2017).

(6) It may be related to blood type (Naish et al., 2011).

(7) It may be because you were not breastfed (Oddy, 2012) or because you as a nursing mother stopped breastfeeding too soon (McCarthy, 2018).

(8) It can be the result of insufficient sound energy reaching the left hemisphere of the brain (one of the symptoms of chronic fatigue syndrome, known for causing weight gain) (Tallman, 2010, p. 389) that gradually dissipates when the function of the right ear is normalized.

(9) It can be caused by the use of some psychiatric medications, such as Risperdal (Tallman, 2010, pp. 193–4).

(10) It may be caused by changes in the hypothalamus in the brain (Marks, 2022).

(11) It may be related to genotype as a response to environmental conditions, which likely explains the physical typology of certain ethnic enclaves, such as Swiss and Alsatian ancestors from mountainous parts of Europe.

(12) It may be the result of coercive parenting regarding finishing offered food by well-intentioned parents who are/were thrilled to have a lot of food or particularly rich food to offer, after having suffered privation themselves. A child coerced to eat will, by the age of five, have lost an inner sense of what and how much to eat to attain satiety.

In fact, obesity may not be abnormal, let alone pathological, according to studies that indicate obese persons who exercise may be healthy regardless of their weight (see, e.g., Kite & Kite, 2022). The Great Depression and World War II, two massive social upheavals associated with food shortages, led to highly successful coercive parenting about food that was accepted and reproduced or rejected (and also led to a pathological condition, anorexia), creating vulnerabilities to medical and commercial applications that have been passed through the generations since then. This vast, vulnerable audience for the theorists obviated their need to actually test their theories in research. As Lindsay Kite (2012) observes, "In 1985, the NIH [National Institutes of Health in the United States] began defining obesity according to BMI [body mass index], which defined the 85th percentile for each sex as the official cutoff for what constitutes 'obese,' based on the standards for underweight, average, overweight and obese that were set by the 1983 Metropolitan Life Insurance Company mortality tables," so that the insurance company could charge more money for "overweight" customers (also see Taylor, 2020).

Posttraumatic stress disorder (PTSD) is often medicalized (see Kleinman, 1995). Suffered especially by those who have experienced the extreme violence of warfare (as soldiers or civilians), violent political oppression, targeting by the police, or crime, PTSD was first diagnosed by Western psychiatrists who traced its origins to bleak, unstable environments in countries such as Cambodia, El Salvador, Tibet, and the former Republic of Yugoslavia. Gradually, the focus of treatment has shifted from the pathology of war and of the environment to the pathology of the individual. Patients are often treated as though their psychobiological reactions to these harrowing circumstances are not normal, as if a psychologically healthy person would not react that way. To be clear, it is not wrong to help people by recognizing that they have suffered psychological trauma, but it is misleading to remove from an individual's story the sickness, threat to life, and horror of the social situation endured.

Ivan Illich: Pioneering Critic of Medicalization

Ivan Illich (1927–2002) introduced the notion of medicalization to sociology. Although Illich was trained as a medieval historian, theologian, and philosopher, sociologists stake claim to him as a public sociologist. Illich developed the concept of medicalization as part of a critique of **radical monopolies** in industrial societies:

> A radical monopoly goes deeper than that of any one corporation or any one government. It can take many forms. . . . Ordinary monopolies corner the market; radical monopolies disable people from doing or

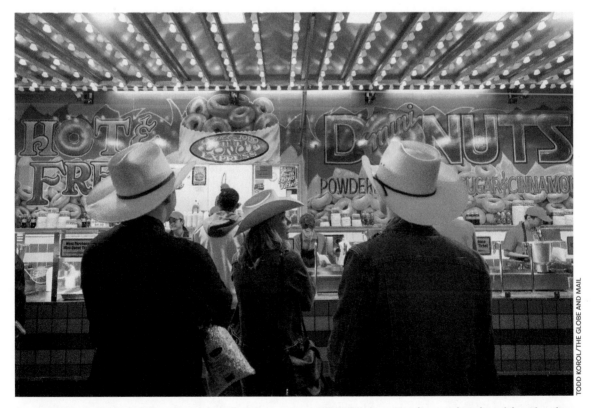

A social determinist might argue that the upward trend in obesity rates is a societal problem having to do with the prevalence of fast-food advertising and the ready availability of cheap, unhealthy food. So if our streets were lined with healthier options, would obesity rates decline? Is obesity a societal problem or an individual one (asks the sociologist with the doughnut problem)? Or is it possible that medical estimates of healthy weight are wrong and that some concerns about weight are a form of "sizeism"?

making things on their own. . . . They impose a society-wide substitution of commodities for use-values by reshaping the milieu and by "appropriating" those of its general characteristics which have enabled people so far to cope on their own. Intensive education turns autodidacts [people who teach themselves] into unemployables, intensive agriculture destroys the subsistence farmer, and the deployment of police undermines the community's self-control. The malignant spread of medicine has comparable results: it turns mutual care and self-medication into misdemeanors or felonies. (Illich, 1976, p. 42)

This passage comes from *Medical Nemesis: The Limits of Medicine*, which opens with the claim that "The medical establishment has become a major threat to health" (1976, p. 1). In the book, Illich describes a "doctor-generated epidemic" that is harming the health of citizens in industrialized society by taking away people's freedom to heal themselves and prevent illness, as well as their freedom to criticize industrial society for the ills of stress, pollution, and general danger that make people sick. Illich's term for this is **iatrogenesis**. He distinguished three different kinds:

- clinical iatrogenesis
- social iatrogenesis
- cultural iatrogenesis.

Clinical iatrogenesis refers to the various ways in which diagnosis and cure cause problems that are as bad as or worse than the health problems they are meant to resolve. This occurs when a patient enters hospital for treatment for, say, a diabetic crisis and becomes infected with hepatitis B originating in the hospital. Or when a cancer treatment has so many side effects it shortens the patient's life or makes them much sicker than he or she would have been without it. Or when a patient prescribed antidepressants commits suicide as a side effect of the drug. A longitudinal study ("longitudinal" being a rare academic luxury) of drugged, somewhat drugged, and not drugged schizophrenics (Harrow et al., 2014) showed that after 20 years the group that had recovered from schizophrenia was the group *not* prescribed psychiatric

medications. The researchers' conclusion is that such medications perpetuate psychosis. For what *sociological* reasons has that discovery not stopped the use of psychiatric drugging by doctors?

Social iatrogenesis occurs when political conditions that "render society unhealthy" are hidden or obscured (Illich, 1976, p. 9). For example, in Canada this happens when lax monitoring by government agencies of laws concerning workplace safety leads to the maiming and death of employees. COVID-19 revealed Canada's poor record compared with other countries: "The proportion of deaths in nursing homes represented 69 per cent of Canada's overall COVID-19 deaths, which is significantly higher than the international average of 41 per cent" (Ireton, 2021). Clearly, many of those deaths could have been avoided. The pandemic brought to light a situation of laxity in most (not all) nursing homes from coast to coast in Canada that flourished in an era of poor monitoring by public health authorities and poorer responses by nursing homes—especially for-profit nursing homes—to citations made by authorities of their inadequacies (Carter, 2021).

Cultural iatrogenesis takes place when the knowledge and abilities of the medical community are extolled or mythologized to the point where the authority of the health profession "tends to mystify and to expropriate the power of the individual to heal himself and to shape his or her environment" (Illich, 1976, p. 9). In other words, patients are given no credit for their role in recovery: it's all the result of the doctor's work. This means, further, that the doctor can do no wrong. Until something goes wrong. Then, the doctor may become quite agile in finding ways to show the negative outcome is entirely the fault of the patient. In fact, medicine increasingly insists on patient "permission" to proceed with treatments for which it requires a medical degree to properly assess the risks involved. Yet the onus is placed upon the patient to make the decision and take full responsibility for it. Formal releases are required in surgeries and other treatments before the doctor or specialist will go ahead with the treatment.

Perhaps the most serious instance of medical culture iatrogenesis is the protection doctors have from prosecution. The systems of law in the United States and in Canada are quite different when a patient believes medical malpractice has occurred and sets out to sue the doctor. In Canada, patients are not allowed the huge claims Americans usually can make for psychological or even physical pain suffered, so forget any impressions you have picked up from US TV and film. In Canada, the disabled patients can sue for time lost from the kind of work they can prove they were capable of doing before the disabling event occurred. They, through their personal injury lawyers, must prove that the injury was caused by malpractice and not through some fault of some other factor or individual. Even if you think it is common knowledge that anatomical event A leads to disabling condition B and that Dr X caused A, a *medical expert* must attest to those supposed facts in that formula. The evidence must be crystal clear, which means you must find believable witnesses willing to testify. It is extremely difficult to find doctors and nurses willing to testify against other doctors and nurses. If the injury takes place in a jail, other inmates may be considered less reliable witnesses than guards, even if the guards destroy evidence. Doctors have relatively infinite funds to pay their own lawyers to defend them. Time is of no consequence to doctors, who are so well paid by comparison with people in other lines of work that they can continue to flourish while they are being sued and while the disabled person cannot work at all. It is impossible to survive on the provincial disability amounts without further support from friends and family, as the movement Basic Income Canada Network, to provide a basic income for all Canadians, attests (Bernstien, 2021).

Big Pharma: The Role of Drug Companies in Medicalization

The term "Big Pharma" is used to refer to the world's large pharmaceutical companies, which reap enormous annual profits from developing, manufacturing, and marketing the drugs used to fight and manage a range of medical conditions, some of them serious (such as HIV), some of them less so (such as insomnia, when this can often be cured through lifestyle changes).

Drug companies invest heavily in research and development. They recover those R&D costs by charging prices far beyond what it costs to manufacture a particular drug product. They can do this when they have a patent on the drug that prevents other companies from copying the product and selling a generic form at lower prices. Note that this system fails to motivate the discovery of inexpensive and simple means of healing that cannot be patented, such as the chemical dichloroacetate.

Consider the case of Roche, the owners of the patent for Tamiflu. Tamiflu is the proprietary term for oseltamivir, the main antiviral medication used against some strains of flu. In 2005, there was an international panic around a new strain of flu, officially known as H5N1 but more commonly known as avian flu or bird flu, because it was first found in birds. Soon after several cases were found in humans, Canada, the United States, Britain, Israel, and Australia bought billions of dollars' worth of Tamiflu to stockpile in case of a serious outbreak. The money was mostly wasted on a pandemic that never emerged (or that never lived up to the hype). Meanwhile, countries that couldn't afford the expensive patented medication, and companies that wanted to provide generic versions of oseltamivir, had to fight to make those cheaper versions of the medication available. In 2009, an Indian company (Cipla Ltd) won the right to produce an alternative version of Tamiflu, called Antiflu, for the world's second most populous country. Canadians were not so fortunate.

Quick Hits

Illich on Medicalization

In every society, medicine, like law and religion, defines what is normal, proper, or desirable. Medicine has the authority to label one man's complaint a legitimate illness, to declare a second man sick though he himself does not complain, and to refuse a third social recognition of his pain, his disability, and even his death. It is medicine which stamps some pain as "merely subjective," some impairment as malingering, and some deaths—though not others—as suicide. (Illich, 1976, p. 45)

Consider another product: the EpiPen device. If you know someone with a serious allergy, or if you have one yourself, you have probably seen an EpiPen. It is used to administer a potentially life-saving dose of the drug epinephrine to someone experiencing a serious allergic reaction. In this case, it is not the drug that is patented but the delivery method: an autoinjector, consisting of a spring-loaded syringe designed to inject the sufferer with the proper dosage of the drug. In the United States, Mylan Pharmaceuticals, which owns the patent, has raised the price of the EpiPen by over 400 per cent since 2009, despite the fact there have been no significant changes to the product to warrant such an increase ("EpiPen Price Furor," 2016). In this case, Canadians *are* lucky: Pfizer, the company with the licence to distribute the product in Canada, has kept the price consistently low, at about Cdn$100–$150 as compared with US$700 (although savings are now available through generics and other discounts for Americans who have insurance), partly because pharmaceutical companies must operate under the oversight of this country's Patent Medicine Prices Review Board.

Big Pharma lobbies hard against generic drugs, which cut into their massive profits, and fiercely defends their patents. But over time, a drug can go off-patent, meaning that the company that developed it no longer holds the right to produce it exclusively. Competition brings the price down—good news for patients—but if the price falls too much, drug companies may decide it is no longer profitable to produce—bad news for patients. This situation is playing out currently in Canada, where there is a shortage of three vital cancer drugs that have recently gone off-patent (Haig, 2019). One of Canada's foremost generic drug firms, Apotex, has been sold to a US company in the wake of the murders of the Canadian owner Barry Sherman and his wife Honey (Donovan, 2022).

Big Pharma's lobby in Canada is strong enough that it affects policy. The flu shot sold in Canada in 2009 had not been through a complete set of clinical trials when it was distributed in the fight against a strain of H1N1 known as "swine flu." Possible side effects were not completely known when the vaccine began to be used. Yet the Canadian government granted GlaxoSmithKline (GSK, a manufacturer of the anti-swine flu vaccine) indemnity, meaning that the government (that is, you, the taxpayer) would cover the cost of any lawsuit filed against the drug maker in the event the drug failed to work or produced fatal complications. GSK might have invested heavily in developing the vaccine, but the government gave the company a deal that carried no financial risk and the promise of huge profits for a company that currently earns an estimated $1.66 billion (US) a year on sales of vaccine.

The pharmaceutical companies, including some new ones, had an unusual opportunity to flex their muscles when COVID-19 spread across the world. This pandemic arrived at a point in the development of new vaccine biotechnologies to turn the world into a gigantic set of trials. Consumers, rigid with terror, were trying to weigh multiple factors in their hope of protecting themselves and their families, as they waited for vaccines to become available. What was the difference between mRNA vaccines, protein subunit vaccines, and the sort of vaccines already familiar for diseases immunized in childhood? How helpful would masks be? What kind were needed and where could they be obtained? How isolated could we become in our various living circumstances in city, suburb, or countryside?

Political and public health leaders were hardly prepared for the magnitude of the threat or the variety of levels of compliance they, at first, guessed at, then, under volleys of criticism from different social sectors, adjusted their stance to—over and over again. And by what turn of fate was the chief spokesperson for public health in Canada a Chinese Canadian with a British accent and a condescending attitude to the inevitably ignorant but by no means unintelligent Canadian masses? An assumption from the beginning that Canadians would not act responsibly if asked to wear masks turned into a self-fulfilling prophecy. Another spokesperson for public health at the provincial level reported with scathing condescension that Liquor Control Board of Ontario retail outlets would be among the few places of business allowed to stay open because "unfortunately some people among us cannot get along without alcohol" or words to that effect. These sorts of interactions with the public were sure to alienate those already out-of-sync with educational systems and they became the core of anti-vaccination resistance. Those vulnerable people in our society fuelled a "Freedom Convoy" to Ottawa and other places and prevails in its resistance today in enclaves likely to be class-related.

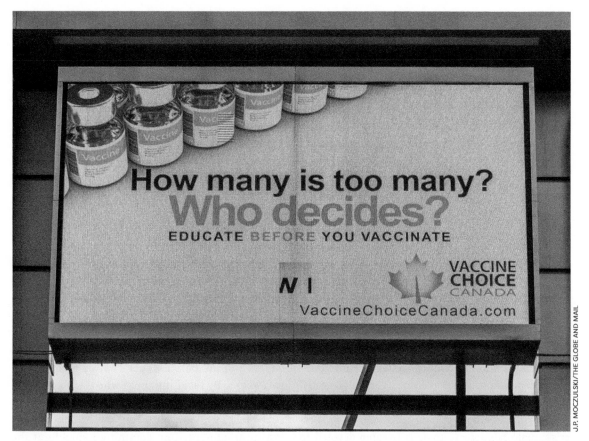

For about one week in February 2019, billboards such as this one popped up in Toronto. They were quickly removed after a public outcry over the anti-vaccine campaign, which critics described as dangerous (Weeks, 2019). A rise in cases of measles in North America has been linked to falling vaccination rates. What are the causes for vaccine hesitancy in Canada? Does it depend on the disease being combatted? Does it depend on the way vaccines are delivered, that is, to very young infants, and targeting multiple diseases in a single shot? And when it comes to getting vaccinated, who should decide—the government or the individual or the parent?

Medicalization and Deaf Culture

One group particularly opposed to medicalization is the Deaf community. Some background here is necessary. Deaf people regard themselves as part of a vibrant cultural group, with their own language, traditions, and history. They embrace the term "Deaf" (capitalized) and do not consider themselves disabled.

Medicalization, as we have seen, is the tendency to define a particular condition as a medical problem requiring intervention. In this context, deafness is regarded medically as an undesirable physical defect that must be "fixed." As Marcel Broesterhuizen (2008) explains, the medicalized approach views Deaf people "as people who lack something, incapable of being fully fledged members of society, less human than others" (Broesterhuizen, 2008, p. 108).

Deaf culture's anti-medicalization stance entails opposition (in certain but not all circumstances) to hearing aids and cochlear implants. A cochlear implant is an electronic device that is surgically implanted in the ear of a Deaf person to transmit sound stimuli electronically to the brain so that it can hear those sounds. Implanting involves removing the non-functional parts of the ear. Opponents in the Deaf community argue that from a medical standpoint, the surgery is risky and not always completely successful. The state of the art of medicine is not so perfect that doctors entirely know what changes they are causing to other parts of the body by implanting the devices. From a social standpoint, losing one's hearing "disability" can interfere with the identity formation of a Deaf person (especially a young Deaf person), depriving the person of membership in the cultural community into which he or she was born (Lane, 1992, 1993). Other medicalized approaches to deafness include the imposition of therapies designed to teach Deaf people to communicate using spoken languages and the denial of access to *or* promotion of sign systems modelled on spoken languages (English, French, etc.) in terms of their structure and vocabulary (CAD, 2012).

Outside of Deaf culture, an awareness of the connection between audio-processing difficulties and behaviour was discovered by a French otolaryngologist, Dr Alfred Tomatis, and further developed by his colleague, Dr Guy Bérard. By using patented equipment that removed the lower frequencies of sound from classical violin concertos, Tomatis had considerable success treating dyslexia, chronic fatigue, depression, and sometimes autism (Tomatis, 1991). He treated Dr Bérard's deafness and restored his hearing, which led to their collaboration in Tomatis's audio laboratory. Tomatis became devoted to

psychiatric theories (Tomatis, 1991, p. 138–9). Then, they parted under a cloud of recriminations by Tomatis (Tomatis, 1991, pp. 120–5).

Bérard took his otolaryngology specialty and developed his own equipment and strategies of research. Studying the "before" and "after" audiograms of his patients led Bérard to identify "distortions" in the patients' perceptions of sound that characterized certain kinds of behaviour (Bérard, 1993). For example, mild depression showed up on the audiogram as peaks of hyperacusis at 1 and 8 kiloHertz; for moderate depression, at 1.5 and 8 kiloHertz; and for severe (suicidal) depression at 2 and 8 kiloHertz. Between those peaks, a trough of less sensitive hearing meant the brain was receiving less sound energy. Most often, the problem was in the left ear, which would more strongly affect the right-brain, but would be most severe when both ears have the same audiogram profile or "curve." Among his 233 patients with severe depression, he cured 90 per cent of them within two weeks. By recalling those who were not cured for further courses of treatment, he brought the cure rate to 97.7 per cent. Four were not cured following treatment. One committed suicide at the beginning of treatment. Among his 1,850 patients with dyslexic syndrome, he cured all of them of their principle symptom of not being able to learn how to read (Bérard & Brockett, 2011, p. 101). While all of these patients were not "deaf" in the ordinary meaning of that word, they had treatable hearing dysfunction. In this emerging field, followers of these two pioneers are finding success or partial success in treating autism, Alzheimer's and other dementias, Parkinson's, a range of mental illnesses, and other supposedly "incurable" conditions. Why have these treatments developed by medical specialists in France not been more widely embraced by their North American medical counterparts?

> **What do *you* think?**
>
> 1. Is deafness primarily a medical problem to be dealt with by medical specialists? Or is it more like seeing problems that can be dealt with by optometrists, who assess the need for and supply glasses, as well as by ophthalmologists, who are medically trained to diagnose and treat more severe eye problems?
> 2. What role should the Deaf community play in dealing with deafness? Do you think that your position might be different if you were Deaf or had a family member or friend who was Deaf?
> 3. Some research shows that deaf children fitted with cochlear implants before the age of two develop spoken language skills much more quickly than children older than two who have had the surgery (Kral & O'Donoghue, 2010). Do you think it is appropriate to have this surgery performed on children before they are old enough to be consulted? How do you think your answer might differ if you were Deaf or a Deaf parent weighing the options?

14.6 Medical Sociology, Race, and Ethnicity

This section looks at how medical sociology examines the way that race and ethnicity affect the delivery of healthcare.

Unemployed Immigrant Doctors: A Problem with Many Standpoints

The Canadian healthcare system faces a shortage of doctors in communities outside of large urban centres. At the same time, the country is welcoming immigrants with medical degrees and general credentials that are considered insufficient to qualify them to practise medicine in Canada. It is a perplexing issue, one that must be considered from a number of standpoints. The sections that follow outline four of these differing standpoints.

Immigrant Doctors

As an immigrant doctor, you came to a country that offered greater financial opportunities for you and your family. On the strength of skills and experience gained in your home country, you scored well in the "point system" used to judge the suitability of candidates for immigration. The Canadian government seemed to welcome your arrival.

As soon as you arrived, problems hit you in the face (New Canadian Media News Desk, 2020). If you chose to settle in Toronto—as many do—you encountered a two-step problem. First, your skills and knowledge were assessed through a training program. The Ontario International Medical Graduate Program takes 48 weeks—close to a year—to complete and has limited space. You managed to gain admission to the program and did well, but then you faced a second, even higher hurdle: a residency program of several years in which you would essentially re-learn everything you needed to know to earn your medical qualifications in the first place. And then you faced the largest problem: the small number of residency positions available. Until recently, you would have been one of more than 1,100 immigrant doctors in Ontario competing for just 36 spots open each year in the residency program. The number of spots has recently increased to 250. Still, the odds are not in your favour.

In the meantime, your family must eat. You might get a job in a medical field, possibly (with training) as a lab assistant. But it is more likely you will end up working as a telemarketer, driving an Uber, delivering meals-to-go, or doing manual labour in factories. Your dream of practising your chosen profession in this country has proven elusive.

Rural Communities

You live in a community that is home to fewer and fewer doctors. The older ones retire; the young graduates opt to take up medical work in the big city. Your family doctor has retired and closed her practice, and you, like her other patients, are scrambling to find another doctor to take you on. But most family doctors are already seeing more patients than they can handle. The trouble is that you're older and therefore more likely to have complicated and time-consuming medical problems. You are more work for a new doctor, who can choose not to take you as a patient. So you put up with minor complaints, knowing that anything more serious will require a trip to the big city, where the bigger research hospitals and more lucrative practices are.

Occasionally, you wonder whether there's something your town should be doing to attract doctors. You don't care where they come from. In Ontario, 214 communities have been designated as "underserved" by the provincial Ministry of Health. Saskatchewan and Newfoundland and Labrador have higher percentages of foreign-trained doctors than other provinces. The reason: they present fewer obstacles for immigrant doctors.

Countries of Origin of Internationally Trained Doctors

You live in a developing country, where, especially in rural areas, there are even fewer doctors per population than there are in Canada's rural communities. The cost of educating medical professionals in your country is prohibitively high. It is much more likely that you will lose trained doctors to emigration than benefit from an influx of health professionals.

In post-apartheid South Africa, the government decided to block doctors immigrating from other African nations to halt the **brain drain**—the exodus of educated professionals—eroding the healthcare systems of those countries. Canada experiences a certain amount of brain drain when some of its medical specialists and nurses go to the United States, but it's nothing compared to the brain drain of doctors leaving developing countries for North America.

Doctors' Associations

Placing restrictions on internationally trained medical graduates gives Canadian-trained doctors more bargaining power as a group. As Linda McQuaig

Quick Hits

Where Do You Go When You Don't Have a Family Doctor?

According to the Canadian Community Health Survey (released 22 October 2020), in 2019, "14.5% of Canadians aged 12 and older (roughly 4.6 million people) reported that they did not have a regular health care provider they see or talk to when they need care or advice for their health" (Statistics Canada, 2020; Figure 14.1). This figure is significantly lower than the 5.6 million Canadians over the age of 12 Canadians without a healthcare provider in 2017 (Statistics Canada, 2017). In all age groups, men were more likely than women to report not having a regular family doctor.

An earlier Statistics Canada report (2013) found that not everyone without a family doctor was looking for one, and 80.6 per cent reported they had a place to go if they needed health advice; these included:

- walk-in clinics (58.9 per cent);
- hospital emergency rooms (13.0 per cent);
- community health centres (8.7 per cent);
- other facilities, including hospital out-patient clinics and telephone health lines (19.3 per cent).

Among those who had looked for family doctor:

- 36.7 per cent said that doctors in their area were not taking new patients.
- 29.7 per cent said their doctor had retired or left the area.
- 25.2 per cent said that no doctors were available in their area.
- 21.2 per cent gave other reasons.

These add up to more than 100 per cent because respondents were permitted to choose more than one option.

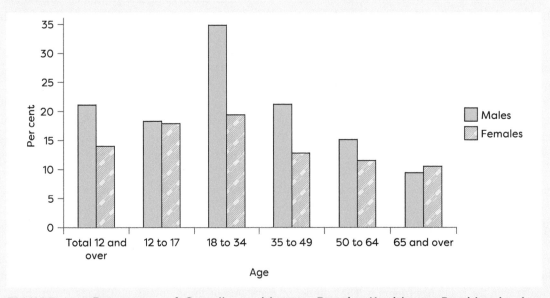

FIGURE 14.1 **Percentage of Canadians without a Regular Healthcare Provider, by Age Category and Sex**

Source: Based on Statistics Canada (2019).

explained in a commentary on the New Brunswick doctors' strike in 2004:

Doctors have managed to maintain enormous bargaining power in Canada by

threatening, from time to time, to abandon us for more prosperous climes. But these threats only have teeth because doctors can rely on the fact that there is no one here to replace them if they go—even when potential replacements are already here and desperate to get to work. (McQuaig, 2004)

On the other side, consider the Ontario Medical Association's "Position Paper on Physician Workforce Policy and Planning," dated April 2002. It addresses the OMA's concerns about "the problem of inadequate physician human resources, and the related consequences for public access to medical treatment." One of the 18 recommendations in the report was to "Temporarily increase the number of fully qualified international medical graduate (IMG) positions." In a 2004 speech, OMA president Dr Larry Erlick, addressing the same problems, noted:

> We . . . need more foreign-trained physicians to practise in Ontario. The fact that we have relied on foreign-trained physicians in the past should come as no surprise, as 25 per cent of physicians practising today in this province are in fact international medical graduates! Some of the red tape has to be cut.

Still, in both documents, helping foreign-trained physicians gain accreditation to practise in Canada was clearly viewed as a secondary solution. The words "temporarily" and "fully qualified" in the first statement leave holes in that support, and Dr Erlick's recommendation was one of a number of "short-term recommendations," given less priority than bringing back Ontario medical graduates now practising elsewhere. More recently, the Association of International Physicians and Surgeons of Ontario headlines the likelihood of foreign-trained doctors finding work in Ontario at 6 per cent. "The success rate of international medical doctors who wish to pursue a career in medicine is six per cent, according to researchers at St. Michael's Hospital in Toronto" (AIPSO, 2018). Nevertheless, Immigration Canada continues to roll out the warm invitations.

The Racialization of Disease: The 2003 SARS Outbreak

A disease becomes **racialized** when it is strongly associated with people of a particular racial or ethnic background, so that people of this background are treated negatively. An example occurred in 2003, when an outbreak of severe acute respiratory syndrome, or SARS, affected Canadians of all races but became primarily associated with Asians.

Canadians began hearing about SARS in March 2003. They quickly learned that the highly contagious

Telling It Like It Is

A Student Point of View

An Account of Systemic Racism from a Black First-Year Nursing Student

I have had my first clinical experience in the nursing profession, and I feel I have already been subjected to systemic racism. Examples of this include disciplinary actions that are different from other student nurses such as when myself and a non-Black student returned late from break. I was pulled aside, and it was stated that the teacher felt sorry for the other student. When I asked "why," it was implied that I coerced her into returning late against her will. Also, vague work appraisals are given, and no specific areas of improvement are suggested. Comments such as, "You seem like a very angry person," and "I have a hard time approaching you and can only imagine how the residents feel," or "Any monkey can be trained to take a blood pressure" are an everyday occurrence. There are many cases where my mistakes are far more noted and exaggerated than those of other students. When defending myself (as I feel I am performing equally well to everyone else), I am labelled as not being "self-aware" and not accepting feedback. Yet when feedback is taken and changes are made, I am told I take things too literally. As a result, I can do no right.

Events like these are commonplace. As a result, promotions as well as workload may not be fairly distributed.

—Nadine Smith

What do *you* think?

1. Who is involved in racializing a disease like SARS or COVID-19? Whose role should it be to challenge the racialization of disease as it is occurring?

2. Can the media be blamed for reporting the association of COVID-19 with Asians? What is the possibility that the virus was accidentally or deliberately released from the virus research facility in the same city as the "wet market" blamed for selling live, potentially virus-carrying animals for meat? What could the media have done to lessen the racial effect of their presentations concerning COVID-19?

3. Can individual Canadians be blamed for altering their purchasing habits to lessen the odds of contracting a virus? Should people be expected to weigh decisions about their personal health against the greater economic and social impact of their decisions?

respiratory ailment with flu-like symptoms was serious, and in about 10 per cent of cases fatal. This made it the focus of widespread media attention throughout the spring and early summer. Over this period, the disease became racialized: because it originated in China, and because members of a Catholic Filipino community were among those who had contracted it, the disease took on a racial identity. Once cases of the disease began to appear in Canada, Chinese and Filipino Canadians became targets of discrimination.

Researchers Carrianne Leung and Jian Guan studied how the mainstream media racialized SARS by portraying Asians as carriers of disease in a way that spread fear among non-Asian Canadians. Table 14.1 summarizes their findings about the content of pictures accompanying news stories in four national newspapers and periodicals (Leung & Guan, 2004, pp. 9, 10).

Leung and Guan found that photographs accompanying stories about SARS tended to feature Asians, particularly Asians wearing masks to reduce the spread of the disease. The researchers noted that the use of frightening words and unreasonable links to the Spanish influenza pandemic of 1918–19 (in which at least 20 million people died over an 18-month period) were also part of media hysteria. Fear surrounding the disease had a devastating economic impact on parts of Canada where the outbreak was prevalent, notably Toronto and, in particular, its various Chinatowns. Media commentators noted that many of the patrons suddenly avoiding Chinese businesses were themselves Chinese, as though this somehow justified similar acts of discrimination by non-Asian Canadians. Regardless, the loss of business occurred because the disease was racialized to the point where many Canadians changed their purchasing habits as a precaution against contracting the virus in communities where it was thought to be prevalent.

Most of you reading this will have seen the same thing happen at the outset of the COVID-19 epidemic, but it became a pandemic so quickly and the countries developing the most severe consequences were the United States and in Europe, which then turned the media spotlight away from Canada. The world would have liked to pin down the origins of the disease, known to have been Chinese, but the world also was so preoccupied with the sick and with efforts to protect those who were not sick that the specific origins faded to a lower priority in the social consciousness. To the time of this writing, the death toll worldwide stood at 6,543,138, with 620,878,405 reported cases.

TABLE 14.1 Photographic Treatment of SARS in the National Media, 2003

Newspaper/ Magazine	Number of SARS Photos	Showing People		Showing Asians		Showing Asians with Masks	
		#	%	#	%	#	%
National Post	120	95	82.0	65	54.2	60	50.0
Globe and Mail	119	68	57.1	52	43.9	41	34.5
Maclean's	27	17	63.0	8	29.6	6	22.2
Time (Canada)	17	15	88.2	8	47.0	6	35.3

Source: Leung & Guan (2004).

THURSDAY, APRIL 3, 2003 ★ TORONTO STAR ★ B3

SARS Outbreak

China admits wider spread of SARS

12 more deaths reported among inland provinces

First cases found in Latin America and Israel

ANN PERRY
STAFF REPORTER

The global death toll from Severe Acute Respiratory Syndrome jumped yesterday as China broke its silence and admitted it had more cases in more provinces than it had previously revealed.

The South China Morning Post reported today that the first victims of the deadly illness were people in China's southern province of Guangdong who ate or handled wild game, confirming earlier reports linking the disease to ducks.

China said it had 1,190 suspected cases through the end of March, and 46 deaths instead of the 34 it had admitted. Cases were reported in Guangxi, Hunan and Sichuan provinces as well as Guangdong for the first time.

In total, the World Health Organization estimated that SARS has infected more than 2,200 people worldwide and killed an estimated 78.

Brazil reported its first suspected case, which, if confirmed, would be the first in Latin America. Israel also reported its first suspected case.

China agreed yesterday to let a team of WHO investigators visit the southern province of Guangdong, where the disease is believed to have started.

The four-member international team, which will leave Beijing today, will take samples from suspected patients to help identify a culprit virus and assess how infectious and virulent it is.

And, for the first time in its 55-

REUTERS
With Hong Kong being the global centre of the SARS outbreak, face masks are common on the city's streets. Some residents strive for their own style amid the crisis. Chinese officials are reporting there are more cases and more deaths than they previously admitted.

year-history, WHO recommended that travellers avoid part of the world because of an infectious disease: Hong Kong and adjoining Guangdong province.

In the first public statement by a senior leader, Chinese Health Minister Zhang Wenkang said the outbreak was "under effective control."

He said 80 per cent of those diagnosed with SARS have recovered.

For weeks, U.N. agency officials have appealed for more co-operation from China.

"Because the mainland is not sharing information . . . the outbreak has been lengthened," Taiwan's Mainland Affairs Council said in a recent report.

Laboratories around the world are racing to come up with a test for SARS.

The U.S. Centers for Disease Control has issued two tests that health officials can give to patients with suspected SARS. Dr. Julie Gerberding, the director of the Atlanta-based centre, said until a large number of people are tested, no one can say whether the disease is caused by the main suspect — a coronavi-

rus.

But she said so far 400 healthy people had been tested for the virus, a previously unknown relative of one of the common cold viruses, and all had tested negative.

Several patients with SARS have tested positive.

"It is not yet proof. There are other viruses still under investigation," she said. In Toronto, Dr. Raymond Tellier of the Hospital for Sick Children, has developed a test that detects this new species of coronavirus. It is currently being used here.

A top health expert in China told a newspaper the earliest SARS patients in Guangdong had close and continuous contact with chickens, ducks, pigeons and owls.

"We will explore further if the disease was passed to human beings from wild animals. You know, Guangdong people like eating exotic animals and I don't find it a healthy practice," said Bi Shengli, a vice-director at the Chinese Centre for Disease Control and Prevention.

The earliest cases of the disease were traced to either chefs or bird vendors, Bi said.

In Thailand yesterday, the government said it would turn back foreigners suspected of having SARS and would force those allowed in from affected countries to wear masks in public.

In the Philippines, which has no confirmed cases, President Gloria Macapagal Arroyo put in place a contingency plan — including air and seaport checks — to prevent an outbreak. Health officials in New Zealand urged indigenous Maori tribesmen to forgo their traditional "hongi" nose-rubbing greeting for visiting Chinese at a convention.

In Hong Kong, the Roman Catholic Church ordered priests to wear masks during Communion and put wafers in the hands of the faithful rather than on the tongue.
FROM STAR WIRE SERVICES

Toronto Star

Telling It Like It Is

A Student Point of View

SARS and Being Chinese

Around the time of the SARS crisis, being Chinese made people look at me in a different way, whether it was at school, at work, or in public places such as the subway and buses. It did not bother me at first, but as more and more individuals died due to SARS, the more I kept my eyes open for tainted looks darting in my direction.

Around that time in school, it wasn't so much the looks, but comments made in class about the situation. What I have learned and understood in this game we call life is that everyone is entitled to his or her opinion. I have also learned and understood that not all opinions are necessarily right or wrong. Unfortunately, not all people consider that their opinions are wrong, hurtful, disrespectful, condescending, and rude.

One incident happened in my math class at college. Our class got off topic, and our focus was turned from present and future value to SARS. Our teacher was reminding us that proper hand washing helps in preventing the spread of infection. One obnoxious fellow who felt he was the

(Continued)

class clown replied to our teacher's comment and stated that to prevent the spread of infection, we need to stay away from all those darn Chinese people. His language use and vocabulary was a little cruder. Being the only Asian person in the class, everyone turned and looked in my direction as if they were expecting me to curse him. I decided to let the one and only authority figure take care of his biased opinion. However, our teacher said absolutely nothing, except to get on with the lesson. His comments offended me and our teacher not correcting him hurt my feelings. It made me pay more attention to the things that were being said in all the rest of my classes. The impact it had on my school life made me more defensive towards what my peers had to say about those of Asian descent. . . .

Ethnicity is a sociological factor that made an impact on my life within that year. Because I have been on the end of a biased opinion at school and indirect discrimination at work, I have further learned another aspect of the game of life: the value and meaning of equality and fairness and that even though there are different ethnicities and races, we are all part of one race called the human race.

—Karin Koo

14.7 Medical Sociology and Gender

This section looks at how issues of gender impact the delivery of healthcare.

Female Doctors and the Feminization of the Medical Profession

We can say that the medical profession is becoming "feminized." This means that the percentage of women practising medicine in Canada is growing. In 1959, women accounted for about 6 per cent of medical school graduates in Canada. They remained a distinct minority over the next two decades, even while their numbers rose. In her preface to an edited collection of articles on female doctors in Canada, Shelley Ross, an associate professor in the Department of Family Medicine at the University of Alberta, explains what has happened since:

> Until the early 1980s, women made up less than one-third of the annual enrolment in Canadian faculties of medicine. Since 1982, however, the number of women enrolling in Canadian medical schools has consistently increased. By 1995, women made up half of those entering medical classes across the country. Since that year, women have been the majority in medical school classes in Canada. Although the high of a 59.1 per cent female incoming cohort across Canada in 2004 has not recurred, the ratio of 55.45 female-to-male has now become the new normal, with some provinces and territories consistently showing even higher proportions of female students in their intake. (Ross, 2019, p. ix)

Male physicians still dominate the profession numerically (52.5 per cent to 47.5 per cent of females), and in terms of influence in provincial and territorial medical associations. In terms of specialties, males dominate at 61.2 per cent compared with females at 38.8 per cent. In 2007, there were roughly twice as many male as female doctors in Canada (Canadian Institute for Health Information, 2007), so the gender gap has narrowed. There is an age group difference: the older the age group, the greater the percentage of male doctors. However, as older doctors retire, the profession becomes more feminized.

Gender matters in an individual's experience of being a doctor. Women and men tend to differ in the types of medicine they practise. Women are more likely to be family physicians than specialists, particularly surgical specialists. In 2019, the percentage of women general surgeons in the age range 35–45 was 41 per cent and in the <35 age range, 47 per cent. It was noted in 2007 that women who specialized went into predictable areas: 71 per cent went into obstetrics and gynecology (OBG), and 67 per cent into pediatrics (Malicki, 2007). In 2019, those percentages are 62 per cent (OBG) and 63 per cent pediatrics; but the entry level (<35 years of age) percentages for females are much lower in both specialties. Some women doctors may feel more comfortable in specialties concerning women because they have "insider information" about their patients. At the same time, specialties *not* already considered "appropriate" for women may be sanctioned by the medical community when females venture into those other areas. It appears that women entering the profession tend to follow their role model predecessors into these same fields of practice, which is growing their percentage in many specialties (CMA, 2022).

Certain stresses are felt more by female doctors than by male doctors. One is the challenge of achieving a satisfying work–life balance. Women are more likely to experience role conflict regarding family life. As a result, they may see fewer patients and work fewer hours. These stresses make them more likely than their male counterparts to take short periods of time off or to retire prematurely (Hedden et al., 2017).

14.8 Medical Marginality: The Intersection of Gender and Race

Medical marginality occurs when a gender or race is blocked from becoming health professionals: doctors and nurses. Throughout the first two and a half centuries of Canadian history doctors were white males and nurses were white females, reflecting the primarily European sources of immigration to the country.

Delayed Doctors: The First Canadian Female Physicians

The first female in the United States to graduate from an American medical school was British-born Elizabeth Blackwell (1821–1910). She was accepted at the Geneva Medical College in New York in 1847, graduating with her medical degree in 1849.

The first female Canadian physician in Canada was Emily Howard Jennings Stowe (1831–1903). She was born in Norwich, Ontario (where an elementary school is named after her). Her path to becoming a medical professional was long and winding. She taught elementary school for seven years starting at age 15. In 1853, she applied to study medicine

> **What do *you* think?**
> 1. Ross (2019, p. 8) comments that there is social resistance to claims that women and men experience medical education and practice differently. Why do you think that is?
> 2. Why might female physicians be less likely to become otolaryngologists or urologists? Consider several reasons.
> 3. Do you think that the feminization of the medical professional might significantly lessen the power differential between doctors and nurses?

at Victoria College in Cobourg but was turned down as a female. She then went to the Provincial Normal School to train as a teacher for a year. Upon graduation, she accepted an appointment as the first Canadian woman to become a principal at an elementary school. She stayed in education for about a decade until she was turned down by the University of Toronto School of Medicine in 1865 because she was female. Emily then moved to the United States to study at the New York Medical College for Women, graduating in homeopathic medicine in 1867. Her youngest two sisters would graduate in medicine at the same college in 1875. (Homeopathic medicine was as fully embraced by most people at that time as allopathic medicine—and is still practised, with modern scientific testing of certain areas showing its success with respiratory disease and pollen allergies.) To receive an official licence in Ontario, she had to take a full course in a recognized Canadian medical school. Finally, in 1870–1, along with Scottish-born Jennie Trout (1841–1921), who would become the first female licensed doctor in Canada in 1875, she was accepted at the Toronto School of Medicine (later, part of the University of Toronto). Neither completed the program due to harassment from male students and professors (e.g., rude drawings, offensive objects placed where they were readily seen, and obnoxious recounts of obscene stories). Emily worked as a physician's assistant until she finally received her Canadian medical licence from the College of Physicians and Surgeons of Ontario in 1880. This made her the second female licensed physician after her former classmate, Jennie Trout.

In 1883, wanting to create physician opportunities for other women, Stowe founded the Ontario Medical College for Women in Toronto, which eventually became Women's College Hospital, a prominent teaching hospital still active in the twenty-first century. In 2018, she was inducted into the Canadian Medical Hall of Fame.

Ann Augusta Stowe (1857–1943), her eldest daughter, was the first Canadian woman trained in Canada to become a physician. She was accepted at the Toronto School of Medicine, graduating in 1883.

In Quebec, Irma Le Vasseur (1877–1964) was the first female French Canadian physician. Her father had to end his medical studies in his third year due to financial reverses in his family but went on to become a noted journalist. When Irma was 10, her parents separated, and her mother moved to New York. Like Emily Stowe, Irma had to go to the United States to be accepted into a school of medicine. She graduated in 1900 from the School of Medicine at Saint Paul University in Minnesota, at age 23, then worked as a doctor in New York.

Returning to Quebec, she petitioned for a private member's bill entitling her to work as a doctor in her home province. It was passed in 1903, making her the twelfth woman in Quebec and the first French Canadian woman licensed to practise medicine in the province. However, in a perhaps surprising pivot, she went to France and Germany to study pediatric medicine. The death of her brothers in infancy may have influenced her interest in pediatric medicine. Three years later, she returned to Quebec, where she became the first French Canadian woman to actively practise medicine there. That year, she co-founded with Justine Lacoste-Beaubien (the wife of a wealthy banker) the first pediatric hospital in Quebec, the Hôpital Sainte-Justine in Montreal, in which she was a director. In 1908, because she qualified as a physician but not as one able to do surgeries, she was sent to work in the pharmaceutical dispensary in an apparent administrative coup.

Her mother had lived in New York since her divorce in 1887, when Irma was 10, so it was not unusual that Irma returned to New York. As a medical inspector of schools, she worked there until an outbreak of typhus in Serbia, in 1915, drew her back to Europe. One of the four doctors who worked alongside her during the first, hard year of the epidemic said, "She was a woman of action who would never become discouraged." They returned to Canada while she remained on the front lines. Toward the end of World War I, she worked in a French military hospital, then returned to New York to work for the Red Cross.

In 1922, aged 43, Irma returned to Quebec, where the infant mortality rate of only one child in four reaching one year of age was second only to the rate in Calcutta. She invested her own money in another pediatric hospital. After disagreements with the administration, she withdrew from that project and founded two more pediatric hospitals, one of which was for children with disabilities. She screened female recruits for service during World War II. She apparently suffered some kind of breakdown for the next decade as she was found to be so malnourished and living in such poor circumstances that, in her late seventies, she was diagnosed with mental illness and hospitalized. She revived sufficiently to fight her diagnosis and was released in 1958. She lived alone and destitute in Quebec City until her death in 1964. In 2018, the government of Canada designated her a Person of National Historic Significance.

Sophia Bethena Jones (1857–1932)

When working on this chapter I had difficulty finding the first female Black Canadian physician. Other than the Chatham-Kent Black Historical Society, which helped me with my research, and the University of Michigan and Spelman College, I saw no other sources that recognized the achievements of Sophia Jones.

Sophia Bethena Jones was born on 16 March 1857 in Chatham, Ontario, a town that was a major northern terminus of the Underground Railroad, known in the 1850s as the "Black mecca of Canada." Consequently, it had a relatively large Black population when Sophia was growing up. She enrolled as an undergraduate at the University of Toronto in 1879. She was ambitious to become a doctor. However, she was not admitted to the medical school there. After teaching for a year, she applied to and was accepted at the University of Michigan Medical School in 1880. In 1885, she became the first Black woman to graduate from that program. This was 21 years after the first African American woman, Rebecca Lee Crumpler, graduated as a doctor in 1864.

Dr Sophia B. Jones went from the University of Michigan Medical School to develop a nursing program at Spelman College, a private institution for Black students in Atlanta, Georgia, founded in 1881. She was the first Black faculty member in 1885, teaching there until 1888. She then taught at Wilberforce University in Ohio, a private institution dedicated to the education of Black students. She continued her teaching career in St. Louis, then at the Frederick Douglass Hospital in Philadelphia, an African American institution that provided the first training school for Black nurses in the city.

In September 1913 she published "Fifty Years of Negro Public Health" in the *Annals of the American Academy of Political and Social Science*. At the time she was the resident physician at the Agricultural and Mechanical College in Greensboro, North Carolina, later to become a branch of the University of North Carolina. This article was the first research publication by a Black woman in the medical field. In the text are the following passages.

> In the course of the past fifty years the Negro race has had to contend against the hostile forces of ignorance, poverty and prejudice while adjusting itself to the new conditions imposed by the life of freedom, and consequently its mortality rate has been excessively high, due largely to pulmonary tuberculosis and infant diseases; but now a marked improvement is apparent, and its mortality rate is declining with that of the general population. (Jones, 1913, p. 145)

When Jones retired, she moved to Monrovia, California, with her sister Anna. They ran an orange grove there. She died in 1932. She never married or had children.

Elizabeth Steinhauer

In 1980, Elizabeth Steinhauer, an Alberta Cree, became the first Canadian Indigenous woman to be licensed as a doctor. That such an achievement happened so recently can be explained in two ways. The residential school system was so traumatic for Indigenous children that it crushed their desire to pursue postsecondary education. Just as significant a deterrent was the Indian Act, which forced Indigenous youth seeking higher education to become enfranchised (being given the federal vote), which also entailed their surrendering their Indian status. To do

What do you think?
1. Why do you think it was difficult to find the first female Black physician, and why has she received so little recognition in Canada?
2. Why do you think she moved so many times in her career?

so, eliminated their treaty and other Indigenous rights, which meant they could be evicted from their home reserve. The two Indigenous men who became doctors in 1866, Peter Edmund Jones, an Anishinaabe leader, and Peter Martin, a Mohawk who went to Oxford University through his contact with Prince Edward, could do so because the Indian Act had not been passed. Susan La Flesche Picott, the first Indigenous woman in the United States to become a doctor, was an Omaha, who graduated from Woman's Medical College of Pennsylvania in 1889. Like Peter Jones and Peter Martin, she had influential contacts who helped her to realize her goals.

The First Black Male Physicians in Canada

Finding out who was the first Black male Canadian doctor has barriers similar to those one confronts when looking for the first Black female physician. This difficulty is addressed in Frank Mackey's 2018 article, "1848, 1861, 1926—Which Came First?" The 1926 date pertains only to McGill University, and refers to Jamaica-born Kenneth Melville (1902–1975). The 1861 graduate was Dr Anderson Ruffin Abbot (1837–1913), who had been accepted as a medical student at the University of Toronto. In the first sources that I consulted Dr Abbot was given as the first, aided by the American-born Dr Alexander Thomas Augusta (1825–1890), who was admitted to the medical program there some time during the 1850s and who received his Bachelor of Science in Medicine in 1860. He had been turned down by American medical schools before he was accepted at the University of Toronto. Both of these Black doctors were honoured in 2022 with plaques on the University of Toronto downtown campus.

What do you think?
Why do you think the Indian Act included an elimination of rights for Indigenous students who went to university?

The 1848 date was when Dr William Wright graduated at 20 years of age from McGill University in medicine. He was born in Quebec City in 1827 to a Black father and a white mother. In the census of 1861, he identified himself as being "creole." In the 1901 census, he referred to himself as "black."

He worked as an assistant to a doctor for the next few years, eventually becoming a surgeon and obstetrician. In 1853 he began teaching at McGill as well as being the chair of the Department of Materia Medica (Pharmacy). Following strong religious views, he was ordained in 1864 as a deacon of the Anglican Church, upgraded to priest in 1871. In 1882, when he was 55, his students complained that he was not keeping up to date with the latest developments in medicine. At that time, medicine was advancing quickly. They boycotted his classes, and he retired the following year. Although in the United States some Black medical teachers received this kind of treatment for racial reasons, there is no concrete evidence that such was the case here.

Notable Nurses

The first nursing training facility in Canada was the General and Marine Hospital in St. Catherines, Ontario. It opened in 1874, just two years later than the first American nursing school, the New England Hospital for Women and Children. Mary Eliza Mahoney was the first Black woman to graduate from that program, doing so in 1879.

A young Canadian Black woman, Bernice Redmon, had to go to St Philip Hospital Medical College in Virginia to achieve her career goal as she was rejected by Canadian nursing schools. She graduated with a nursing diploma in 1945. That year, she returned to Canada and was hired by the Nova Scotia Department of Health, the first Black nurse to practise in public health. Later, she became the first Black woman to be appointed to the Victorian Order of Nurses in Canada.

In 1948, two Black women, Ruth Bailey, from Toronto, and Gwennyth Barton, from Halifax, graduated from the Grace Maternity School of Nursing in Halifax. In 1950, Marissa Scott became the first Black woman to graduate and practise as a nurse in Ontario.

Charlotte Edith Anderson Monture, a Kanienke-haka from the Six Nations in southwestern Ontario, was the first Indigenous woman to become a registered nurse. After being turned down by nursing schools in Canada, she went to New York to be educated at the New Rochelle Nursing School, graduating in 1914. She began her career in that city as a private school nurse. When the United States entered World War I in 1917, she volunteered to serve in the US Army Nurse Corps. In that year, the Canadian government passed the Military Voters Act of 1917. This included giving the federal vote to women who were army nurses in the war. This made Monture the first female status Indian and registered band member to have the federal vote. Otherwise, she would have been "enfranchised," losing her Indigenous status if she had received a university degree in Canada. Status Indians/registered band members did not have the federal vote without losing status until 1960. After the war, she returned to her home community to work as a nurse and midwife in the reserve hospital.

14.9　Medical Sociology and Class

This section looks at how social class affects the delivery of healthcare.

The Inverse Care Law

Dr Julian Tudor Hart studied medicine at Cambridge and interned at the equally prestigious St George's Hospital in London. The natural career move for a British doctor on that path would have been to serve the needs of the wealthier classes in London or some other big city. Instead, he dedicated his life to helping the citizens of a working-class mining village in Wales. Dr Hart became famous among medical sociologists for an article he wrote in 1971. In it he introduced the idea of the inverse care law:

> The availability of good medical care tends to vary inversely with the need for it in the

What do _you_ think?

Do you consider "keeping score" of the "firsts in medicine" among white women and among women in racialized groups is a useful way of illustrating marginality socially in the larger culture? Why or why not?

population served. This inverse care law operates more completely where medical care is most exposed to market forces, and less so where such exposure is reduced. (Hart, 1971, p. 405)

This summary, stated as a "law" of human responses to social needs, means "the more you need it, the more it isn't there." Sadly, Hart was describing a system that, for almost 20 years, had experienced socialized health care similar to Canada's—a system markedly different from the private or market-force system found in the United States. In the British context, the inverse care law was evident in statistics concerning infant mortality from 1949 to 1953, where health outcomes were directly linked to social class. In other words, the death of an infant in its first year of life was far more likely to occur among the lower classes (those engaged in manual labour). This was a product of differences both in the working and living conditions of the different classes and in the medical care available in different areas defined by class. Regarding doctors, Hart observed the following trends:

> In areas with most sickness and death, general practitioners have more work, larger lists [of patients], less hospital support, and inherit more clinically ineffective traditions of consultation [e.g., short visits with little listening to patients' problems] than in the healthiest areas; and hospital doctors shoulder heavier case-loads with less staff and equipment, more obsolete buildings, and suffer recurrent crises in the availability of beds and replacement staff. (Hart, 1971, p. 412)

14.10 The Sociology of Dis/Ability

Like poverty and pollution, **disability** is hard to define precisely. We can probably find consensus on some types of disability, such as paralysis or blindness; as with the homeless poor and oil-contaminated water, the extreme cases are easy to identify. But devising an operational definition—a working definition that we can use for statistical purposes—forces us to consider less obvious cases.

What do *you* think?

1. Do you think the inverse care law holds in Canada? How would you, as a sociologist, go about trying to prove or disprove it?
2. We know that even in Canada, people in certain positions are routinely allowed to "jump the queue" to receive medical procedures faster than most Canadians are normally be able to. (When was the last time you heard of an NHL player having to wait four to six months for an MRI?) Who in your opinion is entitled to priority care? Professional athletes? High-ranking politicians? People who have donated to the hospital? Emergency services professionals (paramedics, police officers, fire fighters)? Hospital workers? Spouses and families of any of the above?

What Is a Disability? The Challenge of Operational Definition

The *Oxford English Dictionary* provides us with a starting point. It defines disability as "any condition—mental or physical, permanent or temporary—that limits a person's ability to participate in regular activities in the home, at work, at school, or in recreational pursuits." But does that mean that a person who cannot drive without glasses is disabled? What about someone with a speech impairment, such as a stutter, or an invisible condition, such as dyslexia? Is disability necessarily a chronic condition, or could we consider someone disabled who for a few months is in a cast with a broken ankle?

An editorial that appeared in a 1999 issue of the eminent medical journal *The Lancet* captures the challenge of establishing an operational definition for disability. The writer reasons that because we all have different degrees of physical and intellectual aptitude, we can all be said to experience disability—in the broadest sense—when it comes to everyday tasks we don't manage as well as our peers do. For me that includes keeping my shoelaces tied, re-sealing Ziploc bags, and doing anything new with a computer.

> All of us could be considered as disabled to some extent. Individuals differ in many ways in the manners in which they cope with the activities of daily living, or have a real but common handicap to which society has adjusted well. Deciding how far ability

has to be impaired to constitute a disability is no easy matter—too vague, and abuse of special opportunities and services may follow; too rigid, and people who may benefit are excluded. ("The Spectrum of Disability," 1999, p. 693)

Postmodernist sociological theory teaches us to be suspicious of **binaries**, those either/or distinctions that are used to separate people into supposedly discrete categories such as male/female, heterosexual/homosexual, Black/white. Postmodernist theorists argued, compellingly, that gender was better viewed as a continuum, with "male" and "female" at the extremes and a lot of territory in between. We could approach the condition of dis/ability the same way. But that won't help us with our operational definition, and as *The Lancet*'s editorial writer points out, disability is an identity with some social and political weight, one that may gain a person access to special resources and services set aside for people with disabilities, as difficult as those often may be to access.

Measuring and Defining Disability

In 2018, Statistics Canada revealed that 6.25 million Canadians aged 15 and over—over 22 per cent of the population—had one or more disabilities that limited their daily activities, based on the 2017 Canadian Survey on Disability (Statistics Canada, 2018). So how does Canada's official data collection bureau define disability? Rather broadly, according to analysts Elisabeth Cloutier, Chantal Grondin, and Amélie Lévesque (2018). The agency uses a social constructionist model of disability that views disability as "the result of the interaction between a person's functional limitation and barriers in the environment, including social and physical barriers that make it harder to function day-to-day" (Cloutier et al., 2018, p. 6). I will have more to say about the social constructionist model shortly, but the key point here is the distinction between an *impairment*, which describes a person's physical or intellectual limitation, and a *disability*, which is the limitation a person experiences because of barriers in the environment. Or, as Statistics Canada puts it, "disability is a social disadvantage that an unsupportive environment imposes on top of an individual's impairment" (Cloutier et al., 2018, p. 6). You may require a wheelchair because of a physical impairment; you experience disability when you have to access an office building with stairs to the front door and no ramp.

Quick Hits

Disability Categories Used by Statistics Canada

In its research on Canadians with disabilities, Statistics Canada recognizes 10 different types of disability, described as follows:

- *hearing*: limitations in the ability to hear, even with a hearing aid or cochlear implant
- *seeing*: limitations in the ability to see, even when wearing eyeglasses or contact lenses
- *mobility*: difficulty in walking on flat surfaces for 15 minutes without rest, or in walking up or down a flight of 12 stairs
- *flexibility*: difficulty bending down or reaching for an object
- *dexterity*: difficulty using the fingers to grasp small objects
- *pain*: limitations because of pain that is constant or recurrent
- *learning*: difficulty learning because of a condition such as dyslexia, hyperactivity, or attention deficit disorder, whether the condition is self-identified or diagnosed by a teacher or health professional
- *memory*: ongoing memory problems or periods of confusion (not including occasional moments of forgetfulness)
- *developmental disabilities*: limitations due to a diagnosed developmental disorder, such as Down syndrome, autism, or Asperger syndrome, or an intellectual impairment caused by a lack of oxygen at birth
- *mental health*: limitations due to an emotional, psychological, or mental health condition, such as anxiety disorder, depression, bipolar disorder, substance abuse, anorexia as well as other conditions.

Source: Cloutier, Grondin, & Lévesque (2018, Appendix B).

What do *you* think?

Among people aged 15–24, the most prevalent type of disability is related to mental health (Figure 14.2). This may not surprise you. What *may* be surprising is that 10.6 per cent of women in this age group report a mental health–related disability compared with just 5.3 per cent of men. The difference is consistent with but greater than the trend in the overall population of Canadians 15 and over, where 8.9 per cent of women and 5.5 per cent of men identified a mental health–related disability (Morris et al., 2018). How do you explain the trend? Are more women mentally ill or are more men undiagnosed?

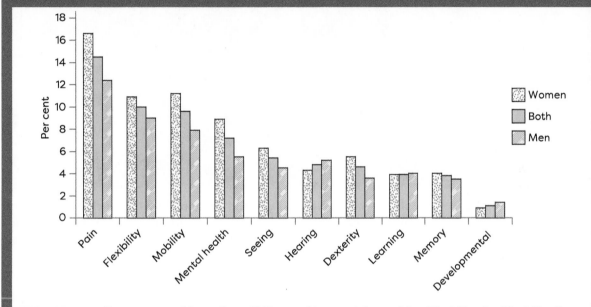

FIGURE 14.2 **Percentage of Canadians 15 Years of Age and Over with a Disability, by Disability Type and Sex (2017)**

Source: Morris, Fawcett, Brisebois, & Hughes (2018, Table 3).

Irving Zola: A Pioneer in the Sociological Study of Disability

Irving K. Zola (1935–1994) has been called the "father" of the sociology of disability, with good reason. He helped establish the Society for Disability Studies, an organization promoting the study of disability as a bona fide academic discipline, and was the founding editor of the society's journal, *Disabilities Studies Quarterly*. As well as being a professor of medical sociology at Brandeis University in Massachusetts, he was an activist for disability rights and a prolific writer on the subject.

Zola's best-known work, *Missing Pieces* (1982), is essentially a sociological diary of a week he spent in Het Dorp ("The Village"), an institutionalized community of 400 people—almost all of them disabled—in the Netherlands. Zola's study combines participant observation—he lived among the people in one of the special apartments provided for residents with disabilities—and

institutional ethnography, since he was writing from the viewpoint of the village's residents, not its administrators. This is not to say that Zola was unremittingly critical of Het Dorp, which was very progressive in a number of ways, or entirely uncritical of its patients, who themselves held some of the anti-disability prejudices Zola observed among the "normals."

Zola's approach shows parallels with the work of postmodernist feminist theorists such as Dorothy Smith, who were, at around the same time, establishing standpoint theory to promote the authority of women's unique and subjective interpretations of their experiences. As a sociologist with a physical disability (he wore a heavy leg brace as a result of childhood polio and a car accident when he was 20), Zola could readily see the need for an academic discipline devoted to the study of disability. As a researcher, he had insider insights as to what questions to ask and what answers might be trusted.

Jo-Mei Games

Released in 2019, *Sea of Solitude* is an adventure game in which players help a character named Kay emerge from a dark, submerged world by coming to terms with a series of traumas she has experienced. Can games such as this really help young people better understand their own mental health?

Telling It Like It Is

A Student's Point of View

Young, Disabled, and Wanting to Transit

As someone with an unsteady gait, no single transit ride is ever the same. I was born with a yet-to-be-diagnosed physical disability characterized by weak legs and poor balance, which is most prominent in my walking, but not so much when I'm sitting. This causes strangers to provide one of the following options when they see me getting onto a bus or SkyTrain: (a) asking if I would like their seat; (b) standing up immediately and walking away from their seat; or, most commonly, (c) looking the other way.

This experience was one that was unique, which happened one summer when my cousin was visiting Canada a few years back. We were en route to the PNE, the seasonal amusement park in Vancouver. As we boarded the bus, we made our way toward the back of the bus, away from the priority and courtesy seats, and sat down. A few stops later, two women, one in her thirties and another who was seemingly her mother, also made their way down to the end. Out of the full bus of everyone sitting, the lady directed my cousin and me to get up and provide our seats to them. I can only assume they selected us because we looked the youngest. Not wanting to start any conflict, we stood up in obedience while everyone stared in glimpses and through the window reflection. It was only when I moved away from my seat that the lady saw how I walked. She developed a pink tinge in her face but was apparently determined to refrain from telling me to sit back down. For the remaining 15 minutes of our ride, the mother sat, my cousin and I stood, and the lady also stood in front of the empty seat. We got off the bus without looking back. Out of all the rides my cousin and I enjoyed on that day, that bus ride was surely the most memorable.

> Visible disability, invisible disability, or no disability at all, appearances do not work as the telltale of a person. As easy as it is to judge someone as "fragile" for having a disability, or "impolite" for not offering the elderly their seat, it is just as easy to not judge someone at all, and to simply ask if you require help.
>
> —Jane Kim

14.11 Models of Disability

Like other areas of concern for the sociologist, disability can be examined from a number of vantage points. In this section we will look at different models used to understand disability.

Medical Models

The **medical model** is a framework for presenting and interpreting disability that is determined and directed by doctors, specialists, and other medical practitioners. It is a **positivist** model in that it reflects the belief that it takes an "expert," using science, to determine the treatments, policies, and programs required to help people living with disabilities.

The medical model guides research that has led to important, life-altering advances in the way disabilities are diagnosed and treated. Its benefits are undeniable. It has been criticized, though, when used without the insights available from people outside the medical community. York University sociologist Karen Anderson outlines some potential weaknesses of research on people with disabilities carried out according to this approach:

> Besides being difficult for the uninitiated to understand . . . it usually leaves out the perspective of the individual person who is being studied, and the meaning of his or her life in any discussion of the design, methods, or results of the research. . . . Medical practitioners often focus on the presenting problem and its treatment without taking into account all aspects of the patient's life or considering if the treatment proposed, and its hoped-for results, will improve the person's life. (Anderson, 1996, p. 386)

Again, this is not to say that this approach has no or little legitimacy. Rather, it is one of several paths of knowledge and causes of action that have legitimacy, and all of them need to be considered.

Economic Models

Economic models of disability view people with disabilities in terms of their contributions to, or drain on, the economy. They can be either sympathetic or unsympathetic toward people with disabilities.

Favourable Economic Models

A sympathetic economic model views people with disabilities in terms of their ability to perform meaningful labour. It looks for ways to maximize the skills of people with disabilities to enable them to become "productive" (i.e., wealth-creating) members of society. Organizations that arrange training and employment opportunities for people with disabilities, and those that fight to remove barriers to employment by promoting accessibility in the workplace, fall into this category.

The economic model has also produced some well-meaning but paternalistic approaches that reflect a limited view of how productive people with disabilities can be. A notorious case involves a program initiated in 1984 by fast-food giant McDonald's to train people with disabilities to work in its restaurants. The McJobs program was like an internship, with prospective employees undergoing both classroom and on-site training under the supervision of a mentor. In television commercials that you can view on YouTube, McDonald's boasted of its success in integrating people with mental and physical disabilities into the workforce.

The program was launched at a time when the kind of employment that McDonald's had come to represent—unchallenging, highly structured, low-paying work with few prospects for career advancement—was coming under scrutiny. Sociologist **Amitai Etzioni** (b. 1929) argued that "McJobs are bad for kids" in an article in which he attacked fast-food restaurants as "breeding grounds for robots working for yesterday's assembly lines, not tomorrow's high-tech posts" (Etzioni, 1986). By 1991, when Canadian author Douglas Coupland popularized the term "McJob" as a "low-pay, low-prestige, low-dignity, low-benefit, no-future job in the service sector" (Coupland, 1991, p. 5), McDonald's had abandoned the McJobs program.

While there may be a tendency to underestimate the skills and potential productivity of people with disabilities, there is also a danger in setting the bar too high. In *Missing Pieces*, Zola comments on how Americans' attitudes toward people with disabilities have been shaped by a version of the economic model that reflects the American dream (Zola, 2003, p. 95). This is the idea that people can overcome adverse circumstances to achieve success through hard work. According to Zola (2003, p. 121), a number of American movies offer a depiction of disability in which the hero with a disability "makes it" in the end, triumphing over the limitations of the disability to become successful. (He cites *The Miracle Worker* and *The Monty Stratton Story*; you can consider Marvel's Professor X, the paraplegic with superhuman abilities, a more recent example.) Zola argues that this kind of portrayal creates unrealistic expectations and reflects negatively on people whose disabilities are not as easily managed. People in mainstream society may be left with the impression that anyone who does not live up to the Hollywood image has essentially failed to realize their full potential and is therefore less deserving of respectful treatment.

Unfavourable Economic Models

Realistic or unrealistic, the economic models described above have one thing in common: they view people with disabilities in terms of the meaningful work they can contribute to society. In contrast to these are economic models that view people with disabilities as a drain on the state. Perhaps the most extreme, and certainly the most cruel, of these involved eugenics, a now discredited approach that we examined in Chapter 6.

A quick recap: eugenics (which means "good genes") is the science of improving the population by controlled breeding to limit the incidence of

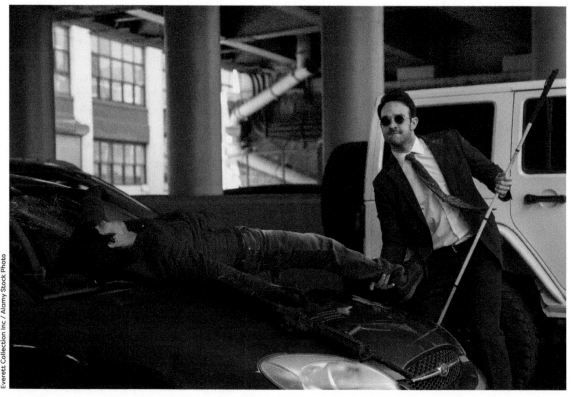

Everett Collection Inc / Alamy Stock Photo

Blinded as a young boy, Matt Murdock, a.k.a. Daredevil, is a lawyer and vigilante who uses his extraordinarily heightened senses to fight crime on the mean streets of New York. Is this an inspiring representation of disability on screen, or does it set unrealistic expectations about what people with visual impairments are capable of?

undesirable heritable characteristics. It is chiefly associated with Francis Galton (pioneer of statistical analysis), Henry Goddard (American psychologist), and the Nazis. As promoted by Goddard especially, eugenics was premised on two mistaken beliefs: that intelligence could be precisely measured, and that intelligence is a heritable characteristic, passed directly from parent to child. Goddard believed he could accurately test a person for "feeble-mindedness" (then, an accepted clinical term), which he was convinced was a hereditary trait. He failed, however, to take into account the social conditions of the person he was testing. Poverty and a lack of formal schooling are no reflection of a person's intellectual capabilities, and yet these could leave a person without the worldly knowledge to succeed on Goddard's vaunted intelligence test.

Despite its now obvious flaws, Goddard's work on eugenics was very influential in the early twentieth century. In Canada, the hype surrounding eugenics inspired two provinces—Alberta in 1928 and British Columbia in 1933—to enact legislation making it legal to have mentally ill people sexually sterilized. Identifying "mental defectives" for sterilization remained an inexact and controversial process, and the legislation victimized not only those with mental health conditions but also those who were marginalized by racialization, ethnicity (especially new immigrants), and sex (many young women were sterilized because they were "sexually promiscuous" or involved in prostitution—two immoral tendencies that were taken as signs of mental defectiveness). The legislation was not repealed until 1972 in Alberta and 1973 in BC.

Despite repeal of the legislation, the issue of whether individuals with mental disabilities could be sterilized without their consent remained a grey area until a 1986 Supreme Court of Canada ruling involving a girl known as Eve (not her real name). Eve had a mental disability that prevented her from communicating and understanding complex thoughts. When she was in her early twenties, her mother tried to get a court order to have Eve sexually sterilized. She was concerned that Eve, who had developed a close relationship with a male student at the boarding school they both attended, might accidentally become pregnant.

The case was first heard in 1978 in the Supreme Court of Prince Edward Island, where the judge felt

that he could not permit an individual to undergo sterilization via hysterectomy—a major surgical procedure—without her consent. The PEI Court of Appeal overturned the decision but did not act on it because the ruling was challenged by Eve and the Canadian Association for the Mentally Retarded (it isn't called that anymore). The Association was motivated to get involved by another incident at the time, in which a 10-year-old with an intellectual disability (legally referred to as "Infant K") had been secretly sterilized because, her parents explained, she reacted hysterically to the sight of blood and was therefore likely to find menstruation emotionally difficult (Hubert, 1985). The Association wanted to ensure that the reproductive rights of people with mental disabilities were preserved. In the case of *E. (Mrs) v. Eve* [1986], the Supreme Court of Canada denied Eve's mother's petition, ruling against the sexual sterilization of a mentally disabled person for non-therapeutic reasons (i.e., for reasons other than the treatment of disease) without the individual's consent.

Social Constructionist Models

A **social constructionist model** begins with the idea that any human social category—race, gender, ability, and so on—is not a totally natural category, but has an important social component. **Critical disability theory** (CDT) is a social constructionist theory that makes a distinction between a *natural impairment*, on the one hand, and *disability*, which can be understood as the barriers set up by society in dealing with that impairment. (We saw this distinction earlier in the definition of disability used by Statistics Canada.) A medical condition that causes paralysis in the legs is a natural impairment until the person born with the condition is denied access to public transit because the nearest subway station has no elevator: then it's a socially constructed disability. For this reason, critical disability theorists place the emphasis on changing society rather than on "curing" the individual.

Activism based on critical disability theory aims for *substantive equality* rather than *formal equality*. A goal of **substantive equality** would be building modifications that guarantee people with natural impairments equal accessibility to and within buildings (e.g., with ramps, automatic doors, and sidewalks with no sudden drops to the road). Under the **formal equality** model, everyone faces and must adapt to the same socially driven architecture that gives advantages to non-disabled people. Full inclusion and participation are the goals of the ideas and practices of critical disability theory.

Another tenet of social constructionist theory is that every culture constructs its own version of social categories such as "disabled." Nora Groce is a medical anthropologist who looks at how different societies treat and theorize about people with disabilities. She argues that "the lives of individuals with disability around the world are usually far more limited by prevailing social, cultural, and economic constraints than by specific physical, sensory, psychological, or intellectual impairments" (Groce, 1999, p. 756).

Groce identifies three main areas in which cultures differ in how they view disability:

1. causality
2. valued and devalued attributes
3. anticipated adult status.

Causality is "the cultural reason for why a disability occurs" (Groce, 1999). Early Europeans, for example, attributed some disabilities (especially those involving epileptic seizures) to demon possession or witchcraft; as you can imagine, they treated people with disabilities with great suspicion and fear. Other cultures have viewed disability as the result of divine judgment, as God's punishment for some act committed by the community, or for "sins" of the parents being visited upon the children. This is an idea that seems to cross cultures and persist over time. But Groce also cites studies by medical anthropologists Benedicte Ingstad (1988) and M. Madiros (1989) showing that among the Tswana people of Botswana (in southern Africa) and among the peasant people of northern Mexico, "the birth of a disabled child is viewed as evidence of God's trust in specific parents' ability to care well for a delicate child" (Groce, 1999, p. 756).

Quick Hits

Master Status and Labelling Theory

In Chapter 4, we considered the statuses that people have at any given time. Remember that a **status** is a position one holds that is recognized by society. Some of the statuses I hold right now are retired professor, writer, husband, stepfather, brother, grandfather, and parrot owner. A person's master status is the one that leads the way in terms of how a person's identity is defined and how others see and interact with that person. Labelling theory, also presented in Chapter 4, explains that society can sometimes turn a negative label into a master status that defines a person. Zola, who wore a leg brace and walked with a cane, gives an example how the label "disabled" was applied to him and became, for many people he met, his master status:

For years I have had the experience of being mistaken for someone else. Usually I was in a new place and a stranger would greet me as Tom, Dick, or Harry. After I explained that I was not he, they would usually apologize, saying "You look just like him." Inevitably I would meet this Tom, Dick, or Harry, and he would be several inches shorter or taller, forty pounds heavier or lighter, a double amputee on crutches or a paraplegic in a wheelchair. I was annoyed and even puzzled how anyone could mistake him for the "unique me." (Zola, 2003, p. 199)

David Morrison is a blogger and college student who has cerebral palsy. In one of his blog posts directed at people without disabilities, he provides four tips to avoid making a person's disability into a master status:

1. Speak to the person, not the wheelchair or the person's assistant.
2. Make eye contact as often as possible.
3. Treat a wheelchair as part of personal space.
4. Assist the person only after asking. (Morrison 2010)

A final tip: avoid labels that emphasize limitation. Referring to someone as a "disabled person" or "an epileptic" is like labelling the whole person with the disability, turning it into a master status. Instead, use descriptive phrases that put the person before the disability, and reserve labels for achievements: "A good friend of mine who has epilepsy," "A brilliant student who uses a wheelchair." Avoid pitying phrases such as "who suffers from" or "who is stricken with," and mention the disability only when it is relevant.

Groce's second point has to do with the "qualities a society finds important." In societies that value physical strength, people with physical disabilities are at a greater disadvantage than they are in a society that values intellectual accomplishments.

How a society regards people with disabilities also depends on what role people with disabilities are expected to occupy (Groce, 1999). If they are expected to participate fully in society, contributing meaningful labour and having families, then society will be willing to provide the resources to make this possible. A society that views its citizens with disabilities as a financial burden, as people in need of looking after and not in a position to contribute meaningfully, will likely be stingy about the resources it allocates to help individuals overcome disability.

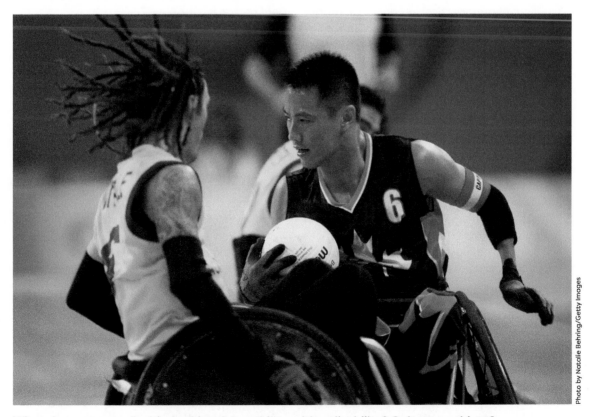

Photo by Natalie Behring/Getty Images

What do you see: a disabled athlete? An athlete with a disability? Or just an athlete?

Wrap It Up

Summary

Congratulations: you're now a doctor! Well, no, that's not quite true. But it's no surprise that a knowledge of sociology is now required to pass the latest (2015) version of the Medical College Admission Test that is used to screen applicants for medical schools in North America. Sociology has a vitally important role to play in the way health care is taught and delivered. Medical sociologists look carefully at the relationships between standard social factors such as class, gender, race and ethnicity, and location, and document inconsistencies in the way patients are treated. They study the social course of disease and record how different illnesses are portrayed in the media.

Canada has a public healthcare system, but make no mistake about it: it's a big business heavily influenced by big business interests. Hospitals grappling with barely adequate budgets make business decisions every day, deciding where best to allocate their funding, while companies ranging in size from huge multinationals selling pharmaceutical products to private clinics offering cosmetic procedures like tummy

tucks have a vested interest in making us feel less healthy and less able than we are, and incapable of improving our health without costly medical interventions.

Like health, ability is a concept that is too often defined without considering all relevant perspectives. The point to keep in mind is that while *people have impairments*, it is *society that constructs disability* as a social category. This is the underlying principle of critical disability theory, where the standpoint of the individual with the limitation is key. Medical professionals approach disability as a condition to be reversed or repaired; that is their job, and health professionals and researchers have made astonishing advances in treating conditions ranging from vision loss and hearing impairment to limited mobility and chronic pain. But if we fail to consider other, non-medicalizing standpoints, we will be missing something critical. Think of Canada's Deaf community, many of whom are fiercely proud of the culture. Who is in the best position to decide if a Deaf person is "disabled"?

Think Back

Questions for Critical Review

1. Choose a particular disease or injury that you have experienced and discuss the social course that you went through to have it diagnosed and treated. Where did you go? Who healed you? How were you socially processed?
2. Identify what biomedicine is and talk about its weaknesses and strengths. In what situations is biomedicine most successful? In what situations does it fail to serve the needs of patients as well as alternative medical approaches?
3. How and why are certain physical conditions medicalized? When is medicalization more harmful than helpful?
4. Describe the situation that faces immigrant doctors upon arriving in Canada. What barriers do they face to practising medicine in this country? Why do these barriers exist? What would happen if they did not exist?
5. How would you say that class affects the social course of disease? Is the relationship between class and the experience of disease different in Canada than in the United States? Why or why not?
6. Explain the concepts of impairment and disability in terms of Deaf culture.
7. Have you ever experienced, or do you currently experience, an impairment of some kind? Consider anything from a mobility-limiting injury (broken arm, ankle sprain) or congenital condition (muscular dystrophy) to a learning disability (dyslexia, attention-deficit disorder). How does your experience connect with what was written in this chapter? Under what circumstances did the impairment become a disability?
8. In "The Country of the Blind" (1904), a short story by H.G. Wells, a mountaineer in Ecuador

stumbles upon an isolated village of people who have never known sight and cannot even imagine what it is like to see. The title comes from the saying, "In the country of the blind, the one-eyed man is king," but the sighted mountaineer soon discovers that the blind villagers have come to survive quite well without the sense of sight—in fact, they interpret his own ability to see as a form of madness, a disability. What lesson does this hold about the social construction of disability in the minds of the villagers? In the mind of the mountaineer? How could a sociologist who happened to know how to cure blindness best approach the villagers?

Read On

Suggested Print and Online Resources

Canadian Association of the Deaf (CAD), http://cad.ca/issues-positions/terminology/
When it comes to disability, like other social conditions, labelling is a thorny issue. This page, from the CAD's website, gives the organization's position on a variety of terms relating to hearing impairment.

Canadian Centre on Disability Studies (CCDS), http://disabilitystudies.ca
The CCDS is dedicated to studying and developing programs with and for people with disabilities. The website has news about current projects and events, as well as published reports on research and completed community projects.

Tania Das Gupta, *Real Nurses and Others: Racism in Nursing* (Halifax: Fernwood, 2009)
Tania Das Gupta is a professor in the Department of Equity Studies at York University. This book is her study of the racism experienced by visible minority nurses in Canada.

Pat Grygier, *A Long Way from Home: The Tuberculosis Epidemic among the Inuit* (Montreal and Kingston: McGill–Queen's University Press, 1994)
Grygier provides an enlightening (and alarming) examination of how Inuit with tuberculosis were treated in Canada during the 1950s.

Nursing Education in Nova Scotia: Male Nurses, http://forms.msvu.ca/library/tutorial/nhdp/history/malenurses.htm
Mount Saint Vincent University is home to a fascinating archive of Nova Scotia's nursing history. This link features a 21-minute recording by Frank Graham, who shares his experiences as a male nursing student in the 1930s.

Eugene Raikhel, "50 Years of Medical Sociology," *Somatosphere*, 2010, http://somatosphere.net/2010/12/50-years-of-medical-sociology-html
In 2010, Eugene Raikhel looked back at some of the key issues that had been tackled in the 50-year history of the *Journal of Health and Social Behavior*. It is effectively an overview of issues in the history of American medical sociology.

Kevin Ryan, "Coming Home," in *Families, Work, and Mobility*, ed. Barbara Neis, Christina Murray, & Nora Spinks, chapter 6 (St John's: Memorial University Press, 2022)
How a Maritime labourer in the Alberta oil fields became a male nurse in Prince Edward Island. For his songs about nursing and PEI: https://kevinryan.ca/

Sally Simpson, Female Indigenous Firsts, https://canadianwomen.org/wp-content/uploads/2022/06/Female-Indigenous-Born-in-Northern-Turtle-Island-aka-Canada-and-Did-it-First-List.pdf
Sally Simpson's list of Indigenous firsts is proof that a sociology assignment can inspire important scholarship that will broaden the knowledge of others.

Society for Disability Studies (SDS), http://disstudies.org/
Established in part by Irving Zola, the SDS is committed to establishing disability studies as a bona fide academic discipline. The website provides information on the organization's mission and current work.

Earle Waugh, Shelley Ross, & Shirley Schipper, *Female Doctors in Canada: Experience and Culture* (Toronto: University of Toronto Press, 2019)
This comprehensive, up-to-date collection of articles looks at how the medical profession is becoming feminized, and what that means to the emerging generation of women doctors in Canada.

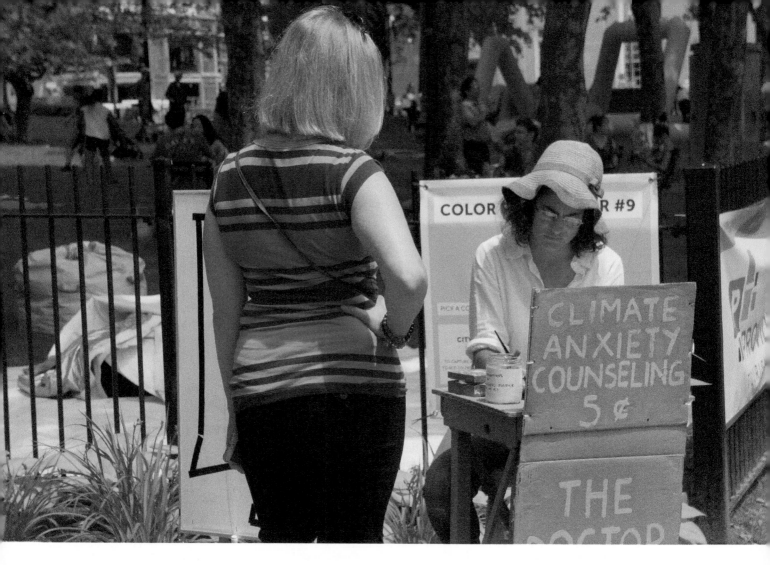

15 Environment and Climate Change

Reading this chapter will help you to . . .

- Describe how race and environmental practices intersect.
- Understand the vested interests that come into play when "scientific judgments" are made about the health of the environment.
- Explain the social ecology position and its relationship to issues of class and race.
- Critically assess the theory that environmental disasters can produce positive social change.
- Identify the environmental effects of the China price.
- Be aware of the sociological implications of proposals to combat climate change.

For Starters

Not in My Country: Rich Countries Dumping Waste in Poor Countries

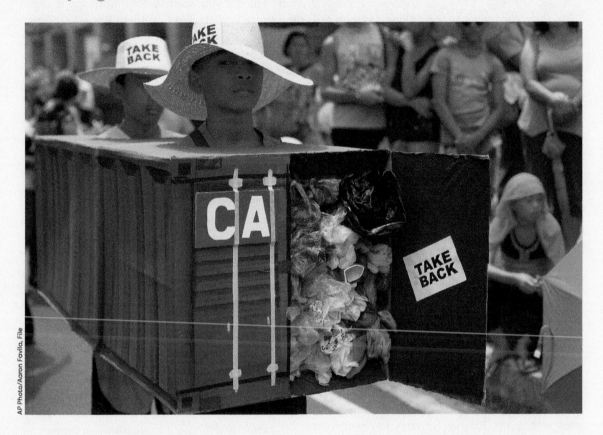

You may be familiar with the acronym NIMBY. It stands for "not in my backyard," and it comes up in the news whenever a community group is attempting to stop an undesirable outsider from setting up shop in the neighbourhood. Group homes, halfway houses, and safe injection sites are among the "social pariahs" that tend to find opposition from NIMBYism. The term is often applied derisively to self-interested residents concerned that their comfortable way of life may be threatened by a project that serves the greater good of the community. In the international context, it describes the very real victimization of vulnerable nations by well-developed countries, including Canada, that are looking for dumping grounds for toxic garbage.

The African coastline, especially the waters of some of the poorer and least powerful countries, has for some time experienced environmental damage resulting from the actions of more powerful countries of the developed North. One reason for the rise of modern piracy off the Somali coast is the decline in ocean food resources—once a staple of the Somali economy—due to the offshore dumping of toxic waste. In 2006, the small West African country of Côte d'Ivoire had a health crisis on its hands owing to massive amounts of toxic waste dumped by a local contractor in some 12 sites in the port city of Abidjan, the country's capital. The culprit was the Netherlands-based oil and commodity shipping company Trafigura Beheer BV, using a ship licensed in Panama.

The Canadian story involves the illegal dumping of 103 40-foot shipping containers filled with what was labelled "heterogeneous plastic scrap materials"—in other words, assorted plastic meant to be recycled. Upon inspection, Philippine customs officials found that about two-thirds of the materials were actually mixed household waste that included rotting food and used diapers (Gutierrez, 2016). The made-in-Canada waste was shipped between 2013 and 2014 from Vancouver to the Philippines by a private firm based in Ontario. The leaking containers presented a significant environmental health hazard to the local Philippine community, but despite international petitions (I signed one) and political pressure from environmental groups and the United Nations, the Canadian government did nothing to remedy the situation or prosecute the offending Canadian company, which argues it was acting in compliance with Canadian (if not international) law. The Philippines, which has received millions of Canadian dollars in tourism grants and disaster relief (following a typhoon that devastated Southeast Asia in 2013), was understandably reluctant to press the matter in international courts (Gutierrez, 2016). Not until the president of the Philippines, Rodrigo Duterte, made a series of public threats ("I will declare war against them. I will advise Canada that your garbage is on the way. Prepare a grand reception. Eat it if you want to. Your garbage is coming home"; quoted in Canadian Press, 2019) did Canada's government finally take responsibility for the mess. In May 2019, Canada hired a ship to return 69 of the containers, destined for a waste disposal facility in Burnaby, BC.

The diversion of Canadian waste to the Philippines is a case of **environmental racism**, which sets a double standard for managing the environment depending on the part of the world affected and the ethnicity of the people harmed. It cannot be blamed on corporate and political actors alone. After all, who's in the best position to keep that wax-lined coffee cup out of the blue bin—and the backyard of people living halfway around the world?

15.1 Introduction: Environmental Sociology: Science or Social Science?

Environmental sociology is a fast-growing subdiscipline that examines our relationship with the environment, focusing especially on where we have gone wrong and looking for ways to reverse our mistakes in the future. A lot of science is involved in environmental studies—in proving climate change, in tracking carbon emissions and weather patterns, in testing the safety of drinking water—but sociology teaches us that the science of the environment is deeply embedded in a social context. The scientific world is intensely political. Scientific facts cannot "speak for themselves"—they have interpreters who are part of the social world and who cannot always be trusted to report "the facts" without a distorting bias based on their place in that world, their **standpoint**.

In the 1970s and 1980s Canadian investigative journalist Lloyd Tataryn researched and wrote on environmental dangers ranging from the formaldehyde in our home insulation (1983) to the uranium mined at Elliot Lake (1976). His investigations often featured places where environmental science and politics collide. In his best-known work, *Dying for a Living*, he wrote:

> The scientific truth must first run a political gauntlet. For after the authorities give their advice, and all the technical data is in, the decision arrived at is ultimately a political verdict and merely masquerades as a purely scientific ruling.
>
> Politicians, corporations, and unions are aware of this environmental fact of life. And since in the long run they must rely upon the combined political and scientific judgement of their technical advisors, they tend to choose as advisors scientists whose biases are similar to their own—scientists who are prone to ask the type of questions that produce answers which most often serve the interests of their employers. . . .
>
> Unfortunately, the public is seldom informed of the political, economic, and scientific biases which scientists in environmental health conflicts bring to their investigations.

Most of us have been led to believe that "science" and "scientists" are above such considerations. (Tataryn, 1979, p. 90)

And sometimes, certainly, the modelling and predictions of scientists from the corporate world are remarkably precise, but then ignored. Beginning in the late 1970s until the early 2000s, climate scientists for the petroleum giant ExxonMobil were uncannily accurate in forecasting the future effects of ongoing fossil fuel consumption. All the while, despite this input, Exxon continued to pour many millions of dollars into advertising to downplay any impact on the environment and climate of burning fossil fuels (Supran, Rahmstorf, & Oreskes, 2023).

15.2 Assessing Environmental Arguments: Two Keys for Social Scientists

Climate change is associated with extreme weather; it is also associated with extreme views, which make for stormy arguments and heated disputes over basic facts. Here are two keys for assessing environmental arguments.

Operational Definitions

In Chapter 3, we looked at the importance of establishing clear operational definitions for variables in social research. Operational definitions are essential to creating policies on social issues. But it can be difficult to take abstract concepts such as poverty and abuse and turn them into concrete, countable entities. All operational definitions "leak": they are imperfect, and sociologists, as scientists, often disagree on the best way to define a term.

Disagreement among academic researchers, provided it is conducted in a civil manner, is healthy for any discipline. Scholarly debate can bring clarity to the issue or issues at hand, especially during the **peer review process**, when the draft of a research article, report, or book undergoes rigorous assessment by other experts in the field to ensure that it is suitable for publication. The author must take into account any and all criticisms before the work can be published. Eventually, through this scientific social process, issues are brought into sharper focus and, in terms of operational definitions, the best of the leaky terms wins out.

Peer review and follow-up are steps in the social process that helps to advance any scientific discipline as a whole. Unfortunately, while the process is familiar to most scientists, it is not always well understood outside the scientific community. Among the outsiders are journalists, politicians, and corporate interest groups, who often are guided by non-scientific social processes and ideas, like the notion that there are two valid sides to every story, and that presenting a "balance of views" is necessary. A classic example is the persistent attempt by American Christian groups to provide "balance" to the discussion of evolution by bringing forward non-scientific arguments in support of creationism and intelligent design (only evolution is scientific). Remember the lesson from Chapter 3: when assessing arguments of this kind, never be afraid to ask, *How do you know that?*

In the study of the environment, the same difficulties are involved, with critical arguments hinging on abstract terms that are difficult to define. How would you begin to devise an operational definition for "pollution"? Where do you set the limits on "safe" versus "dangerous" or "acceptable" versus "unacceptable" levels of exposure to a particular toxin? The stakes are high when millions of dollars and people's lives are involved. Consider the following statement from uranium miner Gus Frobel, who later died from the cancer that he rightfully believed was caused by his working conditions:

> When you read the scientific papers, you find the really knowledgeable scientists, the experts in the field, don't use the term "safe" level of exposure. They know they can't defend it scientifically. They say that to their knowledge there is no "safe" level. Some use the term "acceptable level." Now what's an "acceptable level?" That means some men have to die—but how many? How many deaths are acceptable? (quoted in Tataryn, 1979, p. 100)

Pollution is like poverty. Just as you can tell when someone is very poor (a person sleeping on the street is definitely poor), so you can tell when water or air is extremely polluted: it smells bad, looks horrible, and makes you sick. Extremes are easy to identify. Finding the line that separates "polluted" from "not polluted" is not so easy—it takes a scientific approach

The climate change denier will sometimes pose as a devil's advocate, feigning detachment from a dubious or unpopular position under the pretense of bringing balance to the conversation. When it comes to debating climate change, should both sides be given equal weight?

to get there. It is especially difficult when the damaging effects of pollution may not become apparent for many years. If it takes 20 years for an asbestos mine worker to die from exposure to an unsafe level of asbestos in the air, it could take 20 years for a hypothesis of what constitutes an "unsafe level of exposure" to be proven true, although reasonably sound predictions can be made earlier.

"Operational" definitions thus become key aspects of environmental debates. In any discussion of the environment, look closely for abstract terms. Are they carefully defined? Do the definitions look sound? How were the definitions arrived at? Do the people presenting the information use the words "significant" or "serious" without explaining what they mean by them? The answers to these questions will tell you a lot about whether a particular argument is being fought more on scientific grounds or political ones.

Vested Interests

Even when operational definitions of an environmental argument have been assessed, important sociological questions remain. Who paid for any research studies cited in the argument? Who stands to benefit or lose from a particular test result? Politics are involved in environmental research, especially when some social policy is being proposed, implemented, attacked, or defended. That's why it is

important to identify the **vested interests** surrounding any argument about the environment.

A vested interest is any social or financial interest a party may have in the results of a scientific study and the way those results are interpreted, particularly if the interest is strong enough to override the interest of ensuring those results are accurate, or "truthful." Although scientific measurement can be precise, the *interpretation* of those data can be highly subjective. Give two scientists the same numbers, and they may come up with two very different interpretations.

The way operational definitions are derived may be influenced by the vested interests of the person designing the study or interpreting the results. It is statistically predictable that if one scientist is paid by a mining company, that scientist is likely to have a lower threshold for what constitutes a safe level of exposure to the material being mined, and will be more likely than an impartial scientist to give workers a clean bill of health. A scientist paid by the miners' union or one who is an independent researcher at a local university or hospital will more likely hold a different view that better supports the health of the miners.

A 2018 study by researchers at the University of British Columbia sheds some light on how vested interests can affect operational definitions. The team examined 10 recent environmental impact assessments conducted in BC (Murray et al., 2018). Environmental impact assessments, or EIAs, are commissioned and paid for by a company that is applying for government approval to start or expand a project (e.g., a mine or a pipeline) that could have environmental, social, economic, or health-related consequences for the local community. The EIA is normally carried out by independent professional geoscientists or engineers, *who are paid by the company behind the proposal* to see if any risks to the environment are "significant." Can you see where operational definition and vested interests are about to collide?

The UBC researchers found that in the 10 EIAs they examined, "findings of significant impacts were exceedingly rare" (Murray et al., 2018). Part of the reason for this is that quantitative (i.e., measurable) thresholds of "significance determination" were seldom used in the assessment of health or environmental risks, and when they were, "practitioners

The Point Is . . .

Scientists with Vested Interests Developed the "Tobacco Strategy"

An important work on the subject of vested interests is Naomi Oreskes and Erik Conway's *Merchants of Doubt: How a Handful of Scientists Obscured the Truth on Issues from Tobacco Smoke to Global Warming* (2010). They assert that multinational corporations in different industries use a common set of tactics to manufacture and market doubt about health and environmental concerns raised by scientific researchers. These tactics involve the use of paid scientific researchers to fight "good" science with "bad" science in the name of industry. We can call these "bad science" researchers *scientific mercenaries*.

Stanford Research into the Impact of Tobacco Advertising (SRITA)

Having grown up in an age where the dangers of tobacco use are well established, you might find it easy to scoff at the naiveté of magazine readers in the first half of the twentieth century who found this kind of advertising compelling. But be honest: How often do you find yourself picking up the skincare product, toothpaste, or pain-relief medication that is advertised as "doctor-recommended" or "clinically proven"?

(Continued)

Many of today's scientific mercenaries follow the blueprint drafted in the 1960s by scientists employed to undermine critics of the tobacco industry. By the mid-twentieth century, medical researchers were beginning to understand how damaging cigarette smoking could be to one's health. By the 1960s the community of scholars knew it, but the tobacco industry successfully combatted the growing evidence by hiring teams of scientists to offer their own evidence that minimized the harmful effects of tobacco and, in some cases, pointed to the health benefit of smoking.

Frederick Seitz and Siegfried Singer were scientists who had produced legitimate research in physics before their connections with conservative American government administrations and industry interests seriously affected the scientific credibility of their work. In the following passage from *Merchants of Doubt*, Oreskes and Conway describe their work on behalf of the tobacco industry:

From 1979 to 1985, Fred Seitz directed a program for R.J. Reynolds Tobacco Company that distributed $45 million to scientists around the country for biomedical research that could generate evidence and cultivate experts to be used in court to defend the "product." In the mid-1990s, Fred Singer coauthored a major report attacking the US Environmental Protection Agency [EPA] over the health risks of secondhand smoke. Several years earlier, the US surgeon general had declared that second-hand smoke was hazardous not only to smokers' health, but to anyone exposed to it. Singer attacked this finding, claiming the work was rigged, and that the EPA review of the science—done by leading experts from around the country—was distorted by a political agenda to expand government control over all aspects of our lives. Singer's anti-EPA report was funded by the Tobacco Institute, channeled through a think tank, the [conservative, climate change-denying] Alexis de Tocqueville Institution. (Oreskes & Conway, 2010, pp. 5–6)

What came to be known as the **tobacco strategy** essentially forestalled the onslaught of successful lawsuits against the industry until the 1990s. The tobacco strategy has since been used by other deniers of science to dispute legitimate scientific findings concerning acid rain, ozone layer depletion, and, most recently, human-produced climate change.

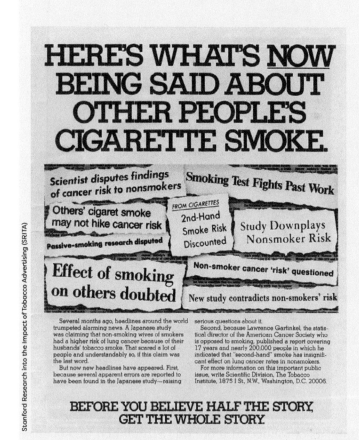

Stanford Research into the Impact of Tobacco Advertising (SRITA)

The Scientific Division of the US Tobacco Institute put out this ad encouraging readers to get the whole story on second-hand smoke. Look at how the argument is crafted. Is it effective?

used a variety of rationales to demote negative impacts to non-significance" (Murray et al., 2018). In other words, as Judith Lavoie explains in her account of the research, "when impacts are likely to exceed established criteria—push past those accepted thresholds—experts find a variety of innovative ways to minimize potential problems" (Lavoie, 2018).

Those innovative ways of downplaying concerns include referencing less-strict guidelines in use in other jurisdictions and expanding the scale of the impacted area from a small, local community to a much larger area. This would be like arguing that the impact of an increase in pollutants on the nearest town is not so significant if you look at how that increase will affect the much larger region the town is situated in. To take another example, in Bolton, the town of 26,000 where I live, late-winter flooding of the Humber River caused great damage to homes of people living in the valley; up on the south hill, where I live, there was no damage. Imagine a study of the impact of the flood on people living in all of Bolton (or the GBA—the Greater Bolton Area—as I like to call it). The percentage of Bolton residents affected would be small, but the impact those valley residents experienced was enormous.

Paid experts are not unbiased: they have a vested interest in pleasing the company that is paying for the report by overlooking or downplaying problems that might call for expensive changes to the proposal or an outright rejection of the application. Expanding the scale of the area impacted by the development and playing fast and loose with the term "significant" are examples of how operational definitions can be manipulated to minimize concerns over dangerous risks to the local community.

When searching for vested interests, it is always important to trace the science back to its social location. Many of the think tanks, institutes, and other organizations that publish reports are funded by large companies, and they tend to be conservative. For example, the climate change–attacking Friends of Science is an organization founded by oil industry geologists and funded by oil companies. They generally take positions that support the big business agenda while downplaying or dismissing potential harm to the environment or industry-related health risks. University researchers are generally more reliable when it comes to environmental issues, but always check first to see who is funding the work.

As we saw in Chapter 13 in the case of Enbridge and the University of Calgary, universities often receive funding from deep-pocketed donors with vested interests.

The Big Business behind the UFFI Disaster: A Case of Vested Interests

Citizens depend on their governments to protect them from the harmful effects of industrial pollution. Government agencies study the health impacts of different manufacturing materials, approving the ones that are safe and recommending bans on the ones that are not. The system fails when government has a vested interest in promoting an unsafe product. A Canadian case in point surrounds the widespread use of urea formaldehyde foam insulation (UFFI) during the late 1970s and 1980s.

Formaldehyde is a chemical with many uses. It is an ingredient of a glue used to bind wood fibres together in such products as particle board, chipboard, and plywood. In Canada in the 1960s, it was introduced as foam insulation.

Complaints about the formaldehyde-based insulation began to surface in the 1970s, primarily in northern European countries such as Denmark, Sweden, and the Netherlands, where governments were generally quick to respond to concerns around industrial pollution. There were reports that the foam encouraged harmful fungal growth. Also, the formaldehyde-based glue used in composite wood products was causing allergic reactions and respiratory problems among people living in mobile homes, where particleboard and plywood were among the principal building materials. What's more, UFFI was not proving effective as an insulation material. Canada's own National Research Council (NRC) had tested the foam and found it liable to shrink, crack, and crumble, greatly decreasing its value as an insulator.

Why then, in the light of these ominous findings, did Canada's government continue to endorse the use of formaldehyde-based products?

A pivotal event occurred in the mid-1970s, when the Organization of Petroleum Exporting Countries (OPEC), representing the world's major oil-producing countries, declared an embargo against the West, creating an oil shortage that led to a sharp rise in North American and European gas and oil prices. The industry solution was to promote greater use of insulation to improve the efficiency of heating in homes and workplaces. Formaldehyde-based insulation was a key part of this proposal, which required the approval of various federal agencies, including the Canadian General Standards Board (CGSB) and the Canada Mortgage and Housing Corporation (CMHC). These government regulatory bodies were ill-prepared to counter the strong-arm tactics of the chemical companies. Moreover, the government itself was in a conflict of interest, as the federally financed Canadian Development Corporation owned 40 per cent of one of the foam-producing chemical companies.

In 1977, the federal government announced the Canadian Home Insulation Program (CHIP), which provided financial incentives to homeowners to upgrade their insulation. Some 80,000 Canadian homeowners registered for CHIP. The government set standards on the percentage of formaldehyde that could be used in UFFI products, but these limits were voluntary, not enforceable, and therefore largely ignored. No consideration was given to the health of contractors installing the insulation.

By 1978, homeowners began to complain about the deteriorating quality of foam insulation and its effects on health. In 1979, Massachusetts became the first jurisdiction to ban UFFI, a move influenced by a scientific study that had found a link between formaldehyde and cancer. Chemical companies responded with an industry-funded conference in 1980, in which 22 of the 26 papers delivered were by industry "experts" who defended the safety and reliability of the product. They argued against any form of regulation.

In December 1980, urea formaldehyde foam insulation was banned in Canada. Homeowners and contractors installing the product were left stranded. People who had installed it in their homes could not resell them until the foam insulation had been removed. Even small amounts could cause headache, nausea, and other allergic reactions to the fumes it emitted.

What do *you* think?
1. What should government agencies and the government have done in this situation?
2. Is there anything that consumers can do in this situation to protect themselves from being overly influenced by chemical corporations and big business? Is it realistic to expect individual consumers to take these precautions?

By permission of Harold Orr.

In 1977, the same year the Canadian Home Insulation Program was announced, an energy-efficient, solar-panelled model home with superior insulation was built in Regina. Funded by the Saskatchewan Research Council, it required so little energy input to heat that it did not even have a furnace. The design became a model for home-building in Europe but was never replicated in Canada. Why do you think the UFFI insulation took off instead of energy-efficient houses? How much of our purchasing decisions are influenced by corporations in ways we don't even realize?

15.3 Social Ecology

The late twentieth century brought a growing awareness of the human role in environmental issues, from the importance of household recycling to the dangers of our carbon emissions. As is written in many self-help books, the first and hardest step is acknowledging you have a problem. This is a key tenet of **social ecology**, a school of thought founded by American thinker and ecologist **Murray Bookchin** (1921–2006). He explained social ecology as follows:

What literally defines social ecology as "social" is its recognition of the often-overlooked fact that nearly all our present ecological problems arise from deep-seated social problems. Conversely, present ecological problems cannot be clearly understood, much less resolved, without resolutely dealing with problems within society. To make this point more concrete: economic, ethnic, cultural, and gender conflicts, among many others, lie at the core of the most serious ecological dislocations we face today. (Bookchin, 1996)

To get a better sense of how a social ecologist might view the relationship between social conflict and environmental issues, we will look at the role of class conflict in the context of industrial pollution.

Industrial Pollution and Social Ecology

We can adopt a social ecology approach to better understand how the exposure of workers to unsafe environmental conditions reflects larger trends in the issue of industrial pollution. First, for workers to be placed in this situation requires the complicity of the employer—the company that requires the work—and sometimes the government, which ultimately is responsible for overseeing environmental protection as well as workplace safety. As Lloyd Tataryn notes:

> Today, people who work and live in contaminated environments serve as early warning systems for toxic substances, much like the ancient royal food tasters and the canaries the coal miners once trundled underground to test the air. Workers and those who live in the shadow of polluting industries are the first people to encounter intense and prolonged exposure to toxic wastes. Much of what is known about environmental health and the consequences of exposure to poisonous and cancer-causing materials has been learned from examining disease patterns among workers and exposed populations. Exposure standards are usually established once an unusual pattern of disease has been detected. In this way workers and people living in industrially contaminated environments act as guinea pigs for the rest of society. (Tataryn, 1979, p. 1)

There appear to be two different ways of interpreting workplace-related illness and injury. The first is the social ecology view, which sees these as essentially *social* in their origin and in the way that they are dealt with. Working conditions are set in place by a company and monitored in varying degrees by the political authorities in an area. This reflects

C. Wright Mills's notion of the sociological imagination, in which individual problems and situations readily connect with the broader social structure and its processes. The workers are not in a position to oppose the company's unsafe environmental practices. This is essentially a class conflict. What does that say about industrial pollution on a larger scale?

A sociologically *uninformed* way of interpreting workplace illness is to keep it individual and personal, reflecting the individual choices and physical constitution of the person afflicted. Far from being symptomatic of broader social processes, a worker's disease is viewed as a result of personal choices taken by the individual worker: smoking, drinking, lack of exercise and poor lifestyle choices in general. With this view, injuries happen at job sites because workers are careless (a viewpoint reflected in early commercials promoting workplace safety as an individual responsibility). It would be wrong to say that individuals are powerless to play a role in workplace safety; however, this second view leans too far in the direction of William Ryan's notion of blaming the victim. It's a recurring theme—watch for it in sections that follow.

The Asbestos Industry: Dying for a Living

It has long been known that asbestos is hazardous to human health. Roman writers in the second century CE noted that those who spun its threads into valuable robes often became sick. By the early twentieth century, some North American insurance companies were refusing to insure asbestos workers, recognizing that these employees had relatively low chances of long-term survival at the job. In 2012, a

> **What do you think?**
> 1. Consider a common workplace setting, such as a warehouse, and a common workplace injury, such as lower back pain. Who should take the greater share of responsibility for ensuring worker safety in this context: the employer or the employee? Now apply the same question to carpal-tunnel syndrome suffered by secretaries whose jobs consist mainly of keyboarding. Is your answer the same?
> 2. What does Tataryn mean when he calls people who work in or live near polluting industries "human canaries"?

consortium of **epidemiology** organizations from around the world issued a position statement on asbestos, declaring that "all types of asbestos fibre are causally implicated in the development of various diseases and premature death" (JPC-SE, 2012, p. 2). These diseases include lung cancer, mesothelioma, and asbestosis.

Canada became a major producer of asbestos in 1879, when the fibrous mineral was first mined in Thetford Mines, Quebec. In the early twentieth century, other jurisdictions began to observe standards of what was considered "acceptable" risk of exposure, a figure first set at 35 fibres per cubic centimetre in 1938, before falling, with further study, to 12, then 5, then 2. By contrast, Thetford Mines, the world's largest producer of asbestos, observed no such standard until 1978, when it finally bowed to media and public pressure by adopting limits of "acceptable" exposure. In the mid-1970s, a worker at another Canadian mine, Paul Formby, discovered levels ranging from 30 to 50 fibres per cubic centimetre where he was working.

It is not just the miners who have been exposed to the environmental hazards of asbestos:

> Towering over the town of Thetford Mines are massive grey piles of asbestos tailings. These tailings poke their way like giant fingers into sections of the town, spilling asbestos waste into the yards of many of the homes. Positioned on top of the tailings are machines called swivel pilers, constantly spraying out clouds of asbestos waste, a practice that Mount Sinai's doctors say would be illegal in the United States. Thetford's tailings daily grow higher and higher, leaving the town covered in grey dust. (Tataryn, 1979, p. 23)

The prevailing attitude in a one-industry town like Thetford Mines is often one that defends the business that brings food to the table, even in the face of environmental health studies with grave conclusions about the health risks to the town's citizens. In a 2007 article, one retired miner, who had worked in the mines for 38 years, articulated this view:

> Those people who had their houses tested [for asbestos] are just whiners, looking for

compensation. . . . We made a very good living in the mines, and I don't regret it for a minute. . . . It's paranoia. It's just like smoking. I know lots of people who smoke and live to be 80 or 90 years old. (cited in Lalonde, 2007)

Although some of his colleagues had died of asbestos-caused illnesses, the miner, according to the article, believed the deaths were owing to "a vulnerability on their part" (Lalonde, 2007).

While studies of the health risks of asbestos exposure were being carried out and debated, the provincial government of Quebec and Canada's federal government continued to promote the use of asbestos products, particularly in developing countries, the destination for 90 per cent of the 150,000 tonnes of asbestos produced in Canada. It was not until September 2012, shortly after the last Canadian asbestos mine closed, that the federal Conservative government announced it would no longer oppose global rules restricting the use and shipment of asbestos (*CBC News*, 2012).

The Canadian government lagged behind other countries in banning asbestos. It was not until July 2015 that Health Canada revised its long-held position that asbestos was dangerous only when inhaled "in significant quantities"; the agency now states plainly that "breathing in asbestos fibres can cause cancer and other diseases" (Grant, 2015). In 2018, the federal government introduced new regulations that would ban the import, sale, or use of asbestos and asbestos-containing products, beginning in 2019. However, the new regulations do not prohibit companies from sifting through the 800 million tonnes of mining residues near the towns of Thetford Mines and Asbestos to extract magnesium and other minerals from the tailings (Rabson, 2018).

A comparable situation surrounds coal mining, which has an ugly history in Canada of unhealthy working conditions (see, for example, the Westray disaster of 1992, in which 26 miners in Nova Scotia died owing to a methane explosion). The burning of coal for electricity contributes significantly to the conditions promoting climate change. There are still major coal mines in British Columbia, Alberta, and Saskatchewan, and 90 per cent of the millions of tonnes mined are burned for electricity across Canada. Coal mining contributes billions of dollars to the

Canadian economy and provides thousands of jobs. Do you think that all of the mines will be shut down during the next 20 years? What about the next 40?

Paul Formby: Environmental Hero in the Fight against Asbestos

After graduating in philosophy from the University of British Columbia, Paul Formby felt the call of the Canadian North. In the early 1970s he travelled to Clinton Creek, Yukon, where he started work in the asbestos mine. He soon wound up in charge of the health and safety committee of the miner's union—an often thankless task—where he encountered significant resistance from the mining company. He explains:

> As far as the company was concerned . . . asbestos dust levels were a taboo subject. From the company's point of view the most important safety measure was safety glasses. As long as we all wore safety glasses everything was supposed to be OK. It was almost as if it was more important to keep the

<table><tr><td>

What do *you* think?

Why do you think Canada's government promoted asbestos use primarily in developing countries? Can Canada's policy be characterized as an instance of environmental racism?

</td></tr></table>

stuff out of our eyes than out of our lungs. By arguing in this way, the company was trying to shift the responsibility for health and safety off of its shoulders and onto ours. The company refused to admit that the work environment it created could possibly be hazardous to its workers. (cited in Tataryn, 1979, p. 20)

At issue was the union's right to test the air for asbestos contamination, as well as the company's questionable claim that the white asbestos (chrysotile) that they were mining was far safer than the dangerous blue asbestos (crocidolite) found in the mines of South Africa and Australia. This is a **red herring**: a logical fallacy in which an irrelevant topic

Francis Vachon/TCPI/The Canadian Press

Rising majestically behind this row of houses in Thetford Mines is a large tailings pile from the town's asbestos quarry. How comfortable would you feel living in one of these houses? Describe the social profile of the typical resident of this street.

is introduced in an argument to divert attention from the original and more important issue (in this case, the hazards of chrysotile). Company management and physicians may have believed in the safety of white asbestos, but their lives were never endangered the way that those of the miners were:

> During contract negotiations the company absolutely refused to discuss the union's right to test the air. . . . The management stated emphatically that asbestos dust levels were not an issue in Clinton Creek. Furthermore, they assured me that the white asbestos found in Canada was so safe I could pour it on my breakfast cereal every morning and suffer no ill effects. The bad stuff, they said, was the blue asbestos that is mined only in South Africa. (Formby, in Tataryn, 1979, p. 21)

Formby remained unconvinced, and decided to take his inquiries further afield. In early 1974 he expressed his concerns in a letter to Dr Irving Selikoff, the head of the environmental sciences laboratory at New York's Mount Sinai Medical School and a leading authority on asbestos-related lung cancer and asbestosis (the scarring of the lung by the body's reaction to the indestructible fibres of asbestos entering the lungs). Selikoff wrote back, confirming that Formby's concerns were valid, and taking issue with the supposed "safety" of the white asbestos.

Formby then asked for and received a leave of absence from work. He travelled across the continent to New York and walked into Mount Sinai Hospital asking to be trained in taking air samples to test for asbestos fibres. Hospital officials were surprisingly sympathetic and accommodating. Rather than treating him like a fanatic, they agreed to train him.

Formby next went to Montreal to contact the union that represented the workers in Thetford Mines, home to Canada's largest asbestos mine. There he spoke with the union's health and safety representative about testing for asbestos particles in the air. Formby was well received, and was assisted in carrying out tests on the air quality at the mine.

For Formby, it was then back to Clinton Creek, where he secretly tested the air there—and then quit. After then he went south to conduct air quality tests at the mine in Cassiar, British Columbia (closed, since 1992, after 40 years in existence). Living out of a suitcase and occasionally sleeping in his old car, Formby went back to Thetford Mines, where he trained the miners to collect air samples. They had to do this in secret, as their actions were considered by the company as grounds for suspension or dismissal.

Formby had samples from the three mines sent to Mount Sinai Hospital for testing. The union at Thetford Mines arranged to have a team of doctors and technical experts, Canadian and American, visit the mine to examine the workers for signs of asbestosis and cancer. Although the miners had previously received class "A" health ratings from the doctors who worked for the mining company, the independent experts found many sick, some dying.

Paul Formby significantly raised the profile of the dangers of asbestos, both for miners and for other workers (such as builders) exposed to the deadly material. His work spawned awareness-raising documentaries and government actions that have reduced (but not eliminated) the risks of human exposure to asbestos.

In July 2015, Health Canada finally changed the information on its website, which had long maintained that chrysotile was "less potent" and less dangerous than other forms of asbestos (Grant, 2015).

Industrial Communities and the Disposable People of Pollution

The story of Thetford Mines and Asbestos, Quebec—towns whose names are synonymous with the industry they revolve around—underlines the fact that it is not just workers who are exposed to the hazardous pollutants produced by environmentally unfriendly companies. Also affected are the communities surrounding these dangerous enterprises. Again, we find the social ecology approach useful in examining how the poor and marginalized communities are usually the ones most powerfully affected. An illustrative case is that of the chemical giant Monsanto and the tiny city of Anniston, Alabama.

The Industrial Contamination of Anniston, Alabama

The following is a classic case of environmental racism. A little background information is necessary. Monsanto, since its founding in 1901, manufactured and distributed some of the most toxic chemicals ever produced. Specifically, the company was

The Point Is . . .

It Takes Courage to Blow the Whistle

John O'Connor started his career as a physician in northern Alberta in 1993, spending much of this time in the oil sands boomtown of Fort McMurray. In 2001 he started working with the Indigenous community of Fort Chipewyan, population 1,200, located a little way downriver from the oil sands. Shortly after beginning to work with the Fort Chipewyan community, whose elders told O'Connor about new deformities they were seeing in fish—a staple of their diet—along with a peculiar oily taste. The doctor began to notice evidence of health problems he hadn't seen in Fort McMurray. Specifically, he observed new cases of cholangio-carcinoma, a rare bile duct cancer that had killed his father, and that often showed up in bile ducts of fish swimming in oil-infested water. He also found a high incidence of liver cancers.

When Dr O'Connor began voicing his concerns, Canada's federal agency, Health Canada, approached the community for its medical files. One government representative even made a very public visit to declare the water fit for consumption. He demonstrated this with a rather unscientific gesture: at the local nursing station, he filled his mouth with water from a tap and announced to an attending *Globe and Mail* reporter: "There's nothing wrong with the water in Fort Chip."

Health Canada presented the findings of its report to the Alberta Energy and Utilities Board in Fort McMurray one week *before* its representatives spoke with members of the Fort Chipewyan community about their experience. After a quick analysis of the data set, which mysteriously omitted statistics from 2004 and 2005, the agency gave the community a clean bill of health.

The agency's work didn't end there, as O'Connor, in a statement given in the House of Commons in June 2009, explained:

> In 2007 I got a large envelope in the mail from the College of Physicians and Surgeons in Edmonton. . . . It was a list of complaints that Health Canada had laid about my activities in Fort Chip. They accused me of blocking access to files, billing irregularities, engendering a sense of

mistrust in government in Fort Chip, and causing undue alarm in the community. (Standing Committee on Environment and Sustainable Development, 2009)

It was the first time that a Canadian government agency had ever used a patient complaint process to attack a physician in this way. The charges were serious and could have led to the suspension—temporary or permanent—of O'Connor's licence to practise medicine. The first three charges were dismissed relatively quickly. The people of Fort Chipewyan, who hadn't been consulted concerning whether they felt "undue alarm," supported him, and in fact requested the dismissal of Health Canada's senior physician. Members of the Alberta Medical Association were unanimous in their support.

In 2008 the Alberta Cancer Board engaged in a more comprehensive study of the community, releasing its findings in February 2009. In the report, the board stated that while the number of cases of cholangiocarcinoma and colon cancer were "within the expected range" during the period of investigation,

> the number of cancer cases overall was higher than expected. In particular, increases of observed over expected were found for biliary tract cancers as a group and cancers of the blood and lymphatic system. These increases were based on a small number of cases and could be due to chance or increased detection. The possibility that the increased rate is due to increased risk in the community, however, cannot be ruled out. (Alberta Cancer Board, 2009, p. 10)

The board concluded that further study was warranted to see if there was any risk associated with living in Fort Chipewyan. In November 2009, the charge against O'Connor of "causing undue alarm" was dropped. In 2015, he was fired from the Nunee Health Board in Fort Chipewyan with no explanation.

involved in the production and sale of polychlorinated biphenyls, or PCBs, from 1929 until the early 1980s, when the substance was effectively banned through a series of regulations. What are PCBs? In the words of journalist Marie-Monique Robin, "for half a century they colonized the planet; they were used as coolants in electric transformers and industrial hydraulic machines, but also as lubricants in applications as varied as plastics, paint, ink, and paper" (Robin, 2010, p. 11).

Monsanto also produced the deadly compound dioxin. It was used as an ingredient in Agent Orange, the notorious broad-based plant killer and defoliant that was dumped in massive quantities on the jungles and people of Vietnam by the United States during the Vietnam War to deprive the enemy fighters of cover. So powerful was Agent Orange that plants still do not grow around an airport in western Newfoundland where the chemical was tested during the 1970s (personal observation, 2013). Then, there are the other deadly D's, including 2,4-D (a component of Agent Orange, used for a time in household weed killers) and the environmentally toxic insecticide DDT.

During the 1980s and 1990s, Monsanto shifted its focus from chemical manufacture to agricultural biotechnology and became a pioneer in the development of genetically modified (GMO) plant crops. In 2018, Monsanto was purchased by German multinational drug producer Bayer AG. Bayer soon found itself on the hook for over $2 billion in damages awarded in May 2019 to a California couple who successfully argued in court that their non-Hodgkin's lymphoma was caused by long-term exposure to glyphosate, a chief ingredient of the Monsanto weed killer Roundup that they had used on their property between 1975 and 2011. Bayer successfully petitioned to have the damages reduced, but this will likely not be the last lawsuit the company faces in relation to Roundup, which remains the market-leading herbicide in the United States.

And now I will tell the story of the small city of Anniston. Situated in Calhoun County, Alabama, Anniston was home to a Monsanto production facility for PCBs beginning in 1929. Most of the workers at Monsanto's plant in Anniston were Black. Many of them lived in the neighbourhoods surrounding the plant, which were likewise predominantly Black. During the 1930s, Monsanto was already receiving and documenting warnings about the deadly risks of PCBs to anyone in close contact with the toxic compound, and the company continued to acquire and file away such information until it stopped producing PCBs in 1971. During that interval of many years, Monsanto did nothing to warn or protect either the workers or the residents of Anniston.

The truth of Anniston's PCB contamination began to leak out in a series of news items in 2002. By 2005, the US Environmental Protection Agency (EPA) was reporting that 60 million pounds of PCBs had been emitted into the atmosphere surrounding Anniston. A nearly equivalent amount—68 million pounds—of PCB-contaminated waste had been dumped at a disposal site in Anniston, while 1.8 million pounds of PCBs had been poured into local streams, where the locals sometimes fished for food. The reported effects on the health of Anniston's residents included rare cancers, brain tumours, miscarriages, and brain damage to infants and children caused by contaminated breast milk.

Monsanto had taken steps to limit the legal damage it knew could result from any discovery of the extent of contamination. The company had begun to buy up homes surrounding the disposal site, offering "good money" in exchange for a written promise from any seller not to sue the company. In 1997, Monsanto sold its industrial chemical division, which included the factory in Anniston, to another company, Solutia Inc., in a move widely seen as an attempt to evade financial liability in lawsuits the company was anticipating.

Nevertheless, in 2002, Monsanto and Solutia were successfully sued in a class action suit by former employees and the citizens of Anniston. Money was awarded to the individual plaintiffs based on the quantities of PCB in their blood, with the cut-off being 20 parts per million (ppm)—10 times the acceptable rate. Under these conditions, only 15 per cent of the plaintiffs qualified for compensation, up to a maximum of US$500,000. One of the leaders of the lawsuit, David Barker, whose brother had died of cancer at 17, had a bloodstream PCB level of 341 ppm—170 times the acceptable level—and was awarded $33,000.

As Marie-Monique Robin reports, the jury's decision was unequivocally condemning:

> The legal grounds for the verdict were "negligence, wantonness, fraud, trespass,

French activists demonstrate in front of the Paris headquarters of Bayer AG to protest its production of chemical pesticides. Two months later, French demonstrators joined protesters in other countries in what has become an annual march calling for an end to the use of pesticides and other "agrochemicals." Bayer–Monsanto has been a lightning rod for a resistance to pesticides that is generally much fiercer in Europe than it is in North America. Why do you think that is?

nuisance, and outrage," and it included a harsh judgment of Monsanto's conduct, which was "so outrageous in character and extreme in degree as to go beyond all possible bounds of decency, so as to be regarded as atrocious and utterly intolerable in civilized society." (Robin, 2010, p. 27)

How could a company conduct business in this way? Is it arrogance, cynicism, or plain greed? Sociologists might look at the organizational culture of such a huge corporate entity, whereby the company and the work it does become a part of the individual identity of the employees working there, especially those at the upper level. They might draw on Durkheim's study of religions, drawing on his notion of a moral community, where individuals have shared mutual identities and a commitment to a common purpose. It's a situation that fosters group

loyalty—the kind that is strengthened when the group with which you identify is threatened by outsiders. In war, your first loyalty is to those beside you in the trenches. But the situation can also be viewed as a reflection of prevailing class and race relations, where the majority of those in positions of power—the scientists and administrators who directed company policy—were white, while the non-corporate members, the "other," were predominantly Black and without power, and therefore more disposable.

Monsanto Again: A Canadian Connection

Consider for a moment the different ways of owning the environment. You can own a piece of property. You might (or more commonly do not) own the rights to the resources beneath the surface. You own the plants growing on top. But what about owning an entire biological entity, patenting a life form? The following case involves a Canadian farmer and the chemical giant Monsanto. It's a David and Goliath story, only in this instance, Goliath wins.

Born in Bruno, Saskatchewan, in 1930, Percy Schmeiser grows canola, the oily seed plant formerly known as rapeseed. He had been mayor of his small town and a local member of Saskatchewan's legislative assembly. He worked his 1,500-acre farm for over 50 years.

In 1997, Schmeiser sprayed the ditches bordering his land with Roundup, Monsanto's market-leading (and trademarked) weed killer. Unfortunately, he found that it was ineffective in killing the plants that were threatening to encroach on his canola fields. After consulting with a Monsanto representative, Schmeiser learned the source of his problem: the encroaching plants were a Monsanto-patented "Roundup-Ready Canola," meaning that they were grown from a Monsanto-engineered seed made to be resistant to a Monsanto-engineered weed killer.

The following year, Schmeiser replanted his fields using seeds from the previous year's crops, as is common practice. In August, around harvest time, he was contacted by a Monsanto representative who informed him that inspectors had, without notifying him (much less asking for permission), trespassed on Schmeiser's property and taken a sample of his crops. Laboratory analysis provided evidence that the canola crops were of the patented Monsanto variety. The representative proposed that Schmeiser agree to a settlement for compensation or else be sued by the multinational company.

Schmeiser opted not to settle, and a court battle followed. "Experts" disagreed over the percentage of plants affected. Schmeiser lost the first case, with the judge ruling as follows:

> [A] farmer whose field contains seed or plants originating from seed spilled into them, or blown as seed, in swaths from a neighbor's land, or even growing from germination by pollen carried into his field from elsewhere by insects, birds, or by the wind, may own the seed or plants on his land even if he did not set about to plant them. He does not, however, own the right to the use of the patented gene or cell [since] growth of the seed, reproducing the patented gene and cell, and sale of the harvested crop constitutes taking the essence of the plaintiff's invention and using it without permission. (cited in Robin, 2010, p. 215)

Schmeiser's "crime," in other words, was not for harvesting the Monsanto-patented canola plants that happened to be growing in his field, but for inadvertently using seeds from those plants to plant his next year's crops. The company was awarded damages of $15,450 ($15 per harvested acre), plus the cost of legal fees. Schmeiser's own legal fees were nearly $200,000. Schmeiser appealed his case to the Supreme Court of Canada, which supported the lower court's decision (by a 5–4 margin) but relieved Schmeiser of paying the damages or Monsanto's legal fees.

What this means is that genetically modified plants, which have the capacity to spread like weeds and may have localized evolutionary advantages over traditional organic crops, are working for their masters (usually Monsanto, which owns about 90 per cent of the patents) by taking over the farmlands. The damage to the environment in this case is social and economic, although we haven't yet learned if genetically modified organisms pose significant biological dangers.

It is worth noting that Schmeiser has become something of a folk hero among anti-Monsanto farmers and anti-GMO activists. He has already been the subject of a 2009 documentary, *David versus Monsanto*, and his story is the focus of a 2020 film, *Percy*, starring Christopher Walken as Schmeiser.

What do you think?

Genetically modified plants may be stronger than traditional crops, being more resistant to drought, disease, and damage caused by insects. Farmers stand to gain from such improvements. Should the company that invents these tougher varieties be allowed to profit from their use, even if the plants grow by chance, winning out over inferior varieties? Should companies be allowed to hold patents on living things?

© Copyright The Globe and Mail Inc/The Canadian Press

This genetically modified pig, developed at the University of Guelph, provides a distinct advantage over regular pigs: its pig poo is environmentally friendly! If you're a bacon lover, would you have any reservations about eating meat from a genetically modified pig? If you're a vegetarian, how do you feel about the fact that many soy products are made with genetically modified soybeans? Overall, what are the benefits and dangers of consuming food with genetically modified ingredients?

15.4 The Environment and Race

So far in this chapter, we have seen that pollution can be racialized. Rich, predominantly white nations dump waste in poorer Black and brown nations. More powerful companies dump waste in poorer neighbourhoods. For many years, Canada shipped most of its asbestos to developing nations, where the lethal health risks of the substance were not as widely understood or where safer alternatives were prohibitively expensive. Monsanto employed a large percentage of Black workers to produce PCBs in a predominantly Black neighbourhood of Anniston, Alabama. To this list we add the story of Africville, a Black neighbourhood outside of Halifax, Nova Scotia, that was forced to share space with a series of polluting companies and an open-pit dump.

Africville: An Environmental Racism Disaster

Situated a little north of Halifax, Africville was a Canadian Black village with origins in the eighteenth century. At its peak, it had a population of roughly 400. It was a thriving community that became a haven for those wanting to escape the racism of mainstream society, and during the first half of the twentieth century it became a home for Black culture that attracted visits from internationally prominent Black athletes and musicians. In 1996 it was declared a National History Site.

Despite its social and cultural importance, Africville was constantly dumped upon by mainstream society. It became a place for governments and businesses to locate the most environmentally gruesome operations and substances: a fertilizer plant, a slaughterhouse, a garbage dump,

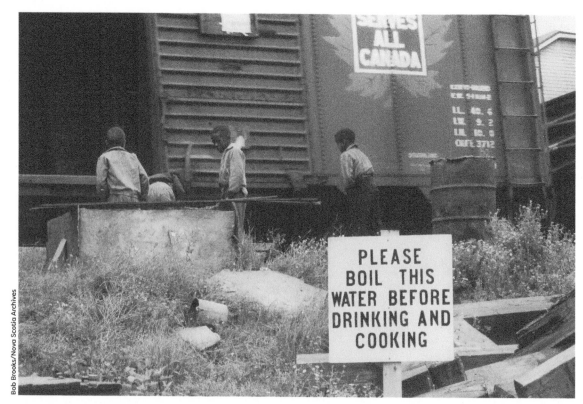

Bob Brooks/Nova Scotia Archives

Young boys play by a CN railcar, along the railway that ran through the heart of Africville. What do you think might have happened to the community had the city of Halifax decided to provide the village with basic services—clean water, waste removal—rather than demolishing it? Do you think it might still be a Black neighbourhood today? Why or why not?

a deposit site for "night soil" (a euphemism for human excrement), and an infectious diseases hospital. Basic municipal services including running water, street lighting, garbage removal, and waste disposal were never provided to the residents of Africville.

During the 1960s, Africville's citizens were forcibly removed from their community, their homes expropriated and demolished. Government officials reasoned that the area was an environmental disaster. Of course, it was, though not through neglect on the part of the community's residents. Displaced people from Africville were given meagre payouts to help them relocate to other parts of Halifax, but many left the region for good. Private homes and a municipal park were built on the former site of the village of Africville.

For those who are interested, there is a rich literature on Africville, both sociological (e.g., Clairmont & Magill, 1999) and more personal accounts by former inhabitants and their descendants (e.g., Grant, 2018).

The Case of Grassy Narrows

In *A Poison Stronger Than Love: The Destruction of an Ojibwa Community* (1985), Anastasia Shkilnyk presents an often-cited case study of how pollution is racialized. It is a sympathetic study of the plight of the Anishinabe, or Ojibwa, people of Grassy Narrows, a First Nations community in northwestern Ontario, near the city of Kenora. However, Shkilnyk's study is flawed in being entrenched in **victimology**: it portrays the people as hapless victims of an industrial attack on the environment, rather than as agents and leaders in the fight against such an attack. For this reason, the incident and Shkilnyk's role in reporting on it are worth studying together as an example both of how environmental issues intersect with race and of how knowledge is produced.

In the mid-twentieth century, fishing was vital to the community of Grassy Narrows, both as a source of food and as a source of income (largely through tourism). Between 1962 and 1970, Reed Paper Company, a British-owned multinational, began dumping huge amounts of mercury—about 20,000 pounds—into the English–Wabigoon river system, about 170 kilometres upstream from Grassy Narrows. In 1970, significantly high amounts of the deadly element were detected in the local fish. Two years later came the first human casualty, a 42-year-old fishing guide.

The people of Grassy Narrows knew that mercury was making the fish and the people who depended on them sick, but the provincial government, with significant financial interests at stake, downplayed the problem. The pulp and paper industry, which was the source of the mercury pollution, was a major employer in northwestern Ontario—so much so, in fact, that the government was supporting Reed Paper with tax rebates. Local tourism, another important industry, stood to suffer if concerns about mercury contamination of the river system became public. There, again, the Ontario government was a stakeholder, having invested large sums in Minaki Lodge, just 45 kilometres west of Grassy Narrows. In 1977 it was revealed that the government had spent about $7.5 million in its acquisition and renovation of the lodge.

The people of Grassy Narrows, led by Chief Andy Keewatin, were not afraid to pursue their case against the company and the government's negligence. In 1975, they contacted the people of Minimata, Japan, a fishing community whose name is now synonymous with a motor and nervous disorder resulting from mercury poisoning (Minimata disease). They paid to have experts from Japan come to assess their situation, and armed with evidence of the river's contamination, they took their fight to the courts. In December of that year, the chiefs and councillors of Grassy Narrows, along with those of neighbouring Whitedog, threatened to deliver

poisoned fish to the homes of Ontario's premier, the ministers of natural resources and of health, the attorney general, the leaders of the opposition parties, and the president of Reed. In a letter sent to these individuals, the representatives of Grassy Narrows clearly articulated their determination not to be victims:

We know that the fish are poisonous. We know that eating the fish can destroy the mind and health and take the life of Indians and whites. This cannot fail to be known by anybody who, for five long years, has watched the growing violence, the deteriorating health, and the declining morale of our people. . . .

For five years, we have fought the bias, indifference and hostility of your minister of natural resources.

It is long enough. Enough have died. Enough people have died. Enough of our people have been destroyed. Enough lack of understanding. Enough pro-polluter bias. Enough indifference. (cited in Hutchison & Wallace, 1977, p. 140)

In 1976, Anastasia Shkilnyk was hired by the Department of Indian Affairs and Northern Development (DIAND) to study the community of Grassy Narrows, which she did over the next two years, returning for follow-up research in 1981 and 1983. She had a genuine interest in helping the people, and her work produced some valuable insights. However, she failed to question seriously the destructive role of the multinational company then fighting the community in the courts and the weak response and motives of both the federal government (her employer) and the provincial government. Further, she failed to accurately represent the active role taken by the people in their effort to resolve the crisis. In her work, the people neither understand their situation nor mount any resistance to the large corporate and governmental players. They are merely victims. There is little Indigenous voice in this book.

Sociology textbooks addressing the circumstances of Grassy Narrows typically give equal weight to two other factors: abuse and alcoholism. They do not mention that the people eventually were able to win $8.7 million in an out-of-court settlement from Reed Pulp and Paper in 1985. They do not talk about the community's fight since 1993 against the environmental impact of the logging practices of Abitibi Consolidated Corporations. They are locked into a time zone of perpetual environmental victimhood.

In 2011, Grassy Narrows First Nation won an Ontario Supreme Court victory stating that the province could not authorize logging operations that would infringe on federal Indigenous rights to hunting and trapping. In spite of the ruling, the provincial government in 2014 denied the community's request to conduct an environmental assessment of Abitibi's commercial timber extraction, even though the people's concerns were supported by locally knowledgeable biologists working for the province.

Meanwhile, the fight over contaminated water is not over. An Ontario government report released in June 2015 revealed that waterways in and around the Grassy Narrows community continue to show high levels of mercury. One year later, another government-funded report acknowledged that there was "an ongoing, yet unknown, source of mercury in the water," rumoured to be a mercury disposal site where dozens of barrels of the poisonous substance are thought to have been dumped (Porter, 2016). In June 2019, the federal minister of Indigenous Services presented the First Nation with a proposal to start construction on a local healthcare facility specializing in the detection and treatment of mercury poisoning; however, the Grassy Narrows leadership rejected it at that time because it did not contain sufficient guarantees of ongoing funding to operate the facility once construction is complete (Prokopchuk, 2019). Ongoing funding was promised from Ottawa in 2021 and the care facility was expected to open in 2023, as both a residence for those debilitated by Minimata disease and as a walk-in clinic for other sufferers (Turner, 2021). On a related issue, the community celebrated a successful 20-year blockade to stop clear-cut logging not long after the international corporation Weyerhauser pledged to refrain from clear-cutting—or any cutting—on Grassy Narrows lands (Turner, 2023).

Jody Porter/CBC

For more than a half-century, the community of Grassy Narrows First Nation has been pushing for governments of all parties (Conservative, Liberal, and New Democratic) at both the provincial and federal levels to do something about the deadly mercury poisoning in the water. To date, no substantial remedial action has been achieved. Why do you think it has taken so long?

The Point Is . . .

Disaster Brings Social Change, But Not Always for the Better

Central to the social ecology viewpoint is the idea that environmental problems reproduce—and even arise from—existing social inequalities. We can consider this idea in the context of "natural" environmental disasters. But can they produce positive social change?

Samuel Henry Prince (1886–1962) was an influential Canadian sociologist who taught in Halifax at King's University (now part of Dalhousie University) from 1924 until 1955. An ordained Anglican minister, Prince received his PhD in sociology in 1919 from Columbia University, where his doctoral dissertation involved pioneering work on "disaster" as a sociological context for social change. His study dealt with the Halifax Explosion of 1917, in which a docked naval vessel carrying explosives caught fire and blew up in Halifax harbour, rocking the city of some 50,000 with blast, fire, and floods that killed nearly 2,000 people and wreaked havoc with infrastructure and housing. Prince's hypothesis was that a disaster can lead to significant social change. In Halifax, he explained,

> the shock resulted in disintegration of social institutions, dislocation of the usual methods of social control and dissolution of the customary; that through the catastrophe the community was thrown into the state of flux which . . . is the logical and natural prerequisite for social change. . . . The shock was of a character such as "to affect all individuals alike at the same time," and to induce that degree of fluidity most favorable to social change. (Prince, 1920)

Prince demonstrated how this disaster led to a broad variety of changes, including the improvement of public transportation and a building code that would gradually replace the previous, wood-dominated housing with buildings using materials less likely to burn. His argument that catastrophe can lead to positive social change is an important and contentious

sociological point, and we will take it up in a moment in the context of Hurricane Katrina, which hit New Orleans in 2005. The Halifax Explosion was nothing like the natural event that Hurricane Katrina was, but it caused environmental devastation on a comparable scale, and Prince's work has great relevance in an investigation of the aftermath of Hurricane Katrina.

First, though, we should point out that Prince's work reflects a greater sense of positivism than one finds in current work taking the social ecology approach. Contemporary studies tend to support the hypothesis that there is a direct connection between social and environmental problems. So-called natural disasters occur in a social context. They have different impacts on groups of people occupying different social locations within the same basic geographical location. The effects of gender, race, ethnicity, class, age, and ability are felt by the victims of natural disasters in varying degrees. The greatest number of victims of Hurricane Katrina were Black, female, poor, and disabled. The greater the number of those social features you possessed (remember the concept of "intersectionality"), the more likely you were to suffer, or even die, from the natural effects of the storm and from the social response to the storm. It illustrates the concept of environmental racism introduced at the start of the chapter.

What can we learn about Prince's hypothesis that disaster brings positive social change? Rebuilding in New Orleans tended to benefit large, well-connected companies that were able to obtain government reconstruction contracts. A 10-year-long project to reinforce the city's levees was completed in May 2018, but less than a year later, a US Army Corp report warned that the system could become obsolete as early as 2023, thanks to rising sea levels (Kaufman, 2019). The city faced its biggest threat since Katrina in July 2019, when a major Gulf Coast weather system swept inland. Fortunately for the city's residents, "Barry" was downgraded to a tropical

(Continued)

depression by the time it made landfall, and New Orleans escaped with relatively minor flooding, with no serious property damage or human injuries. Even though the city is now better protected and prepared for the natural aspects of a future hurricane (the damage from Hurricane Isaac in August 2012 was considerably less), it would be inaccurate to say that Hurricane Katrina has brought significant positive social change to New Orleans, or that the city—particularly the parts of it where the majority of the residents are

African American—is better off than it was before the storm of 2005.

Of note, nearly 80 per cent of white residents of New Orleans, a decade after Katrina, said that Louisiana had "mostly recovered" since the storm, according to a survey from Louisiana State University's Manship School of Mass Communication's Reilly Center for Media and Public Affairs. But nearly 60 per cent of Black people said the opposite—that the state had "mostly not recovered" in their view (Phillip, 2015).

Residents of New Orleans wade through floodwaters from tropical storms in July 2019.

15.5 The Environment and Class

As we have seen already in this chapter, there is a fairly clear relationship between class and the environment. People from the lower classes are more likely than those of the upper classes to live and work in conditions characterized by high levels of pollution or environmental hazards. People from the higher socioeconomic classes can also better afford to eat foods that are healthier and less affected by pollution. The following sections provide two

illustrations of how environmental issues intersect with class.

Walkerton and the Social Politics of Water

In May 2000, the town of Walkerton, Ontario, was hit by an epidemic of the bacterium *Escherichia coli*, commonly known as *E. coli*, which came from their main water supply. In total, an estimated 2,300 people were affected by the outbreak; just over half of them were residents of the town itself, meaning that roughly one-quarter of Walkerton's population became ill. Seven people died as a consequence of the infection.

The tragedy raised questions about whom to trust when it comes to the social management of pollution. The province's Progressive Conservative government had been pursuing a policy of privatizing public-sector government departments, including the one responsible for inspecting the water supply. As a result of granting contracts for testing the water to private companies, the province had drastically reduced its funding to the Ministry of the Environment. Journalist Colin Perkel, in his thorough investigation into the Walkerton tragedy, cites this as evidence of a lack of social responsibility, both on the part of the government and on the part of the American firm, A & L Canada Laboratories East, that filled the government-created vacuum:

> Although A & L Canada Laboratories East, a US-based franchise operation, had never tested for bacteria and was not accredited to do so, it nevertheless accepted water samples from Walkerton. In the absence of updated guidelines or regulations the provincial government felt no need to implement, A & L followed private industry practice in deeming test results to be confidential, to be shared only with the client [i.e., the town workers responsible for monitoring the pollution levels of the water]. (Perkel, 2002, p. 35)

One social product of having a private company do this work was a breakdown in the chain of communication and responsibility between the town and the Ministry of the Environment.

When the story hit the news, the media followed two main storylines. One focused on the personal incompetence and lack of responsibility shown by the Walkerton employee who was primarily responsible for monitoring the water and notifying the Ministry of the Environment of any problems. We can call this the **rotten apple approach**, which aims to argue that the fault lies not with the system but with the individuals who make it up. This non-sociological line of inquiry, which is typical of tabloid-style reporting, dominated certain parts of the media coverage. A bumbling rural official is an easy target for big-city reporters.

The sun rises over Tiananmen Square in Beijing, China.

Photo by Visual China Group via Getty Images/Visual China Group via Getty Images

Sociologists tend to believe that there are no rotten apples, just a bad orchard—the social system surrounding the situation. The second main storyline, exhibited in the work of journalists such as Perkel, took this view, arguing that the *E. coli* epidemic was an inevitable result of the Ministry of the Environment's loss of influence over water testing. The less oversight shown by a large and authoritative social body, the greater the chance that something important will go unnoticed—with tragic consequences, in the case of Walkerton.

The China Price: The True Cost of the Chinese Competitive Advantage

Does it seem like everything you buy is made in China?

According to the US Central Intelligence Agency's World Factbook (CIA, n.d.), China is the world's leading exporter of goods, ahead of the European Union, the United States, and Germany. How did China become the "workshop of the world"? Much of it has to do with what is often called the **China price**. China has a huge competitive advantage in the manufacture and assembly of just about any kind of goods, as it is incredibly cheap to have work done in China. This cheapness comes at the expense of exploited Chinese workers and the environment. Alexandra Harney looked at the China price and, in turn, the price paid by China for its manufacturing success—a price too dear, in Harney's view.

The mechanism of China's global competitive advantage has been called the "survival of the cheapest" (Harney, 2009, p. 40). Less than 20 years ago it was estimated that the average wage for Chinese manufacturing workers was just 57 cents an hour. That has risen recently to $3.60 per hour (in US dollars; Yan, 2017). But despite this recent jump, there are literally millions of migrant workers competing for manufacturing jobs. Tens of millions of them are environmental refugees from farming areas and smaller villages now considered "cancer villages" or "widow towns." The few health benefits that workers can draw on are administered by the household registration system, or *hukou*, which typically favours those from cities over those from villages.

The importance of health benefits to Chinese workers cannot be overstated, since the workplace in China is a major source of pollution. Work-related lung diseases such as silicosis (producing scar tissue in the lungs, and often leading to tuberculosis) claim as many as one million new cases every year (Harney, 2009, p. 57), many of them in industries relating to jewellery manufacture. Perhaps the greatest environmental villain is coal, used to provide power to the ever-growing number of Chinese industries, as well as supplying fuel for household heat and cooking. China is the world's largest producer and consumer of coal, and because of that it emits more carbon dioxide and sulphur dioxide than any other country (Harney, 2009, p. 89). Corrosive acid rain soaks the ground in nearly all parts of the country.

Both the burning of coal and the extraction of coal make it an environmental hazard. In 2006, according to official statistics, 4,746 people died in Chinese coal mines (Harney, 2009, p. 90). However, since much of the coal is produced in relatively small, private, often "illegal" mines, the actual number is probably higher. Owning a coal mine is a lucrative enterprise in China. While China still retains some of the political mechanisms of its earlier period, it is now very much a free-wheeling capitalist economy, with the free, exploitative hand of the market wielding more power in some ways than in most countries of the West.

Officially, China takes strong measures to control the pollution, and it does not lack the resources to improve its air quality when it is sufficiently motivated to do so. Too often, though, this is not the case, as there are huge financial benefits tied to the lack of effective supervision, both in terms of corporate profits and in personal gain for environmental regulators, who take bribes to look the other way. It is easy to blame the Chinese government, but the truth is that Western companies that invest in profitable Chinese businesses regardless of their environmental records make it easy to justify lax oversight of environmental policies.

15.6 The Sociology of Climate Change

In the run-up to the 2019 federal election, Elections Canada issued a warning to charitable organizations dedicated to environmental causes: don't talk about climate change unless you register with us first (McCarthy & Walsh, 2019). Climate change was emerging as a partisan issue, and charitable organizations, unlike political parties and special interest groups registered with Elections Canada, are not allowed to air partisan advertising. Partisan, in this context, refers to any material that could be seen as telling people which party or candidate to vote for or not to vote for.

It is common for organizations promoting environmental causes to encourage voters to speak with local candidates about the environment before marking their ballots. This is not new and has nothing to do with telling people how to vote; it is about asking them to keep the environment in mind when making their ballot decision. So what changed? How did climate change become a partisan issue?

In the months before the 2019 election, all of Canada's major federal parties started announcing their plans to tackle climate change, recognizing that the environment had, for the first time, become the most important issue for a segment of the electorate too large to ignore. Enter Maxime Bernier and his fledgling People's Party of Canada (PPC), which disputes the notion that climate change is influenced by humans and requires urgent action on the part of Canadian voters. Suddenly, a social media campaign about what humans must do to avoid an environmental catastrophe entered the realm of partisan advertising because it could be seen to discredit the official platform of the PPC. Elections Canada later clarified its position—somewhat—but not before creating a lot of confusion about the line between political statement and scientific fact.

Fortunately, aspiring and practising sociologists need not abide by Election Canada rules and the fuzzy distinction between scientific reality and politics. This is a good thing, because climate change has some serious sociological implications. From activists to entrepreneurs, everybody today has a quick fix for global warming, but there's a need for sociologists of today and the future to point to the social impacts of the ideas being proposed. We close out our discussion of the environment by considering just a few of these impacts, some more serious than others.

Have Fewer Children

In an article published in *Environmental Research Letters*, Seth Wynes (a researcher at the University of British Columbia) and Kimberly Nicholas show that among a broad range of individual actions with the potential to substantially reduce personal carbon emissions, having one fewer child has the potential to save 58.6 tonnes of CO_2-equivalent (tCO_2e) emissions per year per person (Wynes & Nicholas, 2017). To put that awkward metric in perspective, consider that number two on their list of high-impact options, living car-free, is likely to save only 2.4 tCO_2e emissions per year, and reducing air travel is likely to save no more annually than 1.6 tCO_2e.

Wynes and Nicholas are not the first to suggest having fewer children as a way to reduce carbon emissions, but what are the sociological implications of such an action? Canada's birth rate at present is just 1.6, well below the replacement level of 2.1 required to keep the population at present levels. What would happen if Canadian families pledged to have just one child rather than two or three? Would the government allow the national population to drop? Or would it open the doors to more immigration, since a dramatic population reduction could have dramatic negative consequences on the country's economy? What would be the social impacts of higher levels of immigration? We could also consider the history of one-child policies in countries like China. Some have argued that the one-child policy in place in China between 1979 and 2015 distorted the natural balance of men and women (because of the social preference for boys that resulted in abortions and infanticides of female babies). According to a CBC report, "Even the government acknowledges the problem and has expressed concern about the tens of millions of young men who won't be able to find brides and may turn to kidnapping women, sex trafficking, other forms of crime or social unrest" (*CBC News*, 2015).

Travel Less

This may have occurred to you already. But what would happen if Canadians dramatically reduced their use of cars? This could be achieved, for instance, if more people worked remotely online or adopted a shorter work week (reducing the number of commuting days). How might this affect the way we work? Would we become less social beings, living much more locally? Or would this effectively strengthen neighbourhoods?

To extend the thought, what if we dramatically reduced our flying time? It is not unreasonable to think there might soon be a significant social stigma attached to non-essential air travel. The notion exists already in Sweden, where Greta Thunberg (see Chapter 6) has brought attention to *flygskam*, or flight shame. One day soon, jetting off to Europe may be something you would not wish to admit to. Will this make us less worldly people, less aware of and sympathetic toward people living in parts of the world we never experience? Or will advances in augmented reality allow us to immerse ourselves in other cultures without having to leave our homes? A technological alternative would be to devote serious research to finding alternative fuels and means of propelling airplanes. Personally, I am hoping for Star Trek transporters. However, the lockdowns of the COVID-19 pandemic proved that

carbon emissions can be drastically reduced when the motivation is strong enough. During 2020, global emissions dropped by 5.4 per cent. However, it did not take long for gains to be exceeded by losses when industry and travel returned to pre-pandemic carbon emission levels in 2021.

Educate More Girls

This is a sociological solution with benefits to the environment, rather than an environmental solution with social impacts. According to Project Drawdown, a multidisciplinary organization researching climate

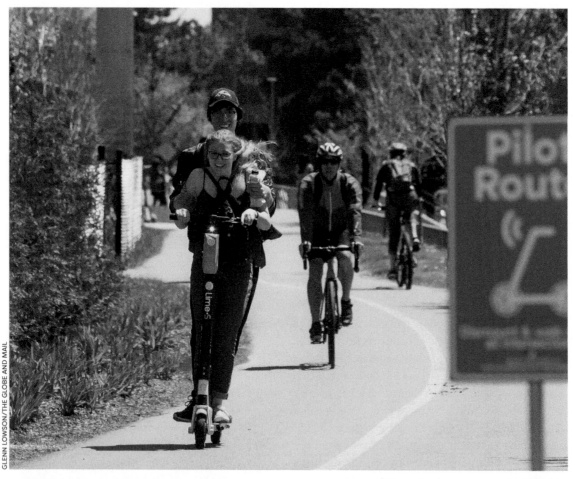

GLENN LOWSON/THE GLOBE AND MAIL

Coming soon to a campus near you: the dockless scooter, seen here in a trial run at the University of Waterloo. Touted as an eco-friendly alternative to driving, the latest mode of micro-transportation may not be as environmentally friendly as its promoters suggest. A 2019 study (Hollingsworth, Copeland, & Johnson, 2019) suggests their benefits may be outweighed by the environmental impact of building, repairing, and picking up the fragile scooters, which passengers are not required to return to the point of departure. While a scooter trip produces fewer carbon emissions than a comparable trip by car, it is as likely to be used as an alternative to walking as it is to driving. If you used a scooter, what mode of transportation would it be replacing?

change solutions, increasing the education rate of girls in the developing world is sixth in a list of the 80 solutions with the greatest potential to reduce climate change between now and 2050 (Basij-Rasikh, 2018). As Shabana Basij-Rasikh explains:

> An educated girl marries later and has fewer and healthier children. She lives longer and enjoys greater economic prosperity. She can be expected to direct a significant amount of her income back to her family. Perhaps most important in the context of global warming, an educated girl is equipped with the skills to withstand and overcome the shocks of extreme weather events and changing weather cycles.

What social outcomes would result from raising education among girls and women in the developing world?

Final Thoughts

Smaller people apparently have a smaller carbon footprint. This is not a joke: if humans were smaller, our metabolic needs would be reduced, which means we would have smaller diets, which means less global food production; we would require smaller articles of clothing and could live in smaller, more fuel-efficient homes and drive smaller, more fuel-efficient vehicles, according to Matthew Liao, Anders Sandberg, and Rebecca Roache (2012). They propose a series of "human engineering" solutions that would involve genetic modifications to the species. Personally, I find that very scary. Maybe we should just ban pizza delivery and offer discounts to people walking home with their order. On the other hand, smaller people have longer lives and may balance out some of those costs over the longer haul.

It is easy to be flippant about some of the proposals for fighting global warming, but climate change is serious, affecting not just our physical environment and well-being but also our mental health, according to Elizabeth Wiley of the Environmental Health Committee of British Columbia (Wiley, 2019). "Specifically," writes Dr Wiley, "climate change has been associated with numerous mental health conditions including posttraumatic stress disorder (PTSD), depression, anxiety, grief, substance use disorders, and suicidal ideation, among many others" (Wiley, 2019). These are grave threats to human health. In that context, sociologists have a role to play in helping understand the implications of all ideas, especially those that involve large corporations or governmental programs, instead of targeting individuals as the chief drivers of climate change.

Wrap It Up

Summary

It is easy to find discouraging evidence concerning the state of the environment, but in this chapter I have tried to find some hope to balance any feelings of despair you might be feeling. Human action is the main cause of environmental degradation, but human action can play the most important role in reversing the process. Natural disasters typically bring about uneven results to different social groups, but they can, in theory, provide opportunities for development that will benefit different social groups equally.

It would take an entire book to provide a comprehensive account of the environmental issues of concern to sociologists today. "The environment" is a hot-button topic, with daily news items about the food we eat and where it comes from, about climate change, about environmental disasters and cleanup, all backed by the latest research and statistics. What I hope I have provided you with here are some sociological tools with which you can assess the issues surrounding the interaction between groups in society and the fate of the environment. These tools include the concepts of social ecology, environmental racism, vested interests, the tobacco strategy, the China price, and, as well, the example of people like Paul Formby and Percy Schmeiser, demonstrating what individuals can do in the fight against socially powerful opponents.

Think Back

Questions for Critical Review

1. In your own words, define environmental racism. Provide two or three examples noted in the chapter, and discuss the extent to which they have been resolved. Are the solutions satisfactory? As our awareness of threats to the environment grows, do you think we will see fewer cases of environmental racism or more?

2. Imagine that a large petroleum-exporting company wanted to run a natural gas pipeline through your community. Who would you trust to give you reliable information on its safety: an engineer employed by the company? Indigenous leaders of people in proximity to the gas line? An environmental regulator working for the federal government (whose job status might be affected by a negative report)? A university professor whose research is funded by a grant? An activist working for a charitable organization dedicated to saving the environment? What are the vested interests of each party?

3. You are a geological engineer who has been hired by a mining company to perform an environmental impact assessment of a proposed mining project in northern BC. What vested interests might you face? What kinds of concepts would you need to operationalize to provide an accurate assessment of environmental risks associated with the project?

4. What is the tobacco strategy, and how does it affect social policy concerning the environment?

5. What is meant by the claim that there is no such thing as a (purely) natural disaster?

6. Pioneering social ecologist Murray Bookchin (1996) wrote that "present ecological problems cannot be clearly understood, much less resolved, without resolutely dealing with problems within society." Apply this statement to the case of Grassy Narrows First Nation.

7. What is wrong with the "rotten apple approach" in dealing with issues of pollution? Why does it not contribute to useful sociology?

8. Consider the following proposals for fighting global warming and assess them from a sociological perspective:
   a. taxing meat products to encourage Canadians to adopt a more plant-based diet
   b. adopting a three-day work week
   c. banning online shopping to encourage more local spending while reducing overall purchases of non-essential consumer goods

Read On

Suggested Print and Online Resources

Mathieu Asselin, *Monsanto: A Photographic Investigation* (Dortmund, Germany: Verlag Kettler, 2017)
Asselin's work includes his own photographs, taken over a seven-year period, as well as archival material and some of Monsanto's own marketing materials. There are many photos of Anniston, Alabama, which was home to one of the company's chemical production plants.

Murray Bookchin, *The Philosophy of Social Ecology: Essays on Dialectical Naturalism* (Montreal: Black Rose Books, 1996)
This work contains the essential ideas of Bookchin's social ecology.

***David vs Monsanto*, www.youtube.com/watch?v=rf0BBDYl6bo**
This is a one-hour documentary film about Saskatchewan farmer Percy Schmeiser's battle with agrichemical company Monsanto.

Alexandra Harney, *The China Price: The True Cost of Chinese Competitive Advantage* (New York: Penguin Books, 2009)
This is an important work outlining the social and environmental cost of the China price. Read it together with her 20-minute TEDx talk: www.youtube.com/watch?v=xMFp8feQbvc

Naomi Oreskes & Erik M. Conway, *Merchants of Doubt: How a Handful of Scientists Obscured the Truth on Issues from Tobacco Smoke to Global Warming* (New York: Bloomsbury, 2010)
The authors outline how a few politically well-connected scientists assist polluting companies in resisting environmental policies.

Colin N. Perkel, *Well of Lies: The Walkerton Water Tragedy* (Toronto: McClelland & Stewart, 2002)

This book describes in detail how the Walkerton tragedy was allowed to occur, and how the drama played out.

Stanford Research into the Impact of Tobacco Advertising (SRITA), http://tobacco.stanford.edu/ tobacco_main/index.php
This interdisciplinary research project draws contributions from Stanford faculty and students in the departments of medicine, history, and anthropology, all looking at the effects of advertising. If you've grown up in the age where tobacco advertising is absent from Canadian magazines and television, you'll likely be astonished by this site's gallery of print and TV ads—particularly those featuring doctor endorsements and those unabashedly targeting teens.

Lloyd Tataryn, *Dying for a Living* **(Ottawa: Deneau and Greenberg, 1979);** *Formaldehyde on Trial: The Politics of Health in a Chemical Society* **(Toronto: Latimer, 1983)**

Two older but still relevant works show how corporate greed and a lack of government oversight create dangerous situations for Canadians.

"The Story of Grassy Narrows," 2016, www.youtube .com/watch?v=9E06pWtCHIg
A seven-minute video tells the story of mercury contamination in the Grassy Narrows community.

Logan Turner, "Grassy Narrows Marks 20 Years of the Blockade Protecting Its Land from Logging," 2 January 2023, *CBC News,* **https:// www.cbc.ca/news/canada/thunder-bay/ grassy-narrows-blockade-20-anniversary-1.6699763**
Indigenous peoples in Canada often have been involved in environmental activism to protect their lands. This article provides a nice outline of what was involved in creating a successful blockade by the Ojibway at Grassy Narrows First Nation. Note that women and youth, as they so often are, have been at the forefront of this activism.

Glossary

Abell, Helen C. (1917–2005) Canadian sociologist considered a founding figure of rural sociology in Canada, particularly regarding the roles women played on the farm.

Abrahamic religions The three major religions—Judaism, Christianity, and Islam—that trace their origin to the Biblical patriarch Abraham.

absolute poverty Poverty calculated in absolute material terms. To exist in absolute poverty is to be without sufficient nutritious food, clean and safe shelter, access to education, etc. *Compare* **relative poverty**.

absolutist Holding or having to do with the view that certain things are always right, good, moral, modern, or beautiful. Ethnocentrism is a negative example of an absolutist position.

access without mobility A buzzword in postsecondary education referring to the availability of online courses to those who would not otherwise be able to attend a college or university because of factors such as cost and family situation. The "without mobility" part is my own addition to the buzzword.

achieved Denoting a **status** that a person has earned but was not born into. Professional titles are an example. *Compare* **ascribed**.

actual culture Social life and institutions as they actually exist. *Compare* **ideal culture**.

Addams, Jane (1860–1935) American social reformer, activist, and sociologist, who in 1889 founded Hull House, a centre for the care and education of the poor in Chicago.

adjunct professor A college or university professor who is employed on a contract basis and who does not enjoy the benefits and job security of a full-time member of staff.

agency The capacity to influence what happens in one's life. *Compare* **victimology**.

agents of socialization The groups that have a significant influence on a person's socialization. Examples include family, **peer group**, community, school, mass media, the legal system, and culture generally.

Algonquian The largest family of Indigenous languages in Canada, including Abenaki, Algonquin, Blackfoot, Cree, Delaware, Maliseet, Mi'kmaw, and Ojibwa.

alienation In Marxist theory, a condition experienced by workers in a capitalist economy when they feel a lack of identity with the products of their labour and a sense of being controlled or exploited.

alternative medicine Any medical treatment or remedy that falls outside of conventional Western medical practices. Examples include traditional Chinese medicine, healing techniques such as acupuncture and massage therapy, and herbal remedies. *See* **biomedicine**, **complementary medicine**.

American dream The mostly unrealistic belief that one can become rich and successful through hard work and determination alone. A naive belief in the American dream is sometimes used to justify punishing others for being poor (the "American nightmare").

androcentrism From *andro*, meaning "man," a form of sexism that views men as central and more important than women.

anomie Durkheim's term for a societal state of breakdown or confusion, or a more personal one based on an individual's lack of connection or contact with society.

anti-colonialism Another term for **postcolonialism**.

aristocrats In Marxist theory, the landowner class of feudal times, who owned the land worked on by the class of **peasants**.

ascribed Denoting a **status** that a person is born into (female, daughter, older sister) or has entered involuntarily (adult, diabetic). *Compare* **achieved**.

assimilation The process by which minorities, Indigenous peoples, and immigrants lose their distinctive cultural characteristics to become like members of the dominant culture. It is a key principle of **melting pot** societies.

authenticity The quality of being true to the traditions of a people. Authenticity is often **contested** by the modern representatives of the people themselves and "experts" from outside the community.

autism spectrum disorder A broad range of neuro-development disorders that involve a relative lack of ability to communicate and generally interact with others. It is also associated with restricted repetitive behaviours, interests, and activities. While it was once attributed to socialization (*see* **refrigerator mothers**), it is now believed to be primarily genetic or biological.

average A statistical figure determined by adding up the numbers for a given phenomenon and dividing the sum by the number of individuals in the statistical population. Five squirrels picked up 24 peanuts from my front porch. The average number of peanuts per squirrel is 24 ÷ 5 = 4.8.

back stage As described by **Goffman**, the site of private, personal, or intimate encounters between individuals. *See* **dramaturgical approach**, **front stage**, **impression management**.

Bales, Robert F. (1916–2004) American social psychologist who taught at Harvard and developed **interaction process analysis**, a framework for studying social interaction in small groups.

bar mitzvah A Jewish **rite of passage** in which a boy becomes a man.

bat mitzvah A Jewish **rite of passage** in which a girl becomes a woman.

Baudrillard, Jean (1929–2007) French sociologist, political commentator and postmodernist cultural theorist, associated with the term **simulacra**.

Beaujot, Roderic (b. 1946) Canadian demographer specializing in the sociology of the family.

Becker, Howard (b. 1928) American sociologist specializing in the sociology of deviance, particularly with regard to **labelling theory**.

behaviourism A school of thought in psychology that emphasizes that behaviour can be studied and explained scientifically not in terms of internal mental states (unlike **psychoanalysis**) but through observing how people's actions are supposedly conditioned by earlier actions and reactions.

behaviour modification An approach to changing someone's behaviour by giving rewards for behaviour that one wishes to encourage and, sometimes, issuing sanctions for behaviour one wishes to discourage. *See* **law of effect**.

Berners-Lee, Tim British computer scientist and professor at Oxford University and Massachusetts Institute of Technology, who is credited with inventing the World Wide Web.

best practices Strategies with a demonstrated history of achieving desired results more effectively or more consistently than similar methods used either in the past by a particular organization or currently by other organizations in the same industry.

Bettelheim, Bruno (1903–1990) Australian-born American child psychologist who, before both his credentials and his work were discredited, became famous for his work with autistic children. *See* **refrigerator mothers**.

binaries Either/or distinctions used to separate people into supposedly discrete categories, such as male/female or able-bodied/disabled, typically when applied to social factors (gender, ability) that are better viewed in terms of a spectrum of possibilities.

biological sex The socially constructed category to which people are assigned at birth based on certain biological criteria, such as the reproductive organs they possess. Western society typically recognizes the biological sexes male, female, and intersex.

biomedicine The application of standard principles of Western scientific disciplines (particularly biology) in the diagnosis and treatment of symptoms of illness. *Compare* **alternative medicine**.

bisexual A person who is sexually attracted to men and women.

blaming the victim William Ryan's term for the process of assigning responsibility to individuals for events or circumstances that have broader social or genetic causes. Example: ascribing unemployment to laziness on the part of unemployed people while failing to consider that job creation is not keeping pace with population increases.

Blumer, Herbert (1900–1987) American sociologist who was a pioneer in social interactionism, as well as a critic of positivist sociological research.

bodily stigmata *See* **stigma**.

Bookchin, Murray (1921–2006) American thinker prominent in the ecology and anarchism movements.

Bott, Elizabeth (1924–2016) Canadian-born anthropologist and social psychologist who specialized in the study of family networks. She is best known for formulating the theory that came to be known as the **Bott hypothesis**.

Bott hypothesis The theory that when a husband's and wife's separate social networks are dense and closely connected, the husband and wife are likely to take on segregated, rather than joint, conjugal roles in the household; joint conjugal roles are more likely to exist where husband and wife do not have close social networks outside of the household.

Bourdieu, Pierre (1930–2002) French sociologist and social critic who introduced the concepts of **cultural capital** and **habitus** to sociology.

bourgeoisie *See* **capitalists.**

boyah (*plural boyat*) A woman living in an Arab country of the Middle East who adopts a masculine style of dress and appearance (e.g., by cutting her hair short) as a way of defying gender norms.

brain drain The exodus of scientists, doctors, and other skilled professionals from a country.

branding The corporate use of marketing as an instrument of socialization to encourage teens and younger children to covet brand-name products linked, via advertising, to the cool or fashionable identity of the day.

broad socialization Socialization in which individualism and independence are promoted. *Compare* **narrow socialization.**

buried knowledge From **Foucault**, that understanding of a nation's past and present that runs counter to the feel-good **master narrative**, in other words, the knowledge carried by the marginalized of events that affected them negatively, whether about slavery in Canada, the high incarceration rates of Indigenous people, the trauma of residential schools for entire communities, or the "discovery" of America.

Butler, Judith (b. 1956) American feminist theorist who examined the way people perform gender roles in an effort to meet society's expectations of what it means to be "male" or "female."

capital Marx's term for the funds and properties necessary for the large-scale manufacture and trade of goods.

capitalists Marx's term for the owners of the means of production (or capital, as these were known during the industrial era). *Also called* **bourgeoisie.**

case study approach A research design that explores a social entity or phenomenon by examining a single representative case or a few selected examples.

Catholic-Traditionalist Angela Robinson's term for Mi'kmaq who adopted Catholicism but incorporated non-Christian elements into their religious practices.

causation The relationship between cause and effect.

China price The true cost of China's competitive advantage in manufacturing, which takes into account the harm done to exploited workers and damage caused to the environment.

cisgender A term used for people who identify with the gender corresponding to their biological sex. *Compare* **transgender.**

Clark, Samuel Delbert (1910–2003) Canadian sociologist whose writings about Canada's social development helped sociology gain respectability in Canada. He founded the sociology department at the University of Toronto.

class Marx's term for a socioeconomic group defined either relationally—that is, in Marxist terms, with respect to their relationship to the **means of production** (e.g., owner, worker)—or absolutely, in terms of access to socially valued goods such as money, education, and respect.

class consciousness Having an awareness of what is in the best interests of one's class.

class reductionism The intellectual fallacy that all forms of oppression are just about class and class differences, a view that wrongly downplays the role of factors such as race, ethnicity, gender, and age.

clinical iatrogenesis Illich's term for the ways in which diagnosis and cure cause problems that are equal to or greater than the health problems they are meant to resolve. An example would be catching a virus while in hospital for minor surgery.

cluttered nest A situation in which adult children continue to live at home with their parents. *Compare* **empty nest.**

cohabiting union (*or couple*) *See* **common-law union.**

Cohen, Albert (1918–2014) American sociologist specializing in criminology. He is most famous for his **subcultural theory** of delinquents (or **delinquent subculture**).

collective consciousness Durkheim's term for shared feeling and understanding among people belonging to a particular religion, fostered by group experiences and rituals.

collectives Another term for **small groups.**

colonialism The policy or practice of acquiring full or partial control over another country, occupying it with settlers, and exploiting it economically or culturally.

colourism Prejudice or discrimination against individuals with a dark skin tone, particularly among people of the same ethnic or racial background.

commodification The tendency to treat something as though it were an object to be bought or sold. For example, the commodification of medicine involves identifying certain conditions that might be normal (though slightly regrettable) as diseases that may be treated with "commodity cures" (such as drugs or surgical procedures).

common-law union (*or couple*) Two people of the same or opposite sex who are living together as a couple but who are not legally married to each other. Also called **cohabiting union.**

companionate conjugal roles The overlapping **conjugal roles** of partners in a marriage who both work outside the home and do work around the house. *Compare* **complementary roles**.

complementary conjugal roles The **conjugal roles** of partners in a marriage when one (traditionally the husband) does paid work, while the other (traditionally the wife) does the unpaid work of childcare and housework.

complementary medicine Alternative medicine practised in conjunction with conventional medicine. *See* **alternative medicine, biomedicine**.

complex household A household in which there are two or more adults who are related but not married to each other.

complicit masculinity Forms of masculinity that do not contribute to or embody male hegemony yet still benefit from it.

Comte, August (1798–1857) French proponent of **positivism** who aimed to develop a truly scientific social science that could be used for social reconstruction.

confirmation A Christian **rite of passage** in which an adult who was baptized as a child or an infant affirms Christian belief and is admitted as a full member of the church.

conflict deviance Behaviour that is subject to debate over whether or not it is deviant. Examples: marijuana use; "creative accounting" on tax returns.

conflict-oriented paradigms ways of understanding society in terms of the production, management, and resolution of different kinds of social contests or competitions, e.g., for status, opportunities, wealth, or other resources.

conflict theory A sociological perspective espousing the view that complex societies are made up of groups in conflict, with one or more groups dominating or oppressing the others.

Confucius (c. 551–479 BCE) Chinese philosopher whose ideas on the importance of practical moral values contain some early sociological insights into topics such as role modelling.

conjugal roles The distinctive roles of spouses that result from the division of labour within the family.

content analysis A study of a set of **cultural artifacts** (e.g., children's books, newspaper articles, internet memes) or events by systematically counting them and interpreting the themes they reflect.

contested Describing a practice whose moral goodness or badness, normalcy or deviance, or general predominance is disputed by some members of society.

control One of four main elements of **Weber**'s model of **formal rationalization**, having to do with the use

of rules, regulations, and a hierarchical structure to keep workers in line. *See* **efficiency, predictability, quantification**.

Cooley, Charles (1864–1929) American sociologist who was an early proponent of **symbolic interactionism**, reflected in his introduction of the concept of the **looking-glass self**.

core need When more than 30 per cent of household income is needed to pay for housing (rental; mortgage), according to a study by Daily Bread Food Bank and North York Harvest Food Bank (2021).

corporate crimes As described by Clinard and Quinney, (1) offences committed by corporate officials on behalf of the corporation they represent, or (2) the offences of the corporation itself. *Compare* **occupational crimes**.

corporate (*or* organic) identity The shared sense of common membership and common purpose that a social group can have.

correlation A mutual relationship or interdependence among variables. *See* **direct correlation, inverse correlation**.

cosmology An account or theory of the origin of the universe.

countercultures Groups that reject selected elements of the dominant culture, such as clothing styles or sexual norms. *Compare* **subculture**.

counter-ideology A set of beliefs that challenges or contests the **dominant ideology** put forward by the dominant culture and the ruling classes.

covert characteristics (of deviance) The unstated qualities that might make a particular group a target for sanctions. *Compare* **overt characteristics (of deviance)**.

credentialism A bias in favour of job candidates with academic degrees, diplomas, or certificates over those without, regardless of their demonstrated knowledge, ability, and experience.

criminology The study of crime in terms of such key sociological elements as causation, prevention, management, or control, and the statistical patterning among certain groups and geographical areas.

critical disability theory (*or* CDT) A social constructionist theory that distinguishes between natural impairment (e.g., paralysis of the legs) and disability, which occurs when society sets up barriers to dealing with impairment (e.g., building stairs without wheelchair-accessible ramps).

critical education An education model that involves the analysis and discussion of ideas. *Compare* **instrumental education**.

critical management studies Research that challenges traditional theories of management by examining previously neglected factors such as the effects of gender, "race," and class on groups and organizations.

critical sociology Sociology that challenges both established sociological theories and the research that sociologists do.

crude marriage rate The number of marriages per 1,000 people in a population.

cultural artifacts Items produced for mass cultural consumption, with value to a researcher engaged in content analysis. Cultural artifacts can include books, articles, websites, advertisements, and other items created to be seen but not specifically to be studied.

cultural capital As described by **Bourdieu**, the knowledge and skills required to develop the sophisticated tastes that mark someone as a person of high culture and upper class.

cultural iatrogenesis As described by **Illich**, a situation in which the knowledge and abilities of health professionals have become so mythologized that individuals lose the capacity to heal themselves.

cultural mosaic A metaphor for any society in which individual ethnic groups are able to maintain distinctive identities. *Compare* **melting pot.**

cultural relativism The view that any aspect of a culture, including its practices and beliefs, is best explained within the context of the culture itself, not by the standard or ways of the researcher's own culture.

cultural reproduction theory The theory that the education system reproduces and reinforces the inequality of the surrounding society.

cultural studies A field of study drawing on both the social sciences (primarily sociology) and the humanities (primarily literature and media studies) to cast academic light on the meanings expressed in popular culture and their significance.

culture A social system (sometimes **contested**) comprising behaviour, beliefs, knowledge, practices, values, and material such as buildings, tools, and sacred items.

culture and personality As described by Ruth Benedict, a now discredited school of thought that argued that every culture has a distinct personality that is encouraged by its cultural practices and beliefs.

cultures of medicine The recognition that different cultures have different ways of practising medicine, including different **social courses of disease**, different techniques, and different physical remedies.

Dawson, Carl Addington (1887–1964) Canadian sociologist trained at the University of Chicago who formed Canada's first postsecondary department of sociology, at McGill University.

decipherment The process of examining a text to discover its true meaning, which often involves looking beyond the explicit message to discover the intent (conscious or unconscious) of the individual or organization that produced it.

deep core need According to a 2021 Toronto food bank study, when more than 50 per cent of household income is needed to pay for housing (rental; mortgage).

definition of the situation In symbolic-interactionist thinking, the notion that different individuals will define a given situation differently, possibly in contradictory ways, based on their own subjective experiences. As a result, understanding how an individual defines a situation is crucial to understanding the individual's actions and responses to it.

degradation ceremony A **rite of passage** designed to strip a person of his or her individuality. Hazing is an example of a degradation ceremony.

delinquent subculture As described by **Albert Cohen**, the subordinate culture of teenage gangs. *See* **subcultural theory.**

democracy A political system that involves a broad-based voting electorate, an opposition that is free to criticize the group in power without fear, freedom of the press and of speech, protection of the rights of minorities, and relative equality of men and women.

dependent variable A variable that is assumed to be affected by an independent variable.

desensitization theory The idea that increased exposure to media violence (e.g., from television, movies, and video games) blunts, or desensitizes, natural feelings of revulsion at the sight or thought of violence.

determinism The belief that personal characteristics, including behaviour and attitudes, are shaped by forces beyond the control, or **agency**, of the individual.

deviance Straying from or different from what is considered usual or normal.

dialect A version of a language, usually with a unique set of features (in terms of vocabulary, grammar, and pronunciation) and a socially identifiable group of speakers. Newfoundland English is an example of a dialect (even though technically there are several Newfoundland dialects).

direct correlation A relationship between two **variables** in which an increase (or decrease) in one causes a corresponding increase (or decrease) in the other. *Compare* **inverse correlation.**

disability Any condition—physical or mental, permanent or temporary—that limits a person's ability to participate in regular activities in the home, at work, at school, or in recreational pursuits.

discourse A conceptual framework with its own internal logic and underlying assumptions. Different disciplines, such as sociology and psychology, have their own discourses.

discourse analysis An approach to analyzing a conversation, a speech, or a written text. The scope of discourse analysis has broadened recently to encompass entire academic disciplines, such as sociology and political philosophy.

discrimination Acts by which individuals are differentially rewarded or punished based on their membership in a social group defined by class, sexual orientation, ethnicity, and so on.

disenchanted Lacking in magic, fantasy, or mystery. **Weber** used the term to characterize the secular, rationalized West.

disinformation A form of false information created and disseminated with the intent to deceive or mislead a person or social group. *Compare* **misinformation**.

disjuncture A gap between knowledges produced from two or more different perspectives (e.g., those of management and employees).

disproportionate representation A situation that occurs when an atypically high or low number of a particular social group is associated with a specific situation. South Asian men are over-represented in the population of cricket players in Canada but are under-represented in the population of professional hockey players: in both cases, disproportionate representation exists.

docile body Foucault's term for a group that has been conditioned, through a specific set of procedures and practices, to behave in a particular, pre-programmed way.

Doctrine of Discovery A Papal Bull issued by Pope Alexander VI in 1493 proclaiming that lands of the "New World" were the possession and under the control of the "discovering" European Christian country, notably Spain.

dominant capitalist class The social class composed primarily of those who own or control the **means of production**.

dominant culture The culture that through its political and economic power is able to impose its values, language, interpretations of events, and ways of behaving on a given society.

dominant ideology A set of beliefs put forward by and in support of the dominant culture and/or ruling classes within a society, to help them justify their dominant position and dominating practices.

dominants The group within a society that has the most political and social power, whose culture or subculture is seen as *the* culture of a country. They make up the **dominant culture**.

double burden (*or ghetto*) A term used to characterize the imbalance in gender roles in situations where a married woman works a paid job during the day and is expected to perform the unpaid domestic work (cleaning house, preparing meals, looking after children, etc.) traditionally associated with women when she comes home. *See* **second shift**.

double ghetto *See* **double burden**.

dramaturgical approach As described by **Goffman**, a way of approaching sociological research as if everyday life were taking place on the stage of a theatre. *See* **back stage, front stage, impression management**.

Du Bois, W.E.B. (1868–1963) African American social philosopher who was among the first to document the experience of American Blacks from a sociological perspective.

Durkheim, Émile (1858–1917) French founding figure of sociology, who studied society in terms of social facts such as ethics, occupations, religion, and suicide.

Ebaugh, Helen Rose Fuchs (b. 1942) American sociologist who specializes in organizational sociology and the sociology of religion. She has studied and written about **role exit**.

economic model (of disability) A way of understanding and representing disabled people in terms of their contribution to or drain on the economy. *Compare* **medical model (of disability)**.

efficiency One of four main elements of **Weber**'s model of **formal rationalization**, having to do with the streamlined movement of people and things. *See* **control, predictability, quantification**.

egalitarianism (*adj.* **egalitarian**) The principle that all people are equal and deserve equal rights and opportunities.

ego As described by **Freud**, the conscious aspect of the individual personality. *Compare* **id, superego**.

Elkind, David (b. 1931) American child psychologist, who has studied culture as an agent of child socialization. He developed the concept of **hurried child syndrome**.

empty nest A situation in which the children of an older couple have grown up and moved out of the family home. *Compare* **cluttered nest**.

endogamy The practice of marrying within one's class, "race," or ethnic group. *Compare* **exogamy**.

Engels, Friedrich (1820–1895) German economist, who co-wrote, with **Marx**, *The Communist Manifesto* (1848).

environmental racism A double standard in attitudes around environmental protection, depending on which "race" or ethnicity prevails in the threatened region. "White" places generally attract a high level of concern and care, while places associated with racial minorities are often neglected.

epidemiology The study of public health, specifically the incidence and spread of diseases in a population.

Erikson, Erik (1902–1994) German-born American psychoanalyst who believed that human identity develops through a series of stages lasting from infancy to old age.

eros As described by **Freud**, the "sexual" or "life" instinct within the **id**.

essentialism The view that every ethnic group is made up of a set of readily identifiable traits that have been passed down from the past to the present with little or no change. Also called **primordialism**.

essentialist feminism A feminist approach that involves looking at differences between the way women and men think while arguing for the equality—and sometimes female superiority—in that difference.

ethics The honourable moral principles that govern sociological research, including respect for the privacy and the rights and concerns of the research subjects.

ethnic entrepreneurs Individuals who manipulate symbols with strong meaning to their ethnic group in order to gain and wield personal power. Examples include Adolf Hitler and Slobodan Milošević.

ethnicity Membership in a social group that shares a common national or cultural tradition.

ethnocentrism The belief that one culture (often one's own, occasionally another considered more powerful or worthy of respect) is the absolute standard by which other cultures should be judged.

ethnography A research method, shared by sociology and social anthropology, in which communities or groups are studied through extensive fieldwork. Ethnography requires the researcher to participate daily in the lives of the subjects, observing their actions and asking questions. *See* **institutional ethnography**.

Etzioni, Amitai (b. 1929) German-born American sociologist and proponent of communitarianism (a belief in the social value of communities) as a response to the individualist mindset encouraged by capitalism.

eugenics The science of improving a population by controlled breeding. The idea was especially popular in the early twentieth century, when people believed that "good traits" and "bad traits" were inherited, and that the poor, the colonized, and other marginalized people should be sterilized to prevent them from reproducing.

Eurocentrism (Eurocentric) Generally, the belief that "European" (i.e., western and northern European, plus North American) culture is superior to other cultures; more specifically in sociology, the use of a European viewpoint to address others, often with the assumption that the audience shares (or would like to share) that viewpoint.

examination A form of disciplinary control that combines the methods of **hierarchical observation** and **normalizing judgment** to condition group behaviour; it is part of a set of tactics used to produce what **Foucault** called a **docile body**.

exogamy The practice of marrying outside of one's class, "race," or ethnic group. *Compare* **endogamy**.

experiential Based on or acquired through one's own experience.

extended family The family beyond mother, father, and children. Use of this term reflects the user's belief that the **nuclear family** is the model of a "normal" family.

fact Something that has been observed, and that as far as can be proven is believed to be true.

false consciousness As described by **Marx**, the belief that something (e.g., capitalism, religion) is in the best interests of one's class when it is not.

Fanon, Frantz (1925–1961) Afro-Caribbean thinker from Martinique, who engaged in pioneering work in **anti-colonialism**.

fecundity A woman's ability to conceive, which changes with age.

feminization The process whereby an occupational sphere becomes dominated by and associated with women (e.g., secretarial work, clerical work). Feminized occupations are usually rewarded with lower salaries and fewer benefits.

folk society As described by Redfield, a rural, small-scale, homogeneous society imbued with a strong sense of the sacred and the personal, usually in contrast to an urban society.

folkways As described by **Sumner**, **norms** that in the usual course of events one *should* not (rather than *must* not) violate. They are the least respected and most weakly sanctioned norms.

food bank A central clearing house run by a non-profit organization to collect, store, and distribute food free of charge to the poor.

food insecurity Inadequate or unreliable access to food in terms of amount, variety, quality, and general desirability.

formal equality In **critical disability theory**, a model according to which everyone faces and must adapt to the same socially driven architecture that gives advantages to people without disabilities. The term is also used in studies of gender and ethnicity, where it refers to the criteria set for job application when these criteria give advantage to applicants who are male and white. This situation existed with the RCMP, where minimum height and weight requirements favoured white, male applicants before minimum strength requirements were put into place. *Compare* **substantive equality**.

formal rationalization (or rationality) As described by **Weber**, a model of improving the effectiveness of an organization or process based on four elements: (1) efficiency, (2) quantification, (3) predictability, and (4) control. Weber was critical of the concept, believing that it led to **disenchantment** and alienation of the individuals involved in the rationalized process or organization.

formal social movement organizations As described by Carol Mueller, a type of feminist organization characterized as professionalized, bureaucratic, and inclusive.

Foucault, Michel (1926–1984) French social theorist who studied and wrote about the relationship between power and the acceptability of different socially placed knowledges. His methodology, known as **archaeology of knowledge**, is a valuable sociological tool.

Frazier, E. Franklin (1894–1962) African American sociologist who is best known for his research on the subject of the "Negro family" in the United States.

Freud, Sigmund (1856–1939) Austrian psychologist and founder of psychoanalysis whose hypotheses about the subconscious and human sexuality remain highly influential and controversial in the popular imagination, and have been largely debunked and dismissed by feminist scholars.

friendly (polite or smiling) racism As described by H. Codjoe, a form of racism that is subtle and seemingly (to the perpetrator) harmless.

front stage As described by **Goffman**, the site of social interactions designed for public display. *See* **backstage, dramaturgical approach, impression management**.

Galton, Francis (1822–1911) English statistician who coined the terms **eugenics** and **correlation**, as well as the phrase "nature vs nurture" (with reference to the two influences of genetics and society).

game stage As described by **Mead**, the third stage of intellectual development, in which the child considers simultaneously the perspective of several roles. *Compare* **play stage, role-taking**.

gay An informal term for someone (male or female) who is sexually attracted to people of the same sex.

gay–straight alliance A student-led club established at a school to provide a safe, supportive environment for LGBTQ2+ youth.

gender As described by **Ann Oakley**, the socially constructed and socially unequal division of masculinity and femininity, as opposed to the biological division of **sex**.

gendered Denoting occupations or postsecondary programs dominated either by men or by women. Examples include early childhood education and interior design for women, firefighting and industrial design for men.

gender role The role that a culture or society assigns as "normal" for boys/men and girls/women.

gender strategy As described by Arlie Hochschild, a way of dealing with situations in different areas of life (work, family, etc.) based on culturally defined **gender roles**. For example, in a dual-income household, the typical gender strategy for caring for infants is for the mother to take time off of work.

genealogy A form of **discourse analysis** that involves tracing the origin and history of modern **discourses** (e.g., the importance of light-coloured skin in South Asian culture). The term is sometimes considered interchangeable with the **archaeology of knowledge**.

general intelligence The mistaken idea that people have a single intelligence level that applies to many areas of life, skills, and abilities. Belief in general intelligence would lead one to conclude that a boy or girl who does not earn high marks at school but has other skills is stupid.

generalized other As described by **Mead**, the attitudes, viewpoints, and general expectations of the society that a child is socialized into.

genocide A set of social practices designed to eliminate or exterminate a people. These practices include warfare, displacement from a homeland, enforced sexual sterilization, separation of family members, and banning languages and other culturally identifiable features, all of which were committed against Indigenous people in Canada.

Gilligan, Carol (b. 1936) American educational psychologist and feminist theorist, who identified stages of moral development in girls and women.

Goffman, Erving (1922–1982) Alberta-born sociologist, best known for his work on **total institutions**, **stigma**, social roles, and **impression management**.

Gramsci, Antonio (1891–1937) Radical Italian Marxist thinker and politician, best known for his concept of **hegemony**.

habitus Bourdieu's term for a set of class-affected or culturally affected and socially acquired characteristics (e.g., opinions, definitions of "manners" and "good taste," leisure pursuits).

haram Forbidden or proscribed under Islamic law, such as foods (e.g., pork) and behaviours (e.g., gambling; drinking alcohol).

Hart, Julian Tudor (1927–2018) British doctor who served the working classes and introduced the **inverse care law**.

hegemonic masculinity As described by Connell, practices and beliefs that normalize and naturalize men's dominance and women's subordination.

hegemony As described by **Gramsci**, a set of relatively non-coercive methods of maintaining power used by the dominant class (e.g., through the various media and the legal system). Often the terms "hegemony" and "hegemonic" are used to refer just to the possession and exercise of power (see, for instance, **hegemonic masculinity**).

heteronormativity Denoting or relating to the norms, mores, rules, and laws that uphold heterosexual standards of identity and behaviour and heterosexuality as natural and universal.

heterosexual A person who is sexually attracted to people of the opposite sex.

hidden curriculum The unstated, unofficial agenda of school system authorities, including elements such as obedience and ranking.

hierarchical observation A form of disciplinary control in which group behaviour is conditioned through observation and surveillance; it is one of three tactics used to produce what **Foucault** called a **docile body**. *Compare* **examination**, **normalizing judgment**.

high culture The culture within a society that is deemed to be sophisticated, civilized, and possessing great taste.

Highland Clearances The eviction by land-owning aristocrats of tenant farmers in Scotland in the late eighteenth and early nineteenth centuries. The clearances, which were carried out to make room for sheep, helped aristocrats capitalize on the rapidly growing textile industry while sending many peasant farmers abroad to find work.

Hill, Daniel G. (1923–2003) American-born Canadian sociologist who specialized in human rights and Black Canadian history, later becoming ombudsman of Ontario.

Hirschi, Travis W. (1935–2017) American criminologist whose social control theory suggests that young people engage in anti-social or delinquent behaviour if their bonds to social institutions—family, religion, school, etc.—are weak or broken.

homosexual A person (male or female) who is sexually attracted to people of the same sex.

Hughes, Everett C. (1897–1983) American sociologist, trained at the University of Chicago, who while working at McGill University explored the ethnic division of labour between French and English in Quebec.

human capital thesis The theory that marginalized groups earn less money than dominant groups because they possess less human capital in the form of education, skill, and experience.

Humphreys, Margaret (b. 1944) English social worker and social activist who drew public attention to the British government's program of forcibly relocating the children of poor families to Australia, Canada, and other countries of the British Commonwealth.

hurried child syndrome As described by **Elkind**, a situation in which a child, pushed to high levels of accomplishment in school and in after-school activities (such as extracurricular sports and clubs), experiences adult-like levels of stress, guilt, and inadequacy.

hypothesis A statement that is verifiable/falsifiable (i.e., that can be proven true or false) and that proposes a specific relationship between or among **variables**. Example: "Playing violent video games makes a person more violent or anti-social."

iatrogenesis As described by **Illich**, health problems that are supposedly caused by health professionals. *See* **clinical iatrogenesis**, **cultural iatrogenesis**, **social iatrogenesis**.

id As described by **Freud**, the instinctive part of the subconscious. (Remember it by the term "inner demons.")

ideal culture Social life and institutions as they ought to exist based on our social norms, values, and goals. *Compare* **actual culture**.

ideology (ideological) A relatively coherent set of interrelated beliefs about society and the people in it. For example, liberal ideology is a set of beliefs that focuses on the individual as an independent player in society and abundant opportunities for social mobility. *See* **dominant ideology**, **counter-ideology**.

Illich, Ivan (1926–2002) Austrian philosopher who was a social critic of the institutions of modern Western society, especially those of education and medicine.

impression management As described by **Goffman**, the ways in which people present themselves publicly in specific roles and social circumstances. *See* **back stage**, **dramaturgical approach**, **front stage**.

independent variable A **variable** that is believed to have some effect on another variable. *Compare* **dependent variable**.

indirect rule A colonial policy in which a European nation uses members of a particular ethnic group as its intermediaries in ruling an area. The policy often leads to dual colonialism and internal colonialism.

Indo-European (1) A language family that includes almost every language spoken in Europe, as well as the languages of Iran, Afghanistan, Pakistan, and India. (2) The prehistoric peoples that swept from a presumed location in Ukraine to where these languages are spoken today.

informant A person knowledgeable in his or her own culture who provides his or her views of the culture to an outside researcher (a sociologist, an anthropologist, or another ethnographer).

informed consent The process whereby fully informed research subjects indicate their understanding and acceptance of the research conditions and formally agree to be studied. Informed consent includes the understanding that permission can be revoked at a later time.

Innis, Harold (1894–1952) Canadian pioneer of **political economy**, who examined the influence of staples (e.g., fish, fur, minerals, wheat) on the economic and social development of Canada.

insider perspectives The viewpoint(s) of those who experience the subject being studied or written about. *Compare* **outsider perspective**. *See also* **standpoint theory**, **subjective**.

institutional ethnography A form of ethnography that challenges the need for a neutral stance in sociological research, claiming instead that any institution or organization can be seen as having two sides: one representing the **ruling interests** of the organization, one representing the interests of those working for the organization (typically in a non-administrative capacity).

institutional racism Another term for **systemic racism**.

instrumental education An education model in which courses are narrowly directed to particular sets of tasks or outcomes, and do not involve challenging or being critical of information received. *Compare* **critical education**.

intake data Basic sociological data that service organizations such as food banks collect from clients when they first appear to avail themselves of the service.

intellectual property Intangible property items such as ideas or artistic works (e.g., literary products, music, films, videos, photographs, drawings, and sculptures) that are the result of a person's creativity.

intelligences A term that expresses the idea that we have different levels of intelligence in different areas of life (e.g., mathematical, computer-related, literary, musical, artistic, culinary, architectural).

interaction process analysis (IPA) A method pioneered by **Bales** and used in the experimental study of small groups; it codes observations in terms of task vs relationship orientation, dominant vs submissive approach, acceptance vs rejection of authority, and so on.

interlocking matrix of domination The effect on an individual or group of gender-based stereotypes when combined with other minoritizing social factors, such as class or ethnicity.

intersectionality The way different social factors—"race" and ethnicity, gender, sexual orientation, class, age, and disability—combine to shape the negative experience of a minoritized group. The greater the number of negatively valued social locations you have, the greater the degree of discrimination you are likely to experience.

intersex A person with both male and female sexual characteristics, as a result of a biological condition that produces either an atypical combination of male and female chromosomes or both male and female genitals/secondary sexual characteristics.

inverse care law The theory, articulated by **Hart**, that good medical care is most available in populations where it is needed the least and least available in populations where it is needed the most.

inverse correlation A relationship between two **variables** in which an increase in one variable causes a decrease in the other, or vice versa. *Compare* **direct correlation**.

joint conjugal roles Conjugal roles in which many tasks, interests, and activities are shared. *Compare* **segregated conjugal roles**.

Kachuck, Beatrice (1926–2014) American educational psychologist and feminist researcher who identified four categories of feminism: **liberal, essentialist, socialist,** and **postmodernist**.

Khaldûn, Ibn (1332–1406) Arab scholar who presented early, insightful analyses of Middle Eastern societies.

labelling theory As described by **Becker**, the theory that individuals and groups outside the mainstream internalize the labels applied to them by the dominant class. The label may, in this way, cause labelled people to act in a way consistent with the label.

latent dysfunctions As described by **Merton**, the unintended negative consequence of a social process or institution. Example: the latent dysfunction of religion is that it divides people into violently opposed groups. *Compare* **manifest function**.

latent functions As described by **Merton**, the largely unintended and unrecognized positive consequence of a social process or institution. Example: a latent function of religion is that it provides social opportunities for older people who might otherwise be socially isolated. *Compare* **manifest function**.

law of effect As described by **Thorndike**, the principle that the likelihood of a person's repeating an action increases if the action is rewarded, while the likelihood decreases if the action is punished or ignored. The law of effect is central to **behaviour modification**.

legitimization of inequality In **cultural reproduction theory**, the validation of streaming that occurs when students accept their categorization as, say, "basic" or "advanced" (a judgment that may reflect that person's class or "race"), thereby reproducing social inequality within the school system.

lesbian A woman who is sexually attracted to other women.

levels of analysis The focus of sociological study, ranging from individuals and small groups to social institutions and society as a whole. **Microsociology** and **macrosociology** represent two different levels of analysis.

liberal feminism A feminist approach that typically involves working toward **pay equity** for women. This form of feminism is criticized as reflecting the concerns of white middle-class Western women while overlooking the concerns of women of different ethnicities and classes.

linguistic determinism (causation) The theory that the way an individual understands the world is shaped by the language he or she speaks. *See* **Sapir–Whorf hypothesis**.

living wage Generally, a salary sufficient to pay for housing, food, and other basic necessities. Any specific definition of this term will be **contested**.

longitudinal studies Studies that continue over time to track changes in the research subjects as they get older.

looking-glass self As described by **Cooley**, the self as defined and reinforced through interactions with others.

low income cut-off (LICO) A measure of poverty derived by calculating the percentage of a family's income spent on food, clothing, and shelter.

lumpenproletariat As described by **Marx**, the group of people in capitalist society who neither own capital nor participate in wage labour. For the most part, they get by with casual/occasional labour, scavenging for food and articles to sell, and crime.

MacLean, Annie Marion (1869–1934) Canadian sociologist, the second woman to receive a PhD in sociology, and a pioneering researcher in using **participant observation**.

macrosociology An approach to sociological inquiry that involves looking at the large-scale structure and dynamics of society as a whole.

Magdalene laundries (*or asylums*) A Church-run institution for prostitutes, unwed mothers, and young women deemed, based on their supposed promiscuity or low intelligence, to be at risk of being led into premarital sexual relationships. The term comes from St Mary Magdalene, identified by some Christian scholars as a reformed prostitute.

Malthus, Thomas (1766–1834) English minister whose contribution to the study of **political economy** and demography was his view that population growth would inevitably be checked by the opposing impact of famine and disease.

manifest function As described by **Robert Merton**, the intended and widely recognized function of a social process or institution. *Compare* **latent function**.

marginalization The experience of being treated as insignificant or of being moved beyond the margin of mainstream society.

marginalized masculinity As described by **Connell**, those forms of masculinity that, owing to class, "race," sexual orientation, and ethnicity, are accorded less respect than other forms of masculinity.

marital roles Another term for **conjugal roles**.

Market Basket Measure (MBM) An estimate of the cost of a specific basket of goods and services for a given year, assuming that all items in the basket were entirely provided for out of the spending of the household. Having an income lower than the MBM constitutes low income or poverty.

Martineau, Harriet (1802–1876) British sociologist who is generally considered to be the first woman in the discipline.

Marx, Karl (1818–1883) Influential German economist and thinker, who viewed society primarily in terms of **class**, and **social change** in terms of economic factors; he was the founder of modern communism.

mass culture The **culture** of the majority, when that culture is produced by big companies and powerful governments.

master narrative A story that a nation or a people constructs about itself. A master narrative typically makes one group (the group that produced it) look heroic while casting other peoples, including minorities within the group, as bad or invisible.

master status The **status** of an individual that dominates all of his or her other statuses in most social contexts, and plays the greatest role in defining the individual's social identity.

McDonaldization As described by Ritzer, the application of principles of **formal rationalization** seen in the fast-food industry to other sectors of society.

Mead, George Herbert (1863–1931) American founding figure of **symbolic interactionism** who looked at how the self is constructed through personal exchanges with others.

mean A statistical figure usually calculated in the same way as the **average**, but for some purposes determined by taking the sum of the highest and lowest figures only and dividing by two. If I have six coffees one day, then two coffees another, and three another, the mean is (6 + 2) ÷ 2 = 4.

means of production As described by **Marx**, the social means required for producing wealth (e.g., land in feudal times; capital—wealth, machinery—during the industrial period).

median The number that falls in the middle of a series of figures for a given population or group. I worked 10 hours on Monday, 10 hours again on Tuesday, 5 hours on Wednesday, 2 hours on Thursday, and 1 hour on Friday. The median of the set 10, 10, 5, 2, 1 is 5.

medicalization The process by which certain behaviours or conditions are defined as medical problems (rather than, say, social problems), and medical intervention becomes the focus of remedy and social control.

medical model (of disability) A positivist view of disability, representing the perspective of doctors, researchers, and others who believe that science can and should be used to determine treatments, policies, and programs for people living with disabilities. Compare **economic model (of disability)**.

medical sociology The use of sociological research and data to analyze and improve public health, focusing primarily on how health care is administered and whether the medical system adequately supports both the providers and the recipients of health care and health services.

melting pot A metaphor for a country in which immigrants are believed or expected to lose their cultural distinctiveness and assimilate into the dominant society. Compare **cultural mosaic**.

Memmi, Albert (1920–2020) French social philosopher of Tunisian Jewish origin, who was one of the foundational writers on the subject of **anti-colonialism**.

meritocratic Describing the tendency to award power or rewards to people based on their demonstrated ability or achievements.

Merton, Robert K. (1910–2003) American sociologist whose many contributions to the discipline include his work in the sociology of science and his coining of important terms such as **reference group**, **role model**, and **status set**.

Métis People of mixed First Nations and European ethnicity (usually Cree or Saulteaux and French) who took on a sense of nationality as well as a distinct legal status.

microsociology An approach to sociology that focuses not on the grand scale of society but on the plans, motivations, and actions of the individual or a specific group. Compare **macrosociology**.

middle class The social class made up primarily of small-scale business people, educated professionals, and salaried employees possessing certifiable credentials.

Mills, C. Wright (1916–1962) Influential American sociologist engaged in issues of class, whose work embraced **public sociology**, and who introduced the important concept of the **sociological imagination**.

Miner, Horace (1912–1993) Chicago school American sociologist and anthropologist whose work put the study of French Canada at the forefront of Canadian sociology.

misinformation A form of false information not created or shared with the intention of causing harm. Compare **disinformation**.

mismatch A situation in which a person with postsecondary education is working at a job that requires a high school education or less. See **underemployment**.

misogyny (misogynous or misogynistic) Practices or beliefs in a patriarchal culture that show contempt for women.

mixed-methods approach A research approach that combines qualitative and quantitative methods.

mobility sports Sports such as soccer and boxing that provide access to socioeconomic mobility for the poorest groups in society. These sports do not require significant funds or access to resources and can be played with little or no equipment.

moral community As described by **Durkheim**, a group of individuals sharing a commitment to a common moral (usually religious) worldview. Durkheim differed from his contemporaries in viewing religion as a communal rather than individual experience.

moral entrepreneur Someone who tries to convince others of the existence of a particular social problem that he or she has defined.

moral panic Widespread concern over an issue believed to threaten both society and the individuals in it. It is typically the product of exaggeration on the part of a manipulative **moral entrepreneur** (e.g., Donald Trump) or sensationalistic mass media (e.g., Fox News).

moral stigmata *See* **stigma.** *Compare* **covert characteristics.**

mores As described by **Sumner,** rules that one *must not* violate. Some of these are enshrined in the criminal code as laws; violation of mores often results in shock, severe disapproval, or punishment.

multiculturalism The set of policies and practices directed toward the respect for cultural differences in a country.

narrative Stories that reflect the lives and views of the tellers.

narrow socialization Socialization in which obedience and conformity to the standards and expectations of the community are emphasized, and punishment for deviation is practised. *Compare* **broad socialization.**

national character A belief now discredited by many sociologists, belonging to the culture and personality school of thought, that people of different countries have distinct personalities unique to their country (e.g., Italians are passionate, Germans are cold).

negative correlation *See* **inverse correlation.**

negative sanction A way of punishing people who contravene cultural norms. Examples include laughing at, isolating, or shaming an individual.

neoliberalism or **neoliberal ideology** A set of financial policies designed to free (i.e., *liberate*) big businesses through tax cuts, deregulating the economy, eliminating tariffs and other barriers to free trade, and weakening labour unions. Also called neoconservatism.

niqab An article of clothing that covers the head and face, with a narrow opening for the eyes, worn by some Muslim women for religious and cultural reasons.

non-utilitarian Denoting actions that are not designed to gain financial rewards or desired possessions.

normalized Made to seem "normal," "right," and "good."

normalizing judgment A form of disciplinary control in which group behaviour is conditioned through a judging system that ranks individual performance in relation to the performance of others, rather than on its intrinsic merits; it is one of three tactics used to produce what **Foucault** called a **docile body.** *Compare* **examination, hierarchical observation.**

norms Rules or standards of behaviour that are expected of a group, society, or culture.

nuclear family A family comprising a mother, a father, and children. The term is used to describe what is typically considered a "normal" family in North American society.

Oakley, Ann (b. 1944) British feminist sociologist and novelist, who was among the first to distinguish the concepts of **sex** and **gender** in a sociological context.

objectivity (objective) A supposed quality of scientific research that is not influenced by emotions, personality, or particular life experiences of the individual scientist. It better applies to the physical sciences—such as physics, chemistry, biology—than to the social sciences.

observational learning theory The theory that children acquire "aggressive scripts" for solving social problems through watching violence on television.

occupational crimes As described by Clinard and Quinney, offences committed by individuals for themselves in the course of their occupations, or by employers against their employees. *Compare* **corporate crimes.**

occupational segregation As described by **Beaujot,** the situation in which women choose (or end up in) occupations that afford them some flexibility and greater tolerance of **work interruptions** necessitated by childcare demands.

operational definition The definition of an abstract quality (e.g., poverty, pollution) in such a way that it can be counted for statistical purposes.

organizational behaviour The study of organizations in terms of the way the individuals within organizations interact.

organizational culture The dynamics of an organization studied in terms of the ritual and symbolic acts carried out by its members.

organizational theory The study of the way organizations operate.

Orientalism As described by **Said**, a romanticized **discourse** about the Middle East and the Far East constructed by outsider "experts" from the West.

Other, the An exotic, often fearful image of a racialized subordinate culture conjured up by the dominant culture.

outsider perspectives The viewpoint(s) of those outside of the group or culture being studied. The outsider perspective was once considered a privileged position, with the outsider viewed as an expert. *Compare* **insider perspective.**

oversocialized As described by **Wrong**, a misleading conception of humans as passive recipients of socialization.

overt characteristics (of deviance) Actions or qualities taken as explicitly violating the cultural.

paradigm A unified set of philosophical or theoretical ideas about how we should try to understand the world around us; sometimes referred to as a "school of thought."

Park, Robert (1864–1944) American urban sociologist who was a founding member of the Chicago school of sociology.

Parsons, Talcott (1902–1979) Influential conservative American sociologist linked with **structural functionalism.**

participant observation A form of research in sociology and anthropology that entails both observing people as an outsider would and actively participating in the various activities of the studied people's lives. It is often used in **ethnographic** research.

passing The practice of downplaying or disowning an ascribed status (typically "race" or sexuality) by claiming a dominant status. Indigenous people, for example, may try to pass for white to avoid discrimination; likewise, gay people may pass for straight for the same reason.

patient role *See* **sick role.**

patriarchal construct A set of social conditions structured in a way that favours men and boys over women and girls.

patriarchy A social system in which men hold political, cultural, and social power. Patriarchy is visible in societies where only male political leaders are elected and where the media and the arts are dominated by male views.

pay equity Compensation paid to women in traditionally female-dominated industries (e.g., childcare, library science, nursing, and secretarial work) where salaries and benefits have been lower than those given to employees in comparable (in terms of educational qualifications, hours worked, and social value) professions dominated by men.

peasants In Marxist thinking, the people who in feudal times worked the land but did not own it.

pecking order A hierarchical arrangement of people or animals within a group.

peer group The social group to which one belongs, or to which one wishes to belong, as a more-or-less equal.

peer pressure The social pressure put on an individual to conform to the ways of a particular group that the individual belongs to or wishes to belong to.

peer review process The rigorous assessment by academic experts of the draft of a scholarly article or book to ensure that the research findings are sound and the work overall is suitable for publication.

petty (*or* petite) bourgeoisie As described by **Marx**, the subclass made up of small-time owners with little capital.

plagiarism A serious form of academic misconduct in which another person's ideas are presented as one's own, whether knowingly or unknowingly.

play stage As described by **Mead**, the second developmental sequence for child socialization, in which pretending is involved. *See* **game stage, role-taking.**

policy sociology The use of sociological research and data to produce social change, especially through government or corporate policy.

political economy An interdisciplinary field of study that involves sociology, political science, economics, law, anthropology, and history. It looks primarily at the relationship between politics and the economics surrounding the production, distribution, and consumption of goods.

polygamy The practice of having more than one husband or wife at the same time.

polygyny The situation in which a man has more than one wife at the same time.

Ponzi schemes Methods of defrauding people by convincing them to invest large sums of money (sometimes, their life savings) in a non-existent enterprise because of the quick and handsome payout of returns to the first investors, which are made out of the money contributed by later investors.

popular culture Commercial culture based on popular taste.

Porter, John (1921–1979) Influential Canadian sociologist who engaged in foundational work looking at social stratification as it relates to ethnicity. His *Vertical Mosaic* is a classic work in Canadian sociology.

positive correlation *See* **direct correlation.**

positive sanction Ways of rewarding people for following the norms of a society (e.g., inclusion into a desired group, career success).

positivism The belief that every rational assertion can be verified by scientific proof.

positivist Based on or influenced by the belief that every rational assertion can be verified by scientific proof.

postcolonialism A theoretical framework developed by **Fanon** and **Memmi** to analyze the destructive impact colonialism has on both the colonizer and the colonized. *Also called* **anti-colonialism.**

postmodernist Based on or having to do with the model of social theory that discourages the application of binaries to the interpretation of social categories such as gender, "race," and ability.

postmodernist feminism A feminist approach that involves looking at women more as subjects (i.e., people with **voices** and **standpoints** of interpretation) who guide research, rather than as objects being researched.

posttraumatic stress disorder (PTSD) A condition in which the sufferer experiences serious psychobiological symptoms stemming from his or her experience of harrowing events, such as warfare, political oppression, or crime. The condition is often medicalized, so that treatment focuses on the pathology of the individual rather than the pathology of the social environment that provides the context for the event experienced by the sufferer. *See* **medicalization.**

potlatch Any of various traditional ceremonies of Indigenous groups of the Northwest Coast. It involves reaffirming traditional values and stories through speaking, acting, dancing, and singing important stories, and reflecting the traditional value of generosity through large-scale giveaway of cherished items.

poverty A state of doing or being without what are considered essentials.

poverty line The arbitrary dividing point, usually based on household income, that separates the poor from the rest of society. It can differ according to the cost of living in the studied environment, and it may differ for urban and rural communities. It can also vary according to the political biases of the person drawing the line.

precariat Flexible workers in the gig economy without job benefits, as identified by British economist Guy Standing; a vulnerable, unstable version of the Marxian working class.

predictability One of four main elements of **Weber**'s model of **formal rationalization**, having to do with setting clear expectations for both the employee and the consumer. *See* **control, efficiency, quantification.**

prejudice The pre-judging of people based on their membership in a particular social group.

preparatory stage As described by **Mead**, the first developmental sequence of child socialization, which involves pure imitation.

presentism An uncritical adherence to present-day values, seen especially in a tendency to judge or interpret past events in terms of modern values.

primary socialization The earliest socialization that a child receives.

primordialism (*or primordiality*) Another term for **essentialism.**

Prince, Samuel Henry (1886–1962) Early Canadian sociologist involved with research of a practical application. His study of the Halifax Explosion of 1917 is a classic work on the sociology of disasters.

profane Not sacred or concerned with religion. *Compare* **sacred.**

professional sociology Sociology that involves research typically designed to generate highly specific information, often with the aim of applying it to a particular problem or intellectual question. Its usual audience is the academic world of sociology departments, academic journals, professional associations, and conferences.

professionalization The process of turning work done by volunteers into paid work.

proletariat *See* **workers.**

Protestant (work) ethic As described by **Weber**, a set of values embodied in early Protestantism, believed to have led to the development of modern capitalism.

psychoanalysis As described by **Freud**, an approach to psychological study that involves hypothesized stages of development and components of the self (*see* **ego, eros, id, superego,** and **thanatos**). It is used by sociologists to look at individual relationships to society and at cultural expression.

public sociology As described by Herbert Gans, sociology that addresses an audience outside of the academy. It is presented in a language that can be understood by the college-educated reader, without the dense style of the academic paper or journal, and expresses concern for a breadth of sociological subjects.

qualitative research The close examination of characteristics that cannot be counted or measured.

quantification One of four main elements of **Weber**'s model of **formal rationalization,** having to do with breaking a process down into a number of quantifiable tasks that can be easily measured to gauge success. *See* **control**, **efficiency**, **predictability**.

quantitative research The close examination of social elements that can be counted or measured, and therefore used to generate statistics.

queer An informal term for someone (male or female) who is sexually attracted to people of the same sex.

queer theory As described by **Judith Butler**, an approach that rejects the idea that gender identity is connected to some biological essence, proposing instead that gender reflects social performance on a continuum, with "male" and "female" at opposite poles.

Quiet Revolution A period in Quebec during the 1960s characterized by province-wide social, economic, and educational reforms, as well as mounting secularization and separatist sentiment.

quintile Each of five ranked groups making up 20 per cent of a total population, used for statistical analysis of such things as household income.

racial bigotry The open, conscious expression of racist views by an individual.

racial profiling Actions undertaken supposedly for reasons of safety, security, or public protection, based on racial stereotypes, rather than on reasonable suspicion.

racialization (racialized) A social process in which groups of people are viewed and judged as essentially different in terms of their intellect, morality, values, and innate worth because of differences of physical type or cultural heritage.

racialized Categorized or judged (in terms of intellect, morality, values, and innate worth) according to cultural heritage or visible racial characteristics (especially skin colour).

racializing deviance The creation of a connection, through various media (television, movies, textbooks), between a racialized group and a form of deviance or crime (e.g., Latinos and drug dealing; Black people and prostitution).

radical monopoly As described by **Illich**, a situation in which professional control work is deemed socially important (e.g., teachers in education; doctors/nurses in health care).

reading The process of analyzing or interpreting narrative texts produced by the culture industry, often in ways not necessarily intended by the creators of the text.

red herring A logical fallacy in which a fundamentally irrelevant topic is presented in an argument in order to divert attention from the original and more important issue. Red herrings also occur in literature, as an apparent villain who isn't really that bad.

Snape, in the *Harry Potter* series, is an example—his character diverts the reader's attention from other, real villains.

reductionist Denoting any unrealistic statement or theory that attempts to explain a set of phenomena by referring to a single cause. In sociology, this includes **class reductionism**, or reducing all inequality to gender, "race," or ethnicity.

refrigerator mothers Women whose lack of maternal affection was thought to be a cause of autism in their sons. The refrigerator mother was a central component of **Bettelheim**'s outdated and now disproven hypothesis surrounding the causes of autism.

reference group A group perceived by another group to be equal but better off.

registered Indian An Indigenous person who bears federal government recognition of his or her legal right to the benefits (and penalties) of being "legally Indian."

relational Denoting the relationship between a class and the means of producing wealth.

relative deprivation A situation in which an individual or the members of a group feel deprived compared to a **reference group** that they see as having no greater entitlement to their relatively better situation.

relative poverty A state of poverty based on a comparison with others in the immediate area or country. *Compare* **absolute poverty**.

replacement rate The rate at which children must be born in order to replace the generation before them.

reproduction As described by **Bourdieu**, the reproduction of social structure refers to the means by which classes, particularly the upper or dominant class, preserve status differences between classes.

research methodology The system of methods a researcher uses to gather data on a particular question.

residential schools A system of educating Indigenous children that involved removing them from their homes and communities, isolating them from their culture, and often abusing them physically, emotionally, and sexually. Underfunded by the federal government, the schools were run by a number of church groups, primarily the Roman Catholic, Anglican, and Presbyterian churches. The system, which began in the late nineteenth century and was formalized in 1910, ended slowly between the 1960s and the 1990s.

resocialization The process of unlearning old ways and learning new ways upon moving into a significantly different social environment.

risk behaviours The social pressure put on an individual to conform to the ways of a particular group that the individual belongs to or wishes to belong to.

rite of passage A ceremony or ritual that marks the passage from one stage of life to another. A wedding is a rite of passage marking the passage from single to married.

ritualized Describing patterns of actions or behaviour that have been established through repetition.

role conflict A situation that occurs when the demands of two separate roles a person has are incompatible. Example: a father who works as a city bus driver cannot pick his sick daughter up from day care because the demands of his job prevent him from leaving work early.

role exit The process of disengaging from a role that has been central to one's identity and establishing a new role. Role exit occurs, for example, when a person leaves a long-held job or a marriage.

role model An influential person whose patterns of behaviour are observed and imitated by others.

role set All of the roles attached to a particular **status**. For example, attached to the status of "professor" are the roles of educator, colleague, writer, and employee.

role strain A situation that occurs when two or more roles associated with one **status** come into conflict. A nurse may experience role strain when his duty to his employer (the hospital) may come into conflict with his obligations to a patient.

role-taking As described by **Mead**, the developmental stage at which children assume the perspective of **significant others**, imagining what they are thinking as they act the way they do. *Compare* **game stage**, **play stage**.

Ross, Aileen (1901–1995) First Canadian woman hired as a sociologist at a Canadian university. Her *The Lost and Lonely* is a classic work in employing **narrative** as a sociological tool.

rotten apple approach An attempt to downplay the systemic problems in a process or an organization by placing the blame on individuals.

ruling interests The interests of an organization, particularly its administration, or the interests of those who are dominant in society, particularly when these trump the interests of the individual.

ruling relations The conformity of workers to the rules and practices of the organization they work for; ruling relations are activated when workers fulfill the organization's **ruling interests**.

Ryan, William American psychologist and author of *Blaming the Victim*.

sacred Describing an act or experience that is positively regarded and deemed worthy of respect and veneration, being associated with religion and set apart from ordinary acts and experiences. *Compare* **profane**.

Said, Edward (1935–2003) Palestinian American cultural critic and public intellectual whose classic work *Orientalism* describes the West's romanticized perception of the Middle East.

sanctions *See* **negative sanctions**, **positive sanctions**.

Sapir–Whorf hypothesis The theory that the structure of a language determines a person's perception of experience. A milder version argues for linguistic relativity, the view that language and culture have a unique relationship in each society. *See* **linguistic determinism**.

Schecter, Stephen Canadian sociological theorist, as well as poet and performance artist, who applies systems theory to the study of society, which he sees as functionally differentiated and highly complex.

scientific classism The use of flawed, pseudo-scientific ideas (e.g., **eugenics**) to justify discriminatory actions against poor people.

scientific management (Taylorism) An approach to workplace efficiency that involves studying the least amount of time, methods, and tools required for a proficient worker to complete a specific task in order to determine the single best way of doing that job (typically from a management perspective, not the worker's). Named for American mechanical engineer **Frederick Taylor**.

scientific method A method of scientific study that consists of systematic observation, measurement, and experiment, and the formulation, testing, and modification of hypotheses.

scientific racism The use of flawed, pseudo-scientific ideas (e.g., **eugenics**, measuring brain sizes) to justify discriminatory actions against certain racialized groups.

second shift The household labour a woman is expected to perform in addition to the labour she performs in the workplace. *See* **double burden**.

secondary socialization Any socialization that occurs later than the **primary socialization** in the life of a child.

secularism (secular) Attitudes and activities with no basis in religion.

segregated conjugal roles **Conjugal roles** in which tasks, interests, and activities are clearly differentiated. *Compare* **joint conjugal roles**.

semi-structured interviews Informal, face-to-face interviews designed to cover specific topics without the rigid structure of a questionnaire but with more structure than an open interview.

service-provider organizations As described by Carol Mueller, a type of feminist organization that combines elements of formal social movement organizations and small groups.

settlement house A building in a low-income, working-class, or immigrant neighbourhood where volunteers offer educational, recreational, and other social services to the community. Hull House, established by Jane Addams in Chicago (1889), was one of the earliest settlement houses in North America. Evangelia House, established in Toronto (1902), was an early Canadian example.

sex The biological differences between boys/men and girls/women, as opposed to the sociological differences (which come under the term gender).

sexuality Feelings of sexual desire and attraction and how these are expressed.

sick role As described by Parsons, the set of expectations that surround a sick person and the experience of being sick.

Siddiqui, Haroon (b. 1942) Indian-born Canadian journalist whose work Being Muslim provides an excellent account of Islam for non-Muslims.

significant others As described by Mead, those key individuals—primarily parents, to a lesser degree older siblings and close friends—whom young children imitate and model themselves after.

Simmel, Georg (1858–1918) German sociologist and initiator of microsociology, which involves studying the way people experience the details of daily life.

simple household A household consisting of unmarried, unrelated adults with or without children.

simulacra As described by Baudrillard, cultural images, often in the form of stereotypes, that are produced and reproduced like material goods or commodities by the media and sometimes by academics.

Sixties Scoop The removal, between the 1960s and the early 1980s, of thousands of Indigenous children from their families, their communities, their home provinces (particularly Manitoba), and sometimes their home country, to place them in non-Indigenous homes.

small groups As described by Carol Mueller, a type of feminist organization with an informal structure, which typically requires large commitments of time and resources from its members. Also called collectives.

Smith, Adam (1723–1790) Scottish founder of modern economics, who advocated minimal state interference in business, making him a pioneer of neoliberalism.

Smith, Dorothy (b. 1926) British-born Canadian feminist sociologist, who pioneered standpoint theory and institutional ethnography.

social change The set of adjustments or adaptations made by a group of people in response to a dramatic change experienced in at least one aspect of their lives.

social constructionism The idea that social identities such as gender, ethnicity, and "race" do not exist naturally but are constructed by individuals or groups for different social purposes; instrumentalism is an example of social constructionism.

social constructionist model A sociological framework based on the idea that any human social category—such as race, gender, ability—is not a strictly natural category but a category with an important social component.

social course (of disease) The social interactions that a sick person goes through in the process of being treated.

social distance A lack of personal familiarity that exists when individuals do not have face-to-face interactions, or any interaction at all. Social distance may exist between students of online courses and their instructors.

social ecology A school of thought, founded by Bookchin, that recognizes the link between environmental issues and social problems, including economic, cultural, ethnic, and gender conflicts.

social fact Durkheim's term for a patterned way of acting, thinking, and feeling that exists outside of the individual but that exerts control over all people.

social gospel A movement in the late nineteenth and early twentieth centuries in Canada, the United States, and various European countries to apply the human welfare principles of Christianity to the social, medical, and psychological ills brought on by industrialization and uncontrolled capitalism.

social iatrogenesis As described by Illich, the deliberate obscuring of political conditions that render society unhealthy.

social inequality The long-term existence of significant differences in access to goods and services among social groups defined by class, ethnicity, etc.

social location Unique vantage point influenced by the important social characteristics of an individual, including class, "race," age, gender, sexual orientation, and degree of ability, that inform the individual's perspective and shape his or her experience.

social mobility The ability to move from one social class into another (usually higher) class.

social order The network of human relationships within society or, more generally, the way society is structured or organized.

social organization The social and cultural principles around which things are structured, ordered, and categorized.

social resources The knowledge and ability required to get what one needs from the system. In the context of law, for example, social resources include knowledge of the legal system, the ability to pay for legal advice, and the ability to present oneself as respectable in a courtroom.

socialist feminists A feminist approach that involves looking at the intersections of oppression between class and gender, focusing mainly on the struggles faced by lower-class women.

sociolinguistics As described by Labov, the study of language (particularly **dialect**) as a social marker of status or general distinctiveness, or the study of how different languages conceptualize the world. *See* **Sapir-Whorf hypothesis.**

sociological imagination As described by **Mills**, the capacity to shift from the perspective of the personal experience to the grander, societal scale that has caused or influenced that personal experience.

sociology The social science that studies the development, structure, and functioning of human society.

Spencer, Herbert (1820–1903) British social thinker who believed that societies evolved like plants and animals do. He coined the term **survival of the fittest** and applied it both within and between societies.

spurious reasoning The perception of a correlation between two factors that are wrongly seen as cause and effect.

standpoint The unique perspective of an individual based on a set of sociological characteristics including age, sex, gender, social class, "race" or ethnic background, employment status, family situation, degree of physical ability, etc.

standpoint theory As described by **Dorothy Smith**, the view that knowledge is developed from a particular lived position, or "standpoint," making **objectivity** impossible.

statistics A science that, in sociology, involves the use of numbers to map social behaviour and beliefs.

status A recognized social position that a person occupies, which comes with a set of responsibilities and expectations. People hold more than one status (husband, stepfather, pet owner, sociology professor, ball fan, garage band drummer, small-town resident), and a person's statuses can and do change over time. More generally, status refers to the relative social standing of a person or group, typically when it is highly regarded.

status consistency *See* **status inconsistency.**

status frustration As described by **Cohen**, a feeling of failure to succeed in middle-class terms or institutions, leading to participation in **delinquent subculture.** *See* **subcultural theory.**

status hierarchy The ranking of **statuses** within the categories of ethnicity, class, age, etc., based on the degree to which they are favoured by society generally. Heterosexuality, for example, is generally ranked above homosexuality and bisexuality in the status hierarchy associated with sexual preference.

status inconsistency A situation in which the **statuses** a person holds do not align in terms of how they are generally ranked by society. A successful First Nations businessman may experience status inconsistency because his ethnic status is not favoured the way his professional and economic statuses are. When an individual's statuses do align, the result is **status consistency.**

status set The complete set of **statuses** held by an individual.

Steger, Manfred (b. 1961) Austrian-born sociologist who specializes in the study of globalization.

stigma (stigmata) As described by **Goffman**, a human attribute that is seen to discredit an individual's social identity: **bodily stigmata** are any of various physical deformities; **moral stigmata** are perceived flaws in the character of an individual; **tribal stigmata** relate to being of a particular lineage or family that has been stigmatized (e.g., the family of a murderer or gang member).

strain theory As described by Robert **Merton**, the theory that individuals are drawn to crime because of the frustration they feel at being prevented by their real-life circumstances from attaining society's culturally defined goals (expressed as the **American dream**).

strata (stratum) Social classes in ranked layers, with no specific relationship to the means of producing wealth.

structural-functionalist A sociological approach that examines the way social systems operate by viewing those systems in terms of the various parts or structures of which they are made. The structural-functionalist approach views society as being like a human body, made up of different structures, with each having a vital function in ensuring the survival of the whole body.

subcultural theory As described by **Cohen**, the theory that youths drawn to crime are those who, having failed to succeed in middle-class institutions (specifically school), become socialized into a **delinquent subculture** in which the values of middle-class institutions are inverted. Cohen's theory builds on Merton's **strain theory**.

subculture A group organized around occupations or hobbies differing from those of the **dominant culture** but that is not engaged in any significant opposition to the dominant culture. People involved in furry fandom, a fascination with anthropomorphic animal characters and costumes, constitute a subculture.

subjectivity How we understand ourselves as individuals in terms of our consciousness, our potential to act in and on the world, and our sense of self as an individual and as a member of society.

subordinate masculinity As described by Connell, behaviours and presentations of self that can threaten the legitimacy of hegemonic masculinity. The usual examples given are gay or effeminate men, and those whose lives and beliefs challenge traditional definitions of male success.

substantive equality In **critical disability theory**, a model according to which architectural modifications guarantee people with physical limitations equal accessibility to and within buildings. More generally, the term applies to situations in which social disadvantages are reduced or eliminated so that all groups have access to a valued good. Compare **formal equality**.

substantive rationalization (or **rationality)** A model of corporate rationality that emphasizes values and ethical norms, rather than the efficiency of business practices. Compare **formal rationality**.

Sumner, William Graham (1840–1910) The first American professor of sociology, who introduced to the discipline such terms as **ethnocentrism** and **folkways**.

superego As described by **Freud**, the human conscience or moral sense.

survival of the fittest As described by **Herbert Spencer**, the principle, wrongly attributed to Charles Darwin, that only the biggest and strongest survive, both in nature and in human society.

Sutherland, Edwin (1883–1950) American criminal sociologist and **symbolic interactionist**, who introduced the idea of **white-collar crime**.

swaddling hypothesis As described by Gorer and Richman, a hypothesis that attributed the presumed "moodiness" of Russian citizens to their having been too tightly swaddled or wrapped up as infants.

symbol An aspect of a culture that has many strings of meaning that are unique to that culture. Examples include the flag for Americans, hockey for Canadians, centuries-old Scottish ballads and some contemporary songs by Dougie MacLean and by the Proclaimers for Scots.

symbolic interactionism A view of social behaviour that looks at the meaning of daily social interactions, including the words and gestures we use and how these are interpreted by others.

systemic racism Racist practices, rules, and laws that have become institutionalized or made "part of the system." People who benefit from this type of racism tend to be blind to its existence. Also called **institutional racism**.

taboo A **norm** so deeply ingrained that the mere thought or mention of it is enough to arouse disgust or revulsion. Examples include incest and cannibalism.

tabula rasa The idea that every human is born as a "blank slate" upon which the culture writes or inscribes a personality, values, and/or a set of abilities.

Taylor, Frederick W. (1856–1915) American mechanical engineer who developed what is termed **scientific management** or **Taylorism**.

Taylorism An approach to workplace efficiency that involves studying the least amount of time, methods, and tools required for a proficient worker to complete a specific task in order to determine the single best way of doing that job (typically from a management perspective, not the worker's). Named for American mechanical engineer **Frederick Taylor**. Also called **scientific management**.

team approach A business approach that encourages workers to feel greater involvement in the operation of the company by inviting their ideas and input.

thanatos As described by **Freud**, the violent death instinct within the **id**.

theocracy A system of government in which the leaders rule in the name of a god or gods.

theory An attempt to explain something that has been observed.

third variable A variable that explains the connection or correlation between two other variables.

Thomas theorem The notion that individuals interpret shared experiences differently, and that an individual's view of a particular situation will influence the way she reacts to it.

Thorndike, Edward (1874–1949) American psychologist involved in the establishment of the psychological school of **behaviourism**, largely through his development of the **law of effect**.

Thrasher, Frederic (1892–1962) American sociologist, part of the University of Chicago school of sociology, involved with studying gangs and juvenile delinquency.

tobacco strategy A marketing strategy in which a medical professional or other scientific "expert" is paid by a company to endorse the company's product on scientific grounds. The tactic was first used by tobacco producers, who hired medical researchers to combat public concerns about the health risks of cigarettes.

total fertility rate An estimate of the average number of children that a woman between the ages of 15 and 49 will have in her lifetime if current age-specific fertility rates remain constant during her reproductive years.

total institution As described by **Goffman**, institutions such as the military, hospitals, and asylums that regulate all aspects of an individual's life.

totem From the Ojibwa word *ndotem*, meaning "my clan," an animal or natural object that has spiritual significance for a group and is adopted as the group's emblem. **Durkheim** viewed the totem as symbolic both of a particular society and of its god, leading him to conclude that *god = society*.

transgender A person (male or female) who either (a) does not conform to the gender role associated with their biological sex, or (b) does not self-identity with the biological sex assigned to them at birth.

transgender man (*or transman*) A female-body person who identifies as a man.

transgender woman (*or transwoman*) A male-body person who feels a greater connection to the gender role associated with being a woman.

transsexual A person who either (a) has the physical characteristics of one sex and a persistent desire to belong to the other, or (b) has had surgery (or is undergoing surgery) to have his or her sex changed surgically.

triangulation The use of at least three narratives, theoretical perspectives, or investigators to examine the same phenomenon.

tribal stigmata *See* **stigma**.

trickle-down theory The misleading notion that if wealthy corporations are permitted to operate unfettered by trade restrictions and high corporate taxes, they will generate greater revenues, some of which will "trickle down" to society's poorer citizens in the form of more jobs and higher wages. It is a central pillar of **neoliberalism**.

Two-Spirit people The umbrella term to describe those who identify with one of the many gender roles beyond male and female recognized by Indigenous groups across North America.

underemployment A situation in which a person does not have enough paid work or else has paid work that does not make full use of the person's abilities and experience. A person with a medical degree earned outside of North America who earns a living as a cab driver because he or she has not been licensed to practise medicine in Canada may be considered underemployed. (It does make a taxicab a good place to give birth.)

values Those features held up by a culture as good, right, desirable, and admirable. Values are typically **contested**.

Veblen, Thorstein (1857–1929) American economist and social critic best known for critiquing *conspicuous consumption* in the United States.

variable A factor or element that is likely to vary or change according to the circumstances governing it. *See* **dependent variable**, **independent variable**.

vertical mosaic Porter's metaphor to describe a society or nation in which there is a hierarchy of higher and lower ethnic groups. *See* **cultural mosaic**.

vested interests A personal interest in a situation from which an individual or group stands to gain in some way. A vested interest can contribute to bias if it is strong enough to override an individual's interest in learning and presenting the truth.

victimology Generally, the study of victims of crime and the psychological effects on them of their experience; in sociology, it often refers to the way a person is portrayed as the victim of some event or situation in a way that downplays or denies the person's **agency**.

visible minorities According to Canadian law, people of non-Caucasian ethnicity, non-white skin colour, and non-Indigenous ancestry. As of the 2011 National Household Survey, the three largest visible-minority groups in Canada are South Asians, Chinese, and Blacks.

vision quest In traditional Indigenous cultures, a **rite of passage** in which an adolescent leaves the community for a brief period in the hopes of having a vision that will reveal his or her guardian spirit, personal songs, and other things.

voice The expression of *a* (not *the*) viewpoint that comes from occupying a particular **social location**.

Watson, John B. (1878–1958) American psychologist and researcher who was a pioneer in **behaviourism**, which he applied to the study of animal behaviour, the raising of children, and advertising.

Weber, Max (1864–1920) German founding figure in sociology, best known for identifying a set of values, the **Protestant (work) ethic**, which he identified as central to the rise of capitalism.

white-collar crime As described by **Sutherland**, non-violent crime committed by a person of the middle or upper middle class in the course of his or her job. Examples include embezzlement and fraud. *See* **corporate crimes**, **occupational crimes.**

workers As described by **Marx**, the people who work for wages and do not own capital, the means of production, in an industrial, capitalist society. Also called **proletariat.**

working class The social class made up primarily of those who lack resources or skills apart from their own labour power.

work interruptions As described by **Baudrillard**, time taken off work, typically by a woman, to care for an infant (i.e., during maternity or paternity leave) or a child who is sick.

Wrong, Dennis H. (1923–2018) Canadian-born sociologist who specialized in writing about the nature of power and of socialization.

XYY males Men and boys who differ from the "normal" XY chromosome pattern. They are associated with above-average height, a tendency to have acne, impulsive or anti-social behaviour, and slightly lower intelligence than "normal" men and boys.

Zola, Irving K. (1935–1994) American sociologist, activist, and pioneer of disability studies, whose ethnography *Missing Pieces* (1982) chronicles his time spent living in a Dutch community for people with disabilities.

References

Chapter 1

Addams, Jane (1893). "The Subjective Necessity for Social Settlements." In *Philanthropy and Social Progress*, ed. Henry C. Adams. New York: Thomas Y. Crowell.

Addams, Jane (ed.) (1896). *Hull-House Maps and Papers: A Presentation of Nationalities and Wages in a Congested District of Chicago, Together with Comments and Essays on Problems Growing out of the Social Conditions*. New York: Thomas Y. Crowell.

Burgess, Ernest (1928). "Factors Determining Success or Failure on Parole." In Illinois, Committee on Indeterminate-Sentence Law and Parole, *The Workings of the Indeterminate-Sentence Law and the Parole System in Illinois*, pp. 203–49. Springfield, IL: Division of Pardons and Paroles.

Burgess, Ernest, & Leonard Cottrell (1939). *Predicting Success or Failure in Marriage*. New York: Prentice-Hall.

Canseco, Marie (2021, Apr. 19). "Most Canadians Not Ready to Expand Drug Legalization beyond Cannabis: Poll." *North Shore News*. https://www.nsnews.com/.

Clark, S.D. (1962). *The Developing Canadian Community*. Toronto: University of Toronto Press.

Clark, S.D. (1976). *Canadian Society in Historical Perspective*. Toronto: McGraw-Hill.

Criado-Perez, Caroline (2019, Feb. 23). "The Deadly Truth about a World Built for Men—From Stab Vests to Car Crashes." *The Guardian* (online).

Dawson, Carl A., & Warren E. Gettys (1948). *An Introduction to Sociology*, 3rd ed. New York: Ronald.

Eichler, Margrit (2001). "Women Pioneers in Canadian Sociology: The Effects of a Politics of Gender and a Politics of Knowledge." *Canadian Journal of Sociology* 26 (3), pp. 375–404.

Estep, Kevin, & Pierce Greenberg (2020, Dec.). "Opting Out: Individualism of Vaccine Refusal in Pockets of Socioeconomic Homogeneity." *American Sociological Review* 85 (6).

Forum Research Inc. (2018, Oct. 15). "Half Approve of Legalized Cannabis." News release. https://poll.forumresearch.com.

Gallagher, James E., & Ronald D. Lambert (eds) (1971). *Social Process and Institution: The Canadian Case*. Toronto: Holt, Rinehart and Winston.

Giroux, Henry (2006). *Beyond the Spectacle of Terrorism: Global Uncertainty and the Challenge of the New Media*. London: Routledge.

Harrison, Deborah (1999). "The Limits of Liberalism in Canadian Sociology: Some Notes on S.D. Clark." In *Images of Change*, ed. Dennis W. Magill & William Michelson. Toronto: Canadian Scholars' Press.

Hiller, Harry H., & Linda Di Luzio (2001). "Text and Context: Another 'Chapter' in the Evolution of Sociology in Canada." *Canadian Journal of Sociology* 26 (3), pp. 487–512.

Hofley, John R. (1992). "Canadianization: A Journey Completed?" In *Fragile Truths: 25 Years of Sociology and Anthropology in Canada*, ed. William K. Carroll et al., pp. 102–22. Ottawa: Carleton University Press.

Hughes, Everett C. ([1943] 1963). *French Canada in Transition*. Chicago: University of Chicago Press.

Khaldûn, Ibn (1981). *The Muqaddimah: An Introduction to History*. Trans. N.J. Dawood. Princeton, NJ: Princeton University Press.

Kaizuka, Shigeki ([1956] 2002). *Confucius: His Life and Thought*. Mineola, NY: Dover.

Lindner, Rolf (1996). *The Reportage of Urban Culture: Robert Park and the Chicago School*. Trans. Adrian Morris. Cambridge: Cambridge University Press.

Lundy, Katherina, & Barbara Warme ([1986] 1990). *Sociology: A Window on the World*. Toronto: Methuen.

MacLean, Annie Marion (1910). *Wage-Earning Women*. New York: Macmillan.

Mills, C. Wright (1948). *The New Men of Power: America's Labor Leaders*. Harcourt, Brace.

Mills, C. Wright (1951). *White Collar: The American Middle Classes*. New York: Oxford University Press.

Mills, C. Wright (1956). *The Power Elite*. New York: Oxford University Press.

Mills, C. Wright (1959). *The Sociological Imagination*. New York: Oxford University Press.

Mills, C. Wright (2000). *Letters and Autobiographical Writings*. Ed. Kathryn Mills and Pamela Mills. Berkeley: University of California Press.

Miner, Horace ([1939] 1963). *St Denis: A French Canadian Parish*. Chicago: University of Chicago Press.

Park, Robert E., & Ernest W. Burgess (1921). *Introduction to the Science of Sociology*. Chicago: University of Chicago Press.

Park, Robert E., Ernest W. Burgess, & Roderick Duncan McKenzie ([1925] 1967). *The City: Suggestions for the Study of Human Nature in the Urban Environment*. Chicago: University of Chicago Press.

Porter, John (1965). *The Vertical Mosaic: An Analysis of Social Class and Power in Canada*. Toronto: University of Toronto Press.

Ross, Aileen (1962). *The Hindu Family in Its Urban Setting*. Toronto: University of Toronto Press.

Ross, Aileen (1982). *The Lost and the Lonely: Homeless Women in Montreal*. Montreal: Canadian Human Rights Commission.

Ryan, Erin Gloria (2013). "Smartphones Are Made for Giant Man-Hands." *Jezebel* (online).

Sandburg, Carl (1914). "Chicago." https://poets.org/poem/chicago.

Sinclair, Upton (1906). *The Jungle*. New York: Doubleday, Page & Co.

Smith, Dorothy (1987). *The Everyday World as Problematic: A Feminist Sociology*. Boston: Northeastern University Press.

Smith, Dorothy (2005). *Institutional Ethnography: A Sociology for People*. Lanham, MD: AltaMira Press.

Steckley, John L. (2003). *Aboriginal Voices and the Politics of Representation in Canadian Sociology Textbooks*. Toronto: Canadian Scholars' Press.

Vermond, Kira (2016, Jan. 19). "Small Change: Women Can Beat the 'Pink Tax' by Buying Guys' Supplies." *Globe and Mail* (online).

Wakefield, Andrew J., et al. (1998). "Ileal-Lymphoid-Nodular Hyperplasia, Non-Specific Colitis, and Pervasive Developmental Disorder in Children." *Lancet* 351 (9103): 637–41.

Weber, Max ([1904] 1930). *The Protestant Ethic and the Spirit of Capitalism*. Trans. Talcott Parsons. New York: Charles Scribner's Sons.

Weber, Max ([1946] 1958). "Essays in Sociology." In *From Max Weber*, ed. M. Weber, H. Gerth, & C.W. Mills. New York: Oxford University Press.

Zhang, Mona (2017, Sept. 30). "The Crimes of Reefer Madness." *High Times*, https://hightimes.com/culture/crimes-reefer-madness.

Chapter 2

Arnott, Richard, & Kenneth Small. (1994, Sept.–Oct.). "The Economics of Traffic Congestion." *American Scientist* 82 (5), pp. 446–55.

Benchetrit, Jenna. (2023, Jan. 3). "By 9:43 a.m., Canada's Richest CEOs Have Already Earned the Average Worker's Annual Salary." *CBC News*. https://www.cbc.ca/news/business/canada-richest-ceo-average-salary-1.6701407.

Bourdieu, Pierre. (1984). *Distinction: A Social Critique of the Judgment of Taste*. Cambridge MA: Harvard University Press.

Bourdieu, Pierre. (2019). *Classification Struggles: General Sociology*, Vol. I. New York: Polity Press.

Burawoy, Michael. (2004). "The Critical Turn to Public Sociology." In *Enriching the Sociological Imagination: How Radical Sociology Changed the Discipline*, ed. Rhonda Levine, pp. 309–22. New York: Routledge, 2004.

Campbell, Marie, & Frances Gregor (2002). *Mapping Social Relations: A Primer in Doing Institutional Ethnography*. Aurora, ON: Garamond.

Davis, Kingsley, & Wilbert E. Moore. (1945). "Some Principles of Stratification." *American Sociological Review* 10 (2), pp. 242–9.

Durkheim, Émile. (1982). *The Rules of Sociological Method*. Ed. Steven Lukes. New York: Free Press.

Feature Upvote. (2022). "Bug vs Feature: What's the Difference and Which to Prioritise?" Feature Upvote blog. https://featureupvote.com/blog/bug-vs-feature/.

Gans, Herbert J. (1989). "Sociology in America: The Discipline and the Public." *American Sociological Review* 54 (1), pp. 1–16.

Horkheimer, Max, & Theodor W. Adorno. (2002). "The Culture Industry: Enlightenment as Mass Deception." In *Dialectic of Enlightenment: Philosophical Fragments*, ed. Gunzelin Schmid Noerr, pp. 94–136. Stanford, CA: Stanford University Press.

Jepperson, Ronald, and John W. Meyer. (2011, Mar.). "Multiple Levels of Analysis and the Limitations of Methodological Individualisms." *Sociological Theory* 29 (1), pp. 54–73.

Kuhn, Thomas S. ([1962] 2012). *The Structure of Scientific Revolutions: 50th Anniversary Edition*. Chicago: University of Chicago Press.

Martin, John Levi. (2015). *Thinking through Theory*. New York: Norton.

Martinussen, Willy. (2017). "Explanatory Practices in Sociology: An Overview." In *Theory in Action: Theoretical Constructionism*, ed. Peter Sholberg & Håkon Leiulfsrud, pp. 160–79. Leiden and Boston: Brill.

Peters, Evelyn J. (2011). "Emerging Themes in Academic Research in Urban Aboriginal Identities in Canada, 1996–2010." *Aboriginal Policy Studies* 1 (1), pp. 78–105.

Piven, Francis Fox, & Richard Cloward. (1993). *Regulating the Poor: The Functions of Public Welfare*. New York: Random House.

Reynolds, Paul Davidson. ([2007] 2016). *A Primer in Theory Construction*. New York: Routledge.

Sears, Alan. (2008). *A Good Book, In Theory: A Guide to Theoretical Thinking*. Toronto: University of Toronto Press.

Smith, Dorothy. (1989). *The Everyday World as Problematic: A Feminist Sociology*. Boston: Northeastern University Press.

Sweet, Matthias. (2011). "Does Traffic Congestion Slow the Economy?" *Journal of Planning Literature* 26 (4). DOI: 10.1177/0885412211409754.

"Top CEOs Raked in Average Worker's Salary before Noon Tuesday." (2023). *The National*. https://www.cbc.ca/player/play/2157803075862.

Tudor, Alyosxa. (2018). "Cross-Fadings of Racialisation and Migratisation: The Postcolonial Turn in Western European Gender and Migration Studies." *Gender, Place & Culture: A Journal of Feminist Geography* 25 (7), pp. 1057–72.

Weber, Max. (1962). *Basic Concepts in Sociology*. New York: Philosophical Library.

Williams, Rob. (2021). "Stephanie Labbé Kept Smiling during Gold Medal Shootout and Canadians Loved It." *The Daily Hive*. https://dailyhive.com/vancouver/stephanie-labbe-smile-canada-olympics-gold-medal-shootout.

Chapter 3

Aboriginal Policing Directorate (1995, July). "Mentor User Guide Gives Aboriginal Youth and Police a Chance to Build Bridges." *First Nations Policing: Update*, 3. Ottawa: Solicitor General Canada. www.publicsafety.gc.ca/lbrr/archives/fnpu%203-1995-eng.pdf.

Best, Joel (2001). *Damned Lies and Statistics: Untangling Numbers from the Media, Politicians, and Activists*. Berkeley: University of California Press.

Campbell, Marie, & Frances Gregor (2002). *Mapping Social Relations: A Primer in Doing Institutional Ethnography*. Aurora, ON: Garamond.

Centers for Disease Control and Prevention (2018, Dec. 19). "Prescription Opioid Data." Atlanta: CDC (online).

Comte, Auguste (1853). *The Positive Philosophy of August Comte*. Trans. & ed. Harriet Martineau. London: Longmans.

Comte, Auguste (1877). *The System of Positive Polity*. London: Longmans, Green.

Coutts, Jane (2022, May 10). "Half of Our Nurses Are Thinking of Quitting: How Can We Keep Them Healthy, Happy and Helping Patients?" Canadian Federation of Nurses Unions. https://nursesunions.ca/

half-of-our-nurses-are-thinking-of-quitting-how-can-we-keep-them-healthy-happy-and-helping-patients/.

Durkheim, Émile ([1897] 1951). *Suicide: A Study in Sociology*. Trans. John A. Spaulding & George Simpson. New York: Free Press of Glencoe.

Esar, Evan (1943). *Esar's Comic Dictionary of Wit and Humour*. New York: Horizon.

Foucault, Michel (1961). *Madness and Civilisation: A History of Insanity in the Age of Reason*. New York: Vintage.

Foucault, Michel (1975). *Discipline and Punish: The Birth of the Prison*. New York: Vintage.

Foucault, Michel (1978). *The History of Sexuality. Vol. 1: An Introduction*. New York: Pantheon.

Gephart, Robert (1988). *Ethnostatistics: Qualitative Foundations for Quantitative Research*. London: Sage.

Giles, Philip. 2004. "Low Income Measurement in Canada," Cat. no. 75F0002MIE, Statistics Canada. https://www150.statcan.gc.ca/n1/pub/75f0002m/75f0002m2004011-eng.pdf.

Goffman, Alice (2014). *On the Run: Fugitive Life in an American City*. Chicago: University of Chicago Press.

Goffman, Erving (1976). *Gender Advertisements*. New York: Harper Torch.

Gomm, Roger, & Patrick McNeil, eds (1982). *Handbook for Sociology Teachers*. London: Heinemann Educational.

Government of Canada (2022; modified Apr. 20). "Towards a Poverty Reduction Strategy—A Backgrounder on Poverty in Canada." https://canada.ca/en/employment-social-development/programs/poverty-reduction/backgrounder.html.

Griswold, Wendy (1994). *Cultures and Societies in a Changing World*. London: Sage.

Guskin, Emily, & Scott Clement (2021, Apr. 28). "Support for New Gun Laws Falls from Peak after Parkland Shooting, Post-ABC Poll Finds." *Washington Post*. https://www.washingtonpost.com/politics/2021/04/28/support-new-gun-laws-falls-peak-after-parkland-shooting-post-abc-poll-finds/.

Hughes, Everett C. ([1943] 1963). *French Canada in Transition*. Chicago: University of Chicago Press.

Humphreys, R.A. Laud (1970). *Tearoom Trade: A Study of Homosexual Encounters in Public Places*. London: Duckworth.

Jhally, Sut (1990). *The Codes of Advertising: Fetishism and the Political Economy of Meaning in the Consumer Society*. New York: Routledge.

Lammam, Charles, & Hugh MacIntyre (2016, Jan.). *An Introduction to the State of Poverty in Canada*. Vancouver: Fraser Institute.

Leung, Pamela T.M., Erin M. Macdonald, Irfan A. Dhalla, & David N. Juurlink (2017, June 1). "A 1980 Letter on the Risk of Opioid Addiction." *New England Journal of Medicine* 376, pp. 2194–5.

Maines, D.R. (1993). "Narrative's Moment and Sociology's Phenomena—Toward a Narrative Sociology." *Sociological Quarterly* 34 (1), pp. 17–37.

Maracle, Brian (1996). *Back on the Rez: Finding the Way Home*. Toronto: Viking Penguin.

Maracle, Lee (1992). *Sundogs*. Penticton, BC: Theytus.

Marshall, Gordon (1998). *Oxford Dictionary of Sociology*. New York: Oxford University Press.

Melendez, Pilar (2022, May 11). "Secret Operation Tests Whether Chipotle's Hiring May Be Racist." *The Daily Beast*. https://www.thedailybeast.com/sting-operation-tests-whether-chipotles-hiring-may-be-racist?ref=scroll.

Miner, Horace ([1939] 1963). *St Denis: A French Canadian Parish*. Chicago: University of Chicago Press.

Pew Research Center (2016, Aug.). "Opinions on Gun Policy and the 2016 Campaign." Washington, DC: Pew (online).

Porter, Jane, & Hershel Jick (1980). "Addiction Rare in Patients Treated with Narcotics." *New England Journal of Medicine* 302, p. 123.

Reinharz, Shulamit (1992). *Feminist Methods in Social Research*. New York: Oxford University Press.

Road Safety Research Office (2016). Preliminary 2016 Ontario Road Safety Annual Report Selected Statistics. Toronto: Ministry of Transportation. www.mto.gov.on.ca/english/publications/pdfs/preliminary-2016-orsar-selected-statistics.pdf.

Ross, Aileen (1961). *Becoming a Nurse*. Toronto: Macmillan.

Ross, Aileen (1982). *The Lost and the Lonely: Homeless Women in Montreal*. Montreal: Canadian Human Rights Commission.

Said, Edward (1979). *Orientalism*. New York: Pantheon.

Sarlo, Christopher (2013, Nov.). "Poverty: Where Do We Draw the Line?" Vancouver: Fraser Institute.

Smith, Joanna (2015, Feb. 8). "High-Paid Chiefs Are Outliers, Data Shows." *Toronto Star* (online).

Smith, Linda Tuhiwai (1999). *Decolonizing Methodologies: Research and Indigenous Peoples*. London: Zed Books.

Sofalvi, Alan J. (2008). "Male Condom Advertising in United States Magazines and on the World Wide Web from 1997–2007: Implications for Media Literacy and Health Literacy." *International Electronic Journal of Health Education* 11, pp. 81–94.

Special Advisory Committee on the Epidemic of Opioid Overdose (2019, June). *National Report: Apparent Opioid-Related Deaths in Canada (January 2016 to December 2018)*. Ottawa: Public Health Agency of Canada. https://health-infobase.canada.ca/datalab/national-surveillance-opioid-mortality.html.

Statistics Canada (2013). "National Household Survey Dictionary, 2011," Cat. no. 99-000-X2011001. Ottawa: Minister of Industry.

Statistics Canada (2017). "Table 4.5: Market Basket Measure (MBM) Thresholds for Economic Families and Persons Not in Economic Families, 2015." *Dictionary, Census of Population, 2016*. https://www12.statcan.gc.ca/census-recensement/2016/ref/dict/tab/t4_5-eng.cfm.

Statistics Canada (2022, Mar. 23). "Market Basket Measure (MBM) for the Reference Family by Market Basket Measure Region, Component and Base Year." Table 11-10-0066-01.

Thompson, Elizabeth, Roberto Rocha, & Albert Leung (2022, Feb. 14). "Hacked Convoy Data Shows More Than Half of Donations Came from U.S." *CBC News*. https://www.cbc.ca/news/politics/convoy-protest-donations-data-1.6351293.

Van der Linden, Clifton, & Alexander G.W. Beyer (2022, Feb. 4). "Most Disagree with Convoy Truckers on Vaccine Mandates and Lockdowns." *The Tyee*. https://thetyee.ca/Analysis/2022/02/04/Most-Disagree-Convoy-Truckers/.

Weaver, R., C. Ferguson, M. Wilbourn, & Y. Salamonson (2014, Apr.). "Men in Nursing on Television: Exposing and Reinforcing Stereotypes." *Journal of Advanced Nursing* 70 (4), pp. 833–42.

Whyte, William F. (1955). *Street-Corner Society: The Social Structure of an Italian Slum*, 2nd ed. Chicago: University of Chicago Press.

Chapter 4

Aguiar, Luis (2001). "'Whiteness' in White Academia." In *Talking about Identity: Encounters in Race, Ethnicity and Language*, 2nd ed., ed. Carl James & Adrienne Shadd, pp. 177–92. Toronto: Between the Lines.

Armstrong, Karen ([1982] 2005). *Through the Narrow Gate: A Memoir of Life in and out of the Convent*. Toronto: Vintage Canada.

Arnett, Jeffrey, & Lene Balle-Jensen (1993). "Cultural Bases of Risk Behavior: Danish Adolescents." *Child Development* 64, pp. 1842–55.

Badcock, Christopher (2010, Apr. 21). "Bruno Bettelheim, Psychotic Savant." *Psychology Today*. https://www.psychologytoday.com/us/blog/the-imprinted-brain/201004/bruno-bettelheim-psychotic-savant.

Bérard, Guy, & Sally Brockett (2011). *Hearing Equals Behavior: Updated and Expanded*. Manchester Center, VT: Shires Press.

Bhanot, Ruchi, & Jasna Jovanovic (2005, May). "Do Parents' Academic Gender Stereotypes Influence Whether They Intrude on Their Children's Homework?" *Sex Roles* 52 (9–10), pp. 597–607.

Boston Globe (2022, June 4). "Sophie Freud, Simmons Professor Who Called Psychoanalysis 'A Narcissistic Indulgence,' Dies at 97." https://www.msn.com/en-us/news/us/sophie-freud-simmons-professor-who-called-psychoanalysis-e2-80-98a-narcissistic-indulgence-e2-80-99-dies-at-97/ar-AAY5y2J.

Bourdieu, Pierre (1996). *On Television*. Trans. Priscilla Parkhurst Ferguson. New York: New Press.

Brown, W. Michael Court (1968). "Males with an XYY Sex Chromosome Complement." *Journal of Medical Genetics* 5 (4), pp. 341–59.

Bushman, Brad J., & L. Rowell Huesmann (2001). "Effects of Televised Violence on Aggression." In *Handbook of Children and the Media*, ed. D. Singer & J. Singer, pp. 223–54. Thousand Oaks, CA: Sage.

CBS News (2019, Mar. 18). "New Zealand Terror Attack: Shooter Acted Alone but May Have Had Support." https://www.cbsnews.com/live-news/new-zealand-mosque-shooting-suspect-brenton-tarrant-christchurch-video-livestream-latest-updates/.

Cooley, Charles Horton (1902). *Human Nature and the Social Order*. New York: Charles Scribner's Sons.

Cooley, Charles Horton (1909). *Social Organization: A Study of the Larger Mind*. New York: Charles Scribner's Sons.

Daniel, Christina, & Oliver J. Mason (2015). "Predicting Psychotic-Like Experiences during Sensory Deprivation." *BioMed Research International*. https://www.hindawi.com/journals/bmri/2015/439379/.

De Trinis, Randall (2010). "A Novice and His Master." https://mertonocso.wordpress.com/2010/06/26/a-novice-and-his-master-part-one-2/.

Doidge, Norman (2015). *The Brain's Way of Healing: Remarkable Discoveries and Recoveries from the Frontiers of Neuroplasticity*. New York: Viking, Penguin Group.

Ebaugh, Helen Rose Fuchs (1988). *Becoming an EX: The Process of Role Exit*. Chicago: University of Chicago Press.

Elkind, David ([1981] 2001). *The Hurried Child: Growing Up Too Fast Too Soon*, 3rd ed. Cambridge, MA: Perseus.

Elkind, David (2003). "The Reality of Virtual Stress." *CIO* (Fall/Winter). www.cio.com/archive/092203/elkind.

Finkel, Michelle A. (2002). "Traumatic Injuries Caused by Hazing Practices." *Journal of Emergency Medicine* 20, pp. 228–33.

Fletcher, Michael A., & Jon Cohen (2011, Feb. 20). "Economy Poll: African Americans, Hispanics Were Hardest Hit but Are Most Optimistic." *Washington Post* (online).

Fowles, Jib (1999). *The Case for Television Violence*. London: Sage.

Fowles, Jib (2001, Mar.). "The Whipping Boy: The Hidden Conflicts Underlying the Campaign against TV." *Reason* (online).

Freud, Sigmund ([1916–17] 1977). *On Sexuality*, vol. 7. London: Penguin.

Frum, David (2017, Oct. 3). "On Gun Control Following the Las Vegas Shooting." *Metro Morning* [Toronto], CBC Radio. www.cbc.ca/news/canada/toronto/programs/metromorning/on-gun-control-following-the-las-vegas-shooting-1.4318401.

Gilligan, Carol (1990). *Making Connections: The Relational Worlds of Adolescent Girls at Emma Willard School*. Cambridge, MA: Harvard University Press.

Goffman, Erving (1961). *Asylums: Essays on the Social Situation of Mental Patients and Other Inmates*. New York: Anchor.

Gorer, Geoffrey, & John Rickman (1949). *The People of Great Russia: A Psychological Study*. New York: Norton.

Grundy, Adam (2020, Oct. 2). "Manufacturing Still among Top Five U.S. Employers." United States Census Bureau. https://www.census.gov/library/stories/2020/10/manufacturing-still-among-top-five-united-states-employers.html.

Hanson, Glen R., Peter J. Hanson, Peter J. Venturelli, & Annette E. Fleckenstein (2009). *Drugs and Society*, 10th ed. New York: Jones and Bartlett.

Hart, Mackenzie, & Garth Davies (2022, July 6). "The Proud Boys Disbanded over a Year Ago, but Far-Right Extremism Still Exists in Canada." *The Conversation*. https://theconversation.com/the-proud-boys-disbanded-over-a-year-ago-but-far-right-extremism-still-exists-in-canada-185670.

Hitchcock, John T., & Leigh Minturn (1963)."The Rajputs of Khalapur." In *Six Cultures: Studies of Child Rearing*, ed. B. Whiting, pp. 203–362. New York: John Wiley & Sons.

Huesmann, L. Rowell, & L.D. Eron (1986). *Television and the Aggressive Child: A Cross-national Comparison*. Mahwah, NJ: Lawrence Erlbaum.

Huesmann, L. Rowell, J. Moise, C.P. Podolski, & L.D. Eron (2003). "Longitudinal Relations between Childhood Exposure to Media Violence and Adult Aggression and Violence: 1977–1992." *Developmental Psychology* 39 (2), pp. 201–21.

Hughes, Everett C. (1945). "Dilemmas and Contractions of Status." *American Journal of Sociology* 50 (5), pp. 353–9.

Jacobs, Patricia A., Muriel Brunton, Marie M. Melville, Robert P. Brittain, & William F. McClemont (1965). "Aggressive Behaviour, Mental Sub-normality and the XYY Male." *Nature* 208 (5017), pp. 1351–2.

Jantz, Gregory L. (2014, Feb. 27). "Brain Differences between Genders." *Psychology Today*. https://www.psychologytoday.com/us/blog/hope-relationships/201402/brain-differences-between-genders.

Jones, Robert P. (2017, July 4). "Trump Can't Reverse the Decline of White Christian America." *The Atlantic* (online).

Kane, P.R., & A.J. Orsini (2003). "The Need for Teachers of Color in Independent Schools." In *The Colors of Excellence: Hiring and Keeping Teachers of Color in Independent Schools*, ed. P.R. Kane & A.J. Orsini, pp. 7–28. New York: Teachers College.

Keilman, John (2013, June 26). "Youth Sports That Don't Keep Score? How Un-American." *Chicago Tribune* (online).

Kirby, Sandra L., & Glen Wintrup (2002). "Running the Gauntlet: An Examination of Initiation/Hazing and Sexual Abuse in Sport." *Journal of Sexual Aggression* 8 (2), pp. 49–68.

Klopfenstein, Kristin (2005). "Beyond Test Scores: The Impact of Black Teacher Role Models on Rigorous Math Taking." *Contemporary Economic Policy* 23, pp. 416–28.

Knockwood, Isabelle (1992). *Out of the Depths: The Experiences of Mi'kmaw Children at the Indian Residential School at Shubenacadie*. Lockeport, NS: Roseway.

Kohn, Melvin L. (1959). "Social Class and Parental Values." *American Journal of Sociology* 64 (4), pp. 337–66.

Kohn, Melvin L. (1977). *Class and Conformity: A Study in Values*, 2nd ed. Chicago: University of Chicago Press.

Lazarus, Joyce (2022, June 7). "A Conversation with Sophie Freud." *BOLLI Banner*. https://blogs.brandeis.edu/bollibanner/2022/06/07/a-conversation-with-sophie-freud-by-joyce-lazarus/.

Leggett, Hadley (2009, Oct. 21). "Out of LSD? Just 15 Minutes of Sensory Deprivation Triggers Hallucinations." *Wired*. https://www.wired.com/2009/10/hallucinations/.

Marshall, Gordon (1998). *Oxford Dictionary of Sociology*. New York: Oxford University Press.

Maté, Gabor (2009). *In the Realm of Hungry Ghosts: Close Encounters with Addictions*. Toronto: Vintage Canada.

McInnis, Opal A., Matthew M. Young, & Student Drug Use Surveys Working Group (2015, Sept.). *Urban and Rural Student Substance Abuse: Technical Report*. Ottawa: Canadian Centre on Substance Abuse.

Mead, George Herbert (1934). *Mind, Self, and Society*. Chicago: University of Chicago Press.

Merton, Robert K. ([1949] 1968). *Social Theory and Social Structure*. New York: Free Press.

Nicolosi, Joseph, & Linda Ames Nicolosi (2002). *A Parent's Guide to Preventing Homosexuality*. Downers Grove, IL: InterVarsity Press.

Ontario Soccer Association (OSA) (2015). *The Ontario Soccer Association Grassroots Festival Guide*. www.ontariosoccer.net/images/publications/2015/about/employment/Grassroots_Festival_Guide_2015.pdf.

Organisation for Economic Co-operation and Development (OECD) (2016). *PISA 2015 Results (Vol. 1): Excellence and Equity in Education*. Paris: OECD.

O'Sullivan, Patrick, with Gare Joyce (2015). *Breaking Away: A Harrowing Story of Resilience, Courage, and Triumph*. Toronto: HarperCollins.

Patai, Raphael ([1973] 2014). *The Arab Mind*, updated ed. New York: Recovery Resources Press.

Postman, Neil (1982). *The Disappearance of Childhood*. New York: Delacorte Press.

Price, William H., & Peter B. Whatmore (1967). "Behaviour Disorders and Pattern of Crime among XYY Males Identified at a Maximum Security Hospital." *British Medical Journal* 2 (5601), pp. 533–6.

Statista (2022). "Manufacturing Sector Employment U.S. 2020." https://www.statista.com/statistics/664993/private-sector-manufacturing-employment-in-the-us/.

Steckley, John, & Brian Rice (1997). "Lifelong Learning and Cultural Identity: A Lesson from Canada's Native People." In *Lifelong Learning: Policies, Programs & Practices*, ed. Michael Hatton, pp. 216–29. Toronto: APEC.

Telfer, Mary A. (1968). "Are Some Criminals Born That Way?" *Think* 34 (6), pp. 24–8.

Thompson, Derek (2016, May 13). "Donald Trump and the Twilight of White America." *The Atlantic* (online).

Thorndike, Edward ([1911] 1999). *Animal Intelligence: Experimental Studies*. Piscataway, NJ: Transaction.

Ungerleider, Charles, Terri Thompson, & Tracy Lavin (2012, Dec. 26). "No Quick Fix for Gender Gap in Education." *Toronto Star* (online).

Voyer, D., & S.D. Voyer (2014, July). "Gender Differences in Scholastic Achievement: A Meta-Analysis." *Psychological Bulletin* 140 (4), pp. 1174–204.

Waldron, J.J., & C.L. Kowalski (2009). "Crossing the Line: Rites of Passage, Team Aspects, and Ambiguity of Hazing." *Research Quarterly for Exercise and Sport* 80 (2), pp. 291–302.

Wang, Jing Hui, & Greg Moreau (2022, Mar. 17). "Police-Reported Hate Crime in Canada, 2020." *Juristat*. Statistics Canada Catalogue no. 85-002-X. https://www150.statcan.gc.ca/n1/pub/85-002-x/2022001/article/00005-eng.htm.

Watson, John B. (1925). *Behaviorism*. New York: Norton.

Watson, John B., & Rosalie Rayner (1920). "Conditioned Emotional Reactions." *Journal of Experimental Psychology* 3 (1), pp. 1–14.

Whiting, Beatrice B. (1963). *Six Cultures: Studies of Child Rearing*. New York: John Wiley.

Willis, Paul E. (1977). *Learning to Labour: How Working Class Kids Get Working Class Jobs*. New York: Columbia University Press.

Wrong, Dennis (1961). "The Oversocialized Conception of Man in Modern Sociology." *American Sociological Review* 26 (2), pp. 183–93.

Chapter 5

Adams, Michael (2003). *Fire and Ice: The United States and the Myth of Converging Values*. Toronto: Penguin Canada.

Adams, Michael (2014, Mar. 14). "Fire and Ice Revisited: American and Canadian Social Values in the Age of Obama and Harper." Speech presented at the Woodrow Wilson Center, Washington, DC.

Adams, Michael (2017, May 27). "Trump, Trudeau and the Patriarchy." *Globe and Mail*, p. F7.

Anderson, Karen L. (1996). *Sociology: A Critical Introduction*. Toronto: Nelson.

Baudrillard, Jean (1983). *Simulations*. Trans. Paul Foss, Paul Patton, & Philip Beitchman. New York: Semiotext[e].

Bissell, Tom (2003). *Chasing the Sea: Lost among the Ghosts of Empire in Central Asia*. New York: Pantheon.

Bohannan, Laura (1966). "Shakespeare in the Bush." *Natural History* (Aug./Sept.). Reprinted in *Annual Editions Anthropology, 1995/1996*, ed. E. Angeloni, pp. 65–9.

Bourdieu, Pierre (1970). *La reproduction: Eléments pour une théorie d'enseignement*. Paris: Éditions de Minuit.

Brean, Joseph (2014, June 17). "Vancouver School Board's Genderless Pronouns—Xe, Xem, Xyr—Not Likely to Stick, If History Is Any Indication." *National Post* (online).

de Certeau, Michel (1984). *The Practice of Everyday Life*. Trans. S. Rendell. Berkeley: University of California Press.

Fadiman, Anne (1997). *The Spirit Catches You and You Fall Down. A Hmong Child, Her American Doctors, and the Collision of Two Cultures*. New York: Farrar, Straus and Giroux.

Fikes, Jay (1996). "A Brief History of the Native American Church." In *One Nation under God: The Triumph of the Native American Church*, ed. Huston Smith & Reuben Snake. Santa Fe, NM: Clear Light Publishers.

Fiske, John (2010). *Understanding Popular Culture*, 2nd ed. London: Routledge.

Gidén, Carl, Patrick Houda, & Jean-Patrice Martel (2014). *On the Origin of Hockey*. Hockey Origin Publishing.

Hodkinson, Paul (2011). "Ageing in a Spectacular Youth Culture: Continuity, Change and Community in the Goth Scene." *British Journal of Sociology* 62, pp. 262–82.

Hodkinson, Paul (2013). "Family and Parenthood in an Ageing 'Youth' Culture: A Collective Embrace of Dominant Adulthood?" *Sociology* 47 (6), pp. 1072–87.

Hoodfar, Homa (2003). "More Than Clothing: Veiling as an Adaptive Strategy." In *The Muslim Veil in North America: Issues and Debates*, ed. Sajida Alvi, H. Hoodfar, & Sheila McDonough, pp. 3–40. Toronto: Women's Press.

Horkheimer, Max, & Theodor Adorno (2002). *Dialectic of Enlightenment*. Trans. Edmund Jephcott. Stanford, CA: Stanford University Press. (Originally published in 1944 as *Philosophische Fragmente* and in 1947 as *Dialektik der Aufklärung*.)

James, Jennifer (2009, Oct.). "Peyote & Mescaline: History Lessons." Cat. no. 133. Do It Now Foundation (online).

LaRocque, Emma (1975). *Defeathering the Indian*. Agincourt, ON: Book Society of Canada.

Lutz, John (2012). "Vanishing the Indians: Aboriginal Labourers in Twentieth-Century British Columbia." In *Aboriginal History: A Reader*, ed. Kristen Burnett & Geoff Read, pp. 305–20. Toronto: Oxford University Press.

MacCannell, Dean ([1976] 1999). *The Tourist: A New Theory of the Leisure Class*. Berkeley: University of California Press.

McGillivray, Anne, & Brenda Comaskey (1999). *Black Eyes All of the Time: Intimate Violence, Aboriginal Women and the Justice System*. Toronto: University of Toronto Press.

Norton, William (2006). *Cultural Geography: Environments, Landscapes, Identities, Inequalities*, 2nd ed. Toronto: Oxford University Press.

Plante, Courtney, Stephen Reysen, Sharon E. Roberts, & Kathleen C. Gerbasi (2016). "Fur Science! A Summary of Five Years of Research from the International Anthropomorphic Research Project." https://furscience.com/wp-content/uploads/2017/10/Fur-Science-Final-pdf-for-Website_2017_10_18.pdf.

Porter, John (1965). *The Vertical Mosaic: An Analysis of Social Class and Power in Canada*. Toronto: University of Toronto.

Ralph, Dan (2013, Aug. 1). "Canadian Families Shunning Hockey, Survey Finds." *Globe and Mail* (online).

Said, Edward (1979). *Orientalism*. New York: Pantheon.

Samuels, Karen (2022). "Motorcycling Together: Mitigating Military Exit." In *Families, Mobility, and Work*, ed. Barbara Neis, Christina Murray, & Nora Spinks, pp. 421–41. St John's: Memorial University Press.

Schonfeld, Zach (2022, Aug. 22). "Threats to Democracy Top List of Issues Facing US: Poll." The Hill. https://thehill.com/homenews/campaign/3610753-threats-to-democracy-top-list-of-issues-facing-us-poll.

Smith, N. (2009). "Beyond the Master Narrative of Youth: Researching Ageing Popular Music Scenes." In *The Ashgate Research Companion to Popular Musicology*, ed. D. Scott. Farnham, UK: Ashgate.

Steger, Manfred B. (2003). *Globalization: A Very Short Introduction*. Oxford: Oxford University Press.

Sumner, William Graham (1906). *Folkways: A Study of the Sociological Importance of Usages, Manners, Customs, Mores, and Morals*. Boston: Ginn and Co.

Chapter 6

Allen, M. (2018). "Police-Reported Crime Statistics in Canada, 2017." *Juristat*. Statistics Canada Catalogue no. 85-002-X.

Becker, Howard (1963). *Outsiders: Studies in the Sociology of Deviance*. New York: Free Press.

Bell, Jim (2020, Jan. 22). "Indigenous Incarceration Rate a 'Travesty,' Canada's Prison Watchdog Says." *Nunatsiaq News*.

Cannabis & Psychosis (2022). https://cannabisandpsychosis.ca.

Clinard, M., & R. Quinney (1973). *Criminal Behavior Systems: A Typology*, 2nd ed. New York: Holt, Rinehart and Winston.

Cohen, Albert K. (1955). *Delinquent Boys: The Culture of the Gang*. Glencoe, IL: Free Press.

Contenta, Sandro, & Jim Rankin (2009, June 6). "Suspended Sentences: Forging a School-to-Prison Pipeline?" *Toronto Star* (online).

Davis, Jonathan (2020). "The Shamanic View of Mental Health: A Holistic Approach." *Integrative Mental Health University*. https://imhu.org/spiritual-emergency/the-shamanic-view-of-mental-health/.

Davis, Lennard J. (2006). "Constructing Normalcy: The Bell Curve, the Novel, and the Invention of the Disabled Body in the Nineteenth Century." In *The Disability Studies Reader*, 2nd ed., ed. Lennard J. David, pp. 3–16. New York: Routledge.

Demerson, Velma (2004). *Incorrigible*. Waterloo, ON: Wilfrid Laurier University Press.

EKOS (2017). *National Justice Survey: Canada's Criminal Justice System*. Ottawa: Department of Justice Canada. http://publications.gc.ca/collections/collection_2018/jus/J4-52-2017-eng.pdf.

Ford, Matt (2016, Apr. 15). "What Caused the Great Crime Decline in the US?" *The Atlantic* (online).

Gaul, Ashleigh (2014, Sept. 20). "Between the Lines: Tracing the Controversial History and Recent Revival of Inuit Facial Tattoos." *Up Here* (online).

Gillis, Charlie (2012, Apr. 19). "The End of the Dry Reserve?" *Maclean's*. https://www.macleans.ca/news/canada/the-end-of-the-dry-reserve/.

Goddard, Henry H. (1911). "Heredity of Feeble-Mindedness." *American Breeders Magazine* 1 (3).

Goffman, Erving (1963). *Stigma: Notes on the Management of Spoiled Identity*. Englewood Cliffs, NJ: Prentice-Hall.

Gramlich, John (2017, Feb. 21). "5 Facts about Crime in the US." *Factank: News in the Numbers*. Washington, DC: Pew Research Center.

Guy, Jack (2022, Aug. 15). "Women in Scotland Now Have a Legal Right to Free Menstrual Products." *CNN*. https://www.cnn.com/2022/08/15/uk/scotland-sanitary-products-law-scli-intl-gbr-wellness/index.html.

Hanlon, Tegan (2015, Oct. 16). "Inupiaq Woman Joins Movement to Revitalize Traditional Tattooing." *Alaska Dispatch News* (online).

Hayes, Chris (2017). *A Colony in a Nation*. New York: Norton.

Herrera, Shaman Elizabeth (2015, July 4). "Schizophrenia—Gift or Illness?" https://blog.shamanelizabeth.com/2015/07/04/schizophrenia-gift-or-illness/.

Hirschi, Travis W. (1969). *Causes of Delinquency*. Berkeley: University of California Press.

Matthews, Dylan (2014, June 5). "How Mid-Century Ireland Dealt with Unwed Mothers and Their Children, and Why We're Talking about It Today." *Vox Media* (online).

Mazón, Mauricio (1984). *The Zoot-Suit Riots: The Psychology of Symbolic Annihilation*. Austin: University of Texas Press.

Merton, Robert K. (1938). "Social Structure and Anomie." *American Sociological Review* 3 (5), pp. 672–82.

Muir, Leilani (2014). *A Whisper Past—Childless after Eugenic Sterilization in Alberta*. Calgary: Friesen Press.

Murphy, Emily ([1922] 1973). *The Black Candle*. Toronto: Coles.

Ontario Human Rights Commission (OHRC) (2003). *Paying the Price: The Human Cost of Racial Profiling*. Inquiry Report. Toronto: OHRC. www.ohrc.on.ca/en/paying-price-human-cost-racial-profiling.

Petrilli, Kat, Shelan Ofori, Lindsey Hines, Gemma Taylor, Sally Adams, & Tom P. Freeman (2022, Sept. 1). "Association of Cannabis Potency with Mental Ill Health and Addiction: A Systematic Review." *The Lancet Psychiatry* 9 (9), pp. 736–50.

Quan, Douglas (2015, Feb. 12). "Harper Vows to Appeal Court Ruling Allowing Women to Wear Niqab during Citizenship Oath, Calls It 'Offensive.'" *National Post* (online).

Reiman, Jeffrey (2007). *The Rich Get Richer and the Poor Get Prison: Ideology, Class, and Criminal Justice*, 8th ed. Boston: Allyn & Bacon.

Rosenberg, Zoe (2016, 29 Aug.). "Trump Management's Shady History of Housing Bias in NYC." *Curbed New York*. https://www.nycurbed.com/2016/8/29/12690262/donald-trump-discrimination-lawsuit-nyc-real-estate.

Rotenberg, Cristine (2016, Apr. 12). *Aboriginal Peoples Survey, 2012: Social Determinants of Health for the Off-Reserve First Nations Population, 15 Years of Age and Older, 2012*. Statistics Canada Cat. no. 89-653-X2016009. Ottawa: Minister of Industry.

Said, Edward (1979). *Orientalism*. New York: Pantheon.

Scull, Andrew (2009). *Hysteria: The Disturbing History*. Oxford: Oxford University Press.

Smith, James M. (2007). *Ireland's Magdalen Laundries and the Nation's Architecture of Containment*. South Bend, IN: University of Notre Dame Press.

Stote, Karen (2015). *An Act of Genocide: Colonialism and the Sterilization of Aboriginal Women*. Halifax: Fernwood.

Sutherland, Edwin (1940). "White Collar Criminality." *American Sociological Review* 5 (1), pp. 1–12.

Sutherland, Edwin (1949). *White Collar Crime*. New York: Holt, Rinehart and Winston.

Swift, Art (2016, Oct. 19). "Support for Legal Marijuana Use Up to 60% in U.S." *Social Issues*. Washington, DC: Gallup.

Tepperman, Lorne, & Michael Rosenberg (1998). *Macro/Micro: A Brief Introduction to Sociology*, 3rd ed. Scarborough, ON: Prentice-Hall, Allyn & Bacon.

Truman, Jennifer L., & Rachel E. Morgan (2016, Oct.). *Criminal Victimization, 2015*. Bureau of Justice Statistics bulletin NCJ 250180. Washington, DC: U.S. Department of Justice.

Usher, Nikki (2016, July 26). "Interview: Why the Public Perception of Crime Exceeds the Reality." *All Things Considered*. National Public Radio.

Venkatesh, Sudhir (2008). *Gang Leader for a Day: A Rogue Sociologist Takes to the Streets*. New York: Penguin.

York, Geoffrey (1990). *The Dispossessed: Life and Death in Native Canada*. Toronto: Lester & Orpen Dennys.

Zimring, Franklin E. (2007). *The Great American Decline*. New York: Oxford University Press.

Chapter 7

Blatchford, Andy (2015, Feb. 1). "'Middle-Class' Politics: Who Belongs to This Vote-Rich Group?" *CBC News* (online).

Blum, William (2003). *Killing Hope: US Military & CIA Interventions since World War II*. London: Zed Books.

Bouw, Brenda (2018, Oct. 23). "Ontario to Freeze Minimum Wage, Eliminate Mandatory Paid Sick Days." *Globe and Mail* (online).

Bregman, Rutger (2016). *Utopia for Realists: The Case for a Universal Basic Income, Open Borders, and a 15-Hour Workweek*. The Correspondent (Kindle edition).

"Canada's Top CEOs Leave the 99% in Their Gold Dust" (2012, Jan. 3). *Toronto Star* (online).

Crehan, Kate (2002). *Gramsci, Culture and Anthropology*. Berkeley: University of California Press.

Cummins, Bryan D. (2003). *Only God Can Own the Land*, Canadian Ethnography Series Vol. 1. Toronto: Pearson.

Curtis, James, Edward Grabb, & Neil Guppy (eds) (1999). *Social Inequality in Canada: Patterns, Problems and Policies*, 3rd ed. Scarborough, ON: Prentice-Hall.

Daily Bread Food Bank and North York Harvest Food Bank (2021). *Who's Hungry 2021. From Crisis to Resilience: A City's Call to Action*. Toronto: Daily Bread Food Bank and North York Harvest Food Bank. https://www.dailybread.ca/research-and-advocacy/whos-hungry-report-2021/.

Dodge, Matt (2022, Apr. 1). "The 2022 Minimum Wage in Canada." https://www.jobillico.com/blog/en/the-2022-minimum-wage-in-canada/.

Dubick, James, Brandon Mathews, & Clare Cady (2016). *Hunger on Campus: The Challenge of Food Insecurity for College Students*. http://studentsagainsthunger.org/wp-content/uploads/2016/10/Hunger_On_Campus.pdf.

Ecocnn (2022, Sept. 15). "Forbes Highest-paid Athletes 2022 World Top 10 List." https://ecocnn.com/forbes-highest-paid-athletes/.

Flavelle, Dana (2012, Jan. 3). "Canada's 0.01%." *Toronto Star*, pp. B1–B3.

Food Banks Canada (2004). *HungerCount 2004: A Comprehensive Report on Hunger and Food Bank Use in Canada, and Recommendations for Change*. Mississauga, ON: Canadian Association of Food Banks.

Food Banks Canada (2019). *HungerCount 2018*. Mississauga, ON: Food Banks Canada.

Food Banks Canada (2021). *HungerCount 2021*. Mississauga, ON: Food Banks Canada.

Forget, Evelyn L. (2011). "The Town with No Poverty: Using Health Administration Data to Revisit Outcomes of a Canadian Guaranteed Annual Income Field Experiment." University of Manitoba (online).

Goldrick-Rab, Sara (2016). "Preface." In James Dubick, Brandon Mathews, & Clare Cady, *Hunger on Campus: The*

Challenge of Food Insecurity for College Students. http://studentsagainsthunger.org/wp-content/uploads/2016/10/Hunger_On_Campus.pdf.

Gramsci, Antonio (1992). *Prison Notebooks,* vol. 1. Ed. Joseph A. Buttligieg. New York: Columbia University Press.

Grattan, E. (2003). "Social Inequality and Stratification in Canada." In *Our Society: Human Diversity in Canada,* 2nd ed., ed. Paul Angelini, pp. 61–86. Scarborough, ON: Thompson-Nelson.

Hodges, David, & Mark Brown (2015, Jan. 27). "Are You in the Middle Class?" *Maclean's* magazine (online).

Hopper, Tristin (2016, Apr. 27). "Why Canadian White People Have So Much Trouble Understanding Why Somebody Wouldn't Want to Leave Attawapiskat." *National Post* (online).

Lemieux, Thomas, & W. Craig Riddell (2015, July 9). *Who Are Canada's Top 1 Percent?* Montreal: Institute for Research on Public Policy. https://irpp.org/research-studies/aots5-riddell-lemieux.

Lowe, Kevin, Stan Fischler, & Shirley Fischler (1988). *Champions: The Making of the Edmonton Oilers.* Scarborough, ON: Prentice-Hall.

Marx, Karl ([1867] 1967). *Capital: A Critique of Political Economy.* Ed. F. Engels. New York: International.

Marx, Karl, & Friedrich Engels ([1848] 1967). *The Communist Manifesto.* New York: Pantheon.

McQuaig, Linda, & Neil Brooks (2012). *Billionaire's Ball: Gluttony and Hubris in an Age of Epic Inequality.* Boston: Beacon Press.

New to Hockey (2018, Aug. 25). "Hockey Equipment Buying Guide—For Parents/Kids." https://newtohockey.com/hockey-equipment-buying-guide-for-kids/.

Ormsby, Mary (2007, Dec. 8). "Why Gear Is Dear." *Toronto Star,* pp. S1, S6.

Rutherford, Kate (2016, Apr. 9). "Attawapiskat Declares State of Emergency over Spate of Suicide Attempts." *CBC News* (online).

Rutherford, Kristina (2009, Jan. 16). "Is the Cost Keeping Kids out of Minor Hockey? Absolutely, Players and Parents Say." *CBC News* (online).

Ryan, William ([1971] 1976). *Blaming the Victim.* New York: Pantheon.

Scoffield, Heather (2011, Nov. 29). "Locals Disagree on Who's to Blame for Attawapiskat Crisis." *Globe and Mail* (online).

Silverthorn, Drew (2016). *Hungry for Knowledge: Assessing the Prevalence of Student Food Insecurity on Five Canadian Campuses.* Toronto: Meal Exchange. http://mealexchange.com.

Smith, Adam ([1759] 1976). *The Theory of Our Moral Sentiments.* Ed. D.D. Raphael & A.L. Macfie. Oxford: Oxford University Press.

Snowden, Jonathan (2013, May 3). "Floyd Mayweather: How His Family's History of Violence Has Shaped Money May." *Bleacher Report* (online).

Standing, Guy (2011). *The Precariat: The New Dangerous Class.* London and New York: Bloomsbury Academic.

Standing, Guy (2014). "The Precariat." *American Sociological Association/Sage Journals* 13 (4). https://doi.org/10.1177/1536504214558209.

Statistics Canada (2018). *Canadian Megatrends: The Fall and Rise of Canada's Top Income Earners.* www150.statcan.gc.ca/n1/pub/11-630-x/11-630-x2016009-eng.htm.

Weber, Max ([1904] 1930). *The Protestant Ethic and the Spirit of Capitalism.* Trans. Talcott Parsons. New York: Charles Scribner's Sons.

Weber, Max ([1946] 1958). "Essays in Sociology." In *From Max Weber,* ed. M. Weber, H. Gerth, & C.W. Mills. New York: Oxford University Press.

Weber, Max ([1914] 1968). *Economy and Society: An Outline of Interpretive Sociology.* New York: Bedminster.

Chapter 8

Adachi, Ken (1976). *The Enemy That Never Was: A History of Japanese Canadians.* Toronto: McClelland & Stewart.

Armstrong, Amelia (2019, Apr. 30). "Police-Reported Hate Crime in Canada, 2017." *Juristat.* Statistics Canada, Catalogue no. 85-002-X.

Backhouse, Constance (1999). *Colour-Coded: A Legal History of Racism in Canada, 1900–1950.* Toronto: University of Toronto Press.

Becerril, Q.O. (2007). "Lucha Cultural por la Dignidad y los Derechos Humanos. Transmigrantes Mexicanos en Canada." PhD diss., Universidad Autónoma Metropolitana—Unidad Iztapalapa.

Burnet, Jean R., & Howard Palmer (1988). *"Coming Canadians": An Introduction to a History of Canada's Peoples.* Toronto: McClelland & Stewart.

Chan, Anthony B. (2019, May 22). "Chinese Canadians." *The Canadian Encyclopedia* (online).

Chrétien, Jean-Pierre (1997). *Le défi de l'ethnisme: Rwanda et Burundi, 1990–1996.* Karthala.

Clow, Julie (2022, Feb. 11). "'No Winning' for N.S. Goalie Who Was Target of Racial Slurs on P.E.I." *CBC News* (online).

Cobb, Russell (2017). "Dreams of a Black Oklahoma: On the Trail of the Forgotten Okies of Alberta." In *Race Reader: A Literary Chronicle of Conflict and Oppression in Middle America,* pp. 15–21. Tulsa, OK: This Land Press.

Codjoe, Henry M. (2001). "Can Blacks Be Racist? Further Reflections on Being 'Too Black and African.'" In *Talking about Identity: Encounters in Race, Ethnicity and Language,* ed. Carl James & Adrienne Shadd, pp. 277–90. Toronto: Between the Lines.

Collins, Patricia Hill (1990). *Black Feminist Thought: Knowledge, Consciousness and the Politics of Empowerment.* Boston: Unwin Hyman.

Dauvergne, Mia, & Shannon Brennan (2011). "Police-Reported Hate Crime in Canada, 2009." *Juristat.* Statistics Canada, Catalogue no. 85-002-X.

Dick, Lyle (2010). "Sergeant Masumi Mitsui and the Japanese Canadian War Memorial." *Canadian Historical Review* 91 (3), pp. 435–63.

Du Bois, W.E.B. (1896). *The Suppression of the African Slave Trade in America.* New York: Longmans, Green.

Du Bois, W.E.B. (1903). *The Souls of Black Folk.* Chicago: A.C. McClurg.

Du Bois, W.E.B. (1935). *Black Reconstruction: An Essay toward a History of the Part which Black Folk Played in the Attempt to Re-Construct Democracy in America.* New York: Harcourt Brace.

Du Bois, W.E.B. (1940). *Dusk of Dawn.* New York: Harcourt, Brace & World.

Du Bois, W.E.B. ([1899] 1967). *The Philadelphia Negro: A Social Study.* New York: Schocken Books.

Fanon, Frantz ([1961] 1965). *The Wretched of the Earth*. New York: Grove.

Fanon, Frantz ([1952] 1967). *Black Skin, White Masks*. New York: Grove.

Firstpost (2022, Sept. 19). "Why Hindus and Muslims Are Fighting on the Streets of UK's Leicester and Who Started It?" https://www.msn.com/en-in/news/world/why-hindus-and-muslims-are-fighting-on-the-streets-of-uk-e2-80-99s-leicester-and-who-started-it/ar-AA11Zde9.

Foucault, Michel ([1972] 1994). *The Archaeology of Knowledge*. London: Routledge.

Freeborn, Jeremy (2008). "Johnny Bright," *The Canadian Encyclopedia*. https://www.thecanadianencyclopedia.ca/en/article/john-dee-bright.

Henao Castrillon, Alexandra (2018). "A Critical Analysis of Mexican Migrant Farm Workers in British Columbia: Language, Oppression, and Resistance." PhD diss., Simon Fraser University.

Hill, Daniel (1960). "Negroes in Toronto: A Sociological Study of a Minority Group." PhD diss., University of Toronto.

Hill, Daniel (1981). *The Freedom Seekers: Blacks in Early Canada*. Agincourt, ON: Book Society of Canada.

Johnston, Hugh (1989). *The Voyage of the Komagata Maru: The Sikh Challenge to Canada's Colour Bar*. Vancouver: University of British Columbia Press.

Jolly, Joanna (2019). *Red River Girl: The Life and Death of Tina Fontaine*. New York: Viking.

LaRocque, Emma (1993). "Three Conventional Approaches to Native People." In *Survival of the Imagination: The Mary Donaldson Memorial Lectures*, ed. Brett Balon & Peter Resch, pp. 209–18. Regina: Coteau.

Lewis, Oscar (1998). "The Culture of Poverty." *Society* 35 (2), pp. 7–9.

Memmi, Albert ([1957] 1991). *The Colonizer and the Colonized*. Boston: Beacon.

Milan, Anne, & Kelly Tran (2004, spring). "Blacks in Canada: A Long History." *Canadian Social Trends*, pp. 2–7.

Newbury, Catharine ([1988] 1993). *The Cohesion of Oppression*. New York: Columbia.

O'Leary, Chris (2018, Aug. 8). "In an Era of Systemic Racism, Bright Found Acceptance in Canada." *cfl.ca*. https://www.cfl.ca/2018/08/08/era-systemic-racism-bright-found-acceptance-canada/.

Ontario Human Rights Commission (OHRC) (2017). "Public Interest Inquiry into Racial Profiling by the Toronto Police Service." https://www.ohrc.on.ca/en/public-inquiry-racial-profiling-and-racial-discrimination-black-persons-toronto-police-service.

Ontario Human Rights Commission (OHRC) (2020, Aug. 10). *A Disparate Impact: Second Interim Report*. Toronto: OHRC.

O'Ree, Willie, & Michael McKinley (2020). *Willie: The Game-Changing Story of the NHL's First Black Player*. Toronto: Penguin Canada.

Owusu-Bempah, Akwasi, & Scot Wortley (2014). "Race, Crime, and Criminal Justice in Canada." In *The Oxford Handbook of Ethnicity, Crime, and Immigration*, ed. Sandra Bucerius & Michael Tonry. New York: Oxford.

Popp, Jesse (2021, Oct. 28). "Want to Reach Out to an Indigenous Scholar? Awesome! But First, Here Are 10 Things to Consider." *The Conversation* (online).

Priest, Lisa (1989). *Conspiracy of Silence: The Riveting Account of the The Pas Murder, Cover-up, and Inquiry*. Toronto: McClelland & Stewart.

Sapers, Howard (2015). *Annual Report of the Office of the Correctional Investigator, 2014–15*. Ottawa: Ministry of Public Safety.

Statistics Canada (2015, Dec. 24). *Aboriginal Statistics at a Glance*, 2nd ed., Catalogue no. 89-645-x2015001. Ottawa: Minister of Industry.

Statistics Canada (2017a, Oct. 25). "Aboriginal Peoples in Canada: Key Results from the 2016 Census." *The Daily* (online). Ottawa: Minister of Industry.

Statistics Canada (2017b, Oct. 25). *Visible Minority and Population Group Reference Guide, Census of Population, 2016*. Catalogue no. 98-500-X2016006. Ottawa: Minister of Industry.

Statistics Canada (2018). *Aboriginal Population Profile, 2016 Census*. Catalogue no. 98-510-X2016001. Ottawa: Minister of Industry.

Statistics Canada (2019, Feb. 27). "Diversity of the Black Population in Canada: An Overview." *Ethnicity, Language, and Immigration Thematic Series*. Catalogue no. 89-657-X2019002. Ottawa: Minister of Industry.

Steckley, John L. (2003). *Aboriginal Voices and the Politics of Representation in Canadian Sociology Textbooks*. Toronto: Canadian Scholars' Press.

Steckley, John L. (2013). *Learning from the Past: Five Cases of Aboriginal Justice*. Whitby, ON: De Sitter Publications.

Takezawa, Yasuko I., Peter Wade, and Audrey Smedley (2020, Nov. 23). "Race." *Encyclopedia Britannica*. https://www.britannica.com/topic/race-human.

Tatum, Beverly Daniel (2003). *"Why Are All the Black Kids Sitting Together in the Cafeteria?" and Other Conversations about Race*, rev. ed. New York: Basic Books.

Taylor, Drew Hayden (1996). *Funny, You Don't Look Like One: Observations from a Blue-Eyed Ojibway*. Penticton, BC: Theytus.

Tuck, Eve, & K. Wayne Yang (2012). "Decolonization Is Not a Metaphor." *Decolonization: Indigeneity, Education & Society* 1 (1), pp. 1–40.

Veenstra, Gerry (2011, Oct.). "Mismatched Racial Identities, Colourism, and Health in Toronto and Vancouver." *Social Science & Medicine* 73 (8), pp. 1152–62.

Venkatesh, Sudhir (2006). *Off the Books: The Underground Economy of the Urban Poor*. Cambridge, MA: Harvard University Press.

Wilson, Shawn (2008). *Research Is Ceremony: Indigenous Research Methods*. Halifax: Fernwood.

Wilson, William Julius (2009). *More Than Just Race: Being Black and Poor in the Inner City*. New York: Norton.

Wortley, Scot (2019, Mar.). *Halifax, Nova Scotia: Street Checks Report*. Halifax: Nova Scotia Human Rights Commission.

Younging, Gregory (2018). *Elements of Indigenous Style*. Edmonton: Brush Education.

Yun, Tom (2022, Mar. 17). "Police-Reported Anti-Asian Hate Crimes in Canada Jumped 300 per cent in 2020: StatCan." *CTV News*. https://www.ctvnews.ca/canada/police-reported-anti-asian-hate-crimes-in-canada-jumped-300-per-cent-in-2020-statcan-1.5823965.

Chapter 9

A Silver Voice from Ireland Blog (2011, July 17). "Margaret Anne Bulkley: The Extraordinary Dr. James Barry." https://thesilvervoice.wordpress.com/2011/07/17/the-most-hardened-creaturedoctor-james-barry/.

Aydin, Banu Kucukemre, Nurcin Saka, Firdevs Bas, Evrim Kiray Bas, Asuman Coban, Sukran Yildirim, Tulay Guran, & Feyza Darendeliler (2019, June). "Frequency of Ambiguous Genitalia in 14,177 Newborns in Turkey," *Journal of the Endocrine Society*, 3 (6), pp. 1185–95.

Azhar, Mobeen (2017). "Pakistan's Traditional Third Gender Isn't Happy with the Trans Movement." *The World*. https://theworld.org/stories/2017-07-29/pakistans-traditional-third-gender-isnt-happy-trans-movement.

Bauer, Greta R., Ayden I. Scheim, Jake Pyne, Robb Travers, & Rebecca Hammond (2015). "Intervenable Factors Associated with Suicide Risk in Transgender Persons: A Respondent Driven Sampling Study in Ontario, Canada." *BMC Public Health* 15, p. 525.

Boom, Kesiena (2015). "4 Tired Tropes Perfectly Explain What Misogynoir Is and How You Can Stop It." https://kesienaboom.journoportfolio.com/about-kesiena/.

Bothelo-Urbanski, Jessica (2016, July 11). "Baby Storm Five Years Later: Preschooler on Top of the World." *Toronto Star* (online).

Brightwell, Laura (2016, May 10). "Attack on Canada's Only Surgery Clinic for Trans People Elicits 'Zero Reaction.'" *Rabble.ca*.

"Bulkley, Margaret Anne." https://www.wikitree.com/wiki/Bulkley-395.

Butler, Judith (1990). *Gender Trouble: Feminism and the Subversion of Identity*. London: Routledge.

Cameron, S. (2010). *On the Farm: Robert William Pickton and the Tragic Story of Vancouver's Missing Women*. Toronto: Knopf Canada.

Canada, Government of (2019). *Reclaiming Power and Place: The Final Report of the National Inquiry into Missing and Murdered Indigenous Women and Girls*.

Chen, Anita Beltran (1998). *From Sunbelt to Snowbelt: Filipinos in Canada*. Calgary: Canadian Ethnic Studies Association.

Cohoon, J.M. (2006). "Just Get Over It or Just Get On with It: Retaining Women in Undergraduate Computing." In *Women in Information Technology: Research on Underrepresentation*, ed. J.M. Cohoon & W. Aspray, pp. 205–37. Cambridge, MA: MIT Press.

Colapinto, John (2000). *As Nature Made Him: The Boy Who Was Raised as a Girl*. New York: HarperCollins.

Connell, R.W. (1995). *Masculinities*. Berkeley: University of California.

Dalton, Lync (2017, June 5). "There's a Lot of Talk about 'Toxic Masculinity.' Is There an Equivalent 'Toxic Femininity'?" *Quora* (online).

DeClerq, Katherine, & Hannah Alberga (2022, Jan. 8). "Female Patients in Ontario Have a 30 per cent Greater Risk of Death after Surgery by a Male Doctor: Study." https://toronto.ctvnews.ca/female-patients-in-ontario-have-a-30-per-cent-greater-risk-of-death-after-surgery-by-a-male-doctor-study-1.5732857.

Elder, Miriam (2013, June 11). "Russia Passes Law Banning Gay 'Propaganda'." *The Guardian* (online).

Feirstein, Bruce (1982). *Real Men Don't Eat Quiche; A Guidebook to All That Is Truly Masculine*. New York: Pocket Books.

FINA (Fédération internationale de natation/International Swimming Federation) (2022, June). *Policy on Eligibility for the Men's and Women's Competiton Categories*.

Frank, Priscilla (2017, Apr. 13). "The Androgenous 'Third Gender' of 17th-Century Japan." *Huffington Post*. https://www.huffpost.com/entry/third-gender-japanese-art_n_58e6a18ce4b0585892c9c078?section=us_queer-voices.

Globe and Mail (2009, Feb. 23) "Defying Gender Expectations through Gender Performance: Boyat in the UAE." (online).

Goldstein, Jerome (2008. Nov. 11). "The Neurobiology of Sexual Orientation—the Gay Brain." Presentation at San Francisco Neurological Society Meeting.

Gonzales, Christina (2015, Aug. 27). "The Nanny Diaries: Toronto's Filipino Caregivers Talk about Low Wages, Long Days and Immigration Delays." *Toronto Life Magazine*.

Goulding, W.D. (2001). *Just Another Indian: A Serial Killer and Canada's Indifference*. Markham, ON: Fifth House.

Hango, Darcy (2013, Dec.). "Gender Differences in Science, Technology, Engineering, Mathematics and Computer Science (STEM) Programs at University." *Insights on Canadian Society*. Statistics Canada Cat. no. 75-006-X. Ottawa: Minister of Industry.

Hochschild, Arlie (1983). *The Managed Heart: Commercialization of Human Feeling*. Berkeley: University of California Press.

Hurst, Mike (2009, Sept. 11). "Caster Semenya Has Male Sex Organs and No Womb or Ovaries." *Daily Telegraph* (London) (online).

Ilada, Janessa, & Ry Mount (2015). "The Third Gender in Thailand—Kathoey." https://maytermthailand.org/2015/04/27/the-third-gender-in-thailand-kathoey/.

Itzkoff, Dave (2019, Nov. 21, updated Nov. 23). "Who Is Julia Sweeney Coming to Terms With? It's Pat." *New York Times*. https://www.nytimes.com/2019/11/21/arts/television/julia-sweeney-pat-snl.html.

Jivani, Jamil (2018). *Why Young Men: Rage, Race, and the Crisis of Identity*. Toronto: HarperCollins.

Kachuck, Beatrice ([1995] 2003). "Feminist Social Theories: Themes and Variations." In *Sociology of Gender: The Challenge of Feminist Sociological Knowledge*, ed. Sharmila Rege. New Delhi: Sage.

Kehoe, Alice (1995). "Blackfoot Persons." In *Women and Power in Native North America*, ed. L. Klein & L. Ackerman. Norman: University of Oklahoma Press.

Khaleeli, Homa (2014, Apr. 16). "India's Third Gender Claims Place in Law." *The Guardian*. https://www.theguardian.com/society/2014/apr/16/india-third-gender-claims-place-in-law.

Knell, Emily (2017, Feb. 2). "Dr. Margaret James Miranda Ann Barry Bulkley," Passion Blog. https://sites.psu.edu/knellpassion2/2017/02/02/11/.

Kruijver, F.P., J.N. Zhou, C.W. Pool, M.A. Hofman, L.J. Gooren, & D.F. Swaab (2000, May). "Male-to-Female Transsexuals Have Female Neuron Numbers in a Limbic Nucleus." *Journal of Clinical Endocrinology and Metabolism* 85 (5), pp. 2034–41.

Leffingwell, William (1925). *Office Management: Principles and Practice*. Chicago: A.W. Shaw.

Lemieux, Jamilah (2015). "Foreword." In Michele Wallace, *Black Macho and the Myth of the Superwoman* (1979, 1990, 2015). New York: Verso.

Lowe, Graham S. (1980). "Women, Work and the Office: The Feminization of Clerical Occupations in Canada, 1901–1931." *Canadian Journal of Sociology* 5 (4), pp. 361–81.

Mangis, Kari (2017). "Okay Men, Let's Talk about Toxic Femininity." The Good Men Project. https://goodmenproject.com/featured-content/talk-about-toxic-femininity-chwm/.

Moyser, Melissa (2017, Mar. 8). *Women in Canada: A Gender-based Statistical Report. Women and Paid Work*. Statistics Canada Cat. no. 89-503-X. Ottawa: Minister of Industry.

Naidoo, Amelia (2010, Jan. 28). "Cross about Cross-Dressing: Is It a Wicked Western Habit That Should Be Stopped?" *The Economist*. www.economist.com/node/154403091.

Naidoo, Amelia (2011, Apr. 21). "Shedding Light on the 'Boyat' Phenomenon: Conference Separates Fact from Fiction on the Issue." http://gulfnews.com/news/gulf/uae/general/shedding-light-on-the-boyat-phenomenon-1.796816.

Oakley, Ann (1972). *Sex, Gender and Society*. London: Temple Smith.

O'Hara, Mary Emily (2014, Nov. 20). "Trans Women of Color Face an Epidemic of Violence and Murder: The Incoherent Response by Cops Is Just Making the Problem Worse." *Vice*. https://www.vice.com/en/article/vdpnxx/trans-women-of-color-face-an-epidemic-of-violence-and-murder-673.

Ontario Medical Association (2021, Sept. 21). "Analysis by Ontario's Doctors Finds Unexplained 13.5 per cent Pay Gap between Male, Female Physicians." News release (online).

Orina, Moses (2021, Sept. 17). "Dr James Miranda Barry: A Woman Ahead of Her Time." https://orinanuggets.com/dr-james-miranda-barry-a-woman-ahead-of-her-time/.

Poisson, Jayme (2013, Nov. 15). "Remember Storm? We Check in on the Baby Being Raised Gender-Neutral." *Toronto Star* (online).

Priest, Lisa (1989). *Conspiracy of Silence*. Toronto: McClelland & Stewart.

Raval, P.J. (2018). *Call Her Ganda* (film). https://www.callherganda.com/.

Rosario, M., E. Scrimshaw, J. Hunter, & L. Braun (2006). "Sexual Identity Development among Lesbian, Gay, and Bisexual Youths: Consistency and Change over Time." *Journal of Sex Research* 43 (1), pp. 46–58.

Ruddick, Sara (1989). *Maternal Thinking: Toward a Politics of Peace*. Boston: Beacon.

Sargent, Paul (2005, Feb.). "The Gendering of Men in Early Childhood Education." *Sex Roles: A Journal of Research* 52 (3/4), pp. 251–9.

Statistics Canada (2016). *2016 Census of Population*. Statistics Canada Cat. no. 98-400-X2016295 to 98-400-X2016298. Ottawa: Minister of Industry.

Statistics Canada (2018a). *Labour Force Survey*. Labour Force Participation in Canada by sex (x 1,000), Select Industries, 2018. Ottawa: Minister of Industry.

Statistics Canada (2018b). *Labour Force Survey*. Labour Force Characteristics by Industry, Annual. Table 14-10-0023-01 (x 1,000). Ottawa: Minister of Industry.

Statistics Canada (2018c). *Labour Force Survey*. Postsecondary Graduates, by Program Type, Credential Type, Classification of Instructional Programs, Primary Grouping (CIP_PG) and Sex. Table 37-10-0012-01. Ottawa: Minister of Industry.

Statistics Canada (2021, June 16). "A Statistical Portrait of Canada's Diverse LGBTQ2+ Communities." https://www150.statcan.gc.ca/n1/daily-quotidien/210615/dq210615a-eng.htm.

Steckley, John (2013). "The Helen Betty Osborne Case." In *Learning from the Past: Five Cases of Aboriginal Justice*, pp. 55–86. Whitby, ON: De Sitter.

Steinbuch, Yaron (2022, Sept. 19). "Iranian Woman Mahsa Amini Dies after Arrest Over Hijab Law." *New York Post*. https://nypost.com/2022/09/19/ranian-woman-mahsa-amini-dies-after-arrest-over-hijab-law/.

Stote, Karen (2015). *An Act of Genocide: Colonialism and the Sterilization of Aboriginal Women*. Halifax: Fernwood.

Tomatis, Alfred (2005). *The Ear and the Voice*. Trans. Roberta Prada. Lanham, MD: Scarecrow Press.

Ubelacker, Sheryl (2015, Apr. 17). "Health Care System Can Often Be a Challenge for Transgender Patients." *Global News* (online).

Uppal, Sharanjit, & Sébastien LaRochelle-Côté (2014, Apr.). "Changes in the Occupational Profile of Young Men and Women in Canada." *Insights on Canadian Society*. Statistics Canada Cat. no. 75-006-X. Ottawa: Minister of Industry.

Village People (1978, 1979). From the album *Macho Man*: "Macho Man" (New York: Sigma Sound Studios, 1978); from the album *Cruisin'*: "Y.M.C.A." (New York: Sigma Sound Studios, 1978); from the album *Go West*: "In the Navy" (New York: Sigma Sound Studios, 1979).

Wareham, Jamier (2021, Nov. 11). "375 Transgender People Murdered In 2021: 'Deadliest Year' Since Records Began." *Forbes* (online).

Warner, Jessica (2002). *Craze: Gin and Debauchery in an Age of Reason*. New York: Basic.

West, Candace, & Don H. Zimmerman (1987, June). "Doing Gender." *Gender and Society* 1 (2), pp. 125–51.

Whitelocks, Sadie (2015, Apr. 17, updated Apr. 29). "I Exist in the Gray: 29-Year-Old Who Looks Like a Woman but Has Male Genitalia Speaks Out about Rare Intersex Condition." *Daily Mail*. https://www.dailymail.co.uk/news/article-3043767/I-exist-gray-29-year-old-looks-like-woman-male-genitalia-speaks-rare-intersex-condition.html.

Wiley Online Library (2015, 20 Apr.). "Xanith" (Oman). https://doi.org/10.1002/9781118896877.wbiehs546.

York, Geoffrey, & Paul Waldie (2019, May 1). "International Sports Court Upholds Testosterone Testing for Women against Caster Semenya Challenge." *Globe and Mail* (online).

Chapter 10

Anderson, Karen L. (1991). *Chain Her by One Foot: The Subjugation of Women in Seventeenth-Century New France*. London: Routledge.

American Psychological Association (APA) (2006, Mar. 22). "When the Boss Is a Woman." https://www.apa.org/topics/women-girls/female-boss.

Aristotle (2000). *Politics*. Mineola, NY: Dover.

Bales, Robert F. (1950). *International Process Analysis: A Method for the Study of Small Groups*. Chicago: University of Chicago Press.

Battiste, Marie (1997). "Mi'kmaq Socialization Patterns." In *Anthology of Mi'kmaq Writers*, ed. L. Choyce & R. Joe. East Lawrencetown, NS: Pottersfield.

Benton-Banai, Edward (1988). *The Mishomis Book: The Voice of the Ojibway*. St Paul, MN: Red School House, Indian Country Communications.

Bogdanich, Walt, & Michael Forsythe (2022). *When McKinsey Comes to Town: The Hidden Influence of the World's Most Powerful Consulting Firm*. New York: Doubleday.

Brym, Robert (2022, Dec. 6). "What the 2021 Census Reveals about Canada's Jewish Community." *Canadian Jewish News* (online).

Brym, Robert, Keith Neuman, & Rhonda Lenton (2018). *2018 Survey of Jews in Canada: Final Report*. Toronto: Environics Institute.

Canada, Government of (2021, Dec. 8). "Preliminary Examination of So-Called 'Honour Killings' in Canada." https://www.justice.gc.ca/eng/rp-pr/cj-jp/fv-vf/hk-ch/p2.html.

Cornelissen, L. (2021, Oct.). "Religiosity in Canada and Its Evolution from 1985 to 2019." *Insights on Canadian Society*. Statistics Canada Cat. no. 75-006-X. Ottawa: Statistics Canada.

Dawson, Lorne L. (1998). *Comprehending Cults: The Sociology of New Religious Movements*. Toronto: Oxford University Press.

Dempsey, L. James (1995). "Alberta's Indians in WWII." In *King and Country, Alberta in the Second World War*, ed. Ken Tingley. Edmonton: Provincial Museum of Alberta.

Durkheim, Émile ([1897] 1951). *Suicide: A Study in Sociology*. Trans. John A. Spaulding & George Simpson. New York: Free Press of Glencoe.

Durkheim, Émile ([1912] 1995). *The Elementary Forms of the Religious Life*. Trans. Karen Fields. New York: Simon & Schuster.

Dusenberry, Verne (1998). *The Montana Cree: A Study in Religious Persistence*. Norman: University of Oklahoma Press.

Etzioni, Amitai (1964). *Modern Organizations*. Englewood Cliffs, NJ: Prentice-Hall.

Fields, Karen (1995). "Introduction." In Karen Fields (trans.), *The Elementary Forms of the Religious Life*, by Émile Durkheim. New York: Simon & Schuster.

Flint, David (1975). *The Hutterites: A Study in Prejudice*. Toronto: Oxford University Press.

Gilbreth, Frank B. Jr, & Ernestine Gilbreth Carey (1948). *Cheaper by the Dozen*. New York: Thomas Y. Crowell.

Hagberg, Lars (2016, July 19). "Anglicans' Shift on Same Sex Marriage Shows Church Is Evolving." Canadian Press. https://www.winnipegfreepress.com/opinion/analysis/anglicans-shift-on-same-sex-marriage-shows-church-is-evolving-387479051.html#&gid=null&pid=1.

Humphreys, Margaret (1995). *Empty Cradles*. New York: Doubleday.

Husain, Mir Zohair (1995). *Global Islamic Politics*. New York: HarperCollins.

Inge, Anabel (2016). "The Making of a Salafi Muslim Woman: Paths to Conversion." *Independent*. https://www.independent.co.uk/news/uk/home-news/young-british-salafi-women-a7436611.html.

Islam, Gazy, & Michael J. Zyphur (2009). "Rituals in Organizations: A Review and Expansion of Current Theory." *Group Organization Management* 34 (114), pp. 114–39.

Jantz, Gregory L. (2014, Feb. 17). "Brain Differences between Genders." *Psychology Today*. https://www.psychologytoday.com/us/blog/hope-relationships/201402/brain-differences-between-genders.

Kushner, David (2009). *Levittown: Two Families, One Tycoon, and the Fight for Civil Rights in America's Legendary Suburb*. New York: Walker & Company.

Ligaya, Armina, & Tara Deschamps (2018, July 31). "The Corporate Climb: Stalled Progress for Women in Canada C-suites." *Toronto Star* (online).

Long, Elizabeth (2003). *Women and the Uses of Reading in Everyday Life*. Chicago: University of Chicago Press.

Love, John F. (1995). *McDonald's: Behind the Arches*, rev. ed. Toronto: Bantam.

Marx, Karl ([1844] 1976). *Introduction to A Contribution to the Critique of Hegel's Philosophy of Right*. Trans. Joseph O'Malley. New York: Oxford.

McClintock, Walter (1910). *The Old North Trail: Life, Legends, and Religion of the Blackfeet Indians*. London: Macmillan.

Merton, Robert K. ([1949] 1968). *Social Theory and Social Structure*. New York: Free Press.

Miller, J.R. (1996). *Shingwauk's Vision: A History of Native Residential Schools*. Toronto: University of Toronto Press.

Mills, Albert J., & Tony Simmons (1995). *Reading Organization Theory: A Critical Approach*. Toronto: Garamond.

Moreau, Greg (2022, Aug. 2). "Police-Reported Crime Statistics in Canada, 2021." Statistics Canada (online).

Mueller, Carol (1995). "The Organizational Basis of Conflict in Contemporary Feminism." In *Feminist Organizations*, ed. Myra Marx Ferree & Patricia Yancey Martin, pp. 263–75. Philadelphia: Temple University Press.

Nembhard, Ingrid M., Lawton R. Burns, & Stephen M. Shortell (2020, Apr. 17). "Responding to COVID-19: Lessons from Management Research." In *NEJM Catalyst, Innovations in Care Delivery*. https://catalyst.nejm.org/doi/full/10.1056/CAT.20.0111.

Nonaka, K., T. Miura, & K. Peter (1993). "Low Twinning Rate and Seasonal Effects on Twinning in a Fertile Population, the Hutterites." *International Journal of Biometeorology* 37 (3), pp. 145–50.

Penny, Laura (2005). *Your Call Is Important to Us: The Truth About Bullshit*. Toronto: McClelland & Stewart.

Poirier, Agnes (2016, Aug. 17). "Burkini Beach Row Puts French Values to Test." *BBC News* (online).

Prentice, Walter (n.d.). "Moral Injury: When McKinsey Comes to Town." University of Texas, McCombs School of Business, Ethics. https://ethicsunwrapped.utexas.edu/moral-injury-when-mckinsey-comes-to-town.

Ritzer, George (2004). *The McDonaldization of Society*, rev. ed. Newbury Park, CA: Pine Forge Press.

Roat, Alyssa (2019, July 5). "What Are Complementarianism and Egalitarianism? What Is the Difference?" *Chistianity.com*. https://www.christianity.com/wiki/christian-terms/what-are-complementarianism-and-egalitarianism-what-s-the-difference.html.

Robinson, Angela (2002). "Ta'n Teli-ktlamsitasit ('Ways of Believing'): Mi'kmaw Religion in Eskasoni, Nova Scotia."

Siddiqui, Haroon (2006). *Being Muslim*. Toronto: Groundwood Books.

Simmel, Georg (1971). "The Problem of Sociology." In *On Individuality and Social Forms*, ed. Donald N. Levine. Chicago: University of Chicago Press.

Smith, James M. (2007). *Ireland's Magdalen Laundries and the Nation's Architecture of Containment*. Notre Dame, IN: University of Notre Dame.

Smith, R.S. (1995). "Giving Credit Where Credit Is Due: Dorothy Swaine Thomas and the 'Thomas Theorem.'" *American Sociologist* 26, pp. 9–28.

Statistics Canada (various years). "GSS Questions Asked." https://www150.statcan.gc.ca/n1/pub/75-006-x/2021001/article/00010-eng.htm.

Statistics Canada (2013). *2011 National Household Survey*, Cat. no. 99-010-X2011032. Ottawa: Minister of Industry.

Steckley, John, & Bryan Cummins (2008). *Full Circle: Canada's First Nations*, 2nd ed. Toronto: Pearson.

Thomas, W.I. (1966). *W.I. Thomas on Social Organization and Social Personality. Selected Papers*. Ed. Morris Janowitz. Chicago: University of Chicago Press.

Thomas, W.I., & Florian Znaniecki ([1918–20] 1996). *The Polish Peasant in Europe and America*. Urbana: University of Illinois Press.

Thrasher, Frederic M. (1927). *The Gang: A Study of 1,313 Gangs in Chicago*. Chicago: University of Chicago Press.

Totten, Mark, (2014). *Gang Life: 10 of the Toughest Tell Their Stories*. Toronto: James Lorimer.

Totten, Mark, & Daniel Totten (2012). *Nasty, Brutish and Short: The Lives of Gang Members in Canada*. Toronto: James Lorimer.

Van Poppel, Frans, & Lincoln H. Day (1996). "A Test of Durkheim's Theory of Suicide—Without Committing the 'Ecological Fallacy.'" *American Sociological Review* 61, pp. 500–7.

Van Tubergen, Frank, Manfred teGrotenhuis, & Wout Ultee (2005). "Denomination, Religious Context, and Suicide: Neo-Durkheimian Multilevel Explanations Tested with Individual and Contextual Data." *American Journal of Sociology* 111 (3), pp. 797–823.

Weber, Max. ([1904] 1930). *The Protestant Ethic and the Spirit of Capitalism*. Trans. Talcott Parsons. New York: Charles Scribner's Sons.

Weber, Max ([1946] 1958). "Essays in Sociology." In *From Max Weber*, ed. M. Weber, H. Gerth, & C.W. Mills. New York: Oxford University Press.

Weber, Max ([1914, 1922] 1978). *Economy and Society: An Outline of Interpretive Sociology*. New York: Bedminster.

Whyte, William F. (1955). *Street-Corner Society: The Social Structure of an Italian Slum*, 2nd ed. Chicago: University of Chicago.

Zolfagharifard, Ellie (2014, Apr. 14). "Was the Gospel of St. Luke 'Written' by Mary?" *Daily Mail*. https://www.dailymail.co.uk/sciencetech/article-2604191/Was-Gospel-St-Luke-written-MARY-Jesus-mother-wrote-biblical-text-claims-writer.html.

Chapter 11

Ansari, Sadiya (2019, Feb. 16). "The Number of Adults Living with Their Parents Has Doubled since 1995. Culture Is a Driving Factor." *Global News* (online).

Armstrong, Pat, & Hugh Armstrong ([1978] 2010). *The Double Ghetto: Canadian Women and Their Segregated Work*. Toronto: Oxford University Press.

Baynes, Chris (2017, July 8). "More than 200,000 Children Married in the US over the Last 15 Years." *The Independent* (online).

Beaujot, Roderic (2000). *Earning and Caring in Canadian Families*. Peterborough, ON: Broadview.

Beaujot, Roderic (2002). "Earning and Caring: Demographic Change and Policy Implications." *Canadian Studies in Population* 29 (2), pp. 195–225.

Beaujot, Roderic (2004, June 15). "Delayed Life Transitions: Trends and Implications." *Vanier Institute of the Family*. www.vifamily.ca/library/cft/delayed_life.html.

Bibby, Reginald (1995). *The Bibby Report: Social Trends Canadian Style*. Toronto: Stoddard.

Bibby, Reginald (2016). Project Canada Survey Series. Lethbridge, Alberta: University of Lethbridge.

Bolaria, B. Singh, & Peter S. Li (1985). *Racial Oppression in Canada*. Toronto: Garamond.

Bott, Elizabeth (1957). *Family and Social Networks: Roles, Norms, and External Relationships in Ordinary Urban Families*. London: Tavistock.

Budgell, Janet (1999). *Our Way Home: A Report to the Aboriginal Healing and Wellness Strategy: Repatriation of Aboriginal People Removed by the Child Welfare System: Final Report*. Prepared by Native Child and Family Services of Toronto, Sevenato and Associates. Toronto: Native Child and Family Services of Toronto.

CTV News (2011, Jan. 27). "Plural Wife Describes Life in Bountiful Commune" (online).

Dasgupta, Sathi (1992). "Conjugal Roles and Social Network in Indian Immigrant Families: Bott Revisited." *Journal of Comparative Family Studies* 23 (3), p. 465.

Dosman, Edgar J. (1972). *Indians: An Urban Dilemma*. Toronto: McClelland & Stewart.

Fournier, S., & E. Crey (1997). *Stolen from Our Embrace*. Vancouver: Douglas & McIntyre.

Frank, Kristyn, & Marc Frenette (2021, Apr.). *Couples' Perceptions of the Division of Household and Child Care Tasks: Are There Differences between Sociodemographic Groups?* Ottawa: Statistics Canada, Analytical Studies Branch Research Paper Series.

Goldscheider, Frances, & Regina Bures (2003). "The Racial Crossover in Family Complexity in the United States." *Demography* 40 (3), pp. 569–87.

Hochschild, Arlie Russell, & Anne Machung (1989). *The Second Shift: Working Parents and the Revolution at Home*. New York: Viking Penguin.

Houle, Patricia, Martin Turcotte, & Michael Wendt (2017, June 1). "Changes in Parents' Participation in Domestic Tasks and Care for Children from 1986 to 2015." *Spotlight on Canadians: Results from the General Social Survey*. Statistics Canada Cat. no. 89-652-X. Ottawa: Minister of Industry.

Human Resources and Skills Development Canada (2014). *Indicators of Well-Being in Canada: Family Life—Marriage*. www4.hrsdc.gc.ca/.3ndic.1t.4r@-eng.jsp?iid=78.

Kelly, Mary Bess (2012). "Divorce Cases in Civil Court, 2010/2011." *Juristat*, Statistics Canada Cat. no. 85-002-X. Ottawa: Minister of Industry.

Kimelman, Edwin C. (1985). *No Quiet Place: Review Committee on Indian and Metis Adoption and Placements*. Winnipeg: Manitoba Community Services.

Larkin, Philip (1974). "This Be the Verse." *High Windows*. London: Faber and Faber.

Leah, Ronnie, & Gwen Morgan (1979). "Immigrant Women Fight Back: The Case of the Seven Jamaican Women." *Resources for Feminist Research* 7 (3), pp. 23–4.

Mandell, Nancy, & Ann Duffy (1995). *Canadian Families: Diversity, Conflict and Change*. Toronto: Harcourt Brace.

Milan, Anne, Hélène Maheux, & Tina Chui (2010). *A Portrait of Couples in Mixed Unions*. Statistics Canada Cat. no. 11-008-X. Ottawa: Minister of Industry.

Miller, J.R. (1996). *Shingwauk's Vision: A History of Native Residential Schools*. Toronto: University of Toronto Press.

Nakhaie, M. Reza (1995). "Housework in Canada: The National Picture." *Journal of Comparative Family Studies* 23 (3), pp. 409–25.

Provencher, Claudine, Anne Milan, Stacey Hallman, & Carol D'Aoust (2018, June 5). "Fertility: Overview 2012 to 2016." *Report on the Demographic Situation in Canada*. Statistics Canada Cat. no. 91-209-X. Ottawa: Minister of Industry.

Rajulton, Fernando, T.R. Balakrishnan, & Zenaida R. Ravanera (1990, June). "Measuring Infertility in Contracepting Populations." Presentation, Canadian Population Society Meetings, Victoria, BC.

Reiss, Fraidy (2015, Oct. 13). "America's Child-Marriage Problem." *New York Times* (online).

Revised Statutes of Canada, c. C-34, s. 43.

Seeley, John, R. Alexander Sim, & E.W. Loosely (1956). *Crestwood Heights: A Study of the Culture of Suburban Life*. Toronto: University of Toronto Press.

Statistics Canada (2011). *Women in Canada: A Gender-Based Statistical Report*. Cat. no. 89-503-X. Ottawa: Minister of Industry.

Statistics Canada (2012). *Portrait of Families and Living Arrangements in Canada: Families, Households, and Marital Status, 2011 Census of Population*. Cat. no. 98-312-X2011001. Ottawa: Minister of Industry.

Statistics Canada (2014). "Mixed Unions in Canada." *National Household Survey (NHS), 2011*. Cat. no. 99-010-X2011003. Ottawa: Minister of Industry.

Statistics Canada (2016). "Fertility: Fewer Children, Older Moms." *The Daily: Canadian Megatrends*. Cat. no. 11-630-X. Ottawa: Minister of Industry.

Statistics Canada (2017a). *2016 Census of Population*. Cat. no. 98-400-X2016028. Ottawa: Minister of Industry.

Statistics Canada (2017b, Aug. 2). "Young Adults Living with Their Parents in Canada in 2016." *Census in Brief*. Cat. no. 98-200-X2016008. Ottawa: Minister of Industry.

Statistics Canada (2017c). *Census in Brief: Same-Sex Couples in Canada in 2016*. Ottawa: Minister of Industry.

Statistics Canada (2019). Table 17-10-0060-01. Estimate of Population as of July 1st, by Marital Status or Legal Marital Status. Ottawa: Minister of Industry.

Statistics Canada (2021, Aug. 19). Family and Household Characteristics of Lesbians, Gay and Bisexual People in Canada.

Statistics Canada (n.d.). *Canadian Vital Statistics, Birth Database, Survey 3231*. Ottawa: Minister of Industry.

Statistics Canada (n.d.). Table 11-10-0017-01. Census Families by Family Type and Family Composition Including before and after-tax Median Income of the Family. Ottawa: Minister of Industry.

Statistics Canada (n.d.). Table 13-10-0416-01. Live Births, by Age of Mother. Ottawa: Minister of Industry.

Tang, Jackie, Nora Galbraith, & Johnny Truong (2019, Mar. 6). "Living Alone in Canada." *Insights on Canadian Society*. Statistics Canada Cat. no. 75-006-X. Ottawa: Minister of Industry.

TNS Canadian Facts (2003). *Public Divided about Definition of Marriage: Results of a Public Opinion Poll on Same-Sex Marriage*. www.tns-cf.com/news/03.09.05-samesex-charts.pdf.

Truth and Reconciliation Commission of Canada, Chairman, Justice Murray Sinclair (2015). *Final Report*, 6 vols. Winnipeg: Truth and Reconciliation Commission.

Truth Commission into Genocide in Canada (2001). *The Untold Story of the Genocide of Aboriginal Peoples by Church and State in Canada*. http://canadiangenocide.nativeweb.org/genocide.pdf.

Chapter 12

Argila, J. (2017). "How to Create Video News That Rocks in Social Media." London: University of Oxford. https://reutersinstitute.politics.ox.ac.uk/our-research/how-create-video-news-rocks-social-media.

Barrera, Jorge (2021, May 16). "Michelle Latimer Breaks Silence, Presents Ancestry Following Questions about Indigenous Identity." *CBC News* (online).

Baym, N.K. (2010). *Personal Connections in the Digital Age*. Cambridge: Polity.

Briziarelli, M. and Armano, E. (2017). *The Spectacle 2.0: Reading Debord in the Context of Digital Capitalism*. London: University of Westminster Press.

Chittley, Jordan (2014, Nov. 5). "Canada's Official Time Signal First Beeped 75 Years Ago Today." *CTV News*. https://www.ctvnews.ca/sci-tech/canada-s-official-time-signal-first-beeped-75-years-ago-today-1.2087778.

Confessore, N. (2018). "Cambridge Analytica and Facebook: The Scandal and the Fallout So Far." *New York Times*. https://www.nytimes.com/2018/04/04/us/politics/cambridge-analytica-scandal-fallout.html.

Cybersecurity & Infrastructure Security Agency (CISA). "Foreign Influence Operations and Disinformation." https://www.cisa.gov/mdm.

Debord, G. (1967). *Society of the Spectacle*. Retrieved Nov. 5, 2020. https://www.marxists.org/reference/archive/debord/society.htm.

Deer, Tracey (2005). *Mohawk Girls*. National Film Board of Canada, https://www.nfb.ca/film/mohawk_girls/.

Dowling, Amber (2021, Jan. 29). "CBC Cancels 'Trickster' Following Director Michelle Latimer's Indigenous Identity Scandal." *Global News* (online).

Giddens, A. (1991). *Modernity and Self-Identity: Self and Society in the Late Modern Age*. Cambridge: Polity.

Habermas, J. (1996). "The Public Sphere." In *Media Studies: A Reader*, ed. Paul Marris & Sue Thornham. Edinburgh: Edinburgh University Press.

Hays, Matthew (2013, July 11). "Mohawk Girls: A Native Take on Sex and the City." *Globe and Mail* (online).

Kavenna, Joanna (2019, Oct. 4). "Shoshana Zuboff: Surveillance Capitalism Is an Assault on Human Autonomy." *The Guardian* (online).

Lewis, J., & S. Cushion (2009). "The Thirst to Be First: An Analysis of Breaking News Stories and Their Impact on the Quality of 24-Hour News Coverage in the UK." *Journalism Practice*, 3 (3), pp. 304–18.

Marwick, A. (2013). "Online Identity." In *Companion to New Media Dynamics*, ed. J. Hartley, J. Burgess, & A. Bruins, pp. 355–64. London: Blackwell.

Marwick, A.E., & Danah Boyd (2011). "I Tweet Honestly, I Tweet Passionately: Twitter Users, Context Collapse, and the Imagined Audience." *New Media & Society* 13 (1), pp. 114–33.

McLuhan, Marshall (1962). *The Gutenberg Galaxy: The Making of Typographic Man*. Toronto: University of Toronto Press.

McLuhan, Marshall (1964). *Understanding Media: The Extensions of Man*. New York: McGraw Hill.

Mills, C.W. (1956). *The Power Elite*. New York: Oxford University Press.

Milmo, D. (2021, Dec. 6). "Rohingya Sue Facebook for £150bn over Myanmar Genocide." *The Guardian*. https://www.theguardian.com/technology/2021/dec/06/rohingya-sue-facebook-myanmar-genocide-us-uk-legal-action-social-media-violence.

Newman, N., R. Fletcher, A. Schulz, S. Andı, & R. Kleis Nielsen (2020). *Reuters Institute Digital News Report 2020*.

O'Neil, C. (2016). *Weapons of Math Destruction: How Big Data Increases Inequality and Threatens Democracy*. New York: Penguin Random House.

Rosenberg, M., C. Caldwalladr, & N. Confessore (2018, Mar. 17). "How Trump Consultants Exploited the

Facebook Data of Millions." *New York Times*. https://www
.nytimes.com/2018/03/17/us/politics/cambridge-analytica-
trump-campaign.html.

Steckley, John L. (2003). *Aboriginal Voices and the Politics of
Representation in Canadian Sociology Textbooks*. Toronto:
Canadian Scholars' Press.

Statista (2022). "Market Share Held by Leading Media
Companies." Statista. https://www.statista.com/statistics/
256349/market-share-held-by-leading-media-companies-
in-canada/.

Strange, Susan (1994). *States and Markets*, 2nd ed. London:
Bloomsbury Publishing.

Taylor, Drew Hayden (2022, Sept. 29). "Identity Wars: What
Makes an Indigenous Person Indigenous, and How Do
'Pretendians' Complicate Things?" *CBC Docs*. https://
www.cbc.ca/documentaries/the-passionate-eye/identity-
wars-what-makes-an-indigenous-person-indignous-
and-how-do-pretendians-complicate-things-1.6595901.

Telefilm Canada (2015). "Audiences in Canada: Trend Report." https://telefilm.ca/wp-content/uploads/audiences-
in-canada-trend-report.pdf.

Vaidhyanathan, Siva (2021). *Anti-Social Media: How Facebook
Disconnects Us and Undermines Democracy*. New York: Oxford University Press.

Winterhalter, Benjamin (2020, Jan. 9). "3 Women Philosophers of the Enlightenment: Emilie du Châtelet, Anne
Conway, and Mary Wollstonecraft," *JSTOR*. https://daily
.jstor.org/3-women-philosophers-of-the-enlightenment/.

Wong, Tony (2014, Nov. 20). "*Mohawk Girls* More Than
Its Sex and the City Aboriginal Billing." *Toronto Star*
(online).

Yarhi, E. (2017). "First Newspapers in Canada." *Canadian
Encyclopedia*. https://www.thecanadianencyclopedia.ca/
en/article/first-newspapers-in-canada.

Zuboff, Shoshana (2019). *The Age of Surveillance Capitalism:
The Fight for a Human Future at the New Frontier of Power*.
New York: PublicAffairs.

Chapter 13

Anyon, Jean (1980). "Social Class and the Hidden Curriculum of Work." *Journal of Education* 162 (1), pp. 67–92.

Archibald, Jo-ann (2008). *Indigenous Storywork: Educating
the Heart, Mind, Body, and Spirit*. Vancouver: University
of British Columbia Press.

Archibald, Jo-ann (2019, Jan. 14). "My Dreams for Indigenous Education in Canada." *The Tyee* (online).

Bowles, S., & H. Gintis (1976). *Schooling in Capitalist America: Educational Reform and Contradictions of Economic
Life*. New York: Basic Books.

Cameron, Linda, & Lee Bartel (2008). *Homework Realities: A
Canadian Study of Parental Opinions and Attitudes*. Technical Report. Toronto: University of Toronto, Ontario Institute for Studies in Education.

Canada, Government of (2022). Immigration and Citizenship. https://www.canada.ca/en/services/immigration-
citizenship.html; https://www.canada.ca/en/immigration-
refugees-citizenship/news/video/express-entry-immigrate-
canada-skilled-worker.html.

Casey, Liam (2015, June 9). "Ontario Teachers Need More
Training on Aboriginal Issues: Report." *CBC News*
(online).

Dei, George (1996). *Anti-Racism Education: Theory and Practice*. Halifax: Fernwood.

Drolet, Marie (2005, Feb.). "Participation in Post-Secondary
Education in Canada: Has the Role of Parental Income
and Education Changed over the 1990s?" Analytical Studies Branch Research Paper Series. Statistics Canada Cat.
no. 11F0019MIE. Ottawa: Minister of Industry.

Drolet, Marie (2017, Nov. 1). "Linking Labour Demand and
Labour Supply: Job Vacancies and the Unemployed."
Insights on Canadian Society. Statistics Canada Cat.
no. 75-006-X. Ottawa: Minister of Industry.

Dubson, Michael, ed. (2001). *Ghosts in the Classroom: Stories
of College Adjunct Faculty—and the Price We All Pay*. Boston: Camel's Back.

El-Assal, Kareem (2022, Mar. 24). "Canada Welcomed
450,000 New International Students in 2021." *CIC News*.

Foucault, Michel (1977). *Discipline and Punish: The Birth of
the Prison*. New York: Pantheon.

Foucault, Michel (1980). "Two Lectures." In *Power/
Knowledge*, ed. Colin Gordon, pp. 78–108. New York:
Pantheon.

Frenette, Marc (2017, Apr. 10). "Postsecondary Enrolment by Parental Income: Recent National and Provincial Trends." *Economic Insights*. Statistics Canada Cat.
no. 11-626-X. Ottawa: Minister of Industry.

Hanbasasa, M., G. Ball, M. Kebbe, A. Farmer, N. Willows,
A. Perez, & K. Maximova (2021). "Food Insecurity among
International Post-Secondary Students Studying on a
Canadian Campus: A Qualitative Descriptive Study." *Can-
adian Journal of Higher Education* 51 (2), pp. 33–45.

Hearn, Alison, & Gus Van Harten (2017, Oct.). *Report of the
CAUT Ad Hoc Investigatory Committee into the Enbridge
Centre for Corporate Sustainability at the University of Cal-
gary*. Ottawa: CAUT.

Helmes-Hayes, Rick (2010). *Measuring the Mosaic: An Intellectual Biography of John Porter*. Toronto: University of
Toronto Press.

Henry, Frances, & Carol Tator (2006). *The Colour of Democracy: Racism in Canada*. Toronto: Nelson Thomson.

Jadhav, Apoorva (2022). "Importance of Plagiarism Laws in Canada." Smart Student Canada.
https://smartstudentcanada.com/importance-of-
plagiarism-laws-in-canada/.

James, Carl (2017). *Towards Race Equity in Education*.
Toronto: York University, 2017. https://edu.yorku
.ca/files/2017/04/Towards-Race-Equity-in-Education-
April-2017.pdf?x38104.

King, Alan, Wendy Warren, & Sharon Miklas (2004). "Study
of Accessibility to Ontario Law Schools." Executive Sum-
mary of the Report Submitted to Deans of Law at Osgood
Hall, York University; University of Ottawa; Queen's
University; University of Western Ontario; University of
Windsor. Kingston: Queen's University Social Program
Evaluation Group.

Lewis, Stephen (1992). *Stephen Lewis Report on Race Relations
in Ontario*. Toronto: Government of Ontario.

Livingstone, David W. (2004). *The Education–Jobs Gap:
Underemployment or Economic Democracy*, 2nd ed. Toronto: Garamond.

Malacrida, Claudia (2015). *A Special Hell: Institutional Life
in Alberta's Eugenic Years*. Toronto: University of Toronto
Press.

McCartney, Kevin D., & Garry Gray (2018). "Big Oil U:
Canadian Media Coverage of Corporate Obstructionism
and Institutional Corruption at the University of Calgary."
Canadian Journal of Sociology 43 (4).

Newson, Janice, & Howard Buchbinder (1988). *The University Means Business: Universities, Corporations and Academic Work.* Toronto: Garamond.

Noble, David (1998). "Digital Diploma Mills: The Automation of Higher Education." *Science as Culture* 7 (3), pp. 355–68.

Noble, David (2002). *Digital Diploma Mills: The Automation of Higher Education.* Toronto: Between the Lines.

Nourpanah, Shiva, & Pauline Gardiner Barber (2022). "'Family. Family. First of All Is Family': Refugee Movements in Eastern Canada." In *Families, Mobility, and Work,* ed. B. Neis, C. Murray, & N. Spinks, pp. 365–88. St John's: Memorial University Press.

Oakes, Jeannie (2005). *Keeping Track: How Schools Structure Inequality,* 2nd ed. New Haven, CT: Yale University Press.

Putman, I. Harold ([1912] 2019). *Egerton Ryerson and Education in Upper Canada.* London: Forgotten Books.

Richards, John, Jennifer Hove, & Kemi Afolabi (2008, Dec.). *Understanding the Aboriginal/Non-Aboriginal Gap in Student Performance: Lessons from British Columbia.* Commentary 276. Toronto: C.D. Howe Institute.

Saewyc, Elizabeth, Chiaki Konishi, Hilary Rose, & Yuko Homma (2014). "School-Based Strategies to Reduce Suicidal Ideation, Suicide Attempts, and Discrimination among Sexual Minority and Heterosexual Adolescents in Western Canada." *International Journal of Child, Youth, and Family Studies* 5 (1).

St. Petersburg College Learning Resources (n.d.) "Plagiarism and Academic Integrity." Instructions for Turnitin. https://spcollege.libguides.com/c.php?g=254383&p=1695459.

Schecter, Stephen (1977). "Capitalism, Class, and Educational Reform in Canada." In *The Canadian State: Political Economy and Political Power,* ed. L. Panitch. Toronto: University of Toronto Press.

Singer, Colin, R. (2019, Jan. 24). "International Students or 'Cash Cows'?" *Immigration.ca.* https://www.immigration.ca/international-students-or-cash-cows/.

Statistics Canada (2018, Dec. 4). "Labour Market Outcomes for College and University Graduates, Class of 2010 to 2014." *The Daily.* Ottawa: Minister of Industry.

Statistics Canada (2019a). "Canadian and International Tuition Fees by Level of Study." Table 37-10-0045-01. Ottawa: Minister of Industry. https://www150.statcan.gc.ca/t1/tbl1/en/tv.action?pid=3710004501

Statistics Canada (2019b). "Canadian Undergraduate Tuition Fees by Field of Study." Table 37-10-0003-01. Ottawa: Minister of Industry.

Statistics Canada (2021, Sept. 8). "Tuition Fees for Degree Programs." *The Daily.*

Thompson, Carol (2006). "Unintended Lessons: Plagiarism and the University." *Teachers College Record* 108 (12), pp. 2439–49.

Wilt, James (2017, Oct. 13). "Five Things We Learned from the Damning Report on the University of Calgary's Connections with Enbridge." *The Narwhal* (online).

Chapter 14

Anderson, Karen (1996). *Sociology: A Critical Introduction.* Toronto: Nelson.

Association of International Physicians and Surgeons of Ontario (AIPSO) (2018). https://aipso.webs.com/.

Bérard, Guy (1993). *Hearing Equals Behaviour.* New Canaan, CT: Keats.

Bérard, Guy, & Sally Brockett (2011). *Hearing Equals Behavior: Updated and Expanded.* Manchester Center, VT: Shires Press.

Bernstien, Jaella (2021, Sept. 19). "What Is Basic Income and Which of Canada's Main Parties Support It?" *CBC News.* https://www.cbc.ca/news/canada-how-basic-income-works-1.6179760.

Bewick, Gavin A. (2012, Oct.). "Bowels Control Brain: Gut Hormones and Obesity." *Biochemical Medicine* (Zagreb) 22 (3), pp. 283–97.

Broesterhuizen, Marcel (2008). "Worlds of Difference: An Ethical Analysis of Choices in the Field of Deafness." *Ethical Perspectives: Journal of the European Centre for Ethics* 15 (1), pp. 103–31.

Canadian Association of the Deaf (CAD) (2012). "Issues and Positions: Deaf Culture vs. Medicalization." www.cad.ca/deaf_culture_vs._medicalization.php.

Canadian Institute for Health Information (2007). "Canada's Health Care Providers, 2007." Ottawa: CIHI.

Canadian Institute for Health Information (2020, Oct. 29). "Physicians in Canada, 2019." https://www.cihi.ca/en/search?query=Number+of+male++physicians.

Canadian Medical Association (CMA) (2022). "Canadian Physician Specialty Profiles." https://www.cma.ca/canadian-physician-specialty-profiles.

Carter, Adam (2021, Jan. 26). "Ontario Health Experts Demand Province Abolish For-Profit Long-Term Care." *CBC News.* https://www.cbc.ca/news/canada/toronto/ontario-long-term-care-1.5888226.

Centers for Disease Control (CDC) (2013, May 17). "Genes and Obesity." https://www.cdc.gov/genomics/resources/diseases/obesity/obesedit.htm.

Chang, Virginia, & Nicholas Christakis (2002). "Medical Modelling of Obesity: A Transition from Action to Experience in a 20th Century American Medical Textbook." *Sociology of Health and Illness* 24 (2), pp. 151–77.

Cloutier, Elisabeth, Chantal Grondin, and Amélie Lévesque (2018, Nov. 28). *Canadian Survey on Disability, 2017: Concepts and Methods Guide.* Statistics Canada Cat. no. 89-654-X2018001. Ottawa: Minister of Industry.

Coupland, Douglas (1991). *Generation X: Tales for an Accelerated Culture.* New York: St Martin's Press.

Donovan, Kevin (2022, Sept. 29). "Apotex, Barry Sherman's 'Fifth Child,' Sold to American Buyer, as Police Still Probe His Murder." *Toronto Star.* https://www.thestar.com/news/canada/2022/09/29/apotex-barry-shermans-fifth-child-sold-to-american-buyer.html.

Emke, Ivan (2002). "Patients in the New Economy: The 'Sick Role' in a Time of Economic Discipline." *Animus: A Philosophical Journal for Our Time* 7, pp. 81–93.

"EpiPen Price Furor Heats Up in US" (2016, Aug. 24). *CBC News* (online).

Etzioni, Amitai (1986, Aug. 24). "The Fast-Food Factories: McJobs Are Bad for Kids." *Washington Post.*

Fadiman, Anne (1997). *The Spirit Catches You and You Fall Down: A Hmong Child, Her American Doctors, and the Collision of Two Cultures.* New York: Farrar, Straus and Giroux.

Groce, Nora E. (1999). "Disability in a Cross-Cultural Perspective: Rethinking Disability." *The Lancet* 354 (9180), pp. 756–7.

Grygier, Pat (1994). *A Long Way from Home: The Tuberculosis Epidemic among the Inuit.* Montreal and Kingston: McGill-Queen's University Press.

Gustafson, T.B., & D.B. Sarwer (2004, Aug. 5). "Childhood Sexual Abuse and Obesity." *Obesity Reviews* 3, pp. 129–35.

Haig, Terry (2019, Aug. 5). "Cancer Professionals Are Worried about Shortage of Some Important Drugs." Radio Canada International.

Harrow, M., T.H. Jobe, & R.N. Faull (2014). "Does Treatment of Schizophrenia with Antipsychotic Medications Eliminate or Reduce Psychosis? A 20-year Multi-follow-up Study." *Psychological Medicine*. doi:10.1017/S0033291714000610.

Hart, Julian Tudor (1971, Feb.). "The Inverse Care Law." *The Lancet* 27, pp. 405–12.

Hedden, Lindsay, M. Ruth Lavergne, Kimberlyn M. McGrail, Michael R. Law, Lucy Cheng, Megan A. Ahuja, & Morris L. Barer (2017, Dec. 11). "Patterns of Physician Retirement and Pre-retirement Activity: A Population-Based Cohort Study." *Canadian Medical Association Journal* 189 (49), pp. 1517–23.

Hubert, Nadine (1985, Aug. 14). "Sterilization and the Mentally Retarded." *The Interim*. www.theinterim.com/issues/bioethics/sterilization-and-the-mentally-retarded/.

Illich, Ivan (1976). *Medical Nemesis: The Limits of Medicine*. London: Penguin.

Ingstad, B. (1988). "Coping Behavior of Disabled Persons and Their Families: Cross-Cultural Perspectives from Norway and Botswana." *International Journal of Rehabilitation Research* 11, pp. 351–9.

Ireton, Julie (2021, Mar. 30). "Canada's Nursing Homes Have Worst Record for COVID-19 Deaths among Wealthy Nations: Report." *CBC News*. https://www.cbc.ca/news/canada/ottawa/canada-record-covid-19-deaths-wealthy-countries-cihi-1.5968749.

Jones, Sophia B. (1913, Sept.). "Fifty Years of Negro Public Health." *Annals of the American Academy of Political and Social Science*.

Kitching, Heather (2022, Apr. 4). "The 'Dire' Doctor Shortage in Rural Northwestern Ontario: 5 Proposed Solutions." *CBC News*. https://www.cbc.ca/news/canada/thunder-bay/nwo-physician-shortage-solutions-1.6408181.

Kite, Lexie, & Lindsay Kite (2022). "Beauty Redefined." https://courses.beautyredefined.org/

Kite, Lindsay (2012). "Healthy Redefined Part 1: Measuring the 'Obesity Crisis'." https://www.morethanabody.org/redefining-health-part-1-measuring-the-obesity-crisis/.

Kleinman, Arthur (1995). *Writing at the Margin: Discourse between Anthropology and Medicine*. Berkeley: University of California Press.

Koos, E.L. (1954). *The Health of Regionsville: What the People Thought and Did about It*. New York: Columbia University Press.

Kral, Andrej, & Gerard M. O'Donoghue (2010). "Profound Deafness in Childhood." *New England Journal of Medicine* 363, pp. 1439–50.

Lane, Harlan L. (1992). *The Mask of Benevolence: Disabling the Deaf Community*. New York: Knopf.

Lane, Harlan L. (1993). "The Medicalisation of Cultural Deafness in Historical Perspective." In *Looking Back: A Reader on the History of Deaf Communities and Their Sign Languages*, ed. Renate Fischer & Harlan L. Lane, pp. 479–94. International Studies on Sign Language and Communication of the Deaf. Hamburg: Signum.

Leung, Carrianne, & Jian Guan (2004). "Yellow Peril Revisited: Impact of SARS on the Chinese and Southeast Asian Canadian Communities." Toronto: Chinese Canadian National Council.

Mackey, Frank (2018, July). "1848, 1861, 1926—Which Came First?" *Connections: Journal of the Quebec Family History Society* 40 (3), pp. 7–10.

Madaule, Paul (1987). "The Dyslexified World." In Tim Gilmore, Paul Madaule, & B. Thompson, *About the Tomatis Method*, trans. from the French by Dr Paula Kacher. Toronto: The Listening Centre Press.

Madiros, M. (1989). "Conception of Childhood Disability among Mexican-American Parents." *Medical Anthropology* 12, pp. 55–68.

Malicki, M. (2007). "Code Blue! (Or Pink!): Perceptions of Men and Women Physicians in Specific Gender-Dominated Medical Subfields." *UW-L Journal of Undergraduate Research* 10, pp. 1–3.

Marks, Julie (2022, June 22). "The Link between Depression, Anxiety, and Obesity." https://psychcentral.com/anxiety/being-overweight-tied-to-anxiety-depression.

McCarthy, Claire M. (2018, Oct. 16). "The Real Link between Breastfeeding and Obesity." Harvard Health blog. https://www.health.harvard.edu/blog/the-real-link-between-breastfeeding-and-preventing-obesity-2018101614998.

McQuaig, Linda (2004). "Closed Shop Gives Doc the Hammer in New Brunswick Strike." *Straight Goods*. www.straightgoods.com/McQuaig/010122.shtml.

Morris, Stuart, Gail Fawcett, Laurent Brisebois, & Jeffrey Hughes (2018, Nov. 28). "A Demographic, Employment, and Income Profile of Canadians with Disabilities Aged 15 Years and Over, 2017." *Canadian Survey on Disability Reports*. Statistics Canada Cat. no. 89-654-X. Ottawa: Minister of Industry.

Morrison, David (2010, Feb. 1). "Should Disability Be Considered a Master Status?" http://disabilities.blogs.starnewsonline.com/10988/should-disability-be-considered-a-master-status/.

Naish, John (2011, Feb. 22). "Yes, Your Blood Group DOES Affect Your Health." *Daily Mail*. http://www.dailymail.co.uk/health/article-1359293/Yes-blood-group-DOES-affect-health.html.

New Canadian Media News Desk (2020, May 11). "Research Shows Canada Has Overlooked Immigrant Doctors." https://newcanadianmedia.ca/research-shows-canada-has-overlooked-immigrant-doctors/.

Noll, J.G., P.K. Trickett, J.D. Long, S. Negriff, E.J. Susman, I. Shalev, J.C. Li, & F.W. Putnam (2017, Jan.). "Childhood Sexual Abuse and Early Timing of Puberty." *Junior Adolescent Health* 60 (1), pp. 65–71.

Oddy, Wendy H. (2012, July). "Infant Feeding and Obesity Risk in the Child." *Breastfeeding Review* 20 (2), pp. 7–12.

Ontario Medical Association (OMA) (2002, Apr.). "Position Paper on Physician Workforce Policy and Planning." Toronto: OMA.

Parsons, Talcott (1951). *The Social System*. New York: Free Press.

Payer, Lynn (1992). *Disease-Mongers: How Doctors, Drug Companies, and Insurers Are Making You Feel Sick*. New York: Wiley.

Ross, Shelley (2019). "The Feminization of Medicine: Issues and Implications." In *Female Doctors in Canada: Experience and Culture*, ed. Earle Waugh, Shelley Ross, & Shirley Schipper, pp. 5–23. Toronto: University of Toronto Press.

Statistics Canada (2013). "National Household Survey Dictionary, 2011." Cat. no. 99-000-X2011001. Ottawa: Minister of Industry.

Statistics Canada (2017, Sept. 27). "Primary Health Care Providers, 2016." *Health Fact Sheets*. Cat. no. 82-625-X. Ottawa: Minister of Industry.

Statistics Canada (2018, Nov. 28). "Canadian Survey on Disability, 2017." *The Daily*. Ottawa: Minister of Industry.

Statistics Canada (2019). "Health Characteristics, Annual Estimates." Table 13-10-0096-01. Ottawa: Minister of Industry.

Statistics Canada (2020, Oct. 22). "Primary Health Care Providers, 2019." *Health Fact Sheets*. Statistics Canada Cat. no. 82-625-X. Ottawa: Ministry of Industry. https://www150.statcan.gc.ca/n1/pub/82-625-x/2020001/article/00004-eng.htm.

Tallman, Laurna (2010). *Listening for the Light: A New Perspective on Integration Disorder*. Marmora, ON: Northern Light Books.

Taylor, Brooke (2021, Dec. 7). "Daily Hive News." https://dailyhive.com/toronto/toronto-neighbourhoods-highest-rates-covid-19.

Taylor, Timothy (2020, Aug. 24). "The Origins of the Body Mass Index." *BBN Times*. https://www.bbntimes.com/global-economy/origins-of-the-body-mass-index.

"The Spectrum of Disability" (1999, Aug. 28). *The Lancet* 354.

Tomatis, Alfred (1987, 1991). *The Ear and the Voice*. Lanham, MD: Scarecrow Press.

Tomatis, Alfred (1991). *The Conscious Ear: My Life of Transformation through Listening*. Barrytown, NY: Station Hill Press.

Weeks, Carly (2019, Feb. 27). "Anti-Vaccine Group Launches Billboard Campaign in Toronto and Surrounding Area." *Globe and Mail* (online).

Welsch, Robert K., & Luis A. Vivanco (2019). *Asking Questions about Cultural Anthropology: A Concise Introduction*. New York: Oxford University Press.

Whigham, Leah D., Richard L. Atkinson, & Barbara A. Israel (2006). "Adipogenic Potential of Multiple Human Adenoviruses In Vivo and In Vitro in Animals." *American Journal of Physiology—Regulatory, Integrative and Comparative Physiology* 290 (1). https://doi.org/10.1152/ajpregu.00479.2005.

Zola, Irving K. (2003). *Missing Pieces: A Chronicle of Living with a Disability*, 2nd ed. Philadelphia: Temple University Press.

Chapter 15

Alberta Cancer Board (2009). *Cancer Incidence in Fort Chipewyan, Alberta, 1995–2006*. Alberta Cancer Board, Division of Population Health and Information Surveillance (online).

Basij-Rasikh, Shabana (2018, Oct. 9). "Want to Fight Climate Change? Educate a Girl." Ted.com. https://ideas.ted.com/want-to-fight-climate-change-educate-a-girl/.

Bookchin, Murray (1996). *The Philosophy of Social Ecology: Essays on Dialectical Naturalism*. Montreal: Black Rose.

Canadian Press (2019, Apr. 23). "'Eat It If You Want To': Filipino President Duterte Lashes Out over Canadian Cargo of Trash." *CBC News* (online).

Carbone, Christopher (2022, Sept. 1). "Most of Great Pacific Garbage Patch's Plastics Come from Five Nations." *Daily Mail*. https://www.msn.com/en-us/news/world/most-of-great-pacific-garbage-patchs-plastics-come-from-five-nations/ar-AA11mZAV.

CBC News (2012, Sept. 14). "Canada Won't Oppose Asbestos Limits: Federal Tories Reverse Course and Won't Veto Substance's Listing in Rotterdam Convention" (online).

CBC News (2015, Oct. 29). "5 Things to Know about China's 1-Child Policy" (online).

Central Intelligence Agency (CIA) (n.d.). "Country Comparison: Exports." World Factbook. www.cia.gov/library/publications/the-world-factbook/rankorder/2078rank.html.

Clairmont, Donald H., & Dennis W. Magill (1999). *Africville: The Life and Death of a Canadian Black Community*. Toronto: Canadian Scholars' Press.

Grant, Shantay (2018). *Africville*. Toronto: Groundwood.

Grant, Tavia (2015, July 1). "Ottawa Reverses Stand on Health Risks of Asbestos in 'Landmark Shift.'" *Globe and Mail* (online).

Gutierrez, Richard (2016, Mar. 2). "Canada's Waste Trade Policy: A Global Concern." *Philippine Daily Inquirer* (online).

Harney, Alexandra (2009). *The China Price: The True Cost of Chinese Competitive Advantage*. New York: Penguin.

Hollingsworth, Joseph, Brenna Copeland, & Jeremiah X. Johnson (2019, Aug. 2). "Are E-Scooters Polluters? The Environmental Impacts of Shared Dockless Electric Scooters." *Environmental Research Letters* 14 (8).

Hutchison, George, & Dick Wallace (1977). *Grassy Narrows*. Toronto: Van Nostrand Rinehold.

Joint Policy Committee of the Societies of Epidemiology (JPC-SE) (2012, June 4). "Position Statement on Asbestos." www.jpc-se.org/documents/01.JPC-SE-Position_Statement_on_Asbestos-June_4_2012-Summary_and_Appendix_A_English.pdf.

Kaufman, Alexander C. (2019, July 12). "New Orleans' Levees Face Biggest Test since Hurricane Katrina." *Huffington Post* (online).

Lalonde, Michelle (2007, Nov. 9). "Town Built on Asbestos Downplays Health Risks." *Montreal Gazette*.

Lavoie, Judith (2018, Dec. 21). "Industry-Hired Experts Downplay Impacts of Major Projects: UBC Study." *The Narwhal*. https://thenarwhal.ca/industry-hired-experts-downplay-impacts-of-major-projects-ubc-study/.

Liao, S. Matthew, Anders Sandberg, & Rebecca Roache (2012). "Human Engineering and Climate Change." *Ethics, Policy, and the Environment* 15 (2), pp. 206–11.

McCarthy, Shawn, & Marieke Walsh (2019, Aug. 20). "Want to Talk about Climate Change during the Federal Election? You'll Have to Register for That." *Globe and Mail* (online).

Murray, Cathryn Clarke, Janson Wong, Gerald G. Singh, Megan Mach, Jackie Lerner, Bernardo Ranieri, Guillaume Peterson St-Laurent, Alice Guimaraes, & Kai M.A. Chan (2018, June). "The Insignificance of Thresholds in Environmental Impact Assessment: An Illustrative Case Study in Canada." *Environmental Management* 61 (6), pp. 1062–71.

Oreskes, Naomi, & Erik M. Conway (2010). *Merchants of Doubt: How a Handful of Scientists Obscured the Truth on Issues from Tobacco Smoke to Global Warming*. New York: Bloomsbury.

Perkel, Colin N. (2002). *Well of Lies: The Walkerton Tragedy*. Toronto: McClelland & Stewart.

Phillip, Abby (2015, Apr. 24). "White People in New Orleans Say They're Better Off since Katrina. Black People Don't." *Washington Post*. https://www.washingtonpost.com/news/post-nation/wp/2015/08/24/white-people-in-new-orleans-say-theyre-better-off-after-katrina-black-people-dont/.

Porter, Jody (2016, June 20). "'Guilt' Drives Former Dryden, Ont. Mill Worker to Reveal His Part in Dumping Toxic Mercury." *CBC News* (online).

Prince, Samuel Henry (1920). *Catastrophe and Social Change: Based upon a Sociological Study of the Halifax Disaster.* New York: Columbia University Press.

Prokopchuk, Matt (2019, June 7). "Grassy Narrows Leadership to Review Ottawa's Latest Mercury Poisoning Care Home Agreement." *CBC News* (online).

Rabson, Mia (2018, Oct. 17). "Canada's Ban on Asbestos to Take Effect but Mining Residues Are Exempt." *Financial Post* (online).

Robin, Marie-Monique (2010). *The World According to Monsanto: Pollution, Politics, and Power; An Investigation into One of the World's Most Controversial Companies.* Melbourne: Spinifex.

Shkilnyk, Anastasia M. (1985). *A Poison Stronger Than Love: The Destruction of an Ojibwa Community.* New Haven, CT: Yale University Press.

Standing Committee on Environment and Sustainable Development (2009, June 11). Evidence. www.parl.gc.ca/House Publications/Publication.aspx?DocId=3983714&Language=E&Mode=1.

Supran, Geoffrey, S. Rahmstorf, & Naomi Oreskes (2023, Jan. 13). "Assessing ExxonMobil's Global Warming Projections." *Science* 379, no. 6628. https://www.science.org/doi.10.1126/science.abk0063.

Tataryn, Lloyd. (1976, June). "The Tortured Future of Elliot Lake." *Saturday Night* [magazine]. Reprinted (2011, Mar. 11) at Republic of Mining. https://republicofmining.com/2011/03/28/the-tortured-future-of-elliot-lake-%E2%80%93-by-lloyd-tataryn-saturday-night-june-1976/.

Tataryn, Lloyd (1979). *Dying for a Living.* Ottawa: Deneau and Greenberg.

Tataryn, Lloyd (1983). *Formaldehyde on Trial: The Politics of Health in a Chemical Society.* Toronto: Lorimer.

Turner, Logan (2021, July 31). "Grassy Narrows Funding Pact for Mercury-Poisoning Care Home Spurs Joy and Bitter Memories." *CBC News* (online).

Turner, Logan (2023, Jan. 2). "Grassy Narrows Marks 20 Years of the Blockade Protecting Its Land from Logging." *CBC News.* https://www.cbc.ca/news/canada/thunder-bay/grassy-narrows-blockade-20-anniversary-1.6699763.

Wetzel, Corryn (2021, Nov. 4). "Global CO_2 Emissions Have Returned to Near Pre-Pandemic Levels." *Smithsonian Magazine.* https://www.smithsonianmag.com/smart-news/global-co2-emissions-have-returned-to-near-pre-pandemic-levels-180979002/.

Wiley, Elizabeth (2019, May). "The Unseen Impacts of Climate Change on Mental Health." *BC Medical Journal* 61 (4).

Wynes, Seth, & Kimberly A. Nicholas (2017). "The Climate Change Mitigation Gap: Education and Government Recommendations Miss the Most Effective Individual Actions." *Environmental Research Letters* 12.

Yan, Sophia (2017, Feb. 27). "'Made in China' Isn't So Cheap Anymore, and That Could Spell Headache for Beijing." *CNBC* (online).

Index

Terms not found in the index may be found in the glossary.